BEHAVIOR SCIENCE BIBLIOGRAPHIES

ETHNOGRAPHIC BIBLIOGRAPHY OF NORTH AMERICA

4th EDITION

Volume 4: Eastern United States

GEORGE PETER MURDOCK
and
TIMOTHY J. O'LEARY

with the assistance of

JOHN BEIERLE
SARAH T. BRIDGES
DONALD HORTON
JOHN B. KIRBY, JR.

ALLISON BUTLER MATTHEWS
JOHN MUSGRAVE
JOAN STEFFENS
FREDERICK W. VOGET

BARBARA A. YANCHEK

HUMAN RELATIONS AREA FILES PRESS
NEW HAVEN
1975

Compilation of this volume has been
financed in part by grant GN35418 from
the National Science Foundation.

CONTENTS

SCHEMATIC TABLE OF CONTENTS
FOR
COMPLETE BIBLIOGRAPHY

Preface to the Fourth Edition

This, the fourth edition of the *Ethnographic Bibliography of North America*, is intended to provide a basic coverage of the published literature on the Native Peoples of North America through the end of the year 1972. This edition differs in a number of ways from the third edition, which was published in 1960. The most obvious change is that the bibliography is now appearing in five volumes. As with every other discipline in the last twenty years, Native American studies has had to cope with an information explosion. Some idea of the magnitude of this explosion can be gained from the fact that while the third edition contained approximately 17,300 bibliographic entries in one volume, the present edition contains close to 40,000 entries in five volumes, most of this increase pertaining to the fourteen-year period 1959-1972, inclusive. Part of the increase, however, also comes from the increased span of coverage of the present edition, which includes a number of subject areas not covered previously.

Another obvious change is in the format of presentation. With one major exception, full bibliographic information has been given for each citation in the bibliography where it has been available. Each citation gives the author's full name, the full title and subtitle, place of publication, publisher, date of publication, etc. If the citation be from a journal, the name of the journal is given in full. This is a major change from previous editions, where such information was compressed as much as possible, using abbreviations for journal names and using short or abbreviated titles wherever possible, all with the idea of saving space so as to be able to include the whole bibliography in one volume. This compression was not necessary in the present edition, since we realized before we started the compilation of citations that there would have to be more than one volume. The major exception noted above is that whereas we have expanded the citations listed in the third edition whenever we could (giving full titles of books, the names of journals in full, etc.) we found it impossible to do a full and thorough job on this expansion, since it would have meant verifying each and every citation in the original. This could not be done with the time and funds allotted to us for the preparation of this edition of the bibliography. As a result, there are some inconsistencies in citation format in the bibliography that follows. It is hoped that for the next edition, all of the pre-1959 citations will have been verified and full information given for each.

The number of ethnic groups covered by the bibliography has been expanded somewhat, especially in the North Mexican area, in order to have the ethnic groups covered in the bibliography correspond more closely to the groups covered in the forthcoming *Handbook of North American Indians*. Also, we have dropped the general use of the word "tribal" when referring to ethnic groups, since many of the groups named in the bibliography are not "tribes" in the traditional sense.

Another major change from the third edition is that this is a computerized bibliography, based on a variation of the Human Relations Area Files Automated Bibliographic System (HABS), which has been developed over the past ten years (see Koh 1973). This computerization will make the preparation of future editions much less expensive, less time-consuming, and far easier to accomplish. Once the bibliographic information has been correctly put into machine-readable form, this inputting should never have to be done again. In addition, with a change in the programming of the computer, new formats can be used and special bibliographies can be printed without the laborious compilation process that was previously necessary. Several people were involved in the adaptation of the HABS for the purposes of this bibliography. HABS programming development has been by John Dow. Programming and computer operations were accomplished by Richard Hart and Joan Steffens. The computer used for the arrangement and printing of the citations was the IBM 370/158 at the Yale University Computer Center. The actual printing was performed with the use of a special IBM print train (developed with the aid of the American Library Association), which carries most of the pertinent diacritics used in a bibliography of this type.

Since the publication of the third edition of this bibliography, a number of individuals have written to us, offering suggestions, additions, and corrections. Such contributions are essential to an undertaking like this, since one individual or organization can neither hope to comprehend all of the requirements of the anticipated users of the bibliography nor control the diversity of the published materials relevant to the purpose of the bibliography. Therefore, we are very pleased to acknowledge the assistance of Lowell John Bean, David M. Brugge,

Harold C. Conklin, Alan Cooke, Gordon M. Day, Alan Dundes, May Ebihara (and her class), James L. Fidelholtz, Don D. Fowler, Stanley A. Freed, Robert F. Heizer, James H. Howard, Dell Hymes, Ira S. Jacknis, Janet Jordan, Luis S. Kemnitzer, Herbert Landar, William S. Lyon, John Moore, Vernon H. Nelson, Wendell Oswalt, Nancy J. Pollock, Bert Salwen, Claude E. Schaeffer, Samuel L. Stanley, Omer C. Stewart, Willard Walker, Margaret Wheat, and Richard B. Woodbury.

Special notes of thanks must go to two people. William C. Sturtevant has been a constant source of encouragement from the beginning of the project, taking time out from his very strenuous duties (among others of editing the forthcoming *Handbook of North American Indians*) to note new books and sources of information, errors in the previous editions, people to contact, etc. June Helm has been of great help in the preparation of the Northern Athabascan bibliographies (Area 2), sending on new versions of her own ongoing computerized bibliography as they became available. They, and the other scholars noted above, receive our most grateful thanks for their assistance. Naturally, they are in no way responsible for whatever deficiencies may remain in the bibliography, but they are very definitely responsible in part for whatever merit it may have for the user.

Most of the actual compilation of this bibliography was accomplished at various libraries within the Yale University system. Our particular thanks go to Harry P. Harrison and the staff of the Circulation Department at the Sterling Memorial Library at Yale, to Robert E. Balay and the staff of the Reference Department at Sterling Memorial Library, and to the staff of the Yale Anthropology Library for courteous and efficient assistance and many kindnesses throughout the period of research.

The compilation of this bibliography was financed in part by a grant (GN-35418) from the National Science Foundation to Frank W. Moore and Timothy J. O'Leary as co-principal investigators. Moore provided institutional coordination and general supervision of the project. O'Leary was responsible for the overall compilation and supervision of the project and for the final printed bibliography. He was very fortunate to be assisted in the compilation by John Beierle, Sarah T. Bridges, John B. Kirby, Jr., Joan Steffens, and Barbara A. Yanchek, all trained researchers with an interest in Native American studies. The data processing of the citations, i.e. the keypunching, proofreading, and editing, which for this bibliography proved to be a far more intellectually demanding task than had originally been envisioned, was very ably carried out by a team under the supervision of Joan Steffens, consisting of Ella Gibson and Lillian Ljungquist, with the assistance of Mary Elizabeth Johnson and Victoria Alexander. Frank W. Moore, who prepared and drew the maps for the 1960 edition, revised them where necessary for this edition.

Our very special thanks, finally, go to George Peter Murdock, who, while not actively engaged in the preparation of this edition of "his" bibliography, has constantly made his influence felt through the guidelines and the general level of excellence he established in the previous editions. While the current set of volumes may present a considerably altered face to the world, in its essentials it has followed the basic pattern of search, selection, and classification that was so ably established by him forty years ago. We certainly hope that he will look with favor on this edition of the bibliography.

Timothy J. O'Leary
New Haven, June 1975

Koh, Hesung C. HABS: a research tool for social science and area studies. Behavior Science Notes, 8(1973):169-199.

Preface to the Third Edition

[This preface is reprinted unchanged from the third edition (1960) in order to give the reader a brief historical background to the compilation of this bibliography. The reader should note that a number of basic changes have been made in the format of the bibliography, and therefore should not take as a guide to the new edition the statements contained in this Preface. The new format is described in the Introduction beginning on p. xi.   TOL]

Some thirty years ago the author began systematically to assemble bibliographical references on primitive and historical cultures with the object, partly of directing distributional and other studies in the classroom, partly of recommending library purchases, and partly of preparing for a projected study which later materialized as the Cross-Cultural Survey at the Institute of Human Relations.[1] By utilizing odd moments of time between appointments, useless for consistent research, to verify references in the Yale University Library, he was able over a period of years to prepare a classified worldwide ethnographic bibliography of considerable size.

This bibliography proved exceedingly useful, to the author and to others, in directing dissertations, making classroom assignments, surveying the existing literature preparatory to field work, and providing ready access to the relevant sources for topical and regional studies of all kinds. A considerable demand was expressed that at least the portion on aboriginal North America be made generally available by publication. The present work in its several editions represents a response to that demand.

The principle of classification by tribal groups having been adopted as the most serviceable to modern anthropologists, the first task was to determine the groups to be used. As a compromise between the segregation of all tribes bearing traditional names, which would have increased the bulk and cost of the work by necessitating frequent repetition of the same references for adjacent peoples, and a classification into a few large areal groups, which would have reduced the usefulness of the volume, it was decided to adopt as a norm the nationally self-conscious tribes of regions with some measure of political development, e.g., those of the Plains. For regions with less extensive political integration, groups of approximately the same degree of linguistic and cultural homogeneity were formed by arbitrarily uniting a number of tribelets or local groups, usually under the name of one of them. Thus under Snuqualmi were lumped the Salishan Dwamish, Nisqualli, Puyallup, Samamish, Skagit, Snohomish, Snuqualmi, and Squaxon of Puget Sound; under Massachuset, the Algonkian Massachuset, Nauset, Nipmuc, and Wampanoag of southeastern New England; and under Wailaki the Athapaskan Kato, Lassik, Mattole, Nongatl, Sinkyone, and Wailaki of Northwestern California. In this way, all of North America as far south as Tehuantepec was divided into 277 tribal groups, a manageable number.

The second task was to prepare a map showing the location of these groups. This was done in 1937 with the cooperation of the students in a graduate class in Systematic Ethnography. The map, which is appended to the present volume, shows, with approximate boundaries, the location of the various tribal groups as of the period of their first extensive contacts with Europeans.[2] It is thus not valid for any single period but represents a shifting date-line, which becomes later as one moves from south to north, from east to west, and from coast to interior. Since the locations of many tribes did not remain constant over three centuries, the shifting date-line made necessary a number of compromises in the fixing of boundaries. Careful mapping by a series of predecessors, notably Kroeber on California, Spier on the Plateau, Osgood on the Mackenzie-Yukon, and Sauer on Mexico, proved of invaluable assistance. Probably the least satisfactory area, because of severe early territorial dislocations, is the Midwest, despite aid generously given by the late Truman Michelson. It is gratifying to note the very high degree of correspondence between our map of North America and those prepared independently by Kroeber and by Driver, et al.[3]

In the selection of names for our 277 groups, established usage was followed in most instances. A few adjectival tribal names, e.g., Costanoan and Salinan, were changed to their nominal forms. Diacritical marks were eliminated. Where several well-known tribes were grouped together, the name of the most important or most familiar was usually given to the cluster. The only radical decision was with regard to names like Apache, Paiute, Shoshoni, and Sioux, which are ambiguous because applied, although commonly with qualifying adjectives, to several different tribal groups. Except in the case of the Eskimo, where it seemed impracticable, such names were either eliminated entirely or confined to a single group. In a few instances this has resulted in a certain arbitrariness in naming. Thus the traditional Coast Miwok have been called Olamentke, the Eastern Dakota are termed Santee, the Owens Valley Paiute of Steward have been grouped with their western congeners as Mono, the Western Apache are dubbed Coyotero, and the Western Shoshoni are named Panamint from their best known sub-group.

The preparation of the map prevented subsequent changes in our groupings, even when clearly advisable. Thus the Eyak, discovered by Birket-Smith and de Laguna, have been classed arbitrarily with the Ahtena (II-1) even though they deserve an independent classification.

The map does not divide the tribal groups into culture areas, but this has been done for the presentation of the bibliography. We have distinguished sixteen areas, adding Oregon Seaboard, Peninsula, Basin, Midwest, Eastern Canada, and Gulf to the ten proposed by Wissler.[4] The decision as to allocation has been close in several instances. Thus the Caddo might well have been placed in the Southeast instead of the Plains, the Klamath in the Plateau instead of in California, the Nanticoke in the Southeast rather than in the Northeast, the Sarsi in the Plains on the basis of culture instead of in the Mackenzie-Yukon on the basis of language, and the Seri in the Southwest rather than in the Peninsula. Mexico, an area embracing 24 tribal groups, though shown on the map, has not been included in the bibliography for the sole reason that pressure of other research has prevented the author from bringing this section of North America to a sufficient degree of completeness to justify publication at the present time. The bibliography therefore covers only 253 of the total of 277 tribal groups distinguished.

The work is organized by areas and within each area by tribal groups arranged in alphabetical order. Under the areal headings are included regional studies, geographical and historical sources, travel accounts, and other works presenting little specific original information on individual tribes. Under the tribal headings are included works pertaining directly to the particular group or its sub-groups. The order of arrangement of items under each heading is alphabetical by author's surname and thereunder by title. One exception is to be noted: standard monographs covering large segments of a tribal culture, or, in default thereof, other general works of considerable scope, are placed ahead of the alphabetical list of other sources. An appendix includes references to works on North America in general or on a number of areas; this list is very incomplete since no special effort was made to assemble such items.

To compress a classified bibliography on a whole continent into a single volume requires selectivity and compactness. The former has been achieved by including only such references as seemed likely to prove of value to an anthropologist desirous of discovering what is known about a particular culture. Works in which the tribe is barely mentioned or in which no new information of value is given have in general been excluded. Compactness has been sought through a standard system of abbreviating references. Space is saved by giving initials rather than full names of authors, by omitting unimportant information such as name of publisher, by using abbreviations for journals, series, and collections which recur frequently,[5] by omitting subtitles except when necessary to indicate the content of a work, and by shortening titles themselves wherever words or phrases could be deleted at the end of a title without loss of meaning or obscuring of content.

Pages have been indicated for all periodical items as a rough indication of quantity of material. For books, similarly, the number of volumes or of pages has been noted in most instances, although frequently the particular pages on which the most relevant information occurs are indicated instead. Diacritical marks are omitted except for a few standard accents. Within a serial volume, the number is noted only when it is separately paginated. Where the indicated date of a volume differs from its actual published date, the former is usually given preference. A few inconsistencies have arisen as a result of changes in the procedure of notation over a period of years. In the earlier years of compilation, for instance, the number of pages of single books was not noted, and the date of actual publication was preferred to the indicated date of a volume in a series. Since these inconsistencies did not seem serious, it was decided to ignore them rather than undertake the vast labor of checking back over all previous work.

Approximately seventy per cent of the works cited have been personally examined by the author, and most of the rest have similarly been seen by his assistants in the course of amassing the references. Perhaps five per cent of the references, including all those that are incomplete, have not been personally assessed—most of them works listed in other bibliographical sources but not available in the Yale University Library.

Effort has been exerted to make the tribal bibliographies as complete as possible on all ethnographical subjects. Works on physical anthropology and linguistics, and on archeology where pertinent to a known historical culture, have been listed whenever obtained in the search for ethnographic items, but no extended canvass for them has been made and the coverage of these subjects, particularly in regard to earlier works, remains incomplete. Complete runs of most of the serials listed in the Key to Abbreviations have been searched for pertinent materials. No consistent search, however, has been made of United States Congressional documents and series, and references to these appear in the Bibliography only when they were obtained incidentally in the search for ethnographic materials. The Bibliography is restricted to published materials, and no reference is made to unpublished manuscripts, dissertations, etc. For such materials, researchers should consult the standard reference works.[6]

In general, fugitive materials and items appearing in popular journals have not been included in this Bibliography, except in cases where they seemed to be of some importance. The cut-off date of this third edition was originally intended to be December, 1958, and the Bibliography is reasonably complete as of that date. However, an effort was made to include materials in the major anthropological journals and important books which have appeared since that time. Coverage of materials appearing in 1959 and early 1960 is, therefore, very incomplete.

Mistakes are inevitable in a work such as this. The frequent recopying incidental to compilation introduces typographical errors which escape even careful proofreading. Important references are overlooked, lost, or misjudged and excluded, and errors of allocation occur in areas with which the author is not especially familiar. The present volume pretends to be only so accurate as reasonable care and effort can make it.

Fortunately there is a remedy for errors and omissions. In future editions, corrections can be made, newly published titles added, overlooked sources noted, the Mexican area included, the general North American appendix expanded, and the archeological,

linguistic, and physical anthropological literature covered as exhaustively as the ethnographical. To accomplish really satisfactory revisions, the author must have the cooperation of his anthropological colleagues. He, therefore, requests that users of this work call his attention to errors and omissions in areas familiar to them.

The first edition of this Bibliography appeared in 1941 as Volume 1 of the Yale Anthropological Series. The second edition appeared in 1953 as a Behavior Science Bibliography published by the Human Relations Area Files. In terms of number of entries, the first edition had approximately 9,400 and the second edition about 12,700. The present edition contains more than 17,300 entries.

The author received valuable assistance from Donald Horton and Frederick W. Voget in the preparation of the first edition, and from Mrs. Allison Butler Matthews and John Musgrave in the preparation of the second edition. In regard to the present or third edition, he is indebted to many colleagues who have supplied new references, and especially to William C. Sturtevant of the Smithsonian Institution for generous advice and assistance. Its actual compilation is almost exclusively the product of the devoted effort of Timothy J. O'Leary.

Yale University
June, 1960   George Peter Murdock

NOTES

1 See G.P. Murdock, "The Cross-Cultural Survey," *American Sociological Review*, V (1940), 361-70.

2 Only 276 groups are actually located. The Seminole of the Southeast, having originated subsequent to intensive white contact, do not appear on the map.

3 See A.L. Kroeber, "Cultural and Natural Areas of Native North America," *University of California Publications in American Archaeology and Ethnology*, XXXVIII (1939), Map 1A; H.E. Driver, et al., "Indian Tribes of North America," *Memoirs of the International Journal of American Linguistics*, IX (1953), end map.

4 C. Wissler, *The American Indian* (2d edit., New York, 1931), p. 219.

5 A key to abbreviations, which precedes the text, presents the full titles and places of publication of these serial works.

6 E.G., F.J. Dockstader, "The American Indian in Graduate Studies; A Bibliography of Theses and Dissertations," CMAI, XV (1957), and W.N. Fenton et al., American Indian and White Relations to 1830, Chapel Hill, 1957.

General Introduction

Background

During the thirty-five years since the publication of the first edition in 1941, this bibliography has served as a standard reference work on the Native Peoples of North America — for the anthropologist in particular and, in general, for all those with a factual interest in learning about the ways of life of these peoples. The bibliography has continuously been expanded in its various editions, both in the types of information included and in the number of works cited, until this fourth edition is more than four times the size of the original. This growth reflects both an expansion of interest by writers and scholars in these peoples and an increase in the efficiency of the reference tools that attempt to control the literature on them.

This bibliography is a selected bibliography of published factual books and articles describing the cultures of the Native Peoples of North America. These peoples are considered to be the Eskimo of Greenland, northern Canada, Alaska, and eastern Siberia; and the Indians of Alaska, Canada, the United States, and Mexico north of the northern boundary of Mesoamerica (the area of "high cultures" in Mexico and Central America). It does not include citations to publications on immigrant ethnic groups settled in this area. For this reason, the title of the bibliography might more properly be reworded as an "Ethnographic Bibliography of the Native North Americans." However, as the present work has been known under its title for so many years, it will remain so in this edition.

The primary focus of the bibliography is on the ethnography of these peoples, i.e. on the description of their cultures and ways of life. The bibliography is restricted to citations of published books and articles. It does not contain references to unpublished manuscripts, to maps, or to sound recordings, films, or other audiovisual materials. An attempt will be made later on in this introduction to provide guidance for those who are interested in locating such materials. In spite of the extent of these volumes, this is a *selected* bibliography, more stringently so for the earlier materials. Many more citations were examined than are listed. Most of those dropped from consideration were peripheral to the scope of the bibliography or were ephemeral in nature (e.g. newspaper articles, broadsides, articles published in commercial house organs, etc.). The bibliography is limited to factual accounts; no fiction about these groups is knowingly listed, except in the very rare cases where experts have agreed that the fictionalized account was in accord with ethnographic fact. These few cases should be obvious on examination.

While the primary focus of the bibliography has remained ethnographic, other subject areas have gradually been added through the various editions until the present one tries to include references to published materials on all subjects relevant to the study of the Native Americans, such as history, psychology, and human biology and medicine, among others. Because of this expansion through the years, not all fields of interest are covered equally thoroughly. Basic ethnographic description remains the most completely covered field, followed by linguistics, by archeology, and then by history, relations of the ethnic groups with the federal governments, education, medicine, human geography, urbanism, and Pan-Indianism. It is to be hoped that eventually all of these subject fields will be covered to the same extent. However, the primary focus will still remain ethnographic description.

In the remainder of this introduction, we will discuss more extensively the subject, area, and ethnic group coverage of this edition; the new format of the bibliography; and the search plan used for its compilation. We will also attempt to provide introductory guides to the location of the types of materials not included in the bibliography, such as most government publications, manuscripts, maps, and audiovisual materials, and also to the use of the Educational Resources Information Center (ERIC). The ERIC will be discussed because of its function in making generally available the results of much research on the Native Americans. Finally, we will provide a brief general discussion of some of the tools used in keeping up with the new literature as it is published, and of going beyond this bibliography in search of older published works.

Coverage

The citations in this edition of the bibliography are restricted to published materials on the Native Peoples of North America issued up to and including the year 1972. It is intended that the bibliography be as exhaustive as possible of those materials which are considered to be of professional quality or which contain valuable data not otherwise available. An effort has been made to have the individual ethnic group bibliographies as complete as possible on the traditional ethnographic subjects. Works on physical anthropology, linguistics, and on archeology where pertinent to a known historical culture have been listed wherever possible. In the earlier editions, no special effort was made to include materials on ethnic history, psychology, education, and other fields peripheral to ethnography. However, for the compilation of this edition we have tried to include everything published during the period 1959-1972 that relates to Native American studies. This broadening of coverage helps to account for the radical increase in the size of the bibliography.

An attempt was made to cover publications in all Western languages, including the Slavic languages. Publications in non-Western languages, however, are covered very sparsely. On the whole, the literature in these latter languages is not very large, although there is a growing body of good ethnographic material in Japanese which has been almost completely missed, since there was no easy way for us to get at it. There may also be material of equal value in other literatures whose languages the compilers were not capable of handling. It is to be hoped that such materials can be included in future editions of this bibliography.

The total number of individual ethnic group bibliographies presented is now 269, compared to the 253 in the earlier editions. The new bibliographies are included so as to make the coverage of the total bibliography more congruent to that of the forthcoming *Handbook of North American Indians* (which will be discussed briefly at the end of the introduction). The additional bibliographies are on the Northern Métis, Red River Métis, Sioux (as a whole), Oklahoma Indians, Middle Atlantic States Mestizos, Lumbee, Southeastern Mestizos, Acaxee, Cazcan, Tepehaun, Totorame, Zacatec, Chichimec, Pame, Cora, and Huichol. They are not as full as those for other ethnic groups in the bibliography, for we did not have the time to make a thorough search of the earlier literature. However, we hope that we have included enough citations to make at least some research on these groups possible.

As in previous editions, no consistent search was made of United States, Canadian or Mexican government publications, and such materials are generally included only when they were obtained incidentally in the search for ethnographic materials. An exception was made for the various publications of the Smithsonian Institution, the Bureau of American Ethnology, and the National Museum of Canada. The field of government publication is the great gap in both this and other bibliographies on the Native Americans. From the sampling we have made during the compilation of this edition, we estimate that

the size of this bibliography would have been nearly doubled if a search of all relevant government publications could have been made and the citations included. However, these publications are generally poorly controlled bibliographically, and very difficult to locate in toto. For the convenience of the users of this bibliography who may want to do research in this field, a brief introduction to locating such publications is given later in the introduction.

It was hoped that citations to films, sound recordings, and maps relating to the Native Americans could be included in this edition, but because of the unexpectedly large amount of printed literature encountered, this part of the compilation process had to be abandoned—with reluctance. We have, however, included a brief discussion of sources of these types of materials.

Neither fugitive materials nor items appearing in popular journals have been included, except in cases where they seemed to be of some special importance. As far as possible, all materials listed in the bibliography have been seen by the compilers. In the case of those not seen, an effort was made to verify the citations by locating them in at least two independent indexing tools. For books and monographs not seen, the standard source for verification was the *National Union Catalog* in its various cumulations. (Unless noted otherwise, titles given in italics will be discussed later in this Introduction.)

Search Pattern

In compiling this edition of the bibliography, a standard search pattern was evolved and followed. Using as a base the list of periodicals in the 1960 edition, as well as lists found in several other bibliographical tools, such as the *International Bibliography of Social and Cultural Anthropology* and the *Social Sciences and Humanities Index*, a search was made of the holdings of periodicals, as well as books, contained in the Yale University library system. Yale University has one of the largest libraries in North America, and it possesses strong holdings in fields related to Native American studies. Searches were also made of several printed library catalogs for materials not encountered in the search of the Yale University Library. These included, among others, the *Library of Congress Catalog. Books: Subjects* for the period 1958-1973, the Harvard Peabody Museum Library catalog, the research catalog of the American Geographical Society, the catalog of the Edward E. Ayer collection of the Newberry Library in Chicago, and the catalog of the History of the Americas Collection of the New York Public Library. Also checked as sources of citations were continuing bibliographical serials, such as the *Arctic*

Bibliography, the *International Bibliography of Social and Cultural Anthropology*, the *Bibliographie Américaniste*, and the *Index to Literature on the American Indian*. A search for relevant citations in *Research in Education, Dissertation Abstracts International*, and the current indexes discussed later in this introduction was also made. Also used as sources of citations to be verified were bibliographies and references contributed by individual correspondents and bibliographies on specific groups, areas, or subjects that had been published during the period 1959-1972.

The citations found during the search were transferred to individual worksheets, verified where necessary, edited, and transferred to keypunched cards for computer manipulation. Approximately 14,000 worksheets were completed during the course of compilation, of which approximately 11,000 were finally utilized. The remainder were withheld for a number of reasons, the two basic ones being a lack of real relevance to the purpose of the bibliography and the presence of obvious inaccuracies that could not be rectified in time for inclusion. These additional worksheets will remain on file at the Human Relations Area Files for further reference and analysis, should this prove necessary. It is estimated that each of the citations included on the worksheets appears twice on the average as an entry in the bibliography (some of the citations contain material on more than twenty groups). This total, when added to the more than 17,000 entries in the 1960 edition, gives the estimated total of 40,000 entries in the present edition that is referred to in the Preface. (It should be noted that the general bibliographies for each of the fifteen culture areas appear twice, once in the general volume and once in a regional volume.) Thus, the present edition is more than twice the size of the 1960 edition.

Format

General Discussion

When preliminary estimates gave the figure of approximately 2,000 pages for the bibliographic entries alone, without introductory materials, maps, or ethnic group lists, it became obvious that the bibliography would have to appear as a multivolume publication. We decided that, while no specific division is ideal, a five-volume format should meet the requirements of most users. The first volume is a general volume, covering all of North America, while the others divide North America into four regional volumes that are approximately equal in size in terms of the number of bibliographical entries—except for the larger final volume, which includes entries on Areas 9 (Plains), 14 (Gulf), and 15 (Southwest).

The first volume includes the general sections from each of the fifteen major areas in the bibliography, which are equivalent to culture areas (e.g. Southwest, Plateau). Into each of these major area bibliographies we have integrated the individual monographs and articles that we feel give the best cultural descriptions of the individual ethnic groups covered in each of the areas. Also included as Area 16 is the bibliography on General North America, which appeared as an appendix in previous editions. This general bibliography now also includes individual bibliographies on Pan-Indianism, Urban Indians, United States Government Relations with the Native Peoples, Canadian Indians in General, and Canadian Government Relations with the Native Peoples. Since these bibliographies are new to this edition, they are not as complete retrospectively as the other bibliographies in the volume. Also included in the first volume are ethnic group maps for each of the areas and the general ethnic group listing that was used in compiling and classifying the bibliography. We hope that this volume can serve as a general introductory bibliography on North American Native Peoples for users who do not feel the need for the finer classifications and more exhaustive listings found in the regional volumes.

Within each of the other four regional volumes is a set of area bibliographies, including detailed bibliographies on individual ethnic groups within the areas, corresponding to the fifteen culture areas established by Murdock (see the Preface to the Third Edition, p. vii). Each of the regional volumes contains bibliographies on a set of contiguous culture areas, which combine to form a major area of North America. Thus, Volume 2, on the Arctic and Subarctic, contains bibliographies covering Area 1 (Arctic Coast), Area 2 (Mackenzie-Yukon), and Area 11 (Eastern Canada). Together, these cover a block of land which forms the northern part of North America. In similar fashion, Volume 3 covers the Far West and Pacific Coast; Volume 4, the eastern part of the United States; and Volume 5, the Plains and Southwest. (See the frontispiece maps and the schematic table of contents for more detailed contents of each volume.) As a result of this regional grouping of bibliographies, the order in which the bibliographies are presented in this edition does not always correspond to the way in which they were presented in earlier editions, but we do not believe that this arrangement will present any grave problems to the user.

The general culture classification closely follows that devised by Murdock for the previous editions. The major difference is that several ethnic group bibliographies have been added for groups or conglomerates of peoples not previously distinguished (e.g. Sioux, Oklahoma Indians, Southeastern Mestizos). In addition, several ethnic group bibliographies have been added to Area 15 (Southwest), so as to have the southern boundary of that area correspond more closely to that used in the *Handbook of North American Indians*. There is a sketch map for each of the fifteen areas, showing the general boundaries and location of groups for which bibliographies have been compiled. As in the previous editions, these maps show the location of the ethnic groups as of the period of their first extensive contacts with Europeans. Since, in addition to the Seminole listed in previous editions, a number of the groups added for this edition of the bibliography originated subsequent to the period of extensive European contact, they are not included on these maps. These ethnic groups are the Northern Métis, the Red River Métis, the Middle Atlantic States Mestizos, Lumbee, Southeastern Mestizos, and the general inclusive category of Oklahoma Indians. The Sioux and the Chichimec also are not located on the ethnic group maps, since the materials included in their respective bibliographies refer to a number of component groups scattered over a large area. An indication of their location is given in the relevant area introductions, however. These latter introductions provide a brief sketch of each area and some information on each of the peoples covered in the individual ethnic group bibliographies, including location, linguistic affiliations, and important monographs and bibliographies which have appeared since 1972, as they are known to the compilers.

In these regional volumes, each areal set of bibliographies contains first a general bibliography pertaining to the culture area as a whole. This general bibliography includes regional studies, general geographical and historical sources, travel accounts, and other materials not specific to any group within the area. The individual ethnic group bibliographies follow in alphabetical order by name of unit, except where new bibliographies have been added (e.g. Lumbee follows Yuchi in Area 13, Southeast). Within each individual bibliography, the entries are arranged in alphabetical order by author's name (surname first). Where an author has more than one entry following his name, they are arranged alphabetically by the first word in the title (*not* by date). Where there is more than one entry for an author, the author's full name is repeated for each entry. Within each individual ethnic group bibliography, any cited bibliography which pertains to that ethnic group has been placed at the beginning of the listing, separated from the main body of entries. In addition, a limited number of works which have been considered by Murdock and/or O'Leary to give a good, basic description of the culture have been asterisked

This separation of bibliographies from the main listing and asterisking of basic cultural descriptions represent major changes in format from previous editions. Formerly, works presenting basic cultural descriptions were placed at the head of each bibliography, and bibliographies as such were not given any special treatment. We have made these changes in the present edition because we felt that bibliographies are important resources, which warrant further checking, since they generally represent viewpoints and present materials not always agreed with or used by the present compilers. We admit that this viewpoint may be debatable, but feel that no essential information is lost, since the basic cultural descriptions are tagged by the asterisks.

So far as the basic cultural descriptions (now asterisked) are concerned, we should note that some reviewers of the previous editions misunderstood the reason for the separate placement, usually noting that "important" works have been separated from the remainder of the listing. That was not the point. While "standard monographs covering large segments of a tribal culture" are certainly important, there are numerous other works in the bibliography not so designated that are certainly "important" as well, but perhaps for different reasons. Examples of these would be Casagrande's "Comanche linguistic acculturation," Lounsbury's "A semantic analysis of the Pawnee kinship usage," and Mead's "The changing culture of an Indian tribe."

Each regional volume concludes with an ethnic group synonymy (or ethnonymy), which pertains to the groups covered in that volume. This ethnonymy is derived from the complete ethnonymy used in the compilation of the bibliography, which may be found in Volume 1. No attempt has been made to list the numerous variant and obsolete spellings for the names that are included. For fuller listings, see Hodge (1910) and Swanton (1952). At the end of each volume is a map of North America, showing the total ethnic group coverage of the complete bibliography.

Formats for Individual Citations

There is a considerable difference between the citation formats used for the third edition of the bibliography and those used for the present edition. In the third edition, because it was desirable to keep the bibliography to one volume, compactness of citation form was a great desideratum. Therefore, a standard system of abbreviating references was followed. Authors' given names were represented by initials; the names of book publishers were omitted; abbreviations were used for the titles of journals, series, and collections that recurred frequently; subtitles were generally omitted; and titles themselves were often shortened.

In this edition, both because it was obvious that it would be impossible to issue the bibliography as a single volume and also because of the impracticability of using the old system for a computerized bibliography, it was decided to present the citations with as full bibliographical information as it was possible to obtain. This meant that the citations in the third edition had to be expanded as fully as possible to correspond to the new citation formats. Since resources were not available for rechecking each of the 17,000 entries in the third edition and thereby making their formats completely consistent with that of the new citations, it was decided to make use only of the information already available. As a result, of the three major citation types in the third edition—i.e. book, book chapter, and journal article—the book citation format is almost identical in the third and fourth editions, while the others show varying amounts of expansion. The expansion has been accomplished mainly by replacing the abbreviations used in the third editon with fuller information. For instance, MA is now given as Minnesota Archaeologist, and MAH as Magazine of American History, etc. This simple replacement procedure does not, of course, take into account the name changes that many of the journals have gone through. However, library catalogs generally cross-reference these varying titles to each other, so we feel the user will not be greatly inconvenienced by this transformation.

As an illustration of the types of format changes that were involved for these citations from the third edition, we will give some examples of the same citations in the two formats. The third edition format will be presented first, then the expanded format for the same citation, as used in this edition.

Book.

>Dobbs, A. An Account of the Countries Adjoining to Hudson's Bay. 211 pp. London, 1744.

>Dobbs, A. An account of the countries adjoining to Hudson's Bay. London, 1744. 211 p.

Note how little the book citation format changed. The differences lie in the capitalization of words within the title, the use of the abbreviation 'p.' to indicate pages, and the moving of the page count to the end of the citation.

Journal article.

>Sapir, E. The Na-dene Languages. AA, n.s., XVII, 535-58. 1915.

>Sapir, Edward. The Na-dene languages. American Anthropologist, n.s., 17 (1915): 535-558.

Note how this citation format changes. Where we knew the first name of the author, it is now generally given in full. Only the first word and proper nouns are capitalized in the title. The name of the journal is written out in full; Roman numerals are changed to Arabic; pagination is given in full; and the year is enclosed within parentheses.

Chapter in a book.

>Service, E. R. The Canadian Eskimo. PPC, 64-85. 1958.

>Service, Elman R. The Canadian Eskimo. In his A Profile of Primitive Culture. New York, 1958: 64-85.

Again the author's full name is given. The title of the book from which the chapter is taken is spelled out, with all significant words having initial capitals, and being preceded by the underlined words "In his," which indicate that the author of the book was Service. The inclusive pagination is moved to the end of the citation.

Within the present volumes, two types of citation format are used in addition to the above. The first is restricted to this introduction. We have used this format, which includes the use of italics, because it provides a visual emphasis of the various titles that are being discussed in the introduction. This emphasis is not needed in the main body of new bibliographic citations in the remainder of the volumes, and, therefore, a different format has been used for these citations. While still fairly compact compared to many other citation styles, these latter formats are much expanded over those used in previous editions of the bibliography. In addition, a fourth citation format type, that for an article in the proceedings of a conference or a congress, has been added. These new individual formats are discussed in order below.

Citation format for books.

>Smith, G. Hubert. Like-a-Fishhook Village and Fort Berthold, Garrison Reservoir, North Dakota. Washington, D.C., National Park Service, 1972. 12, 196 p. illus., maps. (U.S., National Park Service, Anthropological Papers, 2)

This is an example of a monograph which was published as part of a series. The author's name comes first, with the surname and given names reveresed to facilitate alphabetizing. Following the name is the title, which ends with a period. After the title comes the imprint, which consists of the place of publication, the publisher, and the date of publication. Following the imprint comes the collation, which in our format includes the pagination (in this case including both introductory pages and the main body of text), the fact that the monograph is illustrated, and that it contains maps. The phrase within parentheses is the series statement. This indicates that the monograph was the second in the series called Anthropological Papers, which are issued by the U.S. National Park Service. Where applicable, the format may also contain information on the edition cited (if not the first edition by the publisher), on multiple authors, on editors, and on translators. Some other examples of this format are:

Moziño, Jose Mariano. Noticias de Nutka; an account of Nootka Sound in 1792. Translated and edited by Iris Higbie Wilson. Seattle, University of Washington Press, 1970. 54, 142 p. (American Ethnological Society, Monograph, 50)

Waddell, Jack O., ed. The American Indian in urban society. Edited by Jack O. Waddell and O. Michael Watson. Boston, Little, Brown, 1971. 14, 414 p.

Harkins, Arthur M., et al., comps. Modern Native Americans: a selective bibliography. Minneapolis, University of Minnesota, Training Center for Community Programs, 1971. 131 p. ERIC ED054890.

Note that in this last citation, three or more individuals were responsible for the compilation of the bibliography. Only the name of the first compiler (or author) is given, however, together with the phrase "et al." The example previous to this one shows the format for a case where there are two authors, editors, or compilers. Note that the name of the second individual is given, along with the first individual, in a statement following the title. The note ERIC ED054890 in the third citation indicates that the bibliography is also available from the Educational Resources Information Center (ERIC). This organization is discussed later in the introduction.

Citation format for journal articles.

Oswalt, Wendell H. The future of the Caribou Eskimo. By Wendell H. Oswalt and James W. VanStone. Anthropologica, n.s., 2 (1960): 154-176.

The author and title sections here are similar to those in the book citation format. However, in this example there are two authors. This is indicated by the statement following the title. Following this author

statement is the journal citation. It includes the name of the journal; the abbreviation "n.s.," which indicates that it is the new series of the journal which is being referred to; the volume number; the year, enclosed within parentheses, to which the volume number refers (1960), followed by a colon; and the inclusive pagination of the article in full (154-176), followed by a period. Another example of the format is:

Amoss, Pamela Thorsen. The persistence of aboriginal beliefs and practices among the Nooksack Coast Salish. Dissertation Abstracts International, 32 (1971/1972): 6174B. UM 72-15, 064.

The latter citation shows two variations. When the date to which a journal volume refers extends over two or more years, that fact is indicated by listing the beginning year and the ending year and placing a slash (/) between the two years. The note UM 72-15,064 indicates that this citation refers to a dissertation which is available from Xerox University Microfilms. These dissertations are discussed later in the introduction.

Citation format for chapters in books.

Stanton, Max E. A remnant Indian community: the Houma of southern Louisiana. In J. Kenneth Morland, ed. The Not So Solid South. Athens, Ga., Southern Anthropological Society, 1971: 82-92.

The author and title sections here are as in previous examples. Following the title is the name of the book in which the chapter may be found. This section begins with the word "In," underlined, followed by the name of the author(s) or editor(s) of the book, and the title of the book. Then comes the imprint information for the book (place of publication, publisher, and date of publication), followed by a colon, and then the inclusive pagination for the article within the book.

Citation format for articles in the proceedings of conferences or congresses.

Spicer, Edward H. Apuntes sobre el tipo de religión de los Yuto-Aztecas centrales. In Congreso Internacional de Americanistas, 35th. 1962, México. Actas y Memorias, 2. México, D. F., 1964: 27-38.

Rose, A. P. Can religion be treated as a branch of anthropology? In Pacific Science Congress of the Pacific Science Association, 9th. 1957, Bangkok. Proceedings, 3, Anthropology and Social Sciences. Bangkok, The Secretariat, Ninth Pacific Science Congress, 1963: 230-232.

Again, the author and the title are handled like those in the book citation format. Following the title here is the underlined word "In." After this comes the name of the conference or congress as it appears on the title page, and the number of the conference, if it occur regularly. Then comes the date on which the conference was held and the place where it was held. This is followed by the particular title of the volume (if it have one) and the volume number if applicable. Then comes the imprint for that volume, including the place of publication (which may be different from the place where the conference was held), the publisher (if different from the conference), and the date of publication. The date of publication is followed by a colon and then by the inclusive pagination of the article, and is closed by a period.

The preceding examples cover the basic types of the citation formats for the items included in this bibliography. There may be minor additions to the format which include further information, but these will not change the basic form. We believe that these formats are clear and easy to use. The major variation from the bibliographic style with which most researchers are probably familiar lies in the duplication of the author's name in a case where there are two authors. This is done in order to accord with the usual procedure librarians follow in making catalog cards. The book citation format closely follows that of the Library of Congress catalog cards, in order that users may quickly locate books in library catalogs.

Government Publications

As mentioned previously, no specific effort was made to locate and cite government publications. While it had been hoped at the beginning of the compilation process that we would be able to make a thorough search for materials of this type, it proved to be impossible to accomplish with the limited amount of time and other resources we had available. We certainly did not realize at the time the magnitude of the task, the general inaccessibility of these materials, and the great amount of specialized knowledge necessary to locate the materials. However, such publications have been included whenever we encountered them during the course of the compilation. We did, of course, include the standard publications and series relevant to the study of Native American peoples, such as the publications of the Bureau of American Ethnology. Because of their importance, however, we do want to indicate to the user of this bibliography at least how to start doing a bibliographic search for government materials on the Native Americans. Accordingly, we have prepared a brief listing and explanation of the major

reference tools for locating these publications. We will discuss the United States federal, state, and municipal publications first, and then the Canadian. We do not know enough about Mexican government publications to be able to include a discussion of them in this introduction.

The major reference tools for locating United States federal government publications are government publications themselves. They cover the period from 1774 to the present. Until the establishment of the Government Printing Office in 1861, government publications were printed by private contractors. There is still no complete listing of these publications. The closest one can get to such a complete listing is Poore's catalog, referenced as follows:

Poore, Benjamin Perley
　1885 *A descriptive catalogue of the government publications of the United States, September 5, 1775—March 4, 1881, compiled by order of Congress.* Washington, D.C., Government Printing Office. (U.S., 48th Congress, 2d Session, Senate, Miscellaneous Document, 67) [reprint edition available]

The citations in Poore are arranged chronologically by Congress (covering the 1st through the 46th Congresses), and within each Congress by title of the publication (not in any discernible order). There is a large index, with publications on Indians being listed on pages 1302-1304, and individual Indian tribes being listed alphabetically on pages 1303-1304. However, there is no listing on the Eskimo. References in the index are to pages in the body of the bibliography, and not to a specific citation. The approximately fifty items on each page must be scanned until the particular item wanted is found.

John G. Ames compiled an index to United States Government publications for the period 1881-1893, thereby taking up the task where Poore left off. The full citation is:

U.S. Superintendent of Documents
　1905 *Comprehensive index to the publications of the United States Government, 1881-1893.* By John G. Ames. Washington, D.C., Government Printing Office. 2v. (U.S., 58th Congress, 2d Session, House of Representatives, Document, 754) [reprint edition available]

This tool is a combined catalog and index. The index is a list of the documents arranged alphabetically by the key word in the title, e.g. "Indian women marrying white men, legislation prescribing citizenship in U.S. as effect of, recommended"/vol. 1, p. 677/. Eskimos are indexed on page 445 of vol. 1. Indians are indexed on pages 665-677 of vol. 1. An alphabetical list of tribal names appears on page 673 of vol. 1.

For most of the period from 1893 to the present, there are two reference tools that can be used. The first is the permanent and complete catalog of all United States government publications, usually known as the *Document Catalog*, from the binder's title on the spine of each volume. The full citation is:

U.S. Superintendent of Documents
1896- *Catalogue of the public documents of*
1945 *Congress and of all departments of the Government of the United States for the period March 4, 1893-[Dec. 31, 1940].* Washington, D.C., Government Printing Office. 25 v. (SuDocs no. GP3.6:) [reprint edition available]

This catalog provides approximately one volume for each Congress, from the 53d Congress to the 76th Congress, inclusive. It is a dictionary catalog, with the same document appearing under the author, the subject, and the title when necessary. The serial numbers for the documents themselves are usually included only with the main (author) entry. Superintendent of Documents classification numbers are sometimes given. An explanation of these numbers is given later in this section. The major key terms to be checked in each volume are Eskimo, Indian, Indians, and the names of individual tribes.

The second tool to be used for this period is the *Monthly Catalog of United States Government Publications*, which covers the period from 1895 to the present. The full citation is:

U.S. Superintendent of Documents
1895- *Monthly catalog of United States Government publications.* Washington, D.C., Government Printing Office. (SuDocs no. GP3.8:)

This catalog is supposed to be a current bibliography of all publications issued by all branches of the federal government. However, in practice it is essentially a list of all publications printed by the Government Printing Office, in addition to whatever materials the various government agencies send to the Superintendent of Documents. Since most agencies are not compelled to send their publications to the Superintendent of Documents (although they are supposed to), there are large gaps in the listing—one of the reasons why working with government publications can be so difficult. Publications are listed in each monthly issue, alphabetically by the name of the issuing office. Since 1945, there has been a monthly index, and there is an annual index. In 1974 a three-part index, consisting of author, title, and subject indexes, was begun. Again the

most used key terms are Eskimo, Indian, Indians, and the names of individual tribes. A major problem for most users of the index is that the indexing has been very erratic, and it is easy to miss key items. There is now available a cumulated subject index to the *Monthly Catalog* for the period 1900-1971. This is a great time-saver in making retrospective searches through the *Catalog*. The full citation is:

U.S. Superintendent of Documents
1974- *Cumulative subject index to the monthly*
1975 *catalog of United States Government publications, 1900-1971.* Compiled by William W. Buchanan and Edna M. Kanely. Washington, D.C., Carrollton Press. 14 v.

By using the above tools, one can get at least an idea of what has been issued on the Native Peoples in United States government publications. However, the hardest part of the search is actually locating copies of the needed publications. Since, so far as we know, there is no complete set of United States government publications existing anywhere, locating a needed publication can be a very long job for the individual researcher and for the government publications librarian who will have to assist him. A recent directory is certain to be of great assistance in this type of search since it lists more than 1,900 libraries in the United States with government document collections. The citation is:

American Library Association. Government Documents Round Table
1974 *Directory of government document collections & librarians.* Washington, D.C., Congressional Information Service.

For general information concerning the publications of the United States federal government, a good guide is:

Schmeckebier, Laurence F., and Roy B. Eastin
1969 *Government publications and their use.* 2d rev. ed. Washington, D.C., Brookings Institution.

While this is a very useful volume, it can only begin to give the researcher an idea of the complexity and volume of federal government publications. As noted above, most researchers in this field will become highly dependent on their local government publications librarian.

We mentioned Superintendent of Documents classification numbers previously. These refer to the codes of the Superintendent of Documents classification system, which is used in the Public Documents Library of the Government Printing Office. It is an unusual classification, in that its basis is the issuing agency for the individual publications, and not the subjects of the individual publications. An individual code consists of a combination of letters and numbers, which, taken together, are unique to a specific document. The letters, which precede the numbers, designate the issuing agency of the document. The numbers indicate the issuing office within the agency, the particular series of documents issued by that office, and the particular number of the document within that series. Thus GS stands for General Services Administration; HE for the Department of Health, Education, and Welfare; LC for Library of Congress; and Y for the publications of Congress. The SuDocs (the usual abbreviation for Superintendent of Documents) number S12.3:78, for example, is the number for *Bureau of American Ethnology Bulletin* 78 (Kroeber's *Handbook of the Indians of California*). The SI stands for Smithsonian Institution, and the 2 stands for the Bureau of American Ethnology within the Smithsonian Institution, or, alternatively, SI2 stands for Bureau of American Ethnology. The .3 indicates the third type of publication issued by the Bureau of American Ethnology, in this case the *Bulletin* (.1 would indicate the series *Annual Reports*). The colon indicates that the document represented by the number (or sometimes by a combination of letters and numbers) following is issued as part of the preceding series. In the SuDocs numbers given in this bibliography, where a reference is given to a complete series of publications, we have not indicated any number or code after the colon. since by including such a number or code we would be specifying a particular volume in the series. Thus, in the citation in the next paragraph, the SuDocs no. LC30.9: refers to the complete series titled *Monthly checklist of state publications*. If we do include a number or code after the colon, we are specifying a single publication; thus, SuDocs no. CR1.10:33 refers to the *American Indian civil rights handbook*, published in 1972. This is the general form that SuDocs numbers follow, with variations. Many collections of government publications are arranged according to this classification, and the numbers must be used when ordering publications from the Government Printing Office.

Moving from the federal level to the state and municipal levels, the situation immediately becomes much more difficult. There is only one general listing of state publications, which is issued by the Library of Congress. The full citation is:

U.S. Library of Congress. Exchange and Gift Division
   1910- *Monthly checklist of state publications*. Washington, D.C., Government Printing Office. (SuDocs no. LC 30.9:)
This listing is limited to publications received by

the Library of Congress. While the Library makes every effort to ensure that they receive everything, in the course of events this does not happen. Each monthly checklist is arranged alphabetically by states, territories, and insular possessions, with individual publications listed under each category. Each title is accompanied by the necessary cataloging information. The table of contents of an individual publication is sometimes listed, if it is a composite report. There is no monthly index, but there is an annual index published separately. The key terms again are Eskimo, Indian, Indians of North America, and the names of individual tribes.

This is the only recurrent general listing of state publications, and it is incomplete. There is also one general guide to state publications, which is now quite out of date. It may be of some use in the search of the earlier literature, however. The citation is:

Wilcox, Jerome Kear
   1940 *Manual on the use of state publications.* Chicago, American Library Association.

When we turn to municipal publications, the situation is almost hopeless so far as having any bibliographical control is concerned. There is only one recent general index or listing available, and it is, comparatively, quite limited in scope. The citation is:

Index to current Urban Documents
   1972- Westport, Conn., Greewood Press.

This index tries to make available complete and detailed descriptions of the majority of the known official documents issued annually by the largest cities and counties in the United States and Canada. In the 1974 volume, the publications of 173 cities and 26 counties of one million or more inhabitants in the United States (as determined from the 1970 Census), and 23 Canadian cities were surveyed. The two headings to be checked are Indians and Minority Groups. So far, very little has been indexed on the Native Americans.

Aside from the above, there is no general index or listing. Therefore, for each municipality one would have to check with the local library and the city or town hall and go through their holdings. Such a procedure could be very profitable in particular municipalities. Here, the individual researcher is completely on his own so far as this bibliography is concerned. concerned.

When we turn to Canada, we find most of the same problems as with United States government publications. The general bibliographical control of earlier publications is probably not quite as good. The one general guide that discusses publications issued between 1668 and 1935 contains a good index. The citation is:

Higgins, Marion Villiers
    1935 *Canadian government publications; a manual for librarians*. Chicago, American Library Association.

There is one official catalog series, which covers the period 1928 to the present. The citation is:

Canada. Department of Public Printing and Stationery
    1928- *Canadian Government publications: catalogue*. Ottawa. (formerly titled: *Catalogue of official publications of the Parliament and Government of Canada*)

The series is bilingual in English and French, and is now a monthly. It covers parliamentary publications and publications of federal agencies and departments. Key terms to check in the index are Eskimo, Esquimau, Indians, Indiens, and the names of various tribes.

Two other series also cover government publications and offer somewhat better indexing for our purposes. These are:

The Canadian Catalogue of Books Published in Canada, Books about Canada, as Well as Those Written by Canadians
    1921-Toronto, Department of Education of
    1951 Ontario, Public Libraries Branch.

Canadiana. Publications of Canadian Interest Received by the National Library of Canada.
    1950-Ottawa, Information Canada.

These are also bilingual publications, in French and English, and do a somewhat better job of indexing than the *Canadian Government Publications: Catalogue*. *Canadiana* has two sections which index federal and provincial publications. Part VII indexes publications of the government of Canada, and Part VIII indexes publications of the provincial governments of Canada. However, it indexes only those publications received by the National Library and is therefore incomplete.

There are a few catalogs which cover the publications of some of the Canadian provinces. These are:

Bishop, Olga Bernice
    1957 *Publications of the governments of Nova Scotia, Prince Edward Island, New Brunswick, 1758-1852*. Ottawa, National Library of Canada.

Holmes, Marjorie C.
    1950 *Publications of the government of British Columbia, 1871-1947*. Victoria, Provincial Library.

MacDonald, Christine
    1952 *Publications of the governments of the Northwest Territories, 1876-1905 and of the Province of Saskatchewan, 1905-1952*. Regina, Legislative Library.

Unfortunately, however, none of these guides is very helpful for obtaining citations about the Native Peoples of Canada. Beyond these listings, both on the provincial and on the municipal level, there is very little to consult, aside from the *Index to Current Urban Documents*, noted previously.

From the preceding discussion, it can be seen that a great need in the field of Native American studies is a comprehensive, well-indexed bibliography and guide to the government publications of the United States, Canada, and Mexico. To compile such a guide and bibliography would take a great deal in time, money, personnel, and dedication, but the result would well repay the effort involved. We do not see any possibility of such a guide's being published in the near future, however.

Finally, a recent publication provides an extensive sampling of various types of U.S. federal government documents relating to the North American Indian, including Reports of the U.S. Commissioner of Indian Affairs, congressional debates on Indian affairs, treaties, etc. This should give the researcher a good idea of the kind of information contained in these various types of publication. The citation is:

Washburn, Wilcomb E., comp.
    1973 *The American Indian and the United States; a documentary history*. New York, Random House. 4 v.

Indian Claims

Closely related to the preceding is a group of publications partly governmental and partly non-governmental in origin. These relate to the United States Indian Claims Commission and comprise its decisions, the reports of expert testimony before it, and the General Accounting Office reports on its awards. The Indian Claims Commission hears and determines claims against the United States on behalf of any Indian tribe, band, or other identifiable group of American Indians residing within the United States. The Commission was established by Act of Congress of August 13, 1946, and is independent of all other agencies of the U.S. government. A large number of claims has been adjudicated by the Commission since that time. In the course of adjudication, claims have been brought, the testimony of Indians and academic experts (e.g. anthropologists, historians, lawyers) heard, and decisions rendered. Naturally, since these claims involve American Indian groups, all of the information contained in these cases is properly the subject of this bibliography. Unfortunately, until very recently, this information has not been generally available. However, two private companies, both based in New York City, are now in the process of publishing most, if not all, of these data.

Garland Publishing, Inc. has organized reports of expert testimony and findings by tribe into 118 volumes, with the series entitled "American Indian Ethnohistory," being edited by David Agee Horr of Brandeis University. The Clearwater Publishing Company is making available on microfiche the decisions of the Commission and also the reports of expert testimony. Index volumes to each of the series are available in hard copy or on microfiche. The publishers also plan to make available on microfiche the General Accounting Office reports on awards. In additon, individual reports of expert testimony on hard copy (i.e. paper, not microfiche) are available on demand. In general, for information on the availability of all these material, it is a good idea to check the current *Subject Guide to Books in Print* under the heading Indians of North American—Indian Claims, or write the publishers. It might be noted that the total number of pages involved in these cases will probably exceed 150,000 (the equivalent of approximately 500 volumes containing 300 pages each). Having this vast amount of data available should have a great effect on studies of the North American Indian.

ERIC

ERIC (Educational Resources Information Center) is a nationwide, comprehensive information system under the jurisdiction of the Department of Health, Education, and Welfare, which is concerned with the transmittal of the results of research in education and related fields to the government, the public, the education profession, and to commercial and industrial organizations. A network of clearinghouses in different parts of the country under the general supervision of central ERIC in Washington gathers, organizes, indexes, and disseminates the most significant educational research or research-related documents that fall within their specialized subject areas. As part of its function, ERIC publishes the abstract journal *Resources in Education* (formerly *Research in Education*). This journal catalogs, abstracts, and indexes a large number of reports, both published and unpublished, every year. Many of these reports relate directly or indirectly to Native American studies. A very valuable feature of this journal is that nearly all of the items abstracted are available in a reproduced form on microfiche and/or paper copy. For the user, this means that many papers and fugitive documents, which would otherwise be extremely difficult to locate and ac-

quire, are now easily available. In the following bibliography, where it is known that ERIC has made the document available, we have included the ERIC accession number—which is needed for ordering the document—as part of the citation. This accession number appears at the end of the citation as a six-digit number, preceded by the acronym ERIC and the letters ED, e.g. ERIC ED045687. To order an ERIC document, follow the directions given below, which are taken from the May 1975 issue of *Resources in Education*. Since ERIC prices have changed in the past, it is best to check the most recent issue of *Resources in Education* to be certain of the price schedule, but the essentials are listed here. We have tried to be as accurate as possible in transferring the ERIC accession numbers in *Resources in Education* to the citations in this bibliography. However, it is probable that some errors in transcription have crept in during the process. Therefore, it would probably be safest if the user were to check the original abstracts in *Resources in Education* before ordering. The abstracts are listed in accession number order in the journal from 1966 on.

ORDERING ERIC DOCUMENTS

Mail orders to:
ERIC Document Reproduction Service
P.O. Box 190,
Arlington, Virginia 22210

Order by accession number (ED Number)
Specify microfiche (MF) or paper copy (HC)
Use the price schedule below.
Enclose check or money order PAYABLE TO EDRS
Official institution, State, Federal government purchase orders accepted.

MICROFICHE (MF)

Number of microfiche	Price
1 to 5	$ .75
6	.90
7	1.05
8	1.20
Each additional microfiche	.15

Postage: $.18 for up to 60 microfiche
$.08 for each additional 60 fiche

PAPER COPY (HC)

Number of pages	Price
1 to 25	$1.50
26 to 50	1.85
51 to 75	3.15
76 to 100	4.20
Each additional 25 pages	1.20

Postage: $.18 for first 100 pages
$.08 for each additional 100
pages

Note
1. Postage for first class airmail or foreign is extra.
2. Paper copy (HC) will be full page reproductions with heavy paper covers.

Theses and Dissertations

This bibliography classifies and lists published printed materials on Native American studies, but does not attempt to do the same for the many unpublished documents that are available. This is not to say, however, that such materials do not form an important adjunct to Native American studies — in fact, in the case of theses and dissertations, a vitally important one. Fortunately, we have two very useful aids for locating and making available theses and dissertations relating to our subject field. These are the two-volume bibliography compiled by the Dockstaders and the publications of Xerox University Microfilms.

The full citations for the Dockstader volumes are:

Dockstader, Frederick J., comp.
1973 *The American Indian in graduate studies; a bibliography of theses and dissertations.* 2d ed. New York, Museum of the American Indian, Heye Foundation. (Museum of the American Indian, Heye Foundation, Contributions, v. 25, pt. 1)

Dockstader, Frederick J., and Alice W. Dockstader, comps.
1974 *The American Indian in graduate studies; a bibliography of theses and dissertations.* New York, Museum of the American Indian, Heye Foundation. (Museum of the American Indian, Heye Foundation, Contributions, v. 25, pt. 2)

In spite of the title, theses and dissertations on the Eskimos are also included in this bibliography. The two volumes list 7,446 items, covering the period between 1890 and 1970, inclusive. It is well indexed (in part 2) and easy to use, and includes the addresses of the relevant institutions for borrowing purposes. This is the only reference tool that contains a comprehensive listing of master's theses relating to our subject. The listing of dissertations overlaps considerably that in the tools discussed immediately below, but it has the advantages of being specific to our subject and of being available in an easily usable, compact form.

Xerox University Microfilms (XUM) publishes two important aids, which together control the vast number of dissertations issued in the United States and Canada and several other countries as well. These are:

Dissertation Abstracts International
1935- Ann Arbor, Mich., Xerox University Microfilms. (formerly called *Microfilm Abstracts* and *Dissertation Abstracts*)

Comprehensive Dissertation Index, 1861-1972
1973- Ann Arbor, Mich., Xerox University Microfilms. 37 v. (annual cumulations are also issued)

Dissertation Abstracts International is a monthly compilation of abstracts of the doctoral dissertations that have been submitted to XUM by cooperating educational institutions, principally in the United States and Canada. It is, therefore, an incomplete listing, since some institutions do not require that dissertations be sent to XUM, and some institutions make copies of the dissertations available on their own. However, a tremendous number are abstracted and indexed. The journal is issued in two sections: Humanities (A) and Sciences (B), which are paginated separately. Key-word title indexes and author indexes are published in each issue. These monthly indexes are cumulated annually. Each of the sections (A) and (B) is divided into subsections by major academic discipline. Most of the dissertations relevant to Native American studies will be found in the subsections devoted to Anthropology, Education, Geography, and History. However, they are also found scattered through a range of other subsections as disparate as Home Economics and Geology.

A major problem in using *Dissertation Abstracts International* is that what must be used as a subject index is the key-word title index, in which the bibliographic entries are classified and arranged alphabetically by key words contained in the title only. In other words, if a title does not contain the key words Indian, Eskimo, Native American, or the name of a tribal group, the dissertation will not be found under any of these headings in the index. Thus it could be very easy to miss what might be a very important dissertation relating to a particular research subject. The same caution applies to the *Comprehensive Dissertation Index*, which will be discussed below. Because of this problem, the compilers of this edition of the bibliography, in addition to using the various indexes, also checked the abstracts on every page of the most relevant discipline subsections (Anthropology, History, Education, Geography, Geology, Home Economics, Psychology, Social Psychology, Sociology) for the years 1955 to 1972 inclusive in *Dissertation Abstracts International*. Through this procedure, we hope that we have been able to list most of the dissertations relevant to Native American studies. We have been so thorough because we believe that such dissertations contain much of the most important recent work in this field. The citations listed in our bibliography refer to the abstracts in the journal only, and not to the original dissertations. Our citations also include the XUM publication number, which will be found at the end of the citation, e.g. UM 61-23, 609. We have included the publication number, because each dissertation so designated is available from XUM either on microfilm or in Xerographic paper copy. The ordering information for such copies is as follows (information taken from the April 1975 issue of *Dissertation Abstracts International*):

1. Order by publication number and author's name and specify whether a positive microfilm copy or a bound Xerographic paper copy is wanted.

2. Send the order to Xerox University Microfilms, Dissertation Copies, Post Office Box 1764, Ann Arbor, Michigan 48106. The standard charge for any microfilmed dissertation is $5.00; for a Xerographic paper copy, $11.00. Shipping and handling charges and any applicable taxes are additional. Individuals must send checks or money orders with their orders.

While we have made every effort in the compilation of this bibliography to make sure that we have copied the XUM publication numbers correctly, ordinary caution dictates that the abstract itself be rechecked before ordering from XUM.

The *Comprehensive Dissertation Index 1861-1972* covers about 417,000 doctoral dissertations accepted by United States educational institutions and by some foreign universities. It is based both on entries from *Dissertation Abstracts International* and on local school handlists. The indexing system is similar to that in *Dissertation Abstracts International* and has the same inherent problem of the title key-word index. Under each key word, the titles are listed first by the date of the dissertation, with the most recent first, followed alphabetically by the name of the school, and then by the name of the author. This is the most comprehensive listing of dissertations available and is quite useful for that reason. The *Index* is supplemented by annual cumulations.

Manuscripts and Archives

Research with manuscripts and archives is a very special and complicated field, which is outside the scope of this bibliography. However, there is a great fund of information available in these resources, which can be very useful in some specialized studies. Since these types of materials cannot be discussed adequately in the space available here, we will simply list first a general work discussing research in archives, and then a few publications relating to archives and manuscript collections which contain material relevant to Native American studies.

Brooks, Philip Coolidge
   1969 *Research in archives; the use of unpublished primary sources*. Chicago, University of Chicago Press.

This is an introduction for the beginner, which concentrates on research procedures, with emphasis on American archives.

Beers, Henry Putney
   1957 *The French in North America; a bibliographical guide to French archives, reproductions, and research missions*. Baton Rouge, Louisiana State University Press.

   1964 *The French & British in the Old Northwest; a bibliographical guide to archive and manuscript sources*. Detroit, Wayne State University Press.

California. University. Bancroft Library
   1963 *A guide to the manuscript collections*. Edited by Dale L. Morgan and George P. Hammond. Berkeley, Published for the Bancroft Library by the University of California Press. v. 1.

Carnegie Institution, Washington
   1906- [*Guides to manuscript materials for the
   1943   history of the United States.*] Washington, D.C., The Institution. 23 v. (Reprinted in 1965. The title is a collective one, with individual titles varying considerably.)

Canada. Public Archives
   1968 *Union list of manuscripts in Canadian repositories*. Ottawa, Public Archives of Canada.

Fenton, William N., et al.
   1957 *American Indian and White relations to 1830: needs and opportunities for study*. Chapel Hill, University of North Carolina Press.

Fliegel, Carl John
    1970 *Index to the records of the Moravian Mission among the Indians of North America.* New Haven, Research Publications.

Freeman, John Frederick
    1966 *A guide to the manuscripts relating to the American Indian in the library of the American Philosophical Society.* Philadelphia, The Society. (American Philosophical Society, Memoir, 65)

National Union Catalog of Manuscript Collections
    1959- Hamden, Conn., Shoe String Press; Washington, D.C., Library of Congress. (SuDocs no. LC9.8:) (Still in progress; lists a very large number of collections, many relevant to Native American studies.)

Newberry Library, Chicago. Edward E. Ayer Collection
    1937 *A check list of manuscripts in the Edward E. Ayer collection.* Compiled by Ruth Lapham Butler. Chicago, The Library.

U.S. National Archives
    1972 *The American Indian. Select catalog of National Archives microfilm publications.* Washington, D.C., National Archives and Records Service. (U.S. National Archives, Publication 72-27) (SuDocs no. GS4. 2: In 2)

    1974 *Guide to the National Archives of the United States.* Washington, D.C., National Archives and Records Service. (SuDocs no. GS4.6/2:N21)

U.S National Historical Publications Commission
    1961 *A guide to archives and manuscripts in the United States.* Philip M. Hamer, ed. New Haven, Yale University Press. (A basic listing. Look under Indians, American.)

Yale University. Library. Yale University Collection of Western Americana
    1952 *A catalogue of the manuscripts in the Collection of Western Americana founded by William Robertson Coe, Yale University Library.* Compiled by Mary C. Withington. New Haven, Yale University Press.

In addition to the above, the archives catalog of numbered manuscripts of the National Anthropo-logical Archives at the Smithsonian Institution in Washington is scheduled for publication by G. K. Hall in Boston in 1975. The catalog will cover about a quarter of the total collection and will obviously be of great importance to researchers on the Native Americans.

Nonprint Materials and Maps

As noted previously, nonprint materials and maps have not been included in this bibliography. Because of their growing importance and widespread use, however, we will try to indicate in the following section the principal resources to use in locating relevant materials of these types. A general introductory work on reference tools in the audiovisual field is that by Limbacher, which annotates a number of the basic sources. Also basic is the Brigham Young University bibliography, which lists about 1,400 items, covering all types of nonprint instructional materials. The citations are:

Limbacher, James
    1972 *A reference guide to audiovisual information.* New York, R. R. Bowker.

Brigham Young University, Provo, Utah. Instructional Development Program
    1972 *Bibliography of nonprint instructional materials on the American Indian.* Provo, Institute of Indian Services and Research. ERIC ED070310.

The most complete general tools in this field are the *Library of Congress Catalog* and its continuation, the *National Union Catalog*, cited as:

U.S. Library of Congress
    1947- *Library of Congress catalog; a cumu-*
    1955 *lative list of works represented by Library of Congress printed cards. Books: authors.* Washington, D.C., The Library. (SuDocs no. LC30.8:)

National Union Catalog: A Cumulative Author List Representing Library of Congress Printed Cards and Some Titles Reported by Other American Libraries.
    1956- Washington, D.C., The Library. (SuDocs no. LC30.8:)

These two publications list a large number of sound recordings, films, and maps. Beginning in 1953, entries for *Maps and Atlases, Films and Filmstrips*, and *Music and Phonorecords* formed separate parts of the *Library of Congress Catalog*. In the *National Union Catalog, Films and Other Materials for Projection* (formerly *Motion Pictures and Filmstrips*) and *Music and Phonorecords* form separate parts of the catalog, but the section on maps and atlases does not. The *National Union Catalog* is issued monthly, with nine monthly issues and three quarterly cumulations each year, four annual cumulations, and a general cumulation every five years. These latter quinquennial cumulations have been issued for the years 1953-1957, 1958-1962, 1963-1967, and 1968-1972. The sections cited within these cumulations, with their individual subject indexes, form a great bibliographical resource for nonprint materials. The Library of Congress publishes a listing of the subject headings used in its dictionary catalogs and publications. Users of these publications should become familiar with these headings, since they facilitate use of the catalogs and indexes. These headings are discussed more fully on p. xxviii.

Since the above catalogs list only those materials received *and* cataloged by the Library of Congress and the cooperating libraries, the researcher must necessarily use other tools as well, if he wants his search to be as complete as possible. Therefore, we will go on to discuss other reference tools for locating relevant information on sound recordings, films, and maps, in that order.

Sound Recordings

As a brief introduction to the field, the user might want to consult the article by Highwater, which mentions some of the problems involved and the general types of recordings available:

Highwater, Jamake Mamake (J. Marks)
1973 American Indian music; a brief guide to the (recorded) real thing. *Stereo Review*, 30, no. 3: 134-135.

Two major reference tools may be used to keep up with sound recordings generally. The first is:

U.S. Library of Congress
1973- *Music, books on music and sound recordings*. Washington, D.C., The Library. (SuDocs no. LC30.8/6:)

This is a continuing and cumulative list of works that have been cataloged by the Library of Congress and by several North American libraries selected by the Music Library Association as representing a broad spectrum of music collections. It appears semiannually and is cumulated annually, and in the quinquennial cumulations of the *National Union Catalog* (noted above). Check the subject index under the usual Library of Congress subject headings.

The journal *Ethnomusicology*, published by the Society for Ethnomusicology, includes in each issue a current bibliography and discography of ethnic music, as well as reviews of selected sound recordings. Native American materials are listed in the

bibliography under "Americas-recordings."

The National Information Center for Educational Media (NICEM) publishes irregularly two indexes which indicate the availability of a number of specialized sound recordings. These are the *Index to Educational Audio Tapes* and the *Index to Educational Records*. The subject index in each should be checked under the headings Social Science-Indians of North America, Sociology-Anthropology, and History-U.S. The index entries refer back to the main listings, which include information on availability and contents.

For current information on commercially available phonograph recordings, check the semiannual *Schwann-2 Guide* under the heading Indian, American, in the section headed International Popular & Folk Music. The full citation is:

Schwann-2 Record & Tape Guide
1965- Boston, W. Schwann.

Three sources taken together list many of the earlier sound recordings relating to the Native Americans. These are:

International Folk Music Council
1954 *International catalogue of recorded folk music*. Edited by Norman Fraser. London, Published for UNESCO by Oxford University Press. (Archives de la Musique Enregistrée, Série C: Musique Ethnographique et Folklorique, 4)

Kunst, Jaap
1959, *Ethnomusicology, a study of its nature, its problems, methods and representative personalities to which is added a bibliography*. 3d enlarged edition, and supplement. The Hague, Martinus Nijhoff.

U.S. Library of Congress. Music Division
1964 *Folk music; a catalog of folk songs, ballads, dances, instrumental pieces, and folk tales of United States and Latin America on phonograph records*. Washington, D.C., The Library (SuDocs no. LC12.2:F71/3/964)

While the above tools will help the researcher locate information on particular recordings, he still has to find the recordings themselves. The Archive of Folk Song at the Library of Congress has quite a large collection of recordings of Native American music. In addition, the researcher should turn to the following publication, which lists 124 collections in the United States and Canada, most of which have holdings in the music of the Native Americans:

Society for Ethnomusicology
   1971 *Directory of ethnomusicological and sound recording collections in the U.S. and Canada.* Edited by Ann Briegleb. Ann Arbor, Mich., Society for Ethnomusicology. (Society for Ethnomusicology, Special Series, 2)

Films

A basic source of information on films is the Library of Congress publication, *Films and Other Materials for Projection*, whose subject index should be consulted under the usual Library of Congress subject headings. This continuing list of works cataloged by the Library of Congress appears quarterly and is cumulated annually and quinquennially, the latter as part of the *National Union Catalog*. The full citation is:

U.S. Library of Congress
   1953- *Films and other materials for projection.* Washington, D.C., The Library. (SuDocs no. LC30.8/4:) formerly titled *Motion Pictures and Filmstrips*)

There is quite a good listing of 251 "Educational films on the American Indian" compiled by George Hunt and Frank Lobo, on pages 718-744 of Owen et al.'s source book. This title list with annotations presents films available in 1965-1966 and is a good place to begin a search. The full citation is:

Owen, Roger C., et al.
   1967 *The North American Indians: a source book.* New York, Macmillan.

The National Information Center for Educational Media at the University of Southern California in Pasadena has published since 1969 a series of educational film indexes, which include much material relating to the Native Americans. These NICEM Media Indexes, which are revised at irregular intervals, are:

   Index to 16mm. educational films;
   Index to 35mm. educational filmstrips;
   Index to 8mm. motion cartridges;
   Index to educational overhead transparencies;
   Index to educational video tapes.

In the subject indexes, the primary heading to investigate is Social Sciences-Indians of North America. Other headings which should be checked are History-U.S. and Sociology-Anthropology.

In addition to the above, the American Anthropological Association publishes a selected catalog of ethnographic films for teaching purposes. The films are listed alphabetically by title. The listings include technical data, rental and purchase fees, a directory of distributors, a brief description of each film, and bibliographical and review data. Relevant films can be located under North America in the geographical index. The citation is:

Heider, Karl G.
   1972 *Films for anthropological teaching.* 5th ed. Washington, D.C., American Anthropological Association.

Maps

It is not easy to locate relevant maps for research purposes. Maps are included in the printed catalog of the Library of Congress, but except for a few years in the 1950s, they are not listed separately from books. As a result, trying to locate a map in the various card catalogs issued by the Library is a long and tedious process, and is not recommended. Among the many reference tools available, the following would probably be the more helpful to users of this bibliography.

The American Geographical Society has two publications, a retrospective catalog and a current list, which are good places to check for maps in this field. These are:

American Geographical Society of New York
   1938- *Current geographical publications; additions to the research catalogue of the American Geographical Society.* New York, The Society.

   1968, *Index to maps in books and period-*
   1971 *icals.* Boston, G. K. Hall. 10 v. plus one supplement.

The first lists selected maps received by the Society in a separate section in each issue, and is arranged by region and then by subject. Look under the human (cultural) geography numbers (5-57). The second is a bibliography of maps that have appeared in books or articles, not as separate publications. Check under Eskimos, Ethnography, Ethnology, Indians, and the names of various tribes.

Another general retrospective source is the card catalog of the Map Division of the New York Public Library, which has a very large collection. Check under Eskimos, Ethnology (with the names of tribes), and Indians. The citation is:

New York (City) Public Library. Research Libraries
   1971 *Dictionary catalog of the Map Division.* Boston, G. K. Hall. 10 v.

In additon to these American publications, there are two foreign-language current and comprehensive indexes available. These are the *Bibliographie Cartographique Internationale* (French) and *Referativnyi Zhurnal: Geografiia* (Russian), with the former probably being more accessible to American users. The citations are:

Bibliographie Cartographique Internationale
    1938- Paris, Armand Colin.

Referativnyi Zhurnal: Geografiia
    1954- Moskva, Akademiia Nauk SSSR, Institut Nauchnoi Informatsii.

In addition to the above, two other bibliographies may be useful for special purposes. These are:

Wheat, Carl Irving
    1957- *Mapping the Transmississippi West,*
    1963 *1540-1861.* San Francisco, Institute of Historical Cartography. 5 v. in 6.

Wheat, James Clements, and Christian F. Brun
    1969 *Maps and charts published in America before 1800; a bibliography.* New Haven, Yale University Press.

Beyond these, there are several lists and catalogs of individual collections which can be very helpful in locating individual maps. Especially to be noted are those in the National Archives, which contain basic data on Native American groups over a 200-year period.

California. University. Bancroft Library
    1964 *Index to printed maps.* Boston, G. K. Hall.

Newberry Library, Chicago. Edward E. Ayer Collection
    1927 *List of manuscript maps in the Edward E. Ayer collection.* Compiled by Clara A. Smith. Chicago, The Library.

U.S. Library of Congress. Map Division
    1909- *A list of geographical atlases in the*
    1973 *Library of Congress with bibliographical notes.* Compiled by Philip Lee Phillips and Clara Egli LeGear. Washington, D.C., Government Printing Office. 7 v. (in progress) (SuDocs no. LC5.2:G291/)

    1950- *United States atlases; a catalog of*
    1953 *national, state, county, city, and regional atlases in the Library of Congress and cooperating libraries.* Compiled by Clara Egli LeGear. Washington, D.C., Government Printing Office. 2 v. (SuDocs no. LC5.2:Un351/)

U.S. National Archives
    1954 *List of cartographic records of the Bureau of Indian Affairs (Record group 75).* Compiled by Laura E. Kelsay. Washington, D.C., National Archives. (U.S., National Archives, Publications, 55-1; Special Lists, 13) (SuDocs no. GS4.7:13)
    1971 *Guide to cartographic records in the National Archives.* Washington, D.C., National Archives and Records Service. (U.S., National Archives, Publications, 71-16) (SuDocs no. GS4.6/2:C24)
    1974 *Cartographic records in the National Archives of the United States relating to American Indians.* Washington, D.C., National Archives and Records Service. (SuDocs no. GS4.15:71)

In addition to the publications listed above, the reference tools listed in the section on government publications should also be checked, since the United States and Canadian governments publish many maps.

Going Beyond This Bibliography

While this bibliography is certainly a large one, it is still a *selected* bibliography, and it does not pretend to approach completeness on its subject, particularly for the earlier materials. Therefore, if completeness on a particular group or subject is desired, recourse must be made to a large variety of bibliographical reference tools, those used depending upon whether the researcher intend to make a complete retrospective search for all relevant published materials, or whether he/she be interested only in recently published items. If it be the latter, he/she will use recent issues of recurrent periodical and book indexes. If he/she be interested in a complete search, he/she will use these as well as numerous retrospective bibliographies and catalogs. The general approach to library research and use of these bibliographical tools is examined in a number of works. Reference can be made to those listed immediately below, and to the volumes by Freides and Katz listed later in this section.

Cook, Margaret G.
    1963 *The new library key.* 2d ed. New York, H. W. Wilson.

Downs, Robert B.
    1966 *How to do library research.* Urbana, University of Illinois Press.

Frantz, Charles
    1972 *The student anthropologist's handbook; a guide to research, training, and career.* Cambridge, Mass., Schenkman Publishing Company.

Fried, Morton H.

1972 *The study of anthropology.* New York, Thomas Y. Crowell Company.

Hook, Lucyle, and Mary V. Gaver

1969 *The research paper; gathering library material, organizing and preparing the manuscript.* 4th ed. Englewood Cliffs, N.J., Prentice-Hall.

Current Bibliographical Tools

Because this is a retrospective bibliography through the year 1972, and because a new edition is not scheduled to be compiled for several years, we have decided that a brief commentary on what we have found to be the more useful of the recurrent bibliographical tools for obtaining information about the Native Americans might be of benefit to the researcher. The following list of bibliographies and indexes is only a small part of the large number of reference tools that can be used for this type of search. All of those listed, except for the *Current Index to Journals on Education,* the *Social Sciences Index,* the *National Indian Law Library Catalogue,* and the *Internationale Bibliographie des Zeitschriftenliteratur aus allen Gebieten des Wissens,* were utilized in the preparation of the present bibliography. Perhaps the basic tools for anyone doing a bibliographic search of current materials on the Native Americans would be, in order of currentness: *American Book Publishing Record; Public Affairs Information Service Bulletin; Anthropological Index to Current Periodicals Received in the Library of the Royal Anthropological Institute; America: History and Life; Library of Congress Catalog. Books: Subjects; Subject Guide to Books in Print; Index to Literature on the American Indian; International Bibliography of Social and Cultural Anthropology;* and the *Bibliographie Américaniste.* Many of the indexes and bibliographies listed below are discussed in the general reference works, particularly those by Freides and Katz, to be mentioned later.

The indexes and bibliographies discussed below are subject indexed or classified in some way. The most commonly used subject headings are based on the system used by the Library of Congress. However, many indexes follow an arrangement based on the Dewey Decimal Classification. *Resources in Education* and *Current Index to Journals in Education* use a special set of descriptors listed in the *Thesaurus of ERIC Descriptors.* Those not using any of the above usually have their own special classifications and headings, with which the researcher should become familiar before using the indexes and bibliographies. The numerous indexes published by the

H. W. Wilson Company and the R. R. Bowker Company use subject headings based primarily on the Library of Congress list and on the Sears list (see below).

We list below the most relevant headings in each of the three major systems for ease in using the reference tools based on these systems.

Library of Congress Subject Headings:

Aleut
Beadwork
Eskimos
Folk-lore, Eskimo
Folk-lore, Indian
Hymns, [plus tribal name]
Indian Ponies
Indian Warfare
Indians
Indians of North America
Indians of North America as Soldiers
Indians, Civilization of
Moccasins
Numeration, Indian
Picture-writing, Indian
Wampum, Indian
Yuit Language

Dewey Decimal Classification:

016.9701 (bibliography on the American Indian)
497 (American aboriginal languages)
722.91 (architecture, ancient American)
784.751 (songs of Amerindians)
789.91364751 (recordings of Amerindian songs)
897 (literatures in American aboriginal languages)
917.1-917.98 (geography of North America)
970.1 (Indians of North America)
970.3 (specific Indian tribes)
970.4 (Indians in specific places in North America)
970.5 (government relations with Indians)

The terms "Amerindian" and "Indian" used here also include Eskimo.

ERIC Descriptors:

American Indian
American Indians
Bureau of Indian Affairs
Canadian Indians
Canadian Eskimos
Eskimo
Eskimos

The citations for the base documents for these headings are:

Dewey, Melvil
1971 *Decimal classification and relative index.* 18th ed. Lake Placid Club, N.Y., Forest Press, Inc., of Lake Placid Club Education Foundation. 3 v.

Sears, Minnie E.
1972 *Sears list of subject headings.* 10th ed. Edited by Barbara M. Westby. New York, H. W. Wilson.

U.S. Educational Resources Information Center
1974 *Thesaurus of ERIC descriptors.* 5th ed. New York, Macmillan Information.

U.S. Library of Congress. Subject Cataloging Division
1966 *Subject headings used in the dictionary catalogs of the Library of Congress.* 7th ed. Edited by Marguerite V. Quattlebaum. Washington, D.C., The Library. (SuDocs no. LC26.7:7)

The following list of recurrent indexes and bibliographies is divided into several sections, with comments on general reference tools being followed by comments on reference tools in several subject fields. We have indicated in these listings whether the reference tool uses the Library of Congress subject headings (alone or in conjunction with the Sears headings), the Dewey Decimal Classification, or the ERIC Descriptors, by placing the label [LC], [DDC], or [ERIC], respectively, after the title.

Books.

American Book Publishing Record [DDC]
1961- New York, R. R. Bowker.

Canadiana [DDC]
1951- Ottawa, Information Canada.

Bibliografía Mexicana
1967- México, D. F., Biblioteca Nacional de México, Instituto de Investgaciones Bibliográficas.

U.S. Library of Congress [LC]
1950- *Library of Congress catalog. Books: subjects. A cumulated list of works represented by Library of Congress printed cards.* Washington, D.C., The Library. (SuDocs no. LC30.8/3:)

Cumulative Book Index [LC]
1898- New York, H. W. Wilson.

Subject Guide to Forthcoming Books
1967- New York, R. R. Bowker.

These six tools are grouped together because they appear a varying number of times each year. The *American Book Publishing Record* appears monthly, and is cumulated annually and quinquennially in *BPR Cumulative* (not discussed here). It lists books by United States publishers only, but includes some foreign works handled by these publishers. Book titles are classified by subject, with an author and title index. *Canadiana* appears monthly, with annual cumulations. It is concerned with books, pamphlets, and periodicals (but not articles) of Canadian interest. It is a classified list of catalog cards, and has French- and English-language indexes. *Bibliografía Mexicana* appears bimonthly in a classified arrangement with an author-title subject index in the individual issues. It is not cumulated, and refers only to Mexican book publications. Basic headings to check are etnología, costumbres, folclore, and arqueología. The *Library of Congress Catalog. Books: Subjects* appears in three quarterly issues, with annual and quinquennial cumulations. It is international in scope and covers books cataloged during a specified period. Thus it is a retrospective tool as well. The *Cumulative Book Index* is a monthly, with quarterly and annual cumulations. It includes most books published in the English language and is not limited to American publications. The *Subject Guide to Forthcoming Books* appears bimonthly and lists books by American publishers due to appear in the near future. Headings to check are History-U.S. and Sociology, Anthropology, and Archeology-Anthropology.

Subject Guide to Books in Print [LC]
1957- New York, R. R. Bowker.

Subject Guide to Microforms in Print
1962/63- Washington, D.C., Microcard Editions.

These two annual guides provide subject approaches for determining the availability for purchase of in-print books and microforms, respectively. The first is based on *Books in Print*, which provides an author-title approach to currently available United States publications. The *Books in Print Supplement*, an annual that was first issued in 1973, provides an author-title-subject approach to the books published since the last annual issue of *Books in Print*. Thus it also supplements the *Subject Guide to Books in Print*. The *Subject Guide to Microforms in Print* is a classified list of available microfilm, microcards, and microfiche books. Relevant items can be located under 440 (America-General) and 970 (Languages and Literatures-Non-European). These guides are restricted to publications available in the United States.

Articles.

   Reader's Guide to Periodical Literature [LC]
       1905-   New York, H. W. Wilson.

   Canadian Periodical Index
       1948-   Ottawa, Canadian Library Association.

   Essay and General Literature Index [LC]
       1900-   New York, H. W. Wilson.

   Internationale Bibliographie des Zeitschriften-
       literatur aus allen Gebieten des Wissens
       1965-   Osnabrück, Felix Dietrich.

These four tools are concerned with indexing journal articles, together with essays and book chapters
forming parts of collected works. The *Reader's
Guide to Periodical Literature* appears semimonthly,
with quarterly, annual, and biennial cumulations. It
covers about 160 magazines of broad, general, and
popular interest published in the United States. The
Canadian Periodical Index is a monthly subject index
to about 90 general magazines published in Canada
and is approximately equivalent in aims and type
of coverage to the *Reader's Guide to Periodical
Literature*. The *Essay and General Literature Index*
analyzes essays and articles in volumes of English-
language collections of essays and miscellaneous
works written by individual authors in all fields of
the humanities and the social sciences. Individual
chapters are listed by author and subject. Since very
few indexes cover the contents of such collections,
this is the only relatively easy way to get at this
type of material. The *Internationale Bibliographie . . .*
is an attempt at a world periodical index, with more
than 7,500 periodicals being consulted. Headings to
check in the "Schlagwort" index are Eskimo, Eskimo-
ische, Indianer, and Indianische.

Books and articles combined.

   Arctic Institute of North America
       1953-   *Arctic bibliography*. Washington, D.C.,
               and Montreal. (SuDocs no. D1.22:)

   Bibliographie Américaniste
       1914/19-   Paris, Société des Américanistes.

   Vertical File Index [LC]
       1932/34-   New York, H. W. Wilson.

   Index to Literature on the American Indian
       1972-   San Francisco, Indian Historian Press.
               (Covers the literature from 1970 on.)

These four tools index a combination of materials.
The *Arctic Bibliography* appears irregularly and ap-
parently will cease publication in the near future. It
covers and abstracts published materials in all lan-

guages relating to the Arctic, and thus contains
citations relating to Alaska, Greenland, and most of
Canada and eastern Siberia. It is one of the best
available bibliographies in terms of completeness,
coverage, and indexing. The index should be consulted under Aleuts, Eskimos, and Indians. The *Bibliographie Américaniste* appeared annually as part of
the *Journal de la Société des Américanistes* through
vol. 53 (1964), and as a separate publication there-
after. It is classified by major subjects (archéologie,
ethnologie, etc.) and within the major subjects by
major areas (Amérique du Nord, etc.). It is very
good for non-English-language materials, but lags
greatly in publication. The *Vertical File Index* covers
separate publications that are fewer that 49 pages in
length and not usually picked up by the book and
article indexes. It occasionally includes publications
of much greater length. It appears monthly, with
annual cumulations. The *Index to Literature on the
American Indian* is an annual compilation by a group
of Native American scholars which covers both Eskimo and Indian English-language materials. About
150 periodicals are searched and relevant books
listed, usually under a variety of subject categories.
This index, while not pretending to completeness, is
a good place to begin a bibliographic search, because
of its indexing and the completeness of its citations.
Special features of its 1970 and 1971 volumes were
long lists of Native American periodicals, with ordering information. This is a good place to see what was
happening in this special field at that time.

Social Sciences.

   Public Affairs Information Service
       1915-   *Bulletin*. New York, The Service.

   Social Sciences Index [LC]
       1974-   New York, H. W. Wilson.

   Both of these items are general social science indexes, with the first probably being the more useful
at present. The *Public Affairs Information Service
Bulletin*, usually known as *PAIS*, is a weekly index
which is cumulated five times a year and annually.
It is a selected subject index to more than 1,000
periodicals, as well as to some of the books and U.S.
government publications that fall within this very
broad field. Limited to works written in the English
language, its coverage is international. Headings to
check are Eskimos, Indians, and United States-Indian
Affairs Bureau. The Service also publishes a bulletin
surveying foreign-language materials, but it rarely
includes any material on Native Americans in it. The
Social Sciences Index replaced the *Social Sciences
and Humanities Index* in 1974. A quarterly, with
annual cumulations, it indexes 263 of the more
scholarly English and American journals in the social

sciences.

Anthropology.

> Royal Anthropological Institute of Great Britain and Ireland. Library
> 1963- *Anthropological index to current periodicals received in the library of the Royal Anthropological Institute.* London, The Institute.
>
> *International Bibliography of Social and Cultural Anthropology*
> 1955- London, Tavistock; Chicago, Aldine.

These tools cover the general anthropological literature. The *Anthropological Index* appears quarterly, has a worldwide coverage, and indexes about 500 periodicals in all fields of anthropology. Each issue classifies the articles listed by major world areas, and then by broad subject categories (archeology, cultural anthropology, etc.). The key section to check is America. The *International Bibliography of Social and Cultural Anthropology* appears annually and covers the anthropological publications issued during the listed year. Each volume appears two to three years after the listed date, which is understandable, considering its extensive coverage of books and articles in all languages. The citations are arranged in a unique classification scheme, with an author index and subject indexes in English and in French. Subject entry is therefore possible, and at times necessary, in three ways, through the classification and through both indexes, since the latter do not always jibe with each other.

History.

> *America: History and Life*
> 1964- Santa Barbara, Calif., American Bibliographic Center-Clio Press.
>
> *Writings on American History*
> 1906- New York, etc.
>
> *Revue d'Histoire de l'Amérique Française*
> 1947- *Bibliographie d'histoire de l'Amérique française.* Montréal, Institut d'Histoire de l'Amérique Française.

Each of these tools contains numerous citations on the Native Peoples. *America: History and Life* is a quarterly abstract journal of United States and Canadian publications. Originally indexing only periodical literature, it began in 1974 to appear in three parts, A—article abstracts and citations; B—Index to book reviews; and C — American history index (books, articles, and dissertations). Subject headings to check are Eskimos, Indians, and the names of tribes. A cumulation of annotated entries on the

American Indian for the period 1954-1972, totaling 1,687 items, was issued in 1974. The citation is:

> Smith, Dwight L., ed.
> 1974 *Indians of the United States and Canada; a bibliography.* Santa Barbara, Calif., ABC-Clio.

Writings on American History is an annual that has appeared irregularly and has ceased publication at various times in the past. The time lag between date of coverage and publication is now about fifteen years, but efforts are being made to catch up. Attempting a complete listing, it has a very thorough coverage of American publications. Check under Indians in the index. The *Bibliographie d'Histoire de l'Amérique Française* appears quarterly in the *Revue* . . . . Publications on Native America are covered in Section A. 1 ("Les civilisations amérindiennes et les premières découvertes"). The area coverage is limited to French America, but includes many books, articles, and theses that are hard to locate elsewhere.

Other Subjects.

> *Ethnomusicology*
> 1953- *Current bibliography and discography.* Ann Arbor, Mich., Society for Ethnomusicology.
>
> *Music Index*
> 1949- Detroit, Information Coordinators.

These list publications on Native American music. The *Current Bibliography* . . . appears three times a year in the journal *Ethnomusicology*. See the section labeled "Americas." The *Music Index* is a monthly, cumulated annually, giving subject and author entry to about 180 periodicals on music. Check the headings Eskimo Music; Indian, American; Indian Music, American; and Indian Music, North American.

> American Geographical Society of New York
> 1938- *Current geographical publications.* New York, The Society.

This monthly is a classified listing of books, periodical articles, and maps received in the library of the Society. It is arranged by region, then by the Society's subject classification. Check North America and then the codes 5-57 for human (cultural) geography.

> *Art Index* [LC]
> 1929- New York, H. W. Wilson.

This is a quarterly, with annual cumulations. It has a dictionary catalog arrangement and lists materials on many subjects related to the field of art, including, among others, archeology, arts and crafts, art history, and fine arts.

Current Index to Journals in Education [ERIC]
   1969- New York, Macmillan Information.

Education Index [LC]
   1929- New York, H. W. Wilson.

Resources in Education [ERIC]
   1966- Washington, D.C., U.S. Office of Education. (SuDocs no. HE18.10:)

The *Current Index to Journals in Education* (known also as *CIJE*) is a monthly index, cumulated annually, of about 700 United States and foreign education journals, which are scanned, briefly abstracted, and indexed by ERIC descriptors. The *Education Index* is a monthly, cumulated annually, subject index to 200 English-language education journals. There is some, but not a great deal of, overlap with *CIJE*. *Resources in Education* (formerly *Research in Education*) is a monthly listing of abstracts of research reports selected by ERIC clearinghouses and is indexed by ERIC descriptors.

Index Medicus
   1960- Washington, D.C., National Library of Medicine. (SuDocs no. HE20.3612:)

Biological Abstracts
   1926- Philadelphia.

Psychological Abstracts
   1927- Washington, D.C., American Psychological Association.

The *Index Medicus* (cumulated annually by the *Cumulated Index Medicus*, which is not discussed here) is a monthly subject index to the world's medical and medical-related periodical literature. It surveys several thousand periodicals in all languages, with over 200,000 articles being indexed each year. It is a basic index for human biology. It has its own list of subject headings, which is printed as part of each January issue. The two headings to check are Eskimos and Indians, North American. *Biological Abstracts* is a semimonthly abstract journal, covering more than 5,000 periodicals, which has a computer-produced index based on all significant words in the titles and the abstracts. It complements *Index Medicus* for human biology and related fields. *Psychological Abstracts* is a monthly abstract journal of periodical articles and books, with semiannual and annual subject indexes. Relevant citations will generally be found under Ethnology in the index, although this has varied in the past.

Business Periodicals Index [LC]
   1958- New York, H. W. Wilson.

Index to Legal Periodicals [LC]
   1909- New York, H. W. Wilson.

National Indian Law Library
   1973/74- *Catalogue*. Boulder, Colo.

Modern Language Association of America
   1921- *MLA international bibliography of books and articles on the modern languages and literatures*. New York, The Association.

Bibliographie Linguistique de l'Année . . .
   1949- Utrecht, Spectrum, for Comité International Permanent de Linguistique.

Business Periodicals Index is a monthly, cumulated annually, subject index to about 120 business periodicals, most of them not covered by other indexes. The *Index to Legal Periodicals* is a quarterly subject index to about 300 English-language legal periodicals, mainly university law reviews and bar association journals. Many articles are listed on Indian claims and general government relations. The *National Indian Law Library Catalogue* is a new annual index to Indian legal materials and resources. It has not yet been seen by the compilers. The *MLA International Bibliography* . . . is an annual bibliography in four volumes, which are bound together in the library edition. Volume 1 covers folklore, and Volume 3, linguistics. Each contains materials relating to the Native Americans in a classified arrangement, but the indexes are difficult to use. The *Bibliographie Linguistique* . . . is an annual bibliography containing a section on American languages [Langues américaines], with an author index. In spite of the publication lag of about three years, it is probably the first choice for information on Native American languages.

Retrospective Bibliographical Tools

Since this bibliography itself is a retrospective bibliography, and since the major tools for making retrospective searches are to be discussed comprehensively in the forthcoming introductory volume of the *Handbook of North American Indians*, the use of these tools will not be further dicussed here. However, we will list some references which will enable the researcher to make a beginning in this direction. In addition, the bibliographies listed in the area and ethnic bibliographies in the present set of volumes should be perused for additional materials, since not all of the citations contained in them have been utilized in the present bibliography.

Freides, Thelma K.
   1973 *Literature and bibliography of the social sciences*. Los Angeles, Melville Publishing Company.
Katz, William A.
   1974 *Introduction to reference work*. 2d ed. New York, McGraw-Hill Book Company. 2 v.

McInnis, Raymond G., and James W. Scott
    1975   *Social science research handbook.*
           New York, Harper and Row, Barnes
           and Noble Books.

Walford, Arthur J., ed.
    1973   *Guide to reference materials.* 3d ed.
           London, Library Association. 3 v.

White, Carl M., and associates
    1973   *Sources of information in the social
           sciences; a guide to the literature.* 2d
           ed. Chicago, American Library Associ-
           ation.

Winchell, Constance M., ed.
    1967   *Guide to reference books.* 8th ed.
           Chicago, American Library Associ-
           ation. (Three supplements compiled by
           Eugene P. Sheehy covering the years
           1965 through 1970 have also been is-
           sued.)

Winchell and Walford are standard general guides to the reference literature, Winchell with an American and Walford with a European slant. The annotations of reference works in Winchell are more descriptive, while those in Walford are more critical. White and associates discuss social science materials in general and include separate chapters on history, geography, economics and business administration, sociology, anthropology, psychology, education, and political science. Each chapter contains two sections, one a bibliographical essay concentrating on the history of the subject, trends, areas of concern, and important works; the other a guide to the literature, annotating various types of information sources, such as abstracts and summaries, current and retrospective bibliographies, directories and biographical information, and sources of current information. The McInnis and Scott handbook is a bibliographical guide for students and others engaged in social science research. It is in two parts, one devoted to studies by discipline (anthropology, sociology, etc.), the other to area studies. Its orientation is toward the immediate assistance of students engaged in research, while that of White and associates is toward the scrutiny of the general social science information system and the evaluation of its major products. These four works together provide a general characterization of the tools available for bibliographical research, from which the researcher wishing to proceed further in his search for materials on the Native Americans may select the particular tools relevant to his needs. The remaining two works, by Katz and Freides, contain assessments of the general reference and social science literature and information from the librarian's point of view on how to proceed in library research. They form quite a useful adjunct to the detailed guides listed previously.

There remains the problem of actually locating copies of the chosen books and articles, once citations to them have been found. Procedures for doing this at the local library level are given in the guides cited at the beginning of this section (e.g. Cook 1963, Hook and Gaver 1969). If the materials not be in the local library, recourse may be made to the interlibrary loan system, the use of which can be arranged for by the librarian. Locations of library holdings of individual books in the United States and Canada are given in the *National Union Catalog,* while the locations of libraries that contain holdings of particular periodicals are given in the *Union List of Serials* and in *New Serial Titles,* cited below. A good aid for locating libraries with substantial holdings in the field is Ash's guide to subject collections, which lists numerous collections under the two headings: Eskimos and Indians of North America.

Ash, Lee, with the assistance of William Miller and
           Alfred Waltermire, Jr.
    1974   *Subject collections; a guide to special
           book collections and subject emphases
           as reported by university, college, pub-
           lic, and special libraries and museums
           in the United States and Canada.* 4th
           ed. New York, R. R. Bowker.

New Serial Titles
    1950- Washington, D.C., Library of Con-
           gress. (8 issues a year, cumulated
           quarterly and annually) (SuDocs no.
           LC1.23/5:)

New Serial Titles 1950-1970
    1972   New York, R. R. Bowker. 5 v. (cum-
           ulates the preceding)

*Union List of Serials in Libraries of the United
           States and Canada*
    1965   3d ed. Edited by Edna Brown Titus.
           New York, H. W. Wilson. 5 v.

Handbook of North American Indians

Mention has been made a number of times in this introduction of the forthcoming *Handbook of North American Indians.* The *Handbook,* which is under the general editorship of William C. Sturtevant, is scheduled to be issued in 20 large volumes by the Smithsonian Institution Press beginning in 1976. This mammoth enterprise will summarize what is known of the anthropology and history of the Native Americans north of Mesoamerica. It should remain the standard reference work in the field for many years. As of this date, there has been only one generally available published description concerning the *Handbook,* its structure and contents. This is:

Sturtevant, William C.
  1971 Smithsonian plans new Native American handbook. *Indian Historian 4, no. 4:* 5-8.

As noted previously, this edition of the bibliography has been enlarged and generally organized to cover as much as possible the same groups as are discussed in the *Handbook*. However, the fit between them is not particularly close at times, because of the different classificatory systems and emphases of the two works. We should point out that the articles in the *Handbook* will complement this bibliography very directly, in that much of the literature is given a critical discussion in these articles. In addition, the articles themselves will provide extensive bibliographies on the ethnic groups and subject fields discussed. Since the individual bibliographies will have been prepared by experts on these groups and fields, it is inevitable that there will be much in them which is not to be found in this bibliography. Of course, the converse will also be the case. Therefore, it will behoove the conscientious investigator to peruse both the present bibliography and those in the *Handbook* articles, in order to be certain that he/she has defined the general bibliographical parameters of the ethnic groups and subjects that he/she is studying.

Timothy J. O'Leary
June 1975

REFERENCES

Hodge, Frederick Webb, ed.
  1910 *Handbook of American Indians north of Mexico. Pt. 2.* Washington, D.C., Government Printing Office. (U.S., Bureau of American Ethnology, Bulletin, 30, pt. 2) (SuDocs no. SI2.3:30/pt.2)

Swanton, John R.
  1952 *The Indian tribes of North America.* Washington, D.C., Government Printing Office. (U.S., Bureau of American Ethnology, Bulletin, 145) (SuDocs no. SI2.3:145)

Abbreviations

A.D.	Anno Domini	n.p.	no place of publication
Alta.	Alberta	n.s.	new series
app.	appendix	N.Y.	New York
Apr.	April	no.	number
assoc.	association	Nov.	November
B.C.	British Columbia; Before Christ	Nr.	Nummer (number, in German)
Bd.	Band (volume in German)	o.s.	old series
ca.	circum, circa	Oct.	October
Calif.	California	Ont.	Ontario
Co.	Company	Or.	Oregon
col.	column(s)	p.	page, pages
Colo.	Colorado	pt.	part
comp.	compiler(s)	rev.	revised
Conn.	Connecticut	S.D.	South Dakota
D.C.	District of Columbia	Sask.	Saskatchewan
D.F.	Distrito Federal	sec.	section
Dec.	December	Sept.	September
dept.	department	SSSR	Soiuz Sovetskikh Sotsialisticheskikh Respublik (Union of Soviet Socialist Republics)
ed.	editor; edited; edition		
enl.	enlarged	SuDocs	Superintendent of Documents (see discussion on pp. xii-xix)
ERIC	Educational Resources Information Center (see discussion on pp. xxi-xxii)		
		suppl.	supplement
et al.	et alii (and others)	t.	tome (volume, in French)
fasc.	fascicle	tr.	translator; translated; translations
Feb.	February	UM	University Microfilms (see discussion on p. xxii-xxiii)
illus.	illustration(s); illustrated		
Jan.	January	U.S.	United States
Jr.	Junior	v.	volume, volumes
jt.	joint	Vt.	Vermont
Ky.	Kentucky	1st	first
l.	leaves (i.e. pages printed on one side only)	2d	second
		3d	third
Mar.	March	4th	fourth
Mass.	Massachusetts		
Me.	Maine		
mimeo.	mimeographed		
ms., mss.	manuscript, manuscripts		
n.d.	no date of publication		
n.F.	neue Folge (new series, in German)		

It should also be noted that underlining has been used in the citations to indicate that letters or numbers are superscript letters or numbers. Thus, "blood group antigen Di^{a}" is given as "blood group antigen Dia" in the listing.

10 Midwest

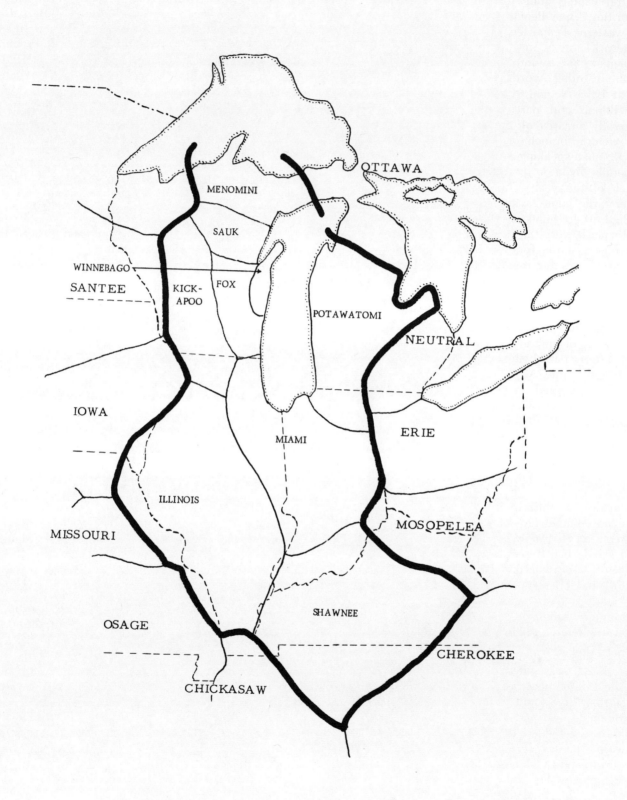

10 Midwest

This area covers the general region of the north-central United States east of the Mississippi River from the Upper Peninsula of Michigan on the north to western Tennessee on the south, eastward to eastern Kentucky, and north along the general Ohio-Indiana boundary into the Lower Peninsula of Michigan. In other words, it is the southern Upper Great Lakes region, together with the drainages of the Illinois and part of the Ohio River. This is generally an area of groups speaking languages of the Central branch of Algonquian, in addition to the Siouan-speaking Winnebago. These groups generally lived in permanent villages and farmed much of the year. They also hunted buffalo and other large game, with many groups having large-scale buffalo hunts in the autumn. Maize, beans, and squash were the principal crops, with wild rice forming a staple food in the northwestern part of the area. Around the Great Lakes, fishing was as important as hunting in the subsistence pattern. Government was generally by a weak village system, with separate civil and war leaders and with village councils. Throughout the historic period there was a great deal of migration in the area, with much of the eastern part being almost unoccupied a good deal of the time. Most of the aboriginal population has been resettled on reservations outside this area, with a group of Kickapoo now living in northern Mexico. Because of these movements, the aboriginal cultures are not well known, and much of the literature consists of historical reconstructions and conjecture, particularly for the southern groups.

10-01. Fox. The Fox (Meskwaki, Mesquakie, Outagami, Red Earth People) lived in the vicinity of Lake Winnebago and the Fox River in eastern Wisconsin. They now live in three areas: on the Sac and Fox Indian Reservation in Tama, Iowa; in Kansas and Nebraska (the Sac and Fox Tribe of Missouri); and on the former Sac and Fox Indian Reservation in east-central Oklahoma. They speak an Algonquian language and, together with the Sauk, they numbered 2,182 in 1970.

10-02. Illinois. The Illinois, including the Cahokia, Kaskaskia, Mascouten, Michigamea, Moingwena, Peoria (Mascouten), and Tamaroa, lived principally along the Illinois and Mississippi Rivers in the states of Illinois, Iowa, and Missouri. The remnants of the Illinois, together with the Wea and Piankashaw, now live on the former Peoria Indian Reservation in northeastern Oklahoma. They spoke an Algonquian language. The Peoria numbered about 400 in 1970, but this total also includes Wea and Piankashaw.

10-03. Kickapoo. The Kickapoo lived in central and southern Wisconsin and northwestern Illinois. They now live on the Kickapoo Indian Reservation in northeastern Kansas, the former Kickapoo Indian Reservation in central Oklahoma, and a reservation in eastern Coahuila, Mexico. They speak an Algonquian language and numbered 1,249 in the United States in 1970, with probably another 500 in Mexico.

10-04. Menomini. The Menomini (Menominee) lived on and near the Menominee River in northeastern Wisconsin. Most of them now live on the former Menominee Indian Reservation in northeastern Wisconsin. They speak an Algonquian language and numbered 4,307 in 1970.

10-05. Miami. The Miami (Twightwees, Meearmeear) lived principally in Indiana and eastern Illinois, but also at earlier times lived in southeastern Wisconsin and southwestern Michigan. Most of the remnants of the group now live (with the Illinois) on the former Peoria Indian Reservation in Oklahoma, with a few still living in the vicinity of Peru, Indiana. They spoke an Algonquian language and numbered 1,090 in 1970.

10-06. Potawatomi. The Potawatomi (Fire Nation) lived on the Lower Peninsula of Michigan and in northeastern Indiana. They now live on a number of reservations, including the Parry Island Reserve in Ontario, the Potawatomi Indian Reservation in Wisconsin, several small reservations in Michigan, the Potawatomi of the Huron and Pogagon Communities in Michigan, the Potawatomi Indian Reservation in northeastern Kansas, and the former Potawatomi and Shawnee Indian Reservation in Oklahoma. A few live with the Mexican Kickapoo in Coahuila, Mexico. They speak and Algonquian language. The Canadian Potawatomi numbered 833 in 1967, and the United States Potawatomi numbered 4,626 in 1970.
4,626 in 1970.

10-07. Sauk. The Sauk (Sac) lived on the upper part of Green Bay and the lower Fox River in northeastern Wisconsin, but were found over a large part of eastern Wisconsin and northwestern Illinois during the historic period. Most of the Sauk now live with the Fox on the Sac and Fox Indian Reservation in Tama, Iowa; the Sac and Fox Tribe of Missouri (living in Kansas and Nebraska); and the former Sac and Fox Indian Reservation in east-central Oklahoma. They speak an Algonquian language and, together with the Fox, numbered 2,182 in 1970.

10-08. Shawnee. The Shawnee lived in the southeastern part of this area in Kentucky and eastern

Tennessee, with settlements being known in Pennsylvania, West Virginia, Ohio, Kansas, Illinois, Maryland, South Carolina, and Georgia. Most of the Shawnee are now living on the former Potawatomi and Shawnee Indian Reservation in central Oklahoma. They speak an Algonquian language and numbered 2,208 in 1970.

10-09. Winnebago. The Winnebago (Hotcangara) lived on the south side of Green Bay, extending inland to Lake Winnebago in northeastern Wisconsin. They now live on the Winnebago Indian Reservation in west-central Wisconsin and on the Winnebago Indian Reservation in northeastern Nebraska. They speak a Siouan language related to Iowa-Oto and numbered 2,832 in 1970.

10-00 Midwest Area Bibliography

Pilling, J. C. Bibliography of the
Algonquian languages. U.S. Bureau of
American Ethnology, Bulletin, 13 (1891):
1-614.

Alberts, R. C. Trade silver and Indian
silver work in the Great Lakes region.
Wisconsin Archeologist, 34 (1953): 1-
121.

Aller, W. F. Aboriginal food utilization
of vegetation by the Indians of the
Great Lakes region as recorded in the
Jesuit Relations. West Virginia
Archaeologist, 35, no. 3 (1954): 59-73.

Anderson, David D. The battle of Fort
Stephenson: the beginning of the end of
the War of 1812 in the Northwest.
Northwest Ohio Quarterly, 33
(1960/1961): 81-90.

Anonymous. Trading on the Missouri and
Upper Mississippi--1831. Museum of the
Fur Trade Quarterly, 2, no. 2 (1966): 7-
10.

Anonymous. Wisconsin Indian state
legislation 1955-1965. Wisconsin Indians
Research Institute, Journal, 2, no. 2
(1966): 68-72.

Anson, Bert. Chief Francis Lafontaine and
the Miami emigration from Indiana.
Indiana Magazine of History, 60 (1964):
241-268.

Antes, John M. A supportive learning
environment. Journal of American Indian
Education, 11, no. 2 (1971/1972): 5-12.

Atwater, C. Remarks made on a tour to
Prairie du Chien. Columbus, 1831.
296 p.

Baerreis, D. A. Trade silver and Indian
silversmiths. Wisconsin Magazine of
History, 34 (1950): 76-82.

Barnhart, John D. Indiana to 1816. The
colonial period. By John D. Barnhart and
Dorothy L. Riker. Indianapolis, Indiana
Historical Bureau and Indiana Historical
Society, 1971. 16, 520 p. illus.,
maps.

Bauman, R. F., ed. The last gathering
under the old council elm. Northwest
Ohio Quarterly, 29 (1957): 145-160.

Bauman, R. F., ed. The removal of Indians
from the Maumee Valley. Northwest Ohio
Quarterly, 30 (1958): 10-25.

Bauman, Robert F. The Ottawa trading
system. Northwest Ohio Quarterly, 36
(1964): 60-78, 146-167.

Beardsley, G. The groundnut as used by
the Indians of eastern North America.
Michigan Academy of Science, Arts and
Letters, Papers, 25, no. 4 (1939): 507-
515.

Beatty, C. The journal of a two-months
tour. London, 1768. 110 p.

Beauchamp, W. M. Indian nations of the
Great Lakes. American Antiquarian and
Oriental Journal, 17 (1895): 321-325.

Beckner, L. The moundbuilders. Filson
Club History Quarterly, 29 (1955): 203-
225.

Birket-Smith, K. A geographic study of
the early history of the Algonquian
Indians. Internationales Archiv für
Ethnographie, 24 (1918): 174-222.

Bloomfield, L. Proto-Algonquian -i·t-
'fellow'. Language, 17 (1941): 292-297.

Braasch, W. F., et al. Survey of medical
care among the Upper Midwest Indians.
American Medical Association, Journal,
139 (1949): 220-225.

Brose, David S. The direct historic
approach to Michigan archaeology.
Ethnohistory, 18 (1971): 51-61.

Brown, C. E. Indian village and camp
sites on the Lower Rock River in
Wisconsin. Wisconsin Archeologist, n.s.,
9 (1929): 7-93.

Brown, C. E. The native copper implements
of Wisconsin. Wisconsin Archeologist, 3
(1904): 49-85.

Brown, C. E. The native copper ornaments
of Wisconsin. Wisconsin Archeologist, 3
(1904): 101-121.

Brown, C. E. The use of earthenware
vessels by the Old Northwest Indians.
Wisconsin Archeologist, n.s., 8 (1929):
69-75.

Brown, C. E. Winabozho. Madison, 1944.
7 p.

Brown, Dorothy M. Indian legends of
historic and sceneic Wisconsin.
Madison, 1969. 69 p.

Brown, Dorothy M. Wisconsin Indian place-
name legends. Madison, 1948. 30 p.

Brown, L. A. Early maps of the Ohio
valley. Pittsburgh, 1960.

Burgess, Charles E.   John Rice Jones,
citizen of many territories. Illinois
State Historical Society, Journal, 61
(1968): 58-82.

Burgess, Charles E.   The De Soto myth in
Missouri. Missouri Historical Society,
Bulletin, 24 (1967/1968): 303-325.

Bushnell, D. I.   Native cemeteries and
forms of burial east of the Mississippi.
U.S. Bureau of American Ethnology,
Bulletin, 71 (1920): 1-160.

Bushnell, D. I.   Native villages and
village sites east of the Mississippi.
U.S. Bureau of American Ethnology,
Bulletin, 69 (1919): 1-111.

Byers, D. S.   The environment of the
Northeast. Robert S. Peabody Foundation
for Archaeology, Papers, 3 (1946): 3-32.

Callender, Charles.   Social organization
of the Central Algonkian Indians.
Milwaukee, 1962.   13, 140 p.   illus.,
maps.   (Milwaukee, Public Museum,
Publications in Anthropology, 7)

Carr, L.   The mounds of the Mississippi
Valley. Smithsonian Institution, Annual
Reports of the Board of Regents (1891):
503-599.

Cartlidge, Anna M.   Colonel John Floyd:
reluctant adventurer. Kentucky
Historical Society, Register, 66 (1968):
317-366.

Carver, J.   Travels through the interior
parts of North America. 2d ed.   London,
1779.

Case, Thomas R.   The battle of Fallen
Timbers. Northwest Ohio Quarterly, 35
(1962/1963): 54-68.

Cass, Lewis.   A memorandum of Lewis Cass:
concerning a system for the regulation
of Indian affairs. Edited by Francis
Paul Prucha and Donald F. Carmony.
Wisconsin Magazine of History, 52
(1968/1969): 35-50.

Chamberlain, L. S.   Plants used by the
Indians of eastern North America.
American Naturalist, 35 (1901): 1-10.

Chambliss, C. E.   The botany and history
of Zizania aquatica L. ("wild rice").
Washington Academy of Sciences, Journal,
30 (1940): 185-205.

Charlevoix, P. F. X. de.   Histoire de la
Nouvelle France.   Paris, 1894.   3 v.

Charlevoix, P. F. X. de.   History and
general description of New France. Ed.

by J. M. Shea.   New York, 1866-1872.
6 v.

Charlevoix, P. F. X. de.   Journal of a
voyage to North America. Ed. by L. P.
Kellogg.   Chicago, 1923.   2 v.

Charlevoix, Pierre F. X. de.   Journal of a
voyage to North America.   Ann Arbor,
University Microfilms, 1966.   2 v.

Clarke, P. D.   Origin and traditional
history of the Wyandotts.   Toronto,
1870.   158 p.

Connelly, Thomas L.   Gateway to Kentucky:
the Wilderness Road, 1748-1792. Kentucky
Historical Society, Register, 59 (1961):
109-132.

Conway, Thomas G.   Potawatomi politics.
Illinois State Historical Society,
Journal, 65 (1972): 395-418.

Cope, Alfred.   A mission to the Menominee:
Alfred Cope's Green Bay diary. Edited by
William Converse Haygood. Wisconsin
Magazine of History, 49 (1965/1966):
302-323; 50 (1966/1967): 18-43, 120-144,
211-241.

Covington, J. W.   The Indian liquor trade
at Peoria, 1824. Illinois State
Historical Society, Journal, 46 (1953):
142-150.

Danziger, Edmund J., Jr.   Civil War
problems in the Central and Dakota
Superintendencies: a case study.
Nebraska History, 51 (1970): 411-424.

Deuel, T.   American Indian ways of life.
Illinois State Museum, Story of Illinois
Series, 9 (1958): 1-76.

Deuel, T.   Basic cultures of the
Mississippi Valley. American
Anthropologist, n.s., 37 (1935): 429-
445.

Dewdney, Selwyn H.   Indian rock paintings
of the Great Lakes. 2d ed. By Selwyn
Dewdney and Kenneth E. Kidd.   Toronto,
Published for the Quetico Foundation by
University of Toronto Press, 1967.   10,
191 p.   illus.   (Quetico Foundation
Series, 4)

Dixon, R. B.   The mythology of the Central
and Eastern Algonkins. Journal of
American Folklore, 22 (1909): 1-9.

Douglas, F. H.   Tribes of the Great Lakes
region. Denver Art Museum, Indian
Leaflet Series, 81 (1937): 121-124.

Dräger, Lothar.   Formen der lokalen
Organisation bei den Stämmen der
Zentral-Algonkin von der Zeit ihrer

Entdeckung bis zur Gegenwart. Eine ethnohistorische Studie. Berlin, Akademie-Verlag, 1968. 161 p. maps. (Leipzig, Museum für Völkerkunde, Veröffentlichungen, 18)

Dräger, Lothar. Formen der lokalen Organisation bei den Stämmen der Zentral-Algonkin von der Zeit ihrer Entdeckung bis zur Gegenwart. Ethnographisch-Archäologische Zeitschrift, 10 (1969): 387-396.

Edmunds, R. David. The Illinois River Potawatomi in the War of 1812. Illinois State Historical Society, Journal, 62 (1969): 341-362.

Essington, J. H. Early inhabitants of the Ohio Valley. West Virginia History, 13 (1952): 277-285.

Faben, W. W. Indians of the tri-state area; the Miamis 1654-1752. Northwest Ohio Quarterly, 41 (1968/1969): 157-162.

Filson, John. The discovery and settlement of Kentucke. Ann Arbor, University Microfilms, 1966. 118 p. map.

Filson, John. The discovery, settlement, and present State of Kentucke. New York, Corinth Books, 1962. 9, 118 p. maps.

Fisher, M. W. The mythology of the Northern and Northeastern Algonkians in reference to Algonkian mythology as a whole. Robert S. Peabody Foundation for Archaeology, Papers, 3 (1946): 226-262.

Fitting, James E. Late prehistoric settlement patterns in the Upper Great Lakes. Ethnohistory, 16 (1969): 289-302.

Ford, J. A. and G. R. Willey. An interpretation of the prehistory of the Eastern United States. American Anthropologist, n.s., 43 (1941): 325-363.

Foreman, G. The last trek of the Indians, 18-88, 159-181, 229-236. Chicago, 1946.

Forsyth, Thomas. Thomas Forsyth to William Clark, St. Louis, December 23, 1812. Edited by Dorothy Libby. Ethnohistory, 8 (1961): 179-195.

Fortier, John. A historical reexamination of Juchereau's Illinois tannery. By John Fortier and Donald Chaput. Illinois State Historical Society, Journal, 62 (1969): 385-406.

Frémont, D. Les aborigènes du nord-ouest canadien au temps de La Vérendrye.

Société Royale du Canada, Mémoires, 43, 3e sér., Sect. 1 (1949): 7-21.

Geary, J. A. Algonquian nasaump and napõpi. Language, 21 (1945): 40-45.

Geary, J. A. Proto-Algonquian *çk. Language, 17 (1941): 304-310.

Geary, J. A. The Proto-Algonquian form for 'I-thee'. Language, 19 (1943): 147-151.

Gerwing, Anselm J. The Chicago Indian Treaty of 1833. Illinois State Historical Society, Journal, 57 (1964): 117-142.

Gifford, Jack Jule. The Northwest Indian War, 1784-1795. Dissertation Abstracts, 24 (1963/1964): 5356. UM 64-6383.

Gille, J. Der Mamabozho-Flutzyklus der Nord-, Nordost-, und Zentral-Algonkin. Göttingen, 1939. 86 p.

Gille, J. Zur Lexikologie des Alt-Algonkin. Zeitschrift für Ethnologie, 71 (1939): 71-86.

Gilman, Rhoda R. Last days of the Upper Mississippi fur trade. Minnesota History, 42 (1970/1971): 123-140.

Glazier, Willard. Down the great river. Edited by William J. Petersen. Palimpsest, 51 (1970): 355-417.

Goddard, Ives. The Eastern Algonquian intrusive nasal. International Journal of American Linguistics, 31 (1965): 206-220.

Governor's Commission on Human Rights. Handbook on Wisconsin Indians. Madison, 1952.

Greenman, Emerson F. The Indians of Michigan. Lansing, Michigan Historical Commission, 1961. 46 p. illus.

Greenman, Emerson F. The Indians of Michigan. Michigan History, 45 (1961): 1-33.

Haas, Mary R. Notes on some PCA stems in /k-/. International Journal of American Linguistics, 24 (1958): 241-245.

Haeger, John D. The American Fur Company and the Chicago of 1812-1835. Illinois State Historical Society, Journal, 61 (1968): 117-139.

Hamilton, Raphael N. Marquette's explorations: the narratives reexamined. Madison, University of Wisconsin Press, 1970. 15, 275 p.

Hanna, Charles A.   The wilderness trail.
New York, AMS Press, 1972. 2 v. illus.

Hanzeli, Victor Eugen.   Early descriptions
by French missionaries of Algonquian and
Iroquoian languages: a study of
seventeenth- and eighteenth-century
practice in linguistics. Dissertation
Abstracts, 22 (1961/1962): 1157. UM 61-
4443.

Hawley, F.   Tree-ring analysis and dating
in the Mississippi drainage. Chicago,
University, Publications in
Anthropology, Occasional Papers, 2
(1941): 1-110.

Hibbard, B. H.   Indian agriculture in
southern Wisconsin. State Historical
Society of Wisconsin, Proceedings, 52
(1904): 145-155.

Hickerson, Harold.   Notes on the post-
contact origin of the Midewiwin.
Ethnohistory, 9 (1962): 404-423.

Hickman, Russell.   The Reeder
Administration inaugurated; part 2--the
census of early 1855. Kansas Historical
Quarterly, 36 (1970): 424-455.

Hildreth, Samuel P.   Pioneer history.   New
York, Arno Press, 1971.   13, 525 p.
illus.

Hinsdale, W. B.   Distribution of the
aboriginal population of Michigan.
Michigan, University, Museum of
Anthropology, Occasional Contributions,
2 (1932): 1-35.

Hinsdale, W. B.   Indian corn culture in
Michigan. Michigan Academy of Science,
Arts and Letters, Papers, 8 (1927): 31-
49.

Hockett, C. F.   Central Algonquian /t/ and
/c/. International Journal of American
Linguistics, 22 (1956): 202-207.

Hockett, C. F.   Central Algonquian
vocabulary stems in /k/. International
Journal of American Linguistics, 23
(1957): 247-268.

Hockett, C. F.   Implications of
Bloomfield's Algonquian studies.
Language, 24 (1948): 117-135.

Hoffman, Bernard G.   The Codex
Canadiensis: an important document for
Great Lakes ethnography. Ethnohistory, 8
(1961): 382-400.

Holmer, N. M.   Lexical and morphological
contacts between Siouan and Algonquian.
Lunds Universitets Arsskrift, n.s., 45
(1949): 1-36.

Holmes, W. H.   Prehistoric textile fabrics
of the United States. U.S. Bureau of
American Ethnology, Annual Reports, 3
(1882): 393-425.

Horsman, R.   British Indian policy in the
Northwest, 1807-1818. Mississippi Valley
Historical Review, 45 (1958): 51-66.

Horsman, Reginald.   American Indian policy
in the Old Northwest, 1783-1812. William
and Mary Quarterly, 3d ser., 18 (1961):
35-53.

Horsman, Reginald.   Wisconsin and the War
of 1812. Wisconsin Magazine of History,
46 (1962): 3-15.

Hrdlička, A.   Catalogue of human crania in
the United States National Museum
collections. United States National
Museum, Proceedings, 69, no. 5 (1927):
1-127.

Hulbert, A. B. and W. N. Schwarze, eds.
Zeisberger's history of Northern
American Indians. Ohio State
Archaeological and Historical Quarterly,
19 (1910): 1-189.

Hulbert, Archer B.   Military roads of the
Mississippi Basin; the conquest of the
Old Northwest. New York, AMS Press,
1971.   237 p. maps.

Hunter, W. A.   The Ohio, the Indian's
land. Pennsylvania History, 21 (1954):
338-350.

Jackson, Donald.   A fort is built.
Palimpsest, 47 (1966): 11-20.

Jackson, Donald.   Black Hawk--the last
campaign. Palimpsest, 42 (1961): 80-94.

Jackson, Donald.   Cast of characters.
Palimpsest, 47 (1966): 21-32.

Jackson, Donald.   Fulfilling the treaty.
Palimpsest, 47 (1966): 1-10.

Jackson, Donald.   The man and his times.
Palimpsest, 42 (1961): 65-79.

Jakle, John A.   The American bison and the
human occupance of the Ohio Valley.
American Philosophical Society,
Proceedings, 112 (1968): 299-305.

Jakle, John Allais.   Salt and the initial
settlement of the Ohio Valley.
Dissertation Abstracts, 28 (1967/1968):
2472B. UM 67-15,110.

Johnson, F., ed.   Man in northeastern
North America. Robert S. Peabody
Foundation for Archaeology, Papers, 3
(1946): 1-347.

Jones, V. H. Notes on the preparation and the uses of basswood fiber by the Indians of the Great Lakes region. Michigan Academy of Science, Arts and Letters, Papers, 22 (1936): 1-14.

Jones, W. Some principles of Algonquian word-formation. American Anthropologist, n.s., 6 (1904): 369-411.

Kellogg, L. P., ed. Early narratives of the Northwest. New York, 1917. 382 p.

Kinietz, V. Notes on the Algonquian family hunting ground system. American Anthropologist, n.s., 42 (1940): 179.

Kinietz, V. Notes on the roached headdress of animal hair among the North American Indians. Michigan Academy of Science, Arts and Letters, Papers, 26 (1940): 463-467.

Knowles, N. The torture of captives by the Indians of eastern North America. American Philosophical Society, Proceedings, 82 (1940): 151-225.

Kuhm, H. W. Indian place-names in Wisconsin. Wisconsin Archeologist, 33 (1952): 1-157.

Kuhm, H. W. The mining and use of lead by the Wisconsin Indians. Wisconsin Archeologist, 32 (1951): 25-38.

Kuhm, H. W. Wisconsin Indian fishing. Wisconsin Archeologist, n.s., 7 (1928): 61-114.

Kuhm, Herbert W. Uses of native herbs by Wisconsin Indians. Wisconsin Archeologist, n.s., 42 (1961): 97-132.

Kurath, G. P. Algonquian ceremonialism and natural resources of the Great Lakes. Bangalore, Indian Institute of Culture, Reprint 22 (1957).

Kurath, G. P. Antiphonal songs of Eastern Woodlands Indians. Musical Quarterly, 42 (1956): 520-526.

Kurath, G. P. Blackrobe and shaman. Michigan Academy of Science, Arts and Letters, Papers, 44 (1959): 209-215.

Kurath, G. P. Catholic hymns of Michigan Indians. Anthropological Quarterly, 30 (1957): 31-44.

Kurath, G. P. Ceremonies, songs and dances of Michigan Indians. Michigan History Magazine, 39 (1955): 466-468.

Kurath, G. P. Pan-Indianism in Great Lakes tribal festivals. Journal of American Folklore, 70 (1957): 179-182.

Kurath, Gertrude P. Michigan Indian festivals. Ann Arbor, Ann Arbor Publishers, 1966. 8, 132 p. illus.

Lahontan, A. L. de D. New voyages to North-America. Ed. by R. G. Thwaites. Chicago, 1905. 2 v.

Lahontan, Louis A. New voyages to North America. New York, Burt Franklin, 1970. 2 v. [93, 797 p.] illus., maps.

Larrabee, Charles. Lieutenant Charles Larrabee's account of the Battle of Tippecanoe, 1811. Indiana Magazine of History, 57 (1961): 225-247.

Laviolette, G. Notes on the aborigines of the Prairie Provinces. Anthropologica, 2 (1956): 107-130.

Lecompte, Janet. Don Benito Vasquez in early Saint Louis. Missouri Historical Society, Bulletin, 26 (1969/1970): 285-305.

Loskiel, G. H. Geschichte der Mission der evangelischen Brüder unter den Indianern in Nordamerika. Barby, 1789. 783 p.

Loskiel, G. H. History of the Mission of the United Brethren among the Indians of North America. London, 1794.

Lurie, Nancy Oestreich. Wisconsin: a natural laboratory for North American Indian studies. Wisconsin Magazine of History, 53 (1969/1970): 3-20.

Lyons, E. J. Isaac McCoy: his plan of and work for Indian colonization. Fort Hayes Kansas State College Bulletin, 35, no. 17 (1945): 1-61.

Mahan, Bruce E. Indian affairs and treaties. Palimpsest, 42 (1961): 472-488.

Mahan, Bruce E. Indian amusements. Palimpsest, 50 (1969): 247-252.

Mahan, Bruce E. The first Fort Crawford. Palimpsest, 42 (1961): 462-471.

Mahan, Bruce E. The second Fort Crawford. Palimpsest, 42 (1961): 489-504.

Mahan, Bruce E. The Upper Mississippi frontier. Palimpsest, 42 (1961): 449-453.

Marquette, J. and L. Joliet. An account of the discovery of some new countries and nations in North America. In B. F. French, ed. Historical Collections of Louisiana and Florida. Vol. 2. 1850: 277-297.

Matthews, G. H. Proto-Siouan kinship terminology. American Anthropologist, 61 (1959): 252-278.

McKern, W. C. An hypothesis for the Asiatic origin of the Woodland culture. American Antiquity, 3 (1937): 138-143.

Michelson, T. Algonquian notes. International Journal of American Linguistics, 9 (1939): 103-112.

Michelson, T. Contributions to Algonquian linguistics. International Journal of American Linguistics, 10 (1939): 75-85.

Michelson, T. Phonetic shifts in Algonquian languages. International Journal of American Linguistics, 8 (1935): 131-171.

Michelson, T. Preliminary report on the linguistic classification of Algonquian tribes. U.S. Bureau of American Ethnology, Annual Reports, 28 (1907): 221-290.

Michelson, T. Some Algonquian kinship terms. American Anthropologist, n.s., 34 (1932): 357-359.

Michelson, T. Terms of relationship and social organization. National Academy of Sciences, Proceedings, 2 (1916): 297-300.

Miller, Wick R. An outline of Shawnee historical phonology. International Journal of American Linguistics, 25 (1959): 16-21.

Mori, John Louis. Material culture and cultural identity: implications for anthropological theory. Dissertation Abstracts International, 34 (1973/1974): 967B. UM 73-21,463.

Nasatir, A. P. Before Lewis and Clark. St. Louis, 1952. 2 v. (882 p.).

Nydahl, T. L. The pipestone quarry and the Indians. Minnesota History, 31 (1950): 193-208.

Olsen, Evelyn G. Indian blood. Parsons, W. Va., McClain, 1967. 253 p. illus., map.

Parkins, A. E. The Indians of the Great Lakes region and their environment. Geographical Review, 6 (1918): 504-512.

Parsons, Joseph A., Jr. Civilizing the Indians of the Old Northwest, 1800-1810. Indiana Magazine of History, 56 (1960): 195-216.

Pearce, N. O. Tuberculosis among Minnesota's Indians. American Indian, 4, no. 1 (1947): 20-23.

Peet, S. D. The location of the Indian tribes. American Antiquarian and Oriental Journal, 1 (1878): 85-98.

Peithmann, Irvin M. Indians of southern Illinois. Springfield, Ill., C. C. Thomas, 1964. 15, 125 p. illus.

Perrot, N. Memoir on the manners, customs, and religion of the savages of North America. In E. H. Blair, ed. The Indian Tribes of the Upper Mississippi Valley. Vol. 1. Cleveland, 1911: 25-272.

Perrot, N. Mémoire sur les moeurs, coutumes et religion des sauvages de l'Amérique septentrionale. Paris, 1864. 341 p.

Petersen, William J. The terms of peace. Palimpsest, 42 (1961): 95-111.

Pike, Zebulon Montgomery. Pike's Mississippi expedition. Edited by William J. Petersen. Palimpsest, 49 (1968): 47-80.

Potherie, B. de la. History of the savage peoples who are allies of New France. In E. H. Blair, ed. The Indian Tribes of the Upper Mississippi Valley. Vol. 1. Cleveland, 1911: 273-372.

Potherie, B. de la. History of the savage peoples who are allies of New France. In E. H. Blair, ed. The Indian Tribes of the Upper Mississippi Valley. Vol. 2. Cleveland, 1912: 13-136.

Prescott, Philander. The recollections of Philander Prescott, frontiersman of the Old Northwest, 1819-1862. Lincoln, University of Nebraska Press, 1966. 11, 272 p. illus., maps.

Quimby, G. I. The archeology of the upper Great Lakes Area. In J. B. Griffin, ed. Archeology of Eastern United States. Chicago, 1952: 99-107.

Quimby, George I. Indian culture and European trade goods. Madison, University of Wisconsin Press, 1966. 14, 217 p. illus., map.

Quimby, George I. Indian life in the Upper Great Lakes, 11,000 B.C. to A.D. 1800. Chicago, University of Chicago Press, 1960. 182 p. illus.

Records, Spencer. Spencer Records' memoir of the Ohio Valley frontier, 1766-1795. Edited by Donald F. Carmony. Indiana Magazine of History, 55 (1959): 323-377.

Reynolds, H. L. Algonkin metal-smiths. American Anthropologist, 1 (1888): 341-352.

Rickey, Don, **Jr.** The British-Indian attack on St. Louis, May 26, 1780. Missouri Historical Review, 55 (1960/1961): 35-45.

Ritzenthaler, *R. E.* Prehistoric Indians of Wisconsin. Public Museum of the City of Milwaukee, Popular Science Handbook, 4 (1953): 1-43.

Ritzenthaler, Robert E. The Woodland Indians of the western Great Lakes. By Robert E. Ritzenthaler and Pat Ritzenthaler. Garden City, Natural History Press, 1970. 16, 178 p. illus., map. (American Museum Science Books, B21)

Rogers, R. A concise account of North America. London, 1765. 264 p.

Schermerhorn, J. F. Report respecting the Indians inhabiting the western parts of the United States. Massachusetts Historical Society, Collections, ser. 2, 2 (1814): 1-45.

Schorer, C. E. Indian tales of C. C. Trowbridge: the bad man. Southern Folklore Quarterly, 36 (1972): 160-175.

Shea, J. G. Discovery and exploration of the Mississippi Valley. 2d ed. Albany, 1903.

Shea, J. G. Early voyages up and down the Mississippi. Albany, 1861. 191 p.

Shea, J. G. The Indian tribes of Wisconsin. State Historical Society of Wisconsin, Collections, 3 (1856): 125-138.

Shetrone, H. C. The mound builders. New York, 1930. 508 p.

Shippen, H. H. A woven bulrush mat from an Indian tribe of the Great Lakes region. Michigan Academy of Science, Arts and Letters, Papers, 39 (1954): 399-406.

Siebert, F. T. Certain Proto-Algonquian consonant clusters. Language, 17 (1941): 298-303.

Siiger, H. Praerieindianerne og Piben. Kobenhavn, Fra Nationalmuseets Arbejdsmark (1946): 24-29.

Silver, Shirley. Natick consonants in reference to Proto-Central Algonquian. International Journal of American Linguistics, 26 (1960): 112-119, 234-241.

Skinner, A. Some aspects of the folk-lore of the Central Algonkin. Journal of American Folklore, 27 (1914): 97-100.

Skinner, A. The Algonkin and the thunderbird. American Museum Journal, 14 (1914): 71-73.

Skinner, A. Traces of the stone age among the eastern and northern tribes. American Anthropologist, n.s., 14 (1912): 391-395.

Smelser, Marshall. Tecumseh, Harrison, and the War of 1812. Indiana Magazine of History, 65 (1969): 25-44.

Smith, Dwight L. Provocation and occurrence of Indian-White warfare in the early American Period in the Old Northwest. Northwest Ohio Quarterly, 33 (1960/1961): 132-147.

Smith, William. Expedition against the Ohio Indians. Ann Arbor, University Microfilms, 1966. 8, 71 p. illus., map.

Sosin, Jack M. Whitehall and the wilderness; the Middle West in British colonial policy, 1760-1775. Lincoln, University of Nebraska Press, 1961. 11, 307 p. maps.

Steeves, T. A. Wild rice. Economic Botany, 6 (1952): 107-142.

Stickney, G. P. The use of maize by Wisconsin Indians. Parkman Club Publications, 13 (1897): 63-87.

Surrey, F. M., ed. Calendar of manuscripts in Paris archives and libraries relating to the history of the Mississippi Valley to 1803. Washington, D.C., 1926-1928. 2 v.

Sylvester, Lorna Lutes. Conner Prairie pioneer settlement and museum. Indiana Magazine of History, 65 (1969): 1-24.

Temple, W. C. Indian villages of the Illinois country. Illinois State Museum, Scientific Papers, 2, no. 2 (1958): 1-218.

Terry, F. T. Aborigines of the Northwest. Parkman Club Publications, 4 (1896): 59-72.

Thomas, C. Burial mounds in the northern sections of the United States. U.S. Bureau of American Ethnology, Annual Reports, 5 (1884): 9-119.

Thwaites, Reuben G., ed. The French regime in Wisconsin [1634-1748]. Madison, 1902, 1906. 2 v. illus.

(Wisconsin, State Historical Society,
Collections, 16-17)

Thwaites, Reuben G., ed. The French
regime in Wisconsin [1743-1760].
Madison, 1908. 25, 1-222 p.
(Wisconsin, State Historical Society,
Collections, 18)

Tonti, H. de. Relation de la Louisianne,
et du Mississipi. Recueil de Voyages au
Nord, 5 (1734): 35-195.

Trail, Robert. Livingston County,
Kentucky--stepping stone to Illinois.
Kentucky Historical Society, Register,
69 (1971): 239-272.

Trumbull, J. H. On the Algonkin verb.
American Philological Association,
Transactions, 7 (1877): 147-171.

Turner, F. J. The character and influence
of the Indian trade in Wisconsin. Johns
Hopkins University Studies in Historical
and Political Science, 9, nos. 11/12
(1891): 3-75.

Ueck, L. P. Material used by the
Southwest Michigan Indians in the
flaking of stone artifacts. Earth
Science Digest, 6, no. 6 (1953): 31-33.

Unger, Robert William. Lewis Cass: Indian
Superintendent of the Michigan
Territory, 1813-1831. A survey of public
opinion as reported by the newspapers of
the old Northwest Territory.
Dissertation Abstracts, 28 (1967/1968):
3621A. UM 68-1994.

U.S., Bureau of Indian Affairs, Fort Wayne
Agency. Letter book of the Indian
Agency at Fort Wayne, 1809-1815. Edited
by Gayle Thornbrough. Indianapolis,
1961. 272 p. map. (Indiana Historical
Society, Publications, 21)

U.S., Congress, Senate, Committee on
Interior and Insular Affairs,
Subcommittee on Indian Affairs. Federal
lands in trust for tribes in Minnesota
and Wisconsin. Hearing, Ninety-second
Congress, first session, on S. 1217
. . . S. 1230 . . . March 26, 1971.
Washington, D.C., Government Printing
Office, 1971. 3, 72 p.

Verwyst, C. Missionary labors of Fathers
Marquette, Menard, and Allouez.
Chicago, 1886. 262 p.

Voegelin, C. F. and E. W. Voegelin.
Linguistic considerations of
northeastern North America. Robert S.
Peabody Foundation for Archaeology,
Papers, 3 (1946): 178-194.

Voegelin, E. W. Indians of Indiana.
Indiana Academy of Science, Proceedings,
50 (1941): 27-32.

Voegelin, E. W. Mortuary customs of the
Shawnee and other eastern tribes.
Indiana Historical Society, Prehistory
Research Series, 2 (1944): 227-444.

Vogel, Virgil J. Indian place names in
Illinois. Springfield, 1963. 179 p.
illus. (Illinois State Historical
Society, Pamphlet Series, 4)

Vogel, Virgil J. Indian place names in
Illinois. Illinois State Historical
Society, Journal, 55 (1962): 45-71, 157-
189, 271-308, 385-458.

Vogel, Virgil J. Wisconsin's name: a
linguistic puzzle. Wisconsin Magazine of
History, 48 (1964): 181-186.

Volwiler, Albert T. George Croghan and
the westward movement, 1741-1782. New
York, AMS Press, 1971. 370 p. maps.

Wakefield, Francis. The elusive
Mascoutens. Michigan History, 50 (1966):
228-234.

Walker, L. J. Indian camp meeting at
Greensky Hill. Journal of American
Folklore, 63 (1950): 96-97.

Walton, I. Indian place names in
Michigan. Midwest Folklore, 5 (1955):
23-34.

Watlington, Patricia. Discontent in
frontier Kentucky. Kentucky Historical
Society, Register, 65 (1967): 77-93.

Wayne, Anthony. Message of Pennsylvania
and New Jersey Quakers to Indians of the
Old Northwest. Edited by Donald F.
Carmony. Indiana Magazine of History, 59
(1963): 51-58.

Wedel, Mildred Mott. Corn horticulture.
Palimpsest, 42 (1961): 561-569.

Wedel, Mildred Mott. Their way of life.
Palimpsest, 42 (1961): 580-592.

Wells, William. William Wells and the
Indian Council of 1793. Edited by Dwight
L. Smith. Indiana Magazine of History,
56 (1960): 217-226.

West, G. A. Copper: its mining and use by
the aborigines of the Lake Superior
region. Public Museum of the City of
Milwaukee, Bulletin, 10 (1929): 1-184.

West, G. A. Uses of tobacco and the
calumet by Wisconsin Indians. Wisconsin
Archeologist, 10 (1911): 5-64.

Whitney, Ellen M., comp. The Black Hawk
War, 1831-1832. Springfield, 1970.
(Illinois State Historical Library,
Collections, 35)

Wilcox, Frank N. Ohio Indian trails.
Edited by William A. McGill. Kent, Kent
State University Press, 1970. 16,
144 p. illus., maps.

Wilson, H. C. A new interpretation of the
wild rice district of Wisconsin.
American Anthropologist, 58 (1956):
1059-1064.

Wisconsin, State Employment Service.
Employability factors and needs of
Wisconsin tribal Indians. Madison,
Wisconsin State Employment Service,
1968. 43 p. ERIC ED021684.

Woehrmann, Paul. At the headwaters of the
Maumee: a history of the forts of Fort
Wayne. Indianapolis, Indiana Historical
Society, 1971. 15, 306 p. illus.

Woehrmann, Paul John. Fort Wayne, Indiana
Territory, 1794-1819: a study of a
frontier post. Dissertation Abstracts,
28 (1967/1968): 4588A. UM 68-6225.

Yarnell, Richard Asa. Aboriginal
relationships between culture and plant
life in the Upper Great Lakes region.
Dissertation Abstracts, 24 (1963/1964):
2217-2218. UM 64-914.

Zeisberger, David, et al. Some remarks
and annotations concerning the
traditions, customs, languages etc. of
the Indians in North America, from the
memoirs of the Reverend David
Zeisberger, and other missionaries of
the United Brethren. Edited by Erminie
Wheeler-Voegelin. Ethnohistory, 6
(1959): 42-69.

Zimmerman, Albright Gravenor. The Indian
trade of colonial Pennsylvania.
Dissertation Abstracts, 28 (1967/1968):
1384A. UM 67-11,752.

10-01 Fox

Anonymous. Cha kä ta ko si: a collection
of Meskwaki manuscripts. Iowa City,
1907.

Armstrong, P. A. The Sauks and the Black
Hawk War. Springfield, 1887. 726 p.

Atkinson, Henry. The Battle of Bad Axe:
General Atkinson's report. Edited by
Roger L. Nichols. Wisconsin Magazine of
History, 50 (1966/1967): 54-58.

Aumann, F. R. The Watchful Fox.
Palimpsest, 46 (1965): 225-236.

Beckwith, H. W. The Illinois and Indiana
Indians. Fergus Historical Series, 27
(1884): 146-162.

Berthrong, D. J. John Beach and the
removal of the Sauk and Fox from Iowa.
Iowa Journal of History and Politics, 54
(1956): 313-334.

Bicknell, A. D. The Tama County Indians.
Annals of Iowa, ser. 3, 4 (1899): 196-
208.

Bloomfield, L. Notes on the Fox language.
International Journal of American
Linguistics, 3 (1925/1926): 219-232; 4
(1926/1927): 181-219.

Boyd, John Paul. The algebra of kinship.
Dissertation Abstracts, 28 (1967/1968):
299A. UM 67-8220.

Briggs, John Ely. The Sacs and Foxes.
Palimpsest, 50 (1969): 223-226.

Bright, William. Reduction rules in Fox
kinship. By William Bright and Jan
Minnick. Southwestern Journal of
Anthropology, 22 (1966): 381-388.

Brown, D. M. Wisconsin Indian corn origin
myths. Wisconsin Archeologist, n.s.,
(1940): 19-27.

Burford, C. C. Sauk and Fox Indian
ceremonials attract large audience and
wide-spread interest. Illinois State
Archaeological Society, Journal, 5
(1947): 24-30.

Busby, A. B. Two summers among the
Musquakies. Vinton, 1886.

Bushnell, D. I. Villages of the
Algonquian, Siouan and Caddoan tribes.
U.S. Bureau of American Ethnology,
Bulletin, 77 (1922): 37-41.

Carman, J. N. and K. S. Pond. The
replacement of the Indian languages of
Kansas by English. Kansas Academy of
Science, Transactions, 58 (1955): 131-
150.

Carney, Richard E. Intelligence test
performance of Indian children as a
function of type of test and age. By
Richard E. Carney and Norma Trowbridge.
Perceptual and Motor Skills, 14 (1962):
511-514.

Chase, Charles Monroe. An editor looks at
early-day Kansas; the letters of Charles
Monroe Chase. Edited by Lela Barnes.
Kansas Historical Quarterly, 26 (1960):
118-151.

Coult, Allan D. Lineage solidarity, transformational analysis and the meaning of kinship terminologies. Man, n.s., 2 (1967): 26-47.

Davidson, Mary Ann Ferrin. An autobiography and a reminiscence. Annals of Iowa, 37 (1964): 241-261.

English, E. H. A Mesquakie chief's burial. Annals of Iowa, 3d ser., 30 (1951): 545-550.

Fay, George E., ed. Charters, constitutions and by-laws of the Indian tribes of North America. Part VI: The Indian tribes of Oklahoma (cont'd.). Greeley, 1968. 5, 129 l. map. (University of Northern Colorado, Museum of Anthropology, Occasional Publications in Anthropology, Ethnology Series, 7) ERIC ED046556.

Fay, George E., ed. Charters, constitutions and by-laws of the Indian tribes of North America. Part XIII: Midwestern tribes. Greeley, 1972. 3, 101 l. map. (University of Northern Colorado, Museum of Anthropology, Occasional Publications in Anthropology, Ethnology Series, 14)

Ferris, I. M. The Sauks and Foxes. Kansas State Historical Society, Collections, 11 (1910): 333-395.

Flannery, R. Two concepts of power. International Congress of Americanists, Proceedings, 29, vol. 3 (1952): 185-189.

Flom, G. T. Syllabus of vowel and consonantal sounds in Meskwaki Indian. Iowa City, 1906.

Foreman, G. The last trek of the Indians, 133-158, 222-229. Chicago, 1946.

Forsyth, T. Account of the manners and customs of the Sauk and Fox nations. In E. H. Blair, ed. The Indian Tribes of the Upper Mississippi Valley. Vol. 2. Cleveland, 1912: 183-245.

Fugle, Eugene. Mesquakie witchcraft lore. Plains Anthropologist, 6 (1961): 31-39.

Gallaher, Ruth A. Realm of spirit. Palimpsest, 50 (1969): 258-263.

Gallaher, Ruth A. The Tama Indians. Palimpsest, 48 (1967): 289-299.

Galland, I. The Indian tribes of the West. Annals of Iowa, 7 (1869): 347-366.

Gates, C. M., ed. Five fur traders of the Northwest. Minneapolis, 1933. 296 p.

Gearing, F. Today's Mesquakies. American Indian, 7, no. 2 (1955): 24-37.

Gearing, Fred, et al., eds. Documentary history of the Fox Project. Chicago, University of Chicago, 1960. 5, 426 p.

*Gearing, Frederick O. The face of the Fox. Chicago, Aldine, 1970. 158 p. illus.

Geary, J. A. The changed conjunct verb (without NI) in Fox. International Journal of American Linguistics, 11 (1945): 169-181.

Geary, J. A. The changed conjunct (with -ni) and the interrogative in Fox. International Journal of American Linguistics, 12 (1946): 66-78.

Geary, J. A. The subjunctive in Fox. International Journal of American Linguistics, 12 (1946): 198-203.

Gilstrap, Harriet Patrick. Memoirs of a pioneer teacher. Chronicles of Oklahoma, 38 (1960): 20-34.

Gilstrap, Harry B., Jr. Colonel Samuel Lee Patrick. Chronicles of Oklahoma, 46 (1968): 58-63.

Goddard, Ives. Proto-Algonquian *nl and *nθ. International Journal of American Linguistics, 39 (1973): 1-6.

Green, O. J. The Mesquaki Indians. Red Man, 5 (1912): 47-52, 104-109.

*Hagan, W. T. The Sac and Fox Indians. Norman, 1958. 301 p.

Hanzeli, Victor E. Missionary linguistics in New France; a study of seventeenth- and eighteenth-century descriptions of American Indian languages. The Hague, Mouton, 1969. 141 p. illus., map. (Janua Linguarum, Series Maior, 29)

Hargrett, L. A bibliography of the constitutions and laws of the American Indians, 102-103. Cambridge, 1947.

Harkins, Arthur M. Indian Americans in Omaha and Lincoln. By Arthur M. Harkins, Mary L. Zemyan, and Richard G. Woods. Minneapolis, University of Minnesota, Training Center for Community Programs, 1970. 42, 24 p. ERIC ED047860.

Harrington, M. R. A bird-quill belt of the Sauk and Fox Indians. Indian Notes and Monographs, 10 (1920): 47-50.

Harrington, M. R. Old Sauk and Fox beaded garters. Indian Notes and Monographs, 10 (1920): 39-41.

Harrington, M. R. Sacred bundles of the Sac and Fox. Pennsylvania, University, University Museum, Anthropological Publications, 4 (1914): 125-262.

Hockett, Charles F. What Algonquian is really like. International Journal of American Linguistics, 32 (1966): 59-73.

House, R. Morton. "The Only Way" Church and the Sac and Fox Indians. Chroncicles of Oklahoma, 43 (1965): 443-466.

Hoyt, Elizabeth E. An approach to the mind of the young Indian. Journal of American Indian Education, 1, no. 1 (1961/1962): 17-23.

Hoyt, Elizabeth E. The children of Tama. Journal of American Indian Education, 3, no. 1 (1963/1964): 15-20.

Hunter, W. A. Refugee Fox settlements among the Senecas. Ethnohistory, 3 (1956): 11-20.

Huot, M. C. Peyote songs. Transition, 24 (1936): 117-119.

Jackson, Donald. Trading with the Indians. Palimpsest, 47 (1966): 42-46.

Jenks, A. E. The wild rice gatherers of the upper lakes. U.S. Bureau of American Ethnology, Annual Reports, 19, vol. 2 (1898): 1013-1137.

Joffe, N. F. The Fox of Iowa. In R. Linton, ed. Acculturation in Seven American Indian Tribes. New York, 1940: 259-332.

Jones, W. Algonquian (Fox). U.S. Bureau of American Ethnology, Bulletin, 40, vol. 1 (1911): 735-873.

Jones, W. An Algonquian syllabary. In Boas Anniversary Volume. New York, 1906: 88-93.

Jones, W. Episodes in the culture-hero myth of the Sauks and Foxes. Journal of American Folklore, 14 (1901): 225-239.

*Jones, W. Ethnography of the Fox Indians. U.S. Bureau of American Ethnology, Bulletin, 125 (1939): 1-156.

Jones, W. Fox texts. American Ethnological Society, Publications, 1 (1907): 1-383.

Jones, W. Mortuary observances and the adoption rites of the Algonkin Foxes of Iowa. International Congress of Americanists, Proceedings, 15, vol. 1 (1906): 263-277.

Jones, W. Notes on the Fox Indians. Journal of American Folklore, 24 (1911): 209-237.

Jones, W. Some principles of Algonquian word-formation. American Anthropologist, n.s., 6 (1904): 369-411.

Jones, W. The Algonkin manitou. Journal of American Folklore, 18 (1905): 183-190.

Jones, W. The heart of the brave. Harvard Monthly, 30 (1900): 99-106.

Kellogg, L. P. The Fox Indians during the French regime. State Historical Society of Wisconsin, Proceedings, 55 (1907): 142-188.

Keyes, Patricia S. Moccasin paths. By Pat and Art Wakolee. Salt Lake City, Deseret Book, 1966. 7, 245 p. illus.

Lasley, M. Sac and Fox tales. Journal of American Folklore, 15 (1902): 170-178.

Lawson, P. V. The Outagamie village at West Menasha. State Historical Society of Wisconsin, Proceedings, 47 (1900): 204-211.

Marsh, C. Expedition to the Sacs and Foxes. State Historical Society of Wisconsin, Collections, 15 (1900): 104-155.

Marston, M. Letter to Reverend Dr. Jedediah Morse. In E. H. Blair, ed. The Indian Tribes of the Upper Mississippi Valley. Vol. 2. Cleveland, 1912: 139-182.

McDermott, John Francis. The Indian as human being. Nebraska History, 52 (1971): 45-49.

McGee, W J. A Muskwaki bowl. American Anthropologist, 11 (1898): 88-91.

Michelson, T. Algonquian linguistic miscellany. Washington Academy of Sciences, Journal, 4 (1914): 402-409.

Michelson, T. Contributions to Algonquian grammar. American Anthropologist, n.s., 15 (1913): 470-476.

Michelson, T. Contributions to Fox ethnology. U.S. Bureau of American Ethnology, Bulletin, 85 (1927): 1-162; 95 (1930): 1-183.

Michelson, T. Field-work among the Catawba, Fox, Sutaio and Sauk Indians. Smithsonian Miscellaneous Collections, 63, no. 8 (1914): 836.

Michelson, T. Fox linguistic notes. In Festschrift Meinhof. Hamburg, 1927: 403-408.

Michelson, T. Fox miscellany. U.S. Bureau of American Ethnology, Bulletin, 114 (1937): 1-124.

Michelson, T. How Meskwaki children should be brought up. In E. C. Parsons, ed. American Indian Life. New York, 1925: 81-86.

Michelson, T. Miss Owen's "Folk-lore of the Musquakie Indians". American Anthropologist, n.s., 38 (1936): 143-145.

Michelson, T. Note on Fox gens festivals. International Congress of Americanists, Proceedings, 23 (1928): 545-546.

Michelson, T. Note on the hunting territories of the Sauk and Fox. American Anthropologist, n.s., 23 (1921): 238-239.

Michelson, T. Notes on Fox mortuary customs and beliefs. U.S. Bureau of American Ethnology, Annual Reports, 40 (1919): 351-496.

Michelson, T. Notes on the Buffalo-Head Dance of the Thunder Gens of the Fox Indians. U.S. Bureau of American Ethnology, Bulletin, 77 (1928): 1-94.

Michelson, T. Notes on the folklore and mythology of the Fox Indians. American Anthropologist, n.s., 15 (1913): 699-700.

Michelson, T. Notes on the Fox society known as Those who worship the Little Spotted Buffalo. U.S. Bureau of American Ethnology, Annual Reports, 40 (1919): 497-539.

Michelson, T. Notes on the Fox Wapanowiweni. U.S. Bureau of American Ethnology, Bulletin, 105 (1932): 1-195.

Michelson, T. Notes on the Great Sacred Pack of the Thunderbird Gens of the Fox Indians. U.S. Bureau of American Ethnology, Bulletin, 95 (1930): 43-183.

Michelson, T. Notes on the social organization of the Fox Indians. American Anthropologist, n.s., 15 (1913): 691-693.

Michelson, T. Observations on the Thunder Dance of the Bear Gens of the Fox Indians. U.S. Bureau of American Ethnology, Bulletin, 89 (1929): 1-73.

Michelson, T. On the future of the independent mode in Fox. American Anthropologist, n.s., 13 (1911): 171-172.

Michelson, T. On the origin of the so-called Dream Dance of the Central Algonkians. American Anthropologist, n.s., 25 (1923): 277-278.

Michelson, T. Revision of Wm. Jones' sketch of Algonquian. U.S. Bureau of American Ethnology, Bulletin, 40, vol. 1 (1911): 737-873.

Michelson, T. Ritualistic origin myths of the Fox Indians. Washington Academy of Sciences, Journal, 6 (1916): 209-211.

Michelson, T. Sol Tax on the social organization of the Fox Indians. American Anthropologist, n.s., 40 (1938): 177-179.

Michelson, T. Some general notes on the Fox Indians. Washington Academy of Sciences, Journal, 9 (1919): 483-494, 521-528, 593-596.

Michelson, T. Studies on the Fox and Ojibwa Indians. Smithsonian Miscellaneous Collections, 78, no. 1 (1926): 111-113.

Michelson, T. The autobiography of a Fox Indian woman. U.S. Bureau of American Ethnology, Annual Reports, 40 (1919): 291-349.

Michelson, T. The changing character of Fox adoption-feasts. American Journal of Sociology, 34 (1929): 890-892.

Michelson, T. The mythical origin of the White Buffalo Dance of the Fox Indians. U.S. Bureau of American Ethnology, Annual Reports, 40 (1919): 23-289.

Michelson, T. The Owl Sacred Pack of the Fox Indians. U.S. Bureau of American Ethnology, Bulletin, 72 (1921): 1-83.

Michelson, T. The so-called stems of Algonquian verbal complexes. International Congress of Americanists, Proceedings, 19 (1915): 541-544.

Michelson, T. The traditional origin of the Fox society known as "The singing around Rite". U.S. Bureau of American Ethnology, Annual Reports, 40 (1919): 541-658.

Michelson, T. Vocalic harmony in Fox. American Journal of Philology, 41 (1920): 181-183.

Michelson, T. What happened to Green Bear who was blessed with a sacred pack. U.S. Bureau of American Ethnology, Bulletin, 119 (1938): 161-176.

Michelson, T. Michelson, T. International Journal of American Linguistics, 1 (1919): 50-57.

Miller, Otis Louis. Indian-White relations in the Illinois country, 1789 to 1818. Dissertation Abstracts International, 33 (1972/1973): 1120A. UM 72-23,975.

Miller, W. B. Two concepts of authority. American Anthropologist, 57 (1955): 271-289.

Miller, Walter B. Two concepts of authority. In Deward E. Walker, Jr., ed. The Emergent Native Americans. Boston, Little, Brown, 1972: 565-583.

Mooney, J. and C. Thomas. Foxes. U.S. Bureau of American Ethnology, Bulletin, 30, vol. 1 (1907): 472-474.

Morgan, L. H. The Indian journals, 1859-62: p. 40, 76-77, 80-81, 83. Ann Arbor, 1959.

Morse, J. A report to the Secretary of War. New Haven, 1922. 400 p.

Nasatir, A. P. Before Lewis and Clark. St. Louis, 1952. 2 v. (882 p.).

Nichols, Roger L. A missionary journey to the Sac-Fox Indians, 1834. Annals of Iowa, 36 (1962): 301-315.

Nichols, Roger L. The founding of Fort Atkinson. Annals of Iowa, 37 (1965): 589-597.

Nichols, Roger L., ed. The Black Hawk War; another view. Annals of Iowa, 36 (1963): 525-533.

Owen, M. A. Algonquins. In J. Hastings, ed. Encyclopaedia of Religion and Ethics. Vol. 1. New York, 1908: 319-326.

Owen, M. A. Folk-lore of the Musquakie Indians. London, 1904. 147 p.

Petersen, William J. Buffalo hunting with Keokuk. Palimpsest, 46 (1965): 257-272.

Petersen, William J. Trailmaking on the frontier. Palimpsest, 44 (1963): 10-27.

Polgar, Steven. Biculturation of Mesquakie teenage boys. American Anthropologist, 62 (1960): 217-235.

Polk, Harry Herndon. Old Fort Des Moines. Annals of Iowa, 36 (1962): 425-436.

Rebok, H. M. The last of the Mus-qua-kies. Iowa Historical Record, 17 (1901): 305-335.

Schmidt, W. Die Foxes. In his Die Ursprung der Göttesidee. Bd. 2. Münster i. W., 1929: 574-580.

Schmidt, W. Die Foxes. In his Die Ursprung der Göttesidee. Bd, 7. Münster i. W., 1940: 761-763.

Schmidt, W. Die Foxes. In his Die Ursprung der Göttesidee. Bd. 5. Münster i. W., 1934: 583-663.

Siebert, Frank T., Jr. Discrepant consonant clusters ending in *-k in Proto-Algonquian, a proposed interpretation of saltatory sound changes. In Contributions to Anthropology: Linguistics I. Ottawa, Queen's Printer, 1967: 48-59. (Canada, National Museum, Bulletin, 214)

Smith, H. H. Ethnobotany of the Meskwaki Indians. Public Museum of the City of Milwaukee, Bulletin, 4 (1928): 175-326.

Smith, H. H. The Red Earth Indians. Public Museum of the City of Milwaukee, Yearbook, 3 (1923): 27-38.

Spencer, Dick, III. Powwow time. Palimpsest, 48 (1967): 300-319.

Steward, J. F. Lost Maramech and earliest Chicago. Chicago, New York, 1903. 390 p.

Stucki, Larry R. Anthropologists and Indians: a new look at the Fox Project. Plains Anthropologist, 12 (1967): 300-317.

Tax, S. The Fox Project. Human Organization, 17, no. 1 (1958): 17-19.

Tax, S. The social organization of the Fox Indians. In F. Eggan, ed. Social Anthropology of North American Tribes. 2d ed. Chicago, 1955: 243-284.

Thwaites, R. G., ed. The Jesuit relations and allied documents. Cleveland, 1896-1901. 74 v.

Vincent, John R. Midwest Indians and frontier photography. Annals of Iowa, 38 (1965): 26-35.

Voorhis, Paul H. New notes on the Mesquakie (Fox) language. International Journal of American Linguistics, 37 (1971): 63-75.

Voorhis, Paul Hantsch. Kickapoo grammar. Dissertation Abstracts, 28 (1967/1968): 4620A. UM 68-6863.

Ward, D. J. H. Meskwakia. Iowa Journal of History and Politics, 4 (1906): 179-189.

Ward, D. J. H. The Meskwaki people of today. Iowa Journal of History and
Politics, 4 (1906): 190-219.

Wied-Neuwied, M. zu. Reise in das innere
Nordamerika. Coblenz, 1839-1841. 2 v.

Wied-Neuwied, M. zu. Travels in the
interior of North America. Early Western
Travels, 22 (1906): 217-230; 24 (1906):
276-277, 294-295.

Wyatt, P. J. Iowas, Sacs and Foxes of
Kansas. Emporia, Kansas State Teachers
College, 1962. 25 p. illus. (Heritage
of Kansas, 6, no. 4)

Wylie, Helen. On the warpath. Palimpsest,
50 (1969): 253-257.

Yarnell, Richard Asa. Aboriginal
relationships between culture and plant
life in the Upper Great Lakes region.
Ann Arbor, University of Michigan, 1964.
6, 218 p. (Michigan, University, Museum
of Anthropology, Anthropological Papers,
23)

Yeast, William E. The Mesquakie memorial
feast. Annals of Iowa, 36 (1963): 591-
598.

Zoltvany, Yves F. New France and the
West, 1701-1713. Canadian Historical
Review, 46 (1965): 301-322.

Zoltvany, Yves F. The frontier policy of
Philippe de Rigaud de Vaudreuil, 1713-
1725. Canadian Historical Review, 48
(1967): 227-250.

10-02   Illinois

Anonymous. Illinois and Miami vocabulary
and Lord's Prayer. U.S. Catholic
Historical Magazine, 3 (1891): 1-9.

Beckwith, H. W. The Illinois and Indiana
Indians. Fergus Historical Series, 27
(1884): 99-106.

Belting, N. M. Illinois names for
themselves and other groups.
Ethnohistory, 5 (1958): 285-291.

Blasingame, E. J. The depopulation of the
Illinois Indians. Ethnohistory, 3
(1956): 193-224, 361-412.

Brown, James Allison, ed. The Zimmerman
Site; a report on excavations at the
Grand Village of Kaskaskia, La Salle
County, Illinois. Springfield, 1961.
86 p. illus. (Illinois, State Museum,
Report of Investigations, 9)

Brown, Margaret Kimball. Cultural
transformation among the Illinois: the
application of a systems model to
archeological and ethnohistorical data.
Dissertation Abstracts International, 34
(1973/1974): 962B-963B. UM 73-20,316.

Brown, Margaret Kimball. Native made
glass pendants from east of the
Mississippi. American Antiquity, 37
(1972): 432-439.

Bushnell, D. I. Native cemeteries and
forms of burial east of the Mississippi.
U.S. Bureau of American Ethnology,
Bulletin, 71 (1920): 39-43.

Carr, L. The Mascoutins. American
Antiquarian Society, Proceedings, n.s.,
13 (1900): 448-462.

Caton, J. D. The last of the Illinois.
Fergus Historical Series, 3 (1876): 1-
55.

Charlevoix, P. F. X. de. Journal of a
voyage to North America. Chicago, 1923.
2 v.

Charlevoix, Pierre F. X. de. Journal of a
voyage to North America. Ann Arbor,
University Microfilms, 1966. 2 v.

Deliette, L. Memoir concerning the
Illinois Country. Ed. by T. C. Pease and
R. C. Werner. Illinois State Historical
Library, Collections, 23 (1934): 302-
395.

Federal Writers' Projects. Wisconsin
Indian place legends: 2-3, 17-18.
Milwaukee, 1936.

Foreman, G. The last trek of the Indians,
204-206. Chicago, 1946.

Fortier, John. A historical reexamination
of Juchereau's Illinois tannery. By John
Fortier and Donald Chaput. Illinois
State Historical Society, Journal, 62
(1969): 385-406.

Goddard, Ives. Historical and
philological evidence regarding the
identification of the Mascouten.
Ethnohistory, 19 (1972): 123-134.

Good, Mary E. Guebert Site: an 18th
century historic Kaskaskia Indian
village in Randolph County, Illinois.
Wood River, Ill., 1972. 16, 194 p.
illus. (Central States Archaeological
Societies, Memoir, 2)

Griffin, James Bennett. The Fort Ancient
aspect: its cultural and chronological
position in Mississippi Valley
archaeology. Ann Arbor, University of
Michigan, 1966. 15, 376 p. illus.

(Michigan, University, Museum of Anthropology, Anthropological Papers, 28)

Hamilton, Raphael. The Marquette death site: the case for Ludington. Michigan History, 49 (1965): 228-248.

Hamy, E. T. Note sur d'anciennes peintures sur peaux des Indiens Illinois. Société des Américanistes, Journal, 2 (1897): 185-195.

Hauser, Raymond E. An ethnohistory of the Illinois Indian tribe, 1673-1832. Dissertation Abstracts International, 34 (1973/1974): 2491A-2492A. UM 73-27,592.

Hennepin, L. A new discovery of a vast country in America. Ed. by R. G. Thwaites. Chicago, 1903. 2 v.

Henson, C. E. Ritual elements in Mississippi River petroglyphs. Folk-Lore, 68 (1957): 405-410.

Holmes, Jack D. L. Spanish-American rivalry over the Chickasaw Bluffs, 1780-1795. East Tennessee Historical Society's Publications, 34 (1962): 26-57.

Jones, A. E. The site of the Mascoutin. State Historical Society of Wisconsin, Proceedings, 54 (1906): 175-182.

Joutel, H. Journal of La Salle's last voyage. New ed. Albany, 1906. 258 p.

Joutel, H. Relation. In P. Margry, ed. Découvertes et Établissements des Français dans l'Ouest et dans le Sud de l'Amérique Septentrionale. Vol. 3. Paris, 1879: 91-534.

Kellogg, L. P., ed. Early narratives of the Northwest, 223-257. New York, 1917.

Kelly, A. R. Some problems of recent Cahokia archaeology. Illinois State Academy of Sciences, Transactions, 25 (1933): 101-103.

Kenton, E., ed. The Indians of North America, Vol. 2: 269-274, 287-289, 356-363, 374-379. New York, 1927.

Kinietz, W. V. The Indian tribes of the western Great Lakes. Michigan, University, Museum of Anthropology, Occasional Contributions, 10 (1940): 161-225, 383-408.

Marquette, J. and L. Joliet. An account of the discovery of some new countries and nations in North America. In B. F. French, ed. Historical Collections of Louisiana and Florida. Vol. 2. 1850: 277-297.

Mereness, N. D., ed. Travels in the American Colonies, 71-74. New York, 1916.

Michelson, T. Notes on Peoria folk-lore and mythology. Journal of American Folklore, 30 (1917): 493-495.

Michelson, T. Once more Mascoutens. American Anthropologist, n.s., 37 (1935): 163-164.

Michelson, T. The identification of the Mascoutens. American Anthropologist, n.s., 36 (1934): 226-233.

Miller, Otis Louis. Indian-White relations in the Illinois country, 1789 to 1818. Dissertation Abstracts International, 33 (1972/1973): 1120A. UM 72-23,975.

Mooney, J. and C. Thomas. Illinois. U.S. Bureau of American Ethnology, Bulletin, 30, vol. 1 (1907): 597-599.

Mooney, J. and C. Thomas. Kaskaskia. U.S. Bureau of American Ethnology, Bulletin, 30, vol. 1 (1907): 661-663.

Mooney, J. and C. Thomas. Mascoutens. U.S. Bureau of American Ethnology, Bulletin, 30, vol. 1 (1907): 810-812.

Mooney, J. and C. Thomas. Michigamea. U.S. Bureau of American Ethnology, Bulletin, 30, vol. 1 (1907): 856-857.

Mooney, J. and C. Thomas. Peoria. U.S. Bureau of American Ethnology, Bulletin, 30, vol. 2 (1910): 228.

Morgan, L. H. Systems of consanguinity and affinity. Smithsonian Contributions to Knowledge, 17 (1871): 291-382.

Morgan, L. H. The Indian journals, 1859-62: p. 40-41. Ann Arbor, 1959.

Nasatir, A. P. Before Lewis and Clark. St. Louis, 1952. 2 v. (882 p.).

Peithmann, I. M. Echoes of the Red Man. New York, 1955. 134 p.

Rainwater, Percy L. Conquistadors, missionaries, and missions. Journal of Mississippi History, 27 (1965): 123-147.

Schmidt, W. Die Mascoutens oder Prärie-Potawatomie. In his Die Ursprung der Göttesidee. Bd. 2. Münster i. W., 1929: 516-538.

Schmidt, W. Die Mascoutens oder Prärie-Potawatomie. In his Die Ursprung der Göttesidee. Bd. 5. Münster i. W., 1934: 580-582.

Shea, J. G. Discovery and exploration of
    the Mississippi Valley. 2d ed. Albany,
    1903.

Silvy, A. Relation par lettres de
    l'Amérique septentrionale, 138-173.
    Paris, 1904.

Skinner, A. An Illinois quilled necklace.
    Indian Notes and Monographs, 10 (1920):
    33-34.

Strong, W. D. The Indian tribes of the
    Chicago region. Field Museum of Natural
    History, Department of Anthropology,
    Leaflets, 24 (1926): 1-13.

Thwaites, R. G., ed. Radisson and
    Groseilliers in Wisconsin. State
    Historical Society of Wisconsin,
    Collections, 11 (1888): 64-96.

Thwaites, R. G., ed. The Jesuit Relations
    and allied documents. Cleveland, 1896-
    1901. 74 v.

Tonti, H. de. An account of Monsieur de
    la Salle's last expedition. New York
    Historical Society, Collections, 2
    (1814): 217-341.

Villiers, M. de. Recettes médicales
    employées dans la région des Illinois
    vers 1724. Société des Américanistes,
    Journal, n.s., 18 (1926): 15-20.

Wakefield, Francis. The elusive
    Mascoutens. Michigan History, 50 (1966):
    228-234.

Winslow, C. S., ed. Indians of the
    Chicago region. Chicago, 1946. 210 p.

Wray, D. E. Archeology of the Illinois
    Valley: 1950. In J. B. Griffin, ed.
    Archeology of Eastern United States.
    Chicago, 1952: 152-164.

Wray, D. E. and H. Smith. An hypothesis
    for the identification of the Illinois
    Confederacy with the Middle Mississippi
    Culture in Illinois. American Antiquity,
    10 (1944): 23-27.

Zoltvany, Yves F. New France and the
    West, 1701-1713. Canadian Historical
    Review, 46 (1965): 301-322.

Zoltvany, Yves F. The frontier policy of
    Philippe de Rigaud de Vaudreuil, 1713-
    1725. Canadian Historical Review, 48
    (1967): 227-250.

                10-03   Kickapoo

Banks, Dean. Civil-War refugees from
    Indian Territory, in the North, 1861-

1864. Chronicles of Oklahoma, 41 (1963):
    286-298.

Basauri, Carlos. Familia "Algonquiniana":
    Kikapoos. In his La Poblacion Indigena
    de Mexico. Tomo 3. Mexico, Secretaria
    de Educacion Publica, 1940: 643-663.

Beckwith, H. W. The Illinois and Indiana
    Indians. Fergus Historical Series, 27
    (1884): 117-137.

Bettarel, Robert Louis. The Moccasin
    Bluff site and the Woodland cultures of
    southwestern Michigan. Dissertation
    Abstracts International, 32 (1971/1972):
    3752B-3753B.   UM 72-4828.

Carman, J. N. and K. S. Pond. The
    replacement of the Indian languages of
    Kansas by English. Kansas Academy of
    Science, Transactions, 58 (1955): 131-
    150.

Dillingham, Betty Ann Wilder. Oklahoma
    Kickapoo. Dissertation Abstracts, 24
    (1963/1964): 2215-2216.   UM 64-806.

Everett, Mark Allen, et al. Light-
    sensitive eruptions in American Indians.
    Archives of Dermatology, 83 (1961): 243-
    248.

Fabila, A. La tribu kikapoo de Coahuiha.
    Mexico, 1945. 94 p.

Farrar, William G. Historic profiles of
    Fort Massac. By William G. and JoAnn S.
    Farrar. Carbondale, Southern Illinois
    University, University Museum, 1970. 3,
    59 p. (Southern Illinois Studies, 5)

Fay, George E., ed. Charters,
    constitutions and by-laws of the Indian
    tribes of North America. Part XIII:
    Midwestern tribes. Greeley, 1972. 3,
    101 l. map. (University of Northern
    Colorado, Museum of Anthropology,
    Occasional Publications in Anthropology,
    Ethnology Series, 14)

Fay, George E., ed. Charters,
    constitutions and by-laws of the Indian
    tribes of North America. Part V: The
    Indian tribes of Oklahoma. Greeley,
    1968. 14, 104 l. map. (University of
    Northern Colorado, Museum of
    Anthropology, Occasional Publications in
    Anthropology, Ethnology Series, 6) ERIC
    ED046555.

Foreman, G. The last trek of the Indians,
    206-217. Chicago, 1946.

Gibson, A. M. An Indian Territory United
    Nations: the Creek Council of 1845.
    Chronicles of Oklahoma, 39 (1961): 398-
    413.

Gibson, Arrell M. The Kickapoos; lords of
the middle border. Norman, University
of Oklahoma Press, 1963. 15, 391 p.
illus., map.

Goggin, J. M. The Mexican Kickapoo
Indians. Southwestern Journal of
Anthropology, 7 (1951): 314-327.

Goodman, Julia Cody. Julia Cody Goodman's
memoirs of Buffalo Bill. Edited by Don
Russell. Kansas Historical Quarterly, 28
(1962): 442-496.

Haas, Mary R. Algonkian-Ritwan: the end
of a controversy. International Journal
of American Linguistics, 24 (1958): 159-
173.

Hoad, L. G. Kickapoo Indian trails.
Caldwell, 1944. 129 p.

Howard, James H. The Kenakuk religion: an
early 19th century revitalization
movement 140 years later. South Dakota,
University, Museum, Museum News, 26,
nos. 11/12 (1965): 1-48.

Hunter, J. D. Memoirs of a captivity
among the Indians of North America.
London, 1823. 447 p.

Hurley, William M. The Kickapoo whistle
system: a speech surrogate. Plains
Anthropologist, 13 (1968): 242-247.

Hutchins, Thomas. Thomas Hutchins,
geographer. Edited by George E. Amick.
Indiana Historical Bulletin, 47 (1970):
15-18.

Hutter, William H. Scenes in (and en
route to) Kansas Territory, autumn,
1854: five letters by William H. Hutter.
Edited by Louise Barry. Kansas
Historical Quarterly, 35 (1969): 312-
336.

Jones, W. Kickapoo ethnological notes.
American Anthropologist, n.s., 15
(1913): 332-335.

Jones, W. Kickapoo tales. American
Ethnological Society, Publications, 9
(1915): 1-142.

Jones, W. The Algonkin Manitou. Journal
of American Folklore, 18 (1905): 183-
190.

Latorre, Dolores. Hasta qué punto los
indios Kickapú se han integrado en la
medicina popular y moderna de México? By
Dolores and Felipe Latorre. Anuario
Indigenista, 29 (1969): 253-267.

Latorre, Dolores L. Research on the
Mexican Kickapoo. Katunob, 5, no. 2/3
(1965): 20.

Latorre, Dolores L. The ceremonial life
of the Mexican Kickapoo Indians. By
Dolores L. Latorre and Felipe A.
Latorre. In International Congress of
Anthropological and Ethnological
Sciences, 8th. 1968, Tokyo and Kyoto.
Proceedings. Vol. 2. Tokyo, Science
Council of Japan, 1969: 268-270.

León-Portilla, Miguel. Panorama de la
población indígena de México. América
Indígena, 19 (1959): 43-73.

Michelson, T. Algonquian tribes of
Oklahoma and Iowa. Smithsonian
Institution, Explorations and Field-Work
(1928): 183-188.

Michelson, T. Studies of the Algonquian
tribes of Iowa and Oklahoma. Smithsonian
Institution, Explorations and Field-Work
(1929): 207-212.

Michelson, T. The punishment of impudent
children among the Kickapoo. American
Anthropologist, n.s., 25 (1923): 281-
283.

Miller, Otis Louis. Indian-White
relations in the Illinois country, 1789
to 1818. Dissertation Abstracts
International, 33 (1972/1973): 1120A.
UM 72-23,975.

Mooney, J. and W. Jones. Kickapoo. U.S.
Bureau of American Ethnology, Bulletin,
30, vol. 1 (1907): 684-686.

Morgan, L. H. Systems of consanguinity
and affinity. Smithsonian Contributions
to Knowledge, 17 (1871): 291-382.

Neighbors, K. F. The Marcy-Neighbors
exploration of the headwaters of the
Brazos and Wichita Rivers in 1854.
Panhandle-Plains Historical Review, 27
(1954): 27-46.

Owen, M. A. Algonquins. In J. Hastings,
ed. Encyclopaedia of Religion and
Ethics. Vol. 1. New York, 1908: 322-
326.

Patton, W. Journal of a visit to the
Indian missions, Missouri Conference.
Missouri Historical Society, Bulletin,
10 (1954): 167-180.

Peterson, F. A. and R. E. Ritzenthaler.
The Kickapoos are still kicking. Natural
History, 64 (1955): 200-206, 224.

Pope, R. K. The withdrawal of the
Kickapoo. American Indian, 8, no. 2
(1958/1959): 17-26.

*Ritzenthaler, R. E. and F. A. Peterson.
The Mexican Kickapoo Indians. Public
Museum of the City of Milwaukee,

Publications in Anthropology, 2 (1956): 1-91.

Ritzenthaler, Robert E.   The Mexican Kickapoo Indians. By Robert E. Ritzenthaler and Frederick A. Peterson. Westport, Greenwood Press, 1970.   91 p. illus., map.

Schmidt, W.   Die Kickapoo und die Shawnee. In his Die Ursprung der Göttesidee. Bd. 2.   Münster i. W., 1929: 599-601.

*Silverberg, J.   The Kickapoo Indians. Wisconsin Archeologist, 38 (1957): 61-181.

Stephens, A. Ray.   The Killough Massacre. Texana, 7 (1969): 322-327.

Townes, Caleb.   From Old Vincennes, 1815. Indiana Magazine of History, 57 (1961): 141-154.

Voorhis, Paul H.   Notes on Kickapoo whistle speech. International Journal of American Linguistics, 37 (1971): 238-243.

Voorhis, Paul Hantsch.   Kickapoo grammar. Dissertation Abstracts, 28 (1967/1968): 4620A.   UM 68-6863.

Wallace, Ben J.   Oklahoma Kickapoo culture change. Plains Anthropologist, 14 (1969): 107-112.

Wallace, Ben J.   The Oklahoma Kickapoo: an ethnographic reconstruction. Wisconsin Archaeologist, n.s., 45 (1964): 1-69.

Wallace, Ernest.   R. S. Mackenzie and the Kickapoos; the raid into Mexico in 1873. By Ernest Wallace and Adrian S. Anderson. Arizona and the West, 7 (1965): 105-126.

Whitehouse, Joseph.   The journal of Private Joseph Whitehouse, a soldier with Lewis and Clark. Edited by Paul Russell Cutright. Missouri Historical Society, Bulletin, 28 (1971/1972): 143-161.

Winfrey, Dorman H., ed.   The Indian papers of Texas and the Southwest, 1825-1916. Edited by Dorman H. Winfrey and James M. Day.   Austin, Pemberton Press, 1966. 412 p.

Wyatt, P. J.   Kickapoos of Kansas. Emporia, Kansas State Teachers College, 1962.   40 p.   illus.   (Heritage of Kansas, 6, no. 3)

Yarnell, Richard Asa.   Aboriginal relationships between culture and plant life in the Upper Great Lakes region. Ann Arbor, University of Michigan, 1964.

6, 218 p.   (Michigan, University, Museum of Anthropology, Anthropological Papers, 23)

10-04   Menomini

Fay, George E.   Bibliography of the Indians of Wisconsin. Wisconsin Indians Research Institute, Journal, 1, no. 1 (1965): 107-132.

Ames, D. W. and B. R. Fisher.   The Menominee termination crisis. Human Organization, 18, no. 3 (1959): 101-111.

Ames, David W.   The Menominee termination crisis: barriers in the way of a rapid cultural transition. By David W. Ames and Burton R. Fisher. Wisconsin Indians Research Institute, Journal, 2, no. 2 (1966): 42-61.

Anonymous.   Agreement with Menominee Indians. Boletín Indigenista, 20 (1960): 33, 35.

Barrett, S. A.   The dream dance of the Chippewa and Menominee Indians. Public Museum of the City of Milwaukee, Bulletin, 1 (1911): 251-406.

Bloomfield, L.   Menomini texts. American Ethnological Society, Publications, 12 (1928): 1-607.

Bloomfield, L.   The Menomini language. International Congress of Americanists, Proceedings, 21 (1924): 336-343.

Bloomfield, Leonard.   The Menomini language. Preface by Charles F. Hockett. New Haven, Yale University Press, 1962. 11, 515 p.

Boas, F.   Zur Anthropologie der nordamerikanischen Indianer. Berliner Gesellschaft für Anthropologie, Ethnologie und Urgeschichte, Verhandlungen (1895): 367-411.

Brown, D. M.   Indian winter legends. Wisconsin Archeologist, n.s., 22 (1941): 49-53.

Bruce, W. H.   Menomonee. In H. R. Schoolcraft, ed. Information respecting the History, Condition, and Prospects of the Indian Tribes of the United States. Vol. 2.   Philadelphia, 1852: 470-481.

Bushnell, D. I.   Sketches by Paul Kane in the Indian Country, 1845-1848. Smithsonian Miscellaneous Collections, 99, no. 1 (1940): 1-25.

Cardenal, Ernesto, tr. Poesía de los indios de Norteamérica. América Indígena, 21 (1961): 355-362.

Cavazos Garza, Israel. Las incursiones de los bárbaros en el noreste de México, durante el siglo XIX. Humanitas (Monterrey), 5 (1964): 343-356.

Cope, Alfred. A mission to the Menominee: Alfred Cope's Green Bay diary. Edited by William Converse Haygood. Wisconsin Magazine of History, 49 (1965/1966): 302-323; 50 (1966/1967): 18-43, 120-144, 211-241.

Curtis, M. E. Folklore of feast and famine among the Menomini. Michigan Academy of Science, Arts and Letters, Papers, 39 (1954): 407-419.

Curtis, M. E. The black bear and the white-tailed deer. Midwest Folklore, 2 (1952): 177-190.

Densmore, F. Menominee music. U.S. Bureau of American Ethnology, Bulletin, 102 (1932): 1-230.

Densmore, F. Music of the Winnebago and Menominee Indians. Smithsonian Institution, Explorations and Field-Work (1928): 189-198.

Densmore, F. Studies of Indian music among the Menomini. Smithsonian Miscellaneous Collections, 78, no. 1 (1926): 119-125.

Densmore, F. Tribal customs of the Menominee Indians. Smithsonian Institution, Explorations and Field-Work (1929): 217-222.

Densmore, Frances. Menominee music. New York, Da Capo Press, 1972. 22, 230 p. illus.

Douglas, F. H. The Menomini Indians. Denver Art Museum, Indian Leaflet Series, 25 (1931): 1-4.

Edgerton, Robert B. Menominee termination: observations on the end of a tribe. Human Organization, 21 (1962/1963): 10-16.

Edgerton, Robert B. Some dimensions of disillusionment in culture contact. Southwestern Journal of Anthropology, 21 (1965): 231-243.

Emmert, Darlene Gay. The Indians of Shiawassee County. Michigan History, 47 (1963): 127-155, 243-272.

Favre, B. La grammaire de la langue ménomonie du P. Antoine-Marie Gachet. Anthropos, 49 (1954): 1094-1100.

Fay, George E., ed. Charters, constitutions and by-laws of the Indian tribes of North America. Part II: The Indian tribes of Wisconsin (Great Lakes Agency). Greeley, 1967. 6, 124 l. illus., map. (University of Northern Colorado, Museum of Anthropology, Occasional Publications in Anthropology, Ethnology Series, 2) ERIC ED046552.

Fay, George E., ed. Charters, constitutions and by-laws of the Indian tribes of Wisconsin. Wisconsin Indians Research Institute, Journal, 3, no. 1 (1967): 1-124.

Fay, George E., ed. Treaties between the Menominee Indians and the United States of America, 1817-1856. Wisconsin Indians Research Institute, Journal, 1, no. 1 (1965): 67-104.

Federal Writers' Projects. Wisconsin Indian place legends: 33-38. Milwaukee, 1936.

Frantz, Donald G. Person indexing in Blackfoot. International Journal of American Linguistics, 32 (1966): 50-58.

Gachet, A. M. Grammaire de la langue ménomonie. Micro-Bibliotheca Anthropos, 21 (1954): 1-456.

Goddard, Ives. Some errata in Bloomfield's Menomini. By Ives Goddard, Charles F. Hockett and Karl V. Teeter. International Journal of American Linguistics, 38 (1972): 1-5.

Goldschmidt, Walter R. A picture technique for the study of values. By Walter Goldschmidt and Robert B. Edgerton. American Anthropologist, 63 (1961): 26-47.

Haas, Mary R. The Menomini terms for playing cards. International Journal of American Linguistics, 34 (1968): 217.

Hamp, Eric P. Assimilation and rule application. Language, 43 (1967): 179-184.

Hanzeli, Victor E. Missionary linguistics in New France; a study of seventeenth- and eighteenth-century descriptions of American Indian languages. The Hague, Mouton, 1969. 141 p. illus., map. (Janua Linguarum, Series Maior, 29)

Hart, Paxton. The making of Menominee County. Wisconsin Magazine of History, 43 (1959): 181-189.

Hilger, M. I. Menomini child life. Société des Américanistes, Journal, n.s., 40 (1951): 167-171.

Hilger, M. Inez. Some early customs of the Menomini Indians. Société des Américanistes (Paris), Journal, n.s., 49 (1960): 45-68.

Hockett, Charles F. What Algonquian is really like. International Journal of American Linguistics, 32 (1966): 59-73.

*Hoffman, W. J. The Menomini Indians. U.S. Bureau of American Ethnology, Annual Reports, 14, vol. 1 (1893): 11-328.

Hoffman, W. J. The mythology of the Menomini Indians. American Anthropologist, 3 (1890): 243-258.

*Hoffman, Walter J. The Menomini Indians. New York, Johnson Reprint, 1970. 328, 615-637 p. illus., map.

Hrdlička, A. Tuberculosis among certain Indian tribes. U.S. Bureau of American Ethnology, Bulletin, 42 (1909): 8-10.

Jenks, A. E. The wild rice gatherers of the upper lakes. U.S. Bureau of American Ethnology, Annual Reports, 19 (1898): 1013-1137.

Keesing, F. M. The Menomini Indians of Wisconsin. American Philosophical Society, Memoirs, 10 (1939): 1-261.

Keesing, Felix M. The Menomini Indians of Wisconsin. New York, Johnson Reprint, 1971. 15, 11, 261 p. illus.

Krautbauer, F. X. Short sketch of the history of the Menominee Indians. American Catholic Historical Researches, 4 (1887): 152-158.

Kurath, G. P. Menomini Indian dance songs in a changing culture. Midwest Folklore, 9 (1959): 31-38.

Kurath, G. P. Wild rice gatherers of today. American Anthropologist, 59 (1957): 713.

LaFave, Reuben. Menominee Indian study committee. Wisconsin Indians Research Institute, Journal, 2, no. 2 (1966): 73-75.

Laird, Melvin R. Plea for justice for the Menominee Indian people. Wisconsin Indians Research Institute, Journal, 1, no. 2 (1965): 65-88.

Lookaround, Phebe Nichols. A letter about the Menominee Indians. Wisconsin Indians Research Institute, Journal, 2, no. 2 (1966): 64-67.

Lookaround, Phebe Nichols. Wisconsin's people of the wild rice. Wisconsin Indians Research Institute, Journal, 2, no. 2 (1966): 61-63.

Lurie, Nancy Oestreich. Menominee termination: from reservation to colony. Human Organization, 31 (1972): 257-270.

Lurie, Nancy Oestreich. Menominee termination. Indian Historian, 4, no. 4 (1971): 33-45.

Mahan, Bruce E. Fort Shelby and Fort McKay. Palimpsest, 42 (1961): 454-461.

Mathews, Edward. An abolitionist in territorial Wisconsin: the journal of Reverend Edward Mathews. Edited by William Converse Haygood. Wisconsin Magazine of History, 52 (1968/1969): 3-18, 117-131, 248-262, 330-343.

McAllester, D. P. Menomini peyote music. American Philosophical Society, Transactions, 42 (1952): 681-700.

Menominee Indian Tribe. Codification of the constitution and by-laws or rules of the Menominee Indian Tribe, advisory and general councils. Wisconsin Indians Research Institute, Journal, 1, no. 2 (1965): 99-103.

Michelson, T. Further remarks on the origin of the so-called dream dance of the Central Algonkians. American Anthropologist, n.s., 26 (1924): 293-294.

Michelson, T. Menominee tales. American Anthropologist, n.s., 13 (1911): 68-88.

Mooney, J. and C. Thomas. Menominee. U.S. Bureau of American Ethnology, Bulletin, 30, vol. 1 (1907): 842-844.

Morgan, L. H. Systems of consanguinity and affinity. Smithsonian Contributions to Knowledge, 17 (1871): 291-382.

National Study of American Indian Education. Community background reports: the formal education of the Menominee Indian children; sociocultural and socioeconomic background factors. Chicago, University of Chicago; Minneapolis, University of Minnesota, 1970. 62 p. (National Study of American Indian Education, Series I, 23) ERIC ED043424.

Neuman, Robert W. Porcupine quill flatteners from central United States. American Antiquity, 26 (1960/1961): 99-102.

Nichols, Phebe Jewell. I knew Chief Oshkosh. Wisconsin Indians Research Institute, Journal, 1, no. 1 (1965): 24-32.

Nichols, Phebe Jewell. Straight as an arrow. Wisconsin Indians Research Institute, Journal, 1, no. 1 (1965): 33-40.

Nichols, Roger L., ed. The Black Hawk War; another view. Annals of Iowa, 36 (1963): 525-533.

Orfield, Gary. Statement on Menominee termination (hearing at Neopit, Wisconsin). Wisconsin Indians Reaearch Institute, Journal, 1, no. 2 (1965): 50-53.

Orfield, Gary. Termination in retrospect: the Menominee experience. In Richard N. Ellis, ed. The Western American Indian. Lincoln, University of Nebraska Press, 1972: 189-195.

Orfield, Gary. The war on Menominee poverty. Wisconsin Indians Research Institute, Journal, 1, no. 2 (1965): 54-63.

Patterson, John D. The plight of the Menominee Indians. Wisconsin Indians Research Institute, Journal, 1, no. 1 (1965): 20-23.

Peet, S. O. Mythology of the Menominees. American Antiquarian and Oriental Journal, 31 (1909): 1-14.

Ritzenthaler, R. and M. Sellars. Indians in an urban situation. Wisconsin Archeologist, 36 (1955): 147-161.

Ritzenthaler, R. E. The Menominee Indian sawmill. Wisconsin Archeologist, 32 (1951): 39-44.

Robertson, Melvin L. A brief story of the Menominee Indians. Wisconsin Indians Research Institute, Journal, 1, no. 1 (1965): 4-19.

Robertson, Melvin L. Chronology of events relating to termination of federal supervision of the Menominee Indian Reservation--Wisconsin. Wisconsin Indians Research Institute, Journal, 1, no. 2 (1965): 7-48.

Robinson, C. D. Legend of the Red Banks. Wisconsin State Historical Society, Annual Report, 2 (1855): 491-494.

Sady, K. R. The Menominee. Human Organization, 6, no. 2 (1947): 1-14.

Schmidt, W. Die Menomini. In his Die Ursprung der Göttesidee. Bd. 2. Münster i. W., 1929: 539-573.

Shames, Deborah, ed. Freedom with reservation; the Menominee struggle to save their land and people. Washington, D.C., National Committee to Save the Menominee People and Forests, 1972. 12, 116 p. illus.

Siebert, Frank T., Jr. Discrepant consonant clusters ending in *-k in Proto-Algonquian, a proposed interpretation of saltatory sound changes. In Contributions to Anthropology: Linguistics I. Ottawa, Queen's Printer, 1967: 48-59. (Canada, National Museum, Bulletin, 214)

Skinner, A. A comparative sketch of the Menomini. American Anthropologist, n.s., 13 (1911): 551-565.

Skinner, A. Associations and ceremonies of the Menomini Indians. American Museum of Natural History, Anthropological Papers, 13 (1915): 167-215.

Skinner, A. Collecting among the Menomini. Wisconsin Archeologist, n.s., 3 (1924): 135-142.

Skinner, A. Little-Wolf joins the medicine lodge. In E. C. Parsons, ed. American Indian Life. New York, 1925: 63-73.

*Skinner, A. Material culture of the Menomini. Indian Notes and Monographs, n.s., 20 (1921): 1-478.

Skinner, A. Medicine ceremony of the Menomini, Iowa, and Wahpeton Dakota. Indian Notes and Monographs, 4 (1920): 15-188.

Skinner, A. Recollections of an ethnologist among the Menomini Indians. Wisconsin Archeologist, 20 (1921): 41-74.

*Skinner, A. Social life and ceremonial bundles of the Menomini Indians. American Museum of Natural History, Anthropological Papers, 13 (1913): 1-165.

Skinner, A. Some Menomini Indian place names in Wisconsin. Wisconsin Archeologist, 18, no. 3 (1919): 97-102.

Skinner, A. Songs of the Menomini medicine ceremony. American Anthropologist, n.s., 27 (1925): 290-314.

Skinner, A. The Menomini game of lacrosse. American Museum Journal, 11 (1911): 139-141.

Skinner, A. The Menomini word "Häwätuk". Journal of American Folklore, 28 (1915): 258-261.

Skinner, A. War customs of the Menomini
Indians. American Anthropologist, n.s.,
13 (1911): 299-312.

Skinner, A. and J. V. Satterlee. Folklore
of the Menomini Indians. American Museum
of Natural History, Anthropological
Papers, 13 (1915): 217-546.

Slotkin, J. S. A case of paranoid
schizophrenia among the Menomini Indians
of Wisconsin. Madison, 1959.
(Microcard Publications of Primary
Records in Culture and Personality, 3)

Slotkin, J. S. Social psychiatry of a
Menomini community. Journal of Abnormal
and Social Psychology, 48 (1953): 10-16.

*Slotkin, J. S. The Menomini powwow.
Public Museum of the City of Milwaukee,
Publications in Anthropology, 4 (1957):
1-166.

Smith, H. H. Ethnobotany of the Menomini
Indians. Public Museum of the City of
Milwaukee, Bulletin, 4 (1923): 1-174.

Smith, H. H. Uses of native plants by the
Menomini. Wisconsin Archeologist, n.s.,
3 (1924): 24-26.

Smith, Huron S. Ethnobotany of the
Menomini Indians. Westport, Greenwood
Press, 1970. 174 p. illus.

Spindler, G. D. Personality and peyotism
in Menomini Indian acculturation.
Psychiatry, 15 (1952): 151-159.

Spindler, G. D. and W. Goldschmidt.
Experimental design in the study of
culture change. Southwestern Journal of
Anthropology, 8 (1952): 68-83.

Spindler, George D. Dreamers without
power. By George D. Spindler and Louise
Spindler. New York, Holt, Rinehart and
Winston, 1971. 14, 208 p. illus.

*Spindler, George D. Sociocultural and
psychological processes in Menomini
acculturation. Berkeley, 1955. 6,
271 p. illus., maps. (California,
University, Publications in Culture and
Society, 5)

Spindler, L. S. Witchcraft in Menomini
acculturation. American Anthropologist,
54 (1952): 593-602.

Spindler, L. S. and G. D. Spindler. Male
and female adaptations in culture
change. American Anthropologist, 60
(1958): 217-233.

Spindler, Louise S. Male and female
adaptations in culture change: Menomini.
By Louise and George Spindler. In Robert

Hunt, ed. Personalities and Cultures.
Garden City, Natural History Press,
1967: 56-78.

Spindler, Louise S. Menomini women and
culture change. Menasha, 1962. 113 p.
illus. (American Anthropological
Association, Memoir, 91)

Szabó, László. Malecite prosodics. In
André Rigault and René Charbonneau, eds.
International Congress of Phonetic
Sciences, 7th. 1971, Montreal.
Proceedings. The Hague, Mouton, 1972:
1032-1034. (Janua Linguarum, Series
Maior, 57)

U.S., Congress. Menominee Indian Timber
Cutting Act. Wisconsin Indians Reaearch
Institute, Journal, 1, no. 1 (1965):
105-106.

U.S., Congress, Senate, Committee on
Interior and Insular Affairs.
Amendments to the Menominee termination
act. Washington, D.C., Government
Printing Office, 1961. 3, 153 p.

U.S., Congress, Senate, Committee on
Interior and Insular Affairs. 1960
amendments to the Menominee Indian
termination act of 1954. Washington,
D.C., Government Printing Office, 1960.
2, 104 p.

U.S., Congress, Senate, Committee on Labor
and Public Welfare, Subcommittee on
Employment, Manpower, and Poverty.
Menominee County aid. Hearings, Eighty-
ninth Congress, first and second
sessions. November 10 and 11, 1965, and
February 17, 1966. Washington, D.C.,
Government Printing Office, 1966. 7,
333 p. illus.

Vizcaya Canales, Isidro. La invasión de
los indios bárbaros al noreste de
México, en los años de 1840 y 1841.
Monterrey, N.L., 1968. 296 p.
(Monterrey, Instituto Tecnologico y de
Estudios Superiores de Monterrey,
Publicaciones, Serie: Historia, 7)

Weidemann, Wayne H. Menominee:
Wisconsin's 72nd County. By Wayne H.
Weidemann and Glenn V. Fuguitt.
Madison, University of Wisconsin,
Department of Rural Sociology, 1963.
38 p. (Population Note, 3) ERIC
ED040781.

Wickham, Woodward A. The Menominees of
Wisconsin. New York, Institute of
Current World Affairs, 1971. 10 p.
(Institute of Current World Affairs, WW-
1)

Wisconsin, Governor's Commission on Human
Rights. Handbook on Wisconsin Indians.

Compiled and written by Joyce M. Erdman. Madison, 1966. 103 p. illus., maps. ERIC ED033816.

Wisconsin, State Legislative Council. Report of Menominee Indian Study Committee. Madison, 1970. 60 p. (Wisconsin, State Legislative Council, Report, 8) ERIC ED047836.

Wisconsin, University, Institute of Governmental Affairs. Report to the Menominee Indian Study Committee, Joint Legislative Council, State of Wisconsin, on county and local government for the Menominee Indian Reservation. Madison, 1956. 9, 95 l. illus., map.

Yarnell, Richard Asa. Aboriginal relationships between culture and plant life in the Upper Great Lakes region. Ann Arbor, University of Michigan, 1964. 6, 218 p. (Michigan, University, Museum of Anthropology, Anthropological Papers, 23)

10-05 Miami

Anonymous. Illinois and Miami vocabulary and Lord's Prayer. U.S. Catholic Historical Magazine, 3 (1891): 1-9.

Anson, Bert. Chief Francis Lafontaine and the Miami emigration from Indiana. Indiana Magazine of History, 60 (1964): 241-268.

*Anson, Bert. The Miami Indians. Norman, University of Oklahoma Press, 1970. 17, 329 p. illus., maps.

Baldwin, C. C. Early Indian migration in Ohio. American Antiquarian and Oriental Journal, 1 (1879): 227-239.

Beckwith, H. W. The Illinois and Indiana Indians. Fergus Historical Series, 27 (1884): 107-117.

Bettarel, Robert Louis. The Moccasin Bluff site and the Woodland cultures of southwestern Michigan. Dissertation Abstracts International, 32 (1971/1972): 3752B-3753B. UM 72-4828.

Bibaud, F. M. Biographie des sagamos illustrés de l'Amérique Septentrionale, 236-242. Montréal, 1848.

Blain, Harry S. Little Turtle's watch. Northwest Ohio Quarterly, 37 (1964/1965): 27-32.

Blasingame, E. J. The Miami prior to the French and Indian War. Ethnohistory, 2 (1955): 1-10.

Brice, W. A. History of Fort Wayne. Fort Wayne, 1868. 324 p.

Corbitt, D. C., tr. and ed. Papers from the Spanish archives relating to Tennessee and the Old Southwest. Translated and edited by D. C. Corbitt and Roberta Corbitt. East Tennessee Historical Society, Publications, 31 (1959): 63-82; 32 (1960): 72-93; 33 (1961): 61-78; 34 (1962): 86-105; 35 (1963): 85-95; 36 (1964): 70-80; 37 (1965): 89-105; 38 (1966): 70-82; 39 (1967): 87-102; 40 (1968): 101-118; 41 (1969): 100-116; 42 (1970): 96-107; 43 (1971): 94-111; 44 (1972): 104-113.

Deliette, L. Memoir concerning the Illinois Country. Ed. T. C. Pease and R. C. Werner. Illinois State Historical Library, Collections, 23 (1934): 302-395.

Dillon, J. B. The national decline of the Miami Indians. Indiana Historical Society Publications, 1 (1897): 121-143.

Dunn, C. Jacob Piatt Dunn: his Miami language studies and Indian manuscript collection. Indiana Historical Society, Prehistory Research Series, 1 no. 2 (1937): 31-59.

Dunn, J. P. True Indian stories. Indianapolis, 1909. 320 p.

Edmunds, R. David. Wea participation in the Northwest Indian wars. Filson Club History Quarterly, 46 (1972): 241-253.

Faben, W. W. Indians of the tri-state area; the Miamis 1654-1752. Northwest Ohio Quarterly, 41 (1968/1969): 157-162.

Fay, George E., ed. Charters, constitutions and by-laws of the Indian tribes of North America. Part V: The Indian tribes of Oklahoma. Greeley, 1968. 14, 104 l. map. (University of Northern Colorado, Museum of Anthropology, Occasional Publications in Anthropology, Ethnology Series, 6) ERIC ED046555.

Foreman, G. The last trek of the Indians, 125-132, 201-204. Chicago, 1946.

Gibson, A. M. An Indian Territory United Nations: the Creek Council of 1845. Chronicles of Oklahoma, 39 (1961): 398-413.

Godfroy, Clarence. Miami Indian stories. Edited by Martha Una McClurg. Winona Lake, Ind., Light and Life Press, 1961. 172 p. illus.

Hamil, Fred C. Michigan in the War of
    1812. Michigan History, 44 (1960): 257-
    291.

Handy, C. N. Miami. In H. R. Schoolcraft,
    ed. Information respecting the History,
    Condition, and Prospects of the Indian
    Tribes of the United States. Vol. 2.
    Philadelphia, 1852: 470-481.

Hanzeli, Victor E. Missionary linguistics
    in New France; a study of seventeenth-
    and eighteenth-century descriptions of
    American Indian languages. The Hague,
    Mouton, 1969. 141 p. illus., map.
    (Janua Linguarum, Series Maior, 29)

Harrison, W. H. A discourse on the
    aborigines of the Ohio Valley. Fergus
    Historical Series, 26 (1883): 1-95.

Henson, C. E. Ritual elements in
    Mississippi River petroglyphs. Folk-
    Lore, 68 (1957): 405-410.

Herr, Remley. Major General Anthony
    Wayne's Indian campaign, 1792-1794.
    Indiana Historical Bulletin, 49 (1972):
    135-138.

Hill, L. U. John Johnston and the Indians
    in the land of the Three Miamis. Piqua,
    1957. 207 p.

Hooton, E. A. Indian village site and
    cemetery near Madisonville Ohio. Harvard
    University, Peabody Museum of American
    Archaeology and Ethnology, Papers, 8,
    no. 1 (1920): 1-137.

Hosmer, H. L. Early history of the Maumee
    Valley. In Toledo Directory. Toledo,
    1858: 9-70.

Huber, John Parker. General Josiah
    Harmar's command: military policy in the
    Old Northwest, 1784-1791. Dissertation
    Abstracts International, 30 (1969/1970):
    247A. UM 69-12,138.

Hundley, W. M. Squawtown. Caldwell,
    1939. 209 p.

Hutchins, Thomas. Thomas Hutchins,
    geographer. Edited by George E. Amick.
    Indiana Historical Bulletin, 47 (1970):
    15-18.

*Kinietz, W. V. The Indian tribes of the
    western Great Lakes. Michigan,
    University, Museum of Anthropology,
    Occasional Contributions, 10 (1940):
    161-225.

Laning, Paul L. Colonial trail blazers
    around western Lake Erie. Inland Seas,
    19 (1963): 266-276.

Mahr, August C. Delaware terms for plants
    and animals in the eastern Ohio country:
    a study in semantics. Anthropological
    Linguistics, 4, no. 5 (1962): 1-48.

Mahr, August C. Semantic evaluation.
    Anthropological Linguistics, 3, no. 5
    (1961): 1-46.

Mary Celeste. The Miami Indians prior to
    1700. Mid-America, n.s., 16 (1934): 225-
    234.

Miller, Otis Louis. Indian-White
    relations in the Illinois country, 1789
    to 1818. Dissertation Abstracts
    International, 33 (1972/1973): 1120A.
    UM 72-23,975.

Mooney, J. Piankashaw. U.S. Bureau of
    American Ethnology, Bulletin, 30, vol. 2
    (1910): 240-241.

Mooney, J. Wea. U.S. Bureau of American
    Ethnology, Bulletin, 30, vol. 2 (1910):
    925-926.

Mooney, J. and C. Thomas. Miami. U.S.
    Bureau of American Ethnology, Bulletin,
    30, vol. 1 (1907): 852-855.

Moorehead, W. K. The Indian tribes of
    Ohio. Ohio State Archaeological and
    Historical Quarterly, 7 (1898): 1-109.

Morgan, L. H. Systems of consanguinity
    and affinity. Smithsonian Contributions
    to Knowledge, 17 (1871): 291-382.

Morgan, L. H. The Indian journals, 1859-
    62: p. 78. Ann Arbor, 1959.

Pattison, William D. The survey of the
    Seven Ranges. Ohio Historical Quarterly,
    68 (1959): 115-140.

Phillips, Edward Hake. Timothy Pickering
    at his best: Indian Commissioner, 1790-
    1794. Essex Institute Historical
    Collections, 102 (1966): 163-201.

Quimby, G. I. European trade articles as
    chronological indicators for the
    archaeology of the historic period in
    Michigan. Michigan Academy of Science,
    Arts and Letters, Papers, 24, no. 4
    (1938): 25-31.

Reves, Haviland F. The Reves Farm--
    private claim 49. Michigan History, 45
    (1961): 237-258.

Robertson, R. S. Burial among the Miamis.
    American Antiquarian and Oriental
    Journal, 2 (1879): 54-55.

Shetrone, H. C. The Indian in Ohio. Ohio
    State Archaeological and Historical
    Quarterly, 27 (1918): 273-510.

Smith, G. H. Three Maimi tales. Journal
of American Folklore, 52 (1939): 194-
208.

Strong, W. D. The Indian tribes of the
Chicago Region. Field Museum of Natural
History, Department of Anthropology,
Leaflets, 24 (1926): 14-16.

Taylor, E. L. The Ohio Indians. Ohio
State Archaeological and Historical
Quarterly, 6 (1898): 72-94.

Thornton, W. Miamis. American Antiquarian
Society, Transactions and Collections, 2
(1836): 305-367.

Townes, Caleb. From Old Vincennes, 1815.
Indiana Magazine of History, 57 (1961):
141-154.

Trent, William. Journal of Captain
William Trent from Logstown to
Pickawillany, A.D. 1752. New York, Arno
Press, 1971. 117 p.

*Trowbridge, C. C. Meearmeear traditions.
Ed. by W. V. Kinietz. Michigan,
University, Museum of Anthropology,
Occasional Contributions, 7 (1938): 1-
91.

Voegelin, C. F. Shawnee stems and the
Jacob P. Dunn Miami dictionary. Indiana
Historical Society, Prehistory Research
Series, 1 (1938/1940): 63-108, 135-167,
345-406, 409-478.

Volney, C. F. C. Tableau du climat et du
sol des États-Unis d'Amérique. Paris,
1803. 2 v.

Volney, C. F. C. View of the climate and
soil of the United States of America,
393-503. London, 1804.

Watts, Florence G. Fort Knox: frontier
outpost on the Wabash, 1787-1816.
Indiana Magazine of History, 62 (1966):
51-78.

Winter, G. Journals and Indian paintings,
1837-1839. Indianapolis, 1948. 208 p.

Yarnell, Richard Asa. Aboriginal
relationships between culture and plant
life in the Upper Great Lakes region.
Ann Arbor, University of Michigan, 1964.
6, 218 p. (Michigan, University, Museum
of Anthropology, Anthropological Papers,
23)

Zoltvany, Yves F. New France and the
West, 1701-1713. Canadian Historical
Review, 46 (1965): 301-322.

10-06   Potawatomi

Fay, George E. Bibliography of the
Indians of Wisconsin. Wisconsin Indians
Research Institute, Journal, 1, no. 1
(1965): 107-132.

Audubon, John James. Birds along the
Missouri. Edited by William J. Petersen.
Palimpsest, 52 (1971): 550-570.

Beckwith, H. The Illinois and Indiana
Indians. Fergus Historical Series, 27
(1884): 162-183.

Bee, Robert L. Potawatomi peyotism: the
influence of traditional patterns.
Southwestern Journal of Anthropology, 22
(1966): 194-205.

Bloodworth, J. Social and economic survey
of Potawatomie jurisdiction.
Washington, D.C., Bureau of Indian
Affairs, 1957. 58 p.

Bolt, Robert. Reverend Leonard Slater in
the Grand River Valley. Michigan
History, 51 (1967): 241-251.

Bourassa, J. N. "The life of Wah-bahn-se:
the warrior chief of the Pottawatamies".
Kansas Historical Quarterly, 38 (1972):
132-143.

Brown, D. M. Indian winter legends.
Wisconsin Archeologist, n.s., 22 (1941):
49-53.

Brown, D. M. Wisconsin Indian corn origin
myths. Wisconsin Archeologist, n.s., 21
(1940): 19-27.

Bryant, Peter. The letters of Peter
Bryant, Jackson County pioneer. Edited
by Donald M. Murray and Robert M.
Rodney. Kansas Historical Quarterly, 27
(1961): 320-352.

Buechner, C. B. The Pokagons. Indiana
Historical Society Publications, 10
(1933): 281-340.

Burke, James M. Early days at St. Mary's
Pottawatomie Mission, from the diary of
Father Maurice Gailland, S.J. Kansas
Historical Quarterly, 20 (1953): 500-
529.

Callan, Louise. Philippine Duchesne,
frontier missionary of the Sacred Heart,
1769-1852. Westminster, Md., Newman
Press, 1957. 13, 805 p.

Carman, J. N. and K. S. Pond. The
replacement of the Indian languages of
Kansas by English. Kansas Academy of

Science, Transactions, 58 (1955): 131-
150.

Caton, J. D. The last of the Illinois and
a sketch of the Pottawatomies. Fergus
Historical Series, 3 (1876): 3-30.

Chapman, B. B. The Pottawatomie and
Absentee Shawnee Reservation. Chronicles
of Oklahoma, 24 (1946): 293-305.

Claspy, Everett. The Potawatomi Indians
of southwestern Michigan. Dowagiac,
Mich., 1966. 5, 43 p.

Clifton, James A. Culture change,
structural stability and factionalism in
the Prairie Potawatomi Reservation
community. Midcontinent American Studies
Journal, 6 (1965): 101-123.

Clifton, James A. Sociocultural dynamics
of the Prairie Potawatomi Drum Cult.
Plains Anthropologist, 14 (1969): 85-93.

Clifton, James A. The Kansas Prairie
Potawatomi: on the nature of a
contemporary Indian community. By James
A. Clifton and Barry Isaac. Kansas
Academy of Science, Transactions, 67
(1964): 1-24.

Collins, Harriet Whitney. The life
history of Harriet Whitney Collins. As
related by herself to her daughter,
Harriet Collins Perry.

Conway, Thomas G. Potawatomi politics.
Illinois State Historical Society,
Journal, 65 (1972): 395-418.

*Deale, V. B. The history of the
Potawotamies before 1722. Ethnohistory,
5 (1958): 305-360.

Dickason, David H. Chief Simon Pokagon:
"The Indian Longfellow". Indiana
Magazine of History, 57 (1961): 127-140.

Dolan, John P. The plight of the
Potawatomi. Neue Zeitschrift für
Missionswissenschaft, 16 (1960): 275-
280.

Drake, Florence. Mary Bourbonnais
organized a Sunday school. Chronicles of
Oklahoma, 40 (1962): 386-389.

Edmunds, R. David. The Illinois River
Potawatomi in the War of 1812. Illinois
State Historical Society, Journal, 62
(1969): 341-362.

Edmunds, R. David. The Prairie Potawatomi
removal of 1833. Indiana Magazine of
History, 68 (1972): 240-253.

Edmunds, Russell David. A history of the
Potawatomi Indians, 1615-1795.

Dissertation Abstracts International, 33
(1972/1973): 5636A. UM 73-9149.

Emmert, Darlene Gay. The Indians of
Shiawassee County. Michigan History, 47
(1963): 127-155, 243-272.

Erickson, Barbara. Patterns of person-
number in Potawatomi. International
Journal of American Linguistics, 31
(1965): 226-236.

Faben, W. W. Indians of the tri-state
area. Northwest Ohio Quarterly, 34
(1961/1962): 168-176.

Faben, W. W. Indians of the tri-state
area, the Potowatomis the removal; 1.
Northwest Ohio Quarterly, 40
(1967/1968): 68-84.

Faben, W. W. Indians of the tri-state
area: the Potowattamis. Northwest Ohio
Quarterly, 30 (1958): 49-53, 100-105.

Farrar, William G. Historic profiles of
Fort Massac. By William G. and JoAnn S.
Farrar. Carbondale, Southern Illinois
University, University Museum, 1970. 3,
59 p. (Southern Illinois Studies, 5)

Farrell, David. Settlement along the
Detroit frontier, 1760-1796. Michigan
History, 52 (1968): 89-107.

Fay, George E., ed. Charters,
constitutions and by-laws of the Indian
tribes of Wisconsin. Wisconsin Indians
Research Institute, Journal, 3, no. 1
(1967): 1-124.

Fay, George E., ed. Charters,
constitutions and by-laws of the Indian
tribes of North America. Part II: The
Indian tribes of Wisconsin (Great Lakes
Agency). Greeley, 1967. 6, 124 l.
illus., map. (University of Northern
Colorado, Museum of Anthropology,
Occasional Publications in Anthropology,
Ethnology Series, 2) ERIC ED046552.

Fay, George E., ed. Charters,
constitutions and by-laws of the Indian
tribes of North America. Part VI: The
Indian tribes of Oklahoma (cont'd.).
Greeley, 1968. 5, 129 l. map.
(University of Northern Colorado, Museum
of Anthropology, Occasional Publications
in Anthropology, Ethnology Series, 7)
ERIC ED046556.

Fay, George E., ed. Charters,
constitutions and by-laws of the Indian
tribes of North America. Part XIII:
Midwestern tribes. Greeley, 1972. 3,
101 l. map. (University of Northern
Colorado, Museum of Anthropology,
Occasional Publications in Anthropology,
Ethnology Series, 14)

Fay, George E., ed. Charters, constitutions and by-laws of the Indian tribes of North America. Part XIV: Great Lakes Agency: Minnesota-Michigan. Greeley, 1972. 4, 84 l. map. (University of Northern Colorado, Museum of Anthropology, Occasional Publications in Anthropology, Ethnology Series, 15)

Fay, George E., ed. Treaties between the Potawatomi tribe of Indians and the United States of America, 1789-1867. Greeley, 1971. 5, 150 l. (University of Northern Colorado, Museum of Anthropology, Occasional Publications in Anthropology, Ethnology Series, 19)

Fay, George E., ed. Treaties between the Potawatomi Tribe of Indians and the United States of America, 1789-1867. Wisconsin Indians Research Institute, Journal, 4, no. 1 (1968): i-ii, 1-150.

Federal Writers' Projects. Wisconsin Indian place legends, 13-14, 17-25, 30-32, 39. Milwaukee, 1936.

Fightmaster, Maxine. Sacred Heart Mission among the Potawatomi Indians. Chronicles of Oklahoma, 50 (1972): 156-176.

Fitting, James E. Settlement analysis in the Great Lakes region. Southwestern Journal of Anthropology, 25 (1969): 360-377.

Foreman, G. The last trek of the Indians, 100-125, 218-222. Chicago, 1946.

Frantz, Donald G. Person indexing in Blackfoot. International Journal of American Linguistics, 32 (1966): 50-58.

Goddard, Ives. Historical and philological evidence regarding the identification of the Mascouten. Ethnohistory, 19 (1972): 123-134.

Hamer, John H. Acculturation stress and the functions of alcohol among the Forest Potawatomi. Quarterly Journal of Studies on Alcohol, 26 (1965): 285-302.

Hamer, John H. Guardian spirits, alcohol, and cultural defense mechanisms. Anthropologica, n.s., 11 (1969): 215-241.

Hamil, Fred C. Michigan in the War of 1812. Michigan History, 44 (1960): 257-291.

Hampton, James E. Pernicious anemia in American Indians. Oklahoma State Medical Association, Journal, 53 (1960): 503-509.

Hanzeli, Victor E. Missionary linguistics in New France; a study of seventeenth- and eighteenth-century descriptions of American Indian languages. The Hague, Mouton, 1969. 141 p. illus., map. (Janua Linguarum, Series Maior, 29)

Harkins, Arthur M. Attitudes and characteristics of selected Wisconsin Indians. By Arthur M. Harkins and Richard G. Woods. Wisconsin Indians Research Institute, Journal, 4, no. 1 (1968): 64-130.

Harkins, Arthur M. Attitudes and characteristics of selected Wisconsin Indians. By Arthur M. Harkins and Richard G. Woods. Minneapolis, University of Minnesota, Training Center for Community Programs, 1969. 89 p. ERIC ED032174.

Harstad, Peter T. Disease and sickness on the Wisconsin frontier: smallpox and other diseases. Wisconsin Magazine of History, 43 (1959): 253-263.

Hockett, C. F. Potawatomi. International Journal of American Linguistics, 14 (1948): 1-10, 63-73, 139-149, 213-225.

Hockett, C. F. Potawatomi syntax. Language, 15 (1939): 235-248.

Hockett, C. F. The conjunct modes in Ojibwa and Potawatomi. Language, 26 (1950): 278-282.

Hockett, C. F. The position of Potawatomi in Central Algonkian. Michigan Academy of Science, Arts and Letters, Papers, 28 (1942): 537-542.

Hockett, Charles F. Language, mathematics and linguistics. The Hague, Mouton, 1967. 243 p. illus. (Janua Linguarum, Series Minor, 60)

Hockett, Charles F. The Potawatomi language. Dissertation Abstracts International, 30 (1969/1970): 2614B. UM 69-20,384.

Hockett, Charles F. What Algonquian is really like. International Journal of American Linguistics, 32 (1966): 59-73.

Howard, James H. Potawatomi mescalism and its relationship to the diffusion of the peyote cult. Plains Anthropologist, 7 (1962): 96.

Howard, James H. Potawatomi mescalism and its relationship to the diffusion of the peyote cult. Plains Anthropologist, 7 (1962): 125-135.

Howard, James H. When they worship the underwater panther: a Prairie Potawatomi bundle ceremony. Southwestern Journal of Anthropology, 16 (1960): 217-224.

Hutter, William H. Scenes in (and en route to) Kansas Territory, autumn, 1854: five letters by William H. Hutter. Edited by Louise Barry. Kansas Historical Quarterly, 35 (1969): 312-336.

Jacobs, Hubert. The Potawatomi mission 1854. Mid-America, 36 (1954): 220-226.

Johnson, F. Notes on the Ojibwa and Potawatomi of the Parry Island Reservation. Indian Notes, 6 (1929): 193-216.

Jones, J. A. The political organization of the three fires. Indiana Academy of Science, Proceedings, 63 (1953): 46.

Karol, Joseph. What happened to the Potawatomi? American Ecclesiastical Review, 129 (1953): 361-367.

Keating, W. H. Narrative of an expedition to the source of St. Peter's River, Vol. 1: 91-138. Philadelphia, 1824.

Kelkar, Ashok R. Participant placement in Algonquian and Georgian. International Journal of American Linguistics, 31 (1965): 195-205.

Kinietz, W. V. The Indian tribes of the western Great Lakes. Michigan, University, Museum of Anthropology, Occasional Contributions, 10 (1940): 308-316.

Kurath, G. P. Wild rice gatherers of today. American Anthropologist, 59 (1957): 713.

Landes, Ruth. Potawatomie medicine. Kansas Academy of Science, Transactions, 66 (1963): 553-599.

*Landes, Ruth. The Prairie Potawatomi; tradition and ritual in the twentieth century. Madison, University of Wisconsin Press, 1970. 12, 420 p. illus.

Larkin, F. A. Dietary patterns and the use of commodity foods in a Potawatomi Indian community. By F. A. Larkin and A. M. Sandretto. Journal of Home Economics, 62 (1970): 385-388.

Lawson, P. V. The Potawatomi. Wisconsin Archeologist, 19 (1920): 41-116.

Longacre, Robert E. Grammar discovery procedures; a field manual. The Hague, Mouton, 1964. 162 p. (Janua Linguarum, Series Minor, 33)

Lykins, J., tr. The gospel according to Matthew and Acts of the Apostles. Louisville, 1844. 240 p.

Mahan, Bruce E. Winnebago and Pottawa Hamie. Palimpsest, 50 (1969): 231-233.

Mathews, Edward. An abolitionist in territorial Wisconsin: the journal of Reverend Edward Mathews. Edited by William Converse Haygood. Wisconsin Magazine of History, 52 (1968/1969): 3-18, 117-131, 248-262, 330-343.

McDonald, D. Removal of the Pottawattomie Indians from northern Indiana. Plymouth, 1899. 59 p.

Metzdorf, W. The Pottawatomi. In E. H. Blair, ed. The Indian Tribes of the Upper Mississippi Valley. Vol. 2. Cleveland, 1912: 287-297.

Meyer, A. H. Circulation and settlement patterns of the Calumet region of Northwest Indiana and Northeast Illinois. Association of American Geographers, Annals, 44 (1954): 245-274.

Michelson, T. The identification of the Mascoutens. American Anthropologist, n.s., 36 (1934): 226-233.

Michelson, T. The linguistic classification of Potawatomi. National Academy of Sciences, Proceedings, 1 (1915): 450-452.

Miller, Otis Louis. Indian-White relations in the Illinois country, 1789 to 1818. Dissertation Abstracts International, 33 (1972/1973): 1120A. UM 72-23,975.

Mooney, J. and J. N. B. Hewitt. Potawatomi. U.S. Bureau of American Ethnology, Bulletin, 30, vol. 2 (1910): 289-293.

Morgan, L. H. Systems of consanguinity and affinity. Smithsonian Contributions to Knowledge, 17 (1871): 291-382.

Morgan, L. H. The Indian journals, 1859-62: p. 35-36, 58, 84. Ann Arbor, 1959.

Morse, J. A report to the Secretary of War. New Haven, 1822. 400 p.

Murphy, Joseph Frances. Potawatomi Indians of the West: origins of the Citizen Band. Dissertation Abstracts, 22 (1961/1962): 1134. UM 61-3062.

Nasatir, A. P. Before Lewis and Clark. St. Louis, 1952. 2 v. (882 p.).

Neumeyer, Elizabeth. Michigan Indians battle against removal. Michigan History, 55 (1971): 275-288.

Nichols, P. V. Wisconsin--what does it mean? América Indígena, 8 (1948): 171-176.

Patton, W. Journal of a visit to the Indian missions, Missouri Conference. Missouri Historical Society, Bulletin, 10 (1954): 167-180.

Petersen, William J. Land of the Fire Makers. Palimpsest, 45 (1964): 321-323.

Pike, Kenneth L. Conflated field structures in Potawatomi and in Arabic. By Kenneth L. Pike and Barbara Erickson. International Journal of American Linguistics, 30 (1964): 201-212.

Pokagon, S. O-gi-maw-kwe mit-i-gwä-ki: queen of the woods. Hartford, 1899.

Pruitt, O. J. John Y. Nelson: plainsman. Annals of Iowa, 35 (1960): 294-303.

Pruitt, O. J. Some Iowa Indian tales. Annals of Iowa, 3d ser., 32 (1953/1955): 203-216.

Quimby, G. I. European trade articles as chronological indicators for the archaeology of the historic period in Michigan. Michigan Academy of Science, Arts and Letters, Papers, 24, no. 4 (1938): 25-31.

Quimby, G. I. Some notes on kinship and kinship terminology among the Potawatomi of the Huron. Michigan Academy of Science, Arts and Letters, Papers, 25 (1939): 553-563.

Quimby, George I. The voyage of the Griffin: 1679. Michigan History, 49 (1965): 97-107.

Ragland, H. D. Potawatomi day schools. Chronicles of Oklahoma, 30 (1952): 270-278.

Rathke, William C. Chief Waubonsie and the Pottawattamie Indians. Annals of Iowa, 35 (1959): 81-100.

Ridgley, Mary H. Reminiscences of the John Bair family. Michigan History, 47 (1963): 363-368.

Ritzenthaler, R. and M. Sellars. Indians in an urban situation. Wisconsin Archeologist, 36 (1955): 147-161.

*Ritzenthaler, R. E. The Potawatomi Indians of Wisconsin. Public Museum of the City of Milwaukee, Bulletin, 19 (1953): 99-174.

Rogers, Edward S. The dugout canoe in Ontario. American Antiquity, 30 (1964/1965): 454-459.

Salzer, Robert J. Bear-walking: a shamanistic phenomenon among the Potawatomi Indians in Wisconsin. Wisconsin Archeologist, n.s., 53 (1972): 110-146.

Schmidt, W. Die Potawatomie (und Ottawa). In his Die Ursprung der Göttesidee. Bd. 2. Münster i. W., 1929: 508-515.

Schoewe, C. G. Uses of wood and bark among the Wisconsin Indians. Wisconsin Archeologist, n.s., 11 (1932): 148-152.

Searcy, Ann McElroy. Contemporary and traditional Prairie Potawatomi child life. Lawrence, 1965. 74 l. (Kansas, University, Potawatomi Study Research Report, 7)

Sibley, George C. George C. Sibley's Journal of a trip to the Salines in 1811. Edited by George R. Brooks. Missouri Historical Society, Bulletin, 21 (1964/1965): 167-207.

Skinner, A. A trip to the Potawatomi. Wisconsin Archeologist, n.s., 3 (1924): 143-150.

Skinner, A. Medicine ceremony of the Menomini, Iowa, and Wahpeton Dakota. Indian Notes and Monographs, 4 (1920): 327-330.

*Skinner, A. The Mascoutens or Prairie Potawatomi Indians. Public Museum of the City of Milwaukee, Bulletin, 6 (1924/1927): 1-411.

*Skinner, Alanson B. The Mascoutens or Prairie Potawatomi Indians; social life and ceremonies. Westport, Greenwood Press, 1970. 262 p. illus.

Smet, P. J. de. Legend of the Potawotomie Indians. Early Western Travels, 29 (1906): 373-380.

Smith, H. H. Among the Potawatomi. Public Museum of the City of Milwaukee, Yearbook, 5 (1925): 68-76.

Smith, H. H. Ethnobotany of the Forest Potawatomi Indians. Public Museum of the City of Milwaukee, Bulletin, 7 (1933): 1-230.

Smith, James. An account of the remarkable occurrences in the life and travels of Col. James Smith, during his captivity with the Indians in the years 1755, '56, '57, '58, and '59, with an appendix of illustrative notes. Edited by Wm. N. Darlington. Cincinnati, R. Clarke, 1870. 12, 190 p. (Ohio Valley Historical Series, 5)

Steele, Charles Hoy. American Indians and urban life: a community study. Dissertation Abstracts International, 33 (1972/1973): 6479A-6480A. UM 73-11,959.

Strong, W. D. The Indian tribes of the Chicago region. Field Museum of Natural History, Department of Anthropology, Leaflets, 24 (1926): 17-34.

Thwaites, R. G., ed. Radisson and Groseilliers in Wisconsin. State Historical Society of Wisconsin, Collections, 11 (1888): 64-96.

Thwaites, R. G., ed. The Jesuit relations and allied documents. Cleveland, 1896-1901. 74 v.

Tiedke, K. E. A study of the Hannahville Indian community. Michigan, State Agricultural Experiment Station, Special Bulletin, 369 (1951): 1-43.

Townes, Caleb. From Old Vincennes, 1815. Indiana Magazine of History, 57 (1961): 141-154.

Vincent, John R. Midwest Indians and frontier photography. Annals of Iowa, 38 (1965): 26-35.

Wakefield, Francis. The elusive Mascoutens. Michigan History, 50 (1966): 228-234.

Watts, Florence G. Fort Knox: frontier outpost on the Wabash, 1787-1816. Indiana Magazine of History, 62 (1966): 51-78.

Wax, Murray L., et al. Indian communities and Project Head Start. Summary and observations in the Dakotas and Minnesota, together with an appraisal of possibilities for a Head Start program among the Potawatomi Indians of Kansas. Washington, D.C., 1967. 65 p. (U.S., Office of Economic Opportunity, Report, 520) ERIC ED016510.

Webb, J. W., ed. Altowan. New York, 1846. 2 v.

Weisenburger, Francis P. Caleb Atwater: pioneer politican and historian. Ohio Historical Quarterly, 68 (1959): 18-37.

Willett, Walter C., et al. A health and nutrition study among Michigan Indians. Michigan Medicine, 69 (1970): 305-311.

Wyatt, P. J. Potawatomies of Kansas. Emporia, Kansas State Teachers College, 1962. 38 p. illus. (Heritage of Kansas Series, 6, no. 2)

Yarnell, Richard Asa. Aboriginal relationships between culture and plant life in the Upper Great Lakes region. Ann Arbor, University of Michigan, 1964. 6, 218 p. (Michigan, University, Museum of Anthropology, Anthropological Papers, 23)

Zoltvany, Yves F. New France and the West, 1701-1713. Canadian Historical Review, 46 (1965): 301-322.

Zurcher, Louis A. The leader and the lost: a case study of indigenous leadership in a poverty program community action committee. Genetic Psychology Monographs, 76 (1967): 23-93.

10-07 Sauk

Anonymous. Indian yarn. Masterkey, 32 (1958): 34.

Armstrong, P. A. The Sauks and the Black Hawk War. Springfield, 1887. 726 p.

Atkinson, Henry. The Battle of Bad Axe: General Atkinson's report. Edited by Roger L. Nichols. Wisconsin Magazine of History, 50 (1966/1967): 54-58.

Aumann, F. R. Indian oratory. Palimpsest, 46 (1965): 251-256.

Aumann, F. R. The Watchful Fox. Palimpsest, 46 (1965): 225-236.

Bass, William M. Human skeletal material from 23AD95, Adair County, Missouri. Plains Anthropologist, 13 (1968): 115-116.

Beckwith, H. W. The Illinois and Indiana Indians. Fergus Historical Series, 27 (1884): 146-162.

Beltrami, J. C. A pilgrimage in Europe and America, Vol. 2: 138-159. London, 1828.

Berrien, Joseph Waring. Overland from St. Louis to the California gold field in 1849: the diary of Joseph Waring Berrien. Edited by Ted and Caryl Hinckley. Indiana Magazine of History, 56 (1960): 273-351.

Berthrong, D. J. John Beach and the removal of the Sauk and Fox from Iowa. Iowa Journal of History and Politics, 54 (1956): 313-334.

Black Hawk. Autobiography. St. Louis, 1882. 208 p.

Briggs, J. E. The council on the Iowa. Palimpsest, 46 (1965): 237-250.

Briggs, John Ely. The Sacs and Foxes. Palimpsest, 50 (1969): 223-226.

Brown, D. M. Wisconsin Indian corn origin myths. Wisconsin Archeologist, n.s., 21 (1940): 19-27.

Burford, C. C. Sauk and Fox Indian ceremonials attract large audience and wide-spread interest. Illinois State Archaeological Society, Journal, 5 (1947): 24-30.

Bushnell, D. I. Villages of the Algonquian, Siouan and Caddoan tribes. U.S. Bureau of American Ethnology, Bulletin, 77 (1922): 37-41.

Carman, J. N. and K. S. Pond. The replacement of the Indian languages of Kansas by English. Kansas Academy of Science, Transactions, 58 (1955): 131-150.

Chase, Charles Monroe. An editor looks at early-day Kansas; the letters of Charles Monroe Chase. Edited by Lela Barnes. Kansas Historical Quarterly, 26 (1960): 118-151.

Donaldson, T. The George Catlin Indian gallery. United States National Museum, Reports (1885): Appendix, 13-39.

Emmert, Darlene Gay. The Indians of Shiawassee County. Michigan History, 47 (1963): 127-155, 243-272.

Fay, George E., ed. Charters, constitutions and by-laws of the Indian tribes of North America. Part XIII: Midwestern tribes. Greeley, 1972. 3, 101 l. map. (University of Northern Colorado, Museum of Anthropology, Occasional Publications in Anthropology, Ethnology Series, 14)

Fay, George E., ed. Charters, constitutions and by-laws of the Indian tribes of North America. Part VI: The Indian tribes of Oklahoma (cont'd.). Greeley, 1968. 5, 129 l. map. (University of Northern Colorado, Museum of Anthropology, Occasional Publications in Anthropology, Ethnology Series, 7) ERIC ED046556.

Ferris, I. M. The Sauks and Foxes. Kansas State Historical Society, Collections, 11 (1910): 333-395.

Field, Gabriel. The Camp Missouri-Chariton Road, 1819: the journal of Lt. Gabriel Field. Edited by Roger L. Nichols. Missouri Historical Society, Bulletin, 24 (1967/1968): 139-152.

Foreman, G. The last trek of the Indians: 133-158, 222-229. Chicago, 1946.

Forsyth, T. Account of the manners and customs of the Sauk and Fox nations. In E. H. Blair, ed. The Indian Tribes of the Upper Mississippi Valley. Vol. 2. Cleveland, 1912: 183-245.

Froncek, Thomas. "I was once a great warrior". American Heritage, 24, no. 1 (Dec. 1972): 16-21, 97-99.

Gallaher, Ruth A. Realm of spirit. Palimpsest, 50 (1969): 258-263.

Gallaher, Ruth A. The Indians at home. Palimpsest, 50 (1969): 240-246.

Galland, I. The Indian tribes of the West. Annals of Iowa, 7 (1869): 347-366.

Gilstrap, Harriet Patrick. Memoirs of a pioneer teacher. Chronicles of Oklahoma, 38 (1960): 20-34.

Gilstrap, Harry B., Jr. Colonel Samuel Lee Patrick. Chronicles of Oklahoma, 46 (1968): 58-63.

*Hagan, W. T. The Sac and Fox Indians. Norman, 1958. 301 p.

Hargrett, L. A bibliography of the constitutions and laws of the American Indians, 102-103. Cambridge, 1947.

Harkins, Arthur M. Indian Americans in Omaha and Lincoln. By Arthur M. Harkins, Mary L. Zemyan, and Richard G. Woods. Minneapolis, University of Minnesota, Training Center for Community Programs, 1970. 42, 24 p. ERIC ED047860.

Harrington, M. R. A bird-quill belt of the Sauk and Fox Indians. Indian Notes and Monographs, 10 (1920): 47-50.

Harrington, M. R. Old Sauk and Fox beaded garters. Indian Notes and Monographs, 10 (1920): 39-41.

Harrington, M. R. Sacred bundles of the Sac and Fox. Pennsylvania, University, University Museum, Anthropological Publications, 4 (1914): 125-262.

Hewitt, J. N. B. Sauk. U.S. Bureau of American Ethnology, Bulletin, 30, vol. 2 (1910): 471-480.

House, R. Morton. "The Only Way" Church and the Sac and Fox Indians. Chronicles of Oklahoma, 43 (1965): 443-466.

Jackson, D. Ma-ka-tai-me-she-kia-kiak, Black Hawk. Urbana, 1955. 206 p.

Jackson, Donald. Trading with the Indians. Palimpsest, 47 (1966): 42-46.

Jenks, A. E.   The wild rice gatherers of the upper lakes. U.S. Bureau of American Ethnology, Annual Reports, 19, vol. 2 (1898): 1013-1137.

Johnston, G.   Osawgenong--A Soc tradition. State Historical Society of Wisconsin, Collections, 15 (1900): 448-451.

Jones, W.   Episodes in the culture-hero myth of the Sauks and Foxes. Journal of American Folklore, 14 (1901): 225-239.

Jones, W.   The Algonkin manitou. Journal of American Folklore, 18 (1905): 183-190.

Kay, Marvin.   Two historic Indian burials from an open site, 23AD95, Adair County, Missouri. Plains Anthropologist, 13 (1968): 103-115.

Keating, W. H.   Narrative of an expedition to the source of St. Peter's River, Vol. 1: 218-232.   Philadelphia, 1824.

Keyes, Patricia S.   Moccasin paths. By Pat and Art Wakolee.   Salt Lake City, Deseret Book, 1966.   7, 245 p.   illus.

Lasley, M.   Sac and Fox tales. Journal of American Folklore, 15 (1902): 170-178.

Marsh, C.   Expedition to the Sacs and Foxes. State Historical Society of Wisconsin, Collections, 15 (1900): 104-155.

Marston, M.   Letter to Reverend Dr. Jedediah Morse. In E. H. Blair, ed. The Indian Tribes of the Upper Mississippi Valley. Vol. 2.   Cleveland, 1912: 139-182.

McDermott, John Francis.   The Indian as human being. Nebraska History, 52 (1971): 45-49.

Michelson, T.   Ethnological researches among the Fox Indians. Smithsonian Miscellaneous Collections, 77, no. 2 (1925): 133-136.

Michelson, T.   Field-work among the Catawba, Fox, Sutaio and Sauk Indians. Smithsonian Miscellaneous Collections, 63, no. 8 (1914): 836.

Michelson, T.   Note on the hunting territories of the Sauk and Fox. American Anthropologist, n.s., 23 (1921): 238-239.

Michelson, T.   Review. American Anthropologist, n.s., 26 (1924): 93-100.

Miller, Otis Louis.   Indian-White relations in the Illinois country, 1789 to 1818. Dissertation Abstracts

International, 33 (1972/1973): 1120A. UM 72-23,975.

Morgan, L. H.   Systems of consanguinity and affinity. Smithsonian Contributions to Knowledge, 17 (1871): 291-382.

Morgan, L. H.   The Indian journals, 1859-62: p. 40, 76-77, 80-81, 83.   Ann Arbor, 1959.

Morse, J.   A report to the Secretary of War.   New Haven, 1822.   400 p.

Mueller, Richard E.   Jefferson Barracks: the early years. Missouri Historical Review, 67 (1972/1973): 7-30.

Nasatir, A. P.   Before Lewis and Clark. St. Louis, 1952.   2 v. (882 p.).

Nichols, Roger L.   A missionary journey to the Sac-Fox Indians, 1834. Annals of Iowa, 36 (1962): 301-315.

Nichols, Roger L.   The founding of Fort Atkinson. Annals of Iowa, 37 (1965): 589-597.

Nichols, Roger L., ed.   The Black Hawk War; another view. Annals of Iowa, 36 (1963): 525-533.

Petersen, William J.   Buffalo hunting with Keokuk. Palimpsest, 46 (1965): 257-272.

Petersen, William J.   Trailmaking on the frontier. Palimpsest, 44 (1963): 10-27.

Polk, Harry Herndon.   Old Fort Des Moines. Annals of Iowa, 36 (1962): 425-436.

Prucha, Francis Paul.   Early Indian peace medals. Wisconsin Magazine of History, 45 (1961): 279-289.

Schmidt, W.   Die Sauk. In his Die Ursprung der Göttesidee. Bd. 2.   Münster i. W., 1929: 581-598.

Sibley, George C.   George C. Sibley's journal of a trip to the Salines in 1811. Edited by George R. Brooks. Missouri Historical Society, Bulletin, 21 (1964/1965): 167-207.

*Skinner, A.   Observations on the ethnology of the Sauk Indians. Public Museum of the City of Milwaukee, Bulletin, 5 (1923/1925): 1-180.

Skinner, A.   Sauk tales. Journal of American Folklore, 41 (1928): 147-171.

Skinner, A.   Sauk war bundles. Wisconsin Archeologist, n.s., 2 (1923): 148-150.

Skinner, A. Some unusual ethnological specimens. Public Museum of the City of Milwaukee, Yearbook, 3 (1923): 103-109.

Skinner, A. Summer among the Sauk and Ioway Indians. Public Museum of the City of Milwaukee, Yearbook, 2 (1922): 6-15.

*Skinner, Alanson B. Observations on the ethnology of the Sauk Indians. Westport, Greenwood Press, 1970. 180 p. illus.

Spencer, Dick, III. Powwow time. Palimpsest, 48 (1967): 300-319.

Steward, J. F. Lost Maramech and earliest Chicago. Chicago, 1903. 390 p.

Thwaites, R. G., ed. The Jesuit relations and allied documents. Cleveland, 1896-1901. 74 v.

Vincent, John R. Midwest Indians and frontier photography. Annals of Iowa, 38 (1965): 26-35.

Voorhis, Paul Hantsch. Kickapoo grammar. Dissertation Abstracts, 28 (1967/1968): 4620A. UM 68-6863.

Wied-Neuwied, M. zu. Reise in das innere Nordamerika. Coblenz, 1839-1841. 2 v.

Wied-Neuwied, M. zu. Travels in the interior of North America. Early Western Travels, 22 (1906): 217-230; 24 (1906): 276-277, 294-295.

Wyatt, P. J. Iowas, Sacs and Foxes of Kansas. Emporia, Kansas State Teachers College, 1962. 25 p. illus. (Heritage of Kansas, 6, no. 4)

Wylie, Helen. On the warpath. Palimpsest, 50 (1969): 253-257.

Yarnell, Richard Asa. Aboriginal relationships between culture and plant life in the Upper Great Lakes region. Ann Arbor, University of Michigan, 1964. 6, 218 p. (Michigan, University, Museum of Anthropology, Anthropological Papers, 23)

Yeast, William E. The Mesquakie memorial feast. Annals of Iowa, 36 (1963): 591-598.

Zolotarevskaîa, I. A. Some materials on the assimilation of Oklahoma Indians. Translated by William Andrews. Edited by William E. Bittle. By I. A. Zolotarevskaja. Plains Anthropologist, 6 (1961): 1-6.

10-08 Shawnee

Alford, T. W. Civilization. Ed. by F. Drake. Norman, 1936. 203 p.

Alford, T. W., tr. The four gospels of our Lord Jesus Christ. Xenia, 1929. 200 p.

Baird, W. David. Fort Smith and the Red Man. Arkansas Historical Quarterly, 30 (1971): 337-348.

Baldwin, C. C. Early Indian migration in Ohio. American Antiquarian and Oriental Journal, 1 (1879): 227-239.

Barlow, William. The coming of the War of 1812 in Michigan Territory. Michigan History, 53 (1969): 91-107.

Beckner, L. Eskippakithiki, the last Indian town in Kentucky. Filson Club History Quarterly, 6 (1932): 355-382.

Benson, Maxine. Schoolcraft, James, and the "White Indian". Michigan History, 54 (1970): 311-328.

Bibaud, F. M. Biographie des sagamas illustrés de l'Amérique Septentrionale, 243-252. Montréal, 1848.

Blain, Harry S. Little Turtle's watch. Northwest Ohio Quarterly, 37 (1964/1965): 27-32.

Brinton, D. G. The Shawnees and their migrations. Historical Magazine, 10 (1866): 1-4.

Brown, James Allison, ed. The Zimmerman Site; a report on excavations at the Grand Village of Kaskaskia, La Salle County, Illinois. Springfield, 1961. 86 p. illus. (Illinois, State Museum, Report of Investigations, 9)

Butler, R. Shawnoes. American Antiquarian Society, Transactions and Collections, 2 (1836): 305-367.

Chalou, George Clifford. The red pawns go to war: British-American Indian relations, 1810-1815. Dissertation Abstracts International, 32 (1971/1972): 5130A. UM 72-9966.

Chapman, B. B. The Potawatomie and Absentee Shawnee Reservation. Chronicles of Oklahoma, 24 (1946): 293-305.

Christian, Thomas. Campaign of 1813 on the Ohio River; sortie at Fort Meigs, May, 1813. Kentucky Historical Society, Register, 67 (1969): 260-268.

Connelly, Thomas Lawrence. Indian warfare
   on the Tennessee frontier, 1776-1794:
   strategy and tactics. East Tennessee
   Historical Society's Publications, 36
   (1964): 3-22.

Corbitt, D. C., tr. and ed. Papers from
   the Spanish archives relating to
   Tennessee and the Old Southwest.
   Translated and edited by D. C. Corbitt
   and Roberta Corbitt. East Tennessee
   Historical Society, Publications, 31
   (1959): 63-82; 32 (1960): 72-93; 33
   (1961): 61-78; 34 (1962): 86-105; 35
   (1963): 85-95; 36 (1964): 70-80; 37
   (1965): 89-105; 38 (1966): 70-82; 39
   (1967): 87-102; 40 (1968): 101-118; 41
   (1969): 100-116; 42 (1970): 96-107; 43
   (1971): 94-111; 44 (1972): 104-113.

Cummings, R. W. Shawnee. In H. R.
   Schoolcraft, ed. Information respecting
   the History, Condition, and Prospects of
   the Indian Tribes of the United States.
   Vol. 2. Philadelphia, 1852: 470-481.

Curtis, E. S. The North American Indian,
   Vol. 19: 19-21. Norwood, 1930.

Dott, Robert H. Lieutenant Simpson's
   California road across Oklahoma.
   Chronicles of Oklahoma, 38 (1960): 154-
   179.

Downes, R. C. Council fires on the upper
   Ohio. Pittsburgh, 1940. 367 p.

Drake, B. Life of Tecumseh, and of his
   brother the Prophet. Cincinnati, 1841.
   235 p.

Drake, Florence. Mary Bourbonnais
   organized a Sunday school. Chronicles of
   Oklahoma, 40 (1962): 386-389.

Draper, Lyman S. Material in Draper "S"
   on 18th- and early 19th-century Indians
   of the Old Northwest. Ethnohistory, 8
   (1961): 281-288.

Dunn, J. P. True Indian stories.
   Indianapolis, 1909. 320 p.

Elliot, James. James Elliot and "The
   garden of North America": a New
   Englander's impressions of the Old
   Northwest. Edited by Eugene L.
   Huddleston. Northwest Ohio Quarterly,
   42, no. 3 (1969/1970): 64-72.

Erskine, Margaret Handley. A captive of
   the Shawnees, 1779-1784. Edited by John
   H. Moore. West Virginia History, 23
   (1961/1962): 287-296.

Fall, Ralph Emmett. Captain Samuel Brady
   (1756-1795), chief of the Rangers, and
   his kin. West Virginia History, 29
   (1967/1968): 203-223.

Fay, George E., ed. Charters,
   constitutions and by-laws of the Indian
   tribes of North America. Part VI: The
   Indian tribes of Oklahoma (cont'd.).
   Greeley, 1968. 5, 129 l. map.
   (University of Northern Colorado, Museum
   of Anthropology, Occasional Publications
   in Anthropology, Ethnology Series, 7)
   ERIC ED046556.

Galloway, W. A. Old Chillicothe, 18-23,
   170-206. Xenia, 1834.

Gibson, A. M. An Indian Territory United
   Nations: the Creek Council of 1845.
   Chronicles of Oklahoma, 39 (1961): 398-
   413.

Gibson, A. M. Joe Kagey: Indian educator.
   Chronicles of Oklahoma, 38 (1960): 12-
   19.

Gibson, A. M. Wyandotte mission.
   Chronicles of Oklahoma, 36 (1958): 137-
   154.

Gilstrap, Harriet Patrick. Memoirs of a
   pioneer teacher. Chronicles of Oklahoma,
   38 (1960): 20-34.

Griffin, James Bennett. The Fort Ancient
   aspect: its cultural and chronological
   position in Mississippi Valley
   archaeology. Ann Arbor, University of
   Michigan, 1966. 15, 376 p. illus.
   (Michigan, University, Museum of
   Anthropology, Anthropological Papers,
   28)

Hagy, James W. The frontier at Castle's
   Woods, 1769-1786. Virginia Magazine of
   History and Biography, 75 (1967): 410-
   428.

Hagy, James William, ed. The lost
   archives of the Cherokee Nation. Edited
   by James William Hagy and Stanley J.
   Folmsbee. East Tennessee Historical
   Society, Publications, 43 (1971): 112-
   122; 44 (1972): 114-125.

Hamil, Fred C. Michigan in the War of
   1812. Michigan History, 44 (1960): 257-
   291.

Hammon, Neal Owen. Early roads into
   Kentucky. Kentucky Historical Society,
   Register, 68 (1970): 91-131.

Hanna, C. A. The wilderness trail,
   Vol. 1: 119-160. New York, 1911.

Hanzeli, Victor E. Missionary linguistics
   in New France; a study of seventeenth-
   and eighteenth-century descriptions of
   American Indian languages. The Hague,
   Mouton, 1969. 141 p. illus., map.
   (Janua Linguarum, Series Maior, 29)

Harris, Frank H. Neosho Agency 1838-1871. Chronicles of Oklahoma, 43 (1965): 35-57.

Harris, Frank H. Seneca Sub-Agency, 1832-1838. Chronicles of Oklahoma, 42 (1964): 75-93.

Harris, Kate. Parkersburg; history of city from time of its settlement to the present in gripping narrative from the pen of the late Miss Kate Harris. West Virginia History, 25 (1963/1964): 241-264.

Harvey, H. History of the Shawnee Indians. Cincinnati, 1855. 316 p.

Herndon, G. Melvin. George Mathews, frontier patriot. Virginia Magazine of History and Biography, 77 (1969): 307-328.

Hickerson, Nancy P. An acoustic analysis of Shawnee. International Journal of American Linguistics, 24 (1958): 20-29, 130-141; 25 (1959): 22-31, 97-104.

Hockett, Charles F. What Algonquian is really like. International Journal of American Linguistics, 32 (1966): 59-73.

Horsman, Reginald. The British Indian Department and the resistance to General Anthony Wayne, 1793-1795. Mississippi Valley Historical Review, 49 (1962/1963): 269-290.

Howe, H. Historical collections of Ohio. Cincinnati, 1848. 3 v.

Howerton, E. H. Logan, the Shawnee Indian capital of West Virginia 1760 to 1780. West Virginia History, 16 (1955): 313-333.

Huber, John Parker. General Josiah Harmar's command: military policy in the Old Northwest, 1784-1791. Dissertation Abstracts International, 30 (1969/1970): 247A. UM 69-12,138.

Huddleston, Eugene L. Indians and literature of the Federalist Era: the case of James Elliot. New England Quarterly, 44 (1971): 221-237.

Hunter, W. A. John Hays' diary and journal of 1760. Pennsylvania Archaeologist, 24 (1954): 63-84.

Hutter, William H. Scenes in (and en route to) Kansas Territory, autumn, 1854: five letters by William H. Hutter. Edited by Louise Barry. Kansas Historical Quarterly, 35 (1969): 312-336.

Jennings, Francis. The Indian trade of the Susquehanna Valley. American Philosophical Society, Proceedings, 110 (1966): 406-424.

Jennings, Francis Paul. Miquon's passing: Indian-European relations in colonial Pennsylvania, 1674-1755. Dissertation Abstracts, 26 (1965/1966): 7281-7282. UM 66-4621.

Johnson, B. A. The Suwanee-Shawnee debate. Florida Anthropologist, 25, no. 2 (1972): 67-72.

Johnston, J. Account of the present state of the Indian tribes inhabiting Ohio. American Antiquarian Society, Transactions and Collections, 1 (1820): 269-299.

Jones, D. A journal of two visits made to some nations of Indians on the west side of the river Ohio. Burlington, 1774. 95 p.

Jones, David. A journal of two visits made to some nations of Indians on the west side of the river Ohio in the years 1772 and 1773. New York, Arno Press, 1971. 127 p.

Joutel, H. Journal of La Salle's last voyage. New ed. Albany, 1906. 258 p.

Joutel, H. Relation. In P. Margry, ed. Découvertes et Établissements des Français dans l'Ouest et dans le Sud de l'Amérique Septentrionale. Vol. 3. Paris, 1879: 89-534.

Kelln, E. E. A seventeenth century mandibular tumor in a North American Indian. By E. E. Kelln, E. V. McMichael, and B. Zimmermann. Oral Surgery, Oral Medicine and Oral Pathology, 23 (1967): 78-81.

Ketcham, Ralph L. Conscience, war, and politics in Pennsylvania, 1755-1757. William and Mary Quarterly, 3d ser., 20 (1963): 416-439.

Klopfenstein, C. G. Westward ho: removal of Ohio Shawnees, 1832-1833. Historical and Philosophical Society of Ohio, Bulletin, 15 (1957): 3-32.

Lane, William Carr. William Carr Lane, diary. Edited by Wm. G. B. Carson. New Mexico Historical Review, 39 (1964): 181-234, 274-332.

Lee, John D. Diary of the Mormon Battalion Mission. Edited by Juanita Brooks. New Mexico Historical Review, 42 (1967): 165-209, 281-332.

Mahan, Joseph Buford, Jr.   Identification
   of the Tsoyaha Waeno, builders of temple
   mounds. Dissertation Abstracts
   International, 31 (1970/1971): 2289A.
   UM 70-21,213.

Mahr, August C.   Delaware terms for plants
   and animals in the eastern Ohio country:
   a study in semantics. Anthropological
   Linguistics, 4, no. 5 (1962): 1-48.

Mahr, August C.   Semantic evaluation.
   Anthropological Linguistics, 3, no. 5
   (1961): 1-46.

Middlebrooks, Audy J.   Holland Coffee of
   Red River. By Audy J. and Glenna
   Middlebrooks. Southwestern Historical
   Quarterly, 69 (1965/1966): 145-162.

Miller, Wick R.   An outline of Shawnee
   historical phonology. International
   Journal of American Linguistics, 25
   (1959): 16-21.

Milling, C. J.   Red Carolinians.   Chapel
   Hill, 1940.   438 p.

Mooney, J.   Shawnee. U.S. Bureau of
   American Ethnology, Bulletin, 30, vol. 2
   (1910): 530-538.

Mooney, J.   The ghost-dance religion. U.S.
   Bureau of American Ethnology, Annual
   Reports, 14, vol. 2 (1893): 670-691.

Moorehead, W. K.   The Indian tribes of
   Ohio. Ohio State Archaeological and
   Historical Quarterly, 7 (1898): 1-109.

Morgan, L. H.   Ancient society, 168-170.
   New York, 1877.

Morgan, L. H.   Systems of consanguinity
   and affinity. Smithsonian Contributions
   to Knowledge, 17 (1871): 291-382.

Morgan, L. H.   The Indian journals, 1859-
   62: p. 28, 44-48, 56, 74-78, 144.   Ann
   Arbor, 1959.

Morse, J.   A report to the Secretary of
   War.   New Haven, 1822.   400 p.

Nasatir, A. P.   Before Lewis and Clark.
   St. Louis, 1952.   2 v. (882 p.).

Nettl, B.   The Shawnee musical style.
   Southwestern Journal of Anthropology, 9
   (1953): 277-285.

Neumann, G. K.   Population statistics
   bearing on a Fort Ancient--Shawnee
   linkage. Indiana Academy of Science,
   Proceedings, 66 (1956): 45.

Nieberding, Velma.   Shawnee Indian
   festival: the Bread Dance. Chronicles of
   Oklahoma, 42 (1964): 253-261.

Nieberding, Velma.   The Nez Perce in the
   Quapaw Agency 1878-1879. Chronicles of
   Oklahoma, 44 (1966): 22-30.

Pattison, William D.   The survey of the
   Seven Ranges. Ohio Historical Quarterly,
   68 (1959): 115-140.

Patton, W.   Journal of a visit to the
   Indian missions, Missouri Conference.
   Missouri Historical Society, Bulletin,
   10 (1954): 167-180.

Perrin du Lac, M.   Travels through the two
   Louisianas.   London, 1807.   106 p.

Perrin du Lac, M.   Voyage dans les deux
   Louisianes.   Lyon, 1805.   472 p.

Phillips, Marie.   Tecumseh's fusil. Museum
   of the Fur Trade Quarterly, 1, no. 1
   (1965): 8-9.

Reves, Haviland F.   The Reves Farm--
   private claim 49. Michigan History, 45
   (1961): 237-258.

Rice, Otis.   The French and Indian War in
   West Virginia. West Virginia History, 24
   (1962/1963): 134-146.

Richardson, J.   Tecumseh and Richardson.
   Toronto, 1924.   124 p.

Robbins, Louise M.   The origin of the
   Shawnee Indians. By Louise M. Robbins
   and Georg K. Neumann. Indiana Academy of
   Sciences, Proceedings, 78 (1968): 93-96.

Robbins, Louise Marie.   The identification
   of the prehistoric Shawnee Indians--the
   description of the population of the
   Fort Ancient Aspect. Dissertation
   Abstracts, 29 (1968/1969): 4007B.   UM
   69-7696.

Royce, C. C.   An inquiry into the identity
   and history of the Shawnee Indians.
   American Antiquarian and Oriental
   Journal, 3 (1881): 178-189.

Schaeffer, C. E.   The grasshopper or
   children's war--a circumboreal legend?
   Pennsylvania Archaeologist, 12 (1942):
   60-61.

Schmidt, W.   Die Kickapoo und die Shawnee.
   In his Die Ursprung der Göttesidee.
   Bd. 2.   Münster i. W., 1929: 599-601.

Shetrone, H. C.   The Indian in Ohio. Ohio
   State Archaeological and Historical
   Quarterly, 27 (1918): 273-510.

Sipe, C. H.   The principal Indian towns in
   western Pennsylvania. Western
   Pennsylvania Historical Magazine, 13
   (1930): 104-122.

Smelser, Marshall. Tecumseh, Harrison, and the War of 1812. Indiana Magazine of History, 65 (1969): 25-44.

Smith, D. L. Shawnee captivity ethnography. Ethnohistory, 2 (1955): 29-41.

Sosin, Jack M. The use of Indians in the War of the American Revolution: a re-assessment of responsibility. Canadian Historical Review, 46 (1965): 101-121.

Spencer, J. Shawnee folk-lore. Journal of American Folklore, 22 (1909): 319-326.

Spencer, J. The Shawnee Indians. Kansas State Historical Society, Transactions, 10 (1908): 382-402.

Stone, Richard G., Jr. Captain Paul Demere at Fort Loudoun, 1757-1760. East Tennessee Historical Society's Publications, 41 (1969): 17-32.

Sunder, John E. British Army officers on the Santa Fe Trail. Missouri Historical Society, Bulletin, 23 (1966/1967): 147-157.

Swanton, J. R. Early history of the Creek Indians and their neighbors. U.S. Bureau of American Ethnology, Bulletin, 73 (1922): 317-320.

Swanton, J. R. Indians of the Southeastern United States. U.S. Bureau of American Ethnology, Bulletin, 137 (1946): 71-832.

Thomas, C. The story of a mound; or, the Shawnees in pre-Columbian times. American Anthropologist, 4 (1891): 109-159, 237-273.

Thomson, Charles. An enquiry into the causes of the alienation of the Delaware and Shawanese Indians from the British interest. St. Claire Shores, Mich., Scholarly Press, 1970. 184 p.

Tracy, Valerie. The Indian in transition: the Neosho Agency, 1850-1861. Chronicles of Oklahoma, 48 (1970): 164-183.

*Trowbridge, C. C. Shawnese traditions. Ed. by W. V. Kinietz and E. W. Voegelin. Michigan, University, Museum of Anthropology, Occasional Contributions, 9 (1939): 1-71.

Tucker, G. Tecumseh: vision of glory. Indianapolis, 1956. 399 p.

Uhler, S. P. Pennsylvania's Indian relations to 1754. Allentown, 1951. 144 p.

Voegelin, C. F. From FL (Shawnee) to TL (English). International Journal of American Linguistics, 19 (1953): 1-25.

Voegelin, C. F. Productive paradigms in Shawnee. In Essays in Anthropology Presented to A. L. Kroeber. Berkeley, 1936: 391-403.

Voegelin, C. F. Shawnee phonemes. Language, 11 (1935): 23-37.

Voegelin, C. F. Shawnee stems and the Jacob P. Dunn Miami dictionary. Indiana Historical Society, Prehistory Research Series, 1 (1938/1940): 63-108, 135-167, 345-406, 409-479.

Voegelin, C. F. The Shawnee female deity. Yale University Publications in Anthropology, 10 (1936): 1-21.

Voegelin, C. F. and E. W. Voegelin. Shawnee name groups. American Anthropologist, n.s., 37 (1935): 617-635.

Voegelin, C. F. and E. W. Voegelin. The Shawnee female deity in historical perspective. American Anthropologist, n.s., 46 (1944): 370-375.

Voegelin, C. F. and J. Yegerlehner. Toward a definition of formal style. Indiana University Publications, Folklore Series, 9 (1957): 141-150.

Voegelin, C. F., et al. From FL (Shawnee) to TL (English). International Journal of American Linguistics, 19 (1953): 106-117.

Voegelin, C. F., et al. Shawnee laws. American Anthropological Association, Memoirs, 79 (1954): 32-46.

Voegelin, Carl F. The Shawnee female deity. New Haven, Human Relations Area Files Press, 1970. 21 p. (Yale University Publications in Anthropology, 10)

Voegelin, E. W. Indians of Indiana. Indiana Academy of Science, Proceedings, 50 (1941): 27-32.

Voegelin, E. W. Mortuary customs of the Shawnee and other eastern tribes. Indiana Historical Society, Prehistory Research Series, 2 (1944): 227-444.

Voegelin, E. W. Shawnee musical instruments. American Anthropologist, n.s., 44 (1942): 463-475.

Voegelin, E. W. Some possible sixteenth and seventeenth century locations of the Shawnee. Indiana Academy of Science, Proceedings, 48 (1939): 13-18.

Voegelin, E. W. The place of agriculture
in the subsistence economy of the
Shawnee. Michigan Academy of Science,
Arts and Letters, Papers, 24 (1941):
513-520.

Voegelin, E. W. and G. K. Neumann.
Shawnee pots and pottery making.
Pennsylvania Archaeologist, 18 (1948):
3-12.

Walker, William A., Jr. Martial sons:
Tennessee enthusiasm for the War of
1812. Tennessee Historical Quarterly, 20
(1961): 20-37.

Wallace, Paul A. W. Indians in
Pennsylvania. Harrisburg, Pennsylvania
Historical and Museum Commission, 1961.
13, 194 p. illus., maps.

Ward, Allen T. Letters of Allen T. Ward,
1842-1851, from the Shawnee and Kaw
(Methodist) Missions. Edited by Lela
Barnes. Kansas Historical Quarterly, 33
(1967): 321-376.

Washington, George. A mystery resolved;
George Washington's letter to Governor
Dinwiddie, June 10, 1754. Edited by
Peter Walne. Virginia Magazine of
History and Biography, 79 (1971): 131-
144.

Watts, Florence G. Fort Knox: frontier
outpost on the Wabash, 1787-1816.
Indiana Magazine of History, 62 (1966):
51-78.

Weslager, C. A. Monongahela woodland
culture and the Shawnee. Pennsylvania
Archaeologist, 18 (1948): 19-22.

White, Lonnie J. Disturbances on the
Arkansas-Texas border, 1827-1831.
Arkansas Historical Quarterly, 19
(1960): 95-110.

Whorf, B. L. Gestalt technique of stem
composition in Shawnee. Indiana
Historical Society, Prehistory Research
Series, 1 (1940): 391-406.

Wickliffe, Charles A. Tecumseh and the
battle of the Thames. Kentucky
Historical Society, Register, 60 (1962):
45-49.

Witthoft, J. and W. A. Hunter. The
seventeenth-century origin of the
Shawnee. Ethnohistory, 2 (1955): 42-57.

Woehrmann, Paul John. The American
invasion of Western Upper Canada in
1813. Northwest Ohio Quarterly, 38
(1965/1966): 74-88; 39, no. 1
(1966/1967): 61-73; 39, no. 4
(1966/1967): 39-48; 40 (1967/1968): 27-
44.

Wright, M. H. and G. H. Shirk. Artist
Mollhausen in Oklahoma, 1853. Chronicles
of Oklahoma, 31 (1953): 392-441.

10-09 Winnebago

Fay, George E. Bibliography of the
Indians of Wisconsin. Wisconsin Indians
Research Institute, Journal, 1, no. 1
(1965): 107-132.

Fay, George E. Bibliography of the
Winnebago Indians. Wisconsin Indians
Research Institute, Journal, 2, no. 1
(1966): 116-121.

Andros, F. The medicine and surgery of
the Winnebago and Dakota Indians.
American Medical Association, Journal, 1
(1883): 116-118.

Anonymous. Fur trade in Minnesota--1856.
Museum of the Fur Trade Quarterly, 1,
no. 1 (1965): 9-10.

Anonymous. Indians are helping
themselves. Boletín Indigenista, 19
(1959): 99, 101, 103.

Anonymous. Medical school: Indian
fashion. Wisconsin Medical Journal, 58
(1959): 668.

Atwater, C. Remarks made on a tour to
Prairie du Chien, 75-180. Columbus,
1831.

Baerreis, D. A. A note on a Winnebago
medical technique. Wisconsin
Archeologist, 34 (1953): 139-143.

Beauchamp, W. M. Indian nations of the
Great Lakes. American Antiquarian and
Oriental Journal, 17 (1895): 321-325.

Becker, David A. Enteric parasites of
Indians and Anglo-Americans, chiefly on
the Winnebago and Omaha Reservations in
Nebraska. Nebraska State Medical
Journal, 53 (1968): 293-296, 347-349,
380-383, 421-423.

Beckwith, H. W. The Illinois and Indiana
Indians. Fergus Historical Series, 27
(1884): 138-145.

Behncke, N. Winnebagoland legends.
Wisconsin Archeologist, n.s., 20 (1939):
31-34.

Berg, David E. Association between serum
and secretory immunoglobins and chronic
otitis media in Indian children. By
David E. Berg, Arden E. Larsen, and C.
T. Yarington, Jr. Annals of Otology,

Rhinology and Laryngology, 80 (1971):
766-772.

Bergen, F. D. Some customs and beliefs of
the Winnebago Indians. Journal of
American Folklore, 9 (1896): 51-54.

Blowsnake, Sam. The autobiography of a
Winnebago Indian. Edited and translated
by Paul Radin. New York, Dover
Publications, 1963. 91 p.

Boas, F. Zur Anthropologie der
nordamerikanischen Indianer. Berliner
Gesellschaft für Anthropologie,
Ethnologie und Urgeschichte,
Verhandlungen (1895): 367-411.

Boas, F. and J. R. Swanton. Siouan. U.S.
Bureau of American Ethnology, Bulletin,
40, vol. 1 (1911): 875-966.

Brown, C. E. Lake Mendota Indian legends.
Madison, 1927.

Brown, D. M. Indian winter legends.
Wisconsin Archeologist, n.s., 22 (1941):
49-53.

Brown, D. M. Wisconsin Indian corn origin
myths. Wisconsin Archeologist, n.s., 21
(1940): 19-27.

Buckstaff, R. N. Painted and incised
pottery fragments of the Winnebagos.
Wisconsin Archeologist, n.s., 22 (1941):
84-86.

Buckstaff, R. N. Serrated shells of the
Winnebago. Wisconsin Archeologist, n.s.,
20 (1939): 23-28.

Bushnell, D. I. Sketches by Paul Kane in
the Indian Country, 1845-1848.
Smithsonian Miscellaneous Collections,
99, no. 1 (1940): 1-25.

Carter, B. F. The weaving technic of
Winnebago bags. Wisconsin Archeologist,
n.s., 12 (1933): 33-47.

Crashing Thunder. The teachings of my
father. In Jesse D. Jennings and E.
Adamson Hoebel, eds. Readings in
Anthropology. 3d ed. New York, McGraw-
Hill, 1972: 229-234.

Curtis, N., ed. The Indians' book, 243-
293. New York, 1907.

DeKaury, S. Narrative of Spoon Decorah.
State Historical Society of Wisconsin,
Collections, 13 (1895): 448-462.

Densmore, F. Music of the Winnebago
Indians. Smithsonian Institution,
Explorations and Field-Work (1927): 183-
188.

Dever, Harry. The Nicolet myth. Michigan
History, 50 (1966): 318-322.

Dorsey, J. O. A study of Siouan cults.
U.S. Bureau of American Ethnology,
Annual Reports, 11 (1890): 423-430.

Dorsey, J. O. On the comparative
phonology of four Siouan languages.
Smithsonian Institution, Annual Reports
of the Board of Regents (1883): 919-929.

Dorsey, J. O. Winnebago folk-lore notes.
Journal of American Folklore, 2 (1889):
140.

Dorsey, J. O. and P. Radin. Winnebago.
U.S. Bureau of American Ethnology,
Bulletin, 30, vol. 2 (1910): 958-961.

Fay, George E., ed. Charters,
constitutions and by-laws of the Indian
tribes of North America. Part II: The
Indian tribes of Wisconsin (Great Lakes
Agency). Greeley, 1967. 6, 124 l.
illus., map. (University of Northern
Colorado, Museum of Anthropology,
Occasional Publications in Anthropology,
Ethnology Series, 2) ERIC ED046552.

Fay, George E., ed. Charters,
constitutions and by-laws of the Indian
tribes of North America. Part XIII:
Midwestern tribes. Greeley, 1972. 3,
101 l. map. (University of Northern
Colorado, Museum of Anthropology,
Occasional Publications in Anthropology,
Ethnology Series, 14)

Fay, George E., ed. Charters,
constitutions and by-laws of the Indian
tribes of Wisconsin. Wisconsin Indians
Research Institute, Journal, 3, no. 1
(1967): 1-124.

Fay, George E., ed. Treaties, and land
cessions, between the bands of the Sioux
and the United States of America, 1805-
1906. Greeley, 1972. 7, 139 l.
(University of Northern Colorado, Museum
of Anthropology, Occasional Publications
in Anthropology, Ethnology Series, 24)

Fay, George E., ed. Treaties between the
Menominee Indians and the United States
of America, 1817-1856. Wisconsin Indians
Research Institute, Journal, 1, no. 1
(1965): 67-104.

Fay, George E., ed. Treaties between the
Winnebago Indians and the United States
of America 1816-1865. Wisconsin Indians
Research Institute, Journal, 2, no. 1
(1966): 7-49.

Federal Writers' Project. Wisconsin
Indian place legends, 4-7, 10, 15-16.
Milwaukee, 1936.

Flannery, R. Algonquian Indian folklore. Journal of American Folklore, 60 (1947): 397-401.

Fletcher, A. C. Phonetic alphabet of the Winnebago Indians. American Association for the Advancement of Science, Proceedings, 38 (1889): 354-357.

Fletcher, A. C. Symbolic earth formations of the Winnebagoes. American Association for the Advancement of Science, Proceedings, 32 (1883): 396-397.

Fletcher, J. E. Manners and customs of the Winnebagoes. In H. R. Schoolcraft, ed. Information respecting the History, Condition, and Prospects of the Indian Tribes of the United States. Vol. 4. Philadelphia, 1854: 51-59.

Fletcher, J. E. Origin and history of the Winnebagoes. In H. R. Schoolcraft, ed. Information respecting the History, Condition, and Prospects of the Indian Tribes of the United States. Vol. 4. Philadelphia, 1854: 227-243.

Fugle, Eugene. An extant Winnebago pirogue in the Sioux City Public Museum. South Dakota, State University, W. H. Over Museum, Museum News, 22, no. 1 (1961): 1-2.

Furnas, Robert W. The Second Nebraska's campaign against the Sioux. By Robert W. Furnas and Henry W. Pierce. Edited by Richard D. Rowen. Nebraska History, 44 (1963): 3-53.

Gallaher, William H. Up the Missouri in 1865; the journal of William H. Gallaher. Edited by James E. Moss. Missouri Historical Review, 57 (1962/1963): 156-183, 261-284.

Gilmore, M. R. Uses of plants by the Indians of the Missouri River region. U.S. Bureau of American Ethnology, Annual Reports, 33 (1912): 43-154.

Greenman, E. F. Chieftainship among Michigan Indians. Michigan History Magazine, 24 (1940): 361-379.

Griffin, James B. A hypothesis for the prehistory of the Winnebago. In Stanley Diamond, ed. Culture in History. New York, Columbia University Press, 1960: 809-865.

Harkins, Arthur M. Attitudes and characteristics of selected Wisconsin Indians. By Arthur M. Harkins and Richard G. Woods. Wisconsin Indians Research Institute, Journal, 4, no. 1 (1968): 64-130.

Harkins, Arthur M. Attitudes and characteristics of selected Wisconsin Indians. By Arthur M. Harkins and Richard G. Woods. Minneapolis, University of Minnesota, Training Center for Community Programs, 1969. 89 p. ERIC ED032174.

Harkins, Arthur M. Indian Americans in Omaha and Lincoln. By Arthur M. Harkins, Mary L. Zemyan, and Richard G. Woods. Minneapolis, University of Minnesota, Training Center for Community Programs, 1970. 42, 24 p. ERIC ED047860.

Harstad, Peter T. Disease and sickness on the Wisconsin frontier: smallpox and other diseases. Wisconsin Magazine of History, 43 (1959): 253-263.

Hayden, F. V. Brief notes on the Pawnee, Winnebago, and Omaha languages. American Philosophical Society, Proceedings, 10 (1868): 411-421.

Hofmann, C. American Indian music in Wisconsin. Journal of American Folklore, 60 (1947): 289-293.

Hurt, Wesley R. Factors in the persistence of peyote in the Northern Plains. Plains Anthropologist, 5 (1960): 16-27.

Hymes, Dell H. Value of the Radin papers for linguistics. In The American Indian. Philadelphia, American Philosophical Society, 1968: 35-45. (American Philosophical Society, Library Publication, 2)

Jenks, A. E. The wild rice gatherers of the upper lakes. U.S. Bureau of American Ethnology, Annual Reports, 19, vol. 2 (1898): 1013-1137.

Jipson, N. W. Winnebago villages and chieftains. Wisconsin Archeologist, n.s., 2 (1923): 125-139.

Kellogg, L. P. Removal of the Winnebago. Wisconsin Academy of Sciences, Arts and Letters, Transactions, 21 (1924): 23-29.

Koenig, M. W. Tuberculosis among the Nebraska Winnebago. Lincoln, 1921. 48 p.

Kurath, G. P. Modern Ottawa dancers. Midwest Folklore, 5 (1955): 15-22.

Kuttner, Robert E. Alcohol and addiction in urbanized Sioux Indians. By Robert E. Kuttner and Albert B. Lorincz. Mental Hygiene, 51 (1967): 530-542.

Kuttner, Robert E. Promiscuity and prostitution in urbanized Indian communities. By Robert E. Kuttner and

Albert B. Lorincz. Mental Hygiene, 54 (1970): 79-91.

Lamere, O. and H. B. Shinn. Winnebago stories. New York, 1928. 165 p.

Lamere, O. and P. Radin. Description of a Winnebago funeral. American Anthropologist, n.s., 13 (1911): 437-444.

Lass, William E. The "Moscow Expedition". Minnesota History, 39 (1964/1965): 227-240.

Lass, William E. The removal from Minnesota of the Sioux and Winnebago Indians. Minnesota History, 38 (1962/1963): 353-364.

Lawson, P. V. Habitat of the Winnebago, 1632-1832. State Historical Society of Wisconsin, Proceedings, 54 (1906): 144-166.

Lawson, P. V. The Winnebago tribe. Wisconsin Archeologist, 6 (1907): 78-162.

Lenders, E. W. Myth des "Wah-ru-hap-ah-rah" oder des heiligen Kriegskeulenbündels. Zeitschrift für Ethnologie, 46 (1914): 404-420.

Lesser, Alexander. Siouan kinship. Dissertation Abstracts, 19 (1958/1959): 208. UM 58-2596.

Lévi-Strauss, Claude. Four Winnebago myths: a structural sketch. In Stanley Diamond, ed. Culture in History. New York, Columbia University Press, 1960: 351-362.

Lipkind, W. Winnebago grammar. New York, 1945. 68 p.

Lowie, R. H., ed. Notes concerning new collections. American Museum of Natural History, Anthropological Papers, 4 (1910): 289-297.

Lurie, N. O. Winnebago berdache. American Anthropologist, 55 (1953): 708-712.

Lurie, Nancy Oestreich. A check list of treaty signers by clan affiliation. Wisconsin Indians Research Institute, Journal, 2, no. 1 (1966): 50-73.

Lurie, Nancy Oestreich. Historical background of the Winnebago people. Prepared by Nancy Oestreich Lurie and Helen Miner Miller for the Wisconsin Winnebago Business Committee. [n.p.] 1965. 10 p. map.

Lurie, Nancy Oestreich. Two dollars. In Solon T. Kimball and James B. Watson,

eds. Crossing Cultural Boundaries. San Francisco, Chandler, 1972: 151-163.

Lurie, Nancy Oestreich. Winnebago protohistory. In Stanley Diamond, ed. Culture in History. New York, Columbia University Press, 1960: 790-808.

Mahan, Bruce E. Fort Shelby and Fort McKay. Palimpsest, 42 (1961): 454-461.

Mahan, Bruce E. Winnebago and Pottawa Hamie. Palimpsest, 50 (1969): 231-233.

Marino, Mary Carolyn. A dictionary of Winnebago: an analysis and reference grammar of the Radin lexical file. Dissertation Abstracts International, 30 (1969/1970): 1997B. UM 69-14,947.

Marten, Anita Elma. The morphophonemics of the Winnebago verbal. Dissertation Abstracts, 25 (1964/1965): 2506. UM 64-10,274.

Mathews, Edward. An abolitionist in territorial Wisconsin: the journal of Reverend Edward Mathews. Edited by William Converse Haygood. Wisconsin Magazine of History, 52 (1968/1969): 3-18, 117-131, 248-262, 330-343.

Matson, G. A. Distribution of blood groups among the Sioux, Omaha, and Winnebago Indians. American Journal of Physical Anthropology, 28 (1941): 313-318.

McBride, Dorothy McFatridge. Hoosier schoolmaster among the Sioux. Montana, the Magazine of Western History, 20, no. 4 (1970): 78-97.

McGee, W J. The Siouan Indians. U.S. Bureau of American Ethnology, Annual Reports, 15 (1894): 157-204.

McKern, W. C. A Winnebago myth. Public Museum of the City of Milwaukee, Yearbook, 9 (1929): 215-230.

McKern, W. C. A Winnebago war-bundle ceremony. Public Museum of the City of Milwaukee, Yearbook, 8, no. 1 (1928): 146-155.

McKern, W. C. Winnebago dog myths. Public Museum of the City of Milwaukee, Yearbook, 10 (1930): 317-322.

Merrill, R. H. The calendar stick of Tshi-zun-hau-kau. Cranbrook Institute of Science, Bulletin, 24 (1945): 1-11.

Michelson, T. Some notes on Winnebago social and political organization. American Anthropologist, n.s., 37 (1935): 446-449.

Miller, Helen Miner. The Wisconsin
   Winnebago people. Rev. ed. By Helen
   Miner Miller, Nadine Day Sieber, and
   Nancy Oestreich Lurie. [n.p.] Wisconsin
   Winnebago Business Committee, 1967.
   15 p. map.

Morgan, L. H. Systems of consanguinity
   and affinity. Smithsonian Contributions
   to Knowledge, 17 (1871): 291-382.

Morgan, L. H. The Indian journals, 1859-
   62: p. 60-61. Ann Arbor, 1959.

Mountain Wolf Woman. Mountain Wolf Woman,
   sister of Crashing Thunder; the
   autobiography of a Winnebago Indian.
   Edited by Nancy Oestreich Lurie. Ann
   Arbor, University of Michigan Press,
   1961. 142 p. illus.

Nichols, Roger L. The founding of Fort
   Atkinson. Annals of Iowa, 37 (1965):
   589-597.

Oestreich, N. Culture change among the
   Wisconsin Winnebago. Wisconsin
   Archeologist, n.s., 25 (1944): 119-125.

Oestreich, N. Trends of change in
   patterns of child care and training
   among the Wisconsin Winnebago. Wisconsin
   Archeologist, n.s., 29 (1948): 39-140.

Peske, G. Richard. Winnebago cultural
   adaptation to the Fox River waterway.
   Wisconsin Archeologist, n.s., 52 (1971):
   62-70.

Petersen, William J. In the neutral
   ground. Palimpsest, 41 (1960): 341-350.

Petersen, William J. Moving the Winnebago
   into Iowa. Iowa Journal of History, 58
   (1960): 357-376.

Petersen, William J. Nicolet and the
   Winnebagoes. Palimpsest, 41 (1960): 325-
   330.

Petersen, William J. The Winnebago leave
   Iowa. Palimpsest, 41 (1960): 351-356.

Petersen, William J. The Winnebago.
   Palimpsest, 41 (1960): 331-340.

Quimby, George I. Omaha kinship
   terminology and spruce-fir pollen.
   American Antiquity, 28 (1962/1963): 91-
   92.

Radin, P. A semi-historical account of
   the war of the Winnebago and the Foxes.
   State Historical Society of Wisconsin,
   Proceedings (1914): 191-207.

Radin, P. A sketch of the peyote cult of
   the Winnebago. Journal of Religious
   Psychology, 7 (1914): 1-22.

Radin, P. Crashing Thunder. New York,
   1926. 202 p.

Radin, P. Literary aspects of Winnebago
   mythology. Journal of American Folklore,
   39 (1926): 18-52.

Radin, P. Monotheistic tendencies among
   the Winnebago Indians. International
   Congress of Americanists, Proceedings,
   32 (1958): 176.

Radin, P. Personal reminiscences of a
   Winnebago Indian. Journal of American
   Folklore, 26 (1913): 293-318.

Radin, P. Some aspects of Winnebago
   archeology. American Anthropologist,
   n.s., 13 (1911): 517-538.

Radin, P. The autobiography of a
   Winnebago Indian. California,
   University, Publications in American
   Archaeology and Ethnology, 16 (1920):
   381-473.

Radin, P. The clan organization of the
   Winnebago. American Anthropologist,
   n.s., 12 (1910): 209-219.

*Radin, P. The evolution of an American
   prose epic. Bollingen Foundation,
   Special Publications, 3 (1954): 1-99; 5
   (1956): 103-148.

Radin, P. The influence of the Whites on
   Winnebago culture. State Historical
   Society of Wisconsin, Proceedings
   (1913): 137-145.

Radin, P. The ritual and significance of
   the Winnebago medicine dance. Journal of
   American Folklore, 24 (1911): 149-208.

*Radin, P. The road of life and death.
   New York, 1945. 345 p.

Radin, P. The social organization of the
   Winnebago Indians. Canada, Department of
   Mines, Geological Survey, Museum
   Bulletin, 10 (1915): 1-40.

Radin, P. The thunderbird warclub, a
   Winnebago tale. Journal of American
   Folklore, 44 (1931): 143-165.

Radin, P. The trickster. New York, 1956.
   221 p.

*Radin, P. The Winnebago tribe. U.S.
   Bureau of American Ethnology, Annual
   Reports, 37 (1916): 33-550.

Radin, P. Thunder-Cloud, a Winnebago
   shaman, relates and prays. In E. C.
   Parsons, ed. American Indian Life. New
   York, 1925: 75-80.

*Radin, P. Winnebago culture as described by themselves. International Journal of American Linguistics, Memoirs, 3 (1950): 1-78.

Radin, P. Winnebago hero cycles. International Journal of American Linguistics, Memoirs, 1 (1948): 1-168.

Radin, P. Winnebago myth cycles. Primitive Culture, 1 (1926): 8-86.

Radin, P. Winnebago tales. Journal of American Folklore, 22 (1909): 288-313.

Radin, P., et al. Der Göttliche Schelm. Zürich, 1954. 219 p.

Radin, Paul. An Indian skeptic takes peyote. In Philip K. Bock, ed. Culture Shock. New York, Knopf, 1970: 316-326.

Radin, Paul. Le fripon divin; un mythe indien. Genève, Georg, 1958. 203 p.

Radin, Paul. Report on the mescaline experience of Crashing Thunder. In Bernard S. Aaronson and Humphrey Osmond, eds. Psychedelics: the Uses and Implications of Hallucinogenic Drugs. Garden City, Doubleday, 1970: 86-90. (Anchor Book)

Radin, Paul. Social organization--general discussion [of the Winnebago]. Wisconsin Indians Research Institute, Journal, 2, no. 1 (1966): 83-101.

Radin, Paul. The trickster, a study in American Indian mythology. New York, Greenwood Press, 1969. 11, 211 p.

*Radin, Paul. The Winnebago tribe. Lincoln, University of Nebraska Press, 1970. 16, 511 p. illus., maps.

*Radin, Paul. The Winnebago tribe. New York, Johnson Reprint, 1970. 37-560 p. illus., maps.

Radin, Paul. Warfare and the council lodge [of the Winnebago]. Wisconsin Indians Research Institute, Journal, 2, no. 1 (1966): 74-83.

Radin, Paul. Winnebago ethical attitudes. In Walter R. Goldschmidt, ed. Exploring the Ways of Mankind. New York, Holt, 1960: 556-560.

Riggs, S. R. Dakota grammar, texts and ethnography. Contributions to North American Ethnology, 9 (1893): xviii-xxix.

Ritzenthaler, R. and M. Sellars. Indians in an urban situation. Wisconsin Archeologist, 36 (1955): 147-161.

Schmidt, W. Die Winnebago. In his Die Ursprung der Göttesidee. Bd. 2. Münster i. W., 1929: 602-647.

Sebeok, T. A. Two Winnebago texts. International Journal of American Linguistics, 13 (1947): 167-170.

Sieber, George W. A 1964 Winnebago funeral. Wisconsin Indians Research Institute, Journal, 2, no. 1 (1966): 102-105.

Smith, H. H. Among the Winnebago. Public Museum of the City of Milwaukee, Yearbook, 8 (1928): 76-82.

Snelling, W. J. Early days at Prairie du Chien. Wisconsin State Historical Society, Reports and Collections, 5, no. 1 (1868): 123-153.

Stacy, J., tr. Bible selections. New York, 1907. 483 p.

Steele, Charles Hoy. American Indians and urban life: a community study. Dissertation Abstracts International, 33 (1972/1973): 6479A-6480A. UM 73-11,959.

Stout, A. B. and H. L. Skavlem. The archaeology of the Lake Koshkonong region. Wisconsin Archeologist, 7 (1908): 47-102.

Susman, A. The accentual system of Winnebago. New York, 1943. 149 p.

Susman, A. Word play in Winnebago. Language, 17 (1941): 342-344.

Swanson, Guy E. Rules of descent: studies in the sociology of parentage. Ann Arbor, University of Michigan, 1969. 5, 108 p. (Michigan, University, Museum of Anthropology, Anthropological Papers, 39)

Vlahcevic, Z. R., et al. Relation of bile acid pool size to the formation of lithogenic bile in female Indians of the Southwest. Gastroenterology, 62 (1972): 73-83.

Voegelin, C. F. A problem in morpheme alternants and their distribution. Language, 23 (1947): 245-254.

Webb, J. W., ed. Altowan. New York, 1846. 2 v.

Weer, P. Preliminary notes on the Siouan Family. Indiana History Bulletin, 14 (1937): 99-120.

Weisenburger, Francis P. Caleb Atwater: pioneer politican and historian. Ohio Historical Quarterly, 68 (1959): 18-37.

Winnebago Indian Tribe. Historical
  background of the Winnebago people.
  Wisconsin Indians Research Institute,
  Journal, 2, no. 1 (1966): 1-6.

Winnebago Tribe of Indians. Laws and
  regulations. Omaha, 1868. 6 p.

Winter, G. Journals and Indian paintings,
  1837-1839. Indianapolis, 1948. 208 p.

Wisconsin, Governor's Commission on Human
  Rights. Handbook on Wisconsin Indians.
  Compiled and written by Joyce M. Erdman.
  Madison, 1966. 103 p. illus., maps.
  ERIC ED033816.

Wisconsin Winnebago Tribe. Constitution
  and Bylaws of the Wisconsin Winnebago
  Tribe. Wisconsin Indians Research
  Institute, Journal, 2, no. 1 (1966):
  106-115.

Wolff, H. Comparative Siouan.
  International Journal of American
  Linguistics, 16 (1950): 61-66.

Yarnell, Richard Asa. Aboriginal
  relationships between culture and plant
  life in the Upper Great Lakes region.
  Ann Arbor, University of Michigan, 1964.
  6, 218 p. (Michigan, University, Museum
  of Anthropology, Anthropological Papers,
  23)

Yeast, William E. The presidential Indian
  peace medal. Annals of Iowa, 37 (1964):
  318-320.

12 Northeast

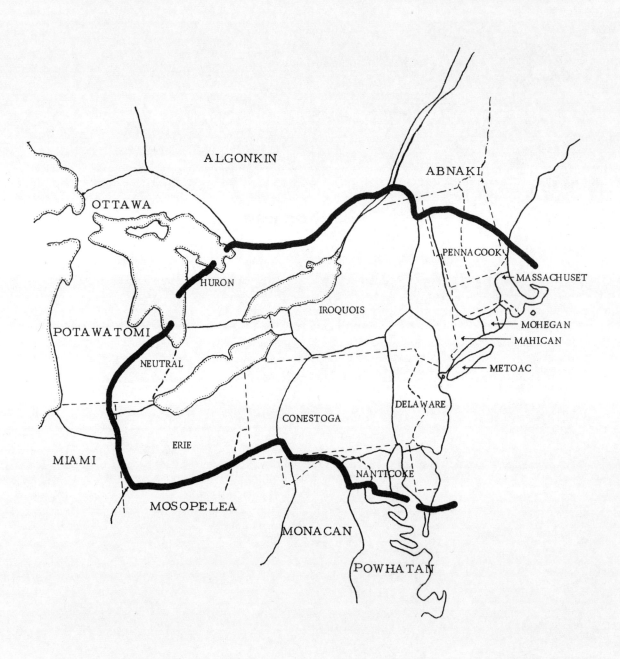

12 Northeast

This area includes the northeastern United States with adjacent areas of Canada. It consists basically of two provinces, the lower Great Lakes region, which contains groups speaking Iroquoian languages, and the North Atlantic coast region, including New England and the Middle Atlantic states, which are inhabited by Algonquian-speaking groups. The whole region is heavily forested, with deciduous species predominating, with no grasslands and little open space. It has a fairly uniform rainfall, not a very bold physiographic relief, and a generally long growing season for crops. It is an area of sedentary farmers, large political units, and large, fortified towns. Subsistence was based on maize, beans, and squash horticulture, with hunting also being important. Gathering of wild plant foods was secondary to hunting and farming. The groups living near the coasts generally spent the summers fishing and collecting shellfish and the winters inland, hunting large game (deer, elk, etc.). Political organization was advanced, with most groups organized in confederacies, the climax being reached with the League of the Iroquois in central New York State. Matrilineal descent was the prevailing form in the area, with leadership often being inherited in this manner. Clans and sibs were strongly developed, and religious and political leadership often went along with membership in these units. There was a great deal of warfare, with torture of captives, cannibalism, and scalping often being part of the pattern. Warfare reached its strongest development with the Iroquois, who used it as an instrument of political policy. Because this was an area of early and heavy European settlement, there are few survivors of the original inhabitants still remaining, except for the New York Iroquois. Most of the other groups are fragmented, removed to distant locations, or extinct.

12-01. Conestoga. The Conestoga (Andaste, White Minqua, Susquehanna, Susquehannock) lived in the Susquehanna River drainage in New York, Pennsylvania, and Maryland. They spoke an Iroquoian language and became extinct in the late eighteenth century.

12-02. Delaware. The Delaware (Lenape, Lenni Lenape), including the Munsee (Minsi), Unami, and Unalachtigo, occupied all of New Jersey, western Long Island, Manhattan Island, and parts of eastern Pennsylvania and Delaware. Their later history is one of continual westward movement, until at present Delaware are living on the Stockbridge-Munsee Indian Reservation in Wisconsin; in the Munsee Delaware Community in Kansas; on the former Cherokee, Wichita, and Caddo Reservations in Oklahoma; and on two reserves in Ontario, Canada. They speak an Algonquian language. The Canadian Delaware numbered 581 in 1967, and the United States Delaware (including the Stockbridge) numbered 2,926 in 1970.

12-03. Erie. The Erie (Cat Nation) lived in northern Ohio, southwestern New York, and northeastern Pennsylvania. They spoke an Iroquoian language and were destroyed as a group in a war with the Iroquois during 1653-1656.

12-04. Huron. The Huron (Wendat), including the Ataronchronon, Tionontati (Tobacco, Petun), Wenrohonronon, and Wyandot (Guyandot), lived in the area from the St. Lawrence River across southern Ontario to Lake Huron. They later were forced to move to southeastern Michigan and northwestern Ohio. Groups of Huron now live at Lorette in Quebec; in a community in Wyandot County, Kansas; and on the former Wyandot Indian Reservation in northeastern Oklahoma. They speak an Iroquoian language. The Canadian Huron numbered 969 in 1967, while the Kansas group numbered 134 and the Oklahoma group numbered 1,157 in 1970.

Heidenreich, Conrad. Huronia; a history and geography of the Huron Indians 1600-1650. Toronto, McClelland and Stewart, 1971. 331 p. illus., maps.

12-05. Iroquois. The Iroquois (Five Nations, Six Nations), including the Cayuga, Mohawk, Oneida, Onondaga, and Seneca, originally lived in the upper Mohawk River Valley and the lake region in New York State. They now live principally on the Allegany, Cattaraugus, Tonawanda, Onondaga, Oneida, and St. Regis Indian Reservations in New York State; the Oneida Indian Reservation in Wisconsin; the former Seneca Indian Reservation in Oklahoma; and the Six Nations, Caughnawaga, and Tyendinaga (Bay of Quinte) Reserves in Canada. They speak Iroquoian languages. The Canadian Iroquois numbered 20,342 in 1967, while the United States Iroquois numbered 21,473 in 1970.

Garrow, Larry, et al. A selected bibliography on the Mohawk people. Minneapolis, National Indian Education Association, 1974. 53 p. ERIC ED093514.

12-06. Mahican. The Mahican (River Indians, Canoe Indians), together with the Wappinger, lived on the Hudson River in eastern New York from Lake Champlain to Manhattan Island and eastward to the Housatonic Valley in Massachusetts and the Connecticut River in Connecticut. Descendants of these groups now live on the Stockbridge-Munsee Indian Reservation in Wisconsin and in the Brotherton Indian Community in Winnebago and Calumet Counties, Wisconsin. They spoke Algonquian languages. The Stockbridge-Munsee numbered 920 in 1970, while the Brotherton Community numbered 254.

12-07. Massachuset. The Massachuset, with the Nauset (Cape Indians), Nipmuc, Wampanoag, and Natick (Praying Indians), lived in eastern Massachusetts from north of Boston to Cape Cod and westward to the eastern shores of Narragansett Bay. Descendants of these groups now live in the Nipmuc Community, near Worcester, Mass.; on Martha's Vineyard (Gay Head); and on Cape Cod (Mashpee). They spoke Algonquian languages and now number about 800.

12-08. Metoac. The Metoac (Long Island Indians), including the Montauk, Corchaug, Shinnecock, Manhasset, Rockaway, and Patchogue, lived in the eastern and central parts of Long Island. Their descendants now live in small communities in the area, including the Poosepatuck and Shinnecock Reservations and the Montauk Indian Village. They spoke Algonquian languages and numbered about 400 in 1970.

12-09. Mohegan. The Mohegan, with the Pequot, Narragansett, and Niantic (Nehantic), lived in western Rhode Island and in Connecticut east of the Connecticut River. They now live on the Eastern and Western Pequot Reservations and the Schaghticoke Reservation, and in the Mohegan Community in Connecticut and the Narragansett Community in Rhode Island. They spoke Algonquian languages and numbered about 600 in 1970.

12-10. Nanticoke. The Nanticoke (Nentego), with the Conoy (Piscataway), lived on the eastern and western shores of Chesapeake Bay and the Potomac River in Maryland, and in southern Delaware. Their descendants now live in the Nanticoke Community in Sussex County, Delaware. They spoke Algonquian languages and numbered 411 in 1970.

12-11. Neutral. The Neutral (Attiwandaron, Attiwandaronk) lived in southeastern Ontario, western New York, northwestern Ohio, and southeastern Michigan. They were destroyed as a group in a war with the Iroquois in the early 1650s. They spoke an Iroquoian language.

12-12. Pennacook. The Pennacook, with the Pocomtuc, lived in the valleys of the Merrimac River in New Hampshire and the Connecticut River in Vermont, New Hampshire, Massachusetts, and northern Connecticut and in the neighboring areas. Their descendants now live with the St. Francis Abnaki in Quebec. They spoke Algonquian languages.

12-13. Middle Atlantic States Mestizos. This bibliographical division includes citations on a number of communities of Mestizos (i.e. racial crosses between Indians and other races) in this general area, including the Ramapo Mountain People, Moors, Sand Hill Indians, Slaughters, Van Guilders, and Wesorts, among others.

Cohen, David Steven. The Ramapo Mountain People. New Brunswick, N.J., Rutgers University Press, 1974. 16, 285 p. illus., maps.

12-00 Northeast Area Bibliography

Anonymous. References on American Indians within the present limits of the State of Delaware. Archaeological Society of Delaware, Bulletin, 1, no. 5 (1934): 18-19.

Guthe, Alfred K., ed. An anthropological bibliography of the eastern seaboard. Vol. 2. Edited by Alfred K. Guthe and Patricia D. Kelly. Trenton, N.J., The Federation, 1963. 82 p. (Eastern States Archaeological Federation, Research Publication, 2)

Pilling, J. C. Bibliography of the Algonquian languages. U.S. Bureau of American Ethnology, Bulletin, 13 (1891): 1-614.

Pilling, J. C. Bibliography of the Iroquoian languages. U.S. Bureau of American Ethnology, Bulletin, 6 (1888): 1-208.

Rouse, I. and D. Horton, eds. A preliminary archaeological bibliography of the eastern United States. Archaeological Society of Connecticut, Bulletin, 9/10 (1939/1940).

Rouse, Irving, ed. An anthropological bibliography of the eastern seaboard. Edited by Irving Rouse and John M. Goggin. New Haven, The Federation, 1947. 174 p. map. (Eastern States Archaeological Federation, Research Publication, 1)

Abbott, C. C. Primitive industry. Salem, 1881. 560 p.

Adams, J. A. English institutions and the American Indian. Johns Hopkins University Studies in Historical and Political Science, 12, no. 10 (1894): 4-59.

Adolf, Leonard. Squanto's role in Pilgrim diplomacy. Ethnohistory, 11 (1964): 247-261.

Alberts, R. C. Trade silver and Indian silver work in the Great Lakes region. Wisconsin Archeologist, 34 (1953): 1-121.

Allen, F. H., et al. Blood groups of eastern American Indians. International Congress of Genetics, Proceedings, 10, vol. 2 (1958): 5.

Allen, L. Siouan and Iroquoian. International Journal of American Linguistics, 6 (1931): 185-193.

Anonymous. New Jersey's place in cultural history. Trenton, 1957. 37 p.

Anonymous. Number of Indians in Rhode-Island, 1774. Massachusetts Historical Society, Collections, ser. 1, 10 (1809): 119.

Anonymous. The number of Indians in Connecticut, 1774. Massachusetts Historical Society, Collections, ser. 1, 10 (1809): 117-118.

Armbruster, E. L. The Indians of New England and New Netherland. New York, 1918. 11 p.

Atkin, Edmond. The Appalachian Indian frontier, the Edmond Atkin report and plan of 1755. Edited by Wilbur R. Jacobs. Lincoln, University of Nebraska Press, 1967. 38, 108 p. illus., maps.

Bailey, Alfred G. The conflict of European and Eastern Algonkian cultures 1504-1700: a study in Canadian civilization. 2d ed. Toronto, University of Toronto Press, 1969. 23, 218 p.

Barbeau, C. M. Indian captivities. American Philosophical Society, Proceedings, 94 (1950): 522-548.

Barbeau, C. M. Indian trade silver. Royal Society of Canada, Proceedings and Transactions, ser. 3, 34, pt. 2 (1940): 27-41.

Barbeau, C. M. and G. Melvin. The Indian speaks. Toronto, 1943. 117 p.

Barbeau, Charles Marius. Legend and history in the oldest geographical names of the St. Lawrence. Inland Seas, 17 (1961): 105-113.

Barber, J. W. The history and antiquities of New England, New York, New Jersey and Pennsylvania, 69-120. Hartford, 1843.

Bauman, Robert F. Claims vs realities: the Anglo-Iroquois partnership. Northwest Ohio Quarterly, 32 (1959/1960): 88-101.

Beardsley, G. The groundnut as used by the Indians of eastern North America. Michigan Academy of Science, Arts and Letters, Papers, 25, no. 4 (1939): 507-515.

Beauchamp, W. M. Indian nations of the Great Lakes. American Antiquarian and Oriental Journal, 17 (1895): 321-325.

Becker, Donald W. Indian place-names in New Jersey. Cedar Grove, N.J., Philips-Campbell, 1964. 9, 111 p. illus.

Beer, David F. Anti-Indian sentiment in early colonial literature. Indian Historian, 2, no. 1 (1969): 29-33, 48.

Beers, H. P. The French in North America. Baton Rouge, 1957.

Benedict, A. L. A medical view of the American Indians of the Northeast. Medical Age, 19 (1901): 767-771.

Bennett, M. K. The food economy of the New England Indians, 1605-1675. Journal of Political Economy, 63 (1955): 369-397.

Biasutti, R. Le razzi e i popoli della terra, 2d ed., Vol. 4: 425-437. Torino, 1957.

Birket-Smith, K. A geographic study of the early history of the Algonquian Indians. Internationales Archiv für Ethnographie, 24 (1918): 174-222.

Birket-Smith, K. Ancient artefacts from eastern United States. Société des Américanistes, Journal, n.s., 12 (1920): 141-169.

Bisbee, E. E., et al. White Mountain scrap heap. Lumenburg, Vermont, 1956. 64 p.

Blackmon, Joab L., Jr. Judge Samuel Sewall's efforts in behalf of the first Americans. Ethnohistory, 16 (1969): 165-176.

Blasingham, E. J. The "New England Indians" in the western Great Lakes region. Indiana Academy of Science, Proceedings, 66 (1956): 47-49.

Blomkvist, E. E. Indeïtsy severo-vostochnogo i prioz ernogo raĭonov SSHA (irokesy i algonkiny). By E. E. Blomkvist and IŪ. P. Averkieva. In A. V. Efimov and S. A. Tokarev, eds. Narody Ameriki. Vol. 1. Moskva, Izdatel'stvo Akademiĩa Nauk SSSR, 1959: 194-227.

Bloomfield, L. Algonquian. Viking Fund Publications in Anthropology, 6 (1946): 85-129.

Bodge, George Madison. Soldiers in King Philip's War. 3d ed. Baltimore, Genealogical Publishing, 1967. 13, 502 p. illus., maps.

Bradley, W. T. Medical practices of the New England aborigines. American Pharmaceutical Association, Journal, 25 (1936): 138-147.

Brasser, T. J. C. The Coastal Algonkians: people of the first frontiers. In Eleanor Burke Leacock and Nancy

Oestreich Lurie, eds. North American Indians in Historical Perspective. New York, Random House, 1971: 64-91.

Braunholtz, H. J. The Sloane Collection: Ethnography. British Museum Quarterly, 18, no. 1 (1953): 23-26.

Burke, Charles T. Puritans at bay; the war against King Philip and the squaw sachems. New York, Exposition Press, 1967. 261 p. illus., map.

Burrage, Henry S., ed. Early English and French voyages, chiefly from Hakluyt, 1534-1608. New York, C. Scribner's Sons, 1906. 22, 451 p. map. (Original Narratives of Early American History, 3)

Bushnell, D. I. Native villages and village sites east of the Mississippi. U.S. Bureau of American Ethnology, Bulletin, 69 (1919): 1-111.

Bushnell, D. I. The use of soapstone by the Indians of the eastern United States. Smithsonian Institution, Annual Reports of the Board of Regents (1939): 471-489.

Bushnell, D. I. Tribal migrations east of the Mississippi. Smithsonian Miscellaneous Collections, 89, no. 12 (1934): 1-9.

Butler, E. L. Algonkian culture and the use of maize in southern New England. Archaeological Society of Connecticut, Bulletin, 22 (1948): 3-39.

Butler, E. L. Some early Indian basket makers of southern New England. Archaeological Society of New Jersey, Research Series, 1 (1947): 34-55.

Butler, E. L. Sweat-houses in the southern New England area. Massachusetts Archaeological Society, Bulletin, 7 (1945): 11-15.

Butler, E. L. The brush or stone memorial heaps of southern New England. Archaeological Society of Connecticut, Bulletin, 19 (1946): 3-12.

Butler, E. L. and W. S. Hadlock. Dogs of the Northeastern Woodland Indians. Massachusetts Archaeological Society, Bulletin, 10 (1949): 17-36.

Butler, E. L. and W. S. Hadlock. Some uses of birch bark in northern New England. Massachusetts Archaeological Society, Bulletin, 18 (1957): 72-75.

Byers, D. S. The environment of the Northeast. Robert S. Peabody Foundation for Archaeology, Papers, 3 (1946): 3-32.

Carpenter, E. S. and R. B. Hassrick. Some notes on arrow poisoning among the tribes of the Eastern Woodlands. Delaware County Institute of Science, Proceedings, 10 (1947): 45-52.

Carr, L. G. K. Interesting animal foods, medicines, and omens of the Eastern Indians. Washington Academy of Sciences, Journal, 41 (1951): 229-235.

Carroll, Peter Neil. Puritanism and the wilderness: the intellectual significance of the New England frontier, 1629-1675. Dissertation Abstracts, 29 (1968/1969): 2172A-2173A. UM 69-1810.

Cartier, Jacques. Voyages de découverte au Canada entre les années 1534 et 1542. Paris, Éditions Anthropos, 1968. 6, 208 p. illus.

Chamberlain, A. F. Maple sugar and the Indians. American Anthropologist, 4 (1891): 381-383.

Chamberlain, A. F. The maple amongst the Algonkian tribes. American Anthropologist, 4 (1891): 39-43.

Chamberlain, L. S. Plants used by the Indians of eastern North America. American Naturalist, 35 (1901): 1-10.

Champlain, Samuel de. Les voyages du Sieur de Champlain. Ann Arbor, University Microfilms, 1966. 325, 52 p. illus., maps.

Charlevoix, P. F. X. de. Histoire de la Nouvelle France. Paris, 1894. 3 v.

Charlevoix, P. F. X. de. History and general description of New France. Ed. J. M. Shea. New York, 1866-1872. 6 v.

Chatard, F. E. An early description of birch-bark canoes. American Neptune, 8 (1948): 91-98.

Clauser, C. E. The relationship between a Coastal Algonkin and a Karankawa cranial series. Indiana Academy of Science, Proceedings, 57 (1948): 18-23.

Company for Propagation of the Gospel in New England and Parts Adjacent in America. Some correspondence between the governors and treasurers of the New England Company in London and the Commissioners of the United Colonies in America, the missionaries of the company, and others between the years 1657 and 1712, to which are added the journals of the Rev. Experience Mayhew in 1713 and 1714. Edited by John W. Ford. New York, B. Franklin, 1970. 32, 127 p.

Connolly, Donald F. X. A chronology of New England Catholicism before the Mayflower landing. American Catholic Historical Society, Records, 70 (1959/1960): 3-17, 88-108.

Cooper, J. M. Land tenure among the Indians of eastern and northern North America. Pennsylvania Archaeologist, 8 (1938): 55-59.

Crèvecoeur, Michel de. Eighteenth-century travels in Pennsylvania and New York. Translated and edited by Percy G. Adams. Lexington, University of Kentucky Press, 1961. 44, 172 p. illus.

Crèvecoeur, Michel de. Journey into northern Pennsylvania and the State of New York. Translated by Clarissa Spencer Bostelmann. Ann Arbor, University of Micigan Press, 1964.

Crocker, J. DeReu. Index to the opinions of the New York State attorney general and the New York State comptroller relating to Indian affairs. Albany, New York State Department of Law, 1961. 9 p.

Daniels, Thomas E. Vermont Indians. Edited by Kathleen Rowlands. Orwell, Vt., Mrs. Thomas E. Daniels, 1963. 63 p. illus.

Darlington, Mary C., ed. History of Col. Henry Bouquet and the western frontiers of Pennsylvania, 1747-1764. New York, Arno Press, 1971. 224 p. illus.

Day, G. M. The Indian as an ecologic factor in the northeastern forest. Ecology, 34 (1953): 329-346.

Day, Gordon M. A St. Francis Abenaki vocabulary. International Journal of American Linguistics, 30 (1964): 371-392.

Day, Gordon M. An Agawam fragment. International Journal of American Linguistics, 33 (1967): 244-247.

Day, Gordon M. English-Indian contacts in New England. Ethnohistory, 9 (1962): 24-40.

Day, Gordon M. Historical notes on New England languages. In Contributions to Anthropology: Linguistics I. Ottawa, Queen's Printer, 1967: 107-112. (Canada, National Museum, Bulletin, 214)

Delabarre, E. B. and H. H. Wilder. Indian corn hills in Massachusetts. American Anthropologist, n.s., 22 (1920): 203-225.

Dexter, F. Extracts from the itineraries and other miscellanies of Ezra Stiles. New Haven, 1916.

Dixon, R. B. The early migrations of the Indians of New England and the Maritime Provinces. American Antiquarian Society, Proceedings, n.s., 24 (1914): 65-76.

Dixon, R. B. The mythology of the Central and Eastern Algonkins. Journal of American Folklore, 22 (1909): 1-9.

Dodge, E. S. Ethnology of northern New England and the Maritime Provinces. Massachusetts Archaeological Society, Bulletin, 18 (1957): 68-71.

Dodge, E. S. Some thoughts on the historic art of the Indians of northeastern North America. Massachusetts Archaeological Society, Bulletin, 13, no. 1 (1951): 1-4.

Douglas, F. H. Iroquoian and Algonkin wampum. Denver Art Museum, Indian Leaflet Series, 31 (1931): 1-4.

Douglas, F. H. New England Indian houses, forts and villages. Denver Art Museum, Indian Leaflet Series, 39 (1932): 1-4.

Douglas, F. H. The New England tribes. Denver Art Museum, Indian Leaflet Series, 27/28 (1931): 1-8.

Douglas-Lithgow, R. A. Dictionary of American Indian place and proper names in New England. Salem, 1909. 400 p.

Drake, S. G. Indian captivities. Auburn, 1850. 367 p.

Du Creux, F. The history of Canada or New France. Champlain Society, Publications, 30/31 (1951/1952): 1-776.

Dunlap, A. R. and C. A. Weslager. Indian place-names in Delaware. Wilmington, 1951. 82 p.

Engberg, R. M. Algonkian sites of Westmoreland and Fayette Counties, Pennsylvania. Western Pennsylvania Historical Magazine, 14 (1931): 143-190.

Essington, J. H. Early inhabitants of the Ohio Valley. West Virginia History, 13 (1952): 277-285.

Feest, Christian F. Tomahawk und Keule im östliche Nordamerika. Archiv für Völkerkunde, 19 (1964/1965): 39-84.

Fenton, W. N. The present state of anthropology in northeastern North America. American Anthropologist, n.s., 50 (1948): 494-515.

Fernow, Berthold. The Ohio Valley in colonial days. New York, Burt Franklin, 1971. 299 p.

Flannery, R. Algonquian Indian folklore. Journal of American Folklore, 60 (1947): 397-401.

Flannery, R. An analysis of Coastal Algonquian culture. Catholic University of America, Anthropological Series, 7 (1939): 1-219.

Forbes, Allan, Jr. Two and a half centuries of conflict: the Iroquois and the Laurentian wars. Pennsylvania Archaeologist, 40, no. 3/4 (1970): 1-20.

Foreman, G. The last trek of the Indians, 17-88, 159-181, 229-236. Chicago, 1946.

Fowler, W. S. Primitive woodworking in the Connecticut Valley. Massachusetts Archaeological Society, Bulletin, 7 (1946): 72-75.

Gerard, W. R. Algonquian names for pickeral. American Anthropologist, n.s., 5 (1903): 581-582.

Gilbert, W. H., Jr. Surviving Indian groups of the eastern United States. Smithsonian Institution, Annual Reports of the Board of Regents (1948): 407-438.

Gille, J. Der Manabozho-Flutzyklus der Nord-, Nordost-, und Zentralalgonkin. Göttingen, 1939. 86 p.

Gille, J. Weskarini und Ur-Algonkin. Göttingen, 1939. 17 p.

Gille, J. Zur Lexikologie des Alt-Algonkin. Zeitschrift für Ethnologie, 71 (1939): 71-86.

Gillette, Charles H. Wampum beads and belts. Indian Historian, 3, no. 4 (1970): 32-38.

Gillingham, H. E. Indian ornaments made by Philadelphia silversmiths. New York, 1936. 26 p.

Goddard, Ives. Algonquian linguistics in the Northeast: 1971. Man in the Northeast, 3 (1972): 55-56.

Goddard, Ives. The Eastern Algonquian intrusive nasal. International Journal of American Linguistics, 31 (1965): 206-220.

Green, Eugene. Generic terms for water and waterways in Algonquian place-names. By Eugene Green and Celia Millward. Anthropological Linguistics, 13 (1971): 33-52.

Griffin, J. B. Aboriginal methods of pottery manufacture in the eastern United States. Pennsylvania Archaeologist, 5 (1935): 19-24.

Haas, M. R. A new linguistic relationship in North America. Southwestern Journal of Anthropology, 14 (1958): 231-264.

Hadlock, W. S. Warfare among the Northeastern Woodland Indians. American Anthropologist, n.s., 49 (1947): 204-221.

Hallett, L. F. Medicine and pharmacy of the New England Indians. Massachusetts Archaeological Society, Bulletin, 17 (1956): 46-49.

Hallowell, A. I. Some psychological characteristics of the Northeastern Indians. Robert S. Peabody Foundation for Archaeology, Papers, 3 (1946): 195-225.

Hallowell, A. Irving. Intelligence of Northeastern Indians. In Robert Hunt, ed. Personalities and Cultures. Garden City, Natural History Press, 1967: 49-55.

Hamilton, K. G. Cultural contributions of Moravian missions among the Indians. Pennsylvania History, 18 (1951): 1-15.

Hanna, Charles A. The wilderness trail. New York, AMS Press, 1972. 2 v. illus.

Hare, Lloyd C. M. Thomas Mayhew, patriarch to the Indians (1593-1682). St. Clair Shores, Mich., Scholarly Press, 1971. 12, 231 p. illus., maps.

Herman, M. W. Wampum as a money in northeastern North America. Ethnohistory, 5 (1958): 21-33.

Hewson, John. Errata in Bloomfield's Algonquian sketch. International Journal of American Linguistics, 38 (1972): 77.

Hildreth, Samuel P. Pioneer history. New York, Arno Press, 1971. 13, 525 p. illus.

Hoffman, Bernard G. Ancient tribes revisited: a summary of Indian distribution and movement in the Northeastern United States from 1534 to 1779. Ethnohistory, 14 (1967): 1-46.

Hoffman, Bernard G. Cabot to Cartier; sources for a historical ethnography of northeastern North America, 1497-1550. Toronto, University of Toronto Press, 1961. 12, 287 p. maps.

Hoffman, Bernard G. Observations on certain ancient Tribes of the Northern Appalachian Province. Washington, D.C., Government Printing Office, 1964. 191-245 p. illus., maps. (U.S., Bureau of American Ethnology, Anthropological Papers, 70. U.S., Bureau of American Ethnology, Bulletin, 191)

Holling, H. C. The book of Indians, 17-44. New York, 1935.

Holmes, W. H. Aboriginal pottery of the eastern United States. U.S. Bureau of American Ethnology, Annual Reports, 20 (1899): 1-201.

Horsman, Reginald. The British Indian Department and the resistance to General Anthony Wayne, 1793-1795. Mississippi Valley Historical Review, 49 (1962/1963): 269-290.

Howe, H. F. Sources of New England Indian history prior to 1620. Massachusetts Archaeological Society, Bulletin, 3 (1942): 19-24.

Howells, W. W. Physical types of the Northeast. Robert S. Peabody Foundation for Archaeology, Papers, 3 (1946): 168-177.

Howes, W. J. The importance of the Connecticut Valley territory of western Massachusetts to the Indians. Massachusetts Archaeological Society, Bulletin, 1, no. 4 (1940): 4-10.

Hrdlička, A. Catalogue of human crania in the United States National Museum collections. United States National Museum, Proceedings, 69, no. 5 (1927): 1-127.

Hrdlička, A. Physical anthropology of the Lenape or Delawares, and of the Eastern Indians in general. U.S. Bureau of American Ethnology, Bulletin, 62 (1916): 110-130.

Hubbard, William. The history of the Indian wars in New England, from the first settlement to the termination of the war with King Philip in 1677. Edited by Samuel G. Drake. New York, B. Franklin, 1971. 31, 292, 303 p. map.

Huden, J. C. Indian place names in Vermont. Burlington, 1957. 32 p.

Huden, John C. Indian place names of New England. New York, 1962. 14, 408 p. (Museum of the American Indian, Heye Foundation, Contributions, 18)

Hunter, W. A. The Ohio, the Indian's land. Pennsylvania History, 21 (1954): 338-350.

Hunter, William A. Forts on the Pennsylvania frontier, 1753-1758. Harrisburg, Pennsylvania Historical and Museum Commission, 1960. 11, 596 p. illus., maps.

Hutslar, Donald A. The log architecture of Ohio. Ohio History, 80 (1971): 177-267.

Jacobs, W. R. The Indian frontier of 1763. Western Pennsylvania Historical Magazine, 34 (1951): 185-198.

Jacobsson, N. Svenskai och Indianer. Stockholm, 1922.

Jeançon, J. A. and F. H. Douglas. Iroquoian and Algonkin wampum. Denver Art Museum, Indian Leaflet Series, 31 (1931): 1-4.

Jennings, Francis. The Indian trade of the Susquehanna Valley. American Philosophical Society, Proceedings, 110 (1966): 406-424.

Jesuits, Letters from Missions (North America). Relations des Jésuites. Montréal, Éditions du Jour, 1972. 6 v.

Johnson, F., ed. Man in northeastern North America. Robert S. Peabody Foundation for Archaeology, Papers, 3 (1946): 1-347.

Josselyn, J. New England's rarities discovered. American Antiquarian Society, Transactions and Collections, 4 (1860): 105-238.

Josselyn, John. New-Englands rarities discovered. Boston, Massachusetts Historical Society, 1972. 114 p. illus.

Kellaway, William. The New England Company, 1649-1776; missionary society to the American Indians. New York, Barnes and Noble, 1962. 303 p. illus.

Kenny, Hamill Thomas. The origin and meaning of the Indian place names of Maryland. Baltimore, Waverly Press, 1961. 19, 186 p. map.

Kinietz, V. Notes on the roached headdress of animal hair among the North American Indians. Michigan Academy of Science, Arts and Letters, Papers, 26 (1940): 463-467.

Klingberg, Frank J. Anglican humanitarianism in colonial New York. Freeport, N.Y., Books for Libraries Press, 1971. 10, 295 p.

Kurath, G. P. Algonquian ceremonialism and natural resources of the Great

Lakes. Bangalore, 1957. (Indian Institute of Culture, Reprint 22)

Kurath, G. P. Antiphonal songs of Eastern Woodlands Indians. Musical Quarterly, 42 (1956): 520-526.

Lahontan, A. L. de D. New voyages to North America. Ed. by R. G. Thwaites. Chicago, 1905. 2 v.

Lahontan, A. L. de D. Nouveaux voyages. La Haye, 1703. 220 p.

Lahontan, Louis A. New voyages to North America. New York, Burt Franklin, 1970. 2 v. [93, 797 p.] illus., maps.

Leach, D. E. Flintlock and tomahawk. New York, 1958. 318 p.

Lincoln, C. H., ed. Narratives of the Indian wars, 1675-1699. New York, 1913. 316 p.

Loskiel, G. H. Geschichte der Mission der evangelischen Brüder unter den Indianern in Nordamerika. Barby, 1789. 783 p.

Loskiel, G. H. History of the mission of the United Brethren among the Indians in North America. London, 1794.

MacNeish, R. S. The archeology of the northeastern United States. In J. B. Griffin, ed. Archeology of Eastern United States. Chicago, 1952: 46-58.

Maine, State Department of Education. Indian education in Maine. Augusta, 1969. 6 p. ERIC ED032995.

Malone, Patrick Mitchell. Indian and English military systems in New England in the seventeenth century. Dissertation Abstracts International, 32 (1971/1972): 5155A-5156A. UM 72-8154.

Mason, John. A brief history of the Pequot War. Ann Arbor, University Microfilms, 1966. 6, 10, 22 p.

Mason, John. A brief history of the Pequot War. With an introduction and some explanatory notes by Thomas Prince. Freeport, N.Y., Books for Libraries Press, 1971. 9, 20 p.

Merwin, B. W. Wampum. Museum Journal, 7 (1916): 125-133.

Michelson, T. Algonquian notes. International Journal of American Linguistics, 9 (1939): 103-112.

Michelson, T. Preliminary report on the linguistic classification of Algonquian tribes. U.S. Bureau of American

Ethnology, Annual Reports, 28 (1907): 221-290.

Moody, Robert Earle. The Maine frontier, 1607 to 1763. Dissertation Abstracts, 28 (1967/1968): 3117A-3118A. UM 65-7515.

Mook, Maurice A. The aboriginal population of Tidewater Virginia. American Anthropologist, n.s., 46 (1944): 193-208.

Morgan, Youngs L. The diary of an early fur trader. Edited by Clarissa Headline and Milton N. Gallup. Inland Seas, 18 (1962): 300-305; 19 (1963): 30-38, 113-122, 227-232, 277-283.

Morris, J. L. Indians of Ontario. Toronto, 1943. 75 p.

Morton, Thomas. New English Canaan. New York, Da Capo Press, 1969. 188 p.

Morton, Thomas. New English Canaan of Thomas Morton. Edited by Charles Francis Adams, Jr. New York, B. Franklin, 1967. 6, 381 p.

New York (Colony). An abridgement of the Indian affairs contained in four folio volumes, transacted in the colony of New York, from the year 1678 to the year 1751, by Peter Wraxall. Edited by Charles Howard McIlwain. New York, B. Blom, 1968. 118, 264 p.

New York (State), State Interdepartmental Committee on Indian Affairs. The Indian today in New York State. 6th ed. Albany, 1969. 3, 17 p. illus., map.

Orr, R. B. North American Indian games--dice. Annual Archaeological Report, being Part of Appendix to the Report of the Minister of Education, Ontario, 27 (1915): 20-34.

Parker, A. C. The role of wampum in the Colonial era. Galleon, 14 (1954): 1-5.

Parsons, Joseph A., Jr. Civilizing the Indians of the Old Northwest, 1800-1810. Indiana Magazine of History, 56 (1960): 195-216.

Pecoraro, Joseph. The effect of a series of special lessons on Indian history and culture upon the attitudes of Indian and non-Indian students. Dissertation Abstracts International, 32 (1971/1972): 1757A. UM 71-26,730.

Peet, S. D. The location of the Indian tribes. American Antiquarian and Oriental Journal, 1 (1878): 85-98.

Penhallow, Samuel. Penhallow's Indian Wars; a facsimile reprint of the first edition. Freeport, N.Y., Books for Libraries Press, 1971. 20, 134, 51 p.

Philhower, C. A. Indian currency and its manufacture. New Jersey Historical Society, Proceedings, n.s., 13 (1928): 310-318.

Philhower, C. A. Wampum, its use and value. New Jersey Historical Society, Proceedings, n.s., 15 (1930): 216-223.

Potherie, B. de la. History of the savage people who are allies of New France. Ed. by E. H. Blair. In E. H. Blair, ed. The Indian Tribes of the Upper Mississippi Valley. Vol. 2. Cleveland, 1912: 13-136.

Potherie, B. de la. History of the savage people who are allies of New France. Ed. by E. H. Blair. In E. H. Blair, ed. The Indian Tribes of the Upper Mississippi Valley. Vol. 1. Cleveland, 1911: 273-372.

Putnam, F. W. The manufacture of soapstone pots by the Indians of New England. Harvard University, Peabody Museum of American Archaeology and Ethnology, Reports, 11, no. 2 (1878): 273-276.

Reynolds, H. L. Algonkin metal-smiths. American Anthropologist, 1 (1888): 341-352.

Ritchie, W. A. A perspective of northeastern archeology. American Antiquity, 4 (1938): 94-112.

Ritchie, W. A. An Algonkian village site near Lavanna. Rochester Museum of Science and Arts, Records of Research, 1 (1928): 1-27.

Ritchie, W. A. An Algonkin-Iroquois contact site on Castle Creek. Rochester Museum of Science and Arts, Records of Research, 2 (1934): 1-58.

Ritchie, W. A. Indian history of New York State. Part III--The Algonkian tribes. Albany, 1956.

Roberts, William I., III. The fur trade of New England in the seventeenth century. Dissertation Abstracts, 19 (1958/1959): 126-127. UM 58-1867.

Rogers, R. A concise account of North America. London, 1765. 264 p.

Rouse, I. Ceramic traditions and sequences in Connecticut. Archaeological Society of Connecticut, Bulletin, 21 (1947): 10-25.

Rouse, I.   Styles of pottery in
    Connecticut. Massachusetts
    Archaeological Society, Bulletin, 7
    (1945): 1-8.

Russell, F. and H. M. Huxley.   A
    comparative study of the physical
    structure of the Labrador Eskimos and
    the New England Indians. American
    Association for the Advancement of
    Science, Proceedings, 48 (1899): 365-
    379.

Salisbury, Noel Emerson.   Conquest of the
    "savage": Puritans, Puritan
    missionaries, and Indians, 1620-1680.
    Dissertation Abstracts International, 32
    (1971/1972): 6905A. UM 72-18,141.

Schmitt, K.   Archeological chronology of
    the Middle Atlantic states. In J. B.
    Griffin, ed. Archeology of Eastern
    United States. Chicago, 1952: 59-70.

Schusky, E.   Pan-Indianism in the eastern
    United States. Anthropology Tomorrow, 6
    (1957): 116-123.

Sherman, C. F.   Habitations, summer and
    winter sites, and reasons for same.
    Massachusetts Archaeological Society,
    Bulletin, 6 (1944): 10-14.

Sherman, C. F.   Winslow's reports of the
    Indians. Massachusetts Archaeological
    Society, Bulletin, 3 (1942): 43-51.

Siebert, Frank T., Jr.   The original home
    of the Proto-Algonquian people. In
    Contributions to Anthropology:
    Linguistics I.   Ottawa, Queen's Printer,
    1967: 13-47. (Canada, National Museum,
    Bulletin, 214)

Skinner, A.   The Algonkin and the
    thunderbird. American Museum Journal, 14
    (1914): 71-73.

Skinner, A.   Traces of the stone age among
    the eastern and northern tribes.
    American Anthropologist, n.s., 14
    (1912): 391-395.

Slotkin, J. S. and K. Schmitt.   Studies of
    wampum. American Anthropologist, n.s.,
    51 (1949): 223-236.

Smith, C. S.   An outline of the
    archaeology of coastal New York.
    Archaeological Society of Connecticut,
    Bulletin, 21 (1947): 3-9.

Smith, C. S.   The archaeology of coastal
    New York. American Museum of Natural
    History, Anthropological Papers, 43,
    no. 2 (1950): 1-105.

Smith, James.   An account of the
    remarkable occurrences in the life and
    travels of Col. James Smith, during his
    captivity with the Indians in the years
    1755, '56, '57, '58, and '59, with an
    appendix of illustrative notes. Edited
    by Wm. N. Darlington. Cincinnati, R.
    Clarke, 1870. 12, 190 p. (Ohio Valley
    Historical Series, 5)

Smith, John.   Captain John Smith's
    America; selections from his writings.
    Edited by John Lankford. New York,
    Harper and Row, 1967. 18, 195 p.
    (Harper Torchbooks, TB 3078)

Smith, John.   The generall historie of
    Virginia, New-England, and the Summer
    Isles. Ann Arbor, University
    Microfilms, 1966. 96, 105-248 p.
    illus., maps.

Smith, John.   Works, 1608-1631. Edited by
    Edward Arber. New York, AMS Press,
    1967. 136, 984 p. illus.

Snyderman, G. S.   The functions of wampum.
    American Philosophical Society,
    Proceedings, 98 (1954): 469-494.

Society for the Propagation of the Gospel
    in New-England.   The New England Company
    of 1649 and John Eliot. Edited by George
    P. Winship. New York, B. Franklin,
    1967. 85, 219 p.

Speck, F. G.   Concerning iconology and the
    masking complex in eastern North
    America. Pennsylvania, University,
    Museum Bulletin, 15 (1950): 6-57.

Speck, F. G.   Dream symbolism and the
    desire motive in floral designs of the
    Northeast. Guardian, 1 (1925): 124-127.

Speck, F. G.   Eastern Algonkian block-
    stamp decoration. Archaeological Society
    of New Jersey, Research Series, 1
    (1947): 1-34.

Speck, F. G.   The family hunting band as
    the basis of Algonkian social
    organization. American Anthropologist,
    n.s., 17 (1915): 289-305.

Speck, F. G.   The functions of wampum
    among the Eastern Algonkian. American
    Anthropological Association, Memoirs, 6
    (1919): 3-71.

Speck, F. G.   The historical approach to
    art in archaeology in the northern
    woodlands. American Antiquity, 8 (1942):
    173-175.

Speck, F. G.   The memorial brush heap in
    Delaware and elsewhere. Archaeological
    Society of Delaware, Bulletin, 4, no. 2
    (1945): 17-23.

Speck, F. G. Wampum in Indian tradition and currency. Numismatic and Antiquarian Society of Philadelphia, Proceedings, 27 (1916): 121-130.

Speck, Frank G. The family hunting band as the basis of Algonkian social organization. In Frederica de Laguna, ed. Selected Papers from the American Anthropologist 1888-1920. Evanston, Row, Peterson, 1960: 607-623.

Spier, L. The Trenton argillite culture. American Museum of Natural History, Anthropological Papers, 22 (1918): 167-226.

Stearns, Martha Genung. Herbs used by the Indians and early settlers of New England. Plants and Gardens, 14 (1958): 170-171.

Steele, Zadock. The Indian captive. New York, B. Blom, 1971. 13, 166 p. map.

Sturtevant, William C. Indian communities in the eastern United States. By William C. Sturtevant and Samuel Stanley. Indian Historian, 1, no. 3 (1967/1968): 15-19.

Sylvester, H. M. Indian wars of New England. Boston, 1910. 3 v.

Thwaites, Reuben G., ed. The French regime in Wisconsin [1634-1748]. Madison, 1902, 1906. 2 v. illus. (Wisconsin, State Historical Society, Collections, 16-17)

Thwaites, Reuben G., ed. The French regime in Wisconsin [1743-1760]. Madison, 1908. 25, 1-222 p. (Wisconsin, State Historical Society, Collections, 18)

Tooker, W. W. The Algonquian terms Patawomeke and Massawomeke. American Anthropologist, 7 (1894): 174-185.

Trelease, Allen W. Indian affairs in colonial New York: the seventeenth century. Ithaca, Cornell University Press, 1960. 15, 379 p. illus., maps.

Trelease, Allen W. Indian affairs in colonial New York: the seventeenth century. Port Washington, Kennikat Press, 1971. 15, 379 p. illus., maps.

Trelease, Allen W. Indian-White contacts in Eastern North America: the Dutch in New Netherland. Ethnohistory, 9 (1962): 137-146.

Trigger, Bruce G. The French presence in Huronia: the structure of Franco-Huron relations in the first half of the seventeenth century. Canadian Historical Review, 49 (1968): 107-141.

Trumbull, B. A compendium of the Indian wars in New England. Ed. by F. B. Hartranft. Hartford, 1926. 61 p.

Trumbull, J. H. On the Algonkin verb. American Philological Association, Transactions, 7 (1877): 147-171.

Trumbull, J. H. The composition of Indian geographical names. Connecticut Historical Society, Collections, 2 (1870): 1-50.

Uhler, S. P. Pennsylvania's Indian relations to 1754. Allentown, 1951. 144 p.

Underhill, John. Newes from America. New York, Da Capo Press, 1971. 44 p. illus.

U.S., Bureau of Indian Affairs. Indians of the eastern seaboard. Washington, D.C., Government Printing Office, 1968. 32 p. ERIC ED028871.

Van Zandt, Roland. Chronicles of the Hudson; three centuries of traveller' accounts. New Brunswick, Rutgers University Press, 1971. 13, 369 p. illus., maps.

Various. King Philip's War narratives. Ann Arbor, University Microfilms, 1966.

Vaughan, Alden T. New England frontier; Puritans and Indians, 1620-1675. Boston, Little, Brown, 1965. 17, 430 p. illus., map.

Vaughan, Alden True. New England Puritans and the American Indian, 1620-1675. Dissertation Abstracts, 28 (1967/1968): 608A-609A. UM 67-10,393.

Voegelin, C. F. and E. W. Voegelin. Linguistic considerations of northeastern North America. Robert S. Peabody Foundation for Archaeology, Papers, 3 (1946): 178-194.

Voegelin, E. W. Mortuary customs of the Shawnee and other eastern tribes. Indiana Historical Society, Prehistory Research Series, 2 (1944): 227-444.

Wallace, A. F. C. Political organization and land tenure among the Northeastern Indians, 1600-1830. Southwestern Journal of Anthropology, 13 (1957): 301-321.

Wallace, P. A. W. Historic Indian paths of Pennsylvania. Pennsylvania Magazine of History and Biography, 76 (1952): 411-439.

Warner, Frederick William. Some aspects of Connecticut Indian culture history.

Dissertation Abstracts International, 31 (1970/1971): 6396B. UM 71-11,452.

Warner, Robert Austin. The Southern New England Indians 1725; a study in culture contact. Dissertation Abstracts International, 30 (1969/1970): 3002B. UM 69-22,078.

Waugh, F. W. Notes on Canadian pottery. Annual Archaeological Report, being Part of Appendix to the Report of the Minister of Education, Ontario, 14 (1901): 108-115.

Wells, Robin F. Castoreum and steel traps in eastern North America. American Anthropologist, 74 (1972): 479-483.

Wells, William. William Wells and the Indian Council of 1793. Edited by Dwight L. Smith. Indiana Magazine of History, 56 (1960): 217-226.

Weslager, C. A. A discussion of the family hunting territory question in Delaware. In L. DeValinger. Indian Land Sales in Delaware. Wilmington, 1941: 14-24.

Weslager, C. A. The non-food use of corn in the domestic economy of the Eastern Indians. Delaware County Institute of Science, Proceedings, 10 (1947): 3-22.

Wherry, E. T. Some little-known food plants of Pennsylvania. Delaware County Institute of Science, Proceedings, 10, no. 2 (1947): 23-27.

White, P. C. T. Lord Selkirk's diary, 1803-04. Champlain Society, Publications, 35 (1958): 1-391.

Willoughby, C. C. Dress and ornaments of the New England Indians. American Anthropologist, n.s., 7 (1905): 499-508.

Willoughby, C. C. Houses and gardens of the New England Indians. American Anthropologist, n.s., 8 (1906): 115-132.

Willoughby, C. C. Textile fabrics of the New England Indians. American Anthropologist, n.s., 7 (1905): 85-93.

Willoughby, C. C. The adze and the ungrooved axe of New England. American Anthropologist, n.s., 9 (1907): 296-306.

Willoughby, C. C. Wooden bowls of the Algonquian Indians. American Anthropologist, n.s., 10 (1908): 423-434.

Winsor, J. The earliest printed books connected with the aborigines of New England, 1630-1700. Massachusetts Historical Society, Proceedings, 10 (1895): 327-359.

Wintemberg, W. J. Archaeological evidence of Algonkian influence on Iroquoian culture. Royal Society of Canada, Proceedings and Transactions, 29, pt. 2 (1935): 331-342.

Wintemberg, W. J. Distinguishing characteristics of Algonkian and Iroquoian cultures. Canada, Department of Mines, National Museum of Canada, Bulletin, 67 (1931): 65-124.

Wintemberg, W. J. The use of shells by the Ontario Indians. Annual Archaeological Report, being Part of Appendix to the Report of the Minister of Education, Ontario (1907): 38-90.

Wood, William. New Englands prospect. New York, Da Capo Press, 1968. 98 p. map.

Wood, William. Wood's New-England's prospect. New York, B. Franklin, 1967. 31, 131 p. illus.

Woodward, A. Wampum. 2d ed. Albany, 1880. 56 p.

Young, R. F. Comenius and the Indians of New England. London, 1929. 27 p.

Zeisberger, David, et al. Some remarks and annotations concerning the traditions, customs, languages etc. of the Indians in North America, from the memoirs of the Reverend David Zeisberger, and other missionaries of the United Brethren. Edited by Erminie Wheeler-Voegelin. Ethnohistory, 6 (1959): 42-69.

Zimmerman, Albright Gravenor. The Indian trade of colonial Pennsylvania. Dissertation Abstracts, 28 (1967/1968): 1384A. UM 67-11,752.

12-01 Conestoga

Alsop, G. A character of the province of Maryland: 71-81. Ed. by J. G. Shea. New York, 1869.

Alsop, George. A character of the Province of Maryland. Edited by Newton D. Mereness. Freeport, N.Y., Books for Libraries Press, 1972. 113 p.

Benson, E. A. The story of the Susquehannocks. Lancaster, Pennsylvania, 1958.

Bozman, J. L. The history of Maryland, Vol. 1: 103-193. Baltimore, 1837.

Cadzow, D. A. Archaeological studies of the Susquehannock Indians. Pennsylvania Historical Commission, Publications, 3, no. 2 (1936): 1-217.

Casselberry, Samuel Emerson. The Schulz-Funck site (36La7): its role in the culture history of the Susquehannock and Shenk's Ferry Indians. Dissertation Abstracts International, 33 (1972/1973): 25B. UM 72-19,283.

Crozier, A. Indian towns near Wilmington, Delaware. Archaeological Society of Delaware, Bulletin, 2, no. 6 (1938): 2-4.

Crozier, A. Notes on the archaeology of Newcastle County, Delaware. Archaeological Society of Delaware, Bulletin, 1, no. 4 (1934): 1-6.

Donehoo, G. P. A short sketch of the Indian trails of Pennsylvania. Wyoming Historical and Geological Society, Proceedings and Collections, 17 (1919): 67-94.

Dunlap, A. R. and C. A. Weslager. Toponymy of the Delaware Valley as revealed by an early seventeenth-century Dutch map. Archaeological Society of New Jersey, Bulletin, 15/16 (1958): 1-13.

Eshleman, H. F. Annals of the Susquehannocks. Lancaster, 1908. 415 p.

Eshleman, H. F. Lancaster County Indians. Lancaster, 1909. 28 p.

Fishwick, Marshall. William Berkeley: unappreciated patriot. West Virginia History, 23 (1961/1962): 195-204.

Franklin, Benjamin. A sermon to the Susquehanna. Indian Historian, 2, no. 2 (1969): 29.

Gamble, Anna Dill. An ancient mission among a great people. American Catholic Historical Society of Philadelphia, Records, 60 (1949): 125-143.

Goldsborough, E. R. The aborigines of the lower Potomac River Valley. Pennsylvania Archaeologist, 8 (1938): 27-36.

Guss, A. L. Early Indian history on the Susquehanna. Harrisburg, 1883. 32 p.

Hanna, C. A. The wilderness trail, Vol. 1: 26-87. New York, 1911.

Heisey, Henry W. Of historic Susquehannock cemeteries. By Henry W. Heisey and J. Paul Witmer. Pennsylvania Archaeologist, 32 (1962): 99-130.

Henretta, J. E., ed. Kane and the Upper Allegheny. Philadelphia, 1929. 357 p.

Hewitt, J. N. B. Conestoga. U.S. Bureau of American Ethnology, Bulletin, 30, vol. 1 (1907): 335-337.

Hewitt, J. N. B. Susquehanna. U.S. Bureau of American Ethnology, Bulletin, 30, vol. 2 (1910): 653-659.

Hill, J. My people the Delawares. Archaeological Society of Delaware, Bulletin, 4, no. 1 (1943): 9-13.

Holzinger, C. H. The Ibaugh Site: a Susquehannock cemetery. Eastern States Archaeological Federation, Bulletin, 17 (1958): 12.

*Jennings, Francis. Glory, death, and transfiguration: the Susquehannock Indians in the seventeenth century. American Philosophical Society, Proceedings, 112 (1968): 15-53.

Kinsey, W. F. A preliminary report on Susquehannock pottery types. Eastern States Archaeological Federation, Bulletin, 17 (1958): 12.

Kinsey, W. F. The Oscar Leibhart Site: a Susquehannock village of 1650-1675. Eastern States Archaeological Federation, Bulletin, 16 (1957): 13.

Landis, D. H. A brief description of Indian life and Indian trade of the Susquehannock Indians. Lancaster, 1929. 48 p.

Lucy, C. L. Notes on a small Andaste burial site and Andaste archaeology. Pennsylvania Archaeologist, 21 (1951): 53-56.

Macaulay, P. S. The legendary Susquehannocks. Pennsylvania Archaeologist, 6 (1936): 43-47.

MacCord, H. A. The Susquehannock Indians in West Virginia, 1630-77. West Virginia History, 13 (1952): 239-253.

Mercer, H. C. Distribution of Indian tribes in Central Pennsylvania in prehistoric times. Antiquarian, 1 (1897): 215-216.

Michels, Joseph W. Settlement pattern and demography at Sheep Rock shelter: their role in culture contact. Southwestern Journal of Anthropology, 24 (1968): 66-82.

Miller, Mary Emily. Port town on the starboard, a history of Frederica, Delaware. Delaware History, 14, no. 2 (1970): 111-134.

Moorehead, W. K. A report of the Susquehanna River expedition. Andover, 1938. 142 p.

Murray, E. The "noble savage". Scientific Monthly, 36 (1933): 251-257.

Murray, L. W. Excavating an Andasta chief. Tioga Point Historical Society, Proceedings and Collections, 1 (1896): 28-32.

Murray, L. W. Selected manuscripts of General John S. Clark relating to the aboriginal history of the Susquehanna. Athens, 1931. 150 p.

Parker, A. C. The influence of the Iroquois on the history and archaeology of the Wyoming Valley. Wyoming Historical and Geological Society, Proceedings and Collections, 11 (1910): 65-102.

Schrabisch, M. Aboriginal rock shelters and other archeological notes of Wyoming Valley and vicinity. Wyoming Historical and Geological Society, Proceedings and Collections, 19 (1926): 47-218.

Shea, J. G. The identity of the Andastes, Minquas, Susquehannas, and Conestogues. Historical Magazine, 2 (1858): 294-297.

Snyderman, George S. The manuscript collections of the Philadelphia yearly meeting of Friends pertaining to the American Indian. American Philosophical Society, Proceedings, 102 (1958): 613-620.

Stephenson, R. L. The prehistoric people of Accokeek Creek. Accokeek, Maryland, 1959. 35 p.

Stephenson, Robert L. The Accokeek Creek site; a Middle Atlantic seaboard culture sequence. By Robert L. Stephenson and Alice L. L. Ferguson. With sections by Henry G. Ferguson. Ann Arbor, University of Michigan, 1963. 10, 215 p. illus. (Michigan, University, Museum of Anthropology, Anthropological Papers, 20)

Stewart, T. B. Andaste camp site. Now and Then, 4 (1930): 76-78.

Strachey, W. The historie of travaile into Virginia Britannia, 39-41. London, 1849.

Streeter, S. F. The fall of the Susquehannocks. Historical Magazine, 1 (1857): 65-73.

Tooker, W. W. The names Susquehanna and Chesapeake, with historical and

ethnological notes. New York, 1901. 63 p.

Uhler, S. P. Pennsylvania's Indian relations to 1754. Allentown, 1951. 144 p.

Wallace, Paul A. W. Indian paths of Pennsylvania. Harrisburg, Pennsylvania Historical and Museum Commission, 1965. 8, 227 p. maps.

Weslager, C. A. Susquehannock Indian religion from an old document. Washington Academy of Sciences, Journal, 36 (1946): 302-305.

Weslager, C. A. The Minquas and their early relations with the Delaware Indians. Archaeological Society of Delaware, Bulletin, 4, no. 1 (1943): 14-23.

Witthoft, J. Archaeological history of Susquehannock Indians and A note on the map-locations of Susquehannock towns. 9 p., unpaginated, mimeographed. Issued with: Archeological Society of Maryland, Newsletter, 4, nos. 1, 2, 4 (1958).

Witthoft, J. and W. F. Kinsey. Susquehannock miscellany. Harrisburg, 1959. 167 p.

Wren, C. A study of North Appalachian Indian pottery. Wyoming Historical and Geological Society, Proceedings and Collections, 13 (1914): 131-222.

Wren, C. Aboriginal pottery of the Wyoming Valley. Wyoming Historical and Geological Society, Proceedings and Collections, 9 (1905): 137-170.

Wren, C. Some Indian graves. Wyoming Historical and Geological Society, Proceedings and Collections, 12 (1912): 199-214.

Wren, C. The stone age. Wyoming Historical and Geological Society, Proceedings and Collections, 8 (1904): 93-115.

Wren, C. Turtle shell rattles and other implements from Indian graves. Wyoming Historical and Geological Society, Proceedings and Collections, 10 (1909): 195-210.

Wysong, T. T. The rocks of Deer Creek. Baltimore, 1879. 78 p.

12-02 Delaware

Abbott, C. C. Idols and idol worship of the Delaware Indians. American Naturalist, 16 (1882): 799-802.

Abbott, C. C. Indians of New Jersey. In F. B. Lee, ed. New Jersey as a Colony and as a State. Vol. 1. New York, 1902: 53-71.

Abbott, C. C. Ten years' diggings in Lenape land. Trenton, 1912. 191 p.

Abbott, C. C. The Delaware Indian as an artist. Popular Science Monthly, 41 (1892): 586-594.

Abbott, C. C. The stone age in New Jersey. Smithsonian Institution, Annual Reports of the Board of Regents (1875): 246-380.

Abbott, C. C. The use of copper by the Delaware Indians. American Naturalist, 19 (1885): 774-777.

Adams, R. C. A Delaware Indian legend. Washington, D.C., 1899. 75 p.

Adams, R. C. A Delaware report. Indian Historian, 2, no. 2 (1969): 25-26.

Adams, R. C. History of the Delaware Indians. In United States, Department of the Interior, Census Office, Eleventh Census, Report on Indians Taxed and Indians not Taxed. Washington, D.C., 1890: 297-300.

Adams, R. C. Legends of the Delaware Indians and picture writing. Washington, D.C., 1905.

Adams, R. C. The adoption of Mew-seu-qua. Washington, D.C., 1917. 52 p.

Adams, R. C. The ancient religion of the Delaware Indians. Washington, D.C., 1904. 43 p.

Allinson, S. Fragmentary history of the New Jersey Indians. New Jersey Historical Society, Proceedings, ser. 2, 4 (1875): 33-50.

Anderson, W. de la R. The Indian legend of Watchung. New Jersey Historical Society, Proceedings, ser. 4, 11 (1926): 45-48.

Anonymous. Presents for the Six Nations-- 1815. Museum of the Fur Trade Quarterly, 4, no. 2 (1968): 6-8.

Anonymous. Walam Olum or red score. Indianapolis, 1954. 393 p.

Armbruster, Henry C. Torrey's trading post. Texana, 2 (1964): 112-131.

Barber, E. A. Notes on the Lenni Lenape. American Antiquarian and Oriental Journal, 6 (1884): 385-389.

Barnholth, William I. Hopocan (Capt. Pipe) the Delaware chieftain. Rev. ed. Akron, Ohio, Summit County Historical Society, 1966. 19 l. maps.

Berlin, A. F. Mode of fishing by the Delaware Indians. American Antiquarian and Oriental Journal, 9 (1887): 167-169.

Bibaud, F. M. Biographie des sagamos illustrés de l'Amérique Septentrionale, 223-226, 231-233. Montréal, 1848.

Bliss, E. F., ed. Diary of David Zeisberger. Cincinnati, 1885. 2 v.

Boas, F. Zur Anthropologie der nordamerikanischen Indianer. Berliner Gesellschaft für Anthropologie, Ethnologie und Urgeschichte, Verhandlungen (1895): 367-411.

Bolton, R. P. Indian life of long ago in the City of New York. New York, 1934. 167 p.

Bolton, R. P. Indian paths in the great metropolis. Indian Notes and Monographs, 23 (1922): 1-279.

Bolton, R. P. New York City in Indian possession. Indian Notes and Monographs, 2 (1920): 225-395.

Bolton, Reginald P. Indian life of long ago in the city of New York. Port Washington, I. J. Friedman, 1971. 16, 167 p. illus.

Brant, C. S. Peyotism among the Kiowa-Apache and neighboring tribes. Southwestern Journal of Anthropology, 6 (1950): 212-222.

Brickell, J. Narrative of John Brickell's captivity among the Delaware Indians. American Pioneer, 1 (1842): 43-56.

Brinton, D. G. Folk-lore of the modern Lenape. In his Essays of an Americanist. Philadelphia, 1890: 181-192.

Brinton, D. G. Lenape conversations. Journal of American Folklore, 1 (1888): 37-43.

Brinton, D. G. and A. S. Anthony, eds. A Lenapé-English dictionary. Philadelphia, 1888. 236 p.

Brinton, Daniel G. The Lenâpé and their
legends. St. Clair Shores, Mich.,
Scholarly Press, 1972. 262 p. illus.

Brinton, Daniel G. The Lenâpé and their
legends. New York, AMS Press, 1969.
262 p. illus.

Brinton, Daniel G. The Lenâpé and their
legends, with the complete text and
symbols of the Walam Olum, a new
translation and an inquiry into its
authenticity. Philadelphia, D. G.
Brinton, 1885. 262 p. illus. (Library
of Aboriginal American Literature, 5)

Brooks, S. T. The question of a Minquas
Indian fort on Iron Hill. Archaeological
Society of Delaware, Bulletin, 4, no. 4
(1947): 27-33.

Brunner, D. B. The Indians of Berks
County. Reading, 1881. 177 p.

Buck, W. J. Lappawinzo and Tishcohan,
chiefs of the Lenni Lenape. Pennsylvania
Magazine of History and Biography, 7
(1883): 215-218.

Bushnell, D. I. Native cemeteries and
forms of burial east of the Mississippi.
U.S. Bureau of American Ethnology,
Bulletin, 71 (1920): 20-24.

Butler, M. Two Lenape rock shelters near
Philadelphia. American Antiquity, 12
(1947): 246-255.

Cross, D. Canoes of the Lenni Lenape.
Archaeological Society of New Jersey,
Newsletter, 3 (1941): 10.

Cross, D. Houses of the Lenni Lenape.
Archaeological Society of New Jersey,
Newsletter, 2 (1940): 11-12.

Cross, D. Pottery making. Archaeological
Society of New Jersey, Newsletter, 5
(1941): 7-9.

Crozier, A. Fishing methods of the
Indians of the Delmarva region.
Archaeological Society of Delaware,
Bulletin, 4, no. 4 (1947): 16-19.

Cummings, R. W. Delaware. In H. R.
Schoolcraft, ed. Information respecting
the History, Condition, and Prospects of
the Indian Tribes of the United States.
Vol. 2. Philadelphia, 1852. 470-481.

De Roo, P. Linape national songs. In
History of America before Columbus.
Vol. 1. Philadelphia, 1900. 585-591.

De Valinger, L. Indian land sales in
Delaware. Archaeological Society of
Delaware, Bulletin, 3, no. 3 (1940): 29-
32; 3, no. 4 (1941): 25-33.

Dencke, C. F., tr. Nek
nechenenawachgissitschik bambilak naga
geschiechauchsitpanna Johannessa
elekhangup. New York, 1818. 21 p.

Dodge, Henry. Journal of Colonel Dodge's
expedition from Fort Gibson to the
Pawnee Pict village. American State
Papers, Military Affairs, 5 (1860): 373-
382.

Donck, Adriaen van der. A description of
the New Netherlands. Edited by Thomas F.
O'Donnell. Syracuse, Syracuse
University Press, 1968. 40, 10, 142 p.

Donehoo, G. P. A short sketch of the
Indian trails of Pennsylvania. Wyoming
Historical and Geological Society,
Proceedings and Collections, 17 (1919):
67-94.

Doren, C. van and J. P. Boyd. Indian
treaties printed by Benjamin Franklin.
Philadelphia, 1938. 340 p.

Downes, R. C. Council fires on the Upper
Ohio. Pittsburgh, 1940. 367 p.

Dragoo, Don W. Archaeological
investigations at Pymatuning Town,
Mercer County, Pennsylvania.
Pennsylvania Archaeologist, 34, no. 2
(1964): 47-52.

Duncan, DeWitt Clinton. An open letter
from Too-Qua-Stee to Congressman Charles
Curtis, 1898. Chronicles of Oklahoma, 47
(1969): 298-304.

Dunlap, A. R. A bibliographical
discussion of the Indian languages of
the Delmarva Peninsula. Archaeological
Society of Delaware, Bulletin, 4, no. 5
(1949): 2-5.

Dunlap, A. R. Contributions to the ethnohistory of the Delaware Indians on the
Brandywine. By A. R. Dunlap and C. A.
Weslager. Pennsylvania Archaeologist, 30
(1960): 18-21.

Dunlap, A. R. Names and places in an
unrecorded Delaware Indian deed, (1681).
By A. R. Dunlap and C. A. Weslager.
Delaware History, 9, no. 3 (1961): 282-
292.

Dunlap, A. R. Two Delaware Valley Indian
place names. By A. R. Dunlap and C. A.
Weslager. Names, 15 (1967): 197-202.

Dunlap, A. R. and C. A. Weslager. Indian
place names in Delaware. Wilmington,
1950.

Dunlap, A. R. and C. A. Weslager.
Toponymy of the Delaware Valley as
revealed by an early seventeenth-century

Dutch map. Archaeological Society of New Jersey, Bulletin, 15/16 (1958): 1-13.

Dunn, J. P. True Indian stories. Indianapolis, 1909. 320 p.

Ely, A. G. A summary of Delaware Indian culture. El Palacio, 52 (1945): 14-19.

Fall, Ralph Emmett. Captain Samuel Brady (1756-1795), chief of the Rangers, and his kin. West Virginia History, 29 (1967/1968): 203-223.

Farley, A. W. The Delaware Indians in Kansas, 1829-1867. Kansas City, 1955. 16 p.

Fay, George E., ed. Charters, constitutions and by-laws of the Indian tribes of North America. Part V: The Indian tribes of Oklahoma. Greeley, 1968. 14, 104 l. map. (University of Northern Colorado, Museum of Anthropology, Occasional Publications in Anthropology, Ethnology Series, 6) ERIC ED046555.

Fay, George E., ed. Treaties between the Stockbridge-Munsee Tribe(s) of Indians and the United States of America 1805-1871. Wisconsin Indians Research Institute, Journal, 4, no. 1 (1968): i-ii, 1-62.

Ferguson, Roger James. The White River Indiana Delawares: an ethnohistoric synthesis, 1795-1867. Dissertation Abstracts International, 33 (1972/1973): 3508A. UM 73-331.

Foreman, G. The last trek of the Indians, 182-190. Chicago, 1946.

Garrett, Minnie A. They called themselves Leni Lenape; a short history of the Delawares. Indian Historian, 1, no. 2 (1967/1968): 33-34.

Gibson, A. M. An Indian Territory United Nations: the Creek Council of 1845. Chronicles of Oklahoma, 39 (1961): 398-413.

Gifford, A. The aborigines of New Jersey. New Jersey Historical Society, Proceedings, 4 (1850): 165-198.

Goddard, Ives. More on the nasalization of PA *a in Eastern Algonquian. International Journal of American Linguistics, 37 (1971): 139-145.

Goddard, Ives. Notes on the genetic classification of the Algonquian languages. In Contributions to Anthropology: Linguistics I. Ottawa, Queen's Printer, 1967: 7-12. (Canada, National Museum, Bulletin, 214)

Goddard, Ives. The ethnohistorical implications of early Delaware linguistic materials. Man in the Northeast, 1 (1971): 14-26.

Goodman, Julia Cody. Julia Cody Goodman's memoirs of Buffalo Bill. Edited by Don Russell. Kansas Historical Quarterly, 28 (1962): 442-496.

Haekel, Josef. Der Hochgottglaube der Delawaren im Lichte ihrer Geschichte. Ethnologica, n.F., 2 (1960): 439-484.

Hanna, C. A. The wilderness trail, Vol. 1: 88-118. New York, 1911.

Hannum, M. F. and F. D. Scull. A study of the Lenni Lenape or Delaware Indians. New York, 1941. 25 p.

Harrington, M. R. A preliminary sketch of Lenape culture. American Anthropologist, n.s., 15 (1913): 208-235.

Harrington, M. R. Dickon among the Lenape Indians. Chicago, 1938. 353 p.

Harrington, M. R. Religion and ceremonies of the Lenape. Indian Notes and Monographs, ser. 2, 19 (1921): 1-249.

Harrington, M. R. Some customs of the Delaware Indians. Museum Journal, 1 (1910): 52-60.

Harrington, M. R. The life of a Lenape boy. Pennsylvania Archaeologist, 3, no. 4 (1933): 3-8.

Harrington, M. R. The thunder power of Rumbling Wings. Pennsylvania Archaeologist, 4, no. 1 (1934): 3-9; 4, no. 2 (1934): 7-12.

Harrington, M. R. The thunder power of Rumbling-Wings. In E. C. Parsons, ed. American Indian Life. New York, 1925: 107-125.

Harrington, M. R. Vestiges of material culture among the Canadian Delawares. American Anthropologist, n.s., 10 (1908): 408-418.

Harris, Z. S. Structural restatements. International Journal of American Linguistics, 13 (1947): 175-186.

Heckewelder, J. G. E. A narrative of the mission of the United Brethren among the Delaware and Mohegan Indians. Philadelphia, 1820.

*Heckewelder, J. G. E. An account of the history, manners, and customs, of the Indian nations, who once inhabited Pennsylvania and the neighbouring states. American Philosophical Society,

Historical and Literary Committee, Transactions, 1 (1819): 1-348.

Heckewelder, J. G. E. Names which the Lenni Lenape or Delaware Indians, who once inhabited this country, had given to rivers, streams, places, etc. American Philosophical Society, Transactions, n.s., 4 (1834): 351-396.

Heckewelder, J. G. E. Words, phrases, and short dialogues, in the language of the Lenni Lenape or Delaware Indians. American Philosophical Society, Historical and Literary Committee, Transactions, 1 (1819): 450-464.

Heckewelder, J. G. E. and P. S. Duponceau. Correspondence. American Philosophical Society, Historical and Literary Committee, Transactions, 1 (1819): 351-448.

Heckewelder, John G. E. A narrative of the mission of the United Brethren among the Delaware and Mohegan Indians. New York, Arno Press, 1971. 429 p.

*Heckewelder, John G. E. History, manners, and customs of the Indian nations who once inhabited Pennsylvania and the neighboring states. New York, Arno Press, 1971. 465 p.

Heckewelder, John G. E. John Heckewelder to Peter S. Du Ponceau, Bethlehem 12th Aug 1818. Edited by Erminie Wheeler-Voegelin. Ethnohistory, 6 (1959): 70-81.

Heller, W. J. The disappearance of the Lenni Lenape from the Delaware and their subsequent migrations. Penn Germania, n.s., 1 (1912): 711-717.

Herman, M. W. A reconstruction of aboriginal Delaware culture from contemporary sources. Kroeber Anthropological Society, Publications, 1 (1950): 45-77.

Heye, G. G. and G. H. Pepper. Exploration of a Munsee cemetery. Museum of the American Indian, Heye Foundation, Contributions, 2, no. 1 (1915): 1-78.

Holm, T. C. A short description of the Province of New Sweden. Historical Society of Pennsylvania, Memoirs, 3 (1834): 112-156.

Hrdlička, A. Physical anthropology of the Lenape or Delawares. U.S. Bureau of American Ethnology, Bulletin, 62 (1916): 1-130.

*Hulbert, A. B. and W. N. Schwarze, eds. Zeisberger's history of northern American Indians. Ohio State

Archaeological and Historical Quarterly, 19 (1910): 1-189.

Hunter, Charles E. The Delaware nativist revival of the mid-eighteenth century. Ethnohistory, 18 (1971): 39-49.

Hunter, W. A. John Hays' diary and journal of 1760. Pennsylvania Archaeologist, 24 (1954): 63-84.

Hunter, W. A. Provincial negotiations with the Western Indians, 1754-58. Pennsylvania History, 18 (1951): 213-219.

Hunter, W. A. Pymatuning. Pennsylvania Archaeologist, 26 (1956): 174-177.

Hutter, William H. Scenes in (and en route to) Kansas Territory, autumn, 1854: five letters by William H. Hutter. Edited by Louise Barry. Kansas Historical Quarterly, 35 (1969): 312-336.

Jennings, Francis. Glory, death, and transfiguration: the Susquehannock Indians in the seventeenth century. American Philosophical Society, Proceedings, 112 (1968): 15-53.

Jennings, Francis Paul. Miquon's passing: Indian-European relations in colonial Pennsylvania, 1674-1755. Dissertation Abstracts, 26 (1965/1966): 7281-7282. UM 66-4621.

Joblin, E. E. M. The education of the Indians of Western Ontario. Ontario, College of Education, Department of Educational Research, Bulletin, 13 (1948): 1-138.

Johnson, A. The Indians and their culture as described in Swedish and Dutch records. International Congress of Americanists, Proceedings, 19 (1915): 277-282.

Johnson, John L. Albert Andrew Exendine: Carlisle coach and teacher. Chronicles of Oklahoma, 43 (1965): 319-331.

Ketcham, Ralph L. Conscience, war, and politics in Pennsylvania, 1755-1757. William and Mary Quarterly, 3d ser., 20 (1963): 416-439.

*Kinietz, W. V. Delaware culture chronology. Indiana Historical Society, Prehistory Research Series, 3 (1946): 1-143.

Kinietz, W. V. European civilization as a determinant of native Indian customs. American Anthropologist, n.s., 42 (1940): 116-121.

Lee, John D. Diary of the Mormon
Battalion Mission. Edited by Juanita
Brooks. New Mexico Historical Review, 42
(1967): 165-209, 281-332.

Leslie, V. E. A tentative catalogue of
Minsi material culture. Pennsylvania
Archaeologist, 21 (1951): 9-20.

Leslie, V. E. An archaeological
reconnaissance of Upper Delaware Valley
sites. Pennsylvania Archaeologist, 16
(1946): 20-30, 59-78, 95-112, 131-141.

Lilly, E. Remarks regarding the
pictographs of the Walum Olum. Indiana
Academy of Science, Proceedings, 49
(1940): 32-33.

Lilly, E. Tentative speculations on the
chronology of the Walam Olum and the
migration route of the Lenape. Indiana
Academy of Science, Proceedings, 54
(1945): 33-40.

Lincoln, A. T. Our Indians of early
Delaware. Delaware Citizens Association,
Historical Bulletin, 1 (1932): 1-42.

Lindeström, P. Geographia Americae, with
an account of the Delaware Indians.
Philadelphia, 1925. 418 p.

Lindeström, Peter Mårtensson. Resa till
Nya Sverige. Stockholm, Natur och
Kultur, 1962. 172 p. illus., maps.

Loskiel, G. H. Geschichte der Mission der
evangelischen Brüder unter den Indianern
in Nordamerika. Barby, 1789. 783 p.

Loskiel, G. H. History of the Mission of
the United Brethren among the Indians of
North America. London, 1794.

Luckenbach, A., tr. Forty-six select
scripture narratives from the Old
Testament. New York, 1838. 304 p.

MacLeod, W. C. The family hunting
territory and Lenape political
organization. American Anthropologist,
n.s., 24 (1922): 448-463.

Mahr, A. C. Aboriginal culture traits as
reflected in 18th century Delaware
Indian tree names. Ohio Journal of
Science, 54 (1954): 380-387.

Mahr, A. C. Eighteenth century
terminology of Delaware Indian
cultivation and use of maize.
Ethnohistory, 2 (1955): 209-240.

Mahr, A. C. Semantic analysis of
eighteenth-century Delaware Indian names
for medicinal plants. Ethnohistory, 2
(1955): 11-28.

Mahr, A. C. Walam Olum, I, 17: a proof of
Rafinesque's integrity. American
Anthropologist, 59 (1957): 705-708.

Mahr, August C. Anatomical terminology of
the eighteenth century Delaware Indians.
Anthropological Linguistics, 2, no. 5
(1960): 1-65.

Mahr, August C. Delaware terms for plants
and animals in the eastern Ohio country:
a study in semantics. Anthropological
Linguistics, 4, no. 5 (1962): 1-48.

Mahr, August C. Semantic evaluation.
Anthropological Linguistics, 3, no. 5
(1961): 1-46.

Mathews, Edward. An abolitionist in
territorial Wisconsin: the journal of
Reverend Edward Mathews. Edited by
William Converse Haygood. Wisconsin
Magazine of History, 52 (1968/1969): 3-
18, 117-131, 248-262, 330-343.

McCracken, H. L. The Delaware big house.
Chronicles of Oklahoma, 34 (1956): 183-
192.

McLean, Malcolm D. Tenoxtitlan, dream
capital of Texas. Southwestern
Historical Quarterly, 70 (1966/1967):
23-43.

Meeussen, A. E. Prefix pluralizers in
Delaware. International Journal of
American Linguistics, 25 (1959): 188-
189.

Mercer, H. C. The Lenape stone. New
York, 1885. 95 p.

Miller, Mary Emily. Port town on the
starboard, a history of Frederica,
Delaware. Delaware History, 14, no. 2
(1970): 111-134.

Mochon, Marion Johnson. Stockbridge-
Munsee cultural adaptations:
"assimilated Indians". American
Philosophical Society, Proceedings, 112
(1968): 182-219.

Mooney, J. Delaware. U.S. Bureau of
American Ethnology, Bulletin, 30, vol. 1
(1907): 385-387.

Mooney, J. Munsee. U.S. Bureau of
American Ethnology, Bulletin, 30, vol. 1
(1907): 957-958.

Mooney, J. Passing of the Delaware
nation. Mississippi Valley Historical
Association, Proceedings, 3 (1911): 329-
340.

Morgan, L. H. Systems of consanguinity
and affinity. Smithsonian Contributions
to Knowledge, 17 (1871): 291-382.

Morgan, L. H.   The Indian journals, 1859-62: p. 28, 49-57, 59.   Ann Arbor, 1959.

Morris, Wayne.   Traders and factories on the Arkansas frontier, 1805-1822. Arkansas Historical Quarterly, 28 (1969): 28-48.

Myers, A. C., ed.   Narratives of early Pennsylvania, western New Jersey, and Delaware.   New York, 1912.   476 p.

Nelson, W.   Indian words, personal names and place names in New Jersey. American Anthropologist, n.s., 4 (1902): 183-192.

Nelson, W.   The Indians of New Jersey. Paterson, 1894.   168 p.

Neumann, Georg K.   A re-examination of the question of the Middle Western origin of the Delaware Indians. Indiana Academy of Science, Proceedings, 79 (1969): 60-61.

Newcomb, W. W.   A note on Cherokee-Delaware pan-Indianism. American Anthropologist, 57 (1955): 1041-1045.

*Newcomb, W. W.   The culture and acculturation of the Delaware Indians. Michigan, University, Museum of Anthropology, Anthropological Papers, 10 (1956): 144 p.

Newcomb, W. W.   The peyote cult of the Delaware Indians. Texas Journal of Science, 8 (1956): 202-211.

Newcomb, W. W.   The Walam Olum of the Delaware Indians in perspective. Texas Journal of Science, 7 (1955): 57-63.

Oklahoma, University, Bureau of Business Research.   The utilization of property of specified Wichita, Caddo, and Delaware Indian tribes' land in Caddo County, Oklahoma.   Norman, 1964.   9, 108 p.   map.

Omwake, H. G.   Delaware Indians in the Far West. Archaeological Society of Delaware, Bulletin, 4, no. 4 (1947): 20-21.

Orchard, W. C.   Porcupine quill ornamentation. Indian Notes, 3 (1926): 59-68.

Pattison, William D.   The survey of the Seven Ranges. Ohio Historical Quarterly, 68 (1959): 115-140.

Patton, W.   Journal of a visit to the Indian Missions, Missouri Conference. Missouri Historical Society, Bulletin, 10 (1954): 168-180.

Peet, S. D.   The Delaware Indians in Ohio. American Antiquarian and Oriental Journal, 2 (1879): 132-144.

Penn, W.   Account of the Lenni Lennape. Ed. by A. C. Myers.   Moylan, 1937. 107 p.

Penn, William.   William Penn's own account of the Lenni Lenape or Delaware Indians. Rev. ed. Edited by Albert Cook Myers. Somerset, N.J., Middle Atlantic Press, 1970.   96 p.   illus.

Petrullo, V.   The diabolic root: a study of peyotism, the new Indian religion, among the Delawares.   Philadelphia, 1934.   185 p.

Philhower, C. A.   Aboriginal inhabitants of New Jersey. In I. S. Kull, ed. New Jersey, a History. Vol. 1.   New York, 1930: 14-53.

Philhower, C. A.   Agriculture and food of the Indians of New Jersey. New Jersey Historical Society, Proceedings, 58 (1940): 93-102, 192-202.

Philhower, C. A.   Foods of the Indians of New Jersey. Archaeological Society of New Jersey, Newsletter, 4 (1941): 5-10.

Philhower, C. A.   Indian days in Middlesex County, New Jersey. New Jersey Historical Society, Proceedings, ser. 4, 12 (1927): 385-405.

Philhower, C. A.   Minisink--its use and significance. New Jersey Historical Society, Proceedings, ser. 4, 11 (1926): 186-190.

Philhower, C. A.   Some personal characteristics of the Lenape Indians. New Jersey Historical Society, Proceedings, n.s., 16 (1931): 138-161.

Philhower, C. A.   South Jersey Indians. New Jersey Historical Society, Proceedings, n.s., 16 (1931): 1-21.

Philhower, C. A.   The aboriginal inhabitants of Monmouth County. New Jersey Historical Society, Proceedings, ser. 4, 9 (1924): 22-40.

Philhower, C. A.   The aboriginal inhabitants of Union County. New Jersey Historical Society, Proceedings, ser. 4, 8 (1923): 124-138.

Philhower, C. A.   The aborigines of Hunterdon County. New Jersey Historical Society, Proceedings, ser. 4, 11 (1926): 508-525.

Philhower, C. A. The art of the Lenape. Archaeological Society of New Jersey, Leaflets, 1 (1932): 1-4.

Philhower, C. A. The earliest account of the Lenape and Narragansett Indians. Archaeological Society of New Jersey, Bulletin, 5 (1952): 10-11.

Philhower, C. A. The Indians of Somerset County. New Jersey Historical Society, Proceedings, ser. 4, 10 (1925): 28-41.

Philhower, C. A. The Indians of the Morris County area. New Jersey Historical Society, Proceedings, 54 (1936): 249-267.

Philhower, C. A. The Munsee-Lenape Site, Sussex County, New Jersey. Eastern States Archaeological Federation, Bulletin, 12 (1953): 9.

Phillips, Edward Hake. Timothy Pickering at his best: Indian Commissioner, 1790-1794. Essex Institute Historical Collections, 102 (1966): 163-201.

Prince, J. D. A modern Delaware tale. American Philosophical Society, Proceedings, 41 (1902): 20-34.

Prince, J. D. An ancient New Jersey Indian jargon. American Anthropologist, n.s., 14 (1912): 508-524.

Prince, J. D. Notes on the modern Minsi-Delaware dialect. American Journal of Philology, 21 (1900): 295-302.

Raynaud, G. Walam Olum (livre des légendes Lenapes). Société Américaine de France, Archives, n.s., 7 (1888): 129-136.

Records, Spencer. Spencer Records' memoir of the Ohio Valley frontier, 1766-1795. Edited by Donald F. Carmony. Indiana Magazine of History, 55 (1959): 323-377.

Rice, Otis. The French and Indian War in West Virginia. West Virginia History, 24 (1962/1963): 134-146.

Rupp, I. D. History of the counties of Berks and Lebanon, 16-32. Lancaster, 1844.

Ruttenber, E. M. History of the Indian tribes of Hudson's River. Albany, 1872. 415 p.

Ruttenber, E. M. Indian geographical names in the valley of Hudson's River, the valley of the Mohawk, and on the Delaware. New York State Historical Association, Proceedings, 6 (1906): 1-241.

Ruttenber, Edward M. History of the Indian tribes of Hudson's River. Port Washington, Kennikat Press, 1971. 5, 415 p. illus.

Rydén, Stig. Discovery in the Skokloster Collection of a 17-century Indian head dress from Delaware. Ethnos, 28 (1963): 107-121.

Schmidt, W. Die Lenape. In his Die Ursprung der Göttesidee. Bd. 5. Münster i. W., 1934: 475-521, 876-882.

Schmidt, W. Die Lenape. In his Die Ursprung der Göttesidee. Bd. 2. Münster i. W., 1929: 408-448.

Schmidt, W. Die Lenape. In his Die Ursprung der Göttesidee. Bd. 7. Münster i. W., 1940: 705-726.

Schrabisch, M. Indian rock-shelters in northern New Jersey and southern New York. American Museum of Natural History, Anthropological Papers, 3 (1909): 141-165.

Schrabisch, M. Mountain haunts of the Coastal Algonquian. American Anthropologist, n.s., 21 (1919): 139-152.

Schrabisch, M. The Indians of New Jersey. Americana, 5 (1910): 877-887.

Scot, G. The model of the government of the Province of East New Jersey. 2d ed. New Jersey Historical Society, Collections, 1 (1874): 359-475.

Shetrone, H. C. The Indian in Ohio. Ohio State Archaeological and Historical Quarterly, 27 (1918): 273-510.

Siebert, Frank T., Jr. Discrepant consonant clusters ending in *-k in Proto-Algonquian, a proposed interpretation of saltatory sound changes. In Contributions to Anthropology: Linguistics I. Ottawa, Queen's Printer, 1967: 48-59. (Canada, National Museum, Bulletin, 214)

Sipe, C. H. The principal Indian towns in western Pennsylvania. Western Pennsylvania Historical Magazine, 13 (1930): 104-122.

Skinner, A. Another Indian village-site on Staten Island. Indian Notes, 2 (1925): 296-297.

Skinner, A. Archaeology of the New York Coastal Algonkin. American Museum of Natural History, Anthropological Papers, 3 (1909): 213-235.

Skinner, A.   The Indians of greater New
    York.   Cedar Rapids, 1915.

Skinner, A.   The Indians of Manhattan
    Island and vicinity. American Museum of
    Natural History, Guide Leaflet Series,
    29 (1909): 5-54; 41 (1915): 5-54.

Skinner, A.   The Indians of Newark before
    the White Men came. Newark, 1915.
    16 p.

Skinner, A.   The Lenapé Indians of Staten
    Island. American Museum of Natural
    History, Anthropological Papers, 3
    (1909): 1-62.

Skinner, A.   Two Lenape stone masks.
    Indian Notes and Monographs, n.s., 3
    (1920): 5-7.

Skinner, A. and M. Schrabisch, eds.   A
    preliminary report of the Archaeological
    Survey of the State of New Jersey. New
    Jersey, Geological Survey, Bulletin, 9
    (1913): 1-94.

Skinner, Alanson B.   The Indians of
    Manhattan Island and vicinity. Port
    Washington, I. J. Friedman, 1961.
    63 p. illus.

Smet, P. J. de.   Western missions and
    missionaries, 218-230. New York, 1863.

Smith, James.   An account of the
    remarkable occurrences in the life and
    travels of Col. James Smith, during his
    captivity with the Indians in the years
    1755, '56, '57, '58, and '59, with an
    appendix of illustrative notes. Edited
    by Wm. N. Darlington. Cincinnati, R.
    Clarke, 1870.   12, 190 p. (Ohio Valley
    Historical Series, 5)

Snyderman, George S.   The manuscript
    collections of the Philadelphia yearly
    meeting of Friends pertaining to the
    American Indian. American Philosophical
    Society, Proceedings, 102 (1958): 613-
    620.

Speck, F. G.   A study of the Delaware big
    house ceremony. Pennsylvania Historical
    Commission, Publications, 2 (1931): 5-
    192.

Speck, F. G.   Bird nomenclature and song
    interpretation of the Canadian Delaware.
    Washington Academy of Sciences, Journal,
    36 (1946): 249-258.

Speck, F. G.   Critical comments on
    "Delaware Culture Chronology". American
    Anthropologist, n.s., 50 (1948): 723-
    724.

Speck, F. G.   Gourds of the Southeastern
    Indians. Boston, 1941. 113 p.

Speck, F. G.   Indian life in Bergen
    County. Bergen County Historical
    Society, Papers and Proceedings, 3
    (1907): 19-28.

Speck, F. G.   Notes on the life of John
    Wilson, the revealer of peyote. General
    Magazine and Historical Chronicle,
    University of Pennsylvania, 25 (1933):
    539-556.

Speck, F. G.   Oklahoma Delaware
    ceremonies, dances and feasts. American
    Philosophical Society, Memoirs, 7
    (1937): 1-161.

Speck, F. G.   Speaking of the Delawares.
    Pennsylvania Archaeologist, 4, no. 4
    (1935): 3-9.

Speck, F. G.   The boy-bear (the bear
    abductor). Anthropos, 36 (1941): 973-
    974.

Speck, F. G.   The Delaware Indians as
    women. Pennsylvania Magazine of History
    and Biography, 70 (1946): 377-389.

Speck, F. G.   The grasshopper war in
    Pennsylvania. Pennsylvania
    Archaeologist, 12 (1942): 31-34.

Speck, F. G.   The great Pennsylvania
    earthquake of Indian days. Pennsylvania
    Archaeologist, 12 (1942): 57-59.

Speck, F. G.   The Wapanachki Delawares and
    the English. Pennsylvania Magazine of
    History and Biography, 67 (1943): 319-
    344.

Speck, F. G. and J. Moses.   The celestial
    bear comes down to earth. Reading,
    Public Museum, Scientific Publications,
    7 (1945): 1-91.

Speck, F. G. and W. C. Orchard.   The Penn
    wampum belts. Museum of the American
    Indian, Heye Foundation, Leaflets, 4
    (1925): 7-20.

Squier, E. G.   Historical and mythological
    traditions of the Algonquins. American
    Review, n.s., 3 (1849): 173-193.

Squier, E. G.   Historical and mythological
    traditions of the Algonquins. In W. W.
    Beach, ed. Indian Miscellany. Albany,
    1877: 9-42.

Stiegerwalt, H. J.   Some Lenape history.
    Archaeological Bulletin, 8 (1917): 3-4.

Swanson, Guy E.   Rules of descent: studies
    in the sociology of parentage. Ann
    Arbor, University of Michigan, 1969.   5,
    108 p. (Michigan, University, Museum of
    Anthropology, Anthropological Papers,
    39)

*Tantaquidgeon, G. A study of Delaware Indian medicine practices and folk beliefs. Harrisburg, 1942. 91 p.

Tantaquidgeon, G. Delaware Indian art designs. Pennsylvania Archaeologist, 20, nos. 1/2 (1950): 24-30.

Tantaquidgeon, Gladys. Folk medicine of the Delaware and related Algonkian Indians. Harrisburg, 1972. 145 p. illus. (Pennsylvania, Historical and Museum Commission, Anthropological Series, 3)

Thomas, C. Migrations of the Lenni Lenape or Delawares. American Antiquarian and Oriental Journal, 19 (1897): 73-80.

Thomas, G. An historical and geographical account of the Province and Country of Pensilvania. London, 1698. 55 p.

Thomson, Charles. An enquiry into the causes of the alienation of the Delaware and Shawanese Indians from the British interest. St. Claire Shores, Mich., Scholarly Press, 1970. 184 p.

Troost, G. Extracts from the voyages of David Pieterszen de Vries. New York Historical Society, Collections, n.s., 1 (1841): 243-280.

Uhler, S. P. Pennsylvania's Indian relations to 1754. Allentown, 1951. 144 p.

Voegelin, C. F. Delaware, an Eastern Algonquian language. Viking Fund Publications in Anthropology, 6 (1946): 130-157.

Voegelin, C. F. Delaware texts. International Journal of American Linguistics, 11 (1945): 105-119.

Voegelin, C. F. Proto-Algonkian clusters in Delaware. Language, 17 (1941): 143-147.

Voegelin, C. F. The Lenape and Munsee dialects of Delaware. Indiana Academy of Science, Proceedings, 49 (1940): 34-37.

Voegelin, C. F. Word distortions in Delaware big house and Walam Olum songs. Indiana Academy of Science, Proceedings, 51 (1942): 48-54.

Voegelin, E. W. Culture parallels to the Delaware Walum Olum. Indiana Academy of Science, Proceedings, 49 (1940): 28-31.

Volkman, A. G. Lenape basketry in Delaware. Archaeological Society of Delaware, Bulletin, 4, no. 5 (1949): 15-18.

Wake, C. S. Migrations of the Algonkins. American Antiquarian and Oriental Journal, 16 (1894): 127-139.

Wake, C. S. The migrations of the Lenape. American Antiquarian and Oriental Journal, 30 (1908): 221-223.

Walker, E. R. The Lenni-Lenape or Delaware Indians. New Jersey Historical Society, Proceedings, ser. 4, 2 (1917): 193-218.

Wallace, A. F. C. King of the Delawares. Philadelphia, 1949. 305 p.

Wallace, A. F. C. New religions among the Delaware Indians, 1600-1900. Southwestern Journal of Anthropology, 12 (1956): 1-21.

Wallace, A. F. C. Some psychological characteristics of the Delaware Indians during the 17th and 18th Centuries. Pennsylvania Archaeologist, 20, nos. 1/2 (1950): 33-39.

Wallace, A. F. C. Woman, land, and society. Pennsylvania Archaeologist, 17 (1947): 1-35.

Wallace, Anthony F. C. King of the Delawares: Teedyuscung, 1700-1763. Freeport, N.Y., Books for Libraries Press, 1970. 13, 305 p. maps.

Wallace, Anthony F. C. New religions among the Delaware Indians, 1600-1900. In Deward E. Walker, Jr., ed. The Emergent Native Americans. Boston, Little, Brown, 1972: 344-361.

Wallace, Paul A. W. Indian paths of Pennsylvania. Harrisburg, Pennsylvania Historical and Museum Commission, 1965. 8, 227 p. maps.

Wallace, Paul A. W. Indians in Pennsylvania. Harrisburg, Pennsylvania Historical and Museum Commission, 1961. 13, 194 p. illus., maps.

Walton, Joseph S. Conrad Weizer and the Indian policy of colonial Pennsylvania. New York, Arno Press, 1971. 420 p. illus.

Washington, George. A mystery resolved; George Washington's letter to Governor Dinwiddie, June 10, 1754. Edited by Peter Walne. Virginia Magazine of History and Biography, 79 (1971): 131-144.

Weer, P. Provenience of the Walam Olum. Indiana Academy of Science, Proceedings, 51 (1942): 55-59.

Weslager, C. A. Delaware Indian villages at Philadelphia. Pennsylvania Archaeologist, 26 (1956): 178-180.

Weslager, C. A. Delaware Indian villages. Pennsylvania Archaeologist, 12 (1942): 53-56.

Weslager, C. A. Further light on the Delaware Indians as women. Washington Academy of Sciences, Journal, 37 (1947): 298-304.

Weslager, C. A. The anthropological position of the Indian tribes of the Delmarva Peninsula. Archaeological Society of Delaware, Bulletin, 4, no. 4 (1947): 3-7.

Weslager, C. A. The Delaware Indians as women. Washington Academy of Sciences, Journal, 34 (1944): 381-388.

Weslager, C. A. The Indians of Lewes, Delaware. Archaeological Society of Delaware, Bulletin, 4, no. 5 (1949): 6-14.

Weslager, C. A. The Minquas and their early relations with the Delaware Indians. Archaeological Society of Delaware, Bulletin, 4, no. 1 (1943): 14-23.

Weslager, Clinton A. The Delaware Indians; a history. New Brunswick, Rutgers University Press, 1972. 19, 546 p. illus.

Westervelt, F. A. The Indians of Bergen County, New Jersey. Hackensack, 1923. 26 p.

Wheeler-Voegelin, E., ed. Some remarks concerning the traditions, customs, languages etc. of the Indians in North America. Ethnohistory, 6 (1959): 42-69, 186.

White, Lonnie J. Disturbances on the Arkansas-Texas border, 1827-1831. Arkansas Historical Quarterly, 19 (1960): 95-110.

Widen, A. Om gudsbegreppet hos Lenape. Ethnos, 2 (1937): 252-265.

Wigglesworth, J. A brief archaeology of the Leni Lenape. Wilmington, Delaware [n.d.]. 12 p.

Wilson, Paul C., Jr. A forgotten mission to the Indians; William Smalley's adventures among the Delaware Indians of Ohio in 1792. Galveston, Tex., 1965. 118 p. illus.

Winfrey, Dorman H., ed. The Indian papers of Texas and the Southwest, 1825-1916.

Edited by Dorman H. Winfrey and James M. Day. Austin, Pemberton Press, 1966. 412 p.

Witthoft, J. Green corn ceremonialism in the eastern woodlands. Michigan, University, Museum of Anthropology, Occasional Contributions, 13 (1949): 11-21.

Witthoft, J. The grasshopper war in Lenape land. Pennsylvania Archaeologist, 16 (1946): 91-94.

Wren, C. A study of North Appalachian Indian pottery. Wyoming Historical and Geological Society, Proceedings and Collections, 13 (1914): 131-222.

Wright, M. H. and G. H. Shirk. Artist Möllhausen in Oklahoma, 1853. Chronicles of Oklahoma, 31 (1953): 392-441.

Zeisberger, D. A grammar of the language of the Lenni Lenape or Delaware Indians. American Philosophical Society, Transactions, n.s., 3 (1830): 65-250.

Zeisberger, D. Delaware Indian and English spelling book. Philadelphia, 1806. 179 p.

Zeisberger, D. Indian dictionary. Cambridge, 1887. 236 p.

Zeisberger, D. Some remarks and annotations concerning the traditions, customs, languages, etc. of the Indians of North America. Olden Time, 1 (1846): 271-281.

Zeisberger, David. Diary of David Zeisberger; a Moravian missionary among the Indians of Ohio. St. Clair Shores, Mich., Scholarly Press, 1972. 2 v.

12-03 Erie

Baldwin, C. C. Early Indian migration in Ohio. American Antiquarian and Oriental Journal, 1 (1879): 227-239.

Braden, J. A. Little brother of the Hudson. New York, 1928. 279 p.

Edson, W. H. The Eries, the nation of the cat. New York State Historical Association, Proceedings, 33 (1935): 36-44.

Hewitt, J. N. B. Erie. U.S. Bureau of American Ethnology, Bulletin, 30, vol. 1 (1907): 430-432.

Hoffman, Bernard G. Observations on certain ancient Tribes of the Northern Appalachian Province. Washington, D.C.,

Government Printing Office, 1964. 191-
245 p. illus., maps. (U.S., Bureau of
American Ethnology, Anthropological
Papers, 70. U.S., Bureau of American
Ethnology, Bulletin, 191)

Houghton, F. The Indian occupancy of the
Niagara Frontier. Buffalo Society of
Natural Sciences, Bulletin, 9 (1908):
263-374.

Moorehead, W. K. The Indian tribes of
Ohio. Ohio State Archaeological and
Historical Quarterly, 7 (1898): 1-109.

Mosely, E. L. Some plants that were
probably brought to northern Ohio from
the West by the Indians. Michigan
Academy of Science, Arts and Letters,
Papers, 13 (1931): 169-172.

Parker, A. C. Excavations in an Erie
Indian village and burial site. New York
State Museum Bulletin, 117 (1907): 459-
554.

Parker, A. C. The origin of the Iroquois
as suggested by their archeology.
American Anthropologist, n.s., 18
(1916): 479-507.

Parker, A. C. The Ripley Erie Site. New
York State Museum Bulletin, 235/238
(1920): 246-306.

Prahl, Earl J. Preliminary archaeological
investigations in the Maumee Valley. By
Earl J. Prahl and M. Joseph Becker.
Northwest Ohio Quarterly, 39, no. 1
(1966/1967): 40-50.

Schmitz, E. Les Eriés on Ka-Kwaks et leur
destruction par les Sénécas.
International Congress of Americanists,
Proceedings, 2, vol. 1 (1878): 360-361.

Silver, D. M. The location of the nations
of Indians called the Wenroes or
Wenrohronons and the Eries. Buffalo,
1923. 19 p.

Thwaites, R. G., ed. The Jesuit Relations
and allied documents. Cleveland, 1896-
1901. 74 v.

Trigger, Bruce G. Settlement as an aspect
of Iroquoian adaptation at the time of
contact. American Anthropologist, 65
(1963): 86-101.

Vietzen, R. C. The immortal Eries.
Elyria, 1945. 387 p.

White, Marian. Ethnic identification and
Iroquois groups in western New York and
Ontario. Ethnohistory, 18 (1971): 19-38.

White, Marian E. Iroquois culture history
in the Niagara Frontier area of New York

State. Ann Arbor, University of
Michigan, 1961. 8, 155 p. illus.
(Michigan, University, Museum of
Anthropology, Anthropological Papers,
16)

Wright, James V. The Middleport horizon.
Anthropologica, n.s., 2 (1960): 113-120.

Wright, James V. The Ontario Iroquois
tradition. Dissertation Abstracts, 24
(1963/1964): 4346-4347. UM 64-7111.

12-04   Huron

Abisch, Roz. 'Twas in the moon of
wintertime, the first American Christmas
carol. Adapted by Roz Abisch. Englewood
Cliffs, Prentice-Hall, 1969. 32 p.
illus.

Abler, Thomas S. Longhouse and palisade:
Northeastern Iroquoian villages of the
seventeenth century. Ontario History, 62
(1970): 17-40.

Anonymous. Grammar of the Huron language.
Ontario, Bureau of Archives, Report, 15
(1920): 25-77.

Anonymous. Huron-Indian ideas about the
unconscious mind. Medical Science, 15,
no. 9 (1964): 52.

Bailey, A. G. The significance of the
identity and disappearance of the
Laurentian Iroquois. Royal Society of
Canada, Proceedings and Transactions,
ser. 3, 27, pt. 2 (1933): 97-108.

Barbeau, C. M. How the Huron-Wyandot
language was saved from oblivion.
American Philosophical Society,
Proceedings, 93 (1949): 226-232.

Barbeau, C. M. Iroquoian clans and
phratries. American Anthropologist,
n.s., 19 (1917): 392-402.

Barbeau, C. M. La croix de Cartier.
Université d'Ottawa, Revue, 11 (1941):
440-443.

Barbeau, C. M. Le mythe de la création
chez les Hurons. Revue Franco-
Américaine, 10 (1913): 492-502.

Barbeau, C. M. Supernatural beings of the
Huron and Wyandot. American
Anthropologist, n.s., 16 (1914): 288-
313.

Barbeau, C. M. Wyandot tales. Journal of
American Folklore, 28 (1915): 83-95.

Barbeau, C. M. and G. Melvin. The Indian
speaks, 17-44, 102-104. Caldwell, 1943.

Barbeau, C. Marius. Huron-Wyandot
traditional narratives: in translations
and native texts. Ottawa, Queen's
Printer, 1960. 6, 338 p. illus., map.
(Canada, National Museum, Bulletin, 165)

Barbeau, C. Marius. The language of
Canada: in the voyages of Jacques
Cartier (1534-1538). In Contributions to
Anthropology 1959. Ottawa, Queen's
Printer, 1961: 108-229. (Canada,
National Museum, Bulletin, 173)

Barbeau, Charles Marius. Dialectes
Hurons-Iroquois. In Internationale
Amerikanistenkongress, 34th. 1960, Wien.
Akten. Horn-Wien, Berger, 1962: 739-
742.

Bauman, Robert F. Iroquois "empire";
Iroquois make all-out effort to destroy
the Hurons and gain control of the Great
Lakes fur trade. Northwest Ohio
Quarterly, 32 (1959/1960): 138-172.

Beauchamp, W. M. Indian nations of the
Great Lakes. American Antiquarian and
Oriental Journal, 17 (1895): 321-325.

Beaugrand-Champagne, A. Le chemin et
l'emplacement de la bourgade
d'Hochelaga. Cahiers des Dix, 12 (1947):
115-160.

Beaugrand-Champagne, A. Le peuple
d'Hochelaga. Cahiers des Dix, 11 (1946):
93-114.

Beaugrand-Champagne, A. Les Hurons.
Cahiers des Dix, 11 (1946): 52-61.

Bibaud, F. M. Biographie des sagamos
illustrés de l'Amérique Septentrionale,
107-110, 185-190. Montreal, 1848.

Biggar, H. P., ed. The works of Samuel de
Champlain, Vol. 3: 114-158. Toronto,
1929.

Blau, Harold. Dream guessing: a
comparative analysis. Ethnohistory, 10
(1963): 233-249.

Boucher, P. Histoire véritable et
naturelle des moeurs et productions du
pays de la Nouvelle France. Paris,
1864.

Bourne, E. G., ed. The voyages and
explorations of Samuel de Champlain,
Vol. 2: 119-144. New York, 1906.

Brebeuf, J. de. Burial ceremonies of the
Hurons. U.S. Bureau of American
Ethnology, Annual Reports, 5 (1884):
110-119.

*Brébeuf, J. de. Relation of the Hurons,
1636. In R. G. Thwaites, ed. The Jesuit

Relations and Allied Documents. Vol. 10.
Cleveland, 1897: 124-317.

Brébeuf, Jean de. Les relations de ce qui
s'est passé au pays des Hurons (1635-
1648). Genève, Librairie E. Droz, 1957.
27, 288 p.

Bushnell, D. I. Native cemeteries and
forms of burial east of the Mississippi.
U.S. Bureau of American Ethnology,
Bulletin, 71 (1920): 73-83.

Campbell, T. S. Pioneer priests of North
America, 1642-1710. New York, 1908,
1910. 2 v.

Carr, L. On the social and political
position of woman among the Huron-
Iroquois tribes. Harvard University,
Peabody Museum of American Archaeology
and Ethnology, Reports, 3 (1887): 207-
232.

Chafe, Wallace L. A challenge for
linguistics today. In Jacob W. Gruber,
ed. The Philadelphia Anthropological
Society; Papers Presented on Its Golden
Anniversary. New York, distributed by
Columbia University Press for Temple
University Publications, 1967: 125-131.

Champlain, Samuel de. Life among the
Hurons. In Milton A. Rugoff, ed. The
Great Travelers. Vol. 2. New York,
Simon and Schuster, 1960: 786-796.

Champlain, Samuel de. Voyages and
discoveries made in New France, from the
year 1615 to the end of the year 1618.
Translated and edited by H. H. Layton
and W. F. Ganong. Toronto, The
Champlain Society, 1929. illus., maps.
(The Works of Samuel de Champlain, 3)

Channen, E. R. The Copeland Site: a
precontact Huron site in Simcoe County,
Ontario. By E. R. Channen and N. D.
Clarke. Ottawa, Queen's Printer, 1965.
27 p. illus., maps. (Canada, National
Museum, Anthropology Papers, 8)

Charlevoix, P. F. X. de. Journal of a
voyage to North America. Chicago, 1923.
2 v.

Chaumonot, J. M. Grammar of the Huron
language. Literary and Historical
Society (Quebec), Transactions, 2
(1831): 94-198.

Clark, Rufus W. Address before the
Society of Colonial Wars of the State of
Michigan. Detroit, Winnard Hammond,
1903. 28 p.

Clarke, P. D. Origin and traditional
history of the Wyandotts. Toronto,
1870. 158 p.

Cleland, Charles E., ed. The Lasanen Site: an historic burial locality in Mackinac County, Michigan. East Lansing, 1971. 11, 147 p. illus. (Michigan State University, Museum, Publications, Anthropological Series, 1, no. 1)

Connelley, W. E. Indian myths. New York, 1928. 167 p.

Connelley, W. E. Notes on the folk-lore of the Wyandots. Journal of American Folklore, 12 (1899): 116-125.

Connelley, W. E. The sword and belt of Orion. Annual Archaeological Report, being Part of Appendix to the Report of the Minister of Education, Ontario (1905): 68-70.

Connelley, W. E. The Wyandots. Annual Archaeological Report, being Part of Appendix to the Report of the Minister of Education, Ontario (1899): 92-141.

Connelley, W. E. Wyandot folk-lore. Topeka, 1899. 116 p.

Cranston, James H. Etienne Brûlé, immortal scoundrel. Toronto, Ryerson Press, 1969. 13, 144 p. illus. (Ryerson Paperbacks, 31)

Desjardins, Paul. La résidence de Sainte-Marie-aux-Hurons. Sudbury, 1966. 46 p. map. (Société Historique du Nouvel-Ontario, Documents Historiques, 48)

Dever, Harry. The Nicolet myth. Michigan History, 50 (1966): 318-322.

Devine, E. J. Old Fort Ste. Marie. Midland, 1942. 56 p.

Draper, Lyman S. Material in Draper "S" on 18th- and early 19th-century Indians of the Old Northwest. Ethnohistory, 8 (1961): 281-288.

Drier, Roy W. The Michigan College of Mining and Technology Isle Royale excavations, 1953-1954. In James B. Griffin. Lake Superior Copper and the Indians: Miscellaneous Studies of Great Lakes Prehistory. Ann Arbor, University of Michigan, 1961: 1-7. (Michigan, University, Museum of Anthropology, Anthropological Papers, 17)

Drury, E. C. All for a beaver hat. Toronto, Ryerson Press, 1959. 160 p.

Duluth, Daniel Greysolon de. Capital punishment in Michigan, 1683: Duluth at Michilimackinac. Michigan History, 50 (1966): 349-360.

Emerson, J. Norman. Problems of Huron origins. Anthropologica, n.s., 3 (1961): 181-201.

Emmert, Darlene Gay. The Indians of Shiawassee County. Michigan History, 47 (1963): 127-155, 243-272.

Faillon, Abbé. The Indian tribes on the St. Lawrence at the time of the arrival of the French. Translated by John Squair. Toronto, Ontario Provincial Museum, Annual Archaeological Report, 34 (1923): 82-88.

Farrell, David. Settlement along the Detroit frontier, 1760-1796. Michigan History, 52 (1968): 89-107.

Fay, George E., ed. Charters, constitutions and by-laws of the Indian tribes of North America. Part VI: The Indian tribes of Oklahoma (cont'd.). Greeley, 1968. 5, 129 l. map. (University of Northern Colorado, Museum of Anthropology, Occasional Publications in Anthropology, Ethnology Series, 7) ERIC ED046556.

Feest, Christian F. Lukas Vischers Beiträge zur Ethnographie Nordamerikas. Archiv für Völkerkunde, 22 (1968): 31-66.

Finley, J. B. History of the Wyandott Mission. Cincinatti, 1840. 432 p.

Finley, J. B. Life among the Indians. Ed. by D. W. Clark. 1868. 548 p.

Fitting, James E. The Huron as an ecotype: the limits of maximization in a western Great Lakes society. Anthropologica, n.s., 14 (1972): 3-18.

Foreman, G. The last trek of the Indians, 92-99, 193-200. Chicago, 1946.

Frohman, Charles E. Fort Sandusky on Sandusky Bay. Inland Seas, 19 (1963): 12-25.

Gendron. Quelques particularitez du pays des Hurons. New ed. Albany, 1868. 26 p.

Gérin, L. The Hurons of Lorette. British Association for the Advancement of Science, Annual Meeting, Report, 70 (1900): 549-568.

Gibson, A. M. Joe Kagey: Indian educator. Chronicles of Oklahoma, 38 (1960): 12-19.

Gibson, A. M. Wyandotte mission. Chronicles of Oklahoma, 36 (1958): 137-154.

Girard, René.   Trois grands Hurons.
Sudbury, Société Historique de Nouvel-
Ontario, 1948.   47 p.

Girault de Villeneuve, E. P. T.   Des
missions.   Québec, 1902.   9 p.

Gray, L. H.   Huron. In J. Hastings, ed.
Encyclopaedia of Religion and Ethics.
Vol. 6.   New York, 1914: 883-886.

Greene, W.   On some processes in use among
the Huron Indians in dyeing. Literary
and Historical Society (Quebec),
Transactions, 2 (1831): 23-25.

Gros-Louis, Max Cné-Onti.   Le "premier"
des Hurons. With Marcel Bellier.
Montréal, Éditions du Jour, 1971.
241 p.   illus.

Gruber, J. W.   Preliminary notes on Huron
dentition. Eastern States Archaeological
Federation, Bulletin, 17 (1958): 9.

Haldeman, S. S.   Phonology of the
Wyandots. American Philosophical
Society, Proceedings, 4 (1846): 268-269.

Hale, H.   A Huron historical legend.
Magazine of American History (1883):
475-483.

Hale, H.   Four Huron wampum records. Royal
Anthropological Institute of Great
Britain and Ireland, Journal, 26 (1896):
221-254.

Hale, H.   Huron folk-lore. Journal of
American Folklore, 1 (1888): 177-183; 2
(1889): 249-254.

Hale, H.   The fall of Hochelaga, a study
of popular tradition. Journal of
American Folklore, 7 (1894): 1-14.

Hamil, Fred C.   Michigan in the War of
1812. Michigan History, 44 (1960): 257-
291.

Hamilton, Raphael N.   Jesuit mission at
Sault Ste. Marie. Michigan History, 52
(1968): 123-132.

Hammond, J. H.   Explanation of the ossuary
burial of the Huron nation. Annual
Archaeological Report, being Part of
Appendix to the Report of the Minister
of Education, Ontario (1923): 95-102.

Hamy, E. T.   Note sur un wampum
représentant les quatre-nations des
Hurons. Société des Américanistes,
Journal, 1 (1897): 163-166.

Hanzeli, Victor E.   Missionary linguistics
in New France; a study of seventeenth-
and eighteenth-century descriptions of
American Indian languages.   The Hague,

Mouton, 1969.   141 p.   illus., map.
(Janua Linguarum, Series Maior, 29)

Hayes, John F.   Wilderness mission; the
story of Sainte-Marie-Among-the-Hurons.
Toronto, Ryerson Press, 1969.   118 p.
illus., map.

Heckewelder, John G. E.   John Heckewelder
to Peter S. Du Ponceau, Bethlehem 12th
Aug 1818. Edited by Erminie Wheeler-
Voegelin. Ethnohistory, 6 (1959): 70-81.

Hegarty, Denis A.   The excavation of the
Indian church at Ste. Marie. Canadian
Catholic Historical Association, Report
(1956): 59-73.

Herman, M. W.   The social aspect of Huron
property. American Anthropologist, 58
(1956): 1044-1058.

Hewitt, J. N. B.   Blood cement used by the
ancient Hurons. American Anthropologist,
6 (1893): 322.

Hewitt, J. N. B.   Huron. U.S. Bureau of
American Ethnology, Bulletin, 30, vol. 1
(1907): 584-591.

Hewitt, J. N. B.   The cosmogonic gods of
the Iroquois. American Association for
the Advancement of Science, Proceedings,
44 (1895): 241-250.

Hickerson, H.   The feast of the dead among
the seventeenth century Algonkians of
the upper Great Lakes. American
Anthropologist, 62 (1960): 81-107.

Hickerson, Harold.   The sociohistorical
significance of two Chippewa
ceremonials. American Anthropologist, 65
(1963): 67-85.

Hirschfelder, C. A.   Burial customs of the
Hurons. American Association for the
Advancement of Science, Proceedings, 40
(1891): 363-365.

Holland, C. P.   From paganism to
mysticism: René Tsondiwane. Martyr's
Shrine Message, 17, no. 1 (1953): 20-21,
23.

Houghton, F.   The Indian occupancy of the
Niagara Frontier. Buffalo Society of
Natural Sciences, Bulletin, 9 (1909):
263-374.

Hrdlička, A.   Ritual ablation of front
teeth in Siberia and America.
Smithsonian Miscellaneous Collections,
99, no. 3 (1940): 1-32.

Hunter, A. F.   Indian village sites in
North and South Orillia townships.
Annual Archaeological Report, being Part
of Appendix to the Report of the

Minister of Education, Ontario (1903): 105-125.

Hunter, A. F. National characteristics and migrations of the Hurons. Canadian Institute, Transactions, 3 (1893): 225-228.

Hunter, A. F. Notes on sites of Huron villages. Annual Archaeological Report, being Part of Appendix to the Report of the Minister of Education, Ontario (1899): 51-82; (1901): 56-100; (1902): 153-183.

James, C. C. The downfall of the Huron nation. Royal Society of Canada, Proceedings and Transactions, ser. 2, 12, pt. 2 (1906): 311-346.

Jenness, D. Indians of Canada. Canada, Department of Mines, National Museum of Canada, Bulletin, 65 (1932): 289-299.

Jones, A. E. Huron Indians. In Catholic Encyclopedia. Vol. 7. New York, 1910: 565-583.

Jones, A. E. Topography of Huronia. International Congress of Americanists, Proceedings, 15, vol. 1 (1907): 299-230.

Jones, A. E. "8endake Ehen," or Old Huronia. Ontario, Province, Bureau of Archives, Report, 5 (1908): 1-505.

Jury, W. Flanagan prehistoric Huron village site. University of Western Ontario, Bulletin of Museums, 6 (1948): 1-9.

Jury, W. and E. M. Jury. Saint Louis: Huron Indian village and Jesuit mission site. University of Western Ontario, Museum of Indian Archaeology, Museum Bulletin, 10 (1955): 1-76.

Jury, W. and W. S. Fox. A pre-White Huron village in Simcoe County, Ontario. Royal Society of Canada, Proceedings and Transactions, ser. 3, 42, pt. 2 (1948): 85-89.

Jury, W. and W. S. Fox. St. Ignace. Royal Society of Canada, Proceedings and Transactions, ser. 3, 41, pt. 2 (1947): 55-78.

Kennedy, J. H. Jesuit and savage in New France. New Haven, 1950. 206 p.

Kenton, E., ed. The Indians of North America, Vol. 1: 211-231, 234-312, 498-523; Vol. 2: 29-46. New York, 1927.

Kenyon, Walter A. Methodist Point. Toronto, 1970. 5, 26 p. illus., map. (Royal Ontario Museum, Art and Archaeology Occasional Paper, 22)

Kerans, P. Murder and atonement in Huronia. Martyrs's Shrine Message, 17, no. 2 (1953): 46-47, 52-53.

Kidd, K. E. Excavation and historical identification of a Huron ossuary. American Antiquity, 18 (1953): 359-379.

Kidd, K. E. Orr Lake pottery. Canadian Institute, Transactions (1951): 165-185.

Kidd, K. E. Sixty years of Ontario archeology. In J. B. Griffin, ed. Archeology of Eastern United States. Chicago, 1952: 71-82.

*Kinietz, W. V. The Indian tribes of the western Great Lakes. Michigan, University, Museum of Anthropology, Occasional Contributions, 10 (1940): 1-160.

Knowles, F. H. S. Physical anthropology of the Roebuck Iroquois. Canada, Department of Mines, National Museum of Canada, Bulletin, 87 (1937): 1-75.

Lahontan, L. A. New voyages to North America. Ed. by R. G. Thwaites. Chicago, 1905. 2 v.

Laning, Paul L. Colonial trail blazers around western Lake Erie. Inland Seas, 19 (1963): 266-276.

Laverdière, C. H., ed. Oeuvres de Champlain. 2d ed. Quebec, 1870. 6 v.

Le Beau, C. Avantures du Sr. C. Le Beau. Amsterdam, 1738. 2 v.

Le Jeune, P. Relation. In R. G. Thwaites, ed. The Jesuit Relations and Allied Documents. Vol. 12. Cleveland, 1898: 1-277.

Le Jeune, P. Relation. In R. G. Thwaites, ed. The Jesuit Relations and Allied Documents. Vol. 11. Cleveland, 1898: 27-279.

LeBlanc, Peter G. Indian-missionary contact in Huronia, 1615-1649. Ontario History, 60 (1968): 133-146.

Lighthall, W. D. Hochelaga and the "Hill of Hochelaga". Royal Society of Canada, Proceedings and Transactions, 3rd ser., 18, pt. 2 (1924): 95.

Lighthall, W. D. Hochelagans and Mohawks. Royal Society of Canada, Proceedings and Transactions, ser. 2, 5, pt. 2 (1899): 199-211.

Lighthall, W. D. New Hochelaga Finds in 1933. Royal Society of Canada, Proceedings and Transactions, 28 (1934): 103-108.

Martin, F. Hurons et Iroquois. Paris, 1877.

McIlwraith, T. F. On the location of Cahiagué. Royal Society of Canada, Proceedings and Transactions, ser. 3, 41, pt. 2 (1947): 99-102.

McIlwraith, T. F. The feast of the dead. Anthropologica, 6 (1958): 83-86.

Merlet, L. V. C. Histoire des relations des Hurons et des Abnaquis du Canada avec Notre-Dame de Chartres. Chartres, 1858. 78 p.

Merwin, B. W. The art of quillwork. Museum Journal, 9 (1918): 50-55.

Mooney, J. Tionontati. U.S. Bureau of American Ethnology, Bulletin, 30, vol. 2 (1910): 755-756.

Morgan, L. H. Systems of consanguinity and affinity. Smithsonian Contributions to Knowledge, 17 (1871): 291-382.

Morgan, L. H. The Indian journals, 1859-62: p. 28, 58-59. Ann Arbor, 1959.

Orr, R. B. The Hurons. Annual Archaeological Report, being Part of Appendix to the Report of the Minister of Education, Ontario (1921/1922): 9-24.

Orr, R. B. The Iroquois in Canada. Annual Archaeological Report, being Part of Appendix to the Report of the Minister of Education, Ontario, 31 (1919): 9-55.

Orr, R. B. The masks or false faces of our Ontario Indians. Annual Archaeological Report, being Part of Appendix to the Report of the Minister of Education, Ontario, 33 (1922): 32-37.

Orr, R. B. Tionnontates. Annual Archaeological Report, being Part of Appendix to the Report of the Minister of Education, Ontario (1914): 7-18.

Parkman, F. The Jesuits in North America. Boston, 1867. 463 p.

Pattison, William D. The survey of the Seven Ranges. Ohio Historical Quarterly, 68 (1959): 115-140.

Peckham, H. H. Thomas Gist's Indian captivity, 1758-1759. Pennsylvania Magazine of History and Biography, 80 (1956): 285-311.

Perrot, N. Memoir on the manners, customs, and religion of the savages of North America. In E. H. Blair, ed. The Indian Tribes of the Upper Mississippi Valley. Vol. 1. Cleveland, 1911: 25-272.

Perrot, N. Mémoire sur les moeurs, coustumes et relligion des sauvages de l'Amérique septentrionale. Paris, 1864. 341 p.

Popham, R. E. Late Huron occupations in Ontario. Ontario History, 42, no. 2 (1950): 81-90.

Potier, P. Elementa grammaticae huronicae. Ontario, Bureau of Archives, Report, 15 (1920): 1-157.

Potier, P. Extraits de l'Evangelé. Ontario, Bureau of Archives, Report, 15 (1920): 457-688.

Potier, P. Radices huronicae. Ontario, Bureau of Archives, Report, 15 (1920): 159-455.

Powell, J. W. Wyandot government. U.S. Bureau of American Ethnology, Annual Reports, 1 (1880): 57-69.

Quimby, George I. The voyage of the Griffin: 1679. Michigan History, 49 (1965): 97-107.

Read, D. B. The Hurons. Canadian Institute, Transactions, ser. 4, 1 (1890): 86-95.

Rice, Otis. The French and Indian War in West Virginia. West Virginia History, 24 (1962/1963): 134-146.

Richardie, F. and P. Potier. Account book of the Huron Mission at Detroit and Sandwich (1740-1751). Ontario, Bureau of Archives, Report, 15 (1920): 689-724.

Ridley, Frank. The Ontario Iroquoian controversy. Ontario History, 55 (1963): 48-59.

Rioux, M. Les Hurons-Iroquois pratiquaient- ils le totemisme? Royal Society of Canada, Proceedings and Transactions, ser. B, 39, pt. 1 (1945): 173-176.

Robinson, P. J. Huron place-names on Lake Erie. Royal Society of Canada, Proceedings and Transactions, ser. 3, 40, pt. 2 (1946): 191-207.

Robinson, P. J. The Huron equivalents of Cartier's second vocabulary. Royal Society of Canada, Proceedings and Transactions, ser. 3, 42 (1948): 127-146.

Robinson, P. J. The origin of the name Hochelaga. Canadian Historical Review, 23 (1942): 295-296.

Rousseau, J. J. La religion primitive des Montagnais et des Hurons. International

Congress of Americanists, Proceedings, 30 (1955): 151-154.

Rousseau, J. J. Les Hochelagas. International Congress of Americanists, Proceeding, 15, vol. 1 (1907): 279-297.

Sagard, Gabriel. Gabriel Sagard, Théodat. Textes choisis par Jean-de-la-Croix Rioux. Montréal, Fides, 1964. 95 p.

Sagard, Gabriel. Histoire du Canada. Nouv. éd. Paris, Librairie Tross, 1866. 4 v.

Sagard, Gabriel. Histoire dv Canada . . . . Paris, C. Sonnivs, 1636. 27, 1,005, 47 p.

Sagard, Gabriel. Le grand voyage du pays des Hurons. Nouv. éd. Paris, Tross, 1865. 25, 268, 12, 148 p.

Sagard, Gabriel. Le grand voyage dv pays des Hvrons. Paris, Chez D. Moreav, 1632. 12, 380, 12, 146 p.

Sagard, Gabriel. Long journey to the country of the Hurons. New York, Greenwood Press, 1968. 47, 411 p. illus., maps. (Champlain Society, Publications, 25)

Sagard, Gabriel. The long journey to the country of the Hurons. Translated by H. H. Langton. Edited by George M. Wrong. Toronto, 1939. 47, 411, 12 p. illus., maps. (Champlain Society, Publications, 25)

Sagard-Théodat, C. Histoire du Canada. New ed. Paris, 1866.

Sargent, M. Seven songs from Lorette. Journal of American Folklore, 63 (1950): 175.

Schlup, E. The Wyandot mission. Ohio State Archaeological and Historical Quarterly, 15 (1906): 163-181.

Scull, G. D., ed. Voyages of Peter Esprit Radisson. Boston, 1885.

Shaw, J. G. Brother Sagard's Huronian triangle. Culture, 3 (1942): 17-30.

Shea, J. G. An historical sketch of the Tionontates. Historical Magazine, 5 (1861): 262-269.

Shetrone, H. C. The Indian in Ohio. Ohio State Archaeological and Historical Quarterly, 26 (1918): 273-510.

Skinner, A. Some Wyandot corn foods. Public Museum of the City of Milwaukee, Yearbook, 3 (1923): 109-112.

Smith, James. An account of the remarkable occurrences in the life and travels of Col. James Smith, during his captivity with the Indians in the years 1755, '56, '57, '58, and '59, with an appendix of illustrative notes. Edited by Wm. N. Darlington. Cincinnati, R. Clarke, 1870. 12, 190 p. (Ohio Valley Historical Series, 5)

Smith, Wallis M. A re-appraisal of the Huron kinship system. Anthropologica, n.s., 12 (1970): 191-206.

Socolofsky, Homer E. Wyandot floats. Kansas Historical Quarterly, 36 (1970): 241-304.

Speck, F. G. Huron hunting territories in Quebec. Indian Notes, 4 (1927): 1-12.

Speck, F. G. Huron moose hair embroidery. American Anthropologist, n.s., 13 (1911): 1-14.

Speck, F. G. Notes on the material culture of the Huron. American Anthropologist, n.s., 13 (1911): 208-228.

Speck, F. G. Some Huron treaty belts. Museum Journal, 2 (1911): 26-27.

Squair, J., tr. The Indian tribes on the St. Lawrence at the time of the arrival of the French. Annual Archaeological Report, being Part of Appendix to the Report of the Minister of Education, Ontario, 34 (1923): 82-88.

Tait, Lyal. The Petuns Tobacco Indians of Canada. Port Borwell, Erie Publishers, 1971. 133 p. illus.

Talbot, F. X. Saint among the Hurons. New York, 1949. 351 p.

Thomas, E. H. Tionnontates (Petun or Tobacco Indian) tools. Pennsylvania Archaeologist, 26 (1956): 43-47.

Thomson, M. M. Excavating Ontario history. Toronto, 1948.

Thwaites, R. G., ed. The Jesuit Relations and allied documents. Cleveland, 1896-1901. 74 v.

*Tooker, Elisabeth. An ethnography of the Huron Indians, 1615-1649. Washington, D.C., Government Printing Office, 1964. 4, 183 p. (U.S., Bureau of American Ethnology, Bulletin, 190)

Tooker, Elisabeth. Northern Iroquoian sociopolitical organization. American Anthropologist, 72 (1970): 90-97.

Tooker, Elisabeth. The Iroquois defeat of
    the Huron: a review of causes.
    Pennsylvania Archaeologist, 33 (1963):
    115-123.

Tooker, Elisabeth. Three aspects of
    Northern Iroquoian culture change.
    Pennsylvania Archaeologist, 30 (1960):
    65-71.

Trigger, Bruce G. Champlain judged by his
    Indian policy: a different view of early
    Canadian history. Anthropologica, n.s.,
    13 (1971): 85-114.

Trigger, Bruce G. Settlement as an aspect
    of Iroquoian adaptation at the time of
    contact. American Anthropologist, 65
    (1963): 86-101.

Trigger, Bruce G. The destruction of
    Huronia. A study in economic and
    cultural change 1609-1630. Royal
    Canadian Institute, Transactions, 33
    (1960): 14-43.

Trigger, Bruce G. The French presence in
    Huronia: the structure of Franco-Huron
    relations in the first half of the
    seventeenth century. Canadian Historical
    Review, 49 (1968): 107-141.

Trigger, Bruce G. The historic location
    of the Hurons. Ontario History, 54
    (1962): 137-148.

Trigger, Bruce G. The Huron farmers of
    the North. New York, Holt, Rinehart and
    Winston, 1969. 12, 130 p. illus.,
    maps.

Trigger, Bruce G. The impact of Europeans
    on Huronia. Vancouver, B.C., Copp
    Clark, 1969. 64 p. map.

Trigger, Bruce G. The Mohawk-Mahican War
    (1624-28): the establishment of a
    pattern. Canadian Historical Review, 51
    (1971): 276-286.

Trigger, Bruce Grahame. Order and freedom
    in Huron society. Anthropologica, n.s.,
    5 (1963): 151-169.

Tylor, E. B. The Hale series of Huron
    wampum belts. Royal Anthropological
    Institute of Great Britain and Ireland,
    Journal, 26 (1896): 248-254.

Walker, B. N. Tales of the bark lodges.
    Oklahoma City, 1919. 107 p.

Walker, B. N. O. Mon-dah-min and the
    Redman's old uses of corn as food.
    Chronicles of Oklahoma, 35 (1957): 194-
    203.

Walker, William. Oregon epic: a letter
    that jarred America. Edited by Ray A.

Billington. Pacific Historian, 12, no. 3
    (1968): 30-37.

Wallace, A. F. C. Mazeway disintegration.
    Human Organization, 15, no. 2 (1957):
    23-27.

Wallace, Anthony F. C. Dreams and the
    wishes of the soul: a type of
    psychoanalytic theory among the
    seventeenth century Iroquois. In John
    Middleton, ed. Magic, Witchcraft, and
    Curing. Garden City, Natural History
    Press, 1967: 171-190.

Washington, George. A mystery resolved;
    George Washington's letter to Governor
    Dinwiddie, June 10, 1754. Edited by
    Peter Walne. Virginia Magazine of
    History and Biography, 79 (1971): 131-
    144.

Waugh, F. W. Notes on Canadian pottery.
    Annual Archaeological Report, being Part
    of Appendix to the Report of the
    Minister of Education, Ontario (1901):
    108-115.

Weer, P. T. Preliminary notes on the
    Iroquoian family. Indiana Historical
    Society, Prehistory Research Series, 1
    (1937): 1-59.

White, Marian. Ethnic identification and
    Iroquois groups in western New York and
    Ontario. Ethnohistory, 18 (1971): 19-38.

White, Marian E. Iroquois culture history
    in the Niagara Frontier area of New York
    State. Ann Arbor, University of
    Michigan, 1961. 8, 155 p. illus.
    (Michigan, University, Museum of
    Anthropology, Anthropological Papers,
    16)

Wilkie, J. Grammar of the Huron language.
    Literary and Historical Society
    (Quebec), Transactions, 2 (1831): 94-
    198.

Wilson, D. The Huron race and its head-
    form. Canadian Journal, n.s., 13 (1871):
    113-134.

Wilson, D. The Huron-Iroquois of Canada.
    Royal Society of Canada, Proceedings and
    Transactions, 2, pt. 2 (1884): 55-106.

Wintemberg, W. J. Bone and horn harpoon
    heads of the Ontario Indians. Annual
    Archaeological Report, being Part of
    Appendix to the Report of the Minister
    of Education, Ontario (1905): 33-56.

Wintemberg, W. J. The Sidey-Mackay
    village site. American Antiquity, 11
    (1946): 154-182.

Wright, James V. An archaeological survey along the north shore of Lake Superior. Ottawa, Queen's Printer, 1963. 9 p. map. (Canada, National Museum, Anthropology Papers, 3)

Wright, James V. The Middleport horizon. Anthropologica, n.s., 2 (1960): 113-120.

Wright, James V. The Ontario Iroquois tradition. Dissertation Abstracts, 24 (1963/1964): 4346-4347. UM 64-7111.

Yarnell, Richard Asa. Aboriginal relationships between culture and plant life in the Upper Great Lakes region. Ann Arbor, University of Michigan, 1964. 6, 218 p. (Michigan, University, Museum of Anthropology, Anthropological Papers, 23)

Zoltvany, Yves F. New France and the West, 1701-1713. Canadian Historical Review, 46 (1965): 301-322.

12-05 Iroquois

Carrière, Gaston. Catalogue des manuscrits en langues indiennes conservés aux archives oblates, Ottawa. Anthropologica, n.s., 12 (1970): 151-179.

Fay, George E. Bibliography of the Indians of Wisconsin. Wisconsin Indians Research Institute, Journal, 1, no. 1 (1965): 107-132.

Fenton, W. N. A calendar of manuscript materials relating to the history of the Six Nations. American Philosophical Society, Proceedings, 97 (1953): 578-595.

Hargrett, L. A bibliography of the constitutions and laws of the American Indians, 106-109. Cambridge, 1947.

Pilling, J. C. Bibliography of the Iroquoian languages. U.S. Bureau of American Ethnology, Bulletin, 6 (1888): 1-208.

Snyderman, G. S. A preliminary survey of American Indian manuscripts in repositories of the Philadelphia area. American Philosophical Society, Proceedings, 97 (1953): 596-610.

Snyderman, G. S. The manuscript collections of the Philadelphia Yearly Meeting of Friends pertaining to the American Indian. American Philosophical Society, Proceedings, 102 (1958): 613-620.

Sturtevant, William C. Iroquois tribes. Indian Historian, 2, no. 2 (1969): 42.

Weinman, Paul L. A bibliography of the Iroquoian literature; partially annotated. Albany, State Education Department, 1969. 9, 254 p. (New York State Museum and Science Service, Bulletin, 411)

Abler, Thomas S. Longhouse and palisade: Northeastern Iroquoian villages of the seventeenth century. Ontario History, 62 (1970): 17-40.

Abler, Thomas S. Moiety exogamy and the Seneca: evidence from Buffalo Creek. Anthropological Quarterly, 44 (1971): 211-222.

Abler, Thomas Struthers. Factional dispute and party conflict in the political system of the Seneca Nation (1845-1895): an ethnohistorical analysis. Dissertation Abstracts International, 31 (1970/1971): 4463B.

Abrams, George H. The Cornplanter Cemetery. Pennsylvania Archaeologist, 35 (1965): 59-73.

Adams, S. L. The longhouse of the Iroquois. Chicago, 1944. 175 p.

Akweks, A. A Mohawk adoption. New York Folklore Quarterly, 6 (1950): 44-46.

Akweks, A. Legend of the wampum bird. Smoke Signals, 6, no. 3 (1954): 9.

Allen, H. E. An Oneida tale. Journal of American Folklore, 57 (1944): 280-281.

American Indian Historical Society. The Iroquois wampum belt controversy. Indian Historian, 3, no. 2 (1970): 4.

Anderson, David D. John Disturnell introduces the Great Lakes to America. Inland Seas, 18 (1962): 96-106.

Anderson, James E. The people of Fairty: an osteological analysis of an Iroquois ossuary. In Contributions to Anthropology 1961-62. Part I. Ottawa, Queen's Printer, 1964: 28-129. (Canada, National Museum, Bulletin, 193)

Angers, Lorenzo. Guerres des Iroquois contre les Montagnais. Bulletin de Recherches Historiques, 45, no. 4 (1939): 102-110.

Anonymous. A law of confiscation; the infamy of New York. Indian Historian, 3, no. 2 (1970): 10.

Anonymous. A Seneca adoption. Masterkey, 26 (1952): 94-96.

Anonymous. Belts of "sacred significance". Indian Historian, 3, no. 2 (1969): 5-9, 50.

Anonymous. Interpretation of three belts of wampum sent to Canada by the Mohawks in 1639. Canadian Antiquarian and Numismatic Journal, 3 (1874/1875): 110-112.

Anonymous. Presents for the Six Nations--1815. Museum of the Fur Trade Quarterly, 4, no. 2 (1968): 6-8.

Anonymous. Supplementary materials on location, numbers and socio-economic conditions of Indians and Eskimos. Eastern Canadian Anthropological Series, 1 (1955): 103-116.

Anonymous. The Cayugas; United States vs Great Britain. Indian Historian, 2, no. 1 (1969): 45-47.

Arnet, Cory. The constitution and the custody law. Indian Historian, 3, no. 2 (1970): 11-12.

Averkieva, IÛlia P. On the role of military democracy in the history of society. In International Congress of Anthropological and Ethnological Sciences, 8th. 1968, Tokyo and Kyoto. Proceedings. Vol. 2. Tokyo, Science Council of Japan, 1969: 194-196.

Bailey, A. G. The significance of the identity and disappearance of the Laurentian Iroquois. Royal Society of Canada, Proceedings and Transactions, ser. 3, 27, no. 2 (1933): 97-107.

Bailey, J. H. An analysis of Iroquoian ceramic types. American Antiquity, 3 (1938): 333-338.

Baldwin, C. C. The Iroquois in Ohio. Western Reserve Historical Society, 2, no. 40 (1878): 25-32.

Barbeau, C. M. Assomption sash. Canada, Department of Mines, National Museum of Canada, Bulletin, 93 (1937): 1-51.

Barbeau, C. M. Iroquoian clans and phratries. American Anthropologist, n.s., 19 (1917): 392-405.

Barbeau, C. M. The dragon myths and ritual songs of the Iroquoians. International Folk Music Council, Journal, 3 (1951): 81-85.

Barbeau, C. Marius. The language of Canada: in the voyages of Jacques Cartier (1534-1538). In Contributions to

Anthropology 1959. Ottawa, Queen's Printer, 1961: 108-229. (Canada, National Museum, Bulletin, 173)

Barbeau, Charles Marius. Dialectes Hurons-Iroquois. In Internationale Amerikanistenkongress, 34th. 1960, Wien. Akten. Horn-Wien, Berger, 1962: 739-742.

Barbé-Marbois, François. Our revolutionary forefathers. Translated by Eugene Parker Chase. Freeport, N.Y., Books for Libraries Press, 1969. 9, 225 p. illus.

Barshied, Willis. Fort Klock--Mohawk trading post. Museum of the Fur Trade Quarterly, 2, no. 2 (1966): 1-2.

Bartram, J. Observations on the inhabitants, climate, soil, rivers, productions, animals, and other matters worthy of notice. London, 1751. 94 p.

Bartram, John. Travels in Pensilvania and Canada. Ann Arbor, University Microfilms, 1966. 94 p. illus.

Bates, E. Our first New York co-operators. Bureau Farmer, 6, no. 2 (1930): 3-25.

Bauman, Richard. An analysis of Quaker-Seneca councils, 1798-1800. Man in the Northeast, 3 (1972): 36-48.

Bauman, Robert F. Claims vs realities: the Anglo-Iroquois partnership. Northwest Ohio Quarterly, 32 (1959/1960): 88-101.

Bauman, Robert F. Iroquois "empire"; Iroquois make all-out effort to destroy the Hurons and gain control of the Great Lakes fur trade. Northwest Ohio Quarterly, 32 (1959/1960): 138-172.

Bauman, Robert F. Ottawa fleets and Iroquois frustration. Northwest Ohio Quarterly, 33 (1960/1961): 6-40.

Bauman, Robert F. The rise of fur trade mastery in the Great Lakes Region. Part 2, the Iroquois fur trade dilemma. Northwest Ohio Quarterly, 32 (1959/1960): 38-64.

Baxter, J. P. A memoir of Jacques Cartier. New York, 1906. 464 p.

Beatty, John Joseph. Mohawk morphology. Dissertation Abstracts International, 33 (1972/1973): 988B. UM 72-24,118.

Beauchamp, W. M. A history of the New York Iroquois. New York State Museum Bulletin, 78 (1905): 125-461.

Beauchamp, W. M. Aboriginal chipped stone implements of New York. New York State Museum Bulletin, 16 (1897): 5-84.

Beauchamp, W. M. Aboriginal occupation of New York. New York State Museum Bulletin, 32 (1900): 5-187.

Beauchamp, W. M. Aboriginal place names of New York. New York State Museum Bulletin, 108 (1907): 5-333.

Beauchamp, W. M. Aboriginal use of wood in New York. New York State Museum Bulletin, 89 (1905): 87-272.

Beauchamp, W. M. An Iroquois condolence. Journal of American Folklore, 8 (1895): 313-316.

Beauchamp, W. M. Cayuga Indian relics. American Naturalist, 23 (1889): 401-406.

Beauchamp, W. M. Champlain and the Oneidas in 1615. American Scenic and Historic Preservation Society, Annual Report, 23 (1918): 625-643.

Beauchamp, W. M. Civil, religious, and mourning councils and ceremonies of adoption of the New York Indians. New York State Museum Bulletin, 113 (1907): 341-451.

Beauchamp, W. M. Earthenware of the New York aborigines. New York State Museum Bulletin, 22 (1898): 75-146.

Beauchamp, W. M. Earthworks and stockades. American Antiquarian and Oriental Journal, 13 (1891): 42-51.

Beauchamp, W. M. Hi-a-wat-ha. Journal of American Folklore, 4 (1891): 295-306.

Beauchamp, W. M. Horn and bone implements of the New York Indians. New York State Museum Bulletin, 50 (1902): 243-350.

Beauchamp, W. M. Indian names in New York. Fayetteville, 1893. 148 p.

Beauchamp, W. M. Indian nations of the Great Lakes. American Antiquarian and Oriental Journal, 17 (1895): 321-325.

Beauchamp, W. M. Iroquois folk lore. Syracuse, 1922. 247 p.

Beauchamp, W. M. Iroquois games. Journal of American Folklore, 9 (1896): 269-277.

Beauchamp, W. M. Iroquois notes. Journal of American Folklore, 4 (1891): 39-46; 5 (1892): 223-229.

Beauchamp, W. M. Iroquois pottery and wampum. Wyoming Historical and Geological Society, Proceedings and Collections, 12 (1912): 55-68.

Beauchamp, W. M. Iroquois women. Journal of American Folklore, 13 (1900): 81-91.

Beauchamp, W. M. Metallic implements of the New York Indians. New York State Museum Bulletin, 55 (1902): 3-92.

Beauchamp, W. M. Metallic ornaments of the New York Indians. New York State Museum Bulletin, 73 (1903): 3-120.

Beauchamp, W. M. Mohawk notes. Journal of American Folklore, 8 (1895): 217-221.

Beauchamp, W. M. Notes on Onondaga dances. Journal of American Folklore, 6 (1893): 181-184.

Beauchamp, W. M. Onondaga customs. Journal of American Folklore, 1 (1888): 195-203.

Beauchamp, W. M. Onondaga Indian names of plants. Torrey Botanical Club, Bulletin, 15 (1888): 262-266.

Beauchamp, W. M. Onondaga names of months. Journal of American Folklore, 2 (1889): 160-161.

Beauchamp, W. M. Onondaga notes. Journal of American Folklore, 8 (1895): 209-216.

Beauchamp, W. M. Onondaga plant names. Journal of American Folklore, 15 (1902): 91-103.

Beauchamp, W. M. Onondaga tale of the Pleiades. Journal of American Folklore, 13 (1900): 281-282.

Beauchamp, W. M. Onondaga tales. Journal of American Folklore, 1 (1888): 44-48; 2 (1889): 261-270; 6 (1893): 173-180.

Beauchamp, W. M. Permanence of early Iroquois clans and sachemships. American Association for the Advancement of Science, Proceedings, 34 (1885): 381-392.

Beauchamp, W. M. Permanency of Iroquois clans and sachemship. American Antiquarian and Oriental Journal, 8 (1886): 82-91.

Beauchamp, W. M. Polished stone articles used by the New York aborigines. New York State Museum Bulletin, 18 (1897): 3-102.

Beauchamp, W. M. The early religion of the Iroquois. American Antiquarian and Oriental Journal, 14 (1892): 344-349.

Beauchamp, W. M.   The good hunter and the
Iroquois medicine. Journal of American
Folklore, 14 (1901): 153-159.

Beauchamp, W. M.   The Iroquois trail.
Fayetteville, 1892.   150 p.

Beauchamp, W. M.   The Iroquois White Dog
Feast. American Antiquarian and Oriental
Journal, 7 (1885): 235-239.

Beauchamp, W. M.   The life of Conrad
Weiser. Syracuse, 1925.   122 p.

Beauchamp, W. M.   The new religion of the
Iroquois. Journal of American Folklore,
10 (1897): 169-180.

Beauchamp, W. M.   The origin and antiquity
of the New York Iroquois. American
Antiquarian and Oriental Journal, 8
(1886): 358-366.

Beauchamp, W. M.   The origin and early
life of the New York Iroquois. Oneida
Historical Society, Transactions
(1887/1889): 119-142.

Beauchamp, W. M.   The origin of the
Iroquois. American Antiquarian and
Oriental Journal, 16 (1894): 61-69.

Beauchamp, W. M.   The principal founders
of the Iroquois League and its probable
date. New York State Historical
Association, Proceedings, 24 (1926): 27-
36.

Beauchamp, W. M.   Wampum and shell
articles used by the New York Indians.
New York State Museum Bulletin, 41
(1901): 328-480.

Beauchamp, W. M.   Wampum belts of the Six
Nations. Smithsonian Institution, Annual
Reports of the Board of Regents (1879):
389-390.

Beauchamp, W. M.   Wampum used in council
and as currency. American Antiquarian
and Oriental Journal, 20 (1898): 1-13.

Beauchamp, William M.   A history of the
New York Iroquois, now commonly called
the Six Nations. Port Washington, I. J.
Friedman, 1961. 337 p. illus.

Beaugrand-Champagne, A. L.   Croyances des
anciens Iroquois. Cahiers des Dix, 6
(1941): 195-210.

Beaugrand-Champagne, A. L.   La poterie
iroquoise. Cahiers des Dix, 8 (1943):
267-284.

Beaugrand-Champagne, A. L.   La stratégie,
la tactique et l'armement des anciens
Iroquois. Cahiers des Dix, 10 (1945):
21-40.

Beaugrand-Champagne, A. L.   Le chemin et
l'emplacement de la bourgade
d'Hochelaga. Cahiers des Dix, 12 (1947):
115-160.

Beaugrand-Champagne, A. L.   Le régime
politique des anciens Iroquois. Cahiers
des Dix, 5 (1940): 217-229.

Beaugrand-Champagne, A. L.   Les anciens
Iroquois de Québec. Cahiers des Dix, 1
(1936): 171-199.

Beaugrand-Champagne, A. L.   Les maladies
et la médicine des anciens Iroquois.
Cahiers des Dix, 9 (1944): 227-242.

Beaugrand-Champagne, A. L.   L'organisation
sociale des anciens Iroquois. Cahiers
des Dix, 4 (1939): 271-289.

Belknap, J.   Report on the Oneida,
Stockbridge and Brotherton Indians,
1796. Indian Notes and Monographs,
ser. 2, 54 (1955): 1-39.

Benedict, Ernest.   Indians and a treaty.
In Waubageshig, ed. The Only Good
Indian. Toronto, new press, 1972: 137-
140.

Berkhofer, Robert F., Jr.   Faith and
factionalism among the Senecas: theory
and ethnohistory. Ethnohistory, 12
(1965): 99-112.

Bibaud, F. M.   Biographie des sagamos
illustrés de l'Amérique Septentrionale,
101-105, 133-134, 161-184, 207-210, 227-
230, 265-270. Montréal, 1848.

Biggar, H. P., ed.   The works of Samuel de
Champlain. Toronto, 1929. 6 v.

Blau, Harold.   Calendric ceremonies of the
New York Onondaga. Dissertation
Abstracts International, 30 (1969/1970):
4470B.   UM 70-7650.

Blau, Harold.   Dream guessing: a
comparative analysis. Ethnohistory, 10
(1963): 233-249.

Blau, Harold.   Historical factors in
Onondaga Iroquois cultural stability.
Ethnohistory, 12 (1965): 250-258.

Blau, Harold.   Mythology, prestige and
politics: a case for Onondaga cultural
persistence. New York Folklore
Quarterly, 23 (1967): 45-51.

Blau, Harold.   Onondaga false face
rituals. New York Folklore Quarterly, 23
(1967): 253-264.

Blau, Harold.   The Iroquois White Dog
Sacrifice: its evolution and symbolism.
Ethnohistory, 11 (1964): 97-119.

Bleeker, S. Indians of the longhouse. New York, 1950. 160 p.

Blomkvist, E. E. Indeĭtsy severo-vostochnogo i prioz ernogo raĭonov SSHA (irokesy i algonkiny). By E. E. Blomkvist and IŪ. P. Averkieva. In A. V. Efimov and S. A. Tokarev, eds. Narody Ameriki. Vol. 1. Moskva, Izdatel'stvo Akademiĭa Nauk SSSR, 1959: 194-227.

Boas, F. Notes on the Iroquois language. In Putnam Anniversary Volume. New York, 1909: 427-460.

Boas, F. Zur Anthropologie der nordamerikanischen Indianer. Berliner Gesellschaft für Anthropologie, Ethnologie und Urgeschichte, Verhandlungen (1895): 367-411.

Bond, R. P. Queen Anne's American kings. Oxford, 1952. 160 p.

Bonvillain, Nancy Lee. A grammar of Akwesasne Mohawk. Dissertation Abstracts International, 33 (1972/1973): 1899B. UM 72-28,017.

Bourgeois, Marie J. Present-day health and illness beliefs and practices of the Seneca Indians. Dissertation Abstracts, 29 (1968/1969): 4488B-4489B. UM 69-9116.

Bourne, E. G., ed. The voyages and explorations of Samuel de Champlain. New York, 1906. 2 v.

Boyd, John Paul. The algebra of kinship. Dissertation Abstracts, 28 (1967/1968): 299A. UM 67-8220.

Boyle, D. Big corn feast. Annual Archaeological Report, being Part of Appendix to the Report of the Minister of Education, Ontario (1899): 34-40.

Boyle, D. Iroquois medicine man's mask. Annual Archaeological Report, being Part of Appendix to the Report of the Minister of Education, Ontario (1899): 27-29.

Boyle, D. On the paganism of the civilised Iroquois of Ontario. Royal Anthropological Institute of Great Britain and Ireland, Journal, 30 (1900): 263-273.

Boyle, D. The Iroquois. Annual Archaeological Report, being Part of Appendix to the Report of the Minister of Education, Ontario (1905): 146-158.

Boyle, D. The making of a Cayuga chief. Annual Archaeological Report, being Part of Appendix to the Report of the

Minister of Education, Ontario (1905): 56-59.

Brant-Sero, J. O. Dekanawideh. Man, 1 (1901): 166-170.

Breysig, K. Die Entstehung des Staates aus der Geschlechtsverfassung bei Tlinkit und Irokesen. Schmollers Jahrbuch für Gesetzgebung, Verwaltung und Volkswirtschaft im Deutschen Reich, 28 (1904): 483-527.

Brigham, A. P. Sites and trails of the Mohawk Indians. New York State Museum Bulletin, 280 (1929): 86-89.

Brodhead, J. R. Wentworth Greenhalgh's journal of a tour to the Indians of western New York. In E. B. O'Callaghan, ed. Documents Relative to the Colonial History of the State of New York. Vol. 3. Albany, 1853: 250-252.

Brown, D. M. Indian winter legends. Wisconsin Archeologist, n.s., 22 (1941): 49-53.

Brown, D. M. Wisconsin Indian corn origin myths. Wisconsin Archeologist, n.s., 21 (1940): 19-27.

Brown, Judith K. Economic organization and the position of women among the Iroquois. Ethnohistory, 17 (1970): 151-167.

Bruemmer, Fred. The Caughnawagas. Beaver, 296, no. 3 (1965/1966): 4-11.

Bruyas, J. Radical words of the Mohawk language with their derivatives. University of the State of New York, Annual Report of the Regents, 16, Appendix E (1863): 1-123.

Buck, J. What is wampum? Annual Archaeological Report, being Part of Appendix to the Report of the Minister of Education, Ontario, 36 (1928): 48-50.

Bulson, Dorwin W. To-wos-scho-hor: the land of the unforgotten Indian; a true story of the Schoharie Creek. [n.p.] 1961. 6, 35 l. illus., maps.

Burke, C. The Indian and his river. Rochester, 1933. 45 p.

Burtin, N. V. Histoire de l'ancien testament traduite en Iroquois. Montreal, 1890. 706 p.

Bushnell, D. I. Native cemeteries and forms of burial east of the Mississippi. U.S. Bureau of American Ethnology, Bulletin, 71 (1920): 70-73, 83-89.

Callihoo, Victoria. The Iroquois in Alberta. Alberta Historical Review, 7, no. 2 (1959): 17-18.

Campbell, T. S. Pioneer priests of North America, 1642-1710. New York, 1908, 1910. 2 v.

Canfield, W. W. The legends of the Iroquois. New York, 1902. 211 p.

Canfield, William W. The legends of the Iroquois: told by "the Cornplanter". Port Washington, I. J. Friedman, 1971. 211 p.

Carpenter, E. S. Iroquoian figurines. American Antiquity, 8 (1942): 105-113.

Carpenter, E. S. Iroquois prehistory. Pennsylvania Archaeologist, 23 (1953): 72-78.

Carpenter, Edmund S. Alcohol in the Iroquois dream quest. American Journal of Psychiatry, 116 (1959): 148-151.

Carr, L. On the social and political position of woman among the Huron-Iroquois tribes. Harvard University, Peabody Museum of American Archaeology and Ethnology, Reports, 3 (1887): 207-232.

Carse, M. R. The Mohawk Iroquois. Archaeological Society of Connecticut, Bulletin, 23 (1949): 3-53.

Caswell, H. S. Our life among the Iroquois Indians. Boston, 1892. 321 p.

Chadwick, E. M. The people of the longhouse. Toronto, 1897. 166 p.

Chafe, Wallace L. A challenge for linguistics today. In Jacob W. Gruber, ed. The Philadelphia Anthropological Society; Papers Presented on Its Golden Anniversary. New York, distributed by Columbia University Press for Temple University Publications, 1967: 125-131.

Chafe, Wallace L. A semantically based sketch of Onondaga. Baltimore, Published at the Waverly Press by Indiana University, 1970. 91 p. (Indiana, University, Publications in Anthropology and Linguistics, Memoir, 25)

Chafe, Wallace L. Another look at Siouan and Iroquoian. American Anthropologist, 66 (1964): 852-862.

Chafe, Wallace L. Handbook of the Seneca language. Albany, State Education Department, 1963. 4, 71 p. (New York State Museum and Science Service, Bulletin, 388)

Chafe, Wallace L. Linguistic evidence for the relative age of Iroquois religious practices. Southwestern Journal of Anthropology, 20 (1964): 278-285.

Chafe, Wallace L. Seneca morphology and dictionary. Washington, D.C., Smithsonian Press, 1967. 6, 126 p. charts. (Smithsonian Contributions to Anthropology, 4)

Chafe, Wallace L. Seneca morphology. Dissertation Abstracts International, 30 (1969/1970): 1544A. UM 69-16,872.

Chafe, Wallace L. Seneca morphology. International Journal of American Linguistics, 26 (1960): 11-22, 123-129, 224-233, 283-289; 27 (1961): 42-45, 114-118, 223-225, 320-328.

Chafe, Wallace L. Seneca thanksgiving rituals. Washington, D.C., 1961. 3, 302 p. (U.S., Bureau of American Ethnology, Bulletin, 183)

Chafe, Wallace L. The classification of morphs in Seneca. Anthropological Linguistics, 1, no. 5 (1959): 1-6.

Chalmers, H. and E. B. Monture. Joseph Brant: Mohawk. Toronto, 1955. 368 p.

Chamberlain, A. F. A Mohawk legend of Adam and Eve. Journal of American Folklore, 2 (1889): 228.

Chamberlain, A. F. Iroquois in northwestern Canada. American Anthropologist, n.s., 6 (1904): 459-463.

Chamberlain, A. F. Notes on Indian child-language. American Anthropologist, 3 (1890): 237-241.

Champlain, Samuel de. Voyages and discoveries made in New France, from the year 1615 to the end of the year 1618. Translated and edited by H. H. Layton and W. F. Ganong. Toronto, The Champlain Society, 1929. illus., maps. (The Works of Samuel de Champlain, 3)

Chaput, Donald. The semantics of nadowa. Names, 15 (1967): 228-234.

Charlevoix, P. F. X. de. Journal of a voyage to North America. Ed. by L. P. Kellogg. Chicago, 1923. 2 v.

Charlton, Thomas H. On Iroquois incest. Anthropologica, n.s., 10 (1968): 29-43.

Churcher, C. S. The Tabor Hill ossuaries: a study in Iroquois demography. By C. S. Churcher and W. A. Kenyon. Human Biology, 32 (1960): 249-273.

Clark, J. V. H. Lights and lines of Indian character. Syracuse, 1854. 375 p.

Clark, J. V. H. Onondaga. Syracuse, 1849. 2 v.

Clark, Joseph. Travels among the Indians, 1797. Doylestown, Pa., C. Ingerman at the Quixott Press, 1968. 42 p.

Clarke, John M. Wampums of the Iroquois Confederacy. New York (State), State Museum, Museum Bulletin, 121 (1908): 85-87.

Clarke, N. T. The Thacher wampum belts. New York State Museum Bulletin, 279 (1929): 53-58.

Clarke, N. T. The wampum belt collection of the New York State Museum. New York State Museum Bulletin, 288 (1931): 85-122.

Clarke, T. W. The bloody Mohawk. New York, 1940. 372 p.

Clarke, Thomas Wood. The bloody Mohawk. Port Washington, I. J. Friedman, 1968. 18, 372 p. illus., maps.

Cleaveland, Moses. General Moses Cleaveland (1754-1806), founder of the City of Cleveland in 1796. Cleveland, Western Reserve Historical Society, 1971.

Coe, Stephen Howard. Cornplanter (Kaiiontwa'/kaN), ca. 1750-1836: Seneca chief. Masters Abstracts, 1, no. 2 (1962): 23. UM M-408.

Coe, Stephen Howard. Indian affairs in Pennsylvania and New York, 1783-1794. Dissertation Abstracts International, 30 (1969/1970): 649A-650A. UM 69-13,646.

Colden, C. History of the Five Indian Nations, continuation, 1707-1720. New York Historical Society, Collections (1935): 359-434.

Colden, C. The history of the Five Indian Nations of Canada. New ed. New York, 1922. 2 v.

Colden, Cadwallader. The history of the five Indian nations of Canada. Toronto, Coles, 1972. 16, 283 p.

Collins, Helen. The League of the Iroquois. Western Pennsylvania Historical Magazine, 55 (1972): 171-178.

Conference on Iroquois Research, Glens Falls, 1965. Iroquois culture, history and prehistory; proceedings. Edited by Elisabeth Tooker. Albany, New York

State Museum and Science Service, 1967. 4, 120 p. illus., maps.

Congdon, Charles E. Allegany Oxbow; a history of Allegany State Park and the Allegany Reserve of the Seneca Nation. Salamanca, N.Y., 1967. 11, 206 p. illus., map.

Congdon, Charles E. The good news of Handsome Lake. New York Folklore Quarterly, 23 (1967): 290-297.

Conklin, H. C. and W. C. Sturtevant. Seneca Indian singing tools at Coldspring Longhouse. American Philosophical Society, Proceedings, 97 (1953): 262-290.

Conover, G. S. Sayerqueraghta, king of the Senecas. Waterloo, Vt., 1885.

Conover, G. S. Seneca Indian villages. Geneva, 1889. 12 p.

Conservation Society of York County. Seneca Indians; home life and culture. York, Pa., Conservation Society of York County, 1944. 12, 125 p. illus., maps.

Converse, H. M. Myths and legends of the New York State Iroquois. Ed. by A. C. Parker. New York State Museum Bulletin, 125 (1908): 5-195.

Converse, H. M. The Iroquois silver brooches. University of the State of New York, Annual Report of the Regents, 54, pt. 1 (1900): r231-r254.

Converse, H. M. The Seneca new-year ceremony and other customs. Indian Notes, 7 (1930): 69-89.

Converse, Harriet M. Myths and legends of the New York Iroquois. Edited by Arthur C. Parker. Port Washington, I. J. Friedman, 1962. 195 p. illus.

Cook, F. Journals of the military expedition of Major General John Sullivan. Auburn, 1887. 580 p.

Cooke, C. A. Iroquois personal names. American Philosophical Society, Proceedings, 96 (1952): 424-438.

Cooper, Johnson Gaylord. Oswego in the French-English struggle in North America 1720-1760. Dissertation Abstracts, 23 (1962/1963): 208-209. UM 62-1095.

Cork, Ella. "The worst of the bargain," concerning the dilemmas inherited from their forefathers along with their lands by the Iroquois Nation of the Canadian Grand River Reserve. San Jacinto, Calif., Foundation for Social Research, 1962. 25, 196 p.

Cornplanter, J. J. Legends of the longhouse. Philadelphia, 1938. 216 p.

Cornplanter, Jesse J. Legends of the Longhouse. Port Washington, I. J. Friedman, 1963. 216 p. illus.

Corwin, R. David. Dilemma of the Iroquois. Natural History, 76, no. 6 (1967): 6-7, 60-66.

Cringan, A. T. Iroquois folk songs. Annual Archaeological Report, being Part of Appendix to the Report of the Minister of Education, Ontario (1902): 137-152.

Cringan, A. T. Pagan dance songs of the Iroquois. Annual Archaeological Report, being Part of Appendix to the Report of the Minister of Education, Ontario (1899): 168-189.

Crocker, J. DeReu. Index to the opinions of the New York State attorney general and the New York State comptroller relating to Indian affairs. Albany, New York State Department of Law, 1961. 9 p.

Crowell, S. The dog sacrifice of the Seneca. In W. W. Beach, ed. Indian Miscellany. Albany, 1877: 323-332.

Cumming, John. A Puritan among the Chippewas. Michigan History, 51 (1967): 213-225.

Cuoq, J. A. Études philologiques sur quelques langues sauvages de l'Amérique. Montréal, 1866. 160 p.

Cuoq, J. A. Kaiatonsera iontewaienstakwa kaiatonseraso: nouveau syllabaire iroquois. Tiohtiake, 1873. 69 p.

Cuoq, J. A. Lexique de la langue iroquoise. Montréal, 1882. 215 p.

Cuoq, Jean André. Études philologiques sur quelques langues sauvages de l'Amérique. New York, Johnson Reprint, 1966. 160 p.

Curtin, J. Seneca Indian myths. New York, 1923. 516 p.

Curtin, J. and J. N. B. Hewitt. Seneca fiction, legends, and myths. U.S. Bureau of American Ethnology, Annual Reports, 32 (1911): 37-819.

Cusick, D. Sketches of ancient history of the Six Nations. Lockport, 1848. 35 p.

Cusick, D. Sketches of the ancient history of the Six Nations. In H. R. Schoolcraft, ed. Information respecting the History, Condition, and Prospects of the Indian Tribes of the United States. Vol. 5. Philadelphia, 1855: 631-646.

Darnell, Regna, ed. Linguistic diversity in Canadian society. Edmonton, Instant Printers, 1971. 307 p. (Linguistic Research, Inc., Sociolinguistics Series, 1)

Day, Gordon M. Iroquois: an etymology. Ethnohistory, 15 (1968): 389-402.

Day, Gordon M. The eastern boundary of Iroquoia: Abenaki evidence. Man in the Northeast, 1 (1971): 7-13.

De Forest, John W. History of the Indians of Connecticut from the earliest known period to 1850. Hamden, Conn., Archon Books, 1964. 48, 509 p. illus., map.

De Forest, John William. History of the Indians of Connecticut from the earliest known period to 1850. St. Clair, Mich., Scholarly Press, 1970. 26, 509 p. illus., map.

Deardorff, M. H. The Cornplanter Grant in Warren County. Western Pennsylvania Historical Magazine, 24 (1941): 1-22.

Deardorff, M. H. The religion of Handsome Lake. U.S. Bureau of American Ethnology, Bulletin, 149 (1951): 77-107.

Deardorff, M. H. Zeisberger's Allegheny River Indian towns: 1767-1770. Pennsylvania Archaeologist, 16 (1946): 2-19.

Deardorff, M. H. and G. S. Snyderman. A nineteenth century journal of a visit to the Indians of New York. American Philosophical Society, Proceedings, 100 (1956): 582-612.

Demirjian, A. A study of the morphology of the glenoid fossa. In Contributions to Anthropology V: Archaeology and Physical Anthropology. Ottawa, Queen's Printer, 1967: 1-25. (Canada, National Museum, Bulletin, 206)

Densmore, F. An Onondaga thanksgiving song. Indian School Journal, 7 (1907): 23-24.

Deserontyon, J. A Mohawk form of ritual of condolence. Indian Notes and Monographs, 10 (1928): 87-110.

Desrosiers, L. P. Iroquoisie, terre française. Cahiers des Dix, 20 (1955): 35-59.

Desrosiers, L. P. Iroquoisie, 1534-1646. Montréal, 1947. 351 p.

Desrosiers, L. P. Les Onnantagués. Cahiers des Dix, 18 (1953): 45-66.

Desrosiers, L. P. Premières missions iroquoises. Revue d'Histoire de l'Amérique Française, 1 (1947): 21-38.

Diamond, Stanley. Memorandum submitted to Subcommittees on Indian Affairs of the Senate and House of Representatives. By Stanley Diamond, William C. Sturtevant, and William N. Fenton. American Anthropologist, 66 (1964): 631-633.

Dodge, E. S. A Cayuga bear society curing rite. Primitive Man, 22 (1949): 65-71.

Dodge, E. S. Notes from the Six Nations on the hunting and trapping of wild turkeys and passenger pigeons. Washington Academy of Sciences, Journal, 35 (1945): 342-343.

Dodge, Henry. Journal of Colonel Dodge's expedition from Fort Gibson to the Pawnee Pict village. American State Papers, Military Affairs, 5 (1860): 373-382.

Doeblin, T. D., et al. Diabetes and hyperglycemia in Seneca Indians. Human Heredity, 19 (1969): 613-627.

Doeblin, Thomas D. The blood groups of the Seneca Indians. By Thomas D. Doeblin and James F. Mohn. American Journal of Human Genetics, 19 (1967): 700-712.

Doeblin, Thomas D., et al. Genetic studies of the Seneca Indians: haptoglobins, transferrins, G-6-PD deficiency, hemoglobinopathy, color blindness, morphological traits and dermatoglyphics. Acta Genetica et Statistica Medica, 18 (1968): 251-260.

Donaldson, T. The George Catlin Indian Gallery. United States National Museum, Reports (1885): 154-196.

Donaldson, T. The Six Nations of New York. In United States, Department of the Interior, Census Office, Eleventh Census. Report on Indians Taxed and Indians not Taxed. Washington, D.C., 1890: 447-498.

Donck, Adriaen van der. A description of the New Netherlands. Edited by Thomas F. O'Donnell. Syracuse, Syracuse University Press, 1968. 40, 10, 142 p.

Donohue, T. The Iroquois and the Jesuits. Buffalo, 1895. 276 p.

Doren, C. van and J. P. Boyd. Indian treaties printed by Benjamin Franklin. Philadelphia, 1938. 340 p.

Doty, L. L. A history of Livingston County, 19-127. Genesee, 1876.

Douglas, F. H. Iroquois foods. Denver Art Museum, Indian Leaflet Series, 26 (1931): 1-4.

Douglas, F. H. Iroquois long house. Denver Art Museum, Indian Leaflet Series, 12 (1930): 1-4.

Dowling, John H. A "rural" Indian community in an urban setting. Human Organization, 27 (1968): 236-240.

Downes, R. C. Council fires on the upper Ohio. Pittsburgh, 1940. 367 p.

Drumm, Judith. Iroquois culture. Albany, State Education Department, State University of New York, 1962. 17 p. (New York, State, Museum and Science Service, State Education Department, Report, EL-5) ERIC ED032986.

Duluth, Daniel Greysolon de. Capital punishment in Michigan, 1683: Duluth at Michilimackinac. Michigan History, 50 (1966): 349-360.

Dunning, R. W. Iroquois feast of the dead. Anthropologica, 6 (1958): 87-118.

Eccles, W. J. Frontenac and the Iroquois. Canadian Historical Review, 36 (1955): 1-16.

Eccles, W. J. The social, economic, and political significance of the military establishment in New France. Canadian Historical Review, 51 (1971): 1-22.

Echeverria, D. The Iroquois visit Rochambeau at Newport in 1780. Rhode Island History, 11 (1952): 73-81.

Eggen, D. Indian tales from western New York. New York Folklore Quarterly, 6 (1950): 240-245.

Emerson, J. N. Understanding Iroquois pottery in Ontario. Toronto, 1956. 64 p.

Emerson, J. Norman. The Payne Site: an Iroquoian manifestation in Prince Edward County, Ontario. In Contributions to Anthropology V: Archaeology and Physical Anthropology. Ottawa, Queen's Printer, 1967: 126-257. (Canada, National Museum, Bulletin, 206)

Emerson, J. Norman. Understanding Iroquois pottery in Ontario: a rethinking. Mississauga, Ontario Archaeological Society, 1968. 4, 132 p. illus.

Emlen, James. The journal of James Emlen
  kept on a trip to Canandaiga, New York;
  September 15 to October 30, 1794 to
  attend the treaty between the United
  States and the Six Nations.
  Ethnohistory, 12 (1965): 279-342.

Engelbrecht, William. The reflection of
  patterned behavior in Iroquois pottery
  decorations. Pennsylvania Archaeologist,
  42, no. 3 (1972): 1-15.

Engelbrecht, William Ernst. A stylistic
  analysis of New York Iroquois pottery.
  Dissertation Abstracts International, 32
  (1971/1972): 6176B. UM 72-14,853.

Ewers, J. C. Gustavus Sohon's portraits
  of Flathead and Pend d'Oreille Indians.
  Smithsonian Miscellaneous Collections,
  110, no. 7 (1948): 54-62.

Ewers, John C. Iroquois Indians in the
  Far West. Montana, the Magazine of
  Western History, 13, no. 2 (1963): 2-10.

Eyman, Frances. Lacrosse and the Cayuga
  Thunder Rite. Expedition, 6, no. 4
  (1964): 15-19.

Fadden, R. The visions of Handsome Lake.
  Pennsylvania History, 22 (1955): 341-
  358.

Faillon, Abbé. The Indian tribes on the
  St. Lawrence at the time of the arrival
  of the French. Translated by John
  Squair. Toronto, Ontario Provincial
  Museum, Annual Archaeological Report, 34
  (1923): 82-88.

Farrell, David. Settlement along the
  Detroit frontier, 1760-1796. Michigan
  History, 52 (1968): 89-107.

Fay, George E., ed. Charters,
  constitutions and by-laws of the Indian
  tribes of Wisconsin. Wisconsin Indians
  Research Institute, Journal, 3, no. 1
  (1967): 1-124.

Fay, George E., ed. Charters,
  constitutions and by-laws of the Indian
  tribes of North America. Part II: The
  Indian tribes of Wisconsin (Great Lakes
  Agency). Greeley, 1967. 6, 124 l.
  illus., map. (University of Northern
  Colorado, Museum of Anthropology,
  Occasional Publications in Anthropology,
  Ethnology Series, 2) ERIC ED046552.

Fay, George E., ed. Charters,
  constitutions and by-laws of the Indian
  tribes of North America. Part VI: The
  Indian tribes of Oklahoma (cont'd.).
  Greeley, 1968. 5, 129 l. map.
  (University of Northern Colorado, Museum
  of Anthropology, Occasional Publications

in Anthropology, Ethnology Series, 7)
  ERIC ED046556.

Feest, Christian F. Lukas Vischers
  Beiträge zur Ethnographie Nordamerikas.
  Archiv für Völkerkunde, 22 (1968): 31-
  66.

Fenstermaker, G. B. Good luck hunting
  charms. National Archaeological News, 1,
  no. 4 (1937): 27-29.

Fenstermaker, G. B. Iroquois animal gods
  or hunting charms. Pennsylvania
  Archaeologist, 6 (1936): 76-78.

Fenstermaker, G. B. Iroquois pottery.
  National Archaeological News, 1, no. 3
  (1937): 3-6, 16-17.

Fenstermaker, G. B. Iroquois pottery.
  Pennsylvania Archaeologist, 6 (1936):
  79-82.

Fenton, W. N. A further quest for
  Iroquois medicines. Smithsonian
  Institution, Explorations and Field-Work
  (1939): 93-96.

Fenton, W. N. An Iroquois condolence
  council for installing Cayuga chiefs in
  1945. Washington Academy of Sciences,
  Journal, 36 (1946): 110-127.

Fenton, W. N. An outline of Seneca
  ceremonies at Coldspring Longhouse. Yale
  University Publications in Anthropology,
  9 (1936): 1-23.

Fenton, W. N. Collecting materials for a
  political history of the Six Nations.
  American Philosophical Society,
  Proceedings, 93 (1949): 233-237.

Fenton, W. N. Contacts between Iroquois
  herbalism and Colonial medicine.
  Smithsonian Institution, Annual Reports
  of the Board of Regents (1941): 503-526.

Fenton, W. N. Fish drives among the
  Cornplanter Seneca. Pennsylvania
  Archaeologist, 12 (1942): 48-52.

Fenton, W. N. Iroquois Indian folklore.
  Journal of American Folklore, 60 (1947):
  383-397.

Fenton, W. N. Iroquois studies at the
  mid-century. American Philosophical
  Society, Proceedings, 95 (1951): 296-
  310.

Fenton, W. N. Iroquois suicide. U.S.
  Bureau of American Ethnology, Bulletin,
  128 (1941): 80-137.

Fenton, W. N. Locality as a basic factor
  in the development of Iroquois social

structure. U.S. Bureau of American Ethnology, Bulletin, 149 (1951): 35-54.

Fenton, W. N. Long-term trends of change among the Iroquois. In V. F. Ray, ed. Cultural Stability and Cultural Change. Seattle, 1957: 30-35.

Fenton, W. N. Masked medicine societies of the Iroquois. Smithsonian Institution, Annual Reports of the Board of Regents (1940): 397-430.

Fenton, W. N. Museum and field studies of Iroquois masks and ritualism. Smithsonian Institution, Explorations and Field-Work (1940): 95-100.

Fenton, W. N. Pennsylvania's remaining Indian settlement. Pennsylvania Park News, 44 (1945): 1-2.

Fenton, W. N. Place names and related activities of the Cornplanter Senecas. Pennsylvania Archaeologist, 15 (1945): 25-29, 42-50, 88-96, 108-118; 16 (1946): 42-57.

Fenton, W. N. Problems arising from the historic northeastern position of the Iroquois. Smithsonian Miscellaneous Collections, 100 (1940): 159-251.

Fenton, W. N. Samuel Crowell's account of a Seneca dog sacrifice. Northwest Ohio Quarterly, 16 (1944): 158-163.

Fenton, W. N. Seneca Indians by Asher Wright. Ethnohistory, 4 (1957): 302-321.

Fenton, W. N. Seth Newhouses's traditional history and constitution of the Iroquois Confederacy. American Philosophical Society, Proceedings, 93 (1949): 185-206.

Fenton, W. N. Simeon Gibson: Iroquois informant, 1889-1943. American Anthropologist, n.s., 46 (1944): 231-234.

Fenton, W. N. Some social customs of the modern Seneca. Social Welfare Bulletin, 7, no. 1 (1936): 4-7.

Fenton, W. N. The concept of locality and the program of Iroquois research. U.S. Bureau of American Ethnology, Bulletin, 149 (1951): 1-12.

Fenton, W. N. The Hiawatha wampum belt of the Iroquois League for Peace. International Congress of the Anthropological and Ethnological Sciences, Acts, 5 (1960): 3-7.

Fenton, W. N. The Hyde de Neuville portraits of New York savages in 1807-1808. New York Historical Society Quarterly, 38 (1954): 118-137.

*Fenton, W. N. The Iroquois eagle dance. U.S. Bureau of American Ethnology, Bulletin, 156 (1953): 1-330.

Fenton, W. N. The roll call of the Iroquois chiefs. Detroit, 1950. 103 p.

Fenton, W. N. The roll call of the Iroquois chiefs. Smithsonian Miscellaneous Collections, 111, no. 15 (1950): 1-75.

Fenton, W. N. The Seneca society of faces. Scientific Monthly, 44 (1937): 215-238.

Fenton, W. N. Tonawanda longhouse ceremonies. U.S. Bureau of American Ethnology, Bulletin, 128 (1941): 140-166.

Fenton, W. N. Toward the gradual civilization of the Indian natives. American Philosophical Society, Proceedings, 100 (1956): 567-581.

Fenton, W. N. Twi'yendagon' (Wood-eater) takes the heavenly path. American Indian, 3, no. 3 (1946): 11-15.

Fenton, W. N. and E. S. Dodge. An elm bark canoe in the Peabody Museum of Salem. American Neptune, 9 (1949): 185-206.

Fenton, W. N. and G. P. Kurath. The feast of the dead, or ghost dance at Six Nations Reserve, Canada. U.S. Bureau of American Ethnology, Bulletin, 149 (1951): 139-166.

Fenton, W. N. and M. H. Deardorff. The last passenger pigeon hunts of the Cornplanter Senecas. Washington Academy of Sciences, Journal, 33 (1943): 289-315.

Fenton, William N. An outline of Seneca ceremonies at Coldspring Longhouse. New Haven, Human Relations Area Files Press, 1970. 23 p. (Yale University Publications in Anthropology, 9)

Fenton, William N. J.-F. Lafitau (1681-1746), precursor of scientific anthropology. Southwestern Journal of Anthropology, 25 (1969): 173-187.

Fenton, William N. Medicinal plant lore of the Iroquois. New York, State, University, Bulletin to the Schools, 35, no. 7 (1949): 233-237.

Fenton, William N. Return to the longhouse. In Solon T. Kimball and James B. Watson, eds. Crossing Cultural

Boundaries. San Francisco, Chandler, 1972: 102-118.

Fenton, William N. The funeral of Tadodáho; Onondaga of today. Indian Historian, 3, no. 2 (1970): 43-47, 66.

Fenton, William N. The Iroquois Confederacy in the twentieth century: a case study of the theory of Lewis H. Morgan in Ancient Society. In Deward E. Walker, Jr., ed. The Emergent Native Americans. Boston, Little, Brown, 1972: 471-484.

Fenton, William N. The Iroquois Confederacy in the twentieth century: a case study of the theory of Lewis H. Morgan in "Ancient Society". Ethnology, 4 (1965): 251-265.

Fenton, William N. The Iroquois in history. In Eleanor Burke Leacock and Nancy Oestreich Lurie, eds. North American Indians in Historical Perspective. New York, Random House, 1971: 129-168.

Fenton, William N. The New York State Wampum Collection: the case for the integrity of cultural treasures. American Philosophical Society, Proceedings, 115 (1971): 437-461.

Fenton, William N. The Seneca green corn ceremony. Conservationist, 18, no. 2 (1963): 20-22, 28.

Festinger, Georges. Nouvelle analyse formelle de la terminologie de parenté Seneca. Homme, 10, no. 1 (1970): 77-93.

Fiddes, G. W. J. He took down his shingle (a backward look at the Indian medicine man). Canadian Journal of Public Health, 56 (1965): 400-401.

Fisher, Carol Ann. A survey of vandalism and its cultural antecedents on four New York State Indian reservations. Dissertation Abstracts, 20 (1959/1960): 2489. UM 59-6303.

Follett, H. C. Seneca burial sites in New York State. Archaeological Bulletin, 6 (1915): 36-37.

Forbes, Allan, Jr. Two and a half centuries of conflict: the Iroquois and the Laurentian wars. Pennsylvania Archaeologist, 40, no. 3/4 (1970): 1-20.

Fox, John W. Dating kaolin pipes from Indian Island. Man in the Northeast, 3 (1972): 20-35.

Fraser, Douglas. Village planning in the primitive world. New York, George Braziller, 1968. 128 p. illus.

Freilich, M. Cultural persistence among the modern Iroquois. Anthropos, 53 (1958): 473-483.

Freilich, Morris. Mohawk heroes and Trinidadian peasants. In Morris Freilich, ed. Marginal Natives: Anthropologists at Work. New York, Harper and Row, 1970: 185-250.

Freilich, Morris. Scientific possibilities in Iroquoian studies: an example of Mohawks past and present. Anthropologica, n.s., 5 (1963): 171-186.

French, M. J. Samuel de Champlain's incursion against the Onondaga nation. Ann Arbor, 1949. 23 p.

Frey, S. L. The historic and prehistoric Mohawks. American Anthropologist, 6 (1893): 277-278.

Frey, S. L. The Mohawks. Oneida Historical Society, Transactions, 8 (1898): 1-41.

Frisch, Jack A. Factionalism, Pan-Indianism, tribalism, and the contemporary political behavior of the St. Regis Mohawks. Man in the Northeast, 2 (1971): 75-81.

Frisch, Jack A. Mohawk color terms. Anthropological Linguistics, 14 (1972): 306-310.

Frisch, Jack A. The Abenakis among the St. Regis Mohawks. Indian Historian, 4, no. 1 (1971): 27-29.

Frisch, Jack A. Tribalism among the St. Regis Mohawks: a search for self-identity. Anthropologica, n.s., 12 (1970): 207-219.

Frisch, Jack Aaron. Revitalization, nativism, and tribalism among the St. Regis Mohawks. Dissertation Abstracts International, 31 (1970/1971): 3816B. UM 71-926.

Frohman, Lawrence A. Diabetes in the Seneca Indians, plasma insulin responses to oral carbohydrate. By Lawrence A. Frohman, Thomas D. Doeblin, and Frank G. Emerling. Diabetes, 18 (1969): 38-43.

Gaudia, Gil. Race, social class, and age of achievement of conservation on Piaget's tasks. Developmental Psychology, 6 (1972): 158-165.

Gaudia, Gil. Race, social class, and age of achievement of conservation on Piaget's tasks. Dissertation Abstracts International, 31 (1970/1971): 5843A-5844A. UM 71-7164.

Ghobashy, Omar Z. The Caughawaga Indians and the St. Lawrence Seaway. New York, Devin-Adair, 1961. 137 p. illus.

Gibson, A. M. Joe Kagey: Indian educator. Chronicles of Oklahoma, 38 (1960): 12-19.

Gibson, A. M. Wyandotte mission. Chronicles of Oklahoma, 36 (1958): 137-154.

Gillette, Charles H. Wampum beads and belts. Indian Historian, 3, no. 4 (1970): 32-38.

Goldenweiser, A. A. Early civilization, 70-82. New York, 1922.

Goldenweiser, A. A. Hanging-Flower, the Iroquois. In E. C. Parsons, ed. American Indian Life. New York, 1925: 99-106.

Goldenweiser, A. A. On Iroquois work. Canada, Geological Survey, Summary Reports (1912): 464-475; (1913): 365-372.

Goldenweiser, A. A. The clan and maternal family of the Iroquois League. American Anthropologist, n.s., 15 (1913): 696-697.

Goldstein, Robert Arnold. French-Iroquois diplomatic and military relations, 1609-1701. Dissertation Abstracts, 22 (1961/1962): 2776-2777. UM 61-5875.

Grassman, T. The Mohawk-Caughnawaga excavations. Pennsylvania Archaeologist, 22 (1952): 33-36.

Grassman, T. The question of the locations of Mohawk Indian village sites existing during the historic period. Pennsylvania Archaeologist, 22 (1952): 98-111.

Grassman, Thomas. The Mohawk Indians and their valley. Schenectady, Eric Hugo Photography and Printing, 1969. 16, 722 p. maps.

Gray, L. H. Iroquois. In J. Hastings, ed. Encyclopaedia of Religion and Ethics. Vol. 7. New York, 1915: 420-422.

Graymont, Barbara. The border war: the Iroquois in the American Revolution. Dissertation Abstracts International, 32 (1971/1972): 6316A-6317A. UM 72-15,574.

Graymont, Barbara. The Iroquois in the American Revolution. Syracuse, Syracuse University Press, 1972. 10, 359 p. illus.

Griffin, J. B. The Iroquois in American prehistory. Michigan Academy of Science,

Arts and Letters, Papers, 29 (1943): 357-374.

Grol, Lini R. Lelawala; a legend of the maid of the mist. Fonthill, Ont., Fonthill Studio, 1971. 39 p. illus.

Guthe, A. K. A possible Seneca house site, A.D. 1600. Pennsylvania Archaeologist, 28 (1958): 33-38.

Guthe, A. K. A possible Seneca house site: 1600 A.D. Eastern States Archaeological Federation, Bulletin, 16 (1957): 13.

Guthe, A. K. The cultural background of the Iroquois. In Essays in the Science of Culture in Honor of Leslie A. White. New York, 1960: 202-215.

Guthe, A. K. The Hummel Site, an early Iroquois occupation. Eastern States Archaeological Federation, Bulletin, 14 (1955): 11.

Hagerty, Gilbert. The iron trade-knife in Oneida territory. Pennsylvania Archaeologist, 33 (1963): 93-114.

Hale, H. A lawgiver of the stone age. American Association for the Advancement of Science, Proceedings, 30 (1881): 324-341.

Hale, H. "Above" and "below". Journal of American Folklore, 3 (1890): 178-190.

Hale, H. An Iroquois condoling council. Royal Society of Canada, Proceedings and Transactions, ser. 2, 1, pt. 2 (1895): 45-65.

Hale, H. Hiawatha and the Iroquois Confederation. Salem, 1881. 20 p.

Hale, H. Indian etymologies. American Anthropologist, 1 (1888): 290-291.

Hale, H. Indian migrations as evidenced by language. American Antiquarian and Oriental Journal, 5 (1883): 18-28.

Hale, H. On some doubtful or intermediate articulations. Royal Anthropological Institute of Great Britain and Ireland, Journal, 14 (1885): 233-243.

Hale, H. The Iroquois book of rites. Philadelphia, 1883. 222 p.

Hale, H. The Iroquois sacrifice of the white dog. American Antiquarian and Oriental Journal, 7 (1885): 7-14.

Hale, Horatio E. The Iroquois Book of rites. 2d ed. Toronto, University of Toronto Press, 1963. 27, 222 p. map.

Hamilton, M. W. Guy Johnson's opinions on
the American Indian. Pennsylvania
Magazine of History and Biography, 77
(1953): 311-327.

Hamilton, Milton W. Sir William Johnson:
interpreter of the Iroquois.
Ethnohistory, 10 (1963): 270-286.

Hamilton, Milton W. Sir William Johnston
and the Indians of New York. Albany,
University of the State of New York,
Office of State History, 1967. 7,
47 p. illus.

Hamilton, Raphael N. Jesuit mission at
Sault Ste. Marie. Michigan History, 52
(1968): 123-132.

Hamilton, T. A., ed. Indian trade guns.
Columbia, Missouri Archaeological
Society, 1960. 8, 226 p. illus.
(Missouri Archaeologist, 22)

Hamori-Torok, Charles. The acculturation
of the Mohawks of the Bay of Quinte.
Dissertation Abstracts, 28 (1967/1968):
1323B.

Hanna, C. A. The wilderness trail, 26-87.
New York, 1911.

Hanson, Charles E., Jr. The Indian garden
project. Museum of the Fur Trade
Quarterly, 2, no. 3 (1966): 3-6.

Hanzeli, Victor E. Missionary linguistics
in New France; a study of seventeenth-
and eighteenth-century descriptions of
American Indian languages. The Hague,
Mouton, 1969. 141 p. illus., map.
(Janua Linguarum, Series Maior, 29)

Hanzeli, Victor E. The Algonquin R-
dialect in historical records. In
International Congress of Linguists,
10th. 1967, Bucarest. Proceedings.
Vol. 2. Bucarest, Éditions de
l'Académie de la République Socialiste
de Roumanie, 1970: 85-89.

Hanzeli, Victor Eugen. Early descriptions
by French missionaries of Algonquian and
Iroquoian languages: a study of
seventeenth- and eighteenth-century
practice in linguistics. Dissertation
Abstracts, 22 (1961/1962): 1157. UM 61-
4443.

Hardcastle, David Paul. The defense of
Canada under Louis XIV, 1643-1701.
Dissertation Abstracts International, 31
(1970/1971): 3470A. UM 70-26,298.

Harkins, Arthur M. Attitudes and
characteristics of selected Wisconsin
Indians. By Arthur M. Harkins and
Richard G. Woods. Wisconsin Indians

Research Institute, Journal, 4, no. 1
(1968): 64-130.

Harkins, Arthur M. Attitudes and
characteristics of selected Wisconsin
Indians. By Arthur M. Harkins and
Richard G. Woods. Minneapolis,
University of Minnesota, Training Center
for Community Programs, 1969. 89 p.
ERIC ED032174.

Harrington, M. R. Hiawatha's peace
league. Pennsylvania Archaeologist, 15
(1945): 70-74.

Harrington, M. R. Iroquois silverwork.
American Museum of Natural History,
Anthropological Papers, 1 (1908): 351-
369.

Harrington, M. R. Some Iroquois wampum.
Masterkey, 32 (1958): 31-32.

Harrington, M. R. Some Seneca corn-foods
and their preparation. American
Anthropologist, n.s., 10 (1908): 575-
590.

Harrington, M. R. Some unusual Iroquois
specimens. American Anthropologist,
n.s., 11 (1909): 85-91.

Harrington, M. R. The dark dance of Ji-
gé-onh. Masterkey, 7 (1933): 76-79.

Harrington, M. R. The story bag.
Masterkey, 5 (1931/1932): 147-152, 179-
183.

Harris, Frank H. Neosho Agency 1838-1871.
Chronicles of Oklahoma, 43 (1965): 35-
57.

Harris, Frank H. Seneca Sub-Agency, 1832-
1838. Chronicles of Oklahoma, 42 (1964):
75-93.

Harris, G. H. Root foods of the Seneca
Indians. Rochester Academy of Science,
Proceedings, 1 (1891): 106-117.

Harris, G. H. The Indian bread root of
the Senecas. Waterloo, 1890. 8 p.

Harris, Kate. Parkersburg; history of
city from time of its settlement to the
present in gripping narrative from the
pen of the late Miss Kate Harris. West
Virginia History, 25 (1963/1964): 241-
264.

Harrison, Samuel A. Memoir of Lieut. Ccl.
Tench Tilghman. New York, New York
Times, 1971. 176 p.

Hatt, R. T. Installing a Cayuga chief.
Cranbrook Institute of Science,
Newsletter, 15 (1946): 65-71.

Havighurst, Walter. Alexander Spotswood; portrait of a governor. Williamsburg, Colonial Williamsburg, 1967. 9, 118 p. illus. (Williamsburg in America Series, 5)

Hawley, C. Early chapters of Cayuga history. Auburn, 1879. 106 p.

Hawley, C. Early chapters of Seneca history. Auburn, 1884.

Hawley, G. Mohawk numbers. Massachusetts Historical Society, Collections, ser. 1, 10 (1809): 137.

Hayes, Charles F., III. Prehistoric Iroquois studies in the Bristol Hills, New York: a summary. Pennsylvania Archaeologist, 33 (1963): 29-34.

Hayes, Charles F., III. The Orringh Stone Tavern and three Seneca sites of the late historic period. Rochester, 1965. 6, 82 p. illus., maps. (Rochester Museum of Arts and Sciences, Research Records, 12)

Heckewelder, J. An account of the history, manners, and customs of the Indian nations. American Philosophical Society, Historical and Literary Committee, Transactions, 1 (1819): 1-348.

Heckewelder, John G. E. History, manners, and customs of the Indian nations who once inhabited Pennsylvania and the neighboring states. New York, Arno Press, 1971. 465 p.

Heckewelder, John G. E. John Heckewelder to Peter S. Du Ponceau, Bethlehem 12th Aug 1818. Edited by Erminie Wheeler-Voegelin. Ethnohistory, 6 (1959): 70-81.

Hendry, Jean. Iroquois masks and maskmaking at Onondaga. Washington, D.C., Government Printing Office, 1964. 349-410 p. illus. (U.S., Bureau of American Ethnology, Anthropological Papers, 74. U.S., Bureau of American Ethnology, Bulletin, 191)

Hennepin, L. A new discovery of a vast country in America. Ed. by R. G. Thwaites. Chicago, 1903. 2 v.

Hennepin, L. Description de la Louisiane. Paris, 1683.

Hennepin, L. Description of Louisiana. Ed. by J. M. Shea. New York, 1880. 407 p.

Hennepin, L. Nouvelle découverte d'un tres grand pays situé dans l'Amérique. Utrecht, 1697.

Henning, C. L. Die Onondaga-Indianer. Globus, 76 (1899): 197-202, 222-226.

Henning, C. L. The origin of the confederacy of the Five Nations. American Association for the Advancement of Science, Proceedings, 47 (1898): 477-480.

Henry, Jeannette. A rebuttal to the five anthropologists on the issue of wampum return. Indian Historian, 3, no. 2 (1970): 15-17.

Henry, T. R. Wilderness messiah. New York, 1955. 285 p.

Herndon, G. Melvin. George Mathews, frontier patriot. Virginia Magazine of History and Biography, 77 (1969): 307-328.

Hertzberg, Hazel W. Teaching a pre-Columbian culture; the Iroquois. Albany, New York State Education Department, Bureau of Secondary Curriculum Development, 1966. 8, 77 p. illus.

Hertzberg, Hazel W. The great tree and the longhouse: the culture of the Iroquois. New York, Macmillan, 1966. 122 p. illus., maps.

Hewitt, J. N. B. A constitutional league of peace in the stone age of America. Smithsonian Institution, Annual Reports of the Board of Regents (1918): 527-545.

Hewitt, J. N. B. A sun-myth and the tree of language of the Iroquois. American Anthropologist, 5 (1892): 61-62.

Hewitt, J. N. B. Era of the formation of the historic League of the Iroquois. American Anthropologist, 7 (1894): 61-67.

Hewitt, J. N. B. Ethnological researches among the Iroquois and Chippewa. Smithsonian Miscellaneous Collections, 78, no. 1 (1925): 114-117.

Hewitt, J. N. B. Ethnological studies among the Iroquois Indians. Smithsonian Miscellaneous Collections, 78, no. 6 (1926): 237-247.

Hewitt, J. N. B. Ethnology of the Iroquois. Smithsonian Miscellaneous Collections, 68, no. 12 (1917): 106-107.

Hewitt, J. N. B. Field researches among the Six Nations of the Iroquois. Smithsonian Institution, Explorations and Field-Work (1930): 201-206.

Hewitt, J. N. B. Field studies among the Iroquois tribes. Smithsonian

Institution, Explorations and Field-Work (1931): 175-178.

Hewitt, J. N. B. Field-work among the Iroquois Indians. Smithsonian Institution, Explorations and Field-Work (1932): 81-84.

Hewitt, J. N. B. Field-work among the Iroquois. Smithsonian Miscellaneous Collections, 70, no. 2 (1911): 103-107.

Hewitt, J. N. B. Iroquoian cosmology. U.S. Bureau of American Ethnology, Annual Reports, 21 (1900): 127-339; 43 (1926): 449-819.

Hewitt, J. N. B. Iroquoian mythologic notes. American Anthropologist, 3 (1890): 290-291.

Hewitt, J. N. B. Iroquois game of lacrosse. American Anthropologist, 5 (1892): 189-191.

Hewitt, J. N. B. Iroquois superstitions. American Anthropologist, 3 (1890): 388-389.

Hewitt, J. N. B. Iroquois. U.S. Bureau of American Ethnology, Bulletin, 30, vol. 1 (1907): 617-620.

Hewitt, J. N. B. Legend of the founding of the Iroquois League. American Anthropologist, 5 (1892): 131-148.

Hewitt, J. N. B. Mohawk. U.S. Bureau of American Ethnology, Bulletin, 30, vol. 1 (1907): 921-926.

Hewitt, J. N. B. New fire among the Iroquois. American Anthropologist, 2 (1889): 319.

Hewitt, J. N. B. Oneida. U.S. Bureau of American Ethnology, Bulletin, 30, vol. 2 (1910): 123-127.

Hewitt, J. N. B. Onondaga. U.S. Bureau of American Ethnology, Bulletin, 30, vol. 2 (1910): 129-135.

Hewitt, J. N. B. Orenda and a definition of religion. American Anthropologist, n.s., 4 (1902): 33-46.

Hewitt, J. N. B. Orenda and a definition of religion. In Frederica de Laguna, ed. Selected Papers from the American Anthropologist 1888-1920. Evanston, Row, Peterson, 1960: 671-684.

Hewitt, J. N. B. Oyaron. U.S. Bureau of American Ethnology, Bulletin, 30, vol. 2 (1910): 178-180.

Hewitt, J. N. B. Sacred numbers among the Iroquois. American Anthropologist, 2 (1889): 165-166.

Hewitt, J. N. B. Seneca. U.S. Bureau of American Ethnology, Bulletin, 30, vol. 2 (1910): 502-508.

Hewitt, J. N. B. Sexual tradition. American Anthropologist, 2 (1889): 346.

Hewitt, J. N. B. Some esoteric aspects of the League of the Iroquois. International Congress of Americanists, Proceedings, 19 (1915): 322-326.

Hewitt, J. N. B. Status of woman in Iroquois polity before 1784. Smithsonian Institution, Annual Reports of the Board of Regents (1932): 475-488.

Hewitt, J. N. B. Teharonhiawagon. U.S. Bureau of American Ethnology, Bulletin, 30, vol. 2 (1910): 718-723.

Hewitt, J. N. B. The cosmogonic gods of the Iroquois. American Association for the Advancement of Science, Proceedings, 44 (1895): 241-250.

Hewitt, J. N. B. The Iroquoian concept of the soul. Journal of American Folklore, 8 (1895): 107-116.

Hewitt, J. N. B. The league of nations of the Iroquois Indians in Canada. Smithsonian Institution, Explorations and Field-Work (1929): 201-206.

Hewitt, J. N. B. The requickening address of the Iroquois Condolence Council. Ed. by W. N. Fenton. Washington Academy of Sciences, Journal, 34 (1944): 65-85.

Hewitt, J. N. B. The requickening address of the League of the Iroquois. In Holmes Anniversary Volume. Washington, D.C., 1916: 163-179.

Hewitt, J. N. B. White dog sacrifice. U.S. Bureau of American Ethnology, Bulletin, 30, vol. 2 (1910): 939-944.

Hewitt, J. N. B. and W. N. Fenton. Some mnemonic pictographs relating to the Iroquois Condolence Council. Washington Academy of Sciences, Journal, 35 (1945): 301-315.

Heye, G. G. Wampum collection. Indian Notes, 7 (1930): 320-324.

Hill, B. E. The Grand River Navigation Company and the Six Nations Indians. Ontario History, 63 (1971): 31-40.

Hill, Peter. A Six Nations' diary, 1891-1894. Edited by Fred Voget. Ethnohistory, 16 (1969): 345-360.

Hinsdale, W. G. Old Iroquois needles of brass. Indian Notes, 4 (1927): 174-176.

Hoffman, Bernard G. Iroquois linguistic classification from historical materials. Ethnohistory, 6 (1959): 160-185.

Holmer, N. M. Seneca. International Journal of American Linguistics, 18 (1952): 217-222, 281-291; 19 (1953): 281-289.

Holmer, N. M. The character of the Iroquoian languages. Uppsala Canadian Studies, 1 (1952): 1-39.

Holmer, N. M. The Seneca language. Uppsala Canadian Studies, 3 (1954): 1-116.

Hopkins, Vivian C. De Witt Clinton and the Iroquois. Ethnohistory, 8 (1961): 113-143, 213-241.

Horsman, Reginald. American Indian policy in the Old Northwest, 1783-1812. William and Mary Quarterly, 3d ser., 18 (1961): 35-53.

Hough, W. Games of Seneca Indians. American Anthropologist, 1 (1888): 134.

Houghton, F. The characteristics of Iroquoian village sites of western New York. American Anthropologist, n.s., 18 (1916): 508-520.

Houghton, F. The Indian inhabitants of the Niagara Frontier. Journal of American History, 16 (1922): 213-228.

Houghton, F. The Indian occupancy of the Niagara Frontier. Buffalo Society of Natural Sciences, Bulletin, 9 (1909): 263-374.

Houghton, F. The migrations of the Seneca nation. American Anthropologist, n.s., 29 (1927): 241-250.

Houghton, F. The Seneca nation from 1655 to 1687. Buffalo Society of Natural Sciences, Bulletin, 10 (1912): 363-476.

Houghton, F. The traditional origin and the naming of the Seneca nation. American Anthropologist, n.s., 24 (1922): 31-43.

Howard, Helen Addison. Hiawatha: co-founder of an Indian United Nations. Journal of the West, 10 (1971): 428-438.

Howard, James H. Cultural persistence and cultural change as reflected in Oklahoma Seneca-Cayuga ceremonialism. Plains Anthropologist, 6 (1961): 21-30.

Howard, James H. Environment and culture; the case of the Oklahoma Seneca-Cayuga. North Dakota Quarterly, 29, no. 3 (1961): 66-71; 29, no. 4 (1961): 113-122.

Howard, James H. Environment and culture: the case of the Oklahoma Seneca-Cayuga. Oklahoma Anthropological Society, Newsletter, 18, no. 6 (1970): 5-13; 18, no. 7 (1970): 5-21.

Howard, James H. Field work among the Oklahoma Seneca-Cayuga. American Philosophical Society, Yearbook (1960): 342-343.

Hrdlička, A. Ritual ablation of front teeth in Siberia and America. Smithsonian Miscellaneous Collections, 99, no. 3 (1940): 1-32.

Hubbard, J. N. An account of Sa-go-ye-wat-ha, or Red-Jacket, and his people. Albany, 1886. 356 p.

Hubbard, John N. An account of Sa-go-ye-wat-ha; or, Red Jacket and his people, 1750-1830. New York, B. Franklin, 1971. 14, 356 p. illus.

Huddleston, Eugene L. Indians and literature of the Federalist Era: the case of James Elliot. New England Quarterly, 44 (1971): 221-237.

Huden, J. C. Iroquois place names in Vermont. Vermont History, 25 (1957): 66-76.

Hudson's Bay Company. Saskatchewan journals and correspondence: Edmonton House 1795-1800; Chesterfield House 1800-1802. Edited by Alice M. Johnson. London, 1967. 102, 368, 14 p. map. (Hudson's Bay Record Society, Publications, 26)

Hughes, David R. Human remains from near Manuels River, Conception Bay, Newfoundland. In Contributions to Anthropology: Archaeology and Physical Anthropology. Ottawa, Queen's Printer, 1969: 195-207. (Canada, National Museum, Bulletin, 224)

Huguenin, C. A. The sacred stone of the Oneidas. New York Folklore Quarterly, 13 (1957): 16-22.

Hulbert, A. B. and W. N. Schwarze, eds. Zeisberger's history of Northern American Indians. Ohio State Archaeological and Historical Quarterly, 19 (1910): 1-189.

Hunt, G. T. The wars of the Iroquois. Madison, 1940. 209 p.

Hunter, W. A.   John Hays' diary and
journal of 1760. Pennsylvania
Archaeologist, 24 (1954): 63-84.

Hunter, W. A.   Refugee Fox settlements
among the Senecas. Ethnohistory, 3
(1956): 11-20.

Huot, M. C.   Some Mohawk words of
acculturation. International Journal of
American Linguistics, 14 (1948): 150-
154.

Isaacs, Hope L.   Orenda: an ethnographic
cognitive study of Seneca medicine and
politics. Dissertation Abstracts
International, 34 (1973/1974): 2428B-
2429B.   UM 73-29,103.

Jackson, E. P.   Indian occupation and use
of the Champlain lowland. Michigan
Academy of Science, Arts and Letters,
Papers, 14 (1931): 113-160.

Jackson, H.   Civilization of the Indian
natives. Philadelphia, 1830. 120 p.

Jameson, Jacob.   Answers to Governor
Cass's questions by Jacob Jameson, a
Seneca [ca. 1821-1825]. Edited by
William N. Fenton. Ethnohistory, 16
(1969): 113-139.

Jamieson, E. and P. Sandiford.   The mental
capacity of Southern Ontario Indians.
Journal of Educational Psychology, 19
(1928): 313-328, 536-551.

Jamieson, N. E.   Indian arts and crafts.
Ontario, 1942.

Jansen, J. V.   Oorlog in een primitieve
maatschappij (de Iroquois). Rotterdam,
1955. 160 p.

Jeancon, J. A. and F. H. Douglas.
Iroquois and Algonkin wampum. Denver Art
Museum, Indian Leaflet Series, 31
(1931): 1-4.

Jenness, D.   Indians of Canada. Canada,
Department of Mines, National Museum of
Canada, Bulletin, 65 (1932): 300-307.

Jenness, D.   Three Iroquois wampum
records. Canada, Department of Mines,
National Museum of Canada, Bulletin, 70
(1932): 25-29.

Jennings, Francis.   Glory, death, and
transfiguration: the Susquehannock
Indians in the seventeenth century.
American Philosophical Society,
Proceedings, 112 (1968): 15-53.

Jennings, Francis.   Goals and functions of
Puritan missions to the Indians.
Ethnohistory, 18 (1971): 197-212.

Jennings, Francis.   The Indian trade of
the Susquehanna Valley. American
Philosophical Society, Proceedings, 110
(1966): 406-424.

Jennings, Francis Paul.   Miquon's passing:
Indian-European relations in colonial
Pennsylvania, 1674-1755. Dissertation
Abstracts, 26 (1965/1966): 7281-7282.
UM 66-4621.

Joblin, E. E. M.   The education of the
Indians of western Ontario. Ontario,
College of Education, Department of
Educational Research, Bulletin, 13
(1948): 1-138.

John, Richard Johnny.   Chronicle:
interview with a Seneca songman. By
Richard Johnny John and Jerome
Rothenberg. Alcheringa, 3 (1971): 82-93.

Johnson, David.   Joseph Brant--
Thayendanagea. Indian Historian, 2,
no. 2 (1969): 35-36.

Johnson, E.   Legends, traditions, and laws
of the Iroquois. Lockport, 1881.

Johnston, Charles M.   Joseph Brant, the
Grand River lands, and the Northwest
crisis. Ontario History, 55 (1963): 267-
282.

Johnston, Charles M., ed.   The valley of
the Six Nations: a collection of
documents on the Indian lands of the
Grand River. Toronto, Champlain
Society, 1964. 96, 344 p. illus., map.
(Champlain Society, Publications,
Ontario Series, 7)

Johnston, Jean.   Ancestry and descendants
of Molly Brant. Ontario History, 63
(1971): 86-92.

Johnston, Jean.   Molly Brant, Mohawk
matron. Ontario History, 56 (1964): 105-
124.

Johnston, Richard B.   Archaeology of Rice
Lake, Ontario. Ottawa, Queen's Printer,
1968. 49 p. illus., map. (Canada,
National Museum, Anthropology Papers,
19)

Jones, Hettie.   Longhouse winter: Iroquois
transformation tales. New York, Holt,
Rinehart and Winston, 1972. illus.

Kardas, Susan.   "The people bought this
and the Clatsop became rich." A view of
nineteenth century fur trade
relationships on the Lower Columbia
between Chinookan speakers, Whites, and
Kanakas. Dissertation Abstracts
International, 32 (1971/1972): 4992B.
UM 72-7442.

Katzer, Bruce. The Caughnawage Mohawks: occupations, residence, and the maintenance of community membership. Dissertation Abstracts International, 33 (1972/1973): 1903B. UM 72-28,057.

Kawashima, Yasu. Jurisdiction of the colonial courts over the Indians in Massachusetts, 1689-1763. New England Quarterly, 42 (1969): 532-550.

Kay, Paul. Correctional notes on cross/parallel. American Anthropologist, 70 (1968): 106.

Kay, Paul. On the multiplicity of cross/parallel distinctions. American Anthropologist, 69 (1967): 83-85.

Kennedy, J. H. Jesuit and savage in New France. New Haven, 1950. 206 p.

Kenton, E., ed. The Indians of North America, Vol. 2: 62-91, 176-181, 186-189. New York, 1927.

Kenyon, Walter A. The origins of the Iroquois. Ontario History, 56 (1964): 1-4.

Keppler, J. Cayuga adoption custom. Indian Notes, 3 (1926): 73-75.

Keppler, J. Comments on certain Iroquois masks. Museum of the American Indian, Heye Foundation, Contributions, 12, no. 4 (1941): 1-40.

Keppler, J. Some Seneca stories. Indian Notes, 6 (1929): 372-376.

Keppler, J. The Peach Tomahawk Algonkian Wampum. Indian Notes, 6 (1929): 130-138.

Ketcham, Ralph L. Conscience, war, and politics in Pennsylvania, 1755-1757. William and Mary Quarterly, 3d ser., 20 (1963): 416-439.

Ketchum, William. An authentic and comprehensive history of Buffalo. St. Clair Shores, Mich., Scholarly Press, 1970. 2 v.

Kidd, K. E. Fashions in tobacco pipes among the Iroquois Indians of Ontario. Toronto, Royal Ontario Museum of Archaeology, Bulletin, 22 (1954): 15-21.

Kimm, S. C. The Iroquois. Middleburgh, 1900. 122 p.

Kirkland, Samuel. The journal of Samuel Kirkland, November 1764-February 1765. Clinton, N.Y., Alexander Hamilton Private Press, 1966. 20 p.

Knowles, F. H. S. Physical anthropology of the Roebuck Iroquois. Canada,

Department of Mines, National Museum of Canada, Bulletin, 87 (1937): 1-75.

Knowles, N. The torture of captives by the Indians of eastern North America. American Philosophical Society, Proceedings, 82 (1940): 151-225.

Knox, William. A project for imperial reform: "Hints respecting the settlement for our American provinces," 1763. Edited by Thomas C. Barrow. William and Mary Quarterly, 3d ser., 24 (1967): 108-126.

Kolinski, Mieczyslaw. An Apache Rabbit Dance song cycle as sung by the Iroquois. Ethnomusicology, 16 (1972): 415-464.

Kolinski, Mieczyslaw. Two Iroquois Rabbit Dance song cycles. Canadian Folk Music Society, Newsletter, 5 (1970): 11-38.

Kraus, B. S. Acculturation. American Antiquity, 9 (1944): 302-318.

Kurath, G. P. An analysis of the Iroquois Eagle Dance and songs. U.S. Bureau of American Ethnology, Bulletin, 156 (1953): 223-306.

Kurath, G. P. Iroquois midwinter medicine rites. International Folk Music Council, Journal, 3 (1951): 96-100.

Kurath, G. P. Local diversity in Iroquois music and dance. U.S. Bureau of American Ethnology, Bulletin, 149 (1951): 109-138.

Kurath, G. P. Matriarchal dances of the Iroquois. International Congress of Americanists, Proceedings, 29, vol. 3 (1952): 123-130.

Kurath, G. P. Onondaga ritual parodies. Journal of American Folklore, 67 (1954): 404-406.

Kurath, G. P. The Iroquois Ohgiwe death feast. Journal of American Folklore, 63 (1950): 361-362.

Kurath, G. P. The Tutelo Fourth Night Spirit Release Singing. Midwest Folklore, 4 (1955): 87-105.

Kurath, Gertrude P. Dance and song rituals of Six Nations Reserve, Ontario. Ottawa, 1968. 14, 205 p. illus. (Canada, National Museum, Bulletin, 220)

Kurath, Gertrude P. Iroquois music and dance: ceremonial arts of two Seneca longhouses. Washington, D.C., Government Printing Office, 1964. 268 p. illus. (U.S., Bureau of American Ethnology, Bulletin, 187)

Lafitau, J. F. Moeurs des sauvages
américuains. Paris, 1724. 2 v.

Laft, F. The snow-snake and the Indian
game of snow-snaking. Annual
Archaeological Report, being Part of
Appendix to the Report of the Minister
of Education, Ontario, 24 (1912): 69-71.

Lammers, Donald Milton. Self concepts of
American Indian adolescents having
segregated and desegregated elementary
backgrounds. Dissertation Abstracts
International, 31 (1970/1971): 930A. UM
70-14,723.

Landy, D. Child training in a
contemporary Iroquois tribe. Boston
University Graduate Journal, 4 (1955):
59-64.

Laning, Paul L. Colonial trail blazers
around western Lake Erie. Inland Seas,
19 (1963): 266-276.

Lankes, Frank J. Reservation supplement;
a collection of memorabilia related to
Buffalo Creek Reservation. West Seneca,
N.Y., West Seneca Historical Society,
1966. 46 p.

Lankes, Frank J. The Senecas on Buffalo
Creek Reservation. West Seneca, N.Y.,
West Seneca Historical Society, 1964.
46 p.

Laviolette, G. Indian bands of the
Province of Quebec. Eastern Canadian
Anthropological Series, 1 (1955): 90-96.

Leach, Douglas Edward. Flintlock and
tomahawk; New England in King Philip's
War. New York, W. W. Norton, 1966. 14,
304 p. illus., maps. (Norton Library,
N340)

League of Women Voters, Appleton,
Wisconsin. The Oneida Indians of
Wisconsin. Wisconsin Indians Research
Institute, Journal, 2, no. 2 (1966): 1-
20.

Leder, L. H., ed. The Livingston Indian
records. Pennsylvania History, 23
(1956): 1-240.

Lenig, Donald. The Oak Hill horizon and
its relation to the development of Five
Nations Iroquois culture. Buffalo,
1965. 5, 114 p. illus., maps. (New
York State Archaeological Association,
Researches and Transactions, 15, no. 1)

Leonard, A. L. The Presque Isle portage
and the Venango trail. Pennsylvania
Archaeologist, 15 (1945): 59-64.

Lighthall, W. D. Hochelagans and Mohawks.
Royal Society of Canada, Proceedings and

Transactions, ser. 2, 5, pt. 2 (1899):
199-211.

Lismer, M. Seneca splint basketry. Indian
Handcrafts, 4 (1941): 1-39.

Loewenthal, J. Der Heilbringer in der
irokesischen und der algonkinischen
Religion. Zeitschrift für Ethnologie, 45
(1913): 65-82.

Loewenthal, J. Irokesische
Wirtschaftsaltertümer. Zeitschrift für
Ethnologie, 52/53 (1920/1921): 171-233.

Long, J. K. Voyages and travels of an
Indian interpreter and trader. London,
1791. 295 p.

Loskiel, G. H. Geschichte der Mission der
evangelischen Brüder unter den Indianern
in Nordamerika. Barby, 1789.

Loskiel, G. H. History of the Mission of
the United Brethren among the Indians of
North America. London, 1794. 3 pts.

Lounsbury, F. G. Oneida verb morphology.
Yale University Publications in
Anthropology, 48, (1953): 1-111.

Lounsbury, F. G. Stray number systems
among certain Indian tribes. American
Anthropologist, n.s., 48 (1946): 672-
675.

Lounsbury, Floyd G. Analyse structurale
des termes de parenté. Translated by
Delphine Perret. Langages, 1 (1966): 75-
99.

Lounsbury, Floyd G. The structural
analysis of kinship semantics. In Paul
Bohannan and John Middleton, eds.
Kinship and Social Organization. Garden
City, Natural History Press, 1968: 125-
148.

Lounsbury, Floyd G. The structural
analysis of kinship semantics. In
International Congress of Linguists,
9th. 1962, Cambridge, Mass. Proceedings.
The Hague, Mouton, 1964: 1073-1093.
(Janua Linguarum, Series Maior, 12)

Lucy, C. L. Notes on a Seneca mask.
Primitive Man, 24 (1951): 35-36.

Lydekker, J. W. The faithful Mohawks.
New York, 1938. 206 p.

Lydekker, John W. The faithful Mohawks.
Port Washington, I. J. Friedman, 1968.
12, 206 p. illus.

Lyford, C. A. Iroquois crafts. Indian
Handcrafts, 6 (1943): 1-97.

MacDonald, Curtis C. Sardis Birchard--
Indian trader. Northwest Ohio Quarterly,
32 (1959/1960): 15-24.

MacGregor, James G. Who was Yellowhead?
Alberta Historical Review, 17, no. 4
(1969): 12-13.

Mackenzie, J. B. The Six-Nations Indians
in Canada. Toronto, 1896. 151 p.

Macleod, Malcolm. Fortress Ontario or
Forlorn Hope? Simcoe and the defence of
Upper Canada. Canadian Historical
Review, 53 (1972): 149-178.

MacLeod, W. C. Trade restrictions in
early society. American Anthropologist,
n.s., 29 (1927): 271-278.

MacNeish, R. S. Iroquois pottery types.
National Museum of Canada, Bulletin, 124
(1952): 1-166.

Mahr, August C. Delaware terms for plants
and animals in the eastern Ohio country:
a study in semantics. Anthropological
Linguistics, 4, no. 5 (1962): 1-48.

Manley, H. S. Buying buffalo from the
Indians. New York History, 28 (1947):
313-329.

Marcoux, J. Catechism in the Mohawk
language. Tiohtiake, 1904. 50 p.

Marcoux, J. Kaiatonsera
ionterennaientakwa ne teieiasontha onkwe
onwe. Caughnawaga, P.Q., 1903. 568 p.

Martin, F. Hurons et Iroquois. Paris,
1877.

Martin, Helen M. How people came to
Mackinac. Michigan History, 44 (1960):
401-404.

Marye, W. B. Warriors' paths.
Pennsylvania Archaeologist, 13 (1943):
4-26; 14 (1944): 4-22.

Mathews, Edward. An abolitionist in
territorial Wisconsin: the journal of
Reverend Edward Mathews. Edited by
William Converse Haygood. Wisconsin
Magazine of History, 52 (1968/1969): 3-
18, 117-131, 248-262, 330-343.

Mathur, Mary E. Fleming. Death, burial,
mourning, among Western Iroquois. Indian
Historian, 4, no. 3 (1971): 37-40, 43.

Mathur, Mary E. Fleming. The Iroquois in
ethnography . . . a time-space concept.
Indian Historian, 2, no. 3 (1969): 12-
18.

Mathur, Mary E. Fleming. The Jay Treaty
and confrontation at St. Regis boundary.

Indian Historian, 3, no. 1 (1970): 37-
40.

Mathur, Mary E. Fleming. The tale of the
lazy Indian. Indian Historian, 3, no. 3
(1970): 14-18.

Mathur, Mary E. Fleming. Tiyanoga of the
Mohawks: father of the United States.
Indian Historian, 3, no. 2 (1970): 59-
62, 66.

Mathur, Mary E. Fleming. Who cares that a
women's work is never done? . . . Indian
Historian, 4, no. 2 (1971): 11-16.

Mathur, Mary Elaine Fleming. The Iroquois
in time and space: a Native American
nationalistic movement. Dissertation
Abstracts International, 32 (1971/1972):
3129B-3130B. UM 71-25,203.

Mayer, J. R. Flintlocks of the Iroquois,
1620-1687. Rochester Museum of Science
and Arts, Records of Research, 6 (1943):
1-59.

McIlwraith, T. F. The feast of the dead.
Anthropologica, 6 (1958): 83-86.

McKelvey, B. The Seneca "time of
trouble". Rochester History, 13, no. 3
(1951): 1-24.

Megapolensis, J. Short sketch of the
Mohawk Indians in New Netherlands. New
York Historical Society, Collections,
ser. 2, 3 (1857): 137-160.

Merrill, A. Have they kept that pledge?
American Indian, 1, no. 1 (1943): 4-14.

Miller, Mary Emily. Port town on the
starboard, a history of Frederica,
Delaware. Delaware History, 14, no. 2
(1970): 111-134.

Mitchell, J. The Mohawks in high steel.
New Yorker, 25, no. 30 (1949): 38-52.

Moeser, Anthony G. The Iroquois water
drum. American Indian Tradition, 9
(1963/1964): 24-26.

Mohawk, John. An Iroquois story.
Introduction by John Trimbur and Dell
Martin. Red Buffalo, 2-3 (1972): 205-
216.

Mohawk, John. Our keepers' brother--the
debate continues. Red Buffalo, 1 (1971):
49-59.

Montgomery, Malcolm. Historiography of
the Iroquois Indians 1925-1963. Ontario
History, 55 (1963): 247-257.

Montgomery, Malcolm. The legal status of the Six Nations Indians in Canada. Ontario History, 55 (1963): 93-105.

Montgomery, Malcolm. The Six Nations Indians and the Macdonald Franchise. Ontario History, 57 (1965): 13-25.

Mooney, J. Cherokee and Iroquois parallels. Journal of American Folklore, 2 (1889): 67.

Mooney, J. and J. N. B. Hewitt. Cayuga. U.S. Bureau of American Ethnology, Bulletin, 30, vol. 1 (1907): 223-224.

Morgan, L. H. Ancient society, 62-150. New York, 1877.

Morgan, L. H. Communications. University of the State of New York, Annual Report of the Regents, 2 (1849): 81-91.

Morgan, L. H. Government and institutions of the Iroquois. Ed. by A. C. Parker. New York State Archaeological Association, Researches and Transactions, 7 (1928): 5-30.

Morgan, L. H. Houses and house-life of the American aborigines. Contributions to North American Ethnology, 4 (1881): 1-281.

Morgan, L. H. Laws of descent of the Iroquois. American Association for the Advancement of Science, Proceedings, 11, no. 2 (1857): 132-148.

*Morgan, L. H. League of the Ho-Dé-No-Sau-Nee or Iroquois. Ed. by H. M. Lloyd. New York, 1901. 2 v.

Morgan, L. H. Letters on the Iroquois, by Skenandoah. American Review, 5 (1847): 177-190, 242-257, 447-461; 6 (1847): 477-490, 626-633.

Morgan, L. H. Report on the fabrics, inventions, implements and utensils of the Iroquois. University of the State of New York, Annual Report of the Regents, 5 (1851): 67-117.

Morgan, L. H. Report to the Regents of the University upon the articles furnished the Indian Collection. University of the State of New York, Annual Report of the Regents, 3 (1850): 65-97.

Morgan, L. H. Systems of consanguinity and affinity. Smithsonian Contributions to Knowledge, 17 (1871): 150-169, 291-382, 511-514.

Morgan, L. H. The fabrics of the Iroquois. American Quarterly Register and Magazine, 4 (1850): 319-343.

*Morgan, Lewis H. League of the Ho-dé-no-sau-nee or Iroquois. Edited by Herbert M. Lloyd. New York, B. Franklin, 1966. 2 v. illus., maps.

*Morgan, Lewis H. League of the Iroquois. New York, Corinth Books, 1962. 477 p. illus.

Morgan, Lewis H. The Iroquois gens. In Paul Bohannan and John Middleton, eds. Kinship and Social Organization. Garden City, Natural History Press, 1968: 161-169.

Morgan, Lewis Henry. Iroquois governance. In Walter R. Goldschmidt, ed. Exploring the Ways of Mankind. New York, Holt, 1960: 381-390.

Mulkearn, L. Half King, Seneca diplomat of the Ohio Valley. Western Pennsylvania Historical Magazine, 37 (1954): 65-81.

Murdock, G. P. Our primitive contemporaries, 291-323. New York, 1934.

Murray, H. Historical and descriptive account of British America, Vol. 1: 73-127. Edinburgh, 1840.

Myrtle, M. The Iroquois. New York, 1855. 317 p.

Nammack, Georgiana C. Fraud, politics, and the dispossession of the Indians; the Iroquois land frontier in the colonial period. Norman, University of Oklahoma Press, 1969. 19, 128 p. maps.

Naroll, Raoul. The causes of the Fourth Iroquois War. Ethnohistory, 16 (1969): 51-81.

Newman, M. T. The physique of the Seneca Indians of western New York. Washington Academy of Sciences, Journal, 47 (1957): 357-362.

Nieberding, V. Seneca-Cayuga green corn feast. Chronicles of Oklahoma, 34 (1956): 231-234.

Nieberding, Velma. The Nez Perce in the Quapaw Agency 1878-1879. Chronicles of Oklahoma, 44 (1966): 22-30.

*Noon, J. A. Law and government of the Grand River Iroquois. Viking Fund Publications in Anthropology, 12 (1949): 1-186.

Norton, John. The journal of Major John Norton, 1816. Edited by Carl F. Klinck and James J. Talman. Toronto, 1970. 124, 391, 19 p. maps. (Champlain Society, Pulications, 46)

Norton, Thomas Elliot. The fur trade in colonial New York, 1636-1776. Dissertation Abstracts International, 33 (1972/1973): 4287A. UM 73-2479.

O'Callaghan, E. B., ed. Documentary history of the State of New York. Albany, 1849-1856. 11 v.

Oneida Industrial Planning Committee. Provisional Overall Economic Development Plan for the Oneida Indian Reservation, Oneida, Wisconsin. Wisconsin Indians Research Institute, Journal, 2, no. 2 (1966): 21-34.

Oneida Tribe of Indians of Wisconsin. Revised constitution and by-laws of the Oneida Tribe of Indians of Wisconsin. Wisconsin Indians Research Institute, Journal, 2, no. 2 (1966): 34-40.

Onion, Daniel K. Corn in the culture of the Mohawk Iroquois. Economic Botany, 18 (1964): 60-66.

Orchard, W. C. Mohawk burden-straps. Indian Notes, 6 (1929): 351-359.

Orchard, W. C. Porcupine-quill ornamentation. Indian Notes, 3 (1926): 59-68.

O'Rielly, Henry. Notices of Sullivan's Campaign. Port Washington, Kennikat Press, 1970. 191 p.

Oronhyatekha. The Mohawk language. Canadian Journal, n.s., 10 (1865): 182-194; 15 (1876): 1-12.

Orr, R. B. The Iroquois in Canada. Annual Archaeological Report, being Part of Appendix to the Report of the Minister of Education, Ontario, 31 (1919): 9-55.

Owl, W. D. The Iroquois temperance league. Narragansett Dawn, 1 (1935): 183-185.

Painter, L. K. Jacob Taylor, Quaker missionary statesman. Niagara Frontier, 6, no. 2 (1959): 33-40.

Palmer, R. A. The North American Indians. Smithsonian Scientific Series, 4 (1929): 70-105.

Parker, A. C. Aboriginal cultures and chronology of the Genesee country. Rochester Academy of Science, Proceedings, 6 (1929): 243-283.

Parker, A. C. Aboriginal inhabitants. In L. R. Doty, ed. History of the Genesee Country. Vol. 1. Chicago, 1925: 145-165.

Parker, A. C. Additional notes on Iroquois silversmithing. American Anthropologist, n.s., 13 (1911): 283-293.

Parker, A. C. An analytical history of the Seneca Indians. New York State Archaeological Association, Researches and Transactions, 6 (1926): 11-158.

Parker, A. C. An early Colonial Seneca site. New York State Archaeological Association, Researches and Transactions, 1, no. 2 (1919): 3-36.

Parker, A. C. Certain Iroquois tree myths and symbols. American Anthropologist, n.s., 14 (1912): 608-620.

Parker, A. C. Champlain's assault on the fortified town of the Oneidas. New York State Museum Bulletin, 207/208 (1918): 165-173.

Parker, A. C. Fundamental factors in Seneca folk lore. New York State Museum Bulletin, 253 (1924): 49-66.

Parker, A. C. Indian medicine and medicine men. Annual Archaeological Report, being Part of Appendix to the Report of the Minister of Education, Ontario (1928): 9-17.

Parker, A. C. Iroquois sun myths. Journal of American Folklore, 23 (1910): 473-478.

Parker, A. C. Iroquois uses of maize and other food plants. New York State Museum Bulletin, 144 (1910): 5-119.

Parker, A. C. League of the Iroquois. Home Geographic Monthly, 2, no. 2 (1932): 7-12.

Parker, A. C. Rumbling Wings and other Indian tales. Garden City, 1928. 279 p.

Parker, A. C. Secret medicine societies of the Seneca. American Anthropologist, n.s., 11 (1909): 161-185.

Parker, A. C. Seneca myths and folk-tales. Buffalo Historical Society Publications, 27 (1923): 1-465.

Parker, A. C. Skunny Wundy and other Indian tales. New York, 1926. 262 p.

Parker, A. C. Snow-snake as played by the Seneca-Iroquois. American Anthropologist, n.s., 11 (1909): 250-256.

Parker, A. C. The amazing Iroquois. Art and Archaeology, 23 (1927): 99-108.

Parker, A. C. The archeological history of New York. New York State Museum Bulletin, 235/238 (1920): 5-743.

Parker, A. C. The civilization of the Red Man. In A. C. Flick, ed. History of the State of New York. Vol. 1. New York, 1933: 99-131.

Parker, A. C. The code of Handsome Lake, the Seneca prophet. New York State Museum Bulletin, 163 (1912): 5-148.

Parker, A. C. The constitution of the Five Nations: a reply. American Anthropologist, n.s., 20 (1918): 120-124.

Parker, A. C. The constitution of the Five Nations. New York State Museum Bulletin, 184 (1916): 7-158.

Parker, A. C. The influence of the Iroquois on the history and archaeology of the Wyoming Valley. Wyoming Historical and Geological Society, Proceedings and Collections, 11 (1910): 65-102.

Parker, A. C. The Iroquois. In A. C. Flick, ed. History of the State of New York. Vol. 1. New York, 1933: 67-97.

Parker, A. C. The Iroquois wampums. New York State Historical Association, Proceedings, 8 (1909): 205-208.

Parker, A. C. The origin of the Iroquois as suggested by their archeology. American Anthropologist, n.s., 18 (1916): 479-507.

Parker, A. C. The peace policy of the Iroquois. Southern Workman, 40 (1911): 691-699.

Parker, A. C. The rise of the Seneca nation. In L. R. Doty, ed. History of the Genesee Country. Vol. 1. Chicago, 1925: 167-189.

Parker, A. C. The Senecas in their own home land. In L. R. Doty, ed. History of the Genesee Country. Vol. 1. Chicago, 1925: 192-222.

Parker, A. C. The status of New York Indians. New York State Museum Bulletin, 253 (1924): 67-82.

Parker, Arthur C. Parker on the Iroquois. Edited by William N. Fenton. Syracuse, Syracuse University Press, 1968. [478 p.] illus., maps.

Parker, Arthur C. The origin of Iroquois silversmithing. American Anthropologist, n.s., 12 (1910): 349-357.

Parker, Arthur Caswell. The history of the Seneca Indians. Port Washington, I. J. Friedman, 1967. 162 p. illus., maps.

Parker, John. The fur trader and the emerging geography of North America. Museum of the Fur Trade Quarterly, 2, no. 3 (1966): 6-10; 2, no. 4 (1966): 7-11.

Parkman, F. The Jesuits in North America. Boston, 1867. 463 p.

Parkman, Francis. The French, the English and the Indians. In John J. TePaske, ed. Three American Empires. New York, Harper and Row, 1967: 127-135.

Parsons, Lee A. A Fiji-Iroquois war club: an unusual case of diffusion. Expedition, 4, no. 1 (1961): 12-13.

Pastore, Ralph Thomas. The Board of Commissioners for Indian Affairs in the Northern Department and the Iroquois Indians, 1775-1778. Dissertation Abstracts International, 33 (1972/1973): 1656A-1657A. UM 72-26,816.

Peck, M. A. Caughnawaga. Canadian Geographical Journal, 10 (1935): 92-100.

Peck, W. F. Semi-centennial history of the City of Rochester. Syracuse, 1884. 736 p.

Peckham, Howard H. Speculations on the colonial wars. William and Mary Quarterly, 3d ser., 17 (1960): 463-472.

Pendergast, James F. Nine small sites on Lake St. Francis representing an early Iroquois horizon in the upper St. Lawrence River valley. Anthropologica, n.s., 6 (1964): 183-221.

Pendergast, James F. The Berry site. In Contributions to Anthropology V: Archaeology and Physical Anthropology. Ottawa, Queen's Printer, 1967: 26-53. (Canada, National Museum, Bulletin, 206)

Pendergast, James F. The Summerstown Station Site. Ottawa, Queen's Printer, 1968. 47 p. illus. (Canada, National Museum, Anthropological Papers, 18)

Pendergast, James F. The Waupoos Site--an Iroquois component in Prince Edward County, Ontario. Pennsylvania Archaeologist, 34, no. 2 (1964): 69-89.

Pendergast, James F. Three prehistoric Iroquois components in eastern Ontario: the Salem, Grays Creek, and Beckstead Sites. Ottawa, 1966. 18, 247 p. illus., map. (Canada, National Museum, Bulletin, 208)

Perrot, N. Memoir on the manners, customs, and religion of the savages of North America. In E. H. Blair, ed. The Indian Tribes of the Upper Mississippi Valley. Vol. 1. Cleveland, 1911: 25-272.

Perrot, N. Mémoire sur les moeurs, coustumes et religion des sauvages de l'Amérique septentrionale. Paris, 1864. 341 p.

Peterson, G. W. An Iroquoian story of the beginning of the world. Torrington, 1937. 69 p.

Phillips, Edward Hake. Timothy Pickering at his best: Indian Commissioner, 1790-1794. Essex Institute Historical Collections, 102 (1966): 163-201.

Postal, Paul M. A note on 'understood transitively'. International Journal of American Linguistics, 32 (1966): 90-93.

Postal, Paul M. Boas and the development of phonology: comments based on Iroquoian. International Journal of American Linguistics, 30 (1964): 269-280.

Postal, Paul M. Mohawk prefix generation. In International Congress of Linguists, 9th. 1962, Cambridge, Mass. Proceedings. The Hague, Mouton, 1964: 346-365. (Janua Linguarum, Series Maior, 12)

Postal, Paul M. Mohawk vowel doubling. International Journal of American Linguistics, 35 (1969): 291-298.

Postal, Paul M. Some syntactic rules in Mohawk. Dissertation Abstracts, 25 (1964/1965): 4349-4350. UM 65-1967.

Postal, Susan Koessler. Hoax nativism at Caughnawaga: a control case for the theory of revitalization. Ethnology, 4 (1965): 266-281.

Powers, M. El primer ensayo de paz en América. América Indígena, 6 (1946): 105-125.

Prahl, Earl J. Preliminary archaeological investigations in the Maumee Valley. By Earl J. Prahl and M. Joseph Becker. Northwest Ohio Quarterly, 39, no. 1 (1966/1967): 40-50.

Pratt, Peter P. A criticism of MacNeish's Iroquois pottery types. Pennsylvania Archaeologist, 30 (1960): 106-110.

Pratt, Peter P. A heavily stockaded late prehistoric Oneida Iroquois settlement. Pennsylvania Archaeologist, 33 (1963): 56-92.

Pratt, Peter P. The Bigford Site: late prehistoric Oneida. Pennsylvania Archaeologist, 31 (1961): 46-59.

Pratt, Peter Paul. Archaeology of the Oneida Iroquois as related to early acculturation and to the location of the Champlain-Iroquois battle of 1615. Dissertation Abstracts, 27 (1966/1967): 2232B. UM 66-14,573.

Preston, W. D. and C. F. Voegelin. Seneca I. International Journal of American Linguistics, 15 (1949): 23-44.

Prucha, Francis Paul. Early Indian peace medals. Wisconsin Magazine of History, 45 (1961): 279-289.

Putt, Raymond V. The role of the hereditary chiefs in contemporary Iroquois society: a nativistic movement on the Six Nations Reserve. Na'páo, 3, no. 1 (1971): 11-20.

Quain, B. H. The Iroquois. In M. Mead, ed. Cooperation and Competition among Primitive Peoples. New York, 1937: 240-281.

Radisson, Pierre Esprit. The explorations of Pierre Esprit Radisson. Edited by Arthur T. Adams. Minneapolis, Ross and Haines, 1961. 84, 258 p. illus.

Radisson, Pierre Esprit. Voyages of Peter Esprit Radisson. Edited by Gideon D. Scull. New York, Burt Franklin, 1971. 6, 385 p.

Randle, M. C. Educational problems of Canadian Indians. Food for Thought, 13, no. 6 (1953): 10-14.

Randle, M. C. Iroquois women, then and now. U.S. Bureau of American Ethnology, Bulletin, 149 (1951): 167-180.

Randle, M. C. Psychological types from Iroquois folktales. Journal of American Folklore, 65 (1952): 13-21.

Randle, M. C. The Waugh Collection of Iroquois folktales. American Philosophical Society, Proceedings, 97 (1953): 611-633.

Rarihokwats. An interview with Rarihokwats. Red Buffalo, 1 (1971): 23-33.

Reaman, George Elmore. The trail of the Iroquois Indians. London, Muller, 1967. 19, 138 p. illus., maps.

Records, Spencer. Spencer Records' memoir of the Ohio Valley frontier, 1766-1795. Edited by Donald F. Carmony. Indiana Magazine of History, 55 (1959): 323-377.

Red Jacket. "You have got our country
. . . you want to force your religion
upon us". In Charles Hurd, ed. A
Treasury of Great American Speeches.
New York, Hawthorn Books, 1959: 57-59.

Reid, W. M. Calumet. Records of the Past,
8 (1909): 97-101.

Reid, W. M. Mohawk pottery. Records of
the Past, 3 (1904): 184-188.

Rhoades, G. E. Prehistoric Iroquois
culture. Annual Archaeological Report,
being Part of Appendix to the Report of
the Minister of Education, Ontario
(1923): 89-95.

Ricciardelli, Alex F. The adoption of
White agriculture by the Oneida Indians.
In Deward E. Walker, Jr., ed. The
Emergent Native Americans. Boston,
Little, Brown, 1972: 327-337.

Ricciardelli, Alex F. The adoption of
White agriculture by the Oneida Indians.
Ethnohistory, 10 (1963): 309-328.

Ricciardelli, Alex Frank. Factionalism at
Oneida, an Iroquois Indian community.
Dissertation Abstracts, 22 (1961/1962):
970. UM 61-3546.

Ricciardelli, Catherine Hinckle. Kinship
systems of the Oneida Indians.
Dissertation Abstracts, 27 (1966/1967):
1358B. UM 66-10,663.

Rice, Otis. The French and Indian War in
West Virginia. West Virginia History, 24
(1962/1963): 134-146.

Richards, C. E. Matriarchy or mistake:
the role of Iroquois women through time.
In V. F. Ray, ed. Cultural Stability and
Cultural Change. Seattle, 1957: 36-45.

Ridley, F. Cultural contacts of Iroquian
and Plains. Pennsylvania Archaeologist,
27 (1957): 33-38.

Ridley, Frank. Archaeology of Lake
Abitibi, Ontario-Québec. Anthropological
Journal of Canada, 4, no. 2 (1966): 2-
50.

Ridley, Frank. The Ontario Iroquoian
controversy. Ontario History, 55 (1963):
48-59.

Rife, David C. Dermatoglyphics of
Cherokee and Mohawk Indians. Human
Biology, 44 (1972): 81-85.

Rioux, M. Les Hurons-Iroquois
pratiquaient-ils le totemisme? Royal
Society of Canada, Proceedings and
Transactions, ser. 3, 39, pt. 1 (1945):
173-176.

Rioux, M. Notes autobiographiques d'un
Iroquois Cayuga. Anthropologica, 1
(1955): 18-36.

Rioux, M. Persistence of a Tutelo
cultural trait among the contemporary
Cayuga. National Museum of Canada,
Bulletin, 123 (1951): 72-74.

Rioux, M. Relations between religion and
government among the Longhouse Iroquois
of Grand River, Ontario. National Museum
of Canada, Bulletin, 126 (1952): 94-98.

Rioux, M. Some medical beliefs and
practices of the contemporary Iroquois
Longhouse of the Six Nations Reserve.
Washington Academy of Sciences, Journal,
41 (1951): 152-158.

Ritchie, W. A. Algonkin-Iroquois contacts
in New York State. Archaeological
Society of Delaware, Bulletin, 1, no. 2
(1934): 2-6.

Ritchie, W. A. Dutch Hollow. New York
State Archaeological Federation,
Research Records, 13, no. 1 (1954): 1-
102.

Ritchie, W. A. Dutch Hollow. Rochester
Museum of Science and Arts, Records of
Research, 10 (1954): 1-102.

Ritchie, W. A. Indian history of New York
State. Part II--The Iroquoian tribes. 2d
ed. New York, State Museum, Educational
Leaflet Series, 7 (1953): 1-20.

Ritzenthaler, R. and M. Sellars. Indians
in an urban situation. Wisconsin
Archeologist, 36 (1955): 147-161.

Ritzenthaler, R. E. The Oneida Indians of
Wisconsin. Public Museum of the City of
Milwaukee, Bulletin, 19 (1950): 1-52.

Ritzenthaler, R. E. The Wisconsin Oneida
wake. Wisconsin Archeologist, n.s., 22
(1941): 1-2.

Ritzenthaler, Robert E. Iroquois falseface masks. Milwaukee, 1969. 71 p.
illus. (Milwaukee Public Museum,
Publications in Primitive Art, 3)

Rockey, Randall Earl. Contrastive
analysis of the language structures of
three ethnic groups of children enrolled
in Head Start programs. Dissertation
Abstracts International, 31 (1970/1971):
6585A. UM 71-13,817.

Rogers, Edward S. False Face Society of
the Iroquois. Toronto, Royal Ontario
Museum, 1966. 16 p. illus.

Rogers, Edward S. The Iroquois. Beaver,
301, no. 4 (1970/1971): 46-49.

Rothenberg, Jerome. From Shaking the Pumpkin: songs and other circumstances of the society of the mystic animals: the opening songs. Alcheringa, 1 (1970): 8-13.

Rousseau, J. J. La crainte des Iroquois. Revue d'Histoire de l'Amérique Française, 2 (1948): 13-26.

Rousseau, J. J. L'aurore de l'agriculture. Actualité Économique, 2 (1944): 344-361.

Rousseau, J. J. and M. Raymond. Le folklore botanique de Caughnawaga. Montréal, Université, Institut Botanique, Contributions, 55 (1945): 7-74.

Rousseau, M. La crainte de l'Iroquois au Lac Mistassini. Association Canadienne-Française pour l'Avancement des Sciences, Annales, 13 (1947): 119-120.

Rousseau, M. A. and J. Rousseau. La crainte des Iroquois chez les Mistassini. Revue d'Histoire de l'Amérique Française, 2 (1948): 13-26.

Rousseau, P. Les Hochelagas. International Congress of Americanists, Proceedings, 15 (1906): 279-297.

Ruttenber, E. M. History of the Indian tribes of Hudson's River. Albany, 1872. 415 p.

Ruttenber, E. M. Indian geographical names in the valley of Hudson's River, the valley of the Mohawk, and on the Delaware. New York State Historical Association, Proceedings, 6 (1906): 1-241.

Ruttenber, Edward M. History of the Indian tribes of Hudson's River. Port Washington, Kennikat Press, 1971. 5, 415 p. illus.

Sanborn, J. W. Day-yu-da-gont. Friendship, 1904. 18 p.

Sanborn, J. W. Hymnal in the Seneca language. Batavia, 1884. 48 p.

Sanborn, J. W. Indian stories. Friendship, 1915. 38 p.

Sanborn, J. W. Legends, customs, and social life of the Seneca Indians. Gowanda, 1878.

Schellbach, L. An historic Iroquois warclub. Indian Notes, 5 (1928): 157-166.

Schlesier, Karl-Heinz. Die Eigentumsrechte der Irokesen. Anthropos, 56 (1961): 158-178.

Schoolcraft, H. R. Notes on the Iroquois. New York, 1846. 498 p.

Schumacher, Irene. Gesellschaftsstruktur und Rolle der Frau; das Beispiel der Irokesen. Berlin, Duncker und Humblot, 1972. 149 p.

Scott, D. C. Traditional history of the Confederacy of the Six Nations. Royal Society of Canada, Proceedings and Transactions, ser. 3, 5, no. 2 (1912): 195-246.

Scull, G. D., ed. Voyages of Peter Esprit Radisson. Boston, 1885.

Seaver, J. E. A narrative of the life of Mary Jemison. 4th ed. New York, 1856.

Seaver, James E. A narrative of the life of Mrs. Mary Jemison. Ann Arbor, Allegany Press, 1967. 189 p.

Seaver, James E. A narrative of the life of Mrs. Mary Jemison. New York, Corinth Books, 1961. 190 p. illus.

Selden, Sherman Ward. The legend, myth and code of Deganaweda and their significance to Iroquois cultural history. Dissertation Abstracts, 28 (1967/1968): 165A. UM 66-14,884.

Seneca Nation Educational Foundation. To our Indian youth--generation with a future. Salamanca, N.Y., 1968. 75 p. ERIC ED035474.

Setzler, F. M. Samuel Crowell's account of a Seneca dog sacrifice. Northwest Ohio Quarterly, 16 (1944): 144-146.

Shea, J. G., ed. A French-Onondaga dictionary. New York, 1860. 103 p.

Shimony, Annemarie A. Conservatism among the Iroquois at the Six Nations Reserve. New Haven, Yale University, Department of Anthropology, 1961. 302 p. illus., maps. (Yale University Publications in Anthropology, 65)

Shipman, C. M. Iroquois village site at Fairport, Ohio. National Archaeological News, 1, no. 11 (1937): 2-4.

Silvy, A. Relation par lettres de l'Amérique septentrionale, 182-196. Ed. by C. de. Rochemonteix. Paris, 1904.

Sipa, C. H. The principal Indian towns in western Pennsylvania. Western Pennsylvania Historical Magazine, 13 (1930): 104-122.

Skinner, A.   An antique tobacco-pouch of
the Iroquois. Indian Notes and
Monographs, 2 (1920): 103-108.

Skinner, A.   An Iroquois antler figurine.
Indian Notes and Monographs, 2 (1920):
109-114.

Skinner, A.   An old Seneca warclub. Indian
Notes, 3 (1926): 45-47.

Skinner, A.   Iroquois falseface pipe.
Indian Notes, 2 (1925): 321-322.

Skinner, A.   Notes on Iroquois archeology.
Indian Notes and Monographs, n.s., 18
(1921): 5-216.

Skinner, A.   Seneca charm canoes. Indian
Notes, 3 (1926): 36-38.

Skinner, A.   Some Seneca masks and their
uses. Indian Notes, 2 (1925): 191-207.

Skinner, A.   Some Seneca tobacco customs.
Indian Notes, 2 (1925): 127-130.

Skinner, A.   The Iroquois Indians of
western New York. Southern Workman, 38
(1909): 206-211.

Smith, DeC.   Additional notes on Onondaga
witchcraft and Hon do'-i. Journal of
American Folklore, 2 (1889): 277-281.

Smith, DeC.   Indian experiences.
Caldwell, 1943.   387 p.

Smith, DeC.   Onondaga superstitions.
Journal of American Folklore, 2 (1889):
282-283.

Smith, DeC.   Witchcraft and demonism of
the modern Iroquois. Journal of American
Folklore, 1 (1888): 184-194.

Smith, E. A.   Comparative differences in
the Iroquois group of dialects. American
Association for the Advancement of
Science, Proceedings, 30 (1881): 315-
319.

Smith, E. A.   Disputed points concerning
Iroquois pronouns. American Association
for the Advancement of Science,
Proceedings, 33 (1884): 606-609.

Smith, E. A.   Life among the Mohawks.
American Association for the Advancement
of Science, Proceedings, 32 (1883): 398-
399.

Smith, E. A.   Myths of the Iroquois.
American Antiquarian and Oriental
Journal, 4 (1882): 31-39.

Smith, E. A.   Myths of the Iroquois. U.S.
Bureau of American Ethnology, Annual
Reports, 2 (1881): 47-116.

Smith, E. A.   Studies in the Iroquois
concerning the verb to be and its
substitutes. American Association for
the Advancement of Science, Proceedings,
32 (1883): 399-402.

Smith, E. A.   The customs and the language
of the Iroquois. Royal Anthropological
Institute of Great Britain and Ireland,
Journal, 14 (1884): 244-253.

Smith, E. A.   The significance of flora to
the Iroquois. American Association for
the Advancement of Science, Proceedings,
34 (1885): 404-411.

Smith, J.   Life and travels.
Philadelphia, 1831.   162 p.

Smith, James.   An account of the
remarkable occurrences in the life and
travels of Col. James Smith, during his
captivity with the Indians in the years
1755, '56, '57, '58, and '59, with an
appendix of illustrative notes. Edited
by Wm. N. Darlington.   Cincinnati, R.
Clarke, 1870.   12, 190 p.   (Ohio Valley
Historical Series, 5)

Snyderman, G. S.   Behind the tree of
peace. Pennsylvania Archaeologist, 18
(1948): 2-93.

Snyderman, G. S.   Concepts of land
ownership among the Iroquois and their
neighbors. U.S. Bureau of American
Ethnology, Bulletin, 149 (1951): 13-34.

Snyderman, G. S.   Halliday Jackson's
journal of a visit paid to the Indians
of New York. American Philosophical
Society, Proceedings, 101 (1957): 565-
588.

Snyderman, G. S.   Some ideological aspects
of present day Seneca folklore.
Primitive Man, 24 (1951): 37-46.

Snyderman, G. S.   The functions of wampum.
American Philosophical Society,
Proceedings, 98 (1954): 469-494.

Snyderman, George S.   The function of
wampum in Iroquois religion. American
Philosophical Society, Proceedings, 105
(1961): 571-608.

Snyderman, George S.   The manuscript
collections of the Philadelphia yearly
meeting of Friends pertaining to the
American Indian. American Philosophical
Society, Proceedings, 102 (1958): 613-
620.

Society of Friends.   The case of the
Seneca Indians.   Philadelphia, 1840.

Sohrweide, Anton W.   Two prehistoric
Onondaga pots from eastern New York. By

Anton W. Sohrweide and Ray Fadden. Pennsylvania Archaeologist, 33 (1963): 51-55.

Sosin, Jack M. The use of Indians in the War of the American Revolution: a re-assessment of responsibility. Canadian Historical Review, 46 (1965): 101-121.

Speck, F. G. Algonkian influence upon Iroquois social organization. American Anthropologist, n.s., 25 (1923): 217-227.

Speck, F. G. How the Dew Eagle Society of the Allegany Seneca cured Gahéhdagowa. Primitive Man, 22 (1949): 39-59.

Speck, F. G. Indian apostates. General Magazine and Historical Chronicle, University of Pennsylvania, 44 (1941): 24-27.

Speck, F. G. Midwinter rites of the Cayuga long house. Philadelphia, 1949. 192 p.

Speck, F. G. Northern elements in Iroquois and New England art. Indian Notes, 2 (1925): 1-12.

Speck, F. G. The Cayuga Indian snake game. General Magazine and Historical Chronicle, University of Pennsylvania, 43 (1941): 416-419.

Speck, F. G. The Iroquois. Cranbrook Institute of Science, Newsletter, 15 (1945): 33-36.

*Speck, F. G. The Iroquois. Cranbrook Institute of Science, Bulletin, 23 (1945): 1-94.

Speck, F. G. and C. E. Schaeffer. The mutual aid and volunteer company of the Eastern Cherokee . . . compared with mutual-aid societies of the Northern Iroquois. Washington Academy of Sciences, Journal, 35 (1945): 169-179.

Speck, F. G. and E. S. Dodge. Amphibian and reptile lore of the Six Nations Cayuga. Journal of American Folklore, 58 (1945): 306-309.

Speck, F. G. and H. P. Beck. Old World tales among the Mohawks. Journal of American Folklore, 63 (1950): 285-308.

Speck, F. G. and W. C. Orchard. The Penn Wampum Belts. Museum of the American Indian, Heye Foundation, Leaflets, 4 (1925): 7-20.

Speck, F. Staniford. Niagara Falls and Cayuga Indian medicine. New York Folklore Quarterly, 1 (1945): 205-208.

Spittal, William Guy. A brief note on: Iroquois musical instruments. American Indian Tradition, 7 (1960/1961): 137.

Squair, J., tr. The Indian tribes on the St. Lawrence at the time of the arrival of the French. Annual Archaeological Report, being Part of Appendix to the Report of the Minister of Education, Ontario, 34 (1923): 82-88.

Squier, E. G. Aboriginal monuments of the State of New York. Smithsonian Contributions to Knowledge, 2, no. 9 (1849): 9-188.

Squier, E. G. Antiquities of the State of New York. Buffalo, 1851. 343 p.

Squire, Roger. Wizards and wampum; legends of the Iroquois. London, Abelard-Schuman, 1972. 121 p. illus.

Stanley, George F. G. The significance of the Six Nations participation in the War of 1812. Ontario History, 55 (1963): 215-231.

Stanley, George F. G. The Six Nations and the American Revolution. Ontario History, 56 (1964): 217-232.

Stephens, B. W. Iroquoian pottery pipes. Central States Archaeological Journal, 2 (1956): 6-9.

Stern, B. J. The letters of Asher Wright to Lewis Henry Morgan. American Anthropologist, n.s., 35 (1933): 138-145.

Stillfried, I. Studie zu Kosmogonischen und kultischen Elementen der Algonkonischen und Irokesischen Stämme. Wiener Völkerkundliche Mitteilungen, 4 (1956): 82-85.

Stites, S. H. Economics of the Iroquois. Lancaster, 1905. 159 p.

Stone, W. L. Life of Joseph Brant. New York, 1838. 2 v.

Stone, W. L. The life and times of Red Jacket or Sa-go-ye-wat-ha. New York, 1841. 488 p.

Strickland, William. Journal of a tour in the United States of America, 1794-1795. Edited by Reverend J. E. Strickland. New York, 1971. 23, 335 p. illus., maps. (New-York Historical Society, Collections, 83)

Strong, J. C. Report of the Commissioners of the Land Office in the matter of the Cayuga Indians residing in Canada. Buffalo, 1889. 8 p.

Sturtevant, William C.   An "illusion of religiosity"? By William C. Sturtevant, Donald Collier, Philip Dark, William N. Fenton and Ernest Stanley Dodge. Indian Historian, 3, no. 2 (1970): 13-14.

Sublett, Audrey J.   Osteological analysis of the Van Son Site. In Anthropological Contributions. Buffalo, 1968: 49-65. (Buffalo Society of Natural Sciences, Bulletin, 24)

Sublett, Audrey J.   The Cornplanter Cemetery: skeletal analyses. Pennsylvania Archaeologist, 35 (1965): 74-92.

Sublett, Audrey Jane.   Seneca physical type and changes through time. Dissertation Abstracts, 27 (1966/1967): 1706B.   UM 66-12,133.

Sullivan, Marie St. John, comp.   Truthful hatchet. Compiled by Marie St. John Sullivan and Rex Shanks.   San Antonio, Naylor, 1966.   14, 157 p.

Sulte, B.   The war of the Iroquois. Annual Archaeological Report, being Part of Appendix to the Report of the Minister of Education, Ontario (1899): 124-151.

Swadesh, Morris.   On the unit of translation. Anthropological Linguistics, 2, no. 2 (1960): 39-42.

Taft, G. E.   An Onondaga festival. Records of the Past, 13 (1914): 101-102.

Taft, G. E.   Cayuga indemnity. Records of the Past, 13 (1914): 96-101.

Taft, G. E.   Cayuga notes.   Benton Harbor, 1913.   23 p.

Taft, G. E.   Tarenyagon. Records of the Past, 12 (1913): 169-170.

Taylor, David R.   The Kenté mission, 1668 to 1680. Picton, Ont., Picton Gazette, 1968.   29 p.   illus., map.

Taylor, Donna.   Iroquois wampum: a study in method. Pennsylvania Archaeologist, 30 (1960): 30-32.

Taylor, Robert J.   Trial at Trenton. William and Mary Quarterly, 3d ser., 26 (1969): 521-547.

Taylor, Walter.   The Kinzua Dam and H.R. 1794. Indian Truth, 40 (April 1963): 1-5.

"The Engages".   Indian awls. Museum of the Fur Trade Quarterly, 7, no. 2 (1971): 2-3.

Thompson, David.   David Thompson's narrative 1784-1812. Edited by Richard Glover.   Toronto, 1962.   102, 410 p. map.   (Champlain Society, Publications, 40)

Thompson, J. R. F.   Thayendanegea the Mohawk and his several portraits. Connoisseur, 170 (Jan. 1969): 49-53.

Thompson, S.   The Indian legend of Hiawatha. Modern Language Association, Publications, 37, no. 1 (1922): 128-140.

Tooker, Elisabeth.   Archaeological evidence for seventeenth century Iroquoian dream fulfillment rituals. By Elisabeth Tooker and Marian E. White. Pennsylvania Archaeologist, 34, no. 3/4 (1964): 1-5.

Tooker, Elisabeth.   Northern Iroquoian sociopolitical organization. American Anthropologist, 72 (1970): 90-97.

Tooker, Elisabeth.   On the new religion of Handsome Lake. Anthropological Quarterly, 41 (1968): 187-200.

Tooker, Elisabeth.   The Iroquois ceremonial at midwinter.   Syracuse, Syracuse University Press, 1970.   10, 189 p.   illus., map.

Tooker, Elisabeth.   The Iroquois defeat of the Huron: a review of causes. Pennsylvania Archaeologist, 33 (1963): 115-123.

Tooker, Elisabeth.   The Iroquois White Dog Sacrifice in the latter part of the eighteenth century. Ethnohistory, 12 (1965): 129-140.

Torok, C. H.   Structures and factions in Tyendinaga politics. Anthropologica, n.s., 14 (1972): 31-42.

Torok, C. H.   The Canadian Indian reserves. Indian Historian, 1, no. 4 (1967/1968): 15-16, 23.

Torok, C. H.   The Tyendinaga Mohawks (the village as a basic factor in Mohawk social structure). Ontario History, 57 (1965): 69-77.

Tracy, Valerie.   The Indian in transition: the Neosho Agency, 1850-1861. Chronicles of Oklahoma, 48 (1970): 164-183.

Trelease, Allen W.   The Iroquois and the western fur trade: a problem in interpretation. Mississippi Valley Historical Review, 49 (1962/1963): 32-51.

Trigger, Bruce G.   A reply to Mr. Ridley. Ontario History, 55 (1963): 161-163.

Trigger, Bruce G. Archaeological and other evidence: a fresh look at the "Laurentian Iroquois". American Antiquity, 33 (1968): 429-440.

Trigger, Bruce G. Champlain judged by his Indian policy: a different view of early Canadian history. Anthropologica, n.s., 13 (1971): 85-114.

Trigger, Bruce G. Settlement as an aspect of Iroquoian adaptation at the time of contact. American Anthropologist, 65 (1963): 86-101.

Trigger, Bruce G. The French presence in Huronia: the structure of Franco-Huron relations in the first half of the seventeenth century. Canadian Historical Review, 49 (1968): 107-141.

Trigger, Bruce G. The Mohawk-Mahican War (1624-28): the establishment of a pattern. Canadian Historical Review, 51 (1971): 276-286.

Trigger, Bruce G. Trade and tribal warfare on the St. Lawrence in the sixteenth century. Ethnohistory, 9 (1962): 240-256.

Tuck, James A. Iroquois cultural development in Central New York. Dissertation Abstracts International, 30 (1969/1970): 3961B. UM 70-1975.

Tuck, James A. Onondaga Iroquois prehistory; a study in settlement archaeology. Syracuse, Syracuse University Press, 1971. 13, 255 p. illus.

Tuck, James A. Some recent work on the prehistory of the Onondaga Nation. Pennsylvania Archaeologist, 39 (1969): 40-52.

Tuck, James A. The Iroquois confederacy. Scientific American, 224, no. 2 (1971): 32-42, 130.

Tyler, Stephen A. Parallel/cross: an evaluation of definitions. Southwestern Journal of Anthropology, 22 (1966): 416-432.

Uhler, S. P. Pennsylvania's Indian relations to 1754. Allentown, 1951. 144 p.

U.S., Congress, Senate, Committee on Interior and Insular Affairs. Kinzua Dam (Seneca Indian relocation). Washington, D.C., Government Printing Office, 1964. 4, 199 p. maps.

Vail, R. W. G., ed. The western campaign of 1779. New York Historical Society Quarterly, 41, no. 1 (1952): 34-69.

Van Hoeven, James William. Salvation and Indian removal: the career biography of the Rev. John Freeman Schermerhorn, Indian commissioner. Dissertation Abstracts International, 33 (1972/1973): 1830A. UM 72-26,134.

Van Horn, Elizabeth H. Iroquois silver brooches. Rochester, Rochester Museum and Science Center, 1972. 70 p. illus.

Van Loon, L. G. Tawagonshi, beginning of the treaty era. Indian Historian, 1, no. 3 (1967/1968): 22-26.

Various. Journals of the military expedition of Major General John Sullivan against the Six Nations of Indians in 1779. Glendale, N.Y., Benchmark Publishing, 1970. 2, 329 p. illus., maps.

Vaughan, Alden T. A test of Puritan justice. New England Quarterly, 38 (1965): 331-339.

Vaughan, Alden T. Pequots and Puritans: the causes of the War of 1637. William and Mary Quarterly, 3d ser., 21 (1964): 256-269.

Voget, F. Acculturation at Caughnawaga. American Anthropologist, 53 (1951): 220-231.

Voget, F. Kinship changes at Caughnawaga. American Anthropologist, 55 (1953): 385-394.

Voget, Fred W. American Indian reformations and acculturation. In Contributions to Anthropology 1960. Part II. Ottawa, Queen's Printer, 1963: 1-13. (Canada, National Museum, Bulletin, 190)

Voget, Fred W. Kinship changes at Caughnawaga. In Deward E. Walker, Jr., ed. The Emergent Native Americans. Boston, Little, Brown, 1972: 447-455.

Voget, Fred W. The American Indian in transition: reformation and accommodation. In Deward E. Walker, Jr., ed. The Emergent Native Americans. Boston, Little, Brown, 1972: 645-657.

Wainwright, N. B. George Croghan and the Indians uprising of 1747. Pennsylvania History, 21 (1954): 21-31.

Wait, Mary Van Sickle. The story of the Cayugas, 1609-1809. By Mary Van Sickle Wait and William Heidt, Jr. Ithaca, Dewitt Historical Society of Tompkins County, 1966. map.

Wallace, A. F. C. Dreams and wishes of the soul. American Anthropologist, 60 (1958): 234-248.

Wallace, A. F. C. Halliday Jackson's journal to the Seneca Indians. Pennsylvania History, 19 (1952): 117-147, 325-349.

Wallace, A. F. C. Handsome Lake and the great revival in the West. American Quarterly, 4 (1952): 149-165.

Wallace, A. F. C. Mazeway resynthesis. New York Academy of Sciences, Transactions, ser. 2, 18 (1956): 626-638.

Wallace, A. F. C. Origins of Iroquois neutrality. Pennsylvania History, 24 (1957): 223-235.

Wallace, A. F. C. Some psychological determinants of culture change in an Iroquoian community. U.S. Bureau of American Ethnology, Bulletin, 149 (1951): 55-76.

Wallace, A. F. C. The Dekanawidah myth analyzed as the record of a revitalization movement. Ethnohistory, 5 (1958): 118-130.

Wallace, A. F. C. Woman, land and society. Pennsylvania Archaeologist, 17 (1947): 1-35.

Wallace, Anthony F. C. A day at the office. In Solon T. Kimball and James B. Watson, eds. Crossing Cultural Boundaries. San Francisco, Chandler, 1972: 193-203.

Wallace, Anthony F. C. Dreams and the wishes of the soul: a type of psychoanalytic theory among the seventeenth century Iroquois. In John Middleton, ed. Magic, Witchcraft, and Curing. Garden City, Natural History Press, 1967: 171-190.

*Wallace, Anthony F. C. The death and rebirth of the Seneca. By Anthony F. C. Wallace, with the assistance of Sheila C. Steen. New York, Knopf, 1970. 13, 384, 11 p. illus.

Wallace, P. A. W. Conrad Weiser, 1696-1760, friend of Colonist and Mohawk. Philadelphia, 1945. 648 p.

Wallace, P. A. W. The Five Nations of New York and Pennsylvania. New York Historical Society Quarterly, 37 (1953): 228-250.

Wallace, P. A. W. The Iroquois: a brief outline of their history. Pennsylvania History, 23 (1956): 15-28.

Wallace, P. A. W. The return of Hiawatha. New York History, 29 (1948): 385-403.

Wallace, P. A. W. The white roots of peace. Philadelphia, 1946. 57 p.

Wallace, Paul A. W. Conrad Weiser, 1696-1760, friend of colonist and Mohawk. New York, Russell and Russell, 1971. 14, 648 p. maps.

Wallace, Paul A. W. Indian paths of Pennsylvania. Harrisburg, Pennsylvania Historical and Museum Commission, 1965. 8, 227 p. maps.

Wallace, Paul A. W. Indians in Pennsylvania. Harrisburg, Pennsylvania Historical and Museum Commission, 1961. 13, 194 p. illus., maps.

Wallace, Paul A. W. Logan, the Mingo: a problem in identification. Pennsylvania Archaeologist, 32 (1962): 91-96.

Wallace, Paul A. W. The white roots of peace. Port Washington, I. J. Friedman, 1968. 9, 57 p.

Walton, Joseph S. Conrad Weizer and the Indian policy of colonial Pennsylvania. New York, Arno Press, 1971. 420 p. illus.

Washington, George. A mystery resolved; George Washington's letter to Governor Dinwiddie, June 10, 1754. Edited by Peter Walne. Virginia Magazine of History and Biography, 79 (1971): 131-144.

Waugh, F. W. Iroquois foods and food preparation. Canada, Department of Mines, Geological Survey, Memoirs, 86 (1916): 1-235.

Waugh, F. W. On work in material culture of the Iroquois, 1912. Canada, Geological Survey, Summary Reports (1912): 476-480.

Waugh, F. W. Some notes on ethnobotany. Ottawa Naturalist, 31 (1917): 27-29.

Weast, Donald Ellsworth. Patterns of drinking among Indian youth: the case of a Wisconsin tribe. Dissertation Abstracts International, 31 (1970/1971): 490A. UM 69-22,508.

Weaver, S. M. Smallpox or chickenpox: an Iroquoian community's reaction to crisis, 1901-1902. Ethnohistory, 18 (1971): 361-378.

Weaver, Sally Mae. Health, culture and dilemma: a study of the non-Conservative Iroquois, Six Nations Reserve, Ontario.

Dissertation Abstracts, 29 (1968/1969): 3175B.

Weber, J. Cynthia. Types and attributes in Iroquois pipes. Man in the Northeast, 2 (1971): 51-65.

Weinman, Paul L. The Rip Van Winkle Site. By Paul L. Weinman and Thomas P. Weinman. Pennsylvania Archaeologist, 41, no. 1/2 (1971): 53-60.

Weslager, C. A. Further light on the Delaware Indians as women. Washington Academy of Sciences, Journal, 37 (1947): 298-304.

Weslager, C. A. The Delaware Indians as women. Washington Academy of Sciences, Journal, 34 (1944): 381-388.

Whallon, Robert, Jr. Investigations of late prehistoric social organization in New York State. In Sally R. Binford and Lewis R. Binford, eds. New Perspectives in Archeology. Chicago, Aldine, 1968: 223-244.

Wheeler-Voegelin, E., ed. John Heckewelder to Peter S. Du Ponceau. Ethnohistory, 6 (1959): 70-81.

Wheeler-Voegelin, E., ed. Some remarks concerning the traditions, customs, languages etc. of the Indians in North America. Ethnohistory, 6 (1959): 42-69, 186.

White, M. E. An Iroquois sequence in New York's Niagara Frontier. Pennsylvania Archaeologist, 28 (1958): 145-150.

White, M. E. An Iroquois sequence in New York's Niagara Frontier. Eastern States Archaeological Federation, Bulletin, 16 (1957): 14.

White, Marian. Ethnic identification and Iroquois groups in western New York and Ontario. Ethnohistory, 18 (1971): 19-38.

White, Marian E. A reexamination of the historic Iroquois Van Son cemetery on Grand Island. In Anthropological Contributions. Buffalo, 1968: 1-48. (Buffalo Society of Natural Sciences, Bulletin, 24)

White, Marian E. An early historic Niagara Frontier Iroquois cemetery in Erie County, New York. Rochester, 1967. 6, 91 p. illus. (New York State Archeological Association, Researches and Transactions, 16, no. 1)

White, Marian E. Iroquois culture history in the Niagara Frontier area of New York State. Ann Arbor, University of Michigan, 1961. 8, 155 p. illus.

(Michigan, University, Museum of Anthropology, Anthropological Papers, 16)

Wilcox, R. Feathers in a dark sky. Woodstock, 1941. 223 p.

Willoughby, C. C. A Mohawk (Caughnawaga) halter for leading captives. American Anthropologist, n.s., 40 (1938): 49-50.

Wilson, D. The Huron-Iroquois of Canada. Royal Society of Canada, Proceedings and Transactions, 2, pt. 2 (1884): 55-106.

Wilson, J. G. Arent van Curler and his journal of 1634-35. American Historical Association, Annual Report (1895): 81-101.

Wintemberg, W. J. Culture of a prehistoric Iroquoian site in eastern Ontario. International Congress of Americanists, Proceedings, 19 (1915): 37-42.

Winter, Joseph. A summary of Owasco and Iroquois maize remains. Pennsylvania Archaeologist, 41, no. 3 (1971): 1-11.

Wisconsin, State Employment Service. Employability factors and needs of Wisconsin tribal Indians. Madison, Wisconsin State Employment Service, 1968. 43 p. ERIC ED021684.

Witthoft, J. Cayuga midwinter festival. New York Folklore Quarterly, 2 (1946): 24-39.

Witthoft, J. Green corn ceremonialism in the eastern woodlands. Michigan, University, Museum of Anthropology, Occasional Contributions, 13 (1949): 21-31.

Witthoft, J. Iroquois archaeology at the mid-century. American Philosophical Society, Proceedings, 95 (1951): 311-321.

Witthoft, J. and W. S. Hadlock. Cherokee-Iroquois little people. Journal of American Folklore, 59 (1946): 413-422.

Wolf, M. Iroquois religion and its relation to their morals. New York, 1919.

Wozniak, Chad J. The new western colony schemes: a preview of the United States territorial system. Indiana Magazine of History, 68 (1972): 283-306.

Wray, C. F. Archaeological evidence of the mask among the Seneca. New York State Archaeological Association, Bulletin, 7 (1956): 7-8.

Wray, C. F.   Index traits of the historic
Seneca--1550-1687. Eastern States
Archaeological Federation, Bulletin, 13
(1954): 6.

Wray, C. F.   Seneca tobacco pipes. New
York State Archaeological Association,
Bulletin, 6 (1956): 15-16.

Wray, C. F. and H. L. Schoff.   A
preliminary report on the Seneca
sequence in western New York--1550-1687.
Pennsylvania Archaeologist, 23 (1957):
55-63.

Wray, Charles F.   Ornamental hair combs of
the Seneca Iroquois. Pennsylvania
Archaeologist, 33 (1963): 35-50.

Wren, C.   A study of North Appalachian
Indian pottery. Wyoming Historical and
Geological Society, Proceedings and
Collections, 13 (1914): 131-222.

Wren, C.   Turtle shell rattles and other
implements from Indian graves. Wyoming
Historical and Geological Society,
Proceedings and Collections, 10 (1909):
195-210.

Wright, James V.   An archaeological survey
along the north shore of Lake Superior.
Ottawa, Queen's Printer, 1963. 9 p.
map. (Canada, National Museum,
Anthropology Papers, 3)

Wright, James V.   The application of the
direct historical approach to the
Iroquois and the Ojibwa. Ethnohistory,
15 (1968): 96-111.

Wright, James V.   The Middleport horizon.
Anthropologica, n.s., 2 (1960): 113-120.

Wright, James V.   The Ontario Iroquois
tradition. Ottawa, 1966. 12, 195 p.
illus., maps. (Canada, National Museum,
Bulletin, 210)

Yager, Willard E.   The Onéota; from notes
and memoranda written down by Willard E.
Yager before his death. Edited by
Douglas Earl Bailey. Walton, N.Y.,
Private printing by Reporter Co., 1961.
206 p. illus.

Yawger, R. N.   The Indian and the pioneer.
Syracuse, 1893. 2 v.

Young, James.   Gainoh ne nenodowohga
neuwahnuhdah. New-York, Printed for the
American Tract Society by D. Fanshaw,
1829. 39, 39 p.

Zeisberger, D.   Essay of an Onondaga
grammar. Pennsylvania Magazine of
History and Biography, 11 (1887): 442-
453; 12 (1888): 65-75, 233-239, 325-340.

Zeisberger, D.   Indian dictionary.
Cambridge, 1887. 236 p.

Zoltvany, Yves F.   New France and the
West, 1701-1713. Canadian Historical
Review, 46 (1965): 301-322.

Zoltvany, Yves F.   The frontier policy of
Philippe de Rigaud de Vaudreuil, 1713-
1725. Canadian Historical Review, 48
(1967): 227-250.

                    12-06   Mahican

Fay, George E.   Bibliography of the
Indians of Wisconsin. Wisconsin Indians
Research Institute, Journal, 1, no. 1
(1965): 107-132.

Hargrett, L.   A bibliography of the
constitutions and laws of the American
Indians, 111-112. Cambridge, 1947.

Allen, Charles.   Report on the Stockbridge
Indians to the Legislature. Boston,
1870. 23 p. (Massachusetts,
Legislature of 1870, House Document, 13)

Anonymous.   Chief Daniel Nimham v. Roger
Morris, Beverly Robinson, and Philip
Philipse--an Indian land case in
colonial New York, 1765-1767. Edited by
Oscar Handlin and Irving Mark.
Ethnohistory, 11 (1964): 193-246.

Armbruster, E. L.   The Indians of New
England and New Netherlands. Brooklyn,
1918.

Belknap, J.   Report on the Oneida,
Stockbridge and Brotherton Indians,
1796. Indian Notes and Monographs,
ser. 2, 54 (1955): 1-39.

Birdsey, N.   An account of the Indians in
and about Stratford. Massachusetts
Historical Society, Collections, ser. 1,
10 (1809): 111-112.

Bolton, R. P.   Indian life of long ago in
the City of New York. New York, 1934.
167 p.

Bolton, R. P.   Indian paths in the great
metropolis. Indian Notes and Monographs,
ser. 2, 23 (1922): 1-280.

Bolton, R. P.   New York City in Indian
possession. Indian Notes and Monographs,
2 (1920): 225-395.

Bolton, R. P.   The Indians of Washington
Heights. American Museum of Natural
History, Anthropological Papers, 3
(1909): 77-109.

Brown, R. H. The Housatonic Indians.
Massachusetts Archaeological Society,
Bulletin, 19, no. 3 (1958): 44-50.

Canning, E. W. B. The aborigines of the
Housatonic Valley. Magazine of American
History, 2 (1878): 734-740.

Coffin, C. C. A prehistoric shell heap at
the mouth of the Housatonic.
Archaeological Society of Connecticut,
Bulletin, 5 (1937): 10-19.

Coffin, C. C. An Indian village site at
Cedar Ridge. Archaeological Society of
Connecticut, Bulletin, 7 (1938): 9-11.

Coffin, C. C. Excavations in Southwest
Connecticut. Archaeological Society of
Connecticut, Bulletin, 10 (1940): 33-49.

Coffin, C. C. Impressed shell designs on
Connecticut Indian pottery.
Archaeological Society of Connecticut,
Bulletin, 4 (1936): 2-6.

Curtis, W. C. The basketry of the
Pautatucks and Scatacooks. Southern
Workman, 33 (1904): 385-390.

Davidson, J. N. Muh-he-ka-ne-ok, a
history of the Stockbridge nation.
Milwaukee, 1893. 66 p.

Day, Gordon M. An Agawam fragment.
International Journal of American
Linguistics, 33 (1967): 244-247.

De Forest, J. W. History of the Indians
of Connecticut. Hartford, 1851. 509 p.

De Forest, John W. History of the Indians
of Connecticut from the earliest known
period to 1850. Hamden, Conn., Archon
Books, 1964. 48, 509 p. illus., map.

De Forest, John William. History of the
Indians of Connecticut from the earliest
known period to 1850. St. Clair, Mich.,
Scholarly Press, 1970. 26, 509 p.
illus., map.

Denton, D. A brief description of New
York. Ed. by G. Gurman. New York, 1845.
57 p.

Donck, A. van der. Beschryvinge van
Nieuw-Nederlant. Amsterdam, 1655.
100 p.

Donck, A. van der. Description of the New
Netherlands. New York Historical
Society, Collections, ser. 2, 1 (1841):
125-242.

Edwards, J. Observations on the language
of the Muhhekaneew Indians. New Haven,
1788. 17 p.

Fay, George E., ed. Charters,
constitutions and by-laws of the Indian
tribes of North America. Part II: The
Indian tribes of Wisconsin (Great Lakes
Agency). Greeley, 1967. 6, 124 l.
illus., map. (University of Northern
Colorado, Museum of Anthropology,
Occasional Publications in Anthropology,
Ethnology Series, 2) ERIC ED046552.

Fay, George E., ed. Charters,
constitutions and by-laws of the Indian
tribes of Wisconsin. Wisconsin Indians
Research Institute, Journal, 3, no. 1
(1967): 1-124.

Fay, George E., ed. Treaties between the
Menominee Indians and the United States
of America, 1817-1856. Wisconsin Indians
Research Institute, Journal, 1, no. 1
(1965): 67-104.

Fay, George E., ed. Treaties between the
Stockbridge-Munsee Tribe(s) of Indians
and the United States of America 1805-
1871. Wisconsin Indians Research
Institute, Journal, 4, no. 1 (1968): i-
ii, 1-62.

Finch, J. K. Aboriginal remains on
Manhattan Island. American Museum of
Natural History, Anthropological Papers,
3 (1909): 65-73.

Goddard, Ives. More on the nasalization
of PA *a in Eastern Algonquian.
International Journal of American
Linguistics, 37 (1971): 139-145.

Goddard, Ives. The ethnohistorical
implications of early Delaware
linguistic materials. Man in the
Northeast, 1 (1971): 14-26.

Haas, Mary R. Roger William's sound
shift: a study in Algonkian. In To Honor
Roman Jakobson; Essays on the Occasion
of His Seventieth Birthday. Vol. 1. The
Hague, Mouton, 1967: 816-832. (Janua
Linguarum, Series Maior, 31)

Harrington, M. R. Ancient shell heaps
near New York City. American Museum of
Natural History, Anthropological Papers,
3 (1909): 169-179.

Harrington, M. R. The rock-shelters of
Armonk, New York. American Museum of
Natural History, Anthropological Papers,
3 (1909): 125-138.

Harstad, Peter T. Disease and sickness on
the Wisconsin frontier: smallpox and
other diseases. Wisconsin Magazine of
History, 43 (1959): 253-263.

Heye, G. G. A Mahican wooden cup. Indian
Notes and Monographs, 5 (1921): 15-18.

Hodge, F. W. and W. C. Orchard. John W. Quinney's coat. Indian Notes, 6 (1929): 343-351.

Hopkins, S. Historical memoirs relating to the Housatonic Indians. Magazine of History, Extra Numbers, 17 (1911): 7-198.

Jackson, E. P. Indian occupation and use of the Champlain lowland. Michigan Academy of Science, Arts and Letters, Papers, 14 (1931): 113-160.

Jackson, E. P. Mountains and the aborigines of the Champlain lowland. Appalachia, 24 (1930): 131-136.

Jameson, Jacob. Answers to Governor Cass's questions by Jacob Jameson, a Seneca [ca. 1821-1825]. Edited by William N. Fenton. Ethnohistory, 16 (1969): 113-139.

Juet, R. Extract from the journal of the voyage of the Half-Moon. New York Historical Society, Collections, ser. 2, 1 (1841): 317-332.

Laet, J. de. Extracts from the New World, or a description of the West Indies. New York Historical Society, Collections, ser. 2, 1 (1841): 281-316.

Leder, L. H., ed. The Livingston Indian records, 1666-1723. Pennsylvania History, 23 (1956): 1-240.

Mathews, Edward. An abolitionist in territorial Wisconsin: the journal of Reverend Edward Mathews. Edited by William Converse Haygood. Wisconsin Magazine of History, 52 (1968/1969): 3-18, 117-131, 248-262, 330-343.

Michelson, T. Investigations among the Stockbridge, Brotherton, and Fox Indians. Smithsonian Miscellaneous Collections, 65, no. 6 (1915): 90-94.

Mochon, Marion Johnson. History of the Wisconsin Stockbridge Indians. Wisconsin Archeologist, n.s., 49 (1968): 81-95.

Mochon, Marion Johnson. Stockbridge-Munsee cultural adaptations: "assimilated Indians". American Philosophical Society, Proceedings, 112 (1968): 182-219.

Montanus, A. Description of New Netherland. In E. B. O'Callaghan, ed. Documentary History of the State of New York. Vol. 4. Albany, 1851: 113-132.

Mooney, J. Quinnipiac. U.S. Bureau of American Ethnology, Bulletin, 30, vol. 2 (1910): 344-345.

Mooney, J. Wappinger. U.S. Bureau of American Ethnology, Bulletin, 30, vol. 2 (1910): 913.

Mooney, J. and C. Thomas. Mahican. U.S. Bureau of American Ethnology, Bulletin, 30, vol. 1 (1907): 786-789.

Morgan, L. H. The Indian journals, 1859-62: p. 57. Ann Arbor, 1959.

Nichols, Roger L. A missionary journey to the Sac-Fox Indians, 1834. Annals of Iowa, 36 (1962): 301-315.

Orcutt, S. The Indians of the Housatonic and Naugatuck valleys. Hartford, 1882. 220 p.

Orcutt, S. and A. Beardsley. The history of the old town of Derby, xvii-xcvii. Springfield, 1880.

Orcutt, Samuel. The Indians in the Housatonic and Naugatuck Valleys. Stratford, Conn., J. E. Edwards, 1972. 4, 220 p. illus.

Prince, J. D. A tale in the Hudson River Indian language. American Anthropologist, n.s., 7 (1905): 74-84.

Prince, J. D. and F. G. Speck. Dying American speech-echoes from Connecticut. American Philosophical Society, Proceedings, 42 (1903): 346-352.

Rainey, F. G. A compilation of historical data contributing to the ethnography of Connecticut and southern New England Indians. Archaeological Society of Connecticut, Bulletin, 3 (1936): 1-89.

Ray, L. The aboriginal inhabitants of Connecticut. In W. W. Beach, ed. Indian Miscellany. Albany, 1877: 280-302.

Ruttenber, E. M. History of the Indian tribes of Hudson's River. Albany, 1872. 415 p.

Ruttenber, Edward M. History of the Indian tribes of Hudson's River. Port Washington, Kennikat Press, 1971. 5, 415 p. illus.

Scott, K. and C. E. Baker. Renewals of Governor Nicolls' Treaty of 1665 with the Esopus Indians. New York Historical Society Quarterly, 37 (1953): 251-272.

Silver, Shirley. Natick consonants in reference to Proto-Central Algonquian. International Journal of American Linguistics, 26 (1960): 112-119, 234-241.

Skinner, A. Archaeology of Manhattan Island. American Museum of Natural

History, Anthropological Papers, 3 (1909): 113-121.

Skinner, A. Archaeology of the New York Coastal Algonkin. American Museum of Natural History, Anthropological Papers, 3 (1909): 213-235.

Skinner, A. Notes on Mahican ethnology. Public Museum of the City of Milwaukee, Bulletin, 2 (1925): 87-116.

Skinner, A. Objects from New York City. Indian Notes, 1 (1924): 236-238.

Skinner, A. The Indians of Greater New York. Cedar Rapids, 1915.

Skinner, A. The Indians of Manhattan Island and vicinity. American Museum of Natural History, Guide Leaflet Series, 29 (1909): 5-54; 41 (1915): 5-54.

Skinner, A. The Manhattan Indians. New York State Museum Bulletin, 158 (1912): 199-212.

Skinner, Alanson B. The Indians of Manhattan Island and vicinity. Port Washington, I. J. Friedman, 1961. 63 p. illus.

Smith, C. P. The Housatonic. New York, 1946. 532 p.

Smith, W. F. The quest of an Indian garden. Archaeological Society of Connecticut, Bulletin, 19 (1946): 13-17.

Speck, F. G. Bird nomenclature and song interpretation of the Canadian Delaware. Washington Academy of Sciences, Journal, 36 (1946): 249-258.

Speck, F. G. Decorative art of the Indian tribes of Connecticut. Canada, Department of Mines, Geological Survey, Memoirs, 75 (1915): 1-73.

Speck, F. G. and J. Moses. The celestial bear comes down to earth. Reading, Public Museum, Scientific Publications, 7 (1945): 1-91.

Spiess, M. The Indians of Connecticut. New Haven, Committee on Historical Publications, Tercentenary Commission of the State of Connecticut, 1933. 33 p.

Strickland, William. Journal of a tour in the United States of America, 1794-1795. Edited by Reverend J. E. Strickland. New York, 1971. 23, 335 p. illus., maps. (New-York Historical Society, Collections, 83)

Townshend, C. H. The Quinnipiack Indian and their reservation. New Haven, 1900. 79 p.

Trigger, Bruce G. The Mohawk-Mahican War (1624-28): the establishment of a pattern. Canadian Historical Review, 51 (1971): 276-286.

Troost, G. Extracts from the voyages of David Pieterszen de Vries. New York Historical Society, Collections, ser. 2, 1 (1841): 243-280.

Trumbull, B. A complete history of Connecticut, Vol. 1: 39-57. New Haven, 1818.

Wassenaer, N. van. Description and first settlement of New Netherland. In E. B. O'Callaghan, ed. Documentary History of the State of New York. Vol. 3. Albany, 1850: 27-48.

Weinman, Paul L. The Rip Van Winkle Site. By Paul L. Weinman and Thomas P. Weinman. Pennsylvania Archaeologist, 41, no. 1/2 (1971): 53-60.

Wheeler-Voegelin, E., ed. Some remarks concerning the traditions, customs, languages etc. of the Indians in North America. Ethnohistory, 6 (1959): 42-69, 186.

Willoughby, C. C. Antiquities of the New England Indians. Cambridge, 1935. 314 p.

Willoughby, C. C. Textile fabrics of the New England Indians. American Anthropologist, n.s., 7 (1905): 85-93.

Willoughby, C. C. The wilderness and the Indian. In A. B. Hart, ed. Commonwealth History of Massachusetts. Vol. 1. Cambridge, 1927: 127-158.

Wissler, C., ed. The Indians of Greater New York and the lower Hudson. American Museum of Natural History, Anthropological Papers, 3 (1909): 3-237.

Wolley, C. A two years journal in New York. Ed. by E. B. O'Callaghan. New York, 1860. 97 p.

Woodward, A. Antler implements from New York City. Indian Notes, 4 (1927): 226-231.

12-07 Massachuset

Adams, Thomas Boylston. Bad news from Virginia. Virginia Magazine of History and Biography, 74 (1966): 131-140.

Adolf, Leonard. Squanto's role in Pilgrim diplomacy. Ethnohistory, 11 (1964): 247-261.

Allen, Z. Native Indians of America.
Providence, 1881. 55 p.

Anonymous. A description of Mashpee.
Massachusetts Historical Society,
Collections, ser. 2, 3 (1846): 1-12.

Anonymous. Saconet Indians. Massachusetts
Historical Society, Collections, ser. 1,
10 (1809): 114.

Anonymous. Wunnashowetuckoog. U.S. Bureau
of American Ethnology, Bulletin, 30,
vol. 2 (1910): 975.

Archer, G. The relation of Captain
Gosnold's voyage. Massachusetts
Historical Society, Collections, ser. 3,
8 (1843): 72-81.

Bacon, O. N. A history of Natick, 21-39.
Boston, 1856.

Badger, S. Historical and characteristic
traits of the American Indians in
general and those of the Natick in
particular. Massachusetts Historical
Society, Collections, ser. 1, 5 (1835):
32-45.

Banks, C. E. History of Martha's
Vineyard. Boston, 1911. 3 v.

Bassett, B. Fabulous traditions and
customs of the Indians of Martha's
Vineyard. Massachusetts Historical
Society, Collections, 1 (1792): 139-140.

Bibaud, F. M. Biographie des sagamos
illustrés de l'Amérique Septentrionale,
91-100. Montréal, 1848.

Biggar, H. P., ed. The Works of Samuel de
Champlain, Vol. 1: 338-361. Toronto,
1922.

Bingham, Amelia G. Mashpee, 1870-1970.
Mashpee, Mass., Mashpee Centennial
Committee, 1970. 48 p. illus., map.

Bodge, George Madison. Soldiers in King
Philip's War. 3d ed. Baltimore,
Genealogical Publishing, 1967. 13,
502 p. illus., maps.

Bradford, W. History of the Plymouth
Plantation. Boston, 1912. 2 v.

Brereton, J. A brief and true relation of
the discovery of the north part of
Virginia. Massachusetts Historical
Society, Collections, ser. 3, 8 (1843):
83-94.

Burke, Charles T. Puritans at bay; the
war against King Philip and the squaw
sachems. New York, Exposition Press,
1967. 261 p. illus., map.

Burrage, H. S., ed. Early English and
French voyages, 330-339, 347-351. New
York, 1906.

Burton, A. H. Massasoit. New York, 1896.
270 p.

Carr, L. Notes on the crania of New
England Indians. Boston, 1880. 10 p.

Chase, H. E. Notes on the Wampanoag
Indians. Smithsonian Institution, Annual
Reports of the Board of Regents (1883):
878-907.

Cheever, G. B. The journal of the
Pilgrims at Plymouth. 2d ed. New York,
1849.

Cotton, J. Vocabulary of the
Massachusetts (or Natick) Indian
language. Massachusetts Historical
Society, Collections, ser. 3, 2 (1830):
147-257.

Cowan, William. PA *a°, *k and *t in
Narragansett. International Journal of
American Linguistics, 35 (1969): 28-33.

Crane, J. C. The Nipmucks and their
country. Worcester Society of Antiquity,
Collections, 16 (1912): 3-19.

Day, Gordon M. An Agawam fragment.
International Journal of American
Linguistics, 33 (1967): 244-247.

Day, Gordon M. The name Contoocook.
International Journal of American
Linguistics, 27 (1961): 168-171.

De Forest, John W. History of the Indians
of Connecticut from the earliest known
period to 1850. Hamden, Conn., Archon
Books, 1964. 48, 509 p. illus., map.

De Forest, John William. History of the
Indians of Connecticut from the earliest
known period to 1850. St. Clair, Mich.,
Scholarly Press, 1970. 26, 509 p.
illus., map.

DeForest, J. W. History of the Indians of
Connecticut. Hartford, 1851. 509 p.

Dexter, H. M. The New England Indians.
Sabbath at Home, 2 (1868): 193-206.

Dexter, H. M., ed. Mourt's relation.
Boston, 1865. 176 p.

Dixon, R. B. The early migrations of the
Indians of New England and the Maritime
Provinces. American Antiquarian Society,
Proceedings, n.s., 24 (1914): 65-76.

Drake, S. G., ed. The old Indian
chronicle. Boston, 1867. 333 p.

Dunn, G. C. Indians in Bridgewater. Massachusetts Archaeological Society, Bulletin, 3 (1942): 31-33.

Durocher, F. Aiamieu kukuetshimitun misinaigan. Quebec, 1856. 72 p.

Dwight, T. Travels in New-England and New-York, Vol. 1: 84-102. London, 1823.

Eliot, J. A grammar of the Massachusetts Indian language. New ed. Boston, 1822. 66 p.

Eliot, J. The Indian grammar begun. Old South Leaflets, 3, no. 52 (1896): 1-16.

Eliot, J. The Indian primer. Edinburgh, 1877.

Eliot, J. The logick primer. Cleveland, 1904. 94 p.

Eliot, J. The logick primer. Cambridge, 1672. 94 p.

Ellis, G. E. The Indians of Eastern Massachusetts. In J. Winsor, ed. The Memorial History of Boston. Vol. 1. Boston, 1880: 241-274.

Ellis, G. W. and J. E. Morris. King Philip's war. New York, 1906. 326 p.

Ferguson, C. C. Some observations in regard to our earliest Indian inhabitants. Worcester Historical Society, Proceedings, n.s., 2 (1939): 193-204.

Freeman, F. Civilization and barbarism. Cambridge, 1878. 186 p.

Gahan, L. K. The Nipmucks and their territory. Massachusetts Archaeological Society, Bulletin, 2, no. 4 (1941): 2-6.

Gardner, kussell A. My Sanchekantackett. Edgartown, Mass., Dukes County Historical Society, 1970. 47-76 p. (Dukes County Intelligencer, 12, no. 2)

Geller, L. D. A traditional murder test in King Philip's War. New York Folklore Quarterly, 25 (1969): 195-201.

Goddard, Ives. More on the nasalization of PA *a in Eastern Algonquian. International Journal of American Linguistics, 37 (1971): 139-145.

Goddard, Ives. Notes on the genetic classification of the Algonquian languages. In Contributions to Anthropology: Linguistics I. Ottawa, Queen's Printer, 1967: 7-12. (Canada, National Museum, Bulletin, 214)

Gookin, D. An historical account of the doings and sufferings of the Christian Indians in New England. Archaeologia Americana, Transactions and Collections, 2 (1836): 423-534.

Gookin, D. Historical collections of the Indians of New England. Massachusetts Historical Society, Collections, ser. 1, 1 (1792): 141-227.

Gookin, Daniel. Historical collections of the Indians in New England. [n.p.] Towtaid, 1970. 16, 140 p. maps.

Gregory, J. H. Some Essex County Indians. Essex Antiquarian, 5 (1901): 39-40.

Guernsey, S. J. Notes on explorations of Martha's Vineyard. American Anthropologist, n.s., 18 (1915): 81-97.

Haas, Mary R. Roger William's sound shift: a study in Algonkian. In To Honor Roman Jakobson; Essays on the Occasion of His Seventieth Birthday. Vol. 1. The Hague, Mouton, 1967: 816-832. (Janua Linguarum, Series Maior, 31)

Hale, E. E. The language of the Massachusetts Indians. Records of the Past, 4 (1905): 361-363.

Hallet, L. F. Cultural traits of the Southern New England Indians. Massachusetts Archaeological Society, Bulletin, 15 (1954): 59-64.

Hare, Lloyd C. M. Thomas Mayhew, patriarch to the Indians (1593-1682). St. Clair Shores, Mich., Scholarly Press, 1971. 12, 231 p. illus., maps.

Harris, William. A Rhode Islander reports on King Philip's War; the second William Harris letter of August 1676. Transcribed and edited by Douglas Edward Leach. Providence, Rhode Island Historical Society, 1963. 5, 95 p.

Hawley, G. Mashpee Indians. Massachusetts Historical Society, Collections, ser. 1, 10 (1809): 113-114.

Haynes, H. W. Agricultural implements of the New England Indians. Boston Society of Natural History, Proceedings, 22 (1883): 437-443.

Higginson, F. New England's plantation. Massachusetts Historical Society, Collections, 1 (1806): 117-124.

Hooton, E. A. Notes on skeletal remains from Martha's Vineyard. American Anthropologist, n.s., 18 (1915): 98-104.

Hosmer, J. K., ed. Winthrop's journal. New York, 1908. 2 v.

James, Frank. The Pilgrims and the Wampanoags. Indian Historian, 4, no. 1 (1971): 45-46.

Jennings, Francis. Goals and functions of Puritan missions to the Indians. Ethnohistory, 18 (1971): 197-212.

Johnson, Margery Ruth. The Mayhew mission to the Indians, 1643-1806. Dissertation Abstracts, 27 (1966/1967): 2480A. UM 66-11,757.

Jones, J. W., ed. The relation of John Verarzanus. In R. Hakluyt, ed. Divers Voyages Touching the Discovery of America. London, 1850: 55-90.

Josselyn, J. An account of two voyages to New England. Boston, 1865. 211 p.

Kawashima, Yasu. Jurisdiction of the colonial courts over the Indians in Massachusetts, 1689-1763. New England Quarterly, 42 (1969): 532-550.

Kawashima, Yasu. Legal origins of the Indian reservation in colonial Massachusetts. American Journal of Legal History, 13 (1969): 45-56.

Kittredge, G. L. Letters of Samuel Lee and Samuel Sewell relating to New England and the Indians. Colonial Society of Massachusetts, Publications, 15 (1912): 142-186.

Knight, M. F. Wampanoag Indian tales. Journal of American Folklore, 38 (1925): 134-137.

Knight, M. V. The craniometry of Southern New England Indians. Connecticut Academy of Arts and Sciences, Memoirs, 4 (1915): 1-36.

Labov, William. The social motivation of a sound change. Word, 19 (1963): 273-309.

LaBrosse, J. B. de. Nehiro-iriniui aiamihe massinahigan. Quebec, 1767. 96 p.

Leach, D. E. Flintlock and tomahawk. New York, 1958. 304 p.

Leach, Douglas Edward. Benjamin Batten and the London Gazette report on King Philip's War. New England Quarterly, 36 (1963): 502-517.

Leach, Douglas Edward. Flintlock and tomahawk; New England in King Philip's War. New York, W. W. Norton, 1966. 14, 304 p. illus., maps. (Norton Library, N340)

Leach, Douglas Edward. The "whens" of Mary Rowlandson's captivity. New England Quarterly, 34 (1961): 352-363.

Lechford, T. Plain dealing: or newes from New-England. Massachusetts Historical Society, Collections, ser. 3, 3 (1833): 101-105.

Logan, Robert A. Cree language notes. Lake Charlotte, Nova Scotia, Loganda, 1958. 2, 14 p.

MacCulloch, Susan L. A tripartite political system among Christian Indians of early Massachusetts. Kroeber Anthropological Society Papers, 34 (1966): 63-73.

Macy, Z. A short journal of the first settlement of the island of Nantucket. Massachusetts Historical Society, Collections, ser. 1, 3 (1794): 155-160.

Marashio, Paul. Puritan and Pequot. Indian Historian, 3, no. 3 (1970): 9-13; 3, no. 1 (1970): 54, 66.

Mason, John. A brief history of the Pequot War. Ann Arbor, University Microfilms, 1966. 6, 10, 22 p.

Mason, John. A brief history of the Pequot War. With an introduction and some explanatory notes by Thomas Prince. Freeport, N.Y., Books for Libraries Press, 1971. 9, 20 p.

Mawen, T. A list of the names of the Indians . . . which live in or belong to Natick. Massachusetts Historical Society, Collections, ser. 1, 10 (1809): 134-136.

Mayhew, D. Observations on the Indian language. Boston, 1884. 12 p.

Michelson, T. On the etymology of the Natick word Kompaw. American Anthropologist, n.s., 13 (1911): 339.

Miller, W. J. Notes concerning the Wampanoag tribe of Indians. Providence, 1880. 148 p.

Mooney, J. Martha's Vineyard Indians. U.S. Bureau of American Ethnology, Bulletin, 30, vol. 1 (1907): 810.

Mooney, J. Nipmuc. U.S. Bureau of American Ethnology, Bulletin, 30, vol. 2 (1910): 74-75.

Mooney, J. Wampanoag. U.S. Bureau of American Ethnology, Bulletin, 30, vol. 2 (1910): 903-904.

Mooney, J. and C. Thomas. Massachuset. U.S. Bureau of American Ethnology, Bulletin, 30, vol. 1 (1907): 816-817.

Mooney, J. and C. Thomas. Nauset. U.S. Bureau of American Ethnology, Bulletin, 30, vol. 2 (1910): 40-41.

Morton, T. New England Canaan. In P. Force, ed. Tracts and Other Papers Relating Principally to the Origin, Settlement, and Progress of the Colonies in North America. Vol. 2, no. 5. Washington, D.C., 1838: 1-125.

Phelps, M. Indians of old Brookfield. Massachusetts Archaeological Society, Bulletin, 9 (1948): 80-82.

Prince, J. D. Last living echoes of the Natick. American Anthropologist, n.s., 9 (1907): 493-498.

Rainey, F. G. A compilation of historical data contributing to the ethnography of Connecticut and Southern New England Indians. Archaeological Society of Connecticut, Bulletin, 3 (1936): 1-89.

Ritchie, William A. The archaeology of Martha's Vineyard. Garden City, Natural History Press, 1969. 17, 253 p. illus., maps.

Robbins, M. Historical approach to Titicut. Massachusetts Archaeological Society, Bulletin, 11 (1950): 48-73.

Robbins, M. Indians of the Old Colony. Massachusetts Archaeological Society, Bulletin, 17 (1956): 59-73.

Saville, M. H. The John Eliot Indian Bible. Indian Notes, 3 (1926): 120-123.

Schoolcraft, H. R. Massachusetts Indians. In his Information respecting the History, Condition, and Prospects of the Indian Tribes of the United States. Vol. 1. Philadelphia, 1851: 284-299.

Shepard, T. The day-breaking, if not the sun-rising of the gospell with the Indians of New-England. Massachusetts Historical Society, Collections, ser. 3, 4 (1834): 1-23.

Sherman, C. F. Winslow's reports of the Indians. Massachusetts Archaeological Society, Bulletin, 3 (1942): 43-52; 4 (1942): 15-16.

Siebert, Frank T., Jr. Discrepant consonant clusters ending in *-k in Proto-Algonquian, a proposed interpretation of saltatory sound changes. In Contributions to Anthropology: Linguistics I. Ottawa, Queen's Printer, 1967: 48-59. (Canada, National Museum, Bulletin, 214)

Silver, Shirley. Natick consonants in reference to Proto-Central Algonquian. International Journal of American Linguistics, 26 (1960): 112-119, 234-241.

Speck, F. G. A note on the Hassanamisco band of Nipmuc. Massachusetts Archaeological Society, Bulletin, 4 (1943): 49-57.

Speck, F. G. Mythology of the Wampanoag. El Palacio, 25 (1928): 83-86.

Speck, F. G. Territorial subdivisions and boundaries of the Wampanoag, Massachusett, and Nauset Indians. Indian Notes and Monographs, ser. 2, 44 (1928): 7-152.

Speck, F. G. and R. W. Dexter. Utilization of marine life by the Wampanoag Indians of Massachusetts. Washington Academy of Sciences, Journal, 38 (1948): 257-265.

Stiles, E. An account of the Potenummecut Indians. Massachusetts Historical Society, Collections, ser. 1, 10 (1809): 112-113.

Swadesh, M. Sociologic notes on obsolescent languages. International Journal of American Linguistics, 14 (1948): 226-235.

Tanis, Norman Earl. Education in John Eliot's Indian utopias, 1646-1675. History of Education Quarterly, 10 (1970): 308-323.

Tantaquidgeon, G. Newly discovered straw basketry of the Wampanoag Indians. Indian Notes, 7 (1930): 475-484.

Tantaquidgeon, G. Notes on the Gay Head Indians of Massachusetts. Indian Notes, 7 (1930): 1-26.

Tooker, W. W. The significance of John Eliot's Natick. American Anthropologist, 10 (1897): 281-287.

Travers, M. A. The Wampanoag Indian Federation of the Algonquin Nation. New Bedford, 1957. 245 p.

Travers, Milton A. The Wampanoag Indian federation of the Algonquin Nation; Indian neighbors of the Pilgrims. Rev. ed. Boston, Christopher Publishing House, 1961. 247 p. illus.

Travers, Milton A. The Wampanoag tribute tribes of Martha's Vineyard. New Bedford, Mass., 1960. 78 p. illus.

Trumbull, J. H. Natick dictionary. U.S.
    Bureau of American Ethnology, Bulletin,
    25 (1903): 1-349.

Trumbull, J. H. Origin and early progress
    of Indian missions in New England.
    Worcester, 1874. 50 p.

Uhlenbeck, C. C. Ontwerp van eene
    vergelijkende vormleer van eenige
    Algonkin-talen. Amsterdam, Koninklijke
    Akademie van Wetenschappen, Afdeeling
    Letterkunde, Verhandelingen, n.s., 11,
    no. 3 (1910): 1-67.

Underhill, John. Newes from America. New
    York, Da Capo Press, 1971. 44 p.
    illus.

Various. King Philip's War narratives.
    Ann Arbor, University Microfilms, 1966.

Vaughan, Alden T. Pequots and Puritans:
    the causes of the War of 1637. William
    and Mary Quarterly, 3d ser., 21 (1964):
    256-269.

Vuilleumier, Marion. Indians on olde Cape
    Cod. Taunton, Mass., W. S. Sullwold,
    1970. 96 p. illus., map.

Wall, C. A. The Nipmuck Indians.
    Worcester, 1898. 21 p.

Weeks, A. G. Massasoit of the Wampanoags.
    Fall River, 1920. 270 p.

Wilder, H. H. Notes on the Indians of
    southern Massachusetts. American
    Anthropologist, n.s., 25 (1923): 197-
    218.

Willoughby, C. C. Antiquities of the New
    England Indians. Cambridge, 1935.
    314 p.

Willoughby, C. C. Certain earthworks of
    eastern Massachusetts. American
    Anthropologist, n.s., 13 (1911): 566-
    576.

Willoughby, C. C. Dress and ornaments of
    the New England Indians. American
    Anthropologist, n.s., 7 (1905): 499-508.

Willoughby, C. C. Houses and gardens of
    the New England Indians. American
    Anthropologist, n.s., 8 (1906): 115-132.

Willoughby, C. C. Indian burial place at
    Winthrop. Harvard University, Peabody
    Museum of American Archaeology and
    Ethnology, Papers, 11 (1924): 1-37.

Willoughby, C. C. Pottery of the New
    England Indians. In Putnam Anniversary
    Volume. New York, 1909: 83-101.

Willoughby, C. C. Textile fabrics of the
    New England Indians. American
    Anthropologist, n.s., 7 (1905): 85-93.

Willoughby, C. C. The adze and the
    ungrooved axe of the New England
    Indians. American Anthropologist, n.s.,
    9 (1907): 296-306.

Willoughby, C. C. The wilderness and the
    Indian. In A. B. Hart, ed. Commonwealth
    History of Massachusetts. Vol. 1. New
    York, 1927: 127-158.

Willoughby, C. C. Wooden bowls of the
    Algonquian Indians. American
    Anthropologist, n.s., 10 (1908): 423-
    434.

Willson, Lawrence. Another view of the
    Pilgrims. New England Quarterly, 34
    (1961): 160-177.

Winslow, E. Good news from New England.
    In E. Arber, ed. The Story of the
    Pilgrim Fathers. London, 1897: 581-592.

Winthrop, J. The history of New England.
    Boston, 1825. 2 v.

Wood, W. New England prospect.
    Massachusetts Archaeological Society,
    Bulletin, 8 (1947): 17-22.

Wood, W. New-England's prospect. New ed.:
    63-110. Boston, 1865.

Wright, H. A. Two letters to the editor
    concerning the boundaries of the
    Nipmucks. Massachusetts Archaeological
    Society, Bulletin, 2, no. 4 (1941): 14-
    16.

12-08   Metoac

Bolton, R. P. Indian life of long ago in
    the City of New York. New York, 1934.
    167 p.

Bolton, R. P. New York City in Indian
    possession. Indian Notes and Monographs,
    2 (1920): 225-395.

Bryant, Margaret M. Some Indian and Dutch
    names reflecting the early history of
    Brooklyn. Names, 20 (1972): 106-110.

Carr, L. G. and C. Westez. Surviving
    folktales and herbal lore among the
    Shinnecock Indians of Long Island.
    Journal of American Folklore, 58 (1945):
    113-123.

Denton, D. A brief description of New
    York. Ed. by G. Furman. New York, 1845.
    57 p.

Douglas, F. H. Long Island Indian culture. Denver Art Museum, Indian Leaflet Series, 50 (1932): 1-4.

Douglas, F. H. Long Island Indian tribes. Denver Art Museum, Indian Leaflet Series, 49 (1932): 1-4.

Dyson, Verne. Heather Flower, and other Indian stories of Long Island. Port Washington, I. J. Friedman, 1967. 94 p. illus.

Furman, G. Antiquities of Long Island. New York, 1875. 478 p.

Furman, Gabriel. Antiquities of Long Island. Edited by Frank Moore. Port Washington, I. J. Friedman, 1968. 271 p.

Harrington, M. R. An ancient village site of the Shinnecock Indians. American Museum of Natural History, Anthropological Papers, 22 (1924): 227-283.

Harrington, M. R. Ancient shell heaps near New York City. American Museum of Natural History, Anthropological Papers, 3 (1909): 169-179.

Harrington, M. R. Past and present of the Shinnecock Indians. Southern Workman, 32 (1903): 282-289.

Harrington, M. R. Shinnecock notes. Journal of American Folklore, 16 (1903): 37-39.

Hayne, C. The lost tribes. Narragansett Dawn, 1 (1935): 164-167.

Hunter, L. M. The Shinnecock Indians. Islip, 1950. 90 p.

Jefferson, T. Long Island. American Antiquarian Society, Transactions and Collections, 2 (1836): 305-367.

Macauley, J. The natural, statistical and civil history of the State of New York, Vol. 2: 252-275. Albany, 1829.

Mooney, J. Metoac. U.S. Bureau of American Ethnology, Bulletin, 30, vol. 1 (1907): 851.

Mooney, J. Montauk. U.S. Bureau of American Ethnology, Bulletin, 30, vol. 1 (1907): 934-935.

Morice, J. H. and F. G. Speck. Concerning "An ethnological introduction to the Long Island Indians". Massachusetts Archaeological Society, Bulletin, 7 (1946): 59-62.

Occum, S. An account of the Montauk Indians. Massachusetts Historical Society, Collections, ser. 1, 10 (1809): 106-111.

Orchard, F. P. A Matinecoc site on Long Island. Indian Notes, 5 (1928): 217-231.

Ruttenber, E. M. History of the Indian tribes of Hudson's River. Albany, 1872. 415 p.

Ruttenber, Edward M. History of the Indian tribes of Hudson's River. Port Washington, Kennikat Press, 1971. 5, 415 p. illus.

Saville, F. H. A Montauk cemetery at Easthampton. Indian Notes and Monographs, 2 (1920): 65-102.

Saville, F. H. Cache of blades from Long Island. Indian Notes, 3 (1926): 41-45.

Saville, F. H. Indian wells on Long Island. Indian Notes, 2 (1925): 207-211.

Skinner, A. Archaeology of the New York Coastal Algonkin. American Museum of Natural History, Anthropological Papers, 3 (1909): 213-235.

Solecki, R. S. The archaeological position of historic Fort Corchaug. Archaeological Society of Connecticut, Bulletin, 24 (1950): 3-40.

Tooker, W. W. John Eliot's first Indian teacher and interpreter. New York, 1896. 60 p.

Tooker, W. W. Some Indian fishing stations upon Long Island. Algonquian Series, 7 (1901): 7-62.

Tooker, William W. The Indian place-names on Long Island and islands adjacent with their probable significations. Edited by Alexander F. Chamberlain. Port Washington, I. J. Friedman, 1962. 314 p.

Westez, C. A. H. A study of the Long Island Indian problem. Massachusetts Archaeological Society, Bulletin, 5 (1944): 17-20.

Westez, C. A. H. An ethnological introduction to the Long Island Indians. Massachusetts Archaeological Society, Bulletin, 6 (1945): 39-42.

Williams, Lorraine Elise. Ft. Shantok and Ft. Corchaug: a comparative study of seventeenth century culture contact in the Long Island Sound area. Dissertation Abstracts International, 33 (1972/1973): 5110B-5111B. UM 73-11,788.

Wolley, C. A two years journal in New York. Ed. by E. B. O'Callaghan. New York, 1860. 97 p.

12-09 Mohegan

Adams, F. P. Pipe of peace. Narragansett Dawn, 1 (1935): 157.

Allen, Z. Native Indians of America. Providence, 1881. 55 p.

Anonymous. Extract from an Indian history. Massachusetts Historical Society, Collections, ser. 1, 9 (1804): 99-102.

Anonymous. The Mohegans. Bostonian Magazine (1895): 369-385, 503-513, 671-678.

Apes, W. A son of the forest. New York, 1829. 216 p.

Aubin, George F. Roger Williams: another view. International Journal of American Linguistics, 38 (1972): 266-267.

Aubin, George Francis. A historical phonology of Narragansett. Dissertation Abstracts International, 33 (1972/1973): 4379A. UM 73-2225.

Bacchiani, A. Giovanni da Verrazzano and his discoveries in North America. American Scenic and Historic Preservation Society, Annual Report, 15 (1910): 190-194.

Bartlett, J. R., ed. Letters of Roger Williams. Narragansett Club, Publications, 6 (1874): 1-420.

Beardsley, E. Edwards. The Mohegan land controversy. New Haven Colony Historical Society, Papers, 3 (1882): 205-225.

Bedford, Denton R. The Great Swamp Fight. Indian Historian, 4, no. 2 (1971): 27-41, 58.

Bibaud, F. M. Biographie des sagamos illustrés de l'Amérique Septentrionale, 111-114, 121-131, 135-160. Montréal, 1848.

Bodge, George Madison. Soldiers in King Philip's War. 3d ed. Baltimore, Genealogical Publishing, 1967. 13, 502 p. illus., maps.

Boissevain, E. Factors of Narragansett survival. Eastern States Archaeological Federation, Bulletin, 14 (1955): 12.

Boissevain, E. The detribalization of the Narragansett Indians. Ethnohistory, 3 (1956): 225-245.

Boissevain, Ethel. Detribalization and group identity: the Narragansett Indian case. New York Academy of Sciences, Transactions, ser. 2, 25 (1962/1963): 493-502.

Boissevain, Ethel. Narragansett survival: a study of group persistence through adapted traits. Ethnohistory, 6 (1959): 347-362.

Boissevain, Ethel. Narragansett survival: a study of group persistence through adopted traits. In Deward E. Walker, Jr., ed. The Emergent Native Americans. Boston, Little, Brown, 1972: 658-664.

Boissevain, Ethel. The detribalization of the Narragansett Indians: a case study. In Deward E. Walker, Jr., ed. The Emergent Native Americans. Boston, Little, Brown, 1972: 435-447.

Bradshaw, H. C. The Indians of Connecticut: the effect of English colonization. Deep River, 1935. 64 p.

Brown, M. W. Narragansett words. Narragansett Dawn, 2, no. 6 (1936): 6.

Burke, Charles T. Puritans at bay; the war against King Philip and the squaw sachems. New York, Exposition Press, 1967. 261 p. illus., map.

Butler, E. L. Notes on Indian ethnology and history. Archaeological Society of Connecticut, Bulletin, 27 (1953): 35-47.

Butler, E. L. Sweat-houses in the southern New England area. Massachusetts Archaeological Society, Bulletin, 7 (1945): 11-16.

Champlin, E. From old medicine records marked 1831. Narragansett Dawn, 2 (1936): 35-36.

Chapin, H. M. Indian graves. Rhode Island Historical Society Collections, 20 (1927): 14-32.

Chapin, H. M. Indian implements found in Rhode Island. Rhode Island Historical Society Collections, 17 (1924): 105-124; 18 (1925): 22-32.

Chapin, H. M. Sachems of the Narragansetts. Providence, 1931.

Chapin, H. M. Unusual Indian implements found in Rhode Island. Rhode Island Historical Society Collections, 19 (1926): 117-128.

Coolidge, John.   Hingham builds a
   meetinghouse. New England Quarterly, 34
   (1961): 435-461.

Cowan, William.   Narragansett 126 years
   after. International Journal of American
   Linguistics, 39 (1973): 7-13.

Cowan, William.   PA *a˚, *k and *t in
   Narragansett. International Journal of
   American Linguistics, 35 (1969): 28-33.

Daly, Patricia.   Approaches to faunal
   analysis in archaeology. American
   Antiquity, 34 (1969): 146-153.

Davis, Jefferson.   The Pequot War retold.
   Red Buffalo, 1 (1971): 1-13.

Day, Gordon M.   An Agawam fragment.
   International Journal of American
   Linguistics, 33 (1967): 244-247.

De Forest, J. W.   History of the Indians
   of Connecticut. Hartford, 1851.   509 p.

De Forest, John W.   History of the Indians
   of Connecticut from the earliest known
   period to 1850. Hamden, Conn., Archon
   Books, 1964.   48, 509 p.   illus., map.

De Forest, John William.   History of the
   Indians of Connecticut from the earliest
   known period to 1850.   St. Clair, Mich.,
   Scholarly Press, 1970.   26, 509 p.
   illus., map.

Dexter, H. M.   The New England Indians.
   Sabbath at Home, 2 (1868): 193-206.

Dixon, R. B.   The early migrations of the
   Indians of New England and the Maritime
   Provinces. American Association for the
   Advancement of Science, Proceedings,
   n.s., 24 (1914): 65-76.

Dorr, H. C.   The Narragansett. Rhode
   Island Historical Society Collections, 7
   (1885): 135-233.

Drake, S. G., ed.   The old Indian
   chronicle. Boston, 1867.   333 p.

Dwight, T.   Travels in New-England and
   New-York, Vol. 1: 84-102. London, 1823.

Edwards, J.   Observations on the Mohegan
   language. Massachusetts Historical
   Society, Collections, ser. 2, 10 (1823):
   81-160.

Ellis, G. W. and J. E. Morris.   King
   Philip's war.   New York, 1906.   326 p.

Ferguson, H. L.   Archeological exploration
   of Fishers Island. Indian Notes and
   Monographs, 11 (1935): 1-44.

Fielding, F. A. H.   Text of the Pequot
   sermon. American Anthropologist, n.s., 5
   (1903): 199-212.

Forbes, A.   Indian games. General Magazine
   and Historical Chronicle, University of
   Pennsylvania, 44 (1941): 27-30.

Freeman, F.   Civilization and barbarism.
   Cambridge, 1878.   186 p.

Gardner, L. L.   Relation of the Pequot
   warres. Massachusetts Historical
   Society, Collections, ser. 3, 3 (1833):
   131-160.

Gatschet, Albert S.   Narragansett
   vocabulary collected in 1879.
   International Journal of American
   Linguistics, 39 (1973): 14.

Glasko, F.   Succotash. Narragansett Dawn,
   1 (1935): 22-23.

Glasko, F.   The Narragansett mothers many
   years ago were proud home makers.
   Narragansett Dawn, 1 (1935): 93-94.

Goddard, Ives.   More on the nasalization
   of PA *a in Eastern Algonquian.
   International Journal of American
   Linguistics, 37 (1971): 139-145.

Goddard, Ives.   Notes on the genetic
   classification of the Algonquian
   languages. In Contributions to
   Anthropology: Linguistics I.   Ottawa,
   Queen's Printer, 1967: 7-12.   (Canada,
   National Museum, Bulletin, 214)

Gookin, D.   An historical account of the
   doings and sufferings of the Christian
   Indians in New England. Archaeologia
   Americana, Transactions and Collections,
   2 (1836): 423-534.

Gookin, D.   Historical collections of the
   Indians of New England. Massachusetts
   Historical Society, Collections, 1
   (1792): 141-227.

Gookin, Daniel.   Historical collections of
   the Indians in New England.   [n.p.]
   Towtaid, 1970.   16, 140 p.   maps.

Gookin, W. F.   Indian deeds on the
   Vineyard. Massachusetts Archaeological
   Society, Bulletin, 13, no. 2 (1952): 6-
   7.

Gookin, W. F.   Metsoo'onk. Massachusetts
   Archaeological Society, Bulletin, 12
   (1951): 58-60.

Haas, Mary R.   Roger William's sound
   shift: a study in Algonkian. In To Honor
   Roman Jakobson; Essays on the Occasion
   of His Seventieth Birthday. Vol. 1.   The

128
12 NORTHEAST

Hague, Mouton, 1967: 816-832. (Janua
Linguarum, Series Maior, 31)

Hallet, L. F. Cultural traits of the
Southern New England Indians.
Massachusetts Archaeological Society,
Bulletin, 15 (1954): 59-64.

Hamp, Eric P. On nasalization in
Narragansett. International Journal of
American Linguistics, 36 (1970): 58-59.

Hare, Lloyd C. M. Thomas Mayhew,
patriarch to the Indians (1593-1682).
St. Clair Shores, Mich., Scholarly
Press, 1971. 12, 231 p. illus., maps.

Hayne, C. The lost tribes. Narragansett
Dawn, 1 (1935): 164-167.

Heckewelder, John G. E. A narrative of
the mission of the United Brethren among
the Delaware and Mohegan Indians. New
York, Arno Press, 1971. 429 p.

Hicks, George L. Making a middle way:
problems of Monhegan identity. By George
L. Hicks and David I. Kertzer.
Southwestern Journal of Anthropology, 28
(1972): 1-24.

Holmes, A. A. Additional memoir of the
Moheagans. Massachusetts Historical
Society, Collections, ser. 1, 9 (1804):
75-99.

Howard, James H. A pioneer rheumatism
remedy of Mohegan origin. North Dakota
Quarterly, 25, no. 4 (1957): 121.

Jennings, Francis. Goals and functions of
Puritan missions to the Indians.
Ethnohistory, 18 (1971): 197-212.

Jones, J. W., ed. The relation of John
Verarzanus. In R. Hakluyt, ed. Divers
Voyages Touching the Discovery of
America. London, 1850: 55-90.

Kittredge, G. L. Letters of Samuel Lee
and Samuel Sewall relating to New
England and the Indians. Colonial
Society of Massachusetts, Publications,
14 (1912): 142-186.

Knight, M. V. The craniometry of Southern
New England Indians. Connecticut Academy
of Arts and Sciences, Memoirs, 4 (1915):
1-36.

Leach, D. E. A new view of the
declaration of war against the
Narragansetts, November, 1675. Rhode
Island History, 15 (1956): 33-41.

Leach, D. E. Flintlock and tomahawk. New
York, 1958. 304 p.

Leach, Douglas Edward. Flintlock and
tomahawk; New England in King Philip's
War. New York, W. W. Norton, 1966. 14,
304 p. illus., maps. (Norton Library,
N340)

Leach, Douglas Edward. The "whens" of
Mary Rowlandson's captivity. New England
Quarterly, 34 (1961): 352-363.

Little Bear. Narragansett fires.
Narragansett Dawn, 1 (1935): 115.

Lone Wolf. Birds of prey. Narragansett
Dawn, 1 (1935): 119-120.

Lone Wolf. The baby name. Narragansett
Dawn, 1 (1935): 118.

Lossing, B. J. The last of the Pequods.
In W. W. Beach, ed. Indian Miscellany.
Albany, 1877: 452-460.

MacCulloch, Susan L. A tripartite
political system among Christian Indians
of early Massachusetts. Kroeber
Anthropological Society Papers, 34
(1966): 63-73.

Marashio, Paul. Puritan and Pequot.
Indian Historian, 3, no. 3 (1970): 9-13;
3, no. 1 (1970): 54, 66.

Mason, J. A brief history of the Pequot
war. Massachusetts Historical Society,
Collections, ser. 2, 8 (1819): 120-153.

Mason, John. A brief history of the
Pequot War. Ann Arbor, University
Microfilms, 1966. 6, 10, 22 p.

Mason, John. A brief history of the
Pequot War. With an introduction and
some explanatory notes by Thomas Prince.
Freeport, N.Y., Books for Libraries
Press, 1971. 9, 20 p.

Mason, V. W. Bermuda's Pequots. Harvard
Alumni Bulletin, 39 (1937): 616-620.

Mathews, Edward. An abolitionist in
territorial Wisconsin: the journal of
Reverend Edward Mathews. Edited by
William Converse Haygood. Wisconsin
Magazine of History, 52 (1968/1969): 3-
18, 117-131, 248-262, 330-343.

Means, C. A. Mohegan-Pequot
relationships. Archaeological Society of
Connecticut, Bulletin, 21 (1947): 26-34.

Mooney, J. Mohegan. U.S. Bureau of
American Ethnology, Bulletin, 30, vol. 1
(1907): 926-927.

Mooney, J. Narraganset. U.S. Bureau of
American Ethnology, Bulletin, 30, vol. 2
(1910): 28-30.

Mooney, J. Niantic. U.S. Bureau of American Ethnology, Bulletin, 30, vol. 2 (1910): 68-69.

Mooney, J. Pequot. U.S. Bureau of American Ethnology, Bulletin, 30, vol. 2 (1910): 229-231.

Morgan, L. H. Ancient society, 173-174. New York, 1877.

Morgan, L. H. Systems of consanguinity and affinity. Smithsonian Contributions to Knowledge, 17 (1871): 291-382.

Morgan, L. H. The Indian Journals, 1859-62: p. 135. Ann Arbor, 1959.

Morton, T. New England Canaan. In P. Force, ed. Tracts and Other Papers relating Principally to the Origin, Settlement, and Progress of the Colonies in North America. Vol. 2, no. 5. Washington, D.C., 1838: 1-125.

Neesqutton. The children of Gitche Manitou. Narragansett Dawn, 1 (1935): 187-189.

Orr, C. History of the Pequot war. Cleveland, 1897. 149 p.

Parsons, U. Indian names of places in Rhode-Island. Providence, 1861. 32 p.

Parsons, U. Indian relics recently found in Charlestown. Historical Magazine, ser. 1, 7 (1863): 41-44.

Peale, A. L. Uncas and the Mohegan-Pequot. Boston, 1939.

Peckham, P. The Narragansett Indian Church. Narragansett Dawn, 1 (1935): 8-9.

Philhower, C. A. The earliest account of the Lenape and Narragansett Indians. Archaeological Society of New Jersey, Bulletin, 5 (1952): 10-11.

Pickering, J., ed. Dr. Edwards' observations on the Mohegan language. Massachusetts Historical Society, Collections, ser. 2, 10 (1823): 135-160.

Pine Tree, Chief. A feast for an Indian scout. Narragansett Dawn, 1 (1935): 179.

Pine Tree, Chief. An old Indian cure in measles. Narragansett Dawn, 1 (1935): 159-160.

Prince, J. D. and F. G. Speck. Dying American speech echoes from Connecticut. American Philosophical Society, Proceedings, 42 (1903): 346-352.

Prince, J. D. and F. G. Speck. Glossary of the Mohegan-Pequot language. American Anthropologist, n.s., 6 (1904): 18-45.

Prince, J. D. and F. G. Speck. The modern Pequots and their language. American Anthropologist, n.s., 5 (1903): 193-212.

Rainey, F. G. A compilation of historical data contributing to the ethnography of Connecticut and Southern New England Indians. Archaeological Society of Connecticut, Bulletin, 3 (1936): 1-89.

Ray, L. The aboriginal inhabitants of Connecticut. In W. W. Beach, ed. Indian Miscellany. Albany, 1877: 280-302.

Redwing, P. Art. Narragansett Dawn, 1 (1935): 234-235.

Redwing, P. History of the Indian's religion. Narragansett Dawn, 1 (1935): 195-199.

Redwing, P. Lessons in the Narragansett tongue. Narragansett Dawn, 1 (1935): 18, 44-45, 68, 88-89, 122-123, 138-139, 185-187, 204, 232-233, 259-260, 287; 2 (1936): 5, 29.

Redwing, P. Old beliefs. Narragansett Dawn, 1 (1935): 161.

Redwing, P. Sign language. Narragansett Dawn, 1 (1935): 255-256.

Redwing, P. The corn dance. Narragansett Dawn, 1 (1935): 96-98.

Redwing, P. Totems. Narragansett Dawn, 2 (1936): 12.

Redwing, P. Youth learns the mysteries of life from Gitche Manitou, the great spirit. Narragansett Dawn, 1 (1935): 25-27.

Rider, S. S. The lands of Rhode Island as they were known to Caunounicus and Miantunnomu when Roger Williams came in 1636. Providence, 1904. 297 p.

Salwen, Bert. Cultural inferences from faunal remains: examples from three Northeast coastal sites. Pennsylvania Archaeologist, 40, no. 1/2 (1970): 1-8.

Sherman, C. F. Habitations, summer and winter sites, and reasons for same. Massachusetts Archaeological Society, Bulletin, 6 (1944): 10-14.

Silver, Shirley. Natick consonants in reference to Proto-Central Algonquian. International Journal of American Linguistics, 26 (1960): 112-119, 234-241.

Simmons, William S. Cautantowwit's House;
an Indian burial ground on the island of
Conanicut in Narragansett Bay.
Providence, Brown University Press,
1970. 19, 178 p. illus., map.

Smith, DeC. Martyrs of the Oblong and
Little Nine. Caldwell, 1948. 310 p.

Solecki, R. S. The archaeological
position of historic Fort Corchaug.
Archaeological Society of Connecticut,
Bulletin, 24 (1950): 3-40.

Speck, F. G. A modern Mohegan-Pequot
text. American Anthropologist, n.s., 6
(1904): 469-476.

Speck, F. G. A Mohegan-Pequot witchcraft
tale. Journal of American Folklore, 16
(1903): 104-106.

Speck, F. G. Decorative art of the Indian
tribes of Connecticut. Canada,
Department of Mines, Geological Survey,
Memoirs, 75 (1915): 1-73.

Speck, F. G. Medicine practices of the
Northeastern Algonquians. International
Congress of Americanists, Proceedings,
19 (1915): 303-321.

Speck, F. G. Mohegan beadwork on birch-
bark. Indian Notes, 5 (1928): 295-298.

Speck, F. G. Mohegan traditions of
Muhkeahweesug, "the little men".
Papoose, 1, no. 7 (1903): 11-14.

Speck, F. G. Native tribes and dialects
of Connecticut. U.S. Bureau of American
Ethnology, Annual Reports, 43 (1926):
199-287.

Speck, F. G. Northern elements in
Iroquois and New England art. Indian
Notes, 2 (1925): 1-13.

Speck, F. G. Notes on the Mohegan and
Niantic Indians. American Museum of
Natural History, Anthropological Papers,
3 (1909): 183-210.

Speck, F. G. Remnants of the Nehantics.
Southern Workman, 47 (1918): 65-69.

Speck, F. G. Some Mohegan-Pequot legends.
Journal of American Folklore, 17 (1904):
183-184.

Spiess, M. Podunk Indian sites.
Archaeological Society of Connecticut,
Bulletin, 5 (1937): 2-6.

Spiess, M. The Indians of Connecticut.
New Haven, Committee on Historical
Publications, Tercentenary Commission of
the State of Connecticut, 1933. 33 p.

Stiles, E. Memoir of the Pequots.
Massachusetts Historical Society,
Collections, ser. 1, 10 (1809): 101-103.

Stiles, E. The number of the Nyhantic
tribe of Indians. Massachusetts
Historical Society, Collections, ser. 1,
10 (1809): 103-104; ser. 4, 10 (1857):
103-104.

Swadesh, M. Sociologic notes on
obsolescent languages. International
Journal of American Linguistics, 14
(1948): 226-235.

Tantaquidgeon, G. Mohegan medicinal
practices, weather lore, and
superstitions. U.S. Bureau of American
Ethnology, Annual Reports, 43 (1926):
264-279.

Tantaquidgeon, G. Notes on Mohegan-Pequot
basketry designs. Indians at Work, 2
(1935): 43-45.

Tantaquidgeon, Gladys. Folk medicine of
the Delaware and related Algonkian
Indians. Harrisburg, 1972. 145 p.
illus. (Pennsylvania, Historical and
Museum Commission, Anthropological
Series, 3)

Trumbull, B. A compendium of the Indian
Wars in New England. Ed. by F. B.
Hartranft. Hartford, 1926. 61 p.

Trumbull, B. A complete history of
Connecticut, Vol. 1: 39-57. New Haven,
1818.

Underhill, John. Newes from America. New
York, Da Capo Press, 1971. 44 p.
illus.

Various. King Philip's War narratives.
Ann Arbor, University Microfilms, 1966.

Vaughan, Alden T. A test of Puritan
justice. New England Quarterly, 38
(1965): 331-339.

Vaughan, Alden T. Pequots and Puritans:
the causes of the War of 1637. William
and Mary Quarterly, 3d ser., 21 (1964):
256-269.

Vaughan, Alden T. Pequots and Puritans:
the causes of the war of 1637. In Roger
L. Nichols and George R. Adams, eds. The
American Indian: Past and Present.
Waltham, Xerox College Publishing, 1971:
61-73.

Voight, Virginia F. Mohegan chief; the
story of Harold Tantaquidgeon. New
York, Funk and Wagnalls, 1965. 192 p.
illus.

Wahana. Ancient Narragansett bath houses. Narragansett Dawn, 1 (1935): 265.

Wheeler, R. A. The Pequot Indians. Westerly, 1877. 23 p.

Whipple, Chandler. The Indian in Connecticut. Stockbridge, Mass., Berkshire Traveller Press, 1972. 95 p.

Wilder, H. H. Notes on the Indians of southern Massachusetts. American Anthropologist, n.s., 25 (1923): 197-218.

Wilder, H. H. The physiognomy of the Indians of southern New England. American Anthropologist, n.s., 14 (1912): 415-436.

Williams, Lorraine Elise. Ft. Shantok and Ft. Corchaug: a comparative study of seventeenth century culture contact in the Long Island Sound area. Dissertation Abstracts International, 33 (1972/1973): 5110B-5111B. UM 73-11,788.

*Williams, R. A key into the language of America. London, 1643. 197 p.

Williams, Roger. A key into the language of America, 1643. Menston, Scolar Press, 1971. 21, 200 p.

Williams, Roger. A key into the language of America. 5th ed. Ann Arbor, Gryphon Books, 1971. 205 p.

Willoughby, C. C. Antiquities of the New England Indians. Cambridge, 1935. 314 p.

Willoughby, C. C. Dress and ornaments of the New England Indians. American Anthropologist, n.s., 7 (1905): 499-508.

Willoughby, C. C. Houses and gardens of the New England Indians. American Anthropologist, n.s., 8 (1906): 115-132.

Willoughby, C. C. Wooden bowls of the Algonquian Indians. American Anthropologist, n.s., 10 (1908): 423-434.

Willson, Lawrence. Another view of the Pilgrims. New England Quarterly, 34 (1961): 160-177.

Wood, G. A. The Mohegan Indians east and west. Mississippi Valley Historical Association, Proceedings, 10 (1920/1921): 440-453.

Woodward, Carl. Plantation in Yankeeland: the story of Cocumscussoc, mirror of colonial Rhode Island. Chester, Conn., Pequot Press, 1971. 9, 198 p.

12-10   Nanticoke

Dunlap, A. R. A bibliographical discussion of the Indian languages of the Delmarva Peninsula. Archaeological Society of Delaware, Bulletin, 4, no. 5 (1949): 2-5.

Anonymous. Choptank. U.S. Bureau of American Ethnology, Bulletin, 30, vol. 1 (1907): 291.

Babcock, W. H. The Nanticoke Indians of Indian River. American Anthropologist, n.s., 1 (1899): 277-282.

Bender, H. E. The Nanticoke Indians in Lancaster County. Lancaster County Historical Association, Publications, 23 (1929): 121-130.

Bozman, J. L. The history of Maryland, Vol. 1: 103-193. Baltimore, 1837.

Brinton, D. G. A vocabulary of the Nanticoke dialect. American Philosophical Society, Proceedings, 31 (1893): 325-333.

Brinton, D. G. The Lenapé and their legends, 22-29. Philadelphia, 1885.

Bushnell, D. I. Native cemeteries and forms of burial east of the Mississippi. U.S. Bureau of American Ethnology, Bulletin, 71 (1920): 24-26.

Carr, L. G. Native drinks in the Southeast and their values, with special emphasis on persimmon beer. Delaware County Institute of Science, Proceedings, 10 (1947): 29-43.

Crozier, A. Fishing methods of the Indians of the Delmarva Region. Archaeological Society of Delaware, Bulletin, 4, no. 4 (1947): 16-19.

Crozier, A. The Nanticokes of the Delmarva Peninsula. Archaeological Society of Delaware, Bulletin, 1, no. 5 (1934): 2-6.

Davidson, D. S. Burial customs in the Delmarva Peninsula and the question of their chronology. American Antiquity, 1 (1935): 84-97.

Denny, E. R. Indians of Kent Island. [Stevensville, Md.? 1959]. 20 p.

Ferguson, A. L. L. An ossuary near Piscataway Creek. American Antiquity, 5 (1940): 4-13.

Ferguson, A. L. L.   Moyaone and the
Piscataway Indians. Washington, D.C.,
1935. 44 p.

Ferguson, Alice L. L.   The Piscataway
Indians of southern Maryland. By Alice
L. L. Ferguson and Henry G. Ferguson.
Accokeek, Md., Alice Ferguson
Foundation, 1960. 46 p. illus.

Gilbert, W. H., Jr.   The Wesorts of
southern Maryland. Washington Academy of
Sciences, Journal, 35 (1945): 237-246.

Goldsborough, E. R.   The aborigines of the
lower Potomac River valley. Pennsylvania
Archaeologist, 8 (1938): 27-36.

Hassrick, R. B.   A visit with the
Nanticoke. Archaeological Society of
Delaware, Bulletin, 4, no. 1 (1943): 7-
8.

Holmes, W. H.   Aboriginal shell-heaps of
the Middle Atlantic tidewater region.
American Anthropologist, n.s., 9 (1907):
113-128.

Holmes, W. H.   Stone implements of the
Potomac-Chesapeake tidewater province.
U.S. Bureau of American Ethnology,
Annual Reports, 15 (1897): 3-152.

Lincoln, A. T.   Our Indians of early
Delaware. Delaware Citizens Association,
Historical Bulletin, 1 (1932): 1-42.

MacLeod, W. C.   Piscataway royalty.
Washington Academy of Sciences, Journal,
16 (1926): 301-309.

Marye, W. B.   A Quiakeson house in eastern
Maryland. American Antiquity, 9 (1944):
456.

Marye, W. B.   Indian paths of the Delmarva
Peninsula. Archaeological Society of
Delaware, Bulletin, 2, no. 3 (1936): 5-
22; 2, no. 4 (1936): 4-27; 2, no. 5
(1937): 2-15; 2, no. 6 (1938): 4-11.

Marye, W. B.   Indian towns of the
southeastern part of Sussex County.
Archaeological Society of Delaware,
Bulletin, 3, no. 2 (1939): 18-25; 3,
no. 3 (1940): 21-28.

Marye, W. B.   The Wiccomiss Indians of
Maryland. American Antiquity, 4 (1938):
146-152; 5 (1939): 51-55.

McAllister, James A., comp.   Indian lands
in Dorchester County, Maryland: selected
sources, 1669 to 1870. Cambridge, Md.,
1962. 6, 152 l. maps.

Mooney, J.   Indian tribes of the District
of Columbia. American Anthropologist, 2
(1889): 259-266.

Mooney, J. and C. Thomas. Conoy. U.S.
Bureau of American Ethnology, Bulletin,
30, vol. 1 (1907): 339-341.

Mooney, J. and C. Thomas. Nanticoke. U.S.
Bureau of American Ethnology, Bulletin,
30, vol. 2 (1910): 24-26.

Murray, W. V. Nanticokes. American
Antiquarian Society, Transactions and
Collections, 2 (1836): 305-367.

Neumann, Georg K.   A re-examination of the
question of the Middle Western origin of
the Delaware Indians. Indiana Academy of
Science, Proceedings, 79 (1969): 60-61.

Parker, A. C.   The Nanticoke. Pennsylvania
Archaeologist, 5 (1935): 83-90; 6
(1936): 3-12.

Semmes, R.   Aboriginal Maryland, 1608-
1689. Maryland Historical Magazine, 24
(1929): 157-172, 195-209.

Speck, F. G.   A maker of eel-pots among
the Nanticokes of Delaware.
Archaeological Society of Delaware,
Bulletin, 4, no. 5 (1949): 25-27.

Speck, F. G.   Back again to Indian River,
its people and their games.
Archaeological Society of Delaware,
Bulletin, 3, no. 5 (1942): 17-24.

Speck, F. G.   "Cudgelling rabbits," an old
Nanticoke hunting tradition and its
significance. Archaeological Society of
Delaware, Bulletin, 4, no. 4 (1946): 9-
12.

Speck, F. G.   Gourds of the Southeastern
Indians. Boston, 1941. 113 p.

Speck, F. G.   Indians of the eastern shore
of Maryland. Baltimore, 1922. 15 p.

Speck, F. G.   Medicine practices of the
Northeastern Algonquians. International
Congress of Americanists, Proceedings,
19 (1915): 303-321.

Speck, F. G.   The frolic among the
Nanticoke of Indian River Hundred,
Delaware. Archaeological Society of
Delaware, Bulletin, 4, no. 1 (1943): 2-
4.

Speck, F. G.   The Nanticoke and Conoy
Indians. Historical Society of Delaware,
Papers, n.s., 1 (1927): 1-77.

Speck, F. G.   The Nanticoke community of
Delaware. Museum of the American Indian,
Heye Foundation, Contributions, 2, no. 4
(1915): 1-43.

Speck, F. G. and C. E. Schaeffer. The
deer and the rabbit hunting drive in

Virginia and the Southeast. Southern
Indian Studies, 2 (1950): 3-20.

Stephenson, Robert L. The Accokeek Creek
site; a Middle Atlantic seaboard culture
sequence. By Robert L. Stephenson and
Alice L. L. Ferguson. With sections by
Henry G. Ferguson. Ann Arbor,
University of Michigan, 1963. 10,
215 p. illus. (Michigan, University,
Museum of Anthropology, Anthropological
Papers, 20)

Stewart, Frank H., comp. Indians of
southern New Jersey. Port Washington,
Kennikat Press, 1972. 93 p. illus.

Stewart, T. D. A report on skeletal
remains. American Antiquity, 5 (1940):
13-18.

Tantaquidgeon, G. A study of Delaware
Indian medicine practice and folk
beliefs. Harrisburg, 1942. 91 p.

Toogood, Anna C. Piscataway Park,
Maryland: general historic background
study. Washington, D.C., U.S. Office of
Archeology and Historic Preservation,
1969. 3, 152 l. illus., maps.

Uhler, S. P. Pennsylvania's Indian
relations to 1754. Allentown, 1951.
144 p.

Various. A relation of Maryland. Ann
Arbor, University Microfilms, 1966.
map.

Wallace, Paul A. W. Indian paths of
Pennsylvania. Harrisburg, Pennsylvania
Historical and Museum Commission, 1965.
8, 227 p. maps.

Weslager, C. A. Folklore among the
Nanticokes of Indian River Hundred.
Delaware Folklore Bulletin, 1, no. 5
(1955): 17-18.

Weslager, C. A. Nanticokes and the
buzzard song. Archaeological Society of
Delaware, Bulletin, 4, no. 2 (1945): 14-
17.

Weslager, C. A. The anthropological
position of the Indian tribes of the
Delmarva Peninsula. Archaeological
Society of Delaware, Bulletin, 4, no. 4
(1947): 3-7.

Weslager, C. A. The Nanticoke Indians.
Harrisburg, 1948. 159 p.

Weslager, C. A. The Nanticoke Indians in
early Pennsylvania. Pennsylvania
Magazine of History and Biography, 67
(1943): 345-355.

Weslager, C. A. Wynicaco--a Choptank
Indian chief. American Philosophical
Society, Proceedings, 87 (1944): 398-
402.

Weslager, Clinton A. Delaware's forgotten
folk; the story of the Moors and
Nanticokes. Philadelphia, University of
Pennsylvania Press, 1943. 9, 215 p.
illus., map.

12-11 Neutral

Anderson, R. T. Malahide, Yarmouth and
Bayham Townships. Annual Archaeological
Report, being Part of Appendix to the
Report of the Minister of Education,
Ontario (1902): 79-92.

Beauchamp, W. M. Indian nations of the
Great Lakes. American Antiquarian and
Oriental Journal, 17 (1895): 321-325.

Beauchamp, W. M. The Neutral Nation.
American Antiquarian and Oriental
Journal, 16 (1894): 193-200.

Coyne, J. H. The Southwold earthwork and
the country of the Neutrals. Canadian
Institute, Annual Report, 6 (1893): 22-
34.

Hanzeli, Victor E. Missionary linguistics
in New France; a study of seventeenth-
and eighteenth-century descriptions of
American Indian languages. The Hague,
Mouton, 1969. 141 p. illus., map.
(Janua Linguarum, Series Maior, 29)

Harris, W. R. The flint workers. Annual
Archaeological Report, being Part of
Appendix to the Report of the Minister
of Education, Ontario (1900): 28-36.

Herriott, W. Aboriginal agriculture in
southwestern Ontario. Waterloo
Historical Society, Annual Report, 11
(1923): 18-21.

Hewitt, J. N. B. Neutrals. U.S. Bureau of
American Ethnology, Bulletin, 30, vol. 2
(1910): 60-62.

Houghton, F. Report on the Neuter
Cemetery, Grand Island, N.Y. Buffalo
Society of Natural Sciences, Bulletin, 9
(1909): 377-385.

Houghton, F. The characteristics of
Iroquoian village sites of western New
York. American Anthropologist, n.s., 18
(1916): 508-520.

Houghton, F. The Indian inhabitants of
the Niagara Frontier. Journal of
American History, 16 (1922): 213-228.

Houghton, F. The Indian occupancy of the Niagara Frontier. Buffalo Society of Natural Sciences, Bulletin, 9 (1909): 263-374.

Kenton, E., ed. The Indians of North America, Vol. 1: 417-427. New York, 1927.

Knowles, F. H. S. Physical anthropology of the Roebuck Iroquois. Canada, Department of Mines, National Museum of Canada, Bulletin, 87 (1937): 1-75.

Knowles, F. H. S. The torture of captives by the Indians of eastern North America. American Philosophical Society, Proceedings, 82 (1940): 151-225.

Kraus, B. S. Acculturation. American Antiquity, 9 (1944): 302-318.

Orr, R. B. The Attiwandarons. Annual Archaeological Report, being Part of Appendix to the Report of the Minister of Education, Ontario (1913): 7-20.

Orr, R. B. The Iroquois in Canada. Annual Archaeological Report, being Part of Appendix to the Report of the Minister of Education, Ontario, 31 (1919): 9-55.

Parker, A. C. The origin of the Iroquois as suggested by their archeology. American Anthropologist, n.s., 18 (1916): 479-507.

Reville, F. D. History of the County of Brant, Vol. 1: 15-68. Brantford, 1920.

Ridley, Frank. Archaeology of the Neutral Indians. Islington, Ont., Etobicoke Historical Society, 1961. 66 p. illus.

Ritchie, W. A. Early Huron and Neutral sand knoll sites in western New York. New York State Archaeological Association, Researches and Transactions, 7, no. 3 (1930): 62-78.

Skinner, A. An unusual Canadian disc pipe. Indian Notes, 3 (1926): 39-41.

Thwaites, R. G., ed. The Jesuit Relations and allied documents. Cleveland, 1896-1901. 74 v.

Trigger, Bruce G. Settlement as an aspect of Iroquoian adaptation at the time of contact. American Anthropologist, 65 (1963): 86-101.

Trigger, Bruce G. The French presence in Huronia: the structure of Franco-Huron relations in the first half of the seventeenth century. Canadian Historical Review, 49 (1968): 107-141.

Waugh, F. W. Attiwandaron or Neutral village-sites in Brant County. Annual Archaeological Report, being Part of Appendix to the Report of the Minister of Education, Ontario (1902): 70-79.

White, Marian. Ethnic identification and Iroquois groups in western New York and Ontario. Ethnohistory, 18 (1971): 19-38.

White, Marian E. Iroquois culture history in the Niagara Frontier area of New York State. Ann Arbor, University of Michigan, 1961. 8, 155 p. illus. (Michigan, University, Museum of Anthropology, Anthropological Papers, 16)

Wintemberg, W. J. Bone and horn harpoon heads of the Ontario Indians. Annual Archaeological Report, being Part of Appendix to the Report of the Minister of Education, Ontario (1905): 33-56.

Wintemberg, W. J. Relics of the Attiwandarons. Records of the Past, 4 (1905): 266-275.

Wintemberg, W. J. The Middleport prehistoric village site. Canada, Department of Mines, Geological Survey, Museum Bulletin, 109 (1948): 1-79.

Wright, Gordon K. The Neutral Indians; a source book. Rochester, 1963. 95 p. illus., map. (New York State Archaeological Association, Occasional Papers, 4)

Wright, James V. The Middleport horizon. Anthropologica, n.s., 2 (1960): 113-120.

Wright, James V. The Ontario Iroquois tradition. Dissertation Abstracts, 24 (1963/1964): 4346-4347. UM 64-7111.

Yarnell, Richard Asa. Aboriginal relationships between culture and plant life in the Upper Great Lakes region. Ann Arbor, University of Michigan, 1964. 6, 218 p. (Michigan, University, Museum of Anthropology, Anthropological Papers, 23)

Young, A. W. History of Chautauqua County, 20-34. Buffalo, 1875.

12-12 Pennacook

Allen, W. The history of Chelmsford. Haverhill, 1820. 192 p.

Ballard, E. Character of the Penacooks. New Hampshire Historical Society, Collections, 8 (1866): 428-445.

Ballard, E. Indian mode of applying names. New Hampshire Historical Society, Collections, 8 (1866): 446-452.

Daniels, Thomas E. Vermont Indians. Edited by Kathleen Rowlands. Orwell, Vt., Mrs. Thomas E. Daniels, 1963. 63 p. illus.

Day, Gordon M. An Agawam fragment. International Journal of American Linguistics, 33 (1967): 244-247.

Day, Gordon M. The name Contoocook. International Journal of American Linguistics, 27 (1961): 168-171.

Eckstorm, F. H. The Indians of Maine. In L. C. Hatch, ed. Maine, a History. Vol. 1. New York, 1919: 43-64.

Fowler, W. S. Stone age methods of woodworking in the Connecticut Valley. Archaeological Society of Connecticut, Bulletin, 20 (1946): 1-32.

Gookin, D. Historical collection of the Indians in New England. Massachusetts Historical Society, Collections, ser. 4, 1 (1859): 141-227.

Gookin, D. Historical collection of the Indians in New England. Massachusetts Historical Society, Collections, ser. 1, 1 (1792): 141-227.

Gookin, Daniel. Historical collections of the Indians in New England. [n.p.] Towtaid, 1970. 16, 140 p. maps.

Johnson, F. Indians of New Hampshire. Appalachia, n.s., 6, no. 7 (1940): 3-15.

Kawashima, Yasu. Jurisdiction of the colonial courts over the Indians in Massachusetts, 1689-1763. New England Quarterly, 42 (1969): 532-550.

Knight, M. V. The craniometry of Southern New England Indians. Connecticut Academy of Arts and Sciences, Memoirs, 4 (1915): 1-36.

Leach, Douglas Edward. Flintlock and tomahawk; New England in King Philip's War. New York, W. W. Norton, 1966. 14, 304 p. illus., maps. (Norton Library, N340)

Mooney, J. Pocomtuc. U.S. Bureau of American Ethnology, Bulletin, 30, vol. 2 (1910): 270.

Mooney, J. and C. Thomas. Pennacook. U.S. Bureau of American Ethnology, Bulletin, 30, vol. 2 (1910): 225-226.

Potter, C. E. Indians of New England. In History of Manchester, New Hampshire. Manchester, 1856: 22-100.

Proctor, M. A. The Indians of the Winnipesaukee and Pemigewasset Valleys. Franklin, N.H., 1930. 67 p.

Robbins, M. Indians of the Old Colony. Massachusetts Archaeological Society, Bulletin, 17 (1956): 59-74.

Schoolcraft, H. R. Pennacooks. In his Information respecting the History, Condition, and Prospects of the Indian Tribes of the United States. Vol. 5. Philadelphia, 1855: 217-237.

Stiles, E. Indians on the Connecticut River. Massachusetts Historical Society, Collections, ser. 4, 10 (1857): 104-105.

Stiles, E. Indians on the Connecticut River. Massachusetts Historical Society, Collections, ser. 1, 10 (1809): 104-105.

Thomas, Peter A. Middle Connecticut Valley Indian house types: a cautionary note. Man in the Northeast, 1 (1971): 48-50.

Wilder, H. H. Excavation of Indian graves in western Massachusetts. American Anthropologist, n.s., 7 (1905): 295-300.

Wilder, H. H. Notes on the Indians of southern Massachusetts. American Anthropologist, n.s., 25 (1923): 197-218.

Wilder, H. H. The physiogonomy of the Indians of southern New England. American Anthropologist, n.s., 14 (1912): 415-436.

Wilder, H. H. and R. W. Whipple. The position of the body in aboriginal interments in western Massachusetts. American Anthropologist, n.s., 19 (1917): 372-387.

Willoughby, C. C. Antiquities of the New England Indians. Cambridge, 1935. 314 p.

Willoughby, C. C. The wilderness and the Indian. In A. B. Hart, ed. Commonwealth History of Massachusetts. Vol. 1. Cambridge, 1927: 127-158.

12-13 Middle Atlantic States Mestizos

Anonymous. Community of outcasts. Appleton's Journal of Literature, Science, and Art, 7 (1872): 324-329.

Anonymous. The Jackson Whites. Eugenical
News, 16 (1931): 218.

Beale, Calvin L. American tri-racial
isolates: their status and pertinence to
genetic research. Eugenics Quarterly, 4
(1957): 187-196.

Beale, Calvin L. An overview of the
phenomenon of mixed racial isolates in
the United States. American
Anthropologist, 74 (1972): 704-710.

Beck, Henry C. Fare to midlands;
forgotten towns of Central New Jersey.
New York, Dutton, 1939. 456 p. illus.,
map.

*Berry, Brewton. Almost White. New York,
Macmillan, 1963. 11, 212 p.

Berry, Brewton. America's mestizos. In
Noel P. Gist and Anthony Gary Dworkin,
eds. The Blending of Races. New York,
Wiley-Interscience, 1972: 191-212.

Chanler, David. The Jackson Whites: an
American episode. Crisis, 46 (1939):
138.

Cohen, David Stephen. They walk these
hills: a study of social solidarity
among the racially-mixed people of the
Ramapo Mountains. Dissertation Abstracts
International, 32 (1971/1972): 2222A-
2223A. UM 71-25,992.

Cohen, David Steven. The origin of the
'Jackson Whites': history and legend
among the Ramapo Mountain People.
Journal of American Folklore, 85 (1972):
260-266.

Collins, Daniel. The racially-mixed
people of the Ramapos: undoing the
Jackson White legends. American
Anthropologist, 74 (1972): 1276-1285.

Dunlap, A. R. Trends in the naming of
tri-racial mixed-blood groups in the
eastern United States. By A. R. Dunlap
and C. A. Weslager. American Speech, 22
(1947): 81-87.

Foster, Laurence. Negro-Indian
relationships in the Southeast.
Philadelphia, University of Pennsylvania
Press, 1935. 86 p.

Frazier, Edward Franklin. The Negro
family in the United States. Chicago,
University of Chicago Press, 1939. 32,
686 p. illus.

Gardner, Emelyn E. Folklore from the
Schoharie Hills, New York. Ann Arbor,
University of Michigan Press, 1937. 15,
351 p. illus., maps.

Gilbert, William Harlen, Jr. Memorandum
concerning the characteristics of the
larger mixed-blood racial islands of the
eastern United States. Social Forces, 24
(1945/1946): 438-447.

Gilbert, William Harlen, Jr. Surviving
Indian groups of the eastern United
States. Smithsonian Institution, Annual
Report of the Board of Regents (1948):
407-438.

Gilbert, William Harlen, Jr. The Wesorts
of southern Maryland: an outcasted
group. Washington Academy of Sciences,
Journal, 35 (1945): 237-246.

Greene, Frances Ensign. The Tobacco Road
of the North. American Mercury, 53
(1941): 15-22.

Harris, Mark. America's oldest
interracial community. Negro Digest, 6,
no. 9 (1947/1948): 21-24.

Harte, Thomas J. Trends in mate selection
in a tri-racial isolate. Social Forces,
37 (1958/1959): 215-221.

Johnston, James Hugo. Documentary
evidence of the relations of Negroes and
Indians. Journal of Negro History, 14
(1929): 21-43.

Kaufman, Charles H. An ethnomusicological
survey among the people of the Ramapo
Mountains. New York Folklore Quarterly,
23 (1967): 3-43, 109-131.

Kite, Elizabeth S. The Pineys. Survey, 31
(1913): 7-13, 38-40.

Price, Edward T. A geographic analysis of
White-Negro-Indian racial mixtures in
the eastern United States. Association
of American Geographers, Annals, 43
(1953): 138-155.

Sawyer, Claire Marie. Some aspects of the
fertility of a tri-racial isolate.
Washington, D.C., Catholic University of
America Press, 1961. 13, 69 p. illus.
(Catholic University of America, Studies
in Sociology, 46)

Shapiro, Harry L. The mixed-blood Indian.
In Oliver LaFarge, ed. The Changing
Indian. Norman, University of Oklahoma
Press, 1942: 19-27.

Speck, Frank G. The Jackson Whites.
Southern Workman, 40 (1911): 104-107.

Steward, William. Gouldtown, a very
remarkable settlement of ancient date.
By William Steward and Theophilus G.
Steward. Philadelphia, Press of J. B.
Lippincott, 1913. 237 p. illus.

Storms, John C. The origin of the
Jackson-Whites of the Ramapo Mountains.
2d ed. Park Ridge, N.J., 1945. 30 l.
illus.

Van de Water, Frederic F. Grey riders;
the story of the New York state
troopers. New York, G. P. Putnam's
Sons, 1922. 10, 370 p.

Weller, George. The Jackson Whites. New
Yorker, 14, no. 31 (Sept. 17, 1938): 29-
32, 36, 38-39.

Weslager, Clinton A. Delaware's forgotten
folk; the story of the Moors and
Nanticokes. Philadelphia, University of
Pennsylvania Press, 1943. 9, 215 p.
illus., map.

Witkop, Carl J., Jr., et al. Medical and
dental findings in the Brandywine
isolate. Alabama Journal of Medical
Science, 3 (1966): 382-403.

Yap, Angelita Q. The study of a kinship
system: its structural principles.
Washington, D.C., Catholic University of
America Press, 1961. 11, 76 p.
(Catholic University of America, Studies
in Sociology, 45)

13 Southeast

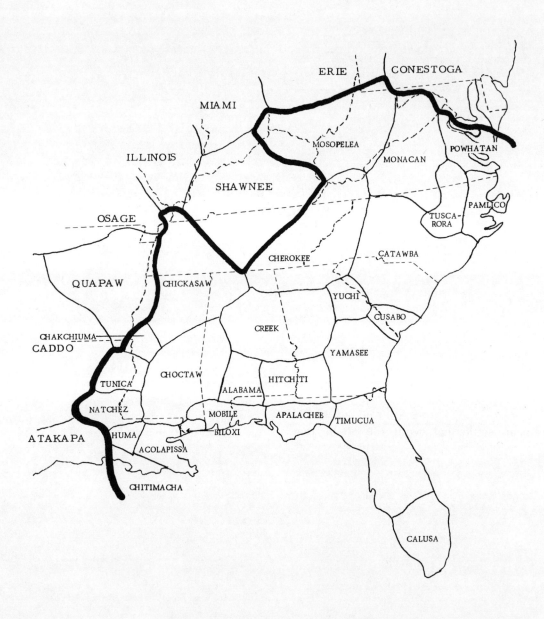

13 Southeast

This is a very large area, consisting generally of all the southeastern United States, running south and west from Chesapeake Bay around the coast to the Mississippi River Delta, north to the confluence of the Ohio River with the Mississippi, and generally northeast from that point, excepting the territory of the Western Shawnee of the lower Ohio River region, which is considered to be a part of the Midwest. The whole area is a region of warm, temperate climate and heavy forest, partly deciduous and partly coniferous. Subsistence was based on maize, beans, and squash horticulture, with hunting being secondary, although important. Fish and shellfish formed a large part of the diet in the coastal areas. Towns were usually permanent, often large, and usually fortified. The ethnic groups were large, with advanced sociopolitical organization, climaxing in the class system of the Natchez in the lower Mississippi valley. There were great confederacies of linguistically related groups, such as those of the "Civilized Tribes," the Cherokee, Creek, Chickasaw, Choctaw, and Seminole. Descent was usually matrilineal, with clans, sibs, moieties, and phratries forming the basis of the political organization. There was a good deal of movement by large groups of native peoples during historic times, such as the move of the Tuscarora from North Carolina to New York State in the eighteenth century, the move of the Mosopelea from the upper Ohio River region to the lower Mississippi region, the numerous moves of the Shawnee over much of the area, and the wide scattering of Yuchi groups at various times. As in the Northeast, this was an area of early and intense European settlement, with the result that most of the aboriginal groups have been destroyed or removed to distant reservations. Most noted of these movements was the forced removal of the Five Civilized Tribes to reservations in the present state of Oklahoma during the 1840s. This was paralleled at the same time by the removal of the tribes of the Midwest from their traditional homeland. There are still large groups of Indians remaining, however, including Cherokee and Creek populations, as well as groups formed during historic times, such as the Seminole in Florida and the Lumbee in North Carolina.

13-01. Acolapissa. The Acolapissa, with the Bayogoula, Chawasha (Chawacha), Mugulasha, Quinipissa, Okelousa (Okalusa), Tangipahoa, and Washa, lived in southeastern Louisiana from the west side of the Mississippi River east to the Pearl River and north to approximately the border of the state of Mississippi. They spoke languages belonging to the Muskogean family, except that the Chawasha and Washa may have spoken languages related to Chitimacha. All of these groups became extinct or merged with other groups in the late eighteenth century.

13-02. Alabama. The Alabama (Alibamu), with the Kaskinampo, Koasati (Alabama-Coushatta), Muklasa, Pawokti, and Tawasa, lived in south-central Alabama and the northwestern tip of Florida. The descendants of these groups now live principally on the Polk County Reservation in Texas (the Alabama-Coushatta Tribe of Texas), in the Alabama-Quassarte Tribal Town in Oklahoma, and in the Coushatta Community in Louisiana. They spoke Muskogean languages. The Alabama-Coushatta Tribe numbered about 450 in 1969, the Coushatta Community 196 in 1966, and the population of the Alabama-Quassarte town was not listed.

13-03. Apalachee. The Apalachee lived in the central part of northwestern Florida in the area of Tallahassee, the present state capital. They spoke a Muskogean language and became extinct as a group in the nineteenth century.

13-04. Biloxi. The Biloxi lived in the lower Pascagoula River area in southeastern Mississippi. There may be a few Biloxi still living in Louisiana. They spoke a Siouan language and are now extinct as a group.

13-05. Calusa. The Calusa, with the Ais (Jece), Guacata, and Tekesta (Tequesta), lived in southern Florida, approximately south of a line through Tampa and Cape Canaveral. They probably spoke languages akin to Timucua and became extinct as groups in the eighteenth and nineteenth centuries.

13-06. Catawba. The Catawba (Issa, Esau), with the Adshusheer, Backhook, Cape Fear Indians, Cheraw (Sara, Saraw, Suali), Congaree, Eno, Hook, Keyauwee, Peedee (Pedee), Santee (Santee Catawba), Sewee, Shoccoree (Shakori), Sissipahaw, Sugeree, Waccamaw, Warrenuncock, Wateree (Chickanee, Guatari), Waxhaw (Wahau), Winyaw, and Woccon, lived on the coast and piedmont of much of North Carolina and South Carolina. The descendants of these groups now live on the former Catawba Indian Reservation and on a state reservation in South Carolina. They spoke a divergent Siouan language and numbered about 700 in 1970.

13-07. Chakchiuma. The Chakchiuma lived in west-central Mississippi on the Yalobusha River. They spoke a Muskogean language and became extinct as a group in the eighteenth century.

13-08. Cherokee. The Cherokee lived in the highest areas of the southern Appalachian Mountains, principally in Tennessee and North Carolina, but also in Virginia, Alabama, Georgia, and South Carolina. They now live mainly on the Cherokee Reservation in western North Carolina (the Eastern Cherokee), and on the former Cherokee Reservation in northeastern Oklahoma. They speak an Iroquoian language and numbered 66,150 in 1970.

13-09. Chickasaw. The Chickasaw lived principally in northern Mississippi, but ranged into northwestern Alabama and western Tennessee. They now live principally on the former Chickasaw Indian Reservation in south-central Oklahoma. They speak a Muskogean language and numbered 5,616 in 1970.

13-10. Chitimacha. The Chitimacha (Shetinasha) live in southern and southwestern Louisiana, principally on the Chitimacha Indian Reservation on Grand Lake near Charenton, Louisiana. They spoke a language isolate in the Macro-Algonquian phylum and numbered about 600 in 1970.

13-11. Choctaw. The Choctaw (Chackta) lived in southeastern Mississippi and the neighboring part of Alabama. They now live principally on the Choctaw Indian Reservation near Philadelphia, Mississippi, the former Choctaw Indian Reservation in southeastern Oklahoma, and in three small communities in Louisiana. They speak a Muskogean language and numbered about 20,000 in 1970.

13-12. Creek. The Creek (Muskogee), including the Coweta, Kasihta, Abihka, and Coosa, among others, lived principally in central Georgia, but had towns in locations from the Atlantic coast and the Savannah River to central Alabama. They now live principally on the former Creek Indian Reservation in east-central Oklahoma and in a community near Atmore, Alabama. They speak a Muskogean language and numbered 17,004 in 1970.

13-13. Cusabo. The Cusabo, including the Ashipoo (Ashepoo), Combahee, Edisto, Etiwaw, Kiawa (Kiawaw), Stono, Wapoo, and Wimbee, lived on the Atlantic coast in southern South Carolina, between Charleston Harbor and the Savannah River. They spoke a Muskogean language and became extinct as a group in the eighteenth century.

13-14. Hitchiti. The Hitchiti (Hichiti), plus the Apalachicola, Chatot, Chiaha (Chehaw), Oconee, Okmulgee, Sawokli, and Tamali (Tamathli), lived in central and southwestern Georgia, southeastern

Alabama, and northwestern Florida. Their descendants are merged with the Creek now living on Oklahoma, and also with the Mikasuki of Florida. They spoke Muskogean languages.

13-15. Huma. The Huma (Houma, Sabine) lived on the east side of the Mississippi River near the present Louisiana-Mississippi border. They are now settled in several communities around Houma, Louisiana, in Terrebonne and Lafourche Parishes. They speak a Muskogean language and numbered 2,221 in 1966.

13-16. Mobile. The Mobile, plus the Naniba (Naniaba), Pascagoula, Pensacola, and Tohome, lived in the lower Tombigbee and Alabama River area in southwestern Alabama and northwestern Florida. Most of these groups merged with the Choctaw, and all are now extinct as groups. They spoke Muskogean languages.

13-17. Monacan. The Monacan, plus the Hassinunga, Manahoac (Mahocks), Ocaneechi (Occaneechi), Nahyssan (Monahassano, Yesan), Ontponea, Saponi, Shackaconia, Stegaraki (Stukanox), Tanxitania (Tanxnitania), Tegninateo, Tutelo (Kattera, Shateras), and Whonkentia (Whonkenti), lived in central Virginia, northeastern West Virginia, and part of north-central North Carolina. In 1753 the Cayuga adopted the Saponi and Tutelo, whose descendants are merged with them. They spoke Siouan languages and are extinct as groups.

13-18. Mosopelea. The Mosopelea (Chonque, Ofo, Ossipee, Ushpee, Ushpi) lived in southwestern Ohio in the seventeenth century, but moved to the lower Yazoo River in western Mississippi before 1700. They spoke a Siouan language and are now extinct as a group.

13-19. Natchez. The Natchez (Sunset Indians), with the Avoyel (Little Taensa, Tassenocogoula) and the Taensa, lived in the vicinity of the present city of Natchez in western Mississippi, with the Taensa to the north around St. Joseph, Louisiana, and the Avoyel to the southwest around Marksville, Louisiana. Both the Avoyel and the Taensa are extinct. There may be a few Natchez [the z is not pronounced] among the Oklahoma Cherokee. They spoke dialects of a language isolate within the Macro-Algonquian phylum.

13-20. Pamlico. The Pamlico (Pomonik, Pomeiock), with the Bear Island Indians, Coree (Coranine), Chowanoc, Hatteras (Croatan), Machapunga, Moratok, Secotan, Weapemeoc (Yeopim), Pasquotank, Perquiman, and Poteskeet, lived on the Atlantic coast in northeastern North Carolina and southeastern Virginia from approximately Cape Lookout in the south to Virginia Beach in the north and inland to the vicinity of Rocky Mount and Kinston, N.C. They spoke Algonquian languages and are extinct as groups.

13-21. Powhatan. The Powhatan, with a large number of subtribes—including the Appomattoc, Chesapeake, Chickahominy, Mattapony, Pamunkey, Piankatank, Potomac, and Rappahannock, among others—lived in the tidewater section of Virginia from the Potomac River to south of the James River, including the eastern shore of Virginia. Their descendants live on the Mattoponi and Pamunkey state reservations and in the Chickahominy, Rappahannock, and Upper Mattaponi communities in Virginia. They spoke an Algonquian language and numbered 1,350 in 1966.

13-22. Seminole. The Seminole, including the Mikasuki (Mikasuke, Miccosukee), lived in northern and central Florida before being forced into the Everglades region of southern Florida in the 1840s. They now live on the former Seminole Indian Reservation in eastern Oklahoma; on the Big Cypress, Brighton, and Hollywood federal reservations and the Miccosukee and Seminole state reservations (all in Florida); and in the Tamiami Trail area in southern Florida. They speak dialects of Muskogean languages and numbered 5,055 in 1960.

13-23. Timucua. The Timucua, with the Acquera (Acuera), Fresh Water Indians, Mococo (Mucoço), Ocale (Etocale), Oçita (Pohoy, Pooy, Uçita), Onathequa, Potano, Saturiwa (Saturiba), Surruque, Tacatacuru, Tocobaga, Utina, Yui, and Yustaga (Hostaqua), lived in central and northeastern Florida. They spoke a language isolate perhaps related to Muskogean and are extinct as a group.

13-24. Tunica. The Tunica, plus the Koroa, Tiou (Tioux), and Yazoo, lived in west-central Mississippi and northeastern Louisiana. Their descendants live in a community near Marksville, Louisiana. They spoke a language isolate of the Macro-Algonquian phylum and numbered 23 in 1966.

13-25. Tuscarora. The Tuscarora (Tuskeruro), with the Meherrin, Neusiok, and Nottaway, lived in southeastern Virginia and northeastern North Carolina. They now live on the Tuscarora Indian Reservation in northeastern New York and on the Six Nations Reserve in southern Ontario. They speak an Iroquoian language. The New York Tuscarora numbered 650 in 1969.

13-26. Yamasee. The Yamasee, with the Guale and the Yamacraw, lived in eastern Georgia from the Savannah River south to the Altamaha River and from the coast inland to the confluence of the Ocmulgee and Oconee Rivers. They spoke Muskogean languages and are now extinct.

13-27. Yuchi. The Yuchi (Hughchee, Uchi), with the Westo, at various times lived in several places in the Southeast from eastern Tennessee to Florida, with three main bands, one on the Tennessee River, one in northwestern Florida, and one in the middle drainage of the Savannah River. Some of their descendants live in the northwestern part of the former Creek Indian Reservation in eastern Oklahoma. They spoke a language isolate within the Macro-Siouan phylum.

13-28. Lumbee. The Lumbee (Croatan Indians, Robeson County Indians) live in southeastern North Carolina, principally in Robeson County with a focus in the city of Lumberton. Since they are a group formed subsequent to the period of extensive White contact, they are not found on the ethnic map for this area. They are a large group, numbering 31,380 in 1970, with some population estimates running as high as 45,000.

13-29. Southeastern Mestizos. This bibliographical division contains citations on a number of communities of Mestizos (i.e. racial crosses between Indians and other races) in this general area, including the Alabama Creoles, Brass Ankles, Carmel Indians, Coe Clan, Dominickers, Haliwa, Melungeons, Person County Indians, Renaview, Turks, Weromo, Win, and Yellowhammers, among others.

13-00 Southeast Area Bibliography

Clark, T. D., ed. Travels in the Old South; a bibliography. Norman, 1956. 2 v. (622 p.).

Duncan, Richard R. Theses and dissertations on Virginia history; a bibliography. By Richard R. Duncan and Dorothy M. Brown. Virginia Magazine of History and Biography, 79 (1971): 55-109.

Guthe, Alfred K., ed. An anthropological bibliography of the eastern seaboard. Vol. 2. Edited by Alfred K. Guthe and Patricia D. Kelly. Trenton, N.J., The Federation, 1963. 82 p. (Eastern States Archaeological Federation, Research Publication, 2)

Jillson, Willard Rouse. A selected bibliography on the American Indian: historic and prehistoric in Kentucky. Frankfort, Roberts, 1964. 42 p.

Pierce, Roy G., comp. Bibliography of the Virginia Indians. Compiled by Roy G. Pierce and Ben C. McCary. Edited by Norman F. Barka. Williamsburg, Archeological Society of Virginia, 1969. 60 p. (Archeological Society of Virginia, Special Publication, 1)

Pilling, J. C. Bibliography of the Muskhogean languages. U.S. Bureau of American Ethnology, Bulletin, 9 (1889): 1-114.

Rouse, Irving, ed. An anthropological bibliography of the eastern seaboard. Edited by Irving Rouse and John M. Goggin. New Haven, The Federation, 1947. 174 p. map. (Eastern States Archaeological Federation, Research Publication, 1)

Surrey, F. M., ed. Calendar of manuscripts in Paris archives and libraries relating to the history of the Mississippi Valley to 1803. Washington, D.C., 1926-1928. 2 v.

Thomas Gilcrease Institute of American History and Art, Tulsa, Okla. Library. The Gilcrease-Hargrett catalogue of imprints. Compiled by Lester Hargrett. Norman, University of Oklahoma Press, 1972. 18, 400 p.

Abel, A. H. The slaveholding Indians. Cleveland, 1915-1925. 3 v.

Adair, J. The history of the American Indians. London, 1775. 464 p.

Adair, James. The history of the American Indians. New York, Johnson Reprint, 1968. 9, 464 p. map.

Adams, J. A. English institutions and the American Indian. Johns Hopkins University, Studies in Historical and Political Science, 12, no. 10 (1894): 4-59.

Alden, J. R. John Stuart and the Southern Colonial frontier. Ann Arbor, 1944. 384 p.

Alden, John Richard. John Stuart and the Southern colonial frontier. New York, Gordian Press, 1966. 14, 384 p. maps.

Alexander, Edward P. An Indian vocabulary from Fort Christanna, 1716. Virginia Magazine of History and Biography, 79 (1971): 303-313.

Allen, Elmo L. The medicine bag--an Indian relic. North Carolina Medical Journal, 26 (1965): 556-558.

Anderson, Robert L. The end of an idyll. Florida Historical Quarterly, 42 (1963/1964): 35-47.

Anonymous. Mémoire sur la Louisiane, ou le Mississippi. Recueil A-Z, 2 (B) (1752): 123-152.

Anonymous. "The Indians in Virginia, 1689". Edited by Stanley Pargellis. William and Mary Quarterly, 3d ser., 16 (1959): 228-243.

Arnade, Charles W. The failure of Spanish Florida. In Congreso Internacional de Americanistas, 33d. 1958, San José. Actas. Tomo 2. San José, Lehmann, 1959: 758-766.

Atkin, Edmond. The Appalachian Indian frontier, the Edmond Atkin report and plan of 1755. Edited by Wilbur R. Jacobs. Lincoln, University of Nebraska Press, 1967. 38, 108 p. illus., maps.

Barbour, Philip. The earliest reconnaissance of the Chesapeake Bay area; Captain John Smith's map and Indian vocabulary. Virginia Magazine of History and Biography, 79 (1971): 280-302.

Barcia Carballido y Zuñiga, A. G. Ensayo cronológico para la historia general de la Florida. Madrid, 1723. 366 p.

Barcia Carballido y Zuñiga, Andrés González de. Barcia's chronological history of the continent of Florida. Translated with an introduction by Anthony Kerrigan. Westport, Greenwood Press, 1970. 9, 426 p.

Barcía Carballido y Zuniga, Andrés Gonzalez. Barcia's chronological history of the continent of Florida. Translated with an introduction by Anthony Kerrigan. Gainesville, University of Florida Press, 1951. 60, 426 p.

Battle, H. B. The domestic use of oil among the Southern aborigines. American Anthropologist, n.s., 24 (1922): 171-182.

Bearss, Edwin C. The Civil War comes to Indian Territory, 1861: the flight of Opothleyoholo. Journal of the West, 11 (1972): 9-42.

Beer, David F. Anti-Indian sentiment in early colonial literature. Indian Historian, 2, no. 1 (1969): 29-33, 48.

Beers, H. P. The French in North America. Baton Rouge, 1957.

Bennett, J. W. Middle American influences upon the cultures of the Southeastern United States. Acta Americana, 2 (1944): 25-50.

Bennett, J. W. Southeastern culture types and Middle American influences. In El Norte de Mexico y el Sur de Estados Unidos. México, 1943: 223-241.

Berquin-Duvallon. Travels in Louisiana and the Floridas. New York, 1806. 181 p.

Beverley, Robert. The history and present state of Virginia. Edited by Louis B. Wright. Charlottesville, Dominion Books, 1968. 35, 366 p. illus.

Beverley, Robert. The history and present state of Virginia; a selection. Indianapolis, Bobbs-Merrill, 1971. 17, 171 p.

Beverly, R. The history and present state of Virginia. Chapel Hill, 1947.

Biasutti, R. Le razzi e i popoli della terra, 2d ed. Vol. 4: 437-440. Torino, 1957.

Biedma, L. F. de. A narrative of the expedition of Hernando de Soto. In B. F. French, ed. Historical Collections of Louisiana and Florida. Vol. 2. 1850: 97-109.

Bierer, Bert W., ed. South Carolina Indian lore. Columbia, S.C., 1972. 164 p. illus., maps.

Binford, Lewis R. Comments on the "Siouan problem". Ethnohistory, 6 (1959): 28-41.

Black, Glenn A. Angel Site: an archaeological, historical, and ethnological study. Indianapolis, Indiana Historical Society, 1967. 2 v. (10, 616 p.) illus., maps.

Blume, G. W. J. Present-day Indians of Tidewater Virginia. Archaeological Society of Virginia, Quarterly Bulletin, 6, no. 4 (1951): 1-11.

Boyd, M. F. Historic sites in and around the Jim Woodruff Reservoir area, Florida-Georgia. U.S. Bureau of American Ethnology, Bulletin, 169 (1958): 195-314.

Brackenridge, H. M. Views of Louisiana. Pittsburgh, 1814. 304 p.

Brannon, P. A. Indian treaties. Alabama Historical Quarterly, 12 (1950): 242-250.

Brannon, P. A. Removal of Indians from Alabama. Alabama Historical Quarterly, 12 (1950): 91-117.

Brannon, P. A. The Pensacola Indian trade. Florida Historical Quarterly, 31 (1952): 1-15.

Brannon, P. A. The Southern Indian trade. Montgomery, 1935. 87 p.

Brasser, T. J. C. The Coastal Algonkians: people of the first frontiers. In Eleanor Burke Leacock and Nancy Oestreich Lurie, eds. North American Indians in Historical Perspective. New York, Random House, 1971: 64-91.

Brinton, Daniel G. The Floridian peninsula. New York, Paladin Press, 1969. 202 p.

Brown, J. A. Panton, Leslie and Company: Indian traders of Pensacola and St. Augustine. Florida Historical Quarterly, 37 (1958/1959): 328-336.

Bullen, R. P. Six sites near the Chattahoochee River in the Jim Woodruff Reservoir area, Florida. U.S. Bureau of American Ethnology, Bulletin, 169 (1958): 315-358.

Burrage, Henry S., ed. Early English and French voyages, chiefly from Hakluyt, 1534-1608. New York, C. Scribner's Sons, 1906. 22, 451 p. map. (Original Narratives of Early American History, 3)

Bushnell, D. I. Aboriginal forms of burial in Eastern United States. In Holmes Anniversary Volume. Washington, D.C., 1916: 31-43.

Bushnell, D. I. Native villages and village sites east of the Mississippi. U.S. Bureau of American Ethnology, Bulletin, 69 (1919): 1-111.

Bushnell, D. I. The use of soapstone by the Indians of the Eastern United States. Smithsonian Institution, Annual Reports of the Board of Regents (1939): 471-489.

Bushnell, D. I. Tribal migrations east of the Mississippi. Smithsonian Miscellaneous Collections, 89, no. 12 (1934): 1-9.

Butler, Joseph T., Jr. The Atakapa Indians: cannibals of Louisiana. Louisiana History, 11 (1970): 167-176.

Calmes, Alan Royce. Indian cultural traditions and European conquest of the Georgia-South Carolina coastal plain, 3000 B.C.-1733 A.D.: a combined archaeological and historical investigation. Dissertation Abstracts, 29 (1968/1969): 533A. UM 68-9770.

Carr, L. Dress and ornaments of certain American Indians. American Antiquarian Society, Proceedings, n.s., 11 (1897): 381-454.

Carr, L. The mounds of the Mississippi Valley. Smithsonian Institution, Annual Reports of the Board of Regents (1891): 503-599.

Carr, L. G. Native drinks in the Southeast and their values. Delaware County Institute of Science, Proceedings, 10, no. 2 (1947): 29-42.

Chard, T. Did the first Spanish horses landed in Florida and Carolina leave progeny? American Anthropologist, n.s., 42 (1940): 90-106.

Charlevoix, P. F. X. de. Histoire de la Nouvelle France. Paris, 1894. 3 v.

Charlevoix, P. F. X. de. History and general description of New France. Ed. by J. M. Shea. New York, 1866-1872. 6 v.

Charlevoix, P. F. X. de. Journal of a voyage to North America. Ed. by L. P. Kellogg. Chicago, 1923. 2 v.

Charlevoix, Pierre F. X. de. Journal of a voyage to North America. Ann Arbor, University Microfilms, 1966. 2 v.

Core, Earl L. Ethnobotany of the southern Appalachian aborigines. Economic Botany, 21 (1967): 198-214.

Coulter, E. Merton. David Meriwether of Virginia and Georgia. Georgia Historical Quarterly, 54 (1970): 320-338.

Coulter, E. Merton. The Okefenokee Swamp, its history and legends. Georgia Historical Quarterly, 48 (1964): 166-192.

Covington, James W. Apalachee Indians, 1704-1763. Florida Historical Quarterly, 50 (1971/1972): 366-384.

Coxe, D. A description of the English Province of Carolana. In B. F. French, ed. Historical Collections of Louisiana and Florida. Vol. 2. 1850: 223-276.

Crane, V. W. The Southern frontier. Philadelphia, 1929. 391 p.

Craven, Wesley Frank. White, Red, and Black: the seventeenth-century Virginian. Charlottesville, University Press of Virginia, 1971. 114 p.

Crockett, B. N. Health conditions in Indian Territory. Chronicles of Oklahoma, 36 (1958): 21-39.

Crockett, B. N. Health conditions in Indian Territory, 1830 to Civil War. Chronicles of Oklahoma, 35 (1957): 80-90.

Crockett, David. Vie et mémoires authentiques. Paris, Club Français du Livre, 1961. 208 p. illus.

Crump, B. L. M. The educability of Indian children in reservation schools. Southeastern State Teachers' College, Contributions to Education, 3 (1932): 1-58.

De Brahm, William Gerard. De Brahm's report of the general survey in the southern district of North America. Edited and with an introduction by Louis De Vorsey, Jr. Columbia, University of South Carolina Press, 1971. 16, 325 p.

De Vorsey, Louis. The Indian boundary in the southern colonies, 1763-1775. Chapel Hill, University of North Carolina Press, 1966. 12, 267 p. maps.

Debo, A. The five civilized tribes. Philadelphia, 1951. 35 p.

Debo, Angie. And still the waters run. New York, Gordian Press, 1966. 10, 417 p. maps.

Delanglez, J. The French Jesuits in Lower Louisiana. Catholic University of America, Studies in American Church History, 21 (1935): 1-573.

Densmore, F. Traces of foreign influence in the music of American Indians. American Anthropologist, n.s., 46 (1944): 106-113.

Deuel, T. Basic cultures of the Mississippi Valley. American Anthropologist, n.s., 37 (1935): 429-445.

Dunn, W. E. Spanish and French rivalry in the Gulf region of the United States, 1678-1702. Texas, University, Studies in History, 1 (1917): 1-238.

Elmendorf, William W. Yukian-Siouan lexical similarities. International Journal of American Linguistics, 29 (1963): 300-309.

Fairbanks, Charles H. The trial ethnohistory project at the University of Florida. By Charles H. Fairbanks and Charles J. Fleener. Florida Anthropologist, 17 (1964): 110-112.

Fairbanks, G. R. History of Florida. Philadelphia, 1871. 350 p.

Feest, Christian F. Tomahawk und Keule im östliche Nordamerika. Archiv für Völkerkunde, 19 (1964/1965): 39-84.

Feest, Christian F. Virginia Indian miscellany I. Archiv für Völkerkunde, 20 (1966): 1-7.

Feest, Christian F. Virginia Indian miscellany II. Archiv für Völkerkunde, 21 (1967): 5-25.

Fernández, Dennis. La Florida del Inca Garcilaso de la Vega (The Florida of the Inca Garcilaso de la Vega). Dissertation Abstracts International, 31 (1970/1971): 4711A. UM 71-7006.

Fischer, LeRoy H. United States Indian agents to the Five Civilized Tribes. Chronicles of Oklahoma, 50 (1972): 410-414.

Fogelson, Raymond David. The Cherokee ball game: a study in Southeastern ethnology. Dissertation Abstracts, 23 (1962/1963): 1488. UM 62-4288.

Ford, J. A. and G. R. Willey. An interpretation of the prehistory of the Eastern United States. American Anthropologist, n.s., 43 (1941): 325-363.

Foreman, G. A traveler in Indian Territory. Cedar Rapids, 1930. 270 p.

Foreman, G. Indian removal. Norman, 1932.

Foreman, Grant. The last trek of the Indians. New York, Russell and Russell, 1972. 382 p. illus.

Franks, Kenny A. An analysis of the Confederate treaties with the Five Civilized Tribes. Chronicles of Oklahoma, 50 (1972): 458-473.

Fuller, A. W. F. An original sixteenth century painting of natives of Florida. International Congress of Americanists, Proceedings, 20, vol. 2 (1928): 191-193.

Fundaburk, E. L. Southeastern Indians, life portraits. Luverne, Ala., 1958. 136 p.

Fundaburk, E. L. and M. D. F. Foreman. Sun circles and human hands. Luverne, Ala., 1957. 232 p.

Fundaburk, Emma L., ed. Southeastern Indians: life portraits. Metuchen, N.J., Scarecrow Reprint, 1969. 135 p. illus., map.

Garcilaso de la Vega el Inca. La florida del Ynca. Madrid, 1723.

Garcilaso de la Vega, el Inca. The Florida of the Inca. Translated and edited by John Grier Varner and Jeannette Johnson Varner. Austin, University of Texas Press, 1951. 45, 655 p. illus., map.

Garth, T. R. A comparison of the intelligence of Mexican and mixed and full blood Indian children. Psychological Review, 30 (1923): 388-401.

Garth, T. R. The intelligence of full blood Indians. Journal of Applied Psychology, 9 (1925): 382-389.

Geary, J. A. Strachey's vocabulary of Indian words used in Virginia, 1612. Works Issued by the Hakluyt Society, Second Series, 103 (1953): 208-214.

Geary, J. A. The language of the Carolina Algonkian tribes. Works Issued by the Hakluyt Society, Second Series, 105 (1955): 873-900.

Gentleman of Elvas. A narrative of the expedition of Hernando de Soto. In B. F. French, ed. Historical Collections of Louisiana and Florida. Vol. 2. 1850: 113-220.

Gentleman of Elvas. True relation of the hardships suffered by Governor Fernando de Soto. Ed. by J. E. Robertson. Deland, 1933. 2 v.

Gifford, J. C. Five native Florida
plants. Tequesta, 4 (1944): 36-44.

Gilbert, W. H. Surviving Indian groups of
the Eastern United States. Smithsonian
Institution, Annual Reports of the Board
of Regents (1948): 403-438.

Goggin, J. M. Style areas in historic
Southeastern art. International Congress
of Americanists, Proceedings, 29, vol. 3
(1951): 172-176.

Goggin, John M. Spanish majolica in the
New World; types of the sixteenth to
eighteenth centuries. New Haven, Yale
University, Department of Anthropology,
1968. 240 p. illus. (Yale University
Publications in Anthropology, 72)

Goode, William H. Outposts of Zion, with
limnings of mission life. Cincinnati,
Poe and Hitchcock, 1863. 464 p.

Goodman, Julia Cody. Julia Cody Goodman's
memoirs of Buffalo Bill. Edited by Don
Russell. Kansas Historical Quarterly, 28
(1962): 442-496.

Gore, J. H. Tuckahoe, or Indian bread.
Smithsonian Institution, Annual Reports
of the Board of Regents (1881): 687-701.

Gosselin, A. Les sauvages du Mississipi
(1698-1708). International Congress of
Americanists, Proceedings, 15, vol. 1
(1907): 31-51.

Gray, L. H. Muskhogeans. In J. Hastings,
ed. Encyclopaedia of Religion and
Ethics. Vol. 9. New York, 1917. 61-62.

Griffin, J. B. Aboriginal methods of
pottery manufacture in the Eastern
United States. Pennsylvania
Archaeologist, 5 (1935): 19-24.

Griffin, J. W., ed. The Florida Indian
and his neighbors. Winter Park, 1949.
168 p.

Gursky, Karl-Heinz. Gulf and Hokan-
Subtiaban: new lexical parallels.
International Journal of American
Linguistics, 34 (1968): 21-41.

Haarmann, Albert W. The Spanish conquest
of British West Florida, 1779-1781.
Florida Historical Quarterly, 39
(1960/1961): 107-134.

Haas, M. R. A new linguistic relationship
in North America. Southwestern Journal
of Anthropology, 14 (1958): 231-264.

Haas, M. R. A proto-Muskogean paradigm.
Language, 22 (1946): 326-332.

Haas, M. R. Development of proto-
Muskogean *kw. International Journal of
American Linguistics, 13 (1947): 135-
137.

Haas, M. R. Noun incorporation in the
Muskogean languages. Language, 17
(1941): 311-315.

Haas, M. R. Southeastern Indian folklore.
Journal of American Folklore, 60 (1947):
403-406.

Haas, M. R. The classification of the
Muskogean languages. In Essays in Memory
of Edward Sapir. Menasha, 1941: 41-46.

Haas, Mary R. Swanton and the Biloxi and
Ofo dictionaries. International Journal
of American Linguistics, 35 (1969): 286-
290.

Haas, Mary R. The last words of Biloxi.
International Journal of American
Linguistics, 34 (1968): 77-84.

Haas, Mary R. The Muskogean and Algonkian
words for skunk. International Journal
of American Linguistics, 29 (1963): 65-
66.

Haggard, J. V. The neutral ground between
Louisiana and Texas. Louisiana
Historical Quarterly, 28 (1945): 1001-
1128.

Hagy, James William. The frontier dreams
of Francois Pierre De Tubeuf. Virginia
Magazine of History and Biography, 77
(1969): 329-335.

Hale, E. M. Ilex cassine, the aboriginal
North American tea. U.S. Department of
Agriculture, Division of Botany,
Bulletin, 14 (1891): 1-22.

Hamor, Ralph. A true discourse of the
present state of Virginia. New York, Da
Capo Press, 1971. 69 p.

Harpe, B. de la. Historical journal of
the establishment of the French in
Louisiana. In B. F. French, ed.
Historical Collections of Louisiana and
Florida. Vol. 3. 1851: 9-118.

Harpe, B. de la. Journal historique de
l'établissement des Français à la
Louisiane. Nouvelle-Orléans, 1831.
412 p.

Havighurst, Walter. Alexander Spotswood;
portrait of a governor. Williamsburg,
Colonial Williamsburg, 1967. 9, 118 p.
illus. (Williamsburg in America Series,
5)

Hawley, F. Tree-ring analysis and dating
in the Mississippi drainage. Chicago,

University, Publications in
Anthropology, Occasional Papers, 2
(1941): 1-110.

Haywood, J. The natural and aboriginal
history of Tennessee. Nashville, 1823.
390 p.

Hendren, S. R. Government and religion of
the Virginia Indians. Johns Hopkins
University, Studies in History and
Political Science, ser. 13, 11/12
(1895): 1-58.

Herndon, G. Melvin. Indian agriculture in
the Southern Colonies. North Carolina
Historical Review, 44 (1967): 283-297.

Hill, William B. The Indians of Axacan
and the Spanish martyrs; the beginnings
of Virginia, 1570. Rev. Clarksville,
Va., Prestwould House, 1970. 17 p.

Hoffman, Bernard G. Ancient tribes
revisited: a summary of Indian
distribution and movement in the
Northeastern United States from 1534 to
1779. Ethnohistory, 14 (1967): 1-46.

Hoffman, Bernard G. Observations on
certain ancient Tribes of the Northern
Appalachian Province. Washington, D.C.,
Government Printing Office, 1964. 191-
245 p. illus., maps. (U.S., Bureau of
American Ethnology, Anthropological
Papers, 70. U.S., Bureau of American
Ethnology, Bulletin, 191)

Holland, C. G. An archeological survey of
southwest Virginia. Washington, D.C.,
Smithsonian Institution Press, 1970.
16, 194 p. illus. (Smithsonian
Contributions to Anthropology, 12)

Holland, James W. Andrew Jackson and the
Creek War: victory at the Horseshoe.
Alabama Review, 21 (1968): 243-275.

Holmes, Jack D. L. Notes on the Spanish
Fort San Esteban de Tombecbé. Alabama
Review, 18 (1965): 281-290.

Holmes, Jack D. L., tr. and ed. Luis
Bertucat and William Agustus Bowles:
West Florida adversaries in 1791.
Translated and edited by Jack D. L.
Holmes and J. Leitch Wright, Jr. Florida
Historical Quarterly, 49 (1970/1971):
49-62.

Holmes, W. H. Aboriginal pottery of the
Eastern United States. U.S. Bureau of
American Ethnology, Annual Reports, 20
(1899): 1-201.

Holmes, W. H. Earthenware of Florida.
Academy of Natural Sciences of
Philadelphia, Journal, ser. 2, 10
(1894): 105-128.

Holmes, W. H. Prehistoric textile art of
the Eastern United States. U.S. Bureau
of American Ethnology, Annual Reports,
13 (1896): 9-46.

Holmes, W. H. Prehistoric textile fabrics
of the United States. U.S. Bureau of
American Ethnology, Annual Reports, 3
(1882): 393-425.

Hough, W. Ceremonial and other practices
in the human body among the Indians.
International Congress of Americanists,
Proceedings, 19 (1915): 283-285.

Householder, J. C. Virginia's Indian
neighbors in 1712. Indiana Academy of
Science, Proceedings, 55 (1946): 23-25.

Howard, J. H. Pan-Indian culture of
Oklahoma. Scientific Monthly, 81 (1955):
215-220.

Howard, Milo B., Jr. The archives and the
study of early Indian-European contacts.
Alabama Academy of Science, Journal, 35
(1964): 93-96.

Hrdlička, A. Ritual ablation of front
teeth in Siberian and America.
Smithsonian Miscellaneous Collections,
99, no. 3 (1940): 1-32.

Hudson, Charles. Acculturative stages in
the Southeast. Working Papers in
Sociology and Anthropology, 1 (1967):
73-83.

Jackson, W. R. Early Florida through
Spanish eyes. Coral Gables, 1954.
179 p.

Jefferson, T. Notes on the State of
Virginia. Chapel Hill, 1955. 315 p.

Jimenez Moreno, W. Relaciones etnológicas
entre Mesoamérica y el Sur de Estados
Unidos. In El Norte de México y el Sur
de Estados Unidos. México, 1943: 286-
300.

Johnson, B. A. The Suwanee-Shawnee
debate. Florida Anthropologist, 25,
no. 2 (1972): 67-72.

Johnson, Cecil. Pensacola in the British
Period: summary and significance.
Florida Historical Quarterly, 37
(1958/1959): 263-280.

Johnson, J. G. The Colonial Southeast,
1732-1763. Colorado, University,
Studies, 19 (1932): 163-225.

Johnston, R. B. Remarks on the physical
type of certain Middle Mississippi and
Southeastern groups. Indiana Academy of
Science, Proceedings, 66 (1956): 50-52.

Jones, C. C. Antiquities of the Southern Indians. New York, 1873. 532 p.

Jones, Charles C. Antiquities of the Southern Indians, particularly of the Georgia tribes. Spartanburg, S.C., Reprint Co., 1972. 16, 582 p. illus.

Joutel, H. Journal of La Salle's last voyage. New ed. Albany, 1906. 258 p.

Kansas City Star. Report on the Five Civilized Tribes 1897. Chronicles of Oklahoma, 48 (1970/1971): 416-430.

Knowles, N. The torture of captives by the Indians of Eastern North America. American Philosophical Society, Proceedings, 82 (1940): 151-225.

Kunkel, P. A. The Indians of Louisiana about 1700. Louisiana Historical Quarterly, 34 (1951): 175-204.

Kurath, G. P. Antiphonal songs of Eastern Woodlands Indians. Musical Quarterly, 43 (1956): 520-526.

La Harpe, Jean-Baptiste Benard de. The historical journal of the establishment of the French in Louisiana. Translated by Joan Cain and Virginia Koenig. Edited by Glen R. Conrad. Lafayette, University of Southwest Louisiana, 1971. 272 p.

Lanning, John T. The Spanish missions of Georgia. St. Clair Shores, Mich., Scholarly Press, 1971. 13, 321 p. illus., map.

Larson, Lewis H., Jr. A Mississippian headdress from Etowah, Georgia. American Antiquity, 25 (1959/1960): 109-112.

Lawson, J. The history of Carolina. Raleigh, 1860. 390 p.

Lawson, John. A new voyage to Carolina. Ann Arbor, University Microfilms, 1966. 258 p. illus., map.

Lawson, John. A new voyage to Carolina. Edited by Hugh Talmage Lefler. Chapel Hill, University of North Carolina Press, 1967. 54, 305 p. illus., maps.

Le Page du Pratz. Histoire de la Louisiane. Paris, 1758. 3 v.

Le Page du Pratz. The history of Louisiana. London, 1763. 2 v.

Leach, Douglas Edward. John Gordon of Gordon's Ferry. Tennessee Historical Quarterly, 18 (1959): 322-344.

Lederer, John. The discoveries of John Lederer. Ann Arbor, University Microfilms, 1966. 27 p. map.

Lee, Enoch L. Indian wars in North Carolina, 1663-1763. Raleigh, Carolina Charter Tercentenary Commission, 1963. 94 p. illus.

Lewis, Clifford M. The Spanish Jesuit mission in Virginia 1570-1572. By Clifford M. Lewis and Albert J. Loomie. Chapel Hill, published for the Virginia Historical Society by the University of North Carolina Press, 1953. 18, 294 p.

Lewis, T. M. N. and M. Kneberg. The prehistory of the Chickamauga Basin in Tennessee. Tennessee Anthropology Papers, 1 (1941): 1-42.

Lewis, T. M. N. and M. Kneberg. Tribes that slumber. Knoxville, 1958. 207 p.

Lorant, Stefan, ed. The New World. Rev. ed. New York, Duell, Sloan and Pearce, 1965. 292 p. illus., maps.

Lowery, W. The Spanish settlements within the present limits of the United States. New York, 1901-1905. 2 v.

Lurie, Nancy Oestreich. Indian cultural adjustment to European civilization. In Roger L. Nichols and George R. Adams, eds. The American Indian: Past and Present. Waltham, Xerox College Publishing, 1971: 42-60.

MacLeod, W. C. Debtor and chattel slavery in aboriginal North America. American Anthropologist, n.s., 27 (1925): 70-78.

MacLeod, W. C. Economic aspects of indigenous American slavery. American Anthropologist, n.s., 30 (1928): 632-650.

MacLeod, W. C. Priests, temples, and the practice of mummification in Southeastern North America. International Congress of Americanists, Proceedings, 22, vol. 2 (1926): 207-230.

Mahan, Joseph Buford, Jr. Identification of the Tsoyaha Waeno, builders of temple mounds. Dissertation Abstracts International, 31 (1970/1971): 2289A. UM 70-21,213.

Mahon, John K. British strategy and southern Indians: War of 1812. Florida Historical Quarterly, 44 (1965/1966): 285-302.

Marambaud, Pierre. William Byrd I; a young Virginia planter in the 1670s. Virginia Magazine of History and Biography, 81 (1973): 131-150.

Martin, Thomas W. The story of Horseshoe Bend National Military Park. New York, Newcomen Society in North America, 1960. 32 p. illus.

Matter, Robert Allen. The Spanish missions of Florida: the friars versus the governors in the "golden age," 1606-1690. Dissertation Abstracts International, 33 (1972/1973): 2296A. UM 72-28,631.

Mattfield, Mary S. Journey to the wilderness: two travelers in Florida, 1694-1774. Florida Historical Quarterly, 45 (1966/1967): 327-351.

Matthews, G. H. Proto-Siouan kinship terminology. American Anthropologist, 61 (1959): 252-278.

Maxwell, H. The use and abuse of forests by the Virginia Indians. William and Mary College Quarterly Historical Magazine, 19 (1910): 73-103.

McAlister, L. N. Pensacola during the second Spanish Period. Florida Historical Quarterly, 37 (1958/1959): 281-327.

McCain, William D. The administration of David Holmes, Governor of the Mississippi Territory, 1809-1817. Journal of Mississippi History, 29 (1967): 328-347.

McCary, B. C. Indians in seventeenth-century Virginia. Williamsburg, 1957. 93 p.

McCoy, Isaac. History of Baptist Indian missions. Washington, D.C., W. M. Morrison; New York, H. and S. Raynor, 1840. 5, 611 p.

McDowell, William L., Jr., ed. Documents relating to Indian affairs, May 21, 1750-August 7, 1754. Columbia, South Carolina Archives Department, 1958. 22, 592 p. (Colonial Records of South Carolina, Series 2)

Miles, William. "Enamoured with colonization": Isaac McCoy's plan of Indian reform. Kansas Historical Quarterly, 38 (1972): 268-286.

Miller, C. F. Revaluation of the Eastern Siouan problem. U.S. Bureau of American Ethnology, Bulletin, 164 (1957): 115-212.

Miller, Carl F. Archeology of the John H. Kerr Reservoir basin, Roanoke River Virginia-North Carolina. Washington, D.C., Government Printing Office, 1962. 16, 447 p. illus., maps. (U.S., Bureau of American Ethnology, River Basin Surveys Papers, 25. U.S., Bureau of American Ethnology, Bulletin, 182)

Milling, C. J. Red Carolinians. Chapel Hill, 1940. 469 p.

Mochon, Marion Johnson. Language, history and prehistory: Mississippian lexico-reconstruction. American Antiquity, 37 (1972): 478-503.

Mochon, Marion Johnson. Toward urbanism: the cultural dynamics of the prehistoric and historic societies of the American Southeast. Dissertation Abstracts International, 33 (1972/1973): 28B. UM 72-18,753.

Montault de Monberaut, Henri. Mémoire justificatif, Indian diplomacy in British West Florida, 1763-1765. Translated by Milo B. Howard, Jr. and Robert R. Rea. University, University of Alabama Press, 1965. 187 p. (Southern Historical Publications, 3)

Mook, Maurice A. The aboriginal population of Tidewater Virginia. American Anthropologist, n.s., 46 (1944): 193-208.

Mooney, James. The Siouan tribes of the East. St. Claire Shores, Mich., Scholarly Press, 1970. 101 p. map.

Moore, J. R. The five great Indian nations. Chronicles of Oklahoma, 29 (1951): 324-336.

Morgan, L. H. Ancient society, 160-165. New York, 1877.

Morton, O. Confederate government relations with the Five Civilized Tribes. Chronicles of Oklahoma, 31 (1953): 189-204, 299-322.

Müller-Tannewitz, Anna. Virginianisches Abenteuer; aus dem ersten Tagen einer Kolonie. Stuttgart, Franck, 1960. 168 p. illus.

Murphy, Christopher. On the problem of intensive agriculture in the aboriginal southeastern United States. By Christopher Murphy and Charles Hudson. Working Papers in Sociology and Anthropology, 2, no. 1 (1968): 24-34.

Myer, W. E. Indian trails of the Southeast. U.S. Bureau of American Ethnology, Annual Reports, 42 (1925): 727-857.

Myron, R. L'art symbolique dans les groupements indiens du sud-Est des États-Unis. Société des Américanistes, Journal, n.s., 47 (1958): 47-54.

Neill, W. T.   Coracles or skin boats of the Southeastern Indians. Florida Anthropologist, 7 (1954): 119-126.

Neill, W. T.   The identity of Florida's "Spanish Indians". Florida Anthropologist, 8 (1955): 43-58.

Neumann, Georg K.   Origins of the Indians of the Middle Mississippi area. Indiana Academy of Sciences, Proceedings, 69 (1959): 66-68.

Ningler, L., tr.   Voyages en Virginie et en Floride. Paris, Chez Duchartre et Van Buggenhoudt, 1927.   311 p.   illus.

O'Callaghan, M. A.   An Indian removal policy in Spanish Louisiana. In Greater America: Essays in Honor of Herbert Eugene Bolton.   Berkeley, 1945: 281-294.

O'Donnell, J. H.   Alexander McGillivray: training for leadership, 1777-1783. Georgia Historical Quarterly, 49 (1965): 172-186.

O'Donnell, James Howlett, III.   The Southern Indians in the War of Independence, 1775-1783. Dissertation Abstracts, 26 (1965/1966): 3911-3912. UM 65-14,145.

Olson, Gary D.   Loyalists and the American Revolution: Thomas Brown and the South Carolina backcountry, 1775-1776. South Carolina Historical Magazine, 68 (1967): 201-219; 69 (1968): 44-56.

Omaechevarria, I.   Martires franciscanoes de Georgia. Missionalia Hispanica, 12 (1955): 5-93, 291-370.

Owen, M. B.   Alabama Indian chiefs. Alabama Historical Quarterly, 13 (1951): 5-90.

Owen, M. B.   Indian trading houses. Alabama Historical Quarterly, 13 (1951): 136-139.

Owen, M. B.   Indian tribes and towns in Alabama. Alabama Historical Quarterly, 12 (1950): 118-241.

Owen, M. B.   Indian wars in Alabama. Alabama Historical Quarterly, 13 (1951): 92-131.

Owen, M. B.   Indians in Alabama. Alabama Historical Quarterly, 12 (1950): 2-90.

Parmley, Ingram Cannon.   A study of marginality in White, Indian, and Negro high school students in Sampson County, North Carolina. Dissertation Abstracts International, 34 (1973/1974): 3586A. UM 73-29,567.

Parsons, Joseph A., Jr.   Civilizing the Indians of the Old Northwest, 1800-1810. Indiana Magazine of History, 56 (1960): 195-216.

Pate, James Paul.   The Chickamauga: a forgotten segment of Indian resistance on the southern frontier. Dissertation Abstracts International, 30 (1969/1970): 2445A. UM 69-19,811.

Pickett, Albert James.   History of Alabama, and incidentally of Georgia and Mississippi, from the earliest period. New York, Arno Press, 1971. 19, 377, 445 p.

Porter, Kenneth W.   Billy Bowlegs (Holata Micco) in the Civil War. Florida Historical Quarterly, 45 (1966/1967): 391-401.

Posey, W. B.   The development of Methodism in the Old Southwest, 1783-1824. Tuscaloosa, 1933.   151 p.

Post, Lauren C.   Some notes on the Attakapas Indians of Southwest Louisiana. Louisiana History, 3 (1962): 221-242.

Prucha, Francis Paul.   Andrew Jackson's Indian policy: a reassessment. Journal of American History, 56 (1969/1970): 527-539.

Randolph, J. Ralph.   British travelers among the Southern Indians, 1660-1763. Norman, University of Oklahoma Press, 1972.   15, 183 p.   illus.

Randolph, Jerry Ralph.   British travelers among the Southern Indians, 1660-1763. Dissertation Abstracts International, 31 (1970/1971): 5333A. UM 71-9285.

Rea, Robert R.   Redcoats and Redskins on the lower Mississippi, 1763-1776: the career of Lt. John Thomas. Louisiana History, 11 (1970): 5-35.

Read, W. A.   Indian place names in Alabama. Louisiana State University, Studies, 9 (1937): 1-84.

Read, W. A.   Indian place-names in Louisiana. Louisiana Historical Quarterly, 11 (1928): 445-462.

Read, W. A.   Indian stream-names in Georgia. International Journal of American Linguistics, 15 (1949): 128-132; 16 (1949): 203-207.

Read, W. A.   Louisiana place names of Indian origin. Louisiana State University, Bulletin, 19 (1927): 1-72.

Read, W. A. Louisiana-French. Louisiana State University, Studies, 5 (1931): 152-158.

Reck, Georg Philipp von. Commissary Von Reck's report on Georgia. Translated by George Fenwick Jones. Georgia Historical Quarterly, 47 (1963): 95-110.

Reynolds, B. D. Indians of Virginia 350 years ago. Virginia Journal of Science, n.s., 8 (1957): 3-18.

Rights, D. L. The American Indian in North Carolina. Winston-Salem, 1957. 318 p.

Rights, D. L. The American Indian in North Carolina. Durham, 1947. 296 p.

Rights, D. L. and W. P. Cumming. The discoveries of John Lederer. Winston-Salem, 1958. 159 p.

Robinson, W. S. Indian education and missions in colonial Virginia. Journal of Southern History, 18 (1952): 152-168.

Robinson, W. S. The legal status of the Indian in Colonial Virginia. Virginia Magazine of History and Biography, 61 (1953): 247-259.

Robinson, W. Stitt. Tributary Indians in Colonial America. Virginia Magazine of History and Biography, 67 (1959): 49-64.

Rogers, R. A concise account of North America. London, 1765. 264 p.

Romans, Bernard. A concise natural history of East and West Florida. Edited by Rembert W. Patrick. Gainesville, University of Florida Press, 1962. illus., maps.

Sams, Conway Whittle. The conquest of Virginia; the forest primeval. New York, G. P. Putnam's Sons, 1916. 23, 432 p. illus., maps.

Schermerhorn, J. F. Report respecting the Indians inhabiting the western parts of the United States. Massachusetts Historical Society, Collections, ser. 2, 2 (1814): 1-45.

Searcy, Margaret Z. The sex of the original Amerind ancestor of part-Indian students at the University of Alabama in Tuscaloosa. Alabama Academy of Science, Journal, 43 (1972): 237.

Shaw, H. L. British administration of the Southern Indians, 1756 to 1783. Lancaster, 1931. 225 p.

Shea, J. G. Discovery and exploration of the Mississippi Valley. 2d ed. Albany, 1903.

Sherzer, Joel. Vowel nasalization in Eastern Algonquian: an areal-typological perspective on linguistic universals. International Journal of American Linguistics, 38 (1972): 267-268.

Shetrone, H. C. The mound builders. New York, 1930. 508 p.

Shipp, B. The history of Hernando de Soto and Florida. Philadelphia, 1881. 689 p.

Sibley, J. A report from Natchitoches in 1807. Indian Notes and Monographs, n.s., 25 (1922): 5-102.

Silver, J. W. Edmund Pendleton Gaines and frontier problems. Journal of Southern History, 1 (1935): 320-344.

Simsa, P. Indianische Königreiche im südöstlichen Nordamerika. International Congress of the Anthropological and Ethnological Sciences, Acts, 4, vol. 2 (1955): 341-346.

Sleight, F. W. Kunti, a food staple of Florida Indians. Florida Anthropologist, 6 (1953): 46-52.

Slotkin, J. S. and K. Schmitt. Studies of wampum. American Anthropologist, n.s., 51 (1949): 223-236.

Small, J. G. Seminole bread. New York Botanical Garden, Journal, 22 (1921): 121-137.

Smith, H. G. The ethnological and archaeological significance of Zamia. American Anthropologist, 53 (1951): 238-244.

Smith, H. G. The European and the Indian. Florida Anthropological Society, Publications, 4 (1956): 1-158.

Smith, John. Captain John Smith's America; selections from his writings. Edited by John Lankford. New York, Harper and Row, 1967. 18, 195 p. (Harper Torchbooks, TB 3078)

Snell, William Robert. Indian slavery in colonial South Carolina, 1671-1795. Dissertation Abstracts International, 34 (1973/1974): 713A. UM 73-19,561.

Sonderegger, Richard Paul. The Southern Frontier from the founding of Georgia to the ending of King George's War. Dissertation Abstracts, 25 (1964/1965): 3546. UM 64-12,688.

South, S'tanley A.   Indians in North
Carolina. Raleigh, State Department of
Archives and History, 1959. 7, 69 p.
illus.

Speck, F. G.   Addendum to "Gourds of the
Southeastern Indians". Gourd Seed, 9
(1948): 15; 10 (1949): 3-6, 8, 11, 16,
24.

Speck, F. G.   Gourds of the Southeastern
Indians. Boston, 1941. 113 p.

Speck, F. G.   Some comparative traits of
the Maskogian languages. American
Anthropologist, n.s., 9 (1907): 470-484.

Speck, F. G.   Some outlines of aboriginal
culture in the Southeastern States.
American Anthropologist, n.s., 9 (1907):
287-295.

Speck, Frank G.   The Catawba nation and
its neighbors. North Carolina Historical
Review, 16 (1939): 404-417.

Stirling, M. W.   Florida cultural
affiliations in relation to adjacent
areas. In Essays in Anthropology
Presented to A. L. Kroeber. Berkeley,
1936: 351-357.

Stirling, M. W.   The historic method as
applied to Southeastern archaeology.
Smithsonian Miscellaneous Collections,
100 (1940): 117-123.

Strachey, W.   The historie of travell into
Virginia Britanica. Works Issued by the
Hakluyt Society, Second Series, 103
(1953): 1-253.

Sturtevant, W. C.   Accomplishments and
opportunities in Florida Indian
ethnology. Florida Anthropology, 2
(1958): 15-56.

Sturtevant, W. C.   Chakaika and the
Spanish Indians. Tequesta, 13 (1953):
35-73.

Sturtevant, William C.   Indian communities
in the eastern United States. By William
C. Sturtevant and Samuel Stanley. Indian
Historian, 1, no. 3 (1967/1968): 15-19.

Sturtevant, William C.   Spanish-Indian
relations in Southeastern North America.
Ethnohistory, 9 (1962): 41-94.

Sturtevant, William C.   The significance
of ethnological similarities between
southeastern North America and the
Antilles. New Haven, Human Relations
Area Files Press, 1970. 58 p. (Yale
University Publications in Anthropology,
64)

Swanton, J. R.   A point of resemblance
between the ball game of the
Southeastern Indians and the ball games
of Mexico and Central America.
Washington Academy of Sciences, Journal,
19 (1929): 304-307.

Swanton, J. R.   Aboriginal culture of the
Southeast. U.S. Bureau of American
Ethnology, Annual Reports, 42 (1925):
673-726.

Swanton, J. R.   De Soto's line of march
from the viewpoint of an ethnologist.
Mississippi Valley Historical
Association, Proceedings, 5 (1912): 147-
157.

Swanton, J. R.   Early history of the
Eastern Siouan tribes. In Essays in
Anthropology Presented to A. L. Kroeber.
Berkeley, 1936: 371-381.

Swanton, J. R.   Ethnological value of the
De Soto narratives. American
Anthropologist, n.s., 34 (1932): 570-
590.

*Swanton, J. R.   Indians of the
Southeastern United States. U.S. Bureau
of American Ethnology, Bulletin, 137
(1946): 1-943.

Swanton, J. R.   Notes on the cultural
province of the Southeast. American
Anthropologist, n.s., 37 (1935): 373-
385.

Swanton, J. R.   Relations between northern
Mexico and the Southeast of the United
States from the point of view of
ethnology and history. In El Norte de
México y el Sur de Estados Unidos.
México, 1943: 259-276.

Swanton, J. R.   Southeastern Indians of
history. In National Research Council,
Conference on Southern Pre-History.
Washington, D.C., 1932: 5-20.

Swanton, J. R.   Sun worship in the
Southeast. American Anthropologist,
n.s., 30 (1928): 206-213.

Swanton, J. R.   The relation of the
Southeast to general cultural problems
of American pre-history. In National
Research Council, Conference on Southern
Pre-History. Washington, D.C., 1932:
60-74.

Swanton, J. R.   The Southern contacts of
the Indians north of the Gulf of Mexico.
International Congress of Americanists,
Proceedings, 20, vol. 1 (1922): 53-59.

Swanton, J. R.   Unclassified languages of
the Southeast. International Journal of
American Linguistics, 1 (1917): 47-49.

*Swanton, John R. The Indians of the southeastern United States. Grosse Pointe, Mich., Scholarly Press, 1969. 13, 943 p. illus., maps.

*Swanton, John R. The Indians of the southeastern United States. New York, Greenwood Press, 1969. 13, 943 p. illus., maps.

Taylor, L. A. Plants used as curatives by certain Southeastern tribes. Cambridge, 1940. 88 p.

Tebeau, Charlton W. A history of Florida. Coral Gables, University of Miami Press, 1971. 14, 502 p. illus.

Texada, David Ker. The administration of Alejandro O'Reilly as governor of Louisiana, 1769-1770. Dissertation Abstracts, 29 (1968/1969): 3086A. UM 69-4504.

Texas, State Library, Austin, Archives Division. Texas Indian papers. Edited by Dorman H. Winfrey, et al. Austin, 1959-1966. 5 v. illus., maps.

Thomas, C. Prehistoric migrations in the Atlantic slope. American Antiquarian and Oriental Journal, 18 (1896): 346-358; 19 (1897): 11-19.

Tonti, H. de. Relation de la Louisianne, et du Mississipi. Recueil de Voyages au Nord, 5 (1734): 35-195.

Toomey, T. N. Proper names from the Muskhogean languages. Hervas Laboratories of American Linguistics, Bulletin, 3 (1917): 1-31.

Torrey, J. Observations on the Tuckahoe or Indian bread of the Southern states. Medical Repository, 21 (1821): 34-44.

Tyler, Lyon G., ed. Narratives of early Virginia, 1606-1625. New York, Charles Scribner's Sons, 1907. 15, 478 p. map. (Original Narratives of Early American History, 5)

Uhler, S. P. Pennsylvania's Indian relations to 1754. Allentown, 1951. 144 p.

Upchurch, John Calhoun. "Middle Florida": an historical geography of the area between the Apalachicola and Suwannee Rivers. Dissertation Abstracts International, 32 (1971/1972): 4666B-4667B. UM 72-5494.

U.S., Bureau of Indian Affairs. Indians of the eastern seaboard. Washington, D.C., Government Printing Office, 1968. 32 p. ERIC ED028871.

U.S., Bureau of Indian Affairs. Indians of the Gulf Coast states. Washington, D.C., Government Printing Office, 1968. 24 p. ERIC ED028866.

Vigneras, L. A. A Spanish discovery of North Carolina in 1566. North Carolina Historical Review, 46 (1969): 398-414.

Villiers du Terrage, M. de. Rapport du Chevalier de Kerlérec. International Congress of Americanists, Proceedings, 15, vol. 1 (1906): 61-86.

Voegelin, C. F. Corrigenda and addenda to thirty extinct languages. American Anthropologist, n.s., 48 (1946): 289.

Voegelin, C. F. Internal relationships of Siouan languages. American Anthropologist, n.s., 43 (1941): 246-249.

Voegelin, C. F. and E. W. Voegelin. Linguistic considerations of northeastern North America. Robert S. Peabody Foundation for Archaeology, Papers, 3 (1946): 178-194.

Voegelin, E. W. Mortuary customs of the Shawnee and other eastern tribes. Indiana Historical Society, Prehistory Research Series, 2 (1944): 227-444.

Watson, Thomas Davis. Merchant adventurer in the Old Southwest: William Panton, the Spanish years, 1783-1801. Dissertation Abstracts International, 33 (1972/1973): 4323A. UM 73-4082.

Weer, P. Preliminary notes on the Muskhogean family. Indiana Historical Society, Prehistory Research Series, 1 (1939): 245-286.

Weer, P. Preliminary notes on the Siouan family. Indiana History Bulletin, 14 (1937): 99-120.

Weitlaner, R. J. Las lenguas del Sur de Estados Unidos y el Norte de México. In El Norte de México y el Sur de Estados Unidos. México, 1943: 181-185.

Wells, Robin F. Castoreum and steel traps in eastern North America. American Anthropologist, 74 (1972): 479-483.

Wells, William. William Wells and the Indian Council of 1793. Edited by Dwight L. Smith. Indiana Magazine of History, 56 (1960): 217-226.

Wenhold, L. L. A 17th century letter of Gabriel Diaz Vara Calderon. Smithsonian Miscellaneous Collections, 95, no. 16 (1936): 1-14.

White, George. Historical collections of Georgia. Baltimore, Genealogical Publishing, 1969. 16, 658, 58 p. illus.

Willey, G. R. Archeology of the Florida Gulf Coast. Smithsonian Miscellaneous Collections, 113 (1949): 1-624.

Williams, John Lee. The Territory of Florida. Gainesville, University of Florida Press, 1962. 15, 304 p. illus., map.

Willis, William S. Divide and rule: Red, White, and Black in the Southeast. In Roger L. Nichols and George R. Adams, eds. The American Indian: Past and Present. Waltham, Xerox College Publishing, 1971: 74-85.

Willis, William S., Jr. Patrilineal institutions in southeastern North America. Ethnohistory, 10 (1963): 250-269.

Willoughby, C. C. Antler-pointed arrows of the South-Eastern Indians. American Anthropologist, n.s., 3 (1901): 431-437.

Willoughby, C. C. Notes on the history and symbolism of the Muskhogeans. In W. C. Moorehead, ed. Etowah Papers. New Haven, 1932: 7-67.

Winston, S. Indian slavery in the Carolina region. Archaeological Society of North Carolina, Bulletin, 3, no. 1 (1936): 3-9.

Withers, A. S. Chronicles of border warfare. Cincinnati, 1895. 447 p.

Witthoft, J. Green corn ceremonialism in the eastern woodlands. Michigan, University, Museum of Anthropology, Occasional Contributions, 13 (1949): 31-77.

Wolf, F. A. The fruiting stage of the Tuckahoe Pachyma cocas. Elisha Mitchell Scientific Society Journal, 38 (1922): 127-137.

Wolff, H. Comparative Siouan. International Journal of American Linguistics, 16 (1950): 61-66.

Wright, Homer Edward. Diplomacy of trade on the Southern Frontier: a case study of the influence of William Panton and John Forbes, 1784-1817. Dissertation Abstracts International, 33 (1972/1973): 3515A-3516A. UM 72-34,170.

Wright, J. Leitch. British designs on the Old Southwest: foreign intrigue on the Florida frontier 1783-1803. Florida Historical Quarterly, 44 (1965/1966): 265-284.

Wright, James Leitch, Jr. English-Spanish rivalry in North America, 1492-1763. Dissertation Abstracts, 19 (1958/1959): 1361. UM 58-5550.

Wright, M. H. A guide to the Indian tribes of Oklahoma. Norman, 1951. 300 p.

Young, Mary E. Indian removal and land allotment: the civilized tribes and Jacksonian justice. In Roger L. Nichols and George R. Adams, eds. The American Indian: Past and Present. Waltham, Xerox College Publishing, 1971: 132-145.

Zolotarevskaía, I. A. IUgo-vostochnye plemena Severnoĭ Ameriki. In A. V. Efimov and S. A. Tokarev, eds. Narody Ameriki. Vol. 1. Moskva, Izdatel'stvo Akademiía Nauk SSSR, 1959: 228-242.

13-01   Acolapissa

Albrechts, A. C. Ethnohistorical data pertaining to the Bayogoula. Southeastern Archaeological Conference, News Letter, 2, no. 4 (1941): 26-29.

Burch, M. C. The indigenous Indians of the lower Trinity area of Texas. Southwestern Historical Quarterly, 60 (1956): 36-52.

Bushnell, D. I. Drawings by A. deBatz in Louisiana. Smithsonian Miscellaneous Collections, 80, no. 5 (1927): 1-14.

Du Ru, Paul. Journal of Paul Du Ru, missionary priest to Louisiana. Translated, with introduction and notes, from a manuscript in the Newberry Library, by Ruth Lapham Butler. Chicago, Printed for the Caxton Club, 1934. 10, 74 p.

Le Moyne d'Iberville, P. Historical Journal. In B. F. French, ed. Historical Collections of Louisiana and Florida. Second Series. Vol. 2. New York, A. Mason, 1875: 31-103.

Margry, P., ed. Découvertes et établissements des Français dans l'Amérique septentrionale, Vol. 5: 463-470. Paris, 1883.

McWilliams, Richebourg Gaillard. Iberville and the Southern Indians. Alabama Review, 20 (1967): 243-262.

Quimby, G. I. The Natchezan culture type. American Antiquity, 7 (1942): 255-275.

Swanton, J. R. Indian tribes of the lower Mississippi Valley and adjacent coast of the Gulf of Mexico. U.S. Bureau of American Ethnology, Bulletin, 43 (1911): 274-284, 297-302.

Swanton, John R. Indian tribes of the Lower Mississippi Valley and adjacent coast of the Gulf of Mexico. New York, Johnson Reprint, 1970. 7, 387 p. illus.

Villiers du Terrage, M. de. Documents concernant l'histoire des Indiens de la région orientale de la Louisiane. Société des Américanistes, Journal, n.s., 14 (1922): 127-140.

13-02 Alabama

Blackwell, R. Quentin. Hemoglobin variant found in Koreans, Chinese, and North American Indians: $a_2\beta^{22}$Glu>Ala. By R. Quentin Blackwell, Ihl-Hyeob Ro, Chen-Sheng Liu, Hung-Ju Yang, Chen-Chang Wang, and Jeanette Tung-Hsiang Huang. American Journal of Physical Anthropology, n.s., 30 (1969): 389-391.

Blackwell, R. Quentin, et al. Hemoglobin variant common to Chinese and North American Indians. Science, 161 (1968): 381-382.

Bludworth, G. T. How the Alabamas came south. Texas Folk-Lore Society, Publications, 13 (1937): 298-299.

Bossu, M. Nouveaux voyages aux Indes Occidentales, Vol. 2: 17-72. Paris, 1768.

Bossu, M. Travels through that part of North America formerly called Louisiana, Vol. 1: 229-277. London, 1771.

Bounds, John H. The Alabama-Coushatta Indians of Texas. Journal of Geography, 70 (1971): 175-182.

Bowman, Barbara H. Hemoglobin G Coushatta: a beta variant with a delta-like substitution. By Barbara H. Bowman, Don R. Barnett, and Rodney Hite. Biochemical and Biophysical Research Communications, 26 (1967): 466-470.

Covington, James W. Federal relations with the Apalachicola Indians: 1823-1838. Florida Historical Quarterly, 42 (1963/1964): 125-141.

Densmore, F. The Alabama Indians and their music. Texas Folk-Lore Society, Publications, 13 (1937): 270-293.

Dickerson, William E. S. The white path. By William E. S. Folsom-Dickerson. San Antonio, Naylor, 1965. 14, 148 p. illus.

Fain, Anna Kilpatrick. Texas Indians; the story of Indian village and the Alabama Indians in Polk County Texas on the Alabama-Coushatti Reservation. Livingstone, Tex., 1960. 21 p. illus.

Fay, George E., ed. Charters, constitutions and by-laws of the Indian tribes of North America. Part V: The Indian tribes of Oklahoma. Greeley, 1968. 14, 104 l. map. (University of Northern Colorado, Museum of Anthropology, Occasional Publications in Anthropology, Ethnology Series, 6) ERIC ED046555.

Garcilaso de la Vega, el Inca. The Florida of the Inca. Translated and edited by John Grier Varner and Jeannette Johnson Varner. Austin, University of Texas Press, 1951. 45, 655 p. illus., map.

Gatschet, A. S. A migration legend of the Creek Indians, 85-90. Philadelphia, 1884.

Gatschet, A. S. and C. Thomas. Alibamu. U.S. Bureau of American Ethnology, Bulletin, 30, vol. 1 (1907): 43-44.

Griffin, William B. Spanish Pensacola, 1700-1763. Florida Historical Quarterly, 37 (1958/1959): 242-262.

Haas, M. R. Men's and women's speech in Koasati. Language, 20 (1944): 142-149.

Haas, Mary R. Historical linguistics and the genetic relationship of languages. In Theoretical Foundations. The Hague, Mouton, 1966: 113-153. (Current Trends in Linguistics, 3)

Harrington, M. R. Among Louisiana Indians. Southern Workman, 37 (1908): 656-661.

Heard, E. Two tales from the Alabamas. Texas Folk-Lore Society, Publications, 13 (1937): 294-298.

Holmes, Jack D. L. Spanish treaties with West Florida Indians, 1784-1802. Florida Historical Quarterly, 48 (1969/1970): 140-154.

Holmes, Jack D. L. Three early Memphis commandants: Beauregard, Deville Degoutin, and Folch. West Tennessee Historical Society, Papers, 18 (1964): 5-38.

Jacobson, Daniel. The origin of the
Koasati community of Louisiana.
Ethnohistory, 7 (1960): 97-120.

Johnson, John E., Jr. Diabetes mellitus
in an American Indian population
isolate. By John E. Johnson, Jr., and C.
Wallace McNutt. Texas Reports on Biology
and Medicine, 22 (1964): 110-125.

Malone, Prairie View. Sam Houston's
Indians: the Alabama-Coushatti. San
Antonio, Naylor, 1960. 63 p.

Martin, H. N. Folktales of the Alabama-
Coushatta Indians. Livingston, 1946.
75 p.

Martin, Howard N. Texas Redskins in
Confederate gray. Southwestern
Historical Quarterly, 70 (1966/1967):
586-592.

McLane, William. William McLane's
narrative of the Magee-Gutierrez
expedition, 1812-1813. Edited by Henry
P. Walker. Southwestern Historical
Quarterly, 66 (1962/1963): 457-479, 569-
588.

Morse, M. Mary E. Heickman; Texas weaver
and teacher to the Alabama-Coushatta
Indian tribe. Handweaver, 17, no. 3
(1966): 18-19.

Pardo, Juan. Journals of the Juan Pardo
expeditions, 1566-1567. Edited by
Stanley J. Folmsbee and Madeline Kneberg
Lewis. Translated by Gerald W. Wade.
East Tennessee Historical Society,
Publications, 37 (1965): 106-121.

Rand, Earl. The structural phonology of
Alabaman, a Muskogean language.
International Journal of American
Linguistics, 34 (1968): 94-103.

Roth, Aline T. Kalita's people; a history
of the Alabama-Coushatta Indians of
Texas. Waco, 1963. 20, 141 p. illus.,
map.

Schneider, R. G., et al. Hemoglobin G
Coushatta: a new variant in an American
Indian family. Science, 143 (1964): 697-
698.

Smither, H. The Alabama Indians of Texas.
Southwestern Historical Quarterly, 36
(1932): 83-108.

Stone, Richard G., Jr. Captain Paul
Demere at Fort Loudoun, 1757-1760. East
Tennessee Historical Society's
Publications, 41 (1969): 17-32.

Swanton, J. R. Animal stories from the
Indians of the Muskhogean stock. Journal
of American Folklore, 26 (1913): 209-
214.

Swanton, J. R. Early history of the Creek
Indians and their neighbors. U.S. Bureau
of American Ethnology, Bulletin, 73
(1922): 137-141, 191-207.

Swanton, J. R. Indian language studies in
Louisiana. Smithsonian Institution,
Explorations and Field-Work (1930): 195-
200.

Swanton, J. R. Koasati. U.S. Bureau of
American Ethnology, Bulletin, 30, vol. 1
(1907): 719-720.

Swanton, J. R. Modern square grounds of
the Creek Indians. Smithsonian
Miscellaneous Collections, 85, no. 8
(1931): 1-46.

Swanton, J. R. Myths and tales of the
Southeastern Indians. U.S. Bureau of
American Ethnology, Bulletin, 88 (1929):
118-213.

Swanton, J. R. Religious beliefs and
medical practices of the Creek Indians.
U.S. Bureau of American Ethnology,
Annual Reports, 42 (1925): 473-672.

Swanton, J. R. Social organization and
social usages of the Indians of the
Creek Confederacy. U.S. Bureau of
American Ethnology, Annual Reports, 42
(1925): 23-472.

Swanton, J. R. The Kaskinampo Indians and
their neighbors. American
Anthropologist, n.s., 32 (1930): 405-
418.

Swanton, John R. Early history of the
Creek Indians and their neighbors. New
York, Johnson Reprint, 1970. 492 p.
maps.

Taylor, L. A. Plants used as curatives by
certain Southeastern Tribes. Cambridge,
1940. 88 p.

Villiers du Terrage, M. de. Documents
concernant l'histoire des Indiens de la
région orientale de la Louisiane.
Société des Américanistes, Journal,
n.s., 14 (1922): 127-140.

Wade, M. D. The Alabama Indians of East
Texas. Livingston, 1936.

Winfrey, Dorman H., ed. The Indian papers
of Texas and the Southwest, 1825-1916.
Edited by Dorman H. Winfrey and James M.
Day. Austin, Pemberton Press, 1966.
412 p.

Wrede, Friedrich Wilhelm von. Sketches of
life in the United States of North

America and Texas. Translated from the German by Chester W. Geue. Waco, Texian Press, 1970. 15, 208 p. illus.

13-03 Apalachee

Arana, Luis Rafael. The Alonso Solana map of Florida, 1683. Florida Historical Quarterly, 42 (1963/1964): 258-266.

Arnade, Charles W. The English invasion of Spanish Florida, 1700-1706. Florida Historical Quarterly, 41 (1962/1963): 29-37.

Bandelier, A. F., ed. The journey of Alvar Nunez Cabeza de Vaca, 25-34. New York, 1922.

Boyd, M. F. Diego Peña's expedition to Apalachee and Apalachicolo in 1716. Florida Historical Quarterly, 28 (1949): 1-27.

Boyd, M. F. Documents describing the second and third expedition of Lieutenant Diego Peña to Apalachee and Apalachicolo in 1717 and 1718. Florida Historical Quarterly, 31 (1952): 109-139.

Boyd, M. F. Further considerations of the Apalachee missions. Americas, 9 (1953): 459-479.

*Boyd, M. F., et al. Here once they stood. Gainesville, Fla., 1951. 189 p.

Brinton, D. G. Notes on the Floridian peninsula, 92-110. Philadelphia, 1859.

Cabeza de Vaca, Alvar Núñez. Adventures in the unknown interior of America. New York, Collier, 1961. 152 p. (Collier Books, AS117)

Covington, James W. Apalachee Indians, 1704-1763. Florida Historical Quarterly, 50 (1971/1972): 366-384.

Covington, James W. The Apalachee Indians move west. Florida Anthropologist, 17 (1964): 221-225.

Fontaneda, H. de Escalante. Memoir. In B. F. French, ed. Historical Collections of Louisiana and Florida. Second Series. Vol. 2. New York, A. Mason, 1875: 235-265.

Fontaneda, H. de Escalante. Mémoire sur la Floride. In H. Ternaux-Compans, ed. Voyages. Vol. 20. Paris, 1841: 9-42.

Gannon, Michael V. Altar and hearth: the coming of Christianity, 1521-1565.

Florida Historical Quarterly, 44 (1965/1966): 17-44.

Garcilaso de la Vega, el Inca. The Florida of the Inca. Translated and edited by John Grier Varner and Jeannette Johnson Varner. Austin, University of Texas Press, 1951. 45, 655 p. illus., map.

Gold, Robert L. Conflict in San Carlos: Indian immigrants in eighteenth-century New Spain. Ethnohistory, 17 (1970): 1-10.

Haas, M. R. The position of Apalachee in the Muskogean family. International Journal of American Linguistics, 15 (1949): 121-127.

Harrison, B. Indian races of Florida. Florida Historical Quarterly, 3 (1924): 29-37.

Jones, B. Calvin. Colonel James Moore and the destruction of the Apalachee missions in 1704. Florida, Bureau of Historic Sites and Properties, Bulletin, 2 (1972): 25-33.

Jones, B. Calvin. Missions reveal state's Spanish-Indian heritage. Archives and History News, 1, no. 2 (1970): 1-3.

Jones, B. Calvin. State archaeologists unearth Spanish mission ruins. Archives and History News, 2, no. 4 (1971): 2.

Jones, B. Calvin. 17th century Spanish mission cemetery is discovered near Tallahassee. Archives and History News, 1, no. 4 (1970): 1-2.

Klingberg, F. J., ed. The Carolina chronicle of Dr. Francis Le Jau, 1706-1717. California, University, Publications in History, 53 (1956): 1-228.

La Roncière, C. G., ed. La Floride française. Paris, 1928. 139 p.

Lazarus, Mrs. W. C. Indians of the Florida panhandle. Fort Walton Beach, Fla., Temple Mound Museum, 1968. 5, 28 p. illus.

Milling, C. J. Red Carolinians. Chapel Hill, 1940. 438 p.

Mooney, J. Apalachee. U.S. Bureau of American Ethnology, Bulletin, 30, vol. 1 (1907): 67-68.

Mooney, J. Pensacola. U.S. Bureau of American Ethnology, Bulletin, 30, vol. 2 (1910): 227.

Morrell, L. Ross. San Juan de Aspalaga (a preliminary architectural study). By L. Ross Morrell and B. Calvin Jones. Florida, Bureau of Historic Sites and Properties, Bulletin, 1 (1970): 23-43.

Oviedo y Valdez, G. F. de. Historia general y natural de las Indias, Vol. 3: 578-586. Madrid, 1853.

Palerm, A. San Carlos de Chachalacas, una fundación de los indios de Florida en Veracruz. Cuadernos Americanos, 61 (1952): 165-184.

Pearson, Fred Lamar, Jr. Spanish-Indian relations in Florida: a study of two visitas, 1657-1678. Dissertation Abstracts, 29 (1968/1969): 1500A-1501A. UM 68-15,502.

Rich, Lou. Wakulla Spring: its setting and literary visitors. Florida Historical Quarterly, 42 (1963/1964): 351-362.

Smith, B. [Documents in the Spanish and two of the early tongues of Florida]. Washington, D.C., 1860. 12 p.

Smith, B. Letter of Hernando de Soto and memoir of Hernando de Escalante Fontaneda. Washington, D.C., 1854. 67 p.

Smith, B. Specimen of the Appalachian language. Historical Magazine, 4 (1860): 40-41.

Swanton, J. R. Early history of the Creek Indians and their neighbors. U.S. Bureau of American Ethnology, Bulletin, 73 (1922): 109-129.

Swanton, John R. Early history of the Creek Indians and their neighbors. New York, Johnson Reprint, 1970. 492 p. maps.

Toomey, T. N. Analysis of a text in the Apalachi language. Hervas Laboratories of American Linguistics, Bulletin, 6 (1918): 1-8.

Wenhold, L. L., ed. The trials of Captain Don Isidoro De Leon. Florida Historical Quarterly, 35 (1957): 246-265.

Willey, G. R. Archeology of the Florida Gulf Coast. Smithsonian Miscellaneous Collections, 113 (1949): 1-624.

13-04 Biloxi

Anonymous. Biloxi. U.S. Bureau of American Ethnology, Bulletin, 30, vol. 1 (1907): 147-148.

Bass, A. James Mooney in Oklahoma. Chronicles of Oklahoma, 32 (1954): 246-262.

Bushnell, D. I. Native cemeteries and forms of burial east of the Mississippi. U.S. Bureau of American Ethnology, Bulletin, 71 (1920): 135-137.

Dorsey, J. O. Preface. Contributions to North American Ethnology, 9 (1893): xviii-xxx.

Dorsey, J. O. Siouan sociology. U.S. Bureau of American Ethnology, Annual Reports, 15 (1894): 243-244.

Dorsey, J. O. The Biloxi Indians of Louisiana. American Association for the Advancement of Science, Proceedings, 42 (1893): 267-287.

Dorsey, J. O. Two Biloxi tales. Journal of American Folklore, 6 (1893): 48-50.

Dorsey, J. O. and J. R. Swanton. A dictionary of the Biloxi and Ofo languages. U.S. Bureau of American Ethnology, Bulletin, 47 (1912): 1-340.

Dumont de Montigny. Memoires historiques sur la Louisiane, Vol. 1: 240-243. Paris, 1753.

Ethridge, A. N. Indians of Grant Parish. Louisiana Historical Quarterly, 23 (1940): 1108-1131.

Gold, Robert L. The East Florida Indians under Spanish and English control: 1763-1765. Florida Historical Quarterly, 44 (1965/1966): 105-120.

Haas, Mary R. Swanton and the Biloxi and Ofo dictionaries. International Journal of American Linguistics, 35 (1969): 286-290.

Haas, Mary R. The last words of Biloxi. International Journal of American Linguistics, 34 (1968): 77-84.

McWilliams, Richebourg Gaillard. Iberville and the Southern Indians. Alabama Review, 20 (1967): 243-262.

Miller, C. F. Revaluation of the Eastern Siouan problem. U.S. Bureau of American Ethnology, Bulletin, 164 (1957): 115-212.

Mooney, J. The Siouan tribes of the East. U.S. Bureau of American Ethnology, Bulletin, 22 (1894): 5-101.

Porter, K. W. A legend of the Biloxi. Journal of American Folklore, 59 (1946): 168-173.

Sturtevant, W. C. Siouan languages in the East. American Anthropologist, 60 (1958): 738-743.

Swanton, J. R. New light on the early history of the Siouan peoples. Washington Academy of Sciences, Journal, 13 (1923): 33-43.

Voegelin, C. F. Ofo-Biloxi sound correspondences. Indiana Academy of Science, Proceedings, 48 (1939): 23-26.

13-05 Calusa

Alegre, F. J. Historia de la Provincia de la Compañia de Jesús de Nueva España. New ed. Rome, 1956-1958. 2 v.

Andrews, C. M. The Florida Indians in the seventeenth century. Tequesta, 1, no. 3 (1943): 36-48.

Arnade, Charles W. Cycles of conquest in Florida. Tequesta, 23 (1963): 23-31.

Brinton, D. G. Notes on the Floridian peninsula, 111-119. Philadelphia, 1859.

Bullen, Ripley P. Southern limit of Timucua territory. Florida Historical Quarterly, 47 (1968/1969): 414-419.

Collins, H. B. Burial of the Calusa Indians. El Palacio, 24 (1928): 223-224.

Collins, H. B. The "lost" Calusa Indians. Smithsonian Institution, Explorations and Field-Work (1928): 151-156.

Covington, J. W. Trade relations between southwestern Florida and Cuba--1600-1840. Florida Historical Quarterly, 38 (1959): 114-128.

Cushing, F. H. Exploration of ancient key dwellers' remains on the Gulf Coast of Florida. American Philosophical Society, Proceedings, 35 (1896): 329-448.

Dickinson, J. God's protecting providence. 7th ed. London, 1790. 136 p.

Dickinson, J. Journal. Ed. by E. W. and C. M. Andrews. Yale Historical Publications, Manuscripts and Edited Texts, 19 (1945): 1-252.

Dickinson, J. Narrative of a shipwreck in the Gulph of Florida. 6th ed. New York, 1803.

Dickinson, Jonathan. Journal; or, God's protecting Providence. Rev. ed. New Haven, printed for the Yale University Press, 1961. 100 p. illus. (Yale Paperbound, Y-50)

DuBois, Bessie Wilson. Jupiter Inlet. Tequesta, 28 (1968): 19-35.

Fewkes, J. W. Aboriginal wooden objects from southern Florida. Smithsonian Miscellaneous Collections, 80, no. 9 (1928): 1-2.

Fontenada, D. de Escalante. Memoir. In B. F. French, ed. Historical Collections of Louisiana and Florida. Second Series. Vol. 2. New York, A. Mason, 1875: 235-265.

Fontenada, D. de Escalante. Memoir respecting Florida. Coral Gables, 1945.

Fontenada, D. de Escalante. Mémoire sur la Floride. In H. Ternaux-Compans, ed. Voyages. Vol. 20. Paris, 1841: 9-42.

Fontenada, D. de Escalante. Memoria de las cosas y costa y Indios de la Florida. Colección de Documentos Inéditos, Relativos al Descubrimiento, Conquista y Colonización de las Posesiones Españolas en América y Oceanía, 5 (1866): 532-548.

Goggin, J. M. The Indians and history of the Matecumbe region. Tequesta, 10 (1950): 13-24.

Goggin, J. M. The Tekesta Indians of southern Florida. Florida Historical Quarterly, 18 (1940): 274-284.

Goggin, J. M. and F. H. Sommer. Excavations on Upper Matecumbe Key, Florida. Yale University Publications in Anthropology, 41 (1949): 1-104.

Griffin, J. W. The Antillean problem in Florida archaeology. Florida Historical Quarterly, 22 (1943): 86-91.

Harrison, B. Indian races of Florida. Florida Historical Quarterly, 3 (1924): 29-37.

Hrdlička, A. The anthropology of Florida. Florida State Historical Society, Publications, 1 (1922): 1-140.

Keegan, G. J. and L. Tormo Sanz. Experiencia misionera en la Florida (siglos XVI y XVII). Missionalia Hispanica, ser. B, 7 (1957): 1-404.

Kenworthy, C. J. Ancient canals in Florida. Smithsonian Institution, Annual Reports of the Board of Regents (1881): 631-635.

Laxson, D. D. Strombus lip shell tools of the Tequesta sub-area. Florida Anthropologist, 17 (1964): 215-220.

Manucy, Albert. The man who was Pedro Menéndez. Florida Historical Quarterly, 44 (1965/1966): 67-80.

McNicoll, R. E. The Caloosa village Tequesta. Tequesta, 1, no. 1 (1941): 11-20.

Mooney, J. Ais. U.S. Bureau of American Ethnology, Bulletin, 30, vol. 1 (1907): 31.

Mooney, J. Calusa. U.S. Bureau of American Ethnology, Bulletin, 30, vol. 1 (1907): 195-196.

Mooney, J. Tequesta. U.S. Bureau of American Ethnology, Bulletin, 30, vol. 2 (1910): 733.

Moore, C. B. Certain antiquities of the Florida West-Coast. Academy of Natural Sciences of Philadelphia, Journal, ser. 2, 11 (1900): 353-394.

Morfi, J. A. de. Memorias for the history of the Province of Texas. Ed. by F. M. Chabot. San Antonio, 1932. 85 p.

Neill, W. T. The identity of Florida's "Spanish Indians". Florida Anthropologist, 8, no. 2 (1955): 43-57.

Pinart, A. L. Geroglificos entre los indios de la Florida. Anthropos, 2 (1907): 133-134.

Read, C. H. Note on ethnological objects excavated at Marco. Royal Anthropological Institute of Great Britain and Ireland, Journal, 25 (1896): 406-407.

Rouse, I. B. A survey of Indian River archeology, Florida. Yale University Publications in Anthropology, 44 (1951): 1-296.

Smith, B., ed. Letter of Hernando de Soto and memoir of Hernando de Escalante Fontaneda. Washington, D.C., 1854. 67 p.

Smith, R. M. Anthropology in Florida. Florida Historical Quarterly, 11 (1933): 151-172.

Stirling, M. W. Florida cultural affiliations in relation to adjacent areas. In Essays in Anthropology Presented to A. L. Kroeber. Berkeley, 1936: 351-357.

Stirling, M. W. Mounds of the vanished Calusa Indians of Florida. Smithsonian

Institution, Explorations and Field-Work (1930): 167-172.

Sturtevant, W. C. Chakaika and the "Spanish Indians". Tequesta, 13 (1953): 35-73.

Swanton, J. R. Early history of the Creek Indians and their neighbors. U.S. Bureau of American Ethnology, Bulletin, 73 (1922): 27-31, 387-398.

Swanton, John R. Early history of the Creek Indians and their neighbors. New York, Johnson Reprint, 1970. 492 p. maps.

Walker, S. T. The aborigines of Florida. Smithsonian Institution, Annual Reports of the Board of Regents (1881): 677-680.

Zubillaga, F. La Florida. Rome, 1941. 473 p.

13-06   Catawba

Adair, J. The history of the American Indians. London, 1775. 464 p.

Alvord, C. W. and L. Bidgood. First explorations of the Trans-Allegheny Region by the Virginians, 1650-1674. Cleveland, 1912. 275 p.

Anghierra, P. M. de. De orbe novo. Tr. by F. A. MacNutt. New York, 1912. 2 v.

Anonymous. Eno. U.S. Bureau of American Ethnology, Bulletin, 30, vol. 1 (1907): 425-426.

Ardrey, W. B. The Catawba Indians. American Antiquarian and Oriental Journal, 16 (1894): 266-269.

Barton, B. S. New views of the origin of the tribes and nations of America, 2d ed.: 77-133. Philadelphia, 1798.

Bradford, W. R. The Catawba Indians of South Carolina. South Carolina, University, Bulletin, n.s., 34 (1946): 1-31.

Brickell, J. The natural history of North-Carolina, 277-408. Dublin, 1737.

Brickell, John. The natural history of North Carolina. Murfreesboro, N.C., Johnson, 1968. 14, 14, 424 p. illus., map.

Brickell, John. The natural history of North-Carolina. New York, Johnson Reprint, 1969. 10, 14, 417 p. illus., map.

Brown, D. S. Catawba land records. South Carolina Historical Magazine, 59 (1958): 64-77, 171-176, 226-233.

Brown, Douglas S. The Catawba Indians, the people of the river. Columbia, University of South Carolina Press, 1966. 8, 400 p. illus., maps.

Bushnell, D. I. Native cemeteries and forms of burial east of the Mississippi. U.S. Bureau of American Ethnology, Bulletin, 71 (1920): 131-135.

Catesby, M. The natural history of Carolina, Florida, and Bahama Islands. London, 1731-1743. 2 v.

Chamberlain, A. F. The Catawba language. Toronto, 1888. 3 p.

Coe, J. L. The cultural sequence of the Carolina Piedmont. In J. B. Griffin, ed. Archeology of Eastern United States. Chicago, 1952: 301-311.

Fewkes, V. J. Catawba pottery-making. American Philosophical Society, Proceedings, 88 (1944): 69-124.

Foreman, G. The last trek of the Indians, 316-320. Chicago, 1946.

Franklin, W. Neil. Act for the better regulation of the Indian trade; Virginia, 1714. Virginia Magazine of History and Biography, 72 (1964): 141-151.

Gardner, Bettie Sue. The Saura Indians of Rockingham County, North Carolina: their origin, language, habitation, and disintegration. Reidsville, N.C., 1962. 27 l.

Gatschet, A. S. Grammatic sketch of the Catawba language. American Anthropologist, n.s., 2 (1900): 527-549.

Gatschet, A. S. Onomatology of the Catawba River basin. American Anthropologist, n.s., 4 (1902): 52-56.

Gregg, A. History of the Old Cheraws, 1-30. New York, 1867.

Gregg, Alexander. History of the old Cheraws. Spartanburg, S.C., Reprint Co., 1965. 8, 546 p. maps. (South Carolina Heritage Series, 9)

Gregg, Alexander. History of the old Cheraws. Baltimore, Genealogical Publishing, 1967. 8, 629 p. illus., maps.

Gregorie, A. K. Notes on Sewee Indians. Charleston Museum, Contributions, 5 (1925): 1-23.

Griffin, J. B. An interpretation of Siouan archaeology in the piedmont of North Carolina and Virginia. American Antiquity, 10 (1945): 321-330.

Hagy, James William, ed. The lost archives of the Cherokee Nation. Edited by James William Hagy and Stanley J. Folmsbee. East Tennessee Historical Society, Publications, 43 (1971): 112-122; 44 (1972): 114-125.

Harrington, M. R. Catawba potters and their work. American Anthropologist, n.s., 10 (1908): 399-407.

Hatton, William. Some short remarkes on the Indian trade in the Charikees and in managment thereof since the year 1717. Edited by Rena Vassar. Ethnohistory, 8 (1961): 401-423.

Hicks, George L. Catawba acculturation and the ideology of race. In June Helm, ed. Symposium on the New Approaches to the Study of Religion. Seattle, University of Washington Press, 1964: 116-124. (American Ethnological Society, Proceedings of the Annual Spring Meeting, 1964)

Hicks, George L. Cultural persistence versus local adaptation: Frank G. Speck's Catawba Indians. Ethnohistory, 12 (1965): 343-354.

Holland, C. G. An archeological survey of southwest Virginia. Washington, D.C., Smithsonian Institution Press, 1970. 16, 194 p. illus. (Smithsonian Contributions to Anthropology, 12)

Holmes, W. H. Aboriginal pottery of the eastern United States. U.S. Bureau of American Ethnology, Annual Reports, 20 (1903): 53-55.

Howe, G. An essay on the antiquities of the Congaree Indians. In H. R. Schoolcraft, ed. Information respecting the History, Condition, and Prospects of the Indian Tribes of the United States. Vol. 4. Philadelphia, 1854: 155-169.

*Hudson, Charles M., Jr. The Catawba Nation. Athens, University of Georgia Press, 1970. 9, 142 p. maps.

Hudson, Charles M., Jr. The Catawba nation: a social history. Dissertation Abstracts, 26 (1965/1966): 3579. UM 65-14,352.

Kingberg, F. J., ed. The Carolina chronicle of Dr. Francis Le Jau, 1706-1717. California, University, Publications in History, 53 (1956): 1-228.

Kirkland, T. J. and R. M. Kennedy.
Historic Camden. Columbia, S.C., 1905.

Lanman, C. Adventures in the wilds of the
United States and British American
Provinces, Vol. 1: 452; Vol. 2: 410-412.
Philadelphia, 1856.

Lawson, John. An account of the Indians
of N. Carolina. In his The History of
Carolina. Raleigh, Strother and Marcom,
1860: 277-390.

Lawson, John. An account of the Indians
of N. Carolina. In Lawson's History of
North Carolina. Richmond, Garrett and
Massie, 1937: 179-259.

Lewis, E. Ceramic analysis of a protohistoric Siouan village. Eastern States
Archaeological Federation, Bulletin, 11
(1953): 9.

Lieber, O. M. Vocabulary of the Catawba
language. South Carolina Historical
Society, Collections, 2 (1858): 327-342.

Matthews, G. Hubert. Catawba texts. By G.
Hubert Matthews and Red Thunder Cloud.
International Journal of American
Linguistics, 33 (1967): 7-24.

McDowell, William L., Jr., ed. Documents
relating to Indian affairs, May 21,
1750-August 7, 1754. Columbia, South
Carolina Archives Department, 1958. 22,
592 p. (Colonial Records of South
Carolina, Series 2)

McDowell, William L., Jr., ed. Documents
relating to Indian affairs: 1754-1765.
Columbia, Published for the South
Carolina Department of Archives and
History by the University of South
Carolina Press, 1970. 55, 657 p.
illus. (Colonial Records of South
Carolina, Series 2, 3)

Michelson, T. Field-work among the
Catawba, Fox, Sutaio and Sauk Indians.
Smithsonian Miscellaneous Collections,
63, no. 8 (1914): 836.

Miller, C. F. Revaluation of the Eastern
Siouan problem. U.S. Bureau of American
Ethnology, Bulletin, 164 (1957): 115-
212.

Milling, C. J. Red Carolinians. Chapel
Hill, 1940. 438 p.

Mills, R. Statistics of South Carolina,
111. 1826.

Mooney, J. Catawba. U.S. Bureau of
American Ethnology, Bulletin, 30, vol. 1
(1907): 213-216.

Mooney, J. Cheraw. U.S. Bureau of
American Ethnology, Bulletin, 30, vol. 1
(1907): 244-245.

Mooney, J. The Siouan tribes of the East.
U.S. Bureau of American Ethnology,
Bulletin, 22 (1894): 5-101.

Pardo, Juan. Journals of the Juan Pardo
expeditions, 1566-1567. Edited by
Stanley J. Folmsbee and Madeline Kneberg
Lewis. Translated by Gerald W. Wade.
East Tennessee Historical Society,
Publications, 37 (1965): 106-121.

Pennypacker, S. W. A note on Catawba
ceramics. Pennsylvania Archaeologist, 7
(1937): 55-56.

Pepper, G. H. Wateree artifacts. Indian
Notes, 1 (1924): 74-75.

Pollitzer, William S. Catawba Indians:
morphology, genetics, and history. By
William S. Pollitzer, David S. Phelps,
Robert E. Waggoner, and Webster C.
Leyshon. American Journal of Physical
Anthropology, n.s., 26 (1967): 5-14.

Potter, E. An account of several nations
of Southern Indians. Massachusetts
Historical Society, Collections, ser. 1,
10 (1809): 119-121.

Quinn, David B. Thomas Hariot and the
Virginia voyages of 1602. William and
Mary Quarterly, 3d ser., 27 (1970): 268-
281.

Rights, D. L. Indian occupation of the
Charlotte area. Archaeological Society
of North Carolina, Bulletin, 2, no. 1
(1935): 10-13.

Rights, D. L. The American Indian in
North Carolina. Winston-Salem, 1957.
318 p.

Rights, D. L. The American Indian in
North Carolina. Durham, 1947. 296 p.

Scaife, H. L. History and condition of
the Catawba Indians. Indian Rights
Association, Publications, ser. 2, 21
(1896): 1-24.

Siebert, F. T., Jr. Linguistic
classification of Catawba. International
Journal of American Linguistics, 11
(1945): 100-104, 211-218.

Smyth, J. F. D. A tour in the United
States of America, Vol. 1: 184-195, 347.
London, 1784.

Speck, F. G. Catawba games and
amusements. Primitive Man, 17 (1944):
19-28.

Speck, F. G. Catawba herbals and curative practices. Journal of American Folklore, 57 (1944): 37-50.

Speck, F. G. Catawba hunting, trapping and fishing. Philadelphia Anthropological Society, Publications, 2 (1946): 1-33.

Speck, F. G. Catawba medicines and curative practices. Philadelphia Anthropological Society, Publications, 1 (1937): 179-197.

Speck, F. G. Catawba religious beliefs, mortuary customs, and dances. Primitive Man, 12 (1939): 21-57.

Speck, F. G. Catawba text. International Journal of American Linguistics, 12 (1946): 64-65.

Speck, F. G. Catawba texts. Columbia University Contributions to Anthropology, 24 (1934): 1-91.

Speck, F. G. Eggan's Yuchi kinship interpretations. American Anthropologist, n.s., 41 (1939): 171-172.

Speck, F. G. Ethnoherpetology of the Catawba and Cherokee Indians. Washington Academy of Sciences, Journal, 36 (1946): 355-360.

Speck, F. G. Recording the Catawba language. El Palacio, 24 (1928): 307-308.

Speck, F. G. Siouan tribes of the Carolinas. American Anthropologist, n.s., 37 (1935): 201-225.

Speck, F. G. Some Catawba texts and folklore. Journal of American Folklore, 26 (1913): 319-330.

Speck, F. G. The cane blowgun in Catawba and Southeastern ethnology. American Anthropologist, n.s., 40 (1938): 198-204.

Speck, F. G. The possible Siouan identity of the words recorded from Francisco of Chicora on the South Carolina coast. Washington Academy of Sciences, Journal, 14 (1924): 303-306.

Speck, F. G. The question of matrilineal descent in the Southeastern Siouan area. American Anthropologist, n.s., 40 (1938): 1-12.

Speck, F. G. and C. E. Schaeffer. Catawba kinship and social organization. American Anthropologist, n.s., 44 (1942): 555-575.

Speck, F. G. and C. E. Schaeffer. The deer and the rabbit hunting drive in Virginia and the Southeast. Southern Indian Studies, 2 (1950): 3-20.

Speck, F. G. and L. G. Carr. Catawba folk tales from Chief Sam Blue. Journal of American Folklore, 60 (1947): 79-84.

Speck, Frank G. Catawba texts. New York, AMS Press, 1969. 18, 91 p. (Columbia University Contributions to Anthropology, 24)

Speck, Frank G. The Catawba nation and its neighbors. North Carolina Historical Review, 16 (1939): 404-417.

Spratt, Zack, comp. Thomas Dryden Spratt's recollections of his family. Washington, D.C., 1962. [125 l.] illus.

Stone, Richard G., Jr. Captain Paul Demere at Fort Loudoun, 1757-1760. East Tennessee Historical Society's Publications, 41 (1969): 17-32.

Sturtevant, W. C. Siouan languages in the East. American Anthropologist, 60 (1958): 738-743.

Swadesh, M. Sociologic notes on obsolescent languages. International Journal of American Linguistics, 14 (1948): 226-238.

Swanton, J. R. Catawba notes. Washington Academy of Sciences, Journal, 8 (1918): 623-629.

Swanton, J. R. Early history of the Eastern Siouan tribes. In Essays in Anthropology Presented to A. L. Kroeber. Berkeley, 1936: 371-381.

Swanton, J. R. New light on the early history of the Siouan peoples. Washington Academy of Sciences, Journal, 13 (1923): 33-43.

Swanton, J. R. The first description of an Indian tribe in the territory of the present United States. In Studies for William A. Read. Baton Rouge, 1940: 326-338.

Talbot, W., ed. The discoveries of John Lederer. New ed. Rochester, 1902. 30 p.

Uhler, S. P. Pennsylvania's Indian relations to 1754. Allentown, 1951. 144 p.

Young, Chester Raymond. The stress of war upon the civilian population of Virginia, 1739-1760. West Virginia History, 27 (1965/1966): 251-277.

13-07   Chakchiuma

Halbert, H. S. The small Indian tribes of
Mississippi. Mississippi Historical
Society, Publications, 5 (1902): 302-
308.

Swanton, J. R. Indian tribes of the lower
Mississippi valley and adjacent coast of
the Gulf of Mexico. U.S. Bureau of
American Ethnology, Bulletin, 43 (1911):
292-297.

Swanton, John R. Indian tribes of the
Lower Mississippi Valley and adjacent
coast of the Gulf of Mexico. New York,
Johnson Reprint, 1970. 7, 387 p.
illus.

13-08   Cherokee

Hargrett, L. A bibliography of the
constitutions and laws of the American
Indians, 3-40. Cambridge, 1947.

Hoyt, Anne K. Bibliography of the
Cherokees. Tahlequah, Okla.,
Northeastern State College, Division of
Library Science, 1968. 4, 57 l. ERIC
ED023533.

Jones, William K. General guide to
documents on the Five Civilized Tribes
in the University of Oklahoma Library
Division of Manuscripts. Ethnohistory,
14 (1967): 47-76.

Pilling, J. C. Bibliography of the
Iroquoian languages. U.S. Bureau of
American Ethnology, Bulletin, 6 (1888):
1-208.

Tennessee, State Library and Archives,
Nashville, Manuscript Division.
Cherokee collection. Nashville, 1966.
(Tennessee, State Library and Archives,
Nashville, Manuscript Division,
Registers, 11)

Adair, J. The history of the American
Indians, 226-256. London, 1775.

Alexander, J. T. A dictionary of the
Cherokee Indian language. Sperry,
Okla., 1971. 359 p.

Allen, Ben. The Wataugans and the
"dangerous example". By Ben Allen and
Dennis T. Lawson. Tennessee Historical
Quarterly, 26 (1967): 137-147.

Allen, I. E. The Cherokee nation: Fort
Mountain, Vann House, Chester Inns, New
Echota. Atlanta [ca. 1958]. 59 p.

Allen, Terry, ed. The whispering wind;
poetry by young American Indians.
Garden City, Doubleday, 1972. 16,
128 p.

Altman, S. Morton. A service program for
teenagers. By S. Morton Altman and
Robert Salmon. Adolescence, 6 (1971):
495-508.

Anonymous. The Sam Houston shoulder
pouch. Tennessee Archaeologist, 11,
no. 2 (1955): 88-89.

Armbruster, Henry C. Torrey's trading
post. Texana, 2 (1964): 112-131.

Ashcraft, Allan C. Confederate Indian
Department conditions in August, 1864.
Chronicles of Oklahoma, 41 (1963): 270-
285.

Ashcraft, Allan C. Confederate Indian
Territory conditions in 1865. Chronicles
of Oklahoma, 42 (1964): 421-428.

Ashcraft, Allan C. Confederate Indian
troop conditions in 1864. Chronicles of
Oklahoma, 41 (1963): 442-449.

Asplin, Ray. A history of Council Grove
in Oklahoma. Chronicles of Oklahoma, 45
(1967): 433-450.

Bailey, C. S. Stories from an Indian
cave. Chicago, 1924. 217 p.

Bailey, Minnie Elizabeth Thomas.
Reconstruction in Indian Territory,
1865-1877. Dissertation Abstracts, 29
(1968/1969): 198A. UM 68-8362.

Baillou, C. D. The Chief Vann house at
Spring Place, Georgia. Early Georgia, 2,
no. 2 (1957): 3-11.

Baillou, C. D. The excavations at New
Echota in 1954. Early Georgia, 1, no. 4
(1955): 18-29.

Baillou, Clemens de. A contribution to
the mythology and conceptual world of
the Cherokee Indians. Ethnohistory, 8
(1961): 93-102.

Baily, Francis. Journal of a tour in
unsettled parts of North America in 1796
and 1797. Edited by Jack D. L. Holmes.
Carbondale, Southern Illinois University
Press, 1969. 26, 336 p. illus.

Baird, W. David. Fort Smith and the Red
Man. Arkansas Historical Quarterly, 30
(1971): 337-348.

Baker, Jack, comp. Cherokee cookbook.
Edited by Jack Gregory and Rennard
Strickland. Fayetteville, Indian
Heritage Association, 1968.

Ballas, Donald J.   Notes on the population, settlement, and ecology of the Eastern Cherokee Indians. Journal of Geography, 59 (1960): 258-267.

Ballas, Donald J.   The livelihood of the Eastern Cherokees. Journal of Geography, 61 (1962): 342-350.

Ballenger, T. L.   Joseph Franklin Johnson. Chronicles of Oklahoma, 30 (1952): 285-291.

Ballenger, T. L.   Spring Frog. Chronicles of Oklahoma, 44 (1966): 2-4.

Ballenger, T. L.   The Andrew Nave letters. Chronicles of Oklahoma, 30 (1952): 2-5.

Ballenger, T. L.   The Illinois River. Chronicles of Oklahoma, 46 (1968): 450-459.

Ballenger, Thomas Lee.   The cultural relations between two pioneer communities. Chronicles of Oklahoma, 34 (1956/1957): 286-295.

Banks, Dean.   Civil-War refugees from Indian Territory, in the North, 1861-1864. Chronicles of Oklahoma, 41 (1963): 286-298.

Barry, A. L.   Yunini's story of the trail of tears. London, 1932. 230 p.

Bartram, W.   Observations on the Creek and Cherokee Indians. American Ethnological Society, Transactions, 3 (1853): 1-81.

Bartram, W.   The travels of William Bartram, naturalist's edition. New Haven, 1958. 788 p.

Bartram, W.   Travels in Georgia and Florida, 1773-74. Ed. by F. Harper. American Philosophical Society, Transactions, n.s., 33 (1943): 126, 172-205, 225.

Bartram, W.   Travels through North and South Carolina. London, 1792.

Bass, A.   Cherokee messenger. Norman, 1936. 348 p.

Bass, Althea.   The real name of the noted Tsali who led the Eastern Cherokee band to hiding in the mountains during the removal in 1838. Chronicles of Oklahoma, 43 (1965): 90-93.

Battey, George M., Jr.   A history of Rome and Floyd County. Atlanta, Webb and Vary, 1922.

Bauer, Fred B.   Land of the North Carolina Cherokees. Brevard, N.C., G. E. Buchanan, 1970. 70 p. illus., map.

Bearss, Edwin C.   General Cooper's CSA Indians threaten Fort Smith. Arkansas Historical Quarterly, 26 (1967): 257-284.

Bearss, Edwin C.   In quest of peace on the Indian border: the establishment of Fort Smith. Arkansas Historical Quarterly, 23 (1964): 123-153.

Bearss, Edwin C.   The Arkansas whiskey war: a Fort Smith case study. Journal of the West, 7 (1968): 143-172.

Bedford, Denton R.   Tsali. San Francisco, Indian Historian Press, 1972. 290 p. illus.

Bell, C.   John Rattling-Gourd of Big Cove. New York, 1955. 103 p.

Bell, George M.   Genealogy of "Old and new Cherokee Indian families". Bartlesville, Okla., 1972. 567 p. illus.

Bell, M. W.   Chick-a-liel-lih. Southern Folklore Quarterly, 17 (1953): 255-258.

Bender, E.   Cherokee. International Journal of American Linguistics, 15 (1949): 223-238.

Bender, E. and Z. S. Harris.   The phonemes of North Carolina Cherokee. International Journal of American Linguistics, 12 (1946): 14-21.

Berkhofer, Robert F., Jr.   The political context of a new Indian history. Pacific Historical Review, 40 (1971): 357-382.

Bibaud, F. M.   Biographie des sagamos illustrés de l'Amérique Septentrionale, 199-205, 274-281. Montréal, 1848.

Bloom, L.   A measure of conservatism. American Anthropologist, n.s., 47 (1945): 630-635.

Bloom, L.   The acculturation of the Eastern Cherokee. North Carolina Historical Review, 19 (1942): 323-358.

Bloom, L.   The Cherokee clan. American Anthropologist, n.s., 41 (1939): 266-268.

Boas, F.   Zur Anthropologie der nordamerikanischen Indianer. Berliner Gesellschaft für Anthropologie, Ethnologie und Urgeschichte, Verhandlungen (1895): 367-411.

Boniol, John Dawson, Jr.   The Walton Road. Tennessee Historical Quarterly, 30 (1971): 402-412.

Boozer, J. D. The legend of Yalloo Falls. Tennessee Archaeologist, 11, no. 2 (1955): 66-67.

Boudinot, Elias. Documents in relation to the validity of the Cherokee Treaty of 1835. Washington, D.C., Blair and Rives, 1838.

Bowers, Lola Garrett. A. Florence Wilson, friend and teacher. By Lola Garrett Bowers and Kathleen Garrett. Tahlequah, Rockett's Printers and Publishers, 1951.

Boyd, G. A. Elias Boudinot. Princeton, 1952.

Broemeling, Carol B. Cherokee Indian agents, 1830-1874. Chronicles of Oklahoma, 50 (1972): 437-457.

Brown, J. P. Old frontiers. Kingsport, 1938. 570 p.

Brown, John P. Old frontiers. New York, Arno Press, 1971. 11, 570 p. illus.

Brown, Jon T. The second trail of tears. Historic Preservation, 24, no. 2 (1972): 40-41.

Brown, Lenard E. John Benjamin Townsend: the Arizona Cherokee. Arizoniana, 2, no. 3 (1961): 29-31.

Brown, T. S. By way of Cherokee. Atlanta, 1944. 127 p.

Buchanan, Robert Wayne. Patterns of organization and leadership among contemporary Oklahoma Cherokees. Dissertation Abstracts International, 33 (1972/1973): 2447B-2448B. UM 72-32,868.

Buice, Sammy David. The Civil War and the Five Civilized Tribes--a study in Federal-Indian relations. Dissertation Abstracts International, 31 (1970/1971): 2815A-2816A. UM 70-23,966.

Bushnell, D. I. Native cemeteries and forms of burial east of the Mississippi. U.S. Bureau of American Ethnology, Bulletin, 71 (1920): 90-93.

Bushnell, D. I. Virginia before Jamestown. Smithsonian Miscellaneous Collections, 100 (1940): 125-158.

Buttrick, D. S. Antiquities of the Cherokee Indians. Vinita, 1884. 20 p.

Caldwell, Joseph R. Cherokee pottery from northern Georgia. American Antiquity, 20 (1954/1955): 277-280.

Cameron, C. M. Cherokee Indian health survey. United States Public Health

Service, Public Health Reports, 71 (1956): 1086-1088.

Carselowey, James M. Cherokee notes. Fayetteville, Ark., Washington County Historical Society, 1960. 73 p. illus.

Carselowey, James M. Cherokee pioneers. Adair, Okla., James Manford Carselowey, 1961. 75 p. illus.

Carselowey, James M. My journal. Adair, Okla., 1962. 83 p. illus.

Cassel, J., J. Gulick, and H. L. Smith. The Cherokee project. Research Reviews, 4, no. 2 (1956): 10-18.

Caywood, E. R. The administration of William C. Rogers. Chronicles of Oklahoma, 30 (1952): 29-37.

Chafe, Wallace L. A challenge for linguistics today. In Jacob W. Gruber, ed. The Philadelphia Anthropological Society; Papers Presented on Its Golden Anniversary. New York, distributed by Columbia University Press for Temple University Publications, 1967: 125-131.

Chafe, Wallace L. Inconsistencies in Cherokee spelling. By Wallace L. Chafe and Jack Frederick Kilpatrick. In Viola E. Garfield and Wallace L. Chafe, eds. Symposium on Language and Culture. Seattle, American Ethnological Society, 1963: 60-63. (American Ethnological Society, Proceedings of the Annual Spring Meeting, 1962)

Chapman, Berlin B. Opening the Cherokee outlet: an archival study. Chronicles of Oklahoma, 40 (1962): 158-181, 253-285.

Chappell, Gordon T. John Coffee: surveyor and land agent. Alabama Review, 14 (1961): 180-195.

Chase, Charles Monroe. The letters of Charles Monroe Chase. Kansas Historical Quarterly, 26 (1960): 267-301.

Cherokee Historical Association. Unto these hills; a drama of the Cherokee Indians. Cherokee, N.C., 1969. 40 p. illus.

Clarke, Mary W. Chief Bowles and the Texas Cherokees. Norman, University of Oklahoma Press, 1971. 17, 154 p. illus., maps.

Cobb, Samuel S. A history of Wagoner, Oklahoma, from S. S. Cobb. By L. W. Wilson. Chronicles of Oklahoma, 50 (1972): 486-496.

Coleman, K. Federal Indian relations in the South, 1781-1789. Chronicles of Oklahoma, 25 (1947): 435-458.

Connelly, Thomas Lawrence. Indian warfare on the Tennessee frontier, 1776-1794: strategy and tactics. East Tennessee Historical Society's Publications, 36 (1964): 3-22.

Corbitt, D. C. Exploring the Southwest Territory in the Spanish Records. East Tennessee Historical Society's Publications, 38 (1966): 109-118.

Corbitt, D. C., tr. and ed. Papers from the Spanish archives relating to Tennessee and the Old Southwest. Translated and edited by D. C. Corbitt and Roberta Corbitt. East Tennessee Historical Society, Publications, 31 (1959): 63-82; 32 (1960): 72-93; 33 (1961): 61-78; 34 (1962): 86-105; 35 (1963): 85-95; 36 (1964): 70-80; 37 (1965): 89-105; 38 (1966): 70-82; 39 (1967): 87-102; 40 (1968): 101-118; 41 (1969): 100-116; 42 (1970): 96-107; 43 (1971): 94-111; 44 (1972): 104-113.

Corkran, D. H. A Cherokee migration fragment. Southern Indian Studies, 4 (1952): 27-28.

Corkran, D. H. Cherokee prehistory. North Carolina Historical Review, 34 (1957): 455-466.

Corkran, D. H. Cherokee sun and fire observances. Southern Indian Studies, 7 (1955): 33-38.

Corkran, D. H. The nature of the Cherokee supreme being. Southern Indian Studies, 8 (1956): 27-35.

Corkran, D. H. The sacred fire of the Cherokees. Southern Indian Studies, 5 (1953): 21-26.

Corkran, David H. The Cherokee frontier: conflict and survival, 1740-62. Norman, University of Oklahoma Press, 1962. 302 p. illus.

Corn, John Franklin. Red Clay and Rattlesnake Springs: a history of the Cherokee Indians of Bradley County, Tennessee. Cleveland, Tenn., the author, 1959.

Cotten, John. The Battle of the Bluffs; from the journal of John Cotten. Edited by J. W. L. Matlock. Tennessee Historical Quarterly, 18 (1959): 252-265.

Cotterill, R. S. The Southern Indians. Norman, 1954. 268 p.

Coulter, D. M. Cherokee weavers used looms over 200 years ago. Handweaver, 18, no. 3 (1967): 17-18.

Coulter, E. Merton. John Howard Payne's visit to Georgia. Georgia Historical Quarterly, 46 (1962): 333-376.

Coulter, E. Merton. Tallulah Falls, Georgia's natural wonder from creation to destruction. Georgia Historical Quarterly, 47 (1963): 121-157.

Crouch, Stella E. C. Story of the Cherokee Indians. Vinita, Okla. [1967?]. 65 p.

Culton, Don Henry. The early Panhandle surveys. Panhandle-Plains Historical Review, 46 (1973): 1-16.

Dale, E. E. and G. Litton. Cherokee cavaliers. Norman, 1940. 308 p.

Davis, J. B. Some Cherokee stories. Annals of Archaeology and Anthropology, 3 (1910): 26-49.

Davis, J. B. The liver-eater: a Cherokee story. Annals of Archaeology and Anthropology, 2 (1909): 134-138.

Davis, J. B. Two Cherokee charms. Annals of Archaeology and Anthropology, 2 (1909): 131-133.

Day, James M. James Kerr: frontier Texian. Texana, 2 (1964): 24-43.

De Brahm, William Gerard. De Brahm's report of the general survey in the southern district of North America. Edited and with an introduction by Louis De Vorsey, Jr. Columbia, University of South Carolina Press, 1971. 16, 325 p.

De Vorsey, Louis, Jr. Indian boundaries in Colonial Georgia. Georgia Historical Quarterly, 54 (1970): 63-78.

De Vorsey, Louis, Jr. The Virginia-Cherokee boundary of 1771. East Tennessee Historical Society's Publications, 33 (1961): 17-31.

Debo, A. And still the waters run. Princeton, 1940. 417 p.

Debo, A. Southern refugees of the Cherokee nation. Southwestern Historical Quarterly, 35 (1932): 255-266.

Debo, Angie. The location of the Battle of Round Mountain. Chronicles of Oklahoma, 41 (1963): 70-104.

Dickeman, Mildred. The integrity of the Cherokee student. In Eleanor B. Leacock, ed. The Culture of Poverty: a Critique.

New York, Simon and Schuster, 1971: 140-179.

Dickens, Roy Selman, Jr. The Pisgah Culture and its place in the prehistory of the Southern Appalachians. Dissertation Abstracts International, 31 (1970/1971): 2430B-2431B. UM 70-21,188.

Dickson, John Lois. The judicial history of the Cherokee nation from 1721 to 1835. Dissertation Abstracts, 25 (1964/1965): 3523. UM 64-13,325.

Dodge, Henry. Journal of Colonel Dodge's expedition from Fort Gibson to the Pawnee Pict village. American State Papers, Military Affairs, 5 (1860): 373-382.

Donaldson, T. Eastern Band of Cherokees of North Carolina. U.S., Census Office, Eleventh Census, Extra Census Bulletin (1892): 7-21.

Doss, Chriss H. Early settlements of Bearmeat Cabin frontier. Alabama Review, 22 (1969): 270-283.

Doster, James F. Land titles and public land sales in early Alabama. Alabama Review, 16 (1963): 108-124.

Downing, A. The Cherokee Indians and their neighbors. American Antiquarian and Oriental Journal, 17 (1895): 307-316.

Dumont, Robert V., Jr. Cherokee children and the teacher. Social Education, 33 (1969): 70-72.

Dumont, Robert V., Jr. Cherokee school society and the intercultural classroom. By Robert V. Dumont, Jr. and Murray L. Wax. Human Organization, 28 (1969): 217-226.

Duncan, DeWitt Clinton. An open letter from Too-Qua-Stee to Congressman Charles Curtis, 1898. Chronicles of Oklahoma, 47 (1969): 298-304.

Durham, Walter T. Kasper Mansker: Cumberland frontiersman. Tennessee Historical Quarterly, 30 (1971): 154-177.

Eaton, R. C. John Ross and the Cherokee Indians. Muskogee, 1921. 153 p.

Eaton, R. C. John Ross and the Cherokee Indians. Menasha, 1914. 212 p.

Edwards, Newton. Economic development of Indian reserves. Human Organization, 20 (1961/1962): 197-202.

Farrar, William G. Historic profiles of Fort Massac. By William G. and JoAnn S. Farrar. Carbondale, Southern Illinois University, University Museum, 1970. 3, 59 p. (Southern Illinois Studies, 5)

Fay, George E., ed. Charters, constitutions and by-laws of the Indian tribes of North America. Part V: The Indian tribes of Oklahoma. Greeley, 1968. 14, 104 l. map. (University of Northern Colorado, Museum of Anthropology, Occasional Publications in Anthropology, Ethnology Series, 6) ERIC ED046555.

Featherstonhaugh, George W. A canoe voyage up the Minnay Sotor. St. Paul, Minnesota Historical Society, 1970. 2 v. maps.

Featherstonhaugh, George W. A canoe voyage up the Minnay Sotor. Vol. 2. London, R. Bentley, 1847.

Fewkes, V. J. Catawba pottery-making. American Philosophical Society, Proceedings, 88 (1944): 69-124.

Field, C. Fine root runner basketry among the Oklahoma Cherokee Indians. Philbrook Art Center, 1 (1943): 1-10.

Filler, Louis, ed. The removal of the Cherokee Nation: manifest destiny or national dishonor? Edited by Louis Filler and Allen Guttmann. Boston, Heath, 1962. 113 p.

Fink, Paul M. Jacob Brown of Nolichucky. Tennessee Historical Quarterly, 21 (1962): 235-250.

Fischer, LeRoy H. Confederate Indian forces outside of Indian Territory. By LeRoy H. Fischer and Jerry Gill. Chronicles of Oklahoma, 46 (1968): 249-284.

Fleischmann, Glen. The Cherokee Removal, 1838. New York, Watts, 1971. 88 p. illus., maps.

Fogelson, Raymond. The Cherokee ballgame cycle. Ethnomusicology, 15 (1971): 327-338.

Fogelson, Raymond David. The Cherokee ball game: a study in Southeastern ethnology. Dissertation Abstracts, 23 (1962/1963): 1488. UM 62-4288.

Foreman, C. T. An early account of the Cherokees. Chronicles of Oklahoma, 34 (1956): 141-158.

Foreman, C. T. Park Hill. Muskogee, Oklahoma, 1948. 186 p.

Foreman, Carolyn Thomas. Cherokee weaving and basketry. Muskogee, Star Printery, 1948.

Foreman, Carolyn Thomas. Indian women chiefs. Muskogee, Okla., Star Printery, 1954. 86 p. illus.

Foreman, Carolyn Thomas. Indians abroad, 1493-1938. Norman, University of Oklahoma Press, 1943. 23, 247 p. illus.

Foreman, Carolyn Thomas. Notes on DeWitt Clinton Duncan and a recently discovered history of the Cherokees. Chronicles of Oklahoma, 47 (1969): 305-311.

Foreman, G. Indians and pioneers. Rev. ed. Norman, 1936. 285 p.

Foreman, G. Sequoyah. Norman, 1938. 90 p.

Foreman, G. The five civilized tribes: 281-426. Norman, 1934.

Foreman, G., ed. A traveler in Indian Territory. Cedar Rapids, 1930. 270 p.

Foreman, Grant. The Five Civilized Tribes; a brief history and a century of progress. Muskogee, Okla., C. T. Foreman, 1966. 58 p. illus.

Foreman, Grant, ed. Indian justice: a Cherokee murder trial at Tahlequah in 1840. Oklahoma City, Harlow, 1934.

Foster, G. E. Literature of the Cherokees. Ithaca, 1889. 138 p.

Foster, G. E. Se-quo-yah. Philadelphia, 1885. 244 p.

Foster, G. E. Story of the Cherokee Bible. Ithaca, 1899. 89 p.

Franklin, W. Neil. Act for the better regulation of the Indian trade; Virginia, 1714. Virginia Magazine of History and Biography, 72 (1964): 141-151.

Fry, Maggie Culver. Kee-too-wah the eternal fire. Oklahoma Today, 19, no. 1 (1963/1964): 34-36.

Gabelentz, H. G. C. von der. Kurze Grammatik der tscherokesischen Sprache. Zeitschrift für die Wissenschaft der Sprache, 3 (1852): 257-300.

Gabler, Mrs. Ina. Lovely's purchase and Lovely County. Arkansas Historical Quarterly, 19 (1960): 31-39.

Gabriel, R. H. Elias Boudinot, Cherokee, and his America. Norman, 1941.

Ganyard, Robert L. Threat from the West: North Carolina and the Cherokee, 1776-1778. North Carolina Historical Review, 45 (1968): 47-66.

Gatschet, A. S. On the affinity of the Cheroki to the Iroquois dialects. American Philological Association, Transactions, 16 (1886): xl-xlv.

Gearing, F. The structural poses of 18th century Cherokee villages. American Anthropologist, 60 (1958): 1148-1157.

Gearing, Fred. On 'uncentralized' political systems. In International Congress of Anthropological and Ethnological Sciences, 6th. 1960, Paris. Tome II, v. 2. Paris, Musée de l'Homme, 1964: 321-327.

Gearing, Frederick O. Priests and warriors; social structures for Cherokee politics in the 18th century. Menasha, 1962. 7, 124 p. illus., map. (American Anthropological Association, Memoir, 93)

Gibbons, Lulu. Indian recipes from Cherokee Indians of eastern Oklahoma. Muskogee, Creek-Seminole Tribes, 1966. 19 p.

Gibson, A. M. An Indian Territory United Nations: the Creek Council of 1845. Chronicles of Oklahoma, 39 (1961): 398-413.

Gilbert, W. H. Eastern Cherokee social organization. In F. Eggan, ed. Social Anthropology of North American Tribes. 2d ed. Chicago, 1955: 285-340.

Gilbert, W. H. The Cherokees of North Carolina. Smithsonian Institution, Annual Report of the Board of Regents, 112 (1957): 529-556.

*Gilbert, W. H. The Eastern Cherokees. U.S. Bureau of American Ethnology, Bulletin, 133 (1943): 169-414.

Gilmer, George R. Sketches of some of the first settlers of Upper Georgia, of the Cherokees, and the author. Indexed ed. Baltimore, Genealogical Publishing, 1965. 463 p. map.

Goode, William H. Outposts of Zion, with limnings of mission life. Cincinnati, Poe and Hitchcock, 1863. 464 p.

Graebner, N. A. Pioneer Indian agriculture in Oklahoma. Chronicles of Oklahoma, 23 (1945/1946): 232-248.

Graebner, N. A. Provincial Indian society in eastern Oklahoma. Chronicles of Oklahoma, 23 (1945/1946): 323-337.

172   13 SOUTHEAST

Graebner, N. A. The public land policy of the five civilized tribes. Chronicles of Oklahoma, 23 (1945/1946): 107-118.

Gregory, Jack. "You didn't have to know English to understand Funny books". By Jack Gregory and Rennard Strickland. Journal of American Indian Education, 11, no. 2 (1971/1972): 1-4.

Gulick, J. Language and passive resistance among the Eastern Cherokees. Ethnohistory, 5 (1958): 60-81.

Gulick, J. Problems of cultural communication--the Eastern Cherokees. American Indian, 8, no. 1 (1958): 20-31.

Gulick, J. The acculturation of Eastern Cherokee community organization. Social Forces, 36 (1958): 246-250.

Gulick, J. The self-corrective circuit and trait-persistence in conservative Eastern Cherokee culture. Research Reviews, 6, no. 3 (1959): 1-10.

*Gulick, John. Cherokees at the crossroads. Chapel Hill, University of North Carolina, Institute for Research in Social Sciences, 1960. 15, 202 p. maps.

Guttmann, Allen. States' rights and Indian removal: the Cherokee Nation v. the State of Georgia. Boston, D. C. Heath, 1965. 11, 94, 14 p. map.

Hagar, S. Cherokee star-lore. In Boas Anniversary Volume. New York, 1906: 354-366.

Hagy, James W. The frontier at Castle's Woods, 1769-1786. Virginia Magazine of History and Biography, 75 (1967): 410-428.

Hagy, James William, ed. The lost archives of the Cherokee Nation. Edited by James William Hagy and Stanley J. Folmsbee. East Tennessee Historical Society, Publications, 43 (1971): 112-122; 44 (1972): 114-125.

Hale, H. Indian migrations as evidenced by language. American Antiquarian and Oriental Journal, 5 (1883): 18-28.

Hampton, James E. Pernicious anemia in American Indians. Oklahoma State Medical Association, Journal, 53 (1960): 503-509.

Hancock, Marvin J. The second battle of Cabin Creek, 1864. Chronicles of Oklahoma, 39 (1961): 414-426.

Harmon, George Dewey. Sixty years of Indian affairs, political, economic, and diplomatic, 1789-1850. Chapel Hill, University of North Carolina Press, 1941. 8, 428 p.

Harrell, D. T. Indian lore. Hobbies, 57 (Nov. 1953): 134-135.

Harrington, M. R. Cherokee and earlier remains on Upper Tennessee River. Indian Notes and Monographs, n.s., 24 (1922): 5-321.

Harrington, M. R. The last of the Iroquois potters. University of the State of New York, Annual Report of the Regents, 62, vol. 1 (1909): 222-227.

Hatfield, Joseph T. Governor William Charles Cole Claiborne, Indians, and outlaws in frontier Mississippi, 1801-1803. Journal of Mississippi History, 27 (1965): 323-350.

Hatton, William. Some short remarks on the Indian trade in the Charikees and in managment thereof since the year 1717. Edited by Rena Vassar. Ethnohistory, 8 (1961): 401-423.

Hawes, Lilla Mills, ed. The frontiers of Georgia in the late eighteenth century: Jonas Fauche to Joseph Vallance Bevan. Georgia Historical Quarterly, 47 (1963): 84-95.

Hawkins, B. Letters, 1796-1806. Georgia Historical Society, Collections, 9 (1916): 1-500.

Haywood, J. The natural and aboriginal history of Tennessee. Nashville, 1823. 390 p.

Heath, Gary N. The first federal invasion of Indian Territory. Chronicles of Oklahoma, 44 (1966/1967): 409-419.

Heimann, Robert K. The Cherokee tobacco case. Chronicles of Oklahoma, 41 (1963): 299-322.

Hemperley, Marion R., ed. Benjamin Hawkins' trip across Georgia in 1796. Georgia Historical Quarterly, 55 (1971): 114-137.

Hemperley, Marion R., ed. Benjamin Hawkins' trip across western and northern Georgia, 1798. Georgia Historical Quarterly, 56 (1972): 415-431.

Hensley, J. C. My father is rich. Nashville, 1956. 214 p.

Herndon, Marcia. The Cherokee ballgame cycle: an ethnomusicologist's view. Ethnomusicology, 15 (1971): 339-352.

Hewes, L. The Oklahoma Ozarks as the land of the Cherokees. Geographical Review, 32 (1942): 269-281.

Hill, W. C. Osman. The soft anatomy of a North American Indian. American Journal of Physical Anthropology, n.s., 21 (1963): 245-269.

Hinkle, L. E. The Cherokee language. Archaeological Society of North Carolina, Bulletin, 2, no. 1 (1935): 1-9.

Holland, James W. Andrew Jackson and the Creek War: victory at the Horseshoe. Alabama Review, 21 (1968): 243-275.

Holland, R. Fount. School in Cherokee and English. Elementary School Journal, 72 (1972): 412-418.

Holland, R. Fount. School in Cherokee and English. Elementary School Journal, 72 (1971/1972): 412-418.

Holland, Reid A. Life in the Cherokee Nation, 1855-1860. Chronicles of Oklahoma, 49 (1971/1972): 284-301.

Holmes, Jack D. L. Spanish treaties with West Florida Indians, 1784-1802. Florida Historical Quarterly, 48 (1969/1970): 140-154.

Holmes, Jack D. L. Spanish-American rivalry over the Chickasaw Bluffs, 1780-1795. East Tennessee Historical Society's Publications, 34 (1962): 26-57.

Holsoe, Svend E. A case of stimulus diffusion? Indian Historian, 4, no. 3 (1971): 56-57.

Holt, E. O. Life with the Cherokee. Cranfills Gap, Texas, 1950. 30 p.

Holway, Hope. Union Mission, 1826-1837. Chronicles of Oklahoma, 40 (1962): 355-378.

Hood, Fred. Twilight of the Confederacy in Indian Territory. Chronicles of Oklahoma, 41 (1963): 425-441.

Hooper, Joseph G., Jr. History is the tribunal; a case in court. Indian Historian, 1, no. 5 (1967/1968): 33-35.

Howard, James H. Bringing back the fire: the revival of a Natchez-Cherokee ceremonial ground. Oklahoma Anthropological Society, Newsletter, 18, no. 4 (1970): 11-17.

Howard, James H. Bringing back the fire: the revival of a Natchez-Cherokee ceremonial ground. American Indian Crafts and Culture, 4, no. 1 (1970): 9-12.

Howard, James H. The Southeastern ceremonial complex and its interpretation. Columbia, 1968. 8, 169 p. illus. (Missouri Archaeological Society, Memoir, 6)

Howard, James H. The Yamasee: a supposedly extinct Southeastern tribe rediscovered. American Anthropologist, 62 (1960): 681-683.

Howard, R. Palmer. A historiography of the Five Civilized Tribes: a chronological approach. Chronicles of Oklahoma, 47 (1969): 312-331.

Howard, R. Palmer. A historiography of the Five Civilized Tribes; a chronological approach. Oklahoma City, Oklahoma Historical Society, 1969. 20 p.

Hudson, Charles. Cherokee concept of natural balance. Indian Historian, 3, no. 4 (1970): 51-54.

Hunter, Kermit. Unto these hills; a drama of the Cherokee. Chapel Hill, University of North Carolina Press, 1951. 4, 100 p. illus.

Hymes, Dell H. Value of the Radin papers for linguistics. In The American Indian. Philadelphia, American Philosophical Society, 1968: 35-45. (American Philosophical Society, Library Publication, 2)

Irvine, A. How the turkey got his beard. Southwestern Lore, 16, no. 2 (1950): 35-36.

Jackson, Joe C. Summer normals in Indian territory after 1898. Chronicles of Oklahoma, 37 (1959): 307-329.

Jacobs, W. R. Indians of the southern colonial frontier. Columbia, South Carolina, 1954.

Jarrett, R. F. Occoneechee. New York, 1916. 284 p.

Jenkins, William H. Alabama forts, 1700-1838. Alabama Review, 12 (1959): 163-180.

Johnson, N. B. A historical relic at Tahlequah. Chronicles of Oklahoma, 44 (1966): 225-227.

Johnson, N. B. The Cherokee orphan asylum. Chronicles of Oklahoma, 44 (1966): 275-280.

Johnson, N. B. The old National Hotel at Tahlequah. Chronicles of Oklahoma, 44 (1966): 227-229.

Jones, Robert L. Houston's politics and the Cherokees, 1829-1833. By Robert L. and Pauline H. Jones. Chronicles of Oklahoma, 46 (1968): 418-432.

Kansas City Star. Report on the Five Civilized Tribes 1897. Chronicles of Oklahoma, 48 (1970): 416-430.

Kate, H. F. C. ten. Legends of the Cherokee. Journal of American Folklore, 2 (1889): 53-55.

Kelley, Paul. Fort Loudoun: the after years, 1760-1960. Tennessee Historical Quarterly, 20 (1961): 303-322.

Kephart, H. The Cherokees of the Smoky Mountains. Ithaca, 1938. 36 p.

Kilpatrick, Anna Gritts. Cherokee bilingual education program: primer for Cherokee (NE 103) elementary. Tahlequah, Okla., Northeastern State College, 1972. 67 p. illus.

Kilpatrick, Anna Gritts. Cherokee conjuration to cure a horse. Southern Folklore Quarterly, 28 (1964): 216-218.

Kilpatrick, Anna Gritts. Chronicles of Wolftown: social documents of the North Carolina Cherokees, 1850-1862. By Anna Gritts Kilpatrick and Jack Frederick Kilpatrick. Washington, D.C., Government Printing Office, 1966. 1-111 p. (U.S., Bureau of American Ethnology, Anthropological Papers, 75. U.S., Bureau of American Ethnology, Bulletin, 196)

Kilpatrick, Anna Gritts. Note on Cherokee wind-controlling magic. Southern Folklore Quarterly, 29 (1965): 204-206.

Kilpatrick, Jack Frederick. An adventure story of the Arkansas Cherokees, 1829. Arkansas Historical Quarterly, 26 (1967): 40-47.

Kilpatrick, Jack Frederick. An etymological note on the tribal name of the Cherokees and certain place and proper names derived from Cherokee. Southern Methodist University, Graduate Research Center, Journal, 30 (1962): 37-41.

Kilpatrick, Jack Frederick. Cherokee burn configurations. By Jack Frederick Kilpatrick and Anna Gritts Kilpatrick. Southern Methodist University, Graduate Research Center, Journal, 33 (1964): 17-21.

Kilpatrick, Jack Frederick. Concerning Kutsche's review of "The shadow of Sequoyah". By Jack Frederick Kilpatrick and Anna Gritts Kilpatrick. American Anthropologist, 69 (1967): 515-516.

Kilpatrick, Jack Frederick. Eastern Cherokee folktales. Reconstructed from the field notes of Frans M. Olbrechts. By Jack Frederick Kilpatrick and Anna Gritts Kilpatrick. Washington, D.C., Government Printing Office, 1966. 379-447 p. illus. (U.S., Bureau of American Ethnology, Anthropological Papers, 80. U.S., Bureau of American Ethnology, Bulletin, 196)

Kilpatrick, Jack Frederick. Echota funeral notices. Southern Methodist University, Graduate Research Center, Journal, 35 (1966): 14-37.

Kilpatrick, Jack Frederick. Friends of Thunder, folktales of the Oklahoma Cherokees. By Jack F. Kilpatrick and Anna G. Kilpatrick. Dallas, Southern Methodist University Press, 1964. 18, 197 p.

Kilpatrick, Jack Frederick. Letters from an Arkansas Cherokee chief (1828-29). By Jack Frederick Kilpatrick and Anna Gritts Kilpatrick. Great Plains Journal, 5 (1965/1966): 26-34.

Kilpatrick, Jack Frederick. Muskhogean charm songs among the Oklahoma Cherokees. By Jack Frederick Kilpatrick and Anna Gritts Kilpatrick. Washington, D.C., Smithsonian Press, 1967. 4, 29-40 p. (Smithsonian Contributions to Anthropology, 2, no. 3)

Kilpatrick, Jack Frederick. Notebook of a Cherokee shaman. By Jack Frederick Kilpatrick and Anna Gritts Kilpatrick. Washington, D.C., Smithsonian Institution Press, 1970. 5, 83-125 p. (Smithsonian Contributions to Anthropology, 2, no. 6)

Kilpatrick, Jack Frederick. Plains Indian motifs in contemporary Cherokee culture. By Jack Frederick Kilpatrick and Anna Gritts Kilpatrick. Plains Anthropologist, 7 (1962): 96.

Kilpatrick, Jack Frederick. Plains Indian motifs in contemporary Cherokee culture. By Jack Frederick Kilpatrick and Anna Gritts Kilpatrick. Plains Anthropologist, 7 (1962): 136-137.

Kilpatrick, Jack Frederick. Run toward the nightland; magic of the Oklahoma Cherokees. By Jack Frederick Kilpatrick and Anna Gritts Kilpatrick. Dallas, Southern Methodist University Press, 1967. 14, 197 p.

Kilpatrick, Jack Frederick. Sequoyah of earth and intellect. Austin, Encino Press, 1965. 7, 25 p.

Kilpatrick, Jack Frederick. "The Foundation of Life": the Cherokee national ritual. By Jack Frederick Kilpatrick and Anna Gritts Kilpatrick. American Anthropologist, 66 (1964): 1386-1391.

Kilpatrick, Jack Frederick. Walk in your soul; love incantations of the Oklahoma Cherokees. By Jack Frederick Kilpatrick and Anna Gritts Kilpatrick. Dallas, Southern Methodist University Press, 1965. 10, 164 p.

Kilpatrick, Jack Frederick, ed. New Echota letters: contributions of Samuel A. Worcester to the Cherokee Phoenix. Edited by Jack Frederick Kilpatrick and Anna Gritts Kilpatrick. Dallas, Southern Methodist University Press, 1968. 130 p.

King, Duane H. Oconastota. By Duane H. King and Danny E. Clinger. American Antiquity, 37 (1972): 222-228.

King, V. O. The Cherokee nation of Indians. Texas State Historical Association Quarterly (1898): 58-72.

Klingberg, F. J., ed. The Carolina chronicle of Dr. Francis Le Jau, 1706-1717. California, University, Publications in History, 53 (1956): 1-228.

Knapp, David, Jr. The Chickamaugas. Georgia Historical Quarterly, 51 (1967): 194-196.

Knepler, A. E. Education in the Cherokee nation. Chronicles of Oklahoma, 21 (1943): 378-401.

Knepler, A. E. Eighteenth century Cherokee educational efforts. Chronicles of Oklahoma, 20 (1942): 55-61.

Knight, O. Cherokee society under the stress of removal. Chronicles of Oklahoma, 32 (1954): 414-428.

Knight, O. History of the Cherokees. Chronicles of Oklahoma, 34 (1956): 159-182.

Krueger, John R. Two early grammars of Cherokee. Anthropological Linguistics, 5, no. 3 (1963): 1-57.

Kupferer, Harriet J. Cherokee change: a departure from lineal models of acculturation. Anthropologica, n.s., 5 (1963): 187-198.

Kupferer, Harriet J. Health practices and educational aspirations as indicators of acculturation and social class among the Eastern Cherokee. Social Forces, 41 (1962/1963): 154-163.

Kupferer, Harriet J. The isolated Eastern Cherokee. Midcontinent American Studies Journal, 6 (1965): 124-134.

Kupferer, Harriet Jane. The "principal people," 1960: a study of cultural and social groups of the Eastern Cherokee. Washington, D.C., Government Printing Office, 1966. 215-325 p. illus., map. (U.S., Bureau of American Ethnology, Anthropological Papers, 78. U.S., Bureau of American Ethnology, Bulletin, 196)

Kupferer, Harriet Jane. The "principal people," 1960: a study of cultural and social groups of the Eastern Cherokee. Dissertation Abstracts, 23 (1962/1963): 394. UM 62-3137.

Kutsche, P. Report on a summer field project in Cherokee, North Carolina. Philadelphia Anthropological Society, Bulletin, 10, no. 1 (1956): 8-11.

Kutsche, Paul. A modified use of the Rorschach Test. In Congreso Internacional de Americanistas, 35th. 1962, Mexico. Actas y Memorias. Tomo 2. Mexico, 1964: 101.

Kutsche, Paul. Cherokee high school dropouts. Journal of American Indian Education, 3, no. 2 (1963/1964): 22-30.

Kutsche, Paul. Southern Appalachian personality. In Congreso Internacional de Americanistas, 35th. 1962, Mexico. Actas y Memorias. Tomo 2. Mexico, 1964: 103-109.

Kutsche, Paul. The Tsali legend: culture heroes and historiography. Ethnohistory, 10 (1963): 329-357.

Lamplugh, George R. Farewell to the Revolution: Georgia in 1785. Georgia Historical Quarterly, 56 (1972): 387-403.

Lane, William Carr. William Carr Lane, diary. Edited by Wm. G. B. Carson. New Mexico Historical Review, 39 (1964): 181-234, 274-332.

Lanman, C. Adventures in the wilds of the United States and British American provinces, Vol. 1: 407-430. Philadelphia, 1856.

Lanman, C. Letters from the Alleghany Mountains, 84-114. New York, 1849.

Lawson, Charles T. Musical life in the Unitas Fratrum Mission at Springplace, Georgia, 1800-1836. [n.p.] 1969. 172 l. illus., map.

Leach, Douglas Edward. John Gordon of Gordon's Ferry. Tennessee Historical Quarterly, 18 (1959): 322-344.

Leftwich, Rodney L. Arts and crafts of the Cherokee. Cullowhee, N.C., Land-of-the-Sky Press, 1970. 13, 160 p. illus.

Leftwich, Rodney L. Cane basketry of the Cherokees. School Arts, 56 (Feb. 1957): 27-30.

Leftwich, Rodney L. Cherokee white oak basketry. School Arts, 54 (Sept. 1954): 23-26.

Leftwich, Rodney L. Did the seventh heaven originate in Indian lore? Hobbies, 63 (June 1958): 113.

Lewis, T. M. N. Early historic Cherokee data. Southeastern Archaeological Conference, News Letter, 3, no. 3 (1953): 28-30.

Lewis, T. M. N. and M. Kneberg. The Cherokee "hothouse". Tennessee Archaeologist, 9, no. 1 (1953): 2-5.

Lewis, Thomas M. N. Oconaluftee Indian village; an interpretation of a Cherokee community of 1750. By T. M. N. Lewis and Madeline Kneberg. Cherokee, N.C., Cherokee Historical Association, 1954. 103 l.

Lewis, Thomas M. N. Tribes that slumber; Indian tribes in the Tennessee region. By T. M. N. Lewis and Madeline Kneberg. Knoxville, University of Tennessee Press, 1958. 11, 196 p. illus., maps.

Lewit, Robert T. Indian missions and antislavery sentiment: a conflict of evangelical and humanitarian ideals. Mississippi Valley Historical Review, 50 (1963/1964): 39-55.

Librik, Leon, et al. Thyrotoxicosis and collagen-like disease in three sisters of American Indian extraction. Journal of Pediatrics, 76 (1970): 64-68.

Lightfoot, B. B. The Cherokee emigrants in Missouri, 1837-1839. Missouri Historical Review, 56 (1961/1962): 156-167.

Littlefield, Daniel F., Jr. The Cherokee Agency Reserve, 1828-1886. By Daniel F. Littlefield, Jr. and Lonnie E. Underhill. Arkansas Historical Review, 31 (1972): 166-180.

Littlefield, Daniel F., Jr. Utopian dreams of the Cherokee fullbloods: 1890-1934. Journal of the West, 10 (1971): 404-427.

Logan, J. H. A history of the upper country of South Carolina. Charleston, 1859. 521 p.

Logan, John Henry. A history of the upper country of South Carolina. Vol. 1. Spartanburg, S.C., Reprint Co., 1960. 521 p.

Loomis, Augustus W. Scenes in the Indian country. Philadelphia, Presbyterian Board of Publication, 1859. 283 p. illus.

Lounsbury, F. G. Stray number systems among certain Indian tribes. American Anthropologist, n.s., 48 (1946): 672-675.

Lumpkin, Wilson. The removal of the Cherokee Indians from Georgia, 1827-1841. New York, A. M. Kelley, 1971.

Lumpkin, Wilson. The removal of the Cherokee Indians from Georgia. New York, Arno Press, 1969.

Mahon, John K. Two Seminole treaties: Payne's Landing, 1832, and Ft. Gibson, 1833. Florida Historical Quarterly, 41 (1962/1963): 1-21.

Mahoney, J. W. and R. Foreman. The Cherokee physician or complete guide to health. Asheville, North Carolina, 1842.

Malone, H. T. Cherokees of the Old South. Athens, 1956. 251 p.

Malone, H. T. Cherokee-White relations on the southern frontier in the early nineteenth century. North Carolina Historical Review, 34 (1957): 1-14.

Malone, H. T. New Echota--capital of the Cherokee nation, 1525-1830. Early Georgia, 1, no. 4 (1955): 6-13.

Malone, H. T. The Cherokee Phoenix. Georgia Historical Quarterly, 34 (1950): 163-188.

Malone, H. T. The Cherokees become a civilized tribe. Early Georgia, 2, no. 2 (1957): 12-15.

Malone, Henry Thompson. A social history of the Eastern Cherokee Indians from the Revolution to removal. Dissertation Abstracts, 19 (1958/1959): 2930-2931. UM 58-5164.

Markman, Robert Paul. The Arkansas Cherokees: 1817-1828. Dissertation Abstracts International, 33 (1972/1973): 1095A. UM 72-23,102.

Marriott, A. Greener fields. New York, 1953. 274 p.

Martin, R. G. The Cherokee Phoenix. Chronicles of Oklahoma, 25 (1947): 102-118.

Mason, R. L. Tree myths of the Cherokees. American Forests and Forest Life, 35 (1929): 259-262, 300.

McAlister, Lyle N. William Augustus Bowles and the State of Muskogee. Florida Historical Quarterly, 40 (1961/1962): 317-328.

McClary, Ben Harris. Nancy Ward: the last beloved woman of the Cherokees. Tennessee Historical Quarterly, 21 (1962): 352-364.

McCoy, Isaac. History of Baptist Indian missions. Washington, D.C., W. M. Morrison; New York, H. and S. Raynor, 1840. 5, 611 p.

McDowell, William L., Jr., ed. Documents relating to Indian affairs, May 21, 1750-August 7, 1754. Columbia, South Carolina Archives Department, 1958. 22, 592 p. (Colonial Records of South Carolina, Series 2)

McDowell, William L., Jr., ed. Documents relating to Indian affairs: 1754-1765. Columbia, Published for the South Carolina Department of Archives and History by the University of South Carolina Press, 1970. 55, 657 p. illus. (Colonial Records of South Carolina, Series 2, 3)

McFadden, Marguerite. Intruders or injustice? Chronicles of Oklahoma, 48 (1970/1971): 431-439.

McGimsey, Charles R., III. Indians of Arkansas. Fayetteville, Arkansas Archeological Survey, 1969. 7, 1-47 p. illus., maps. (Arkansas Archeological Survey, Publications on Archeology, Popular Series, 1)

McGinty, J. R. Symbols of a civilization that perished in its infancy. Early Georgia, 1, no. 4 (1955): 14-17.

McGowan, D. J. Indian secret societies. Historical Magazine, ser. 1, 10 (1866): 139-141.

McLane, William. William McLane's narrative of the Magee-Gutierrez expedition, 1812-1813. Edited by Henry

P. Walker. Southwestern Historical Quarterly, 66 (1962/1963): 457-479, 569-588.

McNeil, Kinneth. Confederate treaties with the tribes of Indian Territory. Chronicles of Oklahoma, 42 (1964): 408-420.

Mellon, Knox, Jr. Christian Priber and the Jesuit myth. South Carolina Historical Magazine, 61 (1960): 75-81.

Middlebrooks, Audy J. Holland Coffee of Red River. By Audy J. and Glenna Middlebrooks. Southwestern Historical Quarterly, 69 (1965/1966): 145-162.

Milam, J. B. The great seal of the Cherokee nation. Chronicles of Oklahoma, 21 (1943): 8-9.

Miles, William. "Enamoured with colonization": Isaac McCoy's plan of Indian reform. Kansas Historical Quarterly, 38 (1972): 268-286.

Milling, C. J. Red Carolinians. Chapel Hill, 1940. 438 p.

Miner, Craig. The struggle for an East-West railway into the Indian Territory, 1870-1882. Chronicles of Oklahoma, 47 (1969): 560-581.

Miner, H. Craig. The Cherokee Oil and Gas Co., 1889-1902: Indian sovereignty and economic change. Business History Review, 46 (1972): 45-66.

Mooney, J. Among the East Cherokee Indians. Smithsonian Miscellaneous Collections, 63, no. 8 (1913): 61-64.

Mooney, J. Cherokee and Iroquois parallels. Journal of American Folklore, 2 (1889): 67.

Mooney, J. Cherokee ball play. American Anthropologist, 3 (1890): 105-132.

Mooney, J. Cherokee mound-building. American Anthropologist, 2 (1889): 167-171.

Mooney, J. Cherokee plant lore. American Anthropologist, 2 (1889): 223-224.

Mooney, J. Cherokee theory and practice of medicine. Journal of American Folklore, 3 (1890): 44-50.

Mooney, J. Cherokee. U.S. Bureau of American Ethnology, Bulletin, 30, vol. 1 (1907): 245-249.

Mooney, J. Evolution in Cherokee personal names. American Anthropologist, 2 (1889): 61-62.

Mooney, J. Improved Cherokee alphabets. American Anthropologist, 5 (1892): 63-64.

Mooney, J. Myths of the Cherokee. U.S. Bureau of American Ethnology, Annual Reports, 19, vol. 1 (1898): 3-548.

Mooney, J. Myths of the Cherokees. Journal of American Folklore, 1 (1888): 97-108.

Mooney, J. The Cherokee river cult. Journal of American Folklore, 13 (1900): 1-10.

Mooney, J. The sacred formulas of the Cherokees. U.S. Bureau of American Ethnology, Annual Reports, 7 (1886): 301-397.

Mooney, J. The Swimmer Manuscript. Ed. by F. M. Olbrechts. U.S. Bureau of American Ethnology, Bulletin, 99 (1932): 1-319.

Mooney, James. Cherokee animal tales. Edited by George F. Scheer. New York, Holiday House, 1968. 79 p. illus.

Mooney, James. Myths of the Cherokee. New York, Johnson Reprint, 1970. 576 p. illus., maps.

Mooney, James. Myths of the Cherokee and Sacred formulas of the Cherokees. Nashville, Tenn., C. Elder, 1972. 576, 301-397 p. illus.

Morgan, L. H. Systems of consanguinity and affinity. Smithsonian Contributions to Knowledge, 17 (1871): 291-382.

Morris, Wayne. Traders and factories on the Arkansas frontier, 1805-1822. Arkansas Historical Quarterly, 28 (1969): 28-48.

Neet, J. Frederick, Jr. Stand Watie; Confederate general in the Cherokee nation. Great Plains Journal, 6 (1966/1967): 36-51.

New, Lloyd. Institute of American Indian Arts. Arizona Highways, 48, no. 1 (1972): 5, 12-15, 44-45.

Nuttall, T. A journal of travels into the Arkansa Territory, 123-137. Philadelphia, 1821.

Nuttall, Thomas. A journal of travels into the Arkansa Territory. Ann Arbor, University Microfilms, 1966. 12, 296 p. illus., map.

O'Donnell, James H. The Virginia Expedition against the Overhill Cherokee, 1776. East Tennessee Historical Society's Publications, 39 (1967): 13-25.

Olbrechts, F. M. Cherokee belief and practice with regard to childbirth. Anthropos, 26 (1931): 17-33.

Olbrechts, F. M. Prophylaxis in Cherokee medicine. Anthropos, 24 (1929): 271-280.

Olbrechts, F. M. Some Cherokee methods of divination. International Congress of Americanists, Proceedings, 23 (1928): 547-552.

Olbrechts, F. M. Some notes on Cherokee treatment of disease. Janus, 33 (1928): 272-280.

Olbrechts, F. M. Two Cherokee texts. International Journal of American Linguistics, 6 (1931): 179-184.

Olbrechts, Frans M. Prophylaxis in Cherokee medicine. Janus, 33 (1929): 18-22.

Olson, Gary D. Thomas Brown, Loyalist partisan, and the Revolutionary War in Georgia, 1777-1782. Georgia Historical Quarterly, 54 (1970): 1-19, 183-208.

Owen, Narcissa. Memoirs of Narcissa Owen, 1831-1907. Washington, D.C., 1907. 126 p. illus.

Painter, C. C. The Eastern Cherokees. Philadelphia, 1888. 16 p.

Palmer, Edward. Alabama notes; made in 1883-1884. Alabama Historical Quarterly, 22 (1960): 244-273.

Pardo, Juan. Journals of the Juan Pardo expeditions, 1566-1567. Edited by Stanley J. Folmsbee and Madeline Kneberg Lewis. Translated by Gerald W. Wade. East Tennessee Historical Society, Publications, 37 (1965): 106-121.

Parker, T. V. The Cherokee Indians. New York, 1907. 116 p.

Parris, John A. Cherokee story. Asheville, N.C., Stephens Press, 1950.

Parris, John A. My mountains, my people. Asheville, N.C., Citizen-Times, 1957. 259 p. illus.

Parris, John A. Roaming the mountains with John Parris. Asheville, N.C., Citizen-Times, 1955. 246 p.

Payne, Betty. Dwight, a history of old Dwight Cherokee Mission, 1820-1953. By Betty Payne and Oscar Payne. Tulsa, Dwight Presbyterian Mission, 1954. 7, 2-33 p. illus., map.

Payne, John Howard. John Howard Payne to his countrymen. Edited by Clemens De Baillou. Athens, University of Georgia Press, 1961. 61 p. (Georgia, University, Libraries, Miscellanea Publications, 2)

Peacock, M. T. Methodist mission work among the Cherokee Indians before the removal. Methodist History, 3 (1965): 20-39.

Peake, G. Ronald. Oklahoma's "five tribes" Indians are improving their living conditions through public housing. Journal of Housing, 28 (1971): 430-432.

Peithmann, Irvin M. Red men of fire; a history of the Cherokee Indians. Springfield, Ill., Thomas, 1964. 15, 165 p. illus., maps.

Peters, Richard. The case of the Cherokee Nation against the State of Georgia; argued and determined at the Supreme Court of the United States, January term 1831. Philadelphia, J. Grigg, 1831. 4, 286 p.

Phelps, Dawson A. The Natchez Trace; Indian trail to parkway. Tennessee Historical Quarterly, 21 (1962): 203-218.

Pickens, A. L. A comparison of Cherokee and pioneer bird-nomenclature. Southern Folklore Quarterly, 7 (1943): 213-221.

Pickering, J. A grammar of the Cherokee language. Boston, 1830. 48 p.

Pickett, A. J. History of Alabama, Vol. 1: 154-163. Charleston, 1851.

Pike, Albert. Albert Pike's journeys in the prairie, 1831-1832. Edited by J. Evetts Haley. Panhandle-Plains Historical Review, 41 (1968): 1-84.

Pollitzer, William S. Analysis of a tri-racial isolate. Human Biology, 36 (1964): 362-373.

Pollitzer, William S. Blood types of the Cherokee Indians. By William S. Pollitzer, Robert C. Hartmann, Hugh Moore, Richard E. Rosenfield, Harry Smith, Shirin Hakim, Paul J. Schmidt, and Webster C. Leyshon. American Journal of Physical Anthropology, n.s., 20 (1962): 33-43.

Pollitzer, William S., et al. Hemoglobin patterns in American Indians. Science, 129 (1959): 216.

Potter, E. An account of several nations of Southern Indians. Massachusetts Historical Society, Collections, ser. 1, 10 (1809): 119-121.

Potts, William S. An account of Alabama Indian Missions and Presbyterian churches in 1828 from the travel diary of William S. Potts. Edited by Joseph G. Smoot. Alabama Review, 18 (1965): 134-152.

Powell, George. A description and history of Blount County. Alabama Historical Quarterly, 27 (1965): 95-132.

Powell, J. W. The Cherokees probably mound builders. U.S. Bureau of American Ethnology, Annual Reports, 5 (1884): 87-107.

Prucha, Francis Paul. Thomas L. McKenney and the New York Indian Board. Mississippi Valley Historical Review, 48 (1961/1962): 635-655.

Rainwater, Percy L. Indian missions and missionaries. Journal of Mississippi History, 28 (1966): 15-39.

Rampp, Lary C. Confederate Indian sinking of the J. R. Williams. Journal of the West, 11 (1972): 43-50.

Rawley, James A. Joseph John Gurney's mission to America, 1837-1840. Mississippi Valley Historical Review, 49 (1962/1963): 653-674.

Reed, Gerard Alexander. The Ross-Watie conflict: factionalism in the Cherokee nation, 1839-1865. Dissertation Abstracts, 28 (1967/1968): 1034A. UM 67-11,088.

Reid, John Phillip. A law of blood; the primitive law of the Cherokee nation. New York, New York University Press, 1970. 8, 340 p. map.

Reyburn, W. D. Cherokee verb morphology. International Journal of American Linguistics, 19 (1953): 172-180, 259-273; 20 (1954): 44-64.

Reynolds, Thurlow W. Cherokee and Creek. Highlands, N.C., 1966. 87 p.

Rice, Otis. The French and Indian War in West Virginia. West Virginia History, 24 (1962/1963): 134-146.

Richardson, Marian M., comp. 1832 Cherokee land lottery. Compiled by Marian M. Richardson and Jessie J. Mize. Danielsville, Ga., Heritage Papers, 1969. 4, 33 p.

Richardson, W. An account of the Presbyterian mission to the Cherokees,

1757-1759. Tennessee Historical Magazine, ser. 2, 1 (1931): 125-128.

Richardson, Willing. The Cherokee pack trail. Annals of Wyoming, 33 (1961): 95.

Rife, David C. Dermatoglyphics of Cherokee and Mohawk Indians. Human Biology, 44 (1972): 81-85.

Rife, David C. Palm patterns and pigmentation in a Cherokee Indian population. Acta Geneticae Medicae et Gemellologiae, 20 (1971): 69-76.

Rights, D. L. The American Indian in North Carolina. 2d ed. Winston-Salem, 1957. 318 p.

Rister, Carl C. Baptist missions among the American Indians. Atlanta, Southern Baptist Convention, Home Mission Board, 1944. 127 p. illus.

Roethler, Michael Donald. Negro slavery among the Cherokee Indians, 1540-1866. Dissertation Abstracts, 25 (1964/1965): 3526. UM 64-13,229.

Roper, James. Fort Adams and Fort Pickering. West Tennessee Historical Society, Papers, 24 (1970): 5-29.

Roper, James. The founding of Memphis; August, 1818, through December, 1820. West Tennessee Historical Society, Papers, 23 (1969): 5-29.

Roper, James E. Isaac Rawlings, frontier merchant. Tennessee Historical Quarterly, 20 (1961): 262-281.

Ross, Mrs. W. P. Life and times of Wm. P. Ross. Fort Smith, 1893. 272 p.

Royce, C. C. The Cherokee nation of Indians. U.S. Bureau of American Ethnology, Annual Reports, 5 (1884): 121-378.

Savage, William W., Jr. Intruders at Chilocco. Chronicles of Oklahoma, 50 (1972): 199-204.

Savage, William W., Jr. Leasing the Cherokee Outlet: an analysis of Indian reaction, 1884-1885. Chronicles of Oklahoma, 46 (1968): 285-292.

Savage, William Woodrow, Jr. The Cherokee Strip Livestock Association: the impact of federal regulation on the cattleman's last frontier. Dissertation Abstracts International, 33 (1972/1973): 682A. UM 72-22,141.

Schmitt, K. and R. E. Bell. Historic Indian pottery from Oklahoma. Oklahoma

Anthropological Society, Bulletin, 2 (1954): 19-30.

Sears, W. H. Creek and Cherokee culture in the 18th century. American Antiquity, 21 (1955): 143-149.

Self, Nancy Hope. The building of the railroads in the Cherokee Nation. Chronicles of Oklahoma, 49 (1971/1972): 180-205.

Self, R. D. Chronology of New Echota. Early Georgia, 1, no. 4 (1955): 3-5.

Senior, Blondel Eslington. A sociometric study of children of different socioeconomic levels in an interracial, interreligious camp. Dissertation Abstracts International, 32 (1971/1972): 4144A. UM 72-2539.

Shadburn, Don L. Cherokee statesmen: the John Rogers family of Chattahoochee. Chronicles of Oklahoma, 50 (1972): 12-40.

Sharp, James Roger. Gov. Daniel Dunklin's Jacksonian democracy in Missouri, 1832-1836. Missouri Historical Review, 56 (1961/1962): 217-229.

Shearer, Ernest C. The mercurial Sam Houston. East Tennessee Historical Society's Publications, 35 (1963): 3-20.

Shoemaker, Arthur. The battle of Chustenahlah. Chronicles of Oklahoma, 38 (1960): 180-184.

Siler, David W. The Eastern Cherokees, a census of the Cherokee Nation in North Carolina, Tennessee, Alabama, and Georgia in 1851. Cottonport, La., Polyanthos, 1972. 122, 38 p.

Siler, M. R. Cherokee Indian lore and Smoky Mountain stories. Bryson City, 1938. 111 p.

Simon, C. M. Younger brother. New York, 1942. 182 p.

Slay, James L. The settlement and organization of Bradley County, Tennessee. East Tennessee Historical Society's Publications, 44 (1972): 3-16.

Smith, James F. The Cherokee land lottery. Vidalia, Georgia Genealogical Reprints, 1968. 6, 413, 73 p. maps.

Smith, James F. The Cherokee land lottery. Baltimore, Genealogical Publishing, 1969. 520 p. maps.

Sockabasin, Allen J., comp. Off-reservation Indian survey Me P-74. Compiled by Allen J. Sockabasin and John

G. Stone. Augusta, Maine Department of Indian Affairs, 1971. 67 p.

Somers, James Earl. Folk medicine in an isolated modern community. North Carolina Medical Journal, 22 (1961): 611-615.

Sosin, Jack M. The use of Indians in the War of the American Revolution: a re-assessment of responsibility. Canadian Historical Review, 46 (1965): 101-121.

Spade, Watt. Cherokee stories. By Watt Spade and Willard Walker. Middletown, Conn., Wesleyan University, Laboratory of Anthropology, 1966. 4, 25 p. illus.

Speck, F. and L. Broom. Cherokee dance and drama. Berkeley, 1951. 121 p.

Speck, F. G. Decorative art and basketry of the Cherokee. Public Museum of the City of Milwaukee, Bulletin, 2 (1920): 53-86.

Speck, F. G. Ethnoherpetology of the Catawba and Cherokee Indians. Washington Academy of Sciences, Journal, 36 (1946): 355-360.

Speck, F. G. Some Eastern Cherokee texts. International Journal of American Linguistics, 4 (1926): 111-113.

Speck, F. G. and C. E. Schaeffer. The mutual-aid and volunteer company of the Eastern Cherokee. Washington Academy of Sciences, Journal, 35 (1945): 169-179.

Spence, L. Cherokees. In J. Hastings, ed. Encyclopaedia of Religion and Ethics. Vol. 3. New York, 1911: 503-508.

Spoehr, A. Changing kinship systems. Field Museum, Anthropological Series, 33 (1947): 153-235.

Starkey, M. L. The Cherokee nation. New York, 1946. 355 p.

Starkey, Marion L. The Cherokee Nation. New York, Russell and Russell, 1972. 355, 6 p. illus.

Starr, E. History of the Cherokee Indians. Oklahoma City, 1921. 680 p.

Starr, Emmet. Old Cherokee families: old families and their genealogy. 2d ed. Norman, University of Oklahoma Press, 1972. 303-476, 94 p. illus.

Starr, Emmet. Starr's History of the Cherokee Indians. Edited by Jack Gregory and Rennard Strickland. Fayetteville, Ark., Indian Heritage Association, 1967. 11, 672 p. illus.

Stealey, John Edmond, 3d. French Lick and the Cumberland Compact. Tennessee Historical Quarterly, 22 (1963): 323-334.

Steen, C. T. The Home for the Insane, Deaf, Dumb and Blind of the Cherokee nation. Chronicles of Oklahoma, 21 (1943): 402-419.

Stein, Jay H., et al. The high prevalence of abnormal glucose tolerance in the Cherokee Indians of North Carolina. Archives of Internal Medicine, 116 (1965): 842-845.

Stephens, A. Ray. The Killough Massacre. Texana, 7 (1969): 322-327.

Stewart, Martha. The Indian Mission Conference of Oklahoma. Chronicles of Oklahoma, 40 (1962): 330-336.

Stone, Richard G., Jr. Captain Paul Demere at Fort Loudoun, 1757-1760. East Tennessee Historical Society's Publications, 41 (1969): 17-32.

Story, I. F. Our Eastern Cherokee Indians. Home Geographic Monthly, 5, no. 6 (1932): 7-12.

Street, O. D. The Indians of Marshall County, Alabama. Alabama Historical Society, Transactions, 4 (1904): 193-210.

Strickland, Rennard. Christian Gotelieb Priber: utopian precursor of the Cherokee government. Chronicles of Oklahoma, 48 (1970/1971): 264-279.

Strickland, Rennard. From clan to court: development of Cherokee law. Tennessee Historical Quarterly, 31 (1972): 316-327.

Stringfield, W. W. North Carolina Cherokee Indians. Raleigh, 1903. 24 p.

Stuart, J. A sketch of the Cherokee and Choctaw Indians. Little Rock, 1837. 42 p.

Terrell, J. W. The demon of consumption. Journal of American Folklore, 5 (1892): 125-126.

Texas, Attorney General's Office. Memorandum to Governor John Connally concerning Cherokee Indian claim relating to lands in Texas. Austin, 1964. 52, 12 p.

Thomas, C. Burial mounds in the northern sections of the United States. U.S. Bureau of American Ethnology, Annual Reports, 5 (1884): 87-107.

Thomas, C. The Cherokees in pre-Columbian times. New York, 1890. 97 p.

Thomas, Daniel H. Fort Toulouse; the French outpost at the Alibamos on the Coosa. Alabama Historical Quarterly, 22 (1960): 137-230.

Thomas, Daniel H. Fort Toulouse--in tradition and fact. Alabama Review, 13 (1960): 243-257.

Thomas, Robert K. Indians, hillbillies and the "education problem". By Robert K. Thomas and Albert L. Wahrhaftig. In Murray L. Wax, et al., eds. Anthropological Perspectives on Education. New York, Basic Books, 1971: 231-251.

Timberlake, H. Memoirs. London, 1762.

Timberlake, Henry. The memoirs of Lieut. Henry Timberlake. New York, Arno Press, 1971. 197 p. illus.

Tinnin, I. W. Influences of the Cherokee national seminaries. Chronicles of Oklahoma, 37 (1959): 59-67.

Tinnin, Ida Wetzel. Educational and cultural influences of the Cherokee seminaries. Chronicles of Oklahoma, 37 (1959): 59-67.

Tooker, W. W. The problems of the Rechaheerian Indians of Virginia. American Anthropologist, 11 (1898): 261-270.

Traveller Bird. Tell them they lie: the Sequoyah myth. Los Angeles, Westernlore Publishers, 1971. 12, 148 p. illus.

Traveller Bird. The path to Snowbird Mountain; Cherokee legends. By Traveller Bird (Tsisghwanai). New York, Farrar, Straus and Giroux, 1972. 5, 87 p. illus.

Tresp, Lothar L., ed. and tr. August, 1748 in Georgia, from the diary of John Martin Bolzius. Georgia Historical Quarterly, 47 (1963): 204-216.

Troper, Harold Martin. The Creek-Negroes of Oklahoma and Canadian immigration, 1909-11. Canadian Historical Review, 53 (1972): 272-288.

Tucker, Norma. Nancy Ward, Ghighau of the Cherokees. Georgia Historical Quarterly, 53 (1969): 192-200.

Tyner, James W. Our people, and where they rest; a visit to eighty-nine old cemeteries in the Old Cherokee Nation. By James W. Tyner and Alice Tyner Timmons. [n.p.] 1969. illus., map.

Ulmer, M. and S. E. Beck, eds. To make my bread. Cherokee, 1951. 72 p.

Urry, J. W. Cherokee colour symbolism. Man, n.s., 4 (1969): 459.

U.S., Bureau of Indian Affairs. Indians of North Carolina. Washington, D.C., Government Printing Office, 1968. 16 p. ERIC ED021677.

U.S., Library of Congress, Legislative Reference Service. The national significance of the Cherokee Indians. By William H. Gilbert and Stephen A. Langone. Washington, D.C., 1962. 117 p.

Van Every, Dale. Disinherited; the lost birthright of the American Indian. New York, Morrow, 1966. 279 p. maps.

Van Hoeven, James William. Salvation and Indian removal: the career biography of the Rev. John Freeman Schermerhorn, Indian commissioner. Dissertation Abstracts International, 33 (1972/1973): 1830A. UM 72-26,134.

Wade, Forest C. Cry of the eagle; history and legends of the Cherokee Indians and their buried treasure. Cumming, Ga., 1969. 151 p. illus., maps.

Wahnenauhi. The Wahnenauhi Manuscript: historical sketches of the Cherokees; together with some of their customs, traditions, and superstitions. Edited by Jack Frederick Kilpatrick. Washington, D.C., Government Printing Office, 1966. 175-214 p. illus. (U.S., Bureau of American Ethnology, Anthropological Papers, 77. U.S., Bureau of American Ethnology, Bulletin, 196)

Wahrhaftig, Albert L. A suggestion for non-reservation Indian communities. Journal of American Indian Education, 5, no. 1 (1965/1966): 1-9.

Wahrhaftig, Albert L. Community and the caretakers. New University Thought, 4 (1966): 54-76.

Wahrhaftig, Albert L. Renaissance and repression: the Oklahoma Cherokee. By Albert L. Wahrhaftig and Robert K. Thomas. Trans-Action, 6, no. 4 (1969): 42-48.

Wahrhaftig, Albert L. Social and economic characteristics of the Cherokee population of eastern Oklahoma. Washington, D.C., 1970. 69 p. illus. (American Anthropological Association, Anthropological Studies, 5)

Wahrhaftig, Albert L. The tribal Cherokee population of eastern Oklahoma. Current Anthropology, 9 (1968): 510-518.

Wahrhaftig, Albert L. The tribal Cherokee population of eastern Oklahoma. In Deward E. Walker, Jr., ed. The Emergent Native Americans. Boston, Little, Brown, 1972: 217-235.

Walker, R. S. Torchlights to the Cherokees. New York, 1931. 339 p.

Walker, Willard. Notes on native writing systems and the design of native literacy programs. Anthropological Linguistics, 11, no. 5 (1969): 148-166.

Wallace, Katherine T. Notes and documents; Elk County, Alabama. Alabama Review, 19 (1966): 227-233.

Wardell, M. L. A political history of the Cherokee nation. Norman, 1938. 383 p.

Warren, Hanna R. Reconstruction in the Cherokee.Nation. Chronicles of Oklahoma, 45 (1967): 180-189.

Washburn, C. Reminiscences of the Indians. Van Buren, Arkansas, 1955. 209 p.

Washburn, C. Reminiscences of the Indians. Richmond, 1869. 236 p.

Washburn, Cephas. Reminiscences of the Indians. New York, Johnson Reprint, 1971. 236 p.

Washington, George. George Washington and the Fairfax family; some new documents. Edited by Peter Walne. Virginia Magazine of History and Biography, 77 (1969): 441-463.

Watts, W. J. Cherokee citizenship. Muldrow, 1895. 144 p.

Wax, Murray L. Indian education in eastern Oklahoma. A report of fieldwork among the Cherokee. Final report. Lawrence, Kansas University, 1969. 276 p. (U.S., Office of Education, Bureau of Research, Bureau, BR-5-0565) ERIC ED029741.

Wax, Murray L. Poverty and interdependency. In Eleanor B. Leacock, ed. The Culture of Poverty: a Critique. New York, Simon and Schuster, 1971: 338-344.

Wax, Murray L. The enemies of the people. By Murray L. Wax and Rosalie H. Wax. In Howard S. Becker, et al., eds. Institutions and the Person. Chicago, Aldine, 1968: 101-118.

Webster, C. L. Prof. D. W. C. Duncan's analysis of the Cherokee language. American Naturalist, 23 (1889): 775-781.

White, Frank L., Jr. The journals of Lieutenant John Pickell, 1836-1837. Florida Historical Quarterly, 38, no. 2 (1959): 142-171.

White, John K. On the revival of printing in the Cherokee language. Current Anthropology, 3 (1962): 511-514.

White, Lonnie J. Arkansas territorial Indian affairs. Arkansas Historical Quarterly, 21 (1962): 193-212.

Wilburn, H. C. Judaculla place-names and the Judaculla tales. Southern Indian Studies, 4 (1952): 23-26.

Wilburn, H. C. Judaculla rock. Southern Indian Studies, 4 (1952): 19-22.

Wilburn, H. C. Nununyi, the Kituhwas, or Mountain Indians and the State of North Carolina. Southern Indian Studies, 2 (1950): 54-64.

Wilkins, Thurman. Cherokee tragedy; the story of the Ridge family and the decimation of a people. New York, Macmillan, 1970. 10, 398 p. maps.

Willey, William J. The second federal invasion of Indian Territory. Chronicles of Oklahoma, 44 (1966/1967): 420-430.

Winfrey, Dorman H. Chief Bowles of the Texas Cherokee. Texana, 2 (1964): 189-202.

Winkler, E. W. The Cherokee Indians in Texas. Texas State Historical Association Quarterly, 7 (1903): 95-165.

Witthoft, J. An early Cherokee ethnobotanical note. Washington Academy of Sciences, Journal, 37 (1947): 73-75.

Witthoft, J. Bird lore of the Eastern Cherokee. Washington Academy of Sciences, Journal, 36 (1946): 372-384.

Witthoft, J. Green corn ceremonialism in the Eastern Woodlands. Michigan, University, Museum of Anthropology, Occasional Contributions, 13 (1949): 31-50.

Witthoft, J. Notes on a Cherokee migration story. Washington Academy of Sciences, Journal, 37 (1947): 304-305.

Witthoft, J. Some Eastern Cherokee bird stories. Washington Academy of Sciences, Journal, 36 (1946): 177-180.

Witthoft, J. Stone pipes of the historic Cherokee. Southern Indian Studies, 1, no. 2 (1949): 43-69.

Witthoft, J. The Cherokee green corn medicine and the green corn festival. Washington Academy of Sciences, Journal, 36 (1946): 213-219.

Witthoft, J. Will West Long, Cherokee informant. American Anthropologist, n.s., 50 (1948): 355-359.

Witthoft, J. and W. S. Hadlock. Cherokee-Iroquois little people. Journal of American Folklore, 59 (1946): 413-422.

Wood, George W. Report of Mr. Wood's visit to the Choctaw and Cherokee missions. 1855. Boston, Press of T. R. Marvin, 1855. 24 p.

Wood, W. W. War and the Eastern Cherokee. Southern Indian Studies, 2 (1950): 47-53.

Woodward, Grace Steele. The Cherokees. Norman, University of Oklahoma Press, 1963. 15, 359 p. illus., maps.

Wright, Bessie L., ed. Diary of a member of the first mule pack train to leave Fort Smith for California in 1849. Panhandle-Plains Historical Review, 42 (1969): 61-119.

Wright, J. Leitch. Creek-American Treaty of 1790: Alexander McGillivray and the diplomacy of the Old Southwest. Georgia Historical Quarterly, 51 (1967): 379-400.

Wright, M. H. American Indian corn dishes. Chronicles of Oklahoma, 36 (1958): 155-166.

Wright, Muriel H. Colonel Cooper's Civil War report on the Battle of Round Mountain. Chronicles of Oklahoma, 39 (1961): 352-397.

Wright, Muriel H. Notes on Colonel Elias C. Boudinot. Chronicles of Oklahoma, 41 (1963): 382-407.

Wright, Muriel H. Seals of the Five Civilized Tribes. Chronicles of Oklahoma, 40 (1962): 214-218.

Young, Chester Raymond. The stress of war upon the civilian population of Virginia, 1739-1760. West Virginia History, 27 (1965/1966): 251-277.

Young, Mary E. Indian removal and land allotment: the civilized tribes and Jacksonian justice. In Roger L. Nichols and George R. Adams, eds. The American

Indian: Past and Present. Waltham, Xerox College Publishing, 1971: 132-145.

Zolotarevskaîa, I. A. Some materials on the assimilation of Oklahoma Indians. Translated by William Andrews. Edited by William E. Bittle. By I. A. Zolotarevskaja. Plains Anthropologist, 6 (1961): 1-6.

13-09   Chickasaw

Hargrett, L. A bibliography of the constitutions and laws of the American Indians, 41-53. Cambridge, 1947.

Jones, William K. General guide to documents on the Five Civilized Tribes in the University of Oklahoma Library Division of Manuscripts. Ethnohistory, 14 (1967): 47-76.

Abbott, M. Indian policy and management in the Mississippi Territory, 1798-1817. Journal of Mississippi History, 14 (1952): 153-169.

Adair, J. The history of the American Indians, 352-373. London, 1775.

Ashcraft, Allan C. Confederate Indian Department conditions in August, 1864. Chronicles of Oklahoma, 41 (1963): 270-285.

Ashcraft, Allan C. Confederate Indian Territory conditions in 1865. Chronicles of Oklahoma, 42 (1964): 421-428.

Ashcraft, Allan C. Confederate Indian troop conditions in 1864. Chronicles of Oklahoma, 41 (1963): 442-449.

Bailey, Minnie Elizabeth Thomas. Reconstruction in Indian Territory, 1865-1877. Dissertation Abstracts, 29 (1968/1969): 198A. UM 68-8362.

Baily, Francis. Journal of a tour in unsettled parts of North America in 1796 and 1797. Edited by Jack D. L. Holmes. Carbondale, Southern Illinois University Press, 1969. 26, 336 p. illus.

Baird, W. David. Fort Smith and the Red Man. Arkansas Historical Quarterly, 30 (1971): 337-348.

Banks, Dean. Civil-War refugees from Indian Territory, in the North, 1861-1864. Chronicles of Oklahoma, 41 (1963): 286-298.

Bartram, W. The travels of William Bartram, naturalist's edition. New Haven, 1958. 788 p.

Bartram, W. Travels through North and South Carolina. London, 1792.

Bearss, Edwin C. The Arkansas whiskey war: a Fort Smith case study. Journal of the West, 7 (1968): 143-172.

Bell, R. E. and D. A. Baerreis. A survey of Oklahoma archeology. Texas Archeological and Paleontological Society, Bulletin, 22 (1951): 7-100.

Boas, F. Zur Anthropologie der nordamerikanischen Indianer. Berliner Gesellschaft für Anthropologie, Ethnologie und Urgeschichte, Verhandlungen (1895): 367-411.

Braden, G. B. The Colberts and the Chickasaw Nation. Tennessee Historical Quarterly, 17 (1958/1959): 222-249, 318-335.

Brinton, D. G. National legend of the Chahta-Muskokee tribes. Morrisania, 1870. 13 p.

Busby, Orel. Buffalo Valley: an Osage hunting ground. Chronicles of Oklahoma, 40 (1962): 22-35.

Bushnell, D. I. Native cemeteries and forms of burial east of the Mississippi. U.S. Bureau of American Ethnology, Bulletin, 71 (1920): 105-108.

Campbell, T. N. Medicinal plants used by Choctaw, Chickasaw and Creek Indians. Washington Academy of Sciences, Journal, 41 (1951): 285-290.

Carney, Champ Clark. The historical geography of the Chickasaw lands of Oklahoma. Dissertation Abstracts, 22 (1961/1962): 1575. UM 61-4427.

Chappell, Gordon T. John Coffee: surveyor and land agent. Alabama Review, 14 (1961): 180-195.

Connelly, Thomas Lawrence. Indian warfare on the Tennessee frontier, 1776-1794: strategy and tactics. East Tennessee Historical Society's Publications, 36 (1964): 3-22.

Corbitt, D. C. Exploring the Southwest Territory in the Spanish Records. East Tennessee Historical Society's Publications, 38 (1966): 109-118.

Corbitt, D. C., tr. and ed. Papers from the Spanish archives relating to Tennessee and the Old Southwest. Translated and edited by D. C. Corbitt

and Roberta Corbitt. East Tennessee Historical Society, Publications, 31 (1959): 63-82; 32 (1960): 72-93; 33 (1961): 61-78; 34 (1962): 86-105; 35 (1963): 85-95; 36 (1964): 70-80; 37 (1965): 89-105; 38 (1966): 70-82; 39 (1967): 87-102; 40 (1968): 101-118; 41 (1969): 100-116; 42 (1970): 96-107; 43 (1971): 94-111; 44 (1972): 104-113.

Cotten, John. The Battle of the Bluffs; from the journal of John Cotten. Edited by J. W. L. Matlock. Tennessee Historical Quarterly, 18 (1959): 252-265.

Cotterill, R. S. The Southern Indians. Norman, 1954. 268 p.

Cushman, H. B. History of the Choctaw, Chickasaw, and Natchez Indians. Greenville, 1899. 607 p.

Cushman, Horatio B. History of the Choctaw, Chickasaw and Natchez Indians. Edited by Angie Debo. New York, Russell and Russell, 1972. 503 p. illus.

Cushman, Horatio B. History of the Choctaw, Chickasaw and Natchez Indians. Edited by Angie Debo. Stillwater, Okla., Redlands Press, 1962. 503 p. illus.

Debo, A. And still the waters run. Princeton, 1940. 417 p.

Debo, Angie. The location of the Battle of Round Mountain. Chronicles of Oklahoma, 41 (1963): 70-104.

Doster, James F. Land titles and public land sales in early Alabama. Alabama Review, 16 (1963): 108-124.

Dumont de Montigny. L'établissement de la province de la Louisiane. Société des Américanistes, Journal, n.s., 23 (1931): 273-440.

Durham, Walter T. Kasper Mansker: Cumberland frontiersman. Tennessee Historical Quarterly, 30 (1971): 154-177.

East, Dennis. New York and Mississippi Land Company and the panic of 1837. Journal of Mississippi History, 33 (1971): 299-331.

Farrar, William G. Historic profiles of Fort Massac. By William G. and JoAnn S. Farrar. Carbondale, Southern Illinois University, University Museum, 1970. 3, 59 p. (Southern Illinois Studies, 5)

Fischer, LeRoy H. Confederate Indian forces outside of Indian Territory. By LeRoy H. Fischer and Jerry Gill.

Chronicles of Oklahoma, 46 (1968): 249-284.

Foreman, G. Indians and pioneers. Rev. ed. Norman, 1936. 285 p.

Foreman, G. The five civilized tribes, 97-144. Norman, 1934.

Foreman, G., ed. A traveler in Indian Territory. Cedar Rapids, 1930. 270 p.

Foreman, Grant. The Five Civilized Tribes; a brief history and a century of progress. Muskogee, Okla., C. T. Foreman, 1966. 58 p. illus.

Gaines, George S. Gaine's reminiscences. Alabama Historical Quarterly, 26 (1964): 133-229.

Gatschet, A. S. A migration legend of the Creek Indians, 90-97. Philadelphia, 1884.

Gatschet, A. S. and C. Thomas. Chickasaw. U.S. Bureau of American Ethnology, Bulletin, 30, vol. 1 (1907): 260-262.

Gibson, A. M. An Indian Territory United Nations: the Creek Council of 1845. Chronicles of Oklahoma, 39 (1961): 398-413.

Gibson, Arrell M. Chickasaw ethnography: an ethnohistorical reconstruction. Ethnohistory, 18 (1971): 99-118.

*Gibson, Arrell M. The Chickasaws. Norman, University of Oklahoma Press, 1971. 15, 312 p. illus., maps.

Graebner, N. A. Pioneer Indian agriculture in Oklahoma. Chronicles of Oklahoma, 23 (1945): 232-248.

Graebner, N. A. Provincial Indian society in eastern Oklahoma. Chronicles of Oklahoma, 23 (1945/1946): 323-337.

Graebner, N. A. The public land policy of the five civilized tribes. Chronicles of Oklahoma, 23 (1945): 107-118.

Hagy, James William, ed. The lost archives of the Cherokee Nation. Edited by James William Hagy and Stanley J. Folmsbee. East Tennessee Historical Society, Publications, 43 (1971): 112-122; 44 (1972): 114-125.

Hatfield, Joseph T. Governor William Charles Cole Claiborne, Indians, and outlaws in frontier Mississippi, 1801-1803. Journal of Mississippi History, 27 (1965): 323-350.

Hawkins, B. Letters, 1796-1806. Georgia Historical Society, Collections, 9 (1916): 1-500.

Haywood, J. The natural and aboriginal history of Tennessee. Nashville, 1823. 390 p.

Hiemstra, W. L. Presbyterian mission schools among the Choctaws and Chickasaws, 1845-1861. Chronicles of Oklahoma, 27 (1949): 33-40.

Hill, A. A. Three examples of unexpectedly accurate Indian lore. Texas Studies in Literature and Language, 6 (1964/1965): 80-83.

Holmes, Jack D. L. Fort Ferdinand of the Bluffs; life on the Spanish-American frontier, 1795-1797. West Tennessee Historical Society, Papers, 13 (1959): 38-54.

Holmes, Jack D. L. Spanish treaties with West Florida Indians, 1784-1802. Florida Historical Quarterly, 48 (1969/1970): 140-154.

Holmes, Jack D. L. Spanish-American rivalry over the Chickasaw Bluffs, 1780-1795. East Tennessee Historical Society's Publications, 34 (1962): 26-57.

Holmes, Jack D. L. The ebb-tide of Spanish military power on the Mississippi: Fort San Fernando de las Barrancas, 1795-1798. East Tennessee Historical Society's Publications, 36 (1964): 23-44.

Holmes, Jack D. L. Three early Memphis commandants: Beauregard, Deville Degoutin, and Folch. West Tennessee Historical Society, Papers, 18 (1964): 5-38.

Holmes, Jack D. L., tr. and ed. The first laws of Memphis: instructions for the commandant of San Fernando de las Barrancas, 1795. West Tennessee Historical Society, Papers, 15 (1961): 93-104.

Hood, Fred. Twilight of the Confederacy in Indian Territory. Chronicles of Oklahoma, 41 (1963): 425-441.

Howard, J. H. Some Chickasaw fetishes. Florida Anthropologist, 12, no. 2 (1959): 47-56.

Howard, R. Palmer. A historiography of the Five Civilized Tribes: a chronological approach. Chronicles of Oklahoma, 47 (1969): 312-331.

Howard, R. Palmer. A historiography of the Five Civilized Tribes; a chronological approach. Oklahoma City, Oklahoma Historical Society, 1969. 20 p.

Howell, Elmo. The Chickasaw queen in William Faulkner's story. Chronicles of Oklahoma, 49 (1971/1972): 334-339.

Howell, George W. The Buttahatchie settlers. Journal of Mississippi History, 34 (1972): 57-72, 159-171, 253-260, 391-399.

Jackson, Joe C. Summer normals in Indian territory after 1898. Chronicles of Oklahoma, 37 (1959): 307-329.

James, Parthena Louise. Reconstruction in the Chickasaw Nation: the Chronicles of Oklahoma, 45 (1967): 44-57. freedman problem.

James, Parthena Louise. The White threat in the Chickasaw Nation. Chronicles of Oklahoma, 46 (1968): 73-85.

Jenkins, William H. Alabama forts, 1700-1838. Alabama Review, 12 (1959): 163-180.

Jennings, J. D. Chickasaw and earlier Indian cultures of Northeast Mississippi. Journal of Mississippi History, 3, no. 3 (1941): 155-226.

Jennings, J. D. Prehistory of the Lower Mississippi Valley. In J. B. Griffin, ed. Archeology of Eastern United States. Chicago, 1952: 256-271.

Kansas City Star. Report on the Five Civilized Tribes 1897. Chronicles of Oklahoma, 48 (1970): 416-430.

Malone, J. B. The Chickasaw Nation. Louisville, 1922. 537 p.

Martin, Martha Philips. Travel through Indian Country in the early 1800's; the memoirs of Martha Philips Martin. Edited by Harriet C. Owsley. Tennessee Historical Quarterly, 21 (1962): 66-81.

McAlister, Lyle N. William Augustus Bowles and the State of Muskogee. Florida Historical Quarterly, 40 (1961/1962): 317-328.

McKee, James W., Jr. William Barksdale and the Congressional election of 1853 in Mississippi. Journal of Mississippi History, 33 (1971): 129-158.

McNeil, Kinneth. Confederate treaties with the tribes of Indian Territory. Chronicles of Oklahoma, 42 (1964): 408-420.

McRill, Leslie. A review of the De Soto expedition in territories of our present southern United States. Chronicles of Oklahoma, 39 (1961): 70-79.

McWilliams, Richebourg Gaillard. Iberville and the Southern Indians. Alabama Review, 20 (1967): 243-262.

Middlebrooks, Audy J. Holland Coffee of Red River. By Audy J. and Glenna Middlebrooks. Southwestern Historical Quarterly, 69 (1965/1966): 145-162.

Milling, C. J. Red Carolinians. Chapel Hill, 1940. 438 p.

Miner, Craig. The struggle for an East-West railway into the Indian Territory, 1870-1882. Chronicles of Oklahoma, 47 (1969): 560-581.

Mitchell, Irene B. The golden age of Bloomfield Academy in the Chickasaw Nation. By Irene B. Mitchell and Ida Belle Renken. Chronicles of Oklahoma, 49 (1971/1972): 412-426.

Morgan, L. H. Systems of consanguinity and affinity. Smithsonian Contributions to Knowledge, 17 (1871): 291-382.

Morris, Cheryl H. Choctaw and Chickasaw Indian agents, 1831-1874. Chronicles of Oklahoma, 50 (1972): 415-436.

Morris, Wayne. Traders and factories on the Arkansas frontier, 1805-1822. Arkansas Historical Quarterly, 28 (1969): 28-48.

Nuttall, T. A journal of travels into the Arkansa Territory. Philadelphia, 1821. 296 p.

Nuttall, Thomas. A journal of travels into the Arkansa Territory. Ann Arbor, University Microfilms, 1966. 12, 296 p. illus., map.

Olson, Gary D. Thomas Brown, Loyalist partisan, and the Revolutionary War in Georgia, 1777-1782. Georgia Historical Quarterly, 54 (1970): 1-19, 183-208.

Osborn, G. C. Relations with the Indians in West Florida during the administration of Governor Peter Chester, 1770-1781. Florida Historical Quarterly, 31 (1953): 239-272.

Parsons, J. E. Letters on the Chickasaw removal of 1837. New York Historical Society Quarterly, 37 (1953): 273-283.

Payne, Mildred Y. Mounds in the mist. By Mildred Y. Payne and Harry Harrison Kroll. South Brunswick, N.J., A. S. Barnes, 1970. 312 p. illus.

Peake, G. Ronald. Oklahoma's "five tribes" Indians are improving their living conditions through public housing. Journal of Housing, 28 (1971): 430-432.

Phelps, D. A. The Chickasaw Agency. Journal of Mississippi History, 14 (1952): 119-137.

Phelps, D. A. The Chickasaw council house. Journal of Mississippi History, 14 (1952): 170-176.

Phelps, D. A. The Chickasaw, the English, and the French, 1699-1744. Tennessee Historical Quarterly, 16 (1957): 117-133.

Phelps, Dawson A. Colbert Ferry and selected documents. Alabama Historical Quarterly, 25 (1963): 203-226.

Phelps, Dawson A. The Natchez Trace; Indian trail to parkway. Tennessee Historical Quarterly, 21 (1962): 203-218.

Pickett, A. J. History of Alabama, Vol. 1: 146-153. Charleston, 1851.

Potter, E. An account of several nations of Southern Indians. Massachusetts Historical Society, Collections, ser. 1, 10 (1809): 119-121.

Rainwater, Percy L. Conquistadors, missionaries, and missions. Journal of Mississippi History, 27 (1965): 123-147.

Rainwater, Percy L. Indian missions and missionaries. Journal of Mississippi History, 28 (1966): 15-39.

Reck, Philipp Georg Friedrich von. Von Reck's second report from Georgia. Edited by George Fenwick Jones. William and Mary Quarterly, 3d ser., 22 (1965): 319-333.

Romans, B. A concise natural history of East and West Florida, 59-71. New York, 1775.

Roper, James. Fort Adams and Fort Pickering. West Tennessee Historical Society, Papers, 24 (1970): 5-29.

Roper, James. The founding of Memphis; August, 1818, through December, 1820. West Tennessee Historical Society, Papers, 23 (1969): 5-29.

Roper, James E. Isaac Rawlings, frontier merchant. Tennessee Historical Quarterly, 20 (1961): 262-281.

Shafer, Harry J. An evaluation of the Natchez occupation at the Fatherland

Site. Journal of Mississippi History, 34 (1972): 215-235.

Smith, H. K. Chickasaws in Humphreys and Benton Counties, Tennessee. Tennessee Archaeologist, 14, no. 1 (1958): 26-30.

Smyth, J. F. D. A tour in the United States of America, Vol. 1: 360-364. London, 1784.

Spalding, Arminta Scott. From the Natchez Trace to Oklahoma: development of Christian civilization among the Choctaws, 1800-1860. Chronicles of Oklahoma, 45 (1967): 2-24.

Sparger, Julia K. Young Ardmore. Chronicles of Oklahoma, 43 (1965): 394-415.

Speck, F. G. Notes on Chickasaw ethnology and folk-lore. Journal of American Folklore, 20 (1907): 50-58.

Steacy, Stephen. The Chickasaw Nation on the eve of the Civil War. Chronicles of Oklahoma, 49 (1971/1972): 51-74.

Stone, Richard G., Jr. Captain Paul Demere at Fort Loudoun, 1757-1760. East Tennessee Historical Society's Publications, 41 (1969): 17-32.

Swanton, J. R. Early history of the Creek Indians and their neighbors. U.S. Bureau of American Ethnology, Bulletin, 73 (1922): 414-420.

*Swanton, J. R. Social and religious beliefs and usages of the Chickasaw Indians. U.S. Bureau of American Ethnology, Annual Reports, 44 (1927): 169-273.

Swanton, J. R. Social organization and social usages of the Indians of the Creek Confederacy. U.S. Bureau of American Ethnology, Annual Reports, 42 (1925): 23-472.

Swanton, John R. Early history of the Creek Indians and their neighbors. New York, Johnson Reprint, 1970. 492 p. maps.

Thomas, Daniel H. Fort Toulouse; the French outpost at the Alibamos on the Coosa. Alabama Historical Quarterly, 22 (1960): 137-230.

Thomas, Daniel H. Fort Toulouse--in tradition and fact. Alabama Review, 13 (1960): 243-257.

Villiers du Terrage, M. de. Documents concernant l'histoire des Indiens de la région orientale de la Louisiane.

Société des Américanistes, Journal,
n.s., 14 (1922): 127-140.

Villiers du Terrage, M. de. Note sur deux
cartes dessinées par les Chickachas.
Société des Américanistes, Journal,
n.s., 13 (1921): 7-9.

Wallace, Katherine T. Notes and
documents; Elk County, Alabama. Alabama
Review, 19 (1966): 227-233.

Warren, H. Chickasaw traditions, customs,
etc. Mississippi Historical Society,
Publications, 8 (1904): 543-553.

Warren, H. Some Chickasaw chiefs and
prominent men. Mississippi Historical
Society, Publications, 8 (1904): 555-
570.

Watts, Charles W. Colbert's Reserve and
the Chickasaw Treaty of 1818. Alabama
Review, 12 (1959): 272-280.

Watts, Florence G. Fort Knox: frontier
outpost on the Wabash, 1787-1816.
Indiana Magazine of History, 62 (1966):
51-78.

Williams, Edward F., 3d. Memphis' early
triumph over its river rivals. West
Tennessee Historical Society, Papers, 22
(1968): 5-27.

Williams, S. C. Beginnings of West
Tennessee. Johnson City, Tenn., 1930.
311 p.

Winfrey, Dorman H., ed. The Indian papers
of Texas and the Southwest, 1825-1916.
Edited by Dorman H. Winfrey and James M.
Day. Austin, Pemberton Press, 1966.
412 p.

Wright, J. B. Ranching in the Choctaw and
Chickasaw nations. Chronicles of
Oklahoma, 37 (1959): 294-300.

Wright, M. H. American Indian corn
dishes. Chronicles of Oklahoma, 36
(1958): 155-166.

Wright, Muriel H. Colonel Cooper's Civil
War report on the Battle of Round
Mountain. Chronicles of Oklahoma, 39
(1961): 352-397.

Wright, Muriel H. Seals of the Five
Civilized Tribes. Chronicles of
Oklahoma, 40 (1962): 214-218.

Young, C. A. A walking tour in the Indian
Territory. Chronicles of Oklahoma, 36
(1958): 167-180.

Young, Mary E. Indian removal and land
allotment: the civilized tribes and
Jacksonian justice. In Roger L. Nichols

and George R. Adams, eds. The American
Indian: Past and Present. Waltham,
Xerox College Publishing, 1971: 132-145.

Young, Mary Elizabeth. Redskins,
ruffleshirts and rednecks; Indian
allotments in Alabama and Mississippi,
1830-1860. Norman, University of
Oklahoma Press, 1961. 217 p. illus.

13-10   Chitimacha

Burch, M. C. The indigenous Indians of
the lower Trinity area of Texas.
Southwestern Historical Quarterly, 60
(1956): 36-52.

Bushnell, D. I. Some new ethnologic data
from Louisiana. Washington Academy of
Sciences, Journal, 12 (1922): 303-307.

Bushnell, D. I. The Chitimacha Indians of
Bayou La Fourche, Louisiana. Washington
Academy of Sciences, Journal, 7 (1917):
301-307.

Densmore, F. A search for songs among the
Chitimacha Indians in Louisiana. U.S.
Bureau of American Ethnology, Bulletin,
133 (1943): 1-16.

Du Ru, Paul. Journal of Paul Du Ru,
missionary priest to Louisiana.
Translated, with introduction and notes,
from a manuscript in the Newberry
Library, by Ruth Lapham Butler.
Chicago, Printed for the Caxton Club,
1934. 10, 74 p.

Dumont de Montigny. Mémoires historiques
sur la Louisiane, Vol. 1: 106-114.
Paris, 1753.

Ethridge, A. N. Indians of Grant Parish.
Louisiana Historical Quarterly, 23
(1940): 1108-1131.

Gatschet, A. S. Chitimacha. U.S. Bureau
of American Ethnology, Bulletin, 30,
vol. 1 (1907): 286.

Gatschet, A. S. Die Schetimascha-Indianer
im südlichen Luisiana. Ausland, 57
(1884): 581-589.

Gatschet, A. S. The Shetimasha Indians of
St. Mary's Parish. Anthropological
Society of Washington, Transactions, 2
(1883): 148-158.

Gursky, Karl-Heinz. A lexical comparison
of Atakapa, Chitimacha, and Tunica
languages. International Journal of
American Linguistics, 35 (1969): 83-107.

Haas, M. R. Natchez and Chitimacha clans
and kinship terminology. American

Anthropologist, n.s., 41 (1939): 597-610.

Haas, Mary R. Historical linguistics and the genetic relationship of languages. In Theoretical Foundations. The Hague, Mouton, 1966: 113-153. (Current Trends in Linguistics, 3)

Haas, Mary R. Tonkawa and Algonkian. Anthropological Linguistics, 1, no. 2 (1959): 1-6.

Harrington, M. R. Among Louisiana Indians. Southern Workman, 37 (1908): 656-661.

Le Page du Pratz, A. S. Histoire de la Louisiane, Vol. 1: 105-117. Paris, 1758.

Merwin, B. W. Basketry of the Chitimacha Indians. Museum Journal, 10 (1919): 29-34.

Post, Lauren C. Some notes on the Attakapas Indians of Southwest Louisiana. Louisiana History, 3 (1962): 221-242.

Stouff, Faye. Sacred Chitimacha Indian beliefs. By Faye Stouff and W. Bradley Twitty. Pompano Beach, Twitty and Twitty, 1971. 79 p.

Swadesh, M. Atakapa-Chitimacha *kw. International Journal of American Linguistics, 13 (1947): 120-121.

Swadesh, M. Chitimacha verbs of derogatory or abusive connotation. Language, 9 (1933): 192-201.

Swadesh, M. Phonologic formulas for Atakapa-Chitimacha. International Journal of American Linguistics, 12 (1946): 113-132.

Swadesh, M. Sociologic notes on obsolescent languages. International Journal of American Linguistics, 14 (1948): 226-235.

Swadesh, M. The phonetics of Chitimacha. Language, 10 (1934): 345-362.

Swanton, J. R. A structural and lexical comparison of the Tunica, Chitimacha, and Atakapa languages. U.S. Bureau of American Ethnology, Bulletin, 68 (1919): 1-56.

Swanton, J. R. Chitimacha myths and beliefs. Journal of American Folklore, 30 (1917): 474-478.

Swanton, J. R. Historic use of the spear-thrower in Southeastern North America. American Antiquity, 3 (1938): 356-358.

Swanton, J. R. Indian tribes of the Lower Mississippi Valley and adjacent coast of the Gulf of Mexico. U.S. Bureau of American Ethnology, Bulletin, 43 (1911): 337-360.

Swanton, J. R. Mythology of the Indians of Louisiana and the Texas Coast. Journal of American Folklore, 20 (1907): 285-289.

Swanton, John R. Indian tribes of the Lower Mississippi Valley and adjacent coast of the Gulf of Mexico. New York, Johnson Reprint, 1970. 7, 387 p. illus.

Toomey, T. N. Relationships of the Chitimachan linguistic family. Hervas Laboratories of American Linguistics, Bulletin, 4 (1914): 1-12.

13-11   Choctaw

Hargrett, L. A bibliography of the constitutions and laws of the American Indians, 54-77. Cambridge, 1947.

Jones, William K. General guide to documents on the Five Civilized Tribes in the University of Oklahoma Library Division of Manuscripts. Ethnohistory, 14 (1967): 47-76.

Abbott, M. Indian policy and management in the Mississippi Territory, 1798-1817. Journal of Mississippi History, 14 (1952): 153-169.

Adair, J. The history of the American Indians, 282-351. London, 1775.

Allen, Virginia R. Medical practices and health in the Choctaw Nation, 1831-1885. Chronicles of Oklahoma, 48 (1970/1971): 60-73.

Anonymous. Indians are helping themselves. Boletín Indigenista, 19 (1959): 99, 101, 103.

Ashcraft, Allan C. Confederate Indian Department conditions in August, 1864. Chronicles of Oklahoma, 41 (1963): 270-285.

Ashcraft, Allan C. Confederate Indian Territory conditions in 1865. Chronicles of Oklahoma, 42 (1964): 421-428.

Ashcraft, Allan C. Confederate Indian troop conditions in 1864. Chronicles of Oklahoma, 41 (1963): 442-449.

Badger, Herbert Andrew. A descriptive grammar of Mississippi Choctaw. Dissertation Abstracts International, 32 (1971/1972): 2663A. UM 71-28,823.

Baily, Francis. Journal of a tour in unsettled parts of North America in 1796 and 1797. Edited by Jack D. L. Holmes. Carbondale, Southern Illinois University Press, 1969. 26, 336 p. illus.

Baird, W. David. Arkansas's Choctaw boundary: a study of justice delayed. Arkansas Historical Quarterly, 28 (1969): 203-222.

Baird, W. David. Fort Smith and the Red Man. Arkansas Historical Quarterly, 30 (1971): 337-348.

Baird, W. David. Peter Pitchlynn: chief of the Choctaws. Norman, University of Oklahoma Press, 1972. 19, 238 p. illus.

Baird, W. David. Spencer Academy, Choctaw Nation, 1842-1900. Chronicles of Oklahoma, 45 (1967): 25-43.

Baird, William David. Peter Pitchlynn: Choctaw delegate. Dissertation Abstracts International, 30 (1969/1970): 1094A. UM 69-13,911.

Bartram, W. The travels of William Bartram, naturalist's edition. New Haven, 1958. 788 p.

Bartram, W. Travels through North and South Carolina. London, 1792.

Baudry des Lozières, L. H. Voyage à la Louisiane. Paris, 1802. 382 p.

Bearss, Edwin C. Fort Smith as the agency for the Western Choctaws. Arkansas Historical Quarterly, 27 (1968): 40-58.

Bearss, Edwin C. General Cooper's CSA Indians threaten Fort Smith. Arkansas Historical Quarterly, 26 (1967): 257-284.

Bearss, Edwin C. The Arkansas whiskey war: a Fort Smith case study. Journal of the West, 7 (1968): 143-172.

Bell, R. E. and D. A. Baerreis. A survey of Oklahoma archeology. Texas Archeological and Paleontological Society, Bulletin, 22 (1951): 7-100.

Benson, H. C. Life among the Choctaw Indians. Cincinnati, 1860. 314 p.

Bossu, Jean B. Travels in the interior of North America, 1751-1762. Translated and edited by Seymour Feiler. Norman,

University of Oklahoma Press, 1962. 17, 243 p. illus., maps.

Bossu, M. Nouveaux voyages aux Indes occidentales, Vol. 2: 87-106. Paris, 1768.

Bossu, M. Travels through that part of North America formerly called Louisiana, Vol. 1: 292-309. London, 1771.

Bounds, Thelma V. Children of Nanih Waiya. San Antonio, Naylor, 1964. 9, 64 p. illus.

Bounds, Thelma V. The story of the Mississippi Choctaws. Chilocco, Interior-Chilocco Press, 1958. 25 p. illus.

Boyd, David French. Journey through Southwest Arkansas, 1858. Edited by Germaine M. Reed. Arkansas Historical Quarterly, 30 (1971): 161-169.

Briceland, Alan V. Ephraim Kirby: Mr. Jefferson's emissary on the Tombigbee-Mobile frontier in 1804. Alabama Review, 24 (1971): 83-113.

Brinton, D. G. National legend of the Chahta-Muskokee tribes. Morrisania, 1870. 13 p.

Brown, C. S. Archeology of Mississippi. University, Mississippi, Mississippi Geological Survey, 1926.

Bryan, F. A Choctaw throwing club. Masterkey, 6 (1933): 178-179.

Bryant, Keith L., Jr. The Choctaw Nation in 1843: a missionary's view. Chronicles of Oklahoma, 44 (1966): 319-321.

Buckner, H. F. Burial among the Choctaws. American Antiquarian and Oriental Journal, 2 (1879): 55-58.

Buice, Sammy David. The Civil War and the Five Civilized Tribes--a study in Federal-Indian relations. Dissertation Abstracts International, 31 (1970/1971): 2815A-2816A. UM 70-23,966.

Burkhalter, Lois Wood. Gideon Lincecum 1793-1874, a biography. Austin, University of Texas Press, 1965. 9, 362 p. illus.

Busby, Orel. Buffalo Valley: an Osage hunting ground. Chronicles of Oklahoma, 40 (1962): 22-35.

Bushnell, D. I. Myths of the Louisiana Choctaw. American Anthropologist, n.s., 12 (1910): 526-535.

Bushnell, D. I.   Native cemeteries and forms of burial east of the Mississippi. U.S. Bureau of American Ethnology, Bulletin, 71 (1920): 94-101.

Bushnell, D. I.   The Choctaw of Bayou Lacomb. U.S. Bureau of American Ethnology, Bulletin, 48 (1909): 1-37.

Bushnell, D. I.   The Choctaw of St. Tammany. Louisiana Historical Quarterly, 1, no. 1 (1917): 11-20.

Byington, C.   A dictionary of the Choctaw language. U.S. Bureau of American Ethnology, Bulletin, 46 (1915): 1-611.

Byington, C.   Grammar of the Choctaw language. Ed. by D. G. Brinton. American Philosophical Society, Proceedings, 11 (1870): 317-367.

Campbell, T. N.   Choctaw subsistence. Florida Anthropologist, 12, no. 1 (1959): 9-24.

Campbell, T. N.   Medicinal plants used by Choctaw, Chickasaw and Creek Indians. Washington Academy of Sciences, Journal, 41 (1951): 285-290.

Campbell, T. N.   The Choctaw afterworld. Journal of American Folklore, 72 (1959): 146-154.

Catlin, G.   Illustrations of the manners, customs and condition of the North American Indians, Vol. 2: 122-128. New York, 1841.

Chappell, Gordon T.   John Coffee: surveyor and land agent. Alabama Review, 14 (1961): 180-195.

Choctaw Nation, Constitution.   The Constitution and laws of the Choctaw Nation. New Haven, 1970. 34 p.

Claiborne, J. F. H.   Mississippi as a province, territory, and state, 483-526. Jackson, 1880.

Collins, H. B.   Additional anthropometric observations on the Choctaw. American Journal of Physical Anthropology, 11 (1928): 353-355.

Collins, H. B.   Anthropometric observations on the Choctaw. American Journal of Physical Anthropology, 8 (1925): 425-436.

Collins, H. B.   Archeological and anthropometrical work in Mississippi. Smithsonian Miscellaneous Collections, 78, no. 1 (1927): 89-95.

Collins, H. B.   Potsherds from Choctaw village sites in Mississippi. Washington

Academy of Sciences, Journal, 17 (1927): 259-263.

Copeland, C. C.   A Choctaw tradition. American Ethnological Society, Transactions, 3, no. 1 (1853): 169-171.

Corwin, Hugh D.   Protestant missionary work among the Comanches and Kiowas. Chronicles of Oklahoma, 46 (1968): 41-57.

Cotterill, R. S.   The Southern Indians. Norman, 1954. 268 p.

Covington, James W., ed.   The Florida Seminoles in 1847. Tequesta, 24 (1964): 49-57.

Culton, Don Henry.   The early Panhandle surveys. Panhandle-Plains Historical Review, 46 (1973): 1-16.

Cushman, H. B.   History of the Choctaw, Chickasaw and Natchez Indians. Greenville, 1899. 607 p.

Cushman, Horatio B.   History of the Choctaw, Chickasaw and Natchez Indians. Edited by Angie Debo. New York, Russell and Russell, 1972. 503 p. illus.

Cushman, Horatio B.   History of the Choctaw, Chickasaw and Natchez Indians. Edited by Angie Debo. Stillwater, Okla., Redlands Press, 1962. 503 p. illus.

Dabney, Lewis M.   Faulkner, the Red, and the Black. Columbia Forum, 1, no. 2 (1972): 52-54.

De Rosier, A. H.   Cyrus Kingsbury; missionary to the Choctaws. Journal of Presbyterian History, 50 (1972): 267-287.

De Rosier, Arthur H., Jr.   The removal of the Choctaw Indians. Knoxville, University of Tennessee Press, 1970. 12, 208 p. illus., maps.

Debo, A.   And still the waters run. Princeton, 1940. 417 p.

Debo, A.   The rise and fall of the Choctaw republic. Norman, 1934. 314 p.

Debo, Angie.   The location of the Battle of Round Mountain. Chronicles of Oklahoma, 41 (1963): 70-104.

Debo, Angie.   The rise and fall of the Choctaw Republic. 2d ed. Norman, University of Oklahoma Press, 1961. 18, 314 p. illus., maps.

Densmore, F. Choctaw music. U.S. Bureau of American Ethnology, Bulletin, 136 (1943): 101-188.

Densmore, Frances. Choctaw music. New York, Da Capo Press, 1972. 101-188 p. illus.

DeRosier, Arthur H., Jr. Negotiations for the removal of the Choctaw: U.S. policies of 1820 and 1830. Chronicles of Oklahoma, 38 (1960): 85-100.

DeRosier, Arthur H., Jr. Pioneers with conflicting ideals: Christianity and slavery in the Choctaw Nation. Journal of Mississippi History, 21 (1959): 174-189.

DeRosier, Arthur H., Jr. The Choctaw removal of 1831: a civilian effort. Journal of the West, 6 (1967): 237-247.

DeRosier, Arthur H., Jr. The removal of the Choctaw Indians from Mississippi. Dissertation Abstracts, 20 (1959/1960): 1337-1338. UM 59-3489.

Donaldson, T. The George Catlin Indian Gallery. United States National Museum, Reports (1885): 212-214.

Doster, James F. Land titles and public land sales in early Alabama. Alabama Review, 16 (1963): 108-124.

Doster, James F., ed. Letters relating to the tragedy of Fort Mims: August-September, 1813. Alabama Review, 14 (1961): 269-285.

Douglas, F. H. A Choctaw pack basket. Denver Art Museum, Material Culture Notes, 4 (1937): 15-18.

Du Bose, Euba Eugenia. The history of Mount Sterling. Alabama Historical Quarterly, 25 (1963): 297-369.

Dundes, Alan. A Choctaw tongue-twister and two examples of Creek word play. International Journal of American Linguistics, 30 (1964): 194-196.

East, Dennis. New York and Mississippi Land Company and the panic of 1837. Journal of Mississippi History, 33 (1971): 299-331.

Edwards, J. The Choctaw Indians in the middle of the nineteenth century. Chronicles of Oklahoma, 10 (1932): 392-425.

Edwards, John. My escape from the South in 1861. Chronicles of Oklahoma, 43 (1965): 58-89.

Edwards, T. A. Early developments in the C and A. Chronicles of Oklahoma, 27 (1949): 148-161.

Eggan, F. Historical changes in the Choctaw kinship system. American Anthropologist, n.s., 39 (1937): 34-52.

Ethridge, A. N. Indians of Grant Parish. Louisiana Historical Quarterly, 23 (1940): 1108-1131.

Everett, Mark Allen, et al. Light-sensitive eruptions in American Indians. Archives of Dermatology, 83 (1961): 243-248.

Farrar, William G. Historic profiles of Fort Massac. By William G. and JoAnn S. Farrar. Carbondale, Southern Illinois University, University Museum, 1970. 3, 59 p. (Southern Illinois Studies, 5)

Feest, Christian F. Lukas Vischers Beiträge zur Ethnographie Nordamerikas. Archiv für Völkerkunde, 22 (1968): 31-66.

Fischer, LeRoy H. Confederate Indian forces outside of Indian Territory. By LeRoy H. Fischer and Jerry Gill. Chronicles of Oklahoma, 46 (1968): 249-284.

Ford, J. A. Analysis of Indian village site collections from Louisiana and Mississippi. Louisiana, Department of Conservation, Anthropological Studies, 2 (1936): 1-285.

Foreman, Carolyn Thomas. St. Agnes Academy for the Choctaws. Chronicles of Oklahoma, 48 (1970/1971): 323-330.

Foreman, G. Indians and pioneers. Rev. ed. Norman, 1936. 285 p.

Foreman, G. The five civilized tribes, 17-94. Norman, 1934.

Foreman, G., ed. A traveler in Indian Territory. Cedar Rapids, 1930. 270 p.

Foreman, Grant. The Five Civilized Tribes; a brief history and a century of progress. Muskogee, Okla., C. T. Foreman, 1966. 58 p. illus.

Gaines, George S. Gaine's reminiscences. Alabama Historical Quarterly, 26 (1964): 133-229.

Gatschet, A. S. A migration legend of the Creek Indians, 100-118. Philadelphia, 1884.

Gibson, A. M. An Indian Territory United Nations: the Creek Council of 1845.

Chronicles of Oklahoma, 39 (1961): 398-413.

Goggin, J. M. Louisiana Choctaw basketry. El Palacio, 46 (1939): 121-123.

Graebner, N. A. Pioneer Indian agriculture in Oklahoma. Chronicles of Oklahoma, 23 (1945): 232-248.

Graebner, N. A. Provincial Indian society in eastern Oklahoma. Chronicles of Oklahoma, 23 (1945/1946): 323-337.

Graebner, N. A. The public land policy of the five civilized tribes. Chronicles of Oklahoma, 23 (1945): 107-118.

Graham, William. Lost among the Choctaws during a tour in the Indian Territory. Chronicles of Oklahoma, 50 (1972): 226-233.

Haag, W. G. Choctaw archeology. Southeastern Archaeological Conference, News Letter, 3, no. 3 (1953): 25-28.

Haas, M. R. The Choctaw word for "rattlesnake". American Anthropologist, n.s., 43 (1941): 129-132.

Haas, Mary R. Historical linguistics and the genetic relationship of languages. In Theoretical Foundations. The Hague, Mouton, 1966: 113-153. (Current Trends in Linguistics, 3)

Halbert, H. S. A Choctaw migration legend. American Antiquarian and Oriental Journal, 16 (1894): 215-216.

Halbert, H. S. Courtship and marriage among the Choctaws. American Naturalist, 16 (1882): 222-224.

Halbert, H. S. District divisions of the Choctaw nation. Alabama Historical Society, Publications, Miscellaneous Collections, 1 (1901): 375-385.

Halbert, H. S. Funeral customs of the Mississippi Choctaws. Mississippi Historical Society, Publications, 3 (1900): 353-366.

Halbert, H. S. Nanih Waiya, the sacred mound of the Choctaws. Mississippi Historical Society, Publications, 2 (1899): 223-234.

Halbert, H. S. Okla Hannali; or the six towns district of the Choctaws. American Antiquarian and Oriental Journal, 15 (1893): 146-149.

Halbert, H. S. Pyramid and old road in Mississippi. American Antiquarian and Oriental Journal, 13 (1891): 348-349.

Halbert, H. S. The Choctaw achahpih (chungkee) game. American Antiquarian and Oriental Journal, 10 (1888): 283-284.

Halbert, H. S. The Choctaw creation legend. Mississippi Historical Society, Publications, 4 (1901): 267-270.

Halbert, H. S. The Choctaw Robin Goodfellow. American Antiquarian and Oriental Journal, 17 (1895): 157.

Hampton, James E. Pernicious anemia in American Indians. Oklahoma State Medical Association, Journal, 53 (1960): 503-509.

Hatfield, Joseph T. Governor William Charles Cole Claiborne, Indians, and outlaws in frontier Mississippi, 1801-1803. Journal of Mississippi History, 27 (1965): 323-350.

Hawkins, B. Letters, 1796-1806. Georgia Historical Society, Collections, 9 (1916): 1-500.

Haynes, Robert V. Early Washington County, Alabama. Alabama Review, 18 (1965): 183-200.

Hefley, A. D. Tobucksy County courthouse. Chronicles of Oklahoma, 48 (1970/1971): 25-38.

Hensley, J. C. My father is rich. Nashville, 1956. 214 p.

Hiemstra, W. L. Presbyterian mission schools among the Choctaws and Chickasaws, 1845-1861. Chronicles of Oklahoma, 27 (1949): 33-40.

Hill, A. A. Three examples of unexpectedly accurate Indian lore. Texas Studies in Literature and Language, 6 (1964/1965): 80-83.

Hodgson, A. Letters from North America, Vol. 1: 215-224, 240-250. London, 1824.

Holmes, Jack D. L. Alabama's forgotten settlers: notes on the Spanish Mobile District, 1780-1813. Alabama Historical Quarterly, 33 (1971): 87-97.

Holmes, Jack D. L. Fort Ferdinand of the Bluffs; life on the Spanish-American frontier, 1795-1797. West Tennessee Historical Society, Papers, 13 (1959): 38-54.

Holmes, Jack D. L. Law and order in Spanish Natchez, 1781-1798. Journal of Mississippi History, 25 (1963): 186-201.

Holmes, Jack D. L. Spanish treaties with West Florida Indians, 1784-1802. Florida

Historical Quarterly, 48 (1969/1970): 140-154.

Holmes, Jack D. L. Spanish-American rivalry over the Chickasaw Bluffs, 1780-1795. East Tennessee Historical Society's Publications, 34 (1962): 26-57.

Holmes, Jack D. L. The Choctaws in 1795. Alabama Historical Quarterly, 30 (1968): 33-49.

Holmes, Jack D. L. The Southern Boundary Commission, the Chattahoochee River, and the Florida Seminoles, 1799. Florida Historical Quarterly, 44 (1965/1966): 312-341.

Holmes, Jack D. L. Three early Memphis commandants: Beauregard, Deville Degoutin, and Folch. West Tennessee Historical Society, Papers, 18 (1964): 5-38.

Holmes, Jack D. L., tr. and ed. The first laws of Memphis: instructions for the commandant of San Fernando de las Barrancas, 1795. West Tennessee Historical Society, Papers, 15 (1961): 93-104.

Hood, Fred. Twilight of the Confederacy in Indian Territory. Chronicles of Oklahoma, 41 (1963): 425-441.

Howard, James H. The Southeastern ceremonial complex and its interpretation. Columbia, 1968. 8, 169 p. illus. (Missouri Archaeological Society, Memoir, 6)

Howard, R. Palmer. A historiography of the Five Civilized Tribes: a chronological approach. Chronicles of Oklahoma, 47 (1969): 312-331.

Howard, R. Palmer. A historiography of the Five Civilized Tribes; a chronological approach. Oklahoma City, Oklahoma Historical Society, 1969. 20 p.

Howell, Elmo. President Jackson and William Faulkner's Choctaws. Chronicles of Oklahoma, 45 (1967): 252-258.

Howell, George W. The Buttahatchie settlers. Journal of Mississippi History, 34 (1972): 57-72, 159-171, 253-260, 391-399.

Jackson, Joe C. Summer normals in Indian territory after 1898. Chronicles of Oklahoma, 37 (1959): 307-329.

Jenkins, William H. Alabama forts, 1700-1838. Alabama Review, 12 (1959): 163-180.

Jennings, J. D. Prehistory of the lower Mississippi Valley. In J. B. Griffin, ed. Archeology of Eastern United States. Chicago, 1952: 256-271.

Kansas City Star. Report on the Five Civilized Tribes 1897. Chronicles of Oklahoma, 48 (1970): 416-430.

Kenaston, Monte Ray. Sharecropping, solidarity, and social cleavage: the genesis of a Choctaw sub-community in Tennessee. Dissertation Abstracts International, 33 (1972/1973): 4088B. UM 73-6220.

Kensell, Lewis Anthony. Phases of reconstruction in the Choctaw Nation, 1865-1870. Chronicles of Oklahoma, 47 (1969): 138-153.

Knight, O. Fifty years of Choctaw law. Chronicles of Oklahoma, 31 (1953): 76-95.

Lanman, C. Adventures in the wilds of the United States and British American provinces, Vol. 2: 429-435. Philadelphia, 1856.

Lewis, A. Pushmataha, American patriot. New York, 1959. 204 p.

Lewit, Robert T. Indian missions and antislavery sentiment: a conflict of evangelical and humanitarian ideals. Mississippi Valley Historical Review, 50 (1963/1964): 39-55.

Lincecum, G. Choctaw traditions about their settlement in Mississippi and the origin of their mounds. Mississippi Historical Society, Publications, 8 (1904): 521-542.

Longacre, Robert E. Grammar discovery procedures; a field manual. The Hague, Mouton, 1964. 162 p. (Janua Linguarum, Series Minor, 33)

Marriott, A. Greener fields. New York, 1953. 274 p.

Martin, Harry W. Correlates of adjustment among American Indians in an urban environment. Human Organization, 23 (1964): 290-295.

Martin, Lawrence M. Cerumen types in Choctaw Indians. By Lawrence M. Martin and John F. Jackson. Science, 163 (1969): 677-678.

Martin, Martha Philips. Travel through Indian Country in the early 1800's; the memoirs of Martha Philips Martin. Edited by Harriet C. Owsley. Tennessee Historical Quarterly, 21 (1962): 66-81.

Martin, Novella Goodman. Choctaw little folk. San Antonio, Naylor, 1970. 10, 82 p. illus.

McAlister, Lyle N. William Augustus Bowles and the State of Muskogee. Florida Historical Quarterly, 40 (1961/1962): 317-328.

McLean, Malcolm D. Tenoxtitlan, dream capital of Texas. Southwestern Historical Quarterly, 70 (1966/1967): 23-43.

McNeil, Kinneth. Confederate treaties with the tribes of Indian Territory. Chronicles of Oklahoma, 42 (1964): 408-420.

McWilliams, Richebourg Gaillard. Iberville and the Southern Indians. Alabama Review, 20 (1967): 243-262.

Milford, L. L. de. Mémoire ou coup-d'oeil rapide sur les différens voyages et mon séjour dans la nation Crëck, 288-317. Paris, 1802.

Miner, Craig. The struggle for an East-West railway into the Indian Territory, 1870-1882. Chronicles of Oklahoma, 47 (1969): 560-581.

Morgan, L. H. Systems of consanguinity and affinity. Smithsonian Contributions to Knowledge, 17 (1871): 291-382.

Morris, Cheryl H. Choctaw and Chickasaw Indian agents, 1831-1874. Chronicles of Oklahoma, 50 (1972): 415-436.

Morris, Wayne. Traders and factories on the Arkansas frontier, 1805-1822. Arkansas Historical Quarterly, 28 (1969): 28-48.

Morrison, J. D. News for the Choctaws. Chronicles of Oklahoma, 27 (1949): 207-222.

Morrison, J. D. Problems in the industrial progress and development of the Choctaw nation. Chronicles of Oklahoma, 32 (1954): 70-91.

Morrison, James D. Notes on abolitionism in the Choctaw nation. Chronicles of Oklahoma, 38 (1960): 78-84.

New, Lloyd. Institute of American Indian Arts. Arizona Highways, 48, no. 1 (1972): 5, 12-15, 44-45.

Nuttall, T. A journal of travels into the Arkansa Territory. Philadelphia, 1821. 296 p.

Nuttall, Thomas. A journal of travels into the Arkansa Territory. Ann Arbor,

University Microfilms, 1966. 12, 296 p. illus., map.

Olson, Gary D. Thomas Brown, Loyalist partisan, and the Revolutionary War in Georgia, 1777-1782. Georgia Historical Quarterly, 54 (1970): 1-19, 183-208.

Osborn, G. C. Relations with the Indians in West Florida during the administration of Governor Peter Chester, 1770-1781. Florida Historical Quarterly, 31 (1953): 239-272.

Peake, G. Ronald. Oklahoma's "five tribes" Indians are improving their living conditions through public housing. Journal of Housing, 28 (1971): 430-432.

Peterson, John H. Community background reports: the Mississippi Choctaws and their educational program. By John H. Peterson and James R. Richburg. Chicago, University of Chicago, 1970. 46 p. (National Study of American Indian Education, Series I, 21, Final Report) ERIC ED042553.

Peterson, John H., Jr. Assimilation, separation, and out-migration in an American Indian group. American Anthropologist, 74 (1972): 1286-1295.

Peterson, John H., Jr. Socio-economic characteristics of the Mississippi Choctaw Indians. State College, 1970. 31 p. maps. (Mississippi, State University, Research Coordinating Unit for Vocational-Technical Education, Report, 34) ERIC ED050869.

Peterson, John Holbrook, Jr. The Mississippi Band of Choctaw Indians: their recent history and current social relations. Dissertation Abstracts International, 31 (1970/1971): 6394B. UM 71-13,106.

Petitot, E. F. S. Six légendes américaines. Missions Catholiques (Lyon), 11 (1879): 21-22, 32-35, 45-48.

Phelps, D. A. The Choctaw mission. Journal of Mississippi History, 14 (1952): 35-62.

Phelps, Dawson A. The Natchez Trace; Indian trail to parkway. Tennessee Historical Quarterly, 21 (1962): 203-218.

Pickett, A. J. History of Alabama, Vol. 1: 134-146. Charleston, 1851.

Pickett, Ben Collins. William L. McClellan, Choctaw Agent, West. Chronicles of Oklahoma, 39 (1961): 42-53.

Plaisance, A. The Choctaw trading house--
  1803-1822. Alabama Historical Quarterly,
  16 (1954): 393-423.

Potter, E. An account of several nations
  of Southern Indians. Massachusetts
  Historical Society, Collections, ser. 1,
  10 (1809): 119-121.

Rainwater, Percy L. Conquistadors,
  missionaries, and missions. Journal of
  Mississippi History, 27 (1965): 123-147.

Rainwater, Percy L. Indian missions and
  missionaries. Journal of Mississippi
  History, 28 (1966): 15-39.

Rea, Robert R. The trouble at Tombeckby.
  Alabama Review, 21 (1968): 21-39.

Read, W. A. Louisiana place names of
  Indian origin. Louisiana State
  University, Bulletin, 19 (1927): 1-72.

Read, W. A. Notes on an Opelousas
  manuscript of 1862. American
  Anthropologist, n.s., 42 (1940): 546-
  548.

Ridaught, H. G. Hell's branch office.
  Citra, Florida, 1957. 240 p.

Romans, B. A concise natural history of
  East and West Florida, 59-71. New York,
  1775.

Roper, James. Fort Adams and Fort
  Pickering. West Tennessee Historical
  Society, Papers, 24 (1970): 5-29.

Roper, James. The founding of Memphis;
  August, 1818, through December, 1820.
  West Tennessee Historical Society,
  Papers, 23 (1969): 5-29.

Roper, James E. Marcus B. Winchester,
  first mayor of Memphis; his later years.
  West Tennessee Historical Society,
  Papers, 13 (1959): 5-37.

Shafer, Harry J. An evaluation of the
  Natchez occupation at the Fatherland
  Site. Journal of Mississippi History, 34
  (1972): 215-235.

Smith, Winston. Early history of
  Demopolis. Alabama Review, 18 (1965):
  83-91.

Smyth, J. F. D. A tour in the United
  States of America, Vol. 2: 7. London,
  1784.

Sonderegger, Richard Paul. The Southern
  Frontier from the founding of Georgia to
  the ending of King George's War.
  Dissertation Abstracts, 25 (1964/1965):
  3546. UM 64-12,688.

Sosin, Jack M. The use of Indians in the
  War of the American Revolution: a re-
  assessment of responsibility. Canadian
  Historical Review, 46 (1965): 101-121.

Spalding, Arminta Scott. From the Natchez
  Trace to Oklahoma: development of
  Christian civilization among the
  Choctaws, 1800-1860. Chronicles of
  Oklahoma, 45 (1967): 2-24.

Speck, F. G. and C. E. Schaeffer. The
  deer and the rabbit hunting drive in
  Virginia and the Southeast. Southern
  Indian Studies, 2 (1950): 3-20.

Spence, L. Choctaws. In J. Hastings, ed.
  Encyclopaedia of Religion and Ethics.
  Vol. 3. New York, 1911: 567-569.

Spoehr, A. Changing kinship systems.
  Field Museum, Anthropological Series, 33
  (1947): 153-235.

Stewart, Martha. The Indian Mission
  Conference of Oklahoma. Chronicles of
  Oklahoma, 40 (1962): 330-336.

Stockham, Richard J. The misunderstood
  Lorenzo Dow. Alabama Review, 16 (1963):
  20-34.

Stuart, J. A sketch of the Cherokee and
  Choctaw Indians. Little Rock, 1837.
  42 p.

Swanton, J. R. An early account of the
  Choctaw Indians. American
  Anthropological Association, Memoirs, 5
  (1918): 53-72.

*Swanton, J. R. Source material for the
  social and ceremonial life of the
  Choctaw Indians. U.S. Bureau of American
  Ethnology, Bulletin, 103 (1931): 1-282.

Swanton, J. R. and C. Thomas. Choctaw.
  U.S. Bureau of American Ethnology,
  Bulletin, 30, vol. 1 (1907): 288-289.

Taylor, L. A. Plants used as curatives by
  certain Southeastern tribes. Cambridge,
  1940. 88 p.

Thomas, Daniel H. Fort Toulouse; the
  French outpost at the Alibamos on the
  Coosa. Alabama Historical Quarterly, 22
  (1960): 137-230.

Thomas, Daniel H. Fort Toulouse--in
  tradition and fact. Alabama Review, 13
  (1960): 243-257.

Tolbert, Charles Madden. A sociological
  study of the Choctaw Indians of
  Mississippi. Dissertation Abstracts, 19
  (1958/1959): 597. UM 58-2856.

Villiers du Terrage, M. de. Documents concernant l'histoire des Indiens de la région orientale de la Louisiane. Société des Américanistes, Journal, n.s., 14 (1904): 397-426.

Villiers du Terrage, M. de. Notes sur les Chactas. Société des Américanistes, Journal, n.s., 15 (1923): 223-250.

Wade, J. W. The removal of the Mississippi Choctaws. Mississippi Historical Society, Publications, 8 (1904): 397-426.

Walker, B. N. O. Mon-dah-min and the Red Man's uses of corn as food. Chronicles of Oklahoma, 35 (1957): 194-203.

Wallace, Katherine T. Notes and documents; Elk County, Alabama. Alabama Review, 19 (1966): 227-233.

Watkins, J. A. A contribution to Chacta history. American Antiquarian and Oriental Journal, 16 (1894): 257-265.

Watkins, J. A. The Choctaws in Mississippi. American Antiquarian and Oriental Journal, 16 (1894): 69-77.

West, Ruth Tenison. Pushmataha's travels. Chronicles of Oklahoma, 37 (1959): 162-174.

White, Lonnie J. Arkansas territorial Indian affairs. Arkansas Historical Quarterly, 21 (1962): 193-212.

White, Lonnie J. The election of 1827 and the Conway-Crittenden duel. Arkansas Historical Quarterly, 19 (1960): 293-313.

Willis, W. S. The nation of bread. Ethnohistory, 4 (1957): 125-149.

Winfrey, Dorman H., ed. The Indian papers of Texas and the Southwest, 1825-1916. Edited by Dorman H. Winfrey and James M. Day. Austin, Pemberton Press, 1966. 412 p.

Wood, George W. Report of Mr. Wood's visit to the Choctaw and Cherokee missions. 1855. Boston, Press of T. R. Marvin, 1855. 24 p.

Wright, A. Choctaws. Missionary Herald, 25 (1828): 182-183.

Wright, Bessie L., ed. Diary of a member of the first mule pack train to leave Fort Smith for California in 1849. Panhandle-Plains Historical Review, 42 (1969): 61-119.

Wright, J. B. Ranching in the Choctaw and Chickasaw nations. Chronicles of Oklahoma, 37 (1959): 294-300.

Wright, M. H. American Indian corn dishes. Chronicles of Oklahoma, 36 (1958): 155-166.

Wright, M. H. and G. H. Shirk. Artist Möllhausen in Oklahoma, 1853. Chronicles of Oklahoma, 31 (1953): 392-441.

Wright, Muriel H. Colonel Cooper's Civil War report on the Battle of Round Mountain. Chronicles of Oklahoma, 39 (1961): 352-397.

Wright, Muriel H. Lee F. Harkins, Choctaw. Chronicles of Oklahoma, 37 (1959): 285-287.

Wright, Muriel H. Seals of the Five Civilized Tribes. Chronicles of Oklahoma, 40 (1962): 214-218.

Young, F. B. Notices of the Chactaw or Choktah Tribe. Edinburgh Journal of Natural and Geographical Science, 2 (1830): 13-17.

Young, Mary E. Indian removal and land allotment: the civilized tribes and Jacksonian justice. In Roger L. Nichols and George R. Adams, eds. The American Indian: Past and Present. Waltham, Xerox College Publishing, 1971: 132-145.

Young, Mary Elizabeth. Redskins, ruffleshirts and rednecks; Indian allotments in Alabama and Mississippi, 1830-1860. Norman, University of Oklahoma Press, 1961. 217 p. illus.

13-12   Creek

Hargrett, L. A bibliography of the constitutions and laws of the American Indians, 78-90. Cambridge, 1947.

Jones, William K. General guide to documents on the Five Civilized Tribes in the University of Oklahoma Library Division of Manuscripts. Ethnohistory, 14 (1967): 47-76.

Adair, J. The history of the American Indians, 257-281. London, 1775.

Anders, Ferdinand. Lukas Vischer (1780-1840): Künstler-Reisender-Sammler. By Ferdinand Anders, Margarete Pfister-Burkhalter, and Christian F. Feest. Hannover, Münstermann-Druck, 1967. 9, 257 p. illus. (Völkerkundliche Abhandlungen, 2)

Anonymous. Coweta Indian mound. Alabama Historical Quarterly, 21 (1959): 95.

Anonymous. Creeks. U.S. Bureau of American Ethnology, Bulletin, 30, vol. 1 (1907): 362-365.

Anonymous. Moffett's Mill. Alabama Historical Quarterly, 21 (1959): 84.

Anonymous. The pole cat, or shell dance. Southern Literary Messenger, 3 (1837): 390-391.

Anonymous. Wetumca council house. Alabama Historical Quarterly, 21 (1959): 106-108.

Anonymous. William McIntosh, Creek chief. Alabama Historical Quarterly, 21 (1959): 73-75.

Ashcraft, Allan C. Confederate Indian Department conditions in August, 1864. Chronicles of Oklahoma, 41 (1963): 270-285.

Ashcraft, Allan C. Confederate Indian troop conditions in 1864. Chronicles of Oklahoma, 41 (1963): 442-449.

Ashley, M. E. A Creek site in Georgia. Indian Notes, 4 (1927): 221-226.

Asplin, Ray. A history of Council Grove in Oklahoma. Chronicles of Cklahoma, 45 (1967): 433-450.

Bailey, Minnie Elizabeth Thomas. Reconstruction in Indian Territory, 1865-1877. Dissertation Abstracts, 29 (1968/1969): 198A. UM 68-8362.

Baily, Francis. Journal of a tour in unsettled parts of North America in 1796 and 1797. Edited by Jack D. L. Holmes. Carbondale, Southern Illinois University Press, 1969. 26, 336 p. illus.

Balman, Gail. The Creek Treaty of 1866. Chronicles of Cklahoma, 48 (1970/1971): 184-196.

Banks, Dean. Civil-War refugees from Indian Territory, in the North, 1861-1864. Chronicles of Cklahoma, 41 (1963): 286-298.

Bareis, C. Two historic Indian burials from Pittsburg County, Oklahoma. Chronicles of Cklahoma, 29 (1951): 408-414.

Barnett, Leona G. Este cate emunkv--"Red man always". Chronicles of Oklahoma, 46 (1968): 20-40.

Barton, B. S. New views of the origin of the tribes and nations of America. 2d ed. Philadelphia, 1798.

Bartram, W. Observations on the Creek and Cherokee Indians. American Ethnological Society, Transactions, 3 (1853): 1-81.

Bartram, W. The travels of William Bartram, naturalist's edition. New Haven, 1958. 788 p.

Bartram, W. Travels in Georgia and Florida, 1773-1774. Ed. by F. Harper. American Philosophical Society, Transactions, n.s., 33 (1943): 126, 172-209, 225.

Bartram, W. Travels through North and South Carolina. London, 1792.

Bass, Althea L. The story of Tullahassee. Oklahoma City, Semco Color Press, 1960. 271 p. illus.

Baynton, Benjamin. Authentic memoirs of William Augustus Bowles. New York, Arno Press, 1971. 6, 79 p.

Bearss, Edwin C. The Civil War comes to Indian Territory, 1861: the flight of Opothleyoholo. Journal of the West, 11 (1972): 9-42.

Beauchamp, Green. Early chronicles of Barbour County. Alabama Historical Quarterly, 33 (1971): 37-74.

Bell, R. E. and D. A. Baerreis. A survey of Oklahoma archeology. Texas Archeological and Paleontological Society, Bulletin, 22 (1951): 7-100.

Benson, Henry C. Life among the Choctaw Indians and sketches of the South-west. New York, Johnson Reprint, 1970. 314 p.

Bittle, George C. Richard Keith Call's 1836 campaign. Tequesta, 29 (1969): 67-72.

Blackmar, A. C. Reference to last residence of Gen. McIntosh. Alabama Historical Quarterly, 21 (1959): 76.

Boas, F. Zur Anthropologie der nordamerikanischen Indianer. Berliner Gesellschaft für Anthropologie, Ethnologie und Urgeschichte, Verhandlungen (1895): 367-411.

Bolster, M. H. "The Smoked Meat Rebellion". Chronicles of Oklahoma, 31 (1953): 37-55.

Boniol, John Dawson, Jr. The Walton Road. Tennessee Historical Quarterly, 30 (1971): 402-412.

200   13   SOUTHEAST

Bonner, J. C. Tustunugee Hutkee and Creek factionalism on the Georgia-Alabama Frontier. Anthropological Records, 10 (1957): 111-125.

Bonner, James C. Chattahoochee old town: a footnote in historiography. Georgia Historical Quarterly, 51 (1967): 443-448.

Bonner, James C. Journal of a mission to Georgia in 1827. Georgia Historical Quarterly, 44 (1960): 74-85.

Boyd, M. F. Historic sites in and around the Jim Woodruff Reservoir area, Florida-Georgia. U.S. Bureau of American Ethnology, Bulletin, 169 (1958): 195-314.

Boyd, M. F. and J. Navarro Latorne. Spanish interest in British Florida. Florida Historical Quarterly, 32 (1953): 92-130.

Brannon, P. A. Creek Indian War, 1836-37. Alabama Historical Quarterly, 13 (1951): 156-158.

Brannon, P. A. The dress of the early Indians of Alabama. Arrow Points, 5, no. 5 (1922): 84-92.

Brannon, Peter A. Russell County place names. Alabama Historical Quarterly, 21 (1959): 96-103.

Brantley, William A., Jr. Battle of Horseshoe Bend in Tallapoosa County, Alabama, March 27, 1814. Birmingham, Southern University Press, 1969. 19, 4 p. illus.

Brearley, David. Fort Mitchell in the Indian uprising of 1818: David Brearley to Andrew Jackson. Alabama Historical Quarterly, 21 (1959): 10.

Briceland, Alan V. Ephraim Kirby: Mr. Jefferson's emissary on the Tombigbee-Mobile frontier in 1804. Alabama Review, 24 (1971): 83-113.

Brinton, D. G. Contributions to a grammar of the Muskokee language. American Philosophical Society, Proceedings, 11 (1870): 301-309.

Brinton, D. G. National legend of the Chahta-Muskokee tribes. Morrisania, 1870. 13 p.

Brinton, D. G. The national legends of the Chahta-Muskokee tribes. Historical Magazine, ser. 2, 7 (1870): 118-126.

Buckner, H. F. and G. Herrod. A grammar of the Maskoke or Creek language. Marion, 1860. 138 p.

Buice, Sammy David. The Civil War and the Five Civilized Tribes--a study in Federal-Indian relations. Dissertation Abstracts International, 31 (1970/1971): 2815A-2816A. UM 70-23,966.

Bullen, R. P. An archaeological survey of the Chattahoochee River Valley in Florida. Washington Academy of Sciences, Journal, 50 (1950): 100-125.

Burckhard, Johann Christian. Partners in the Lord's work; the diary of two Moravian missionaries in the Creek Indian country, 1807-1913. Atlanta, 1969. 3, 77 p. illus., map. (Georgia, State College, Atlanta, School of Arts and Sciences, Research Papers, 21)

Bushnell, D. I. An account of Lamhatty. American Anthropologist, n.s., 10 (1908): 568-574.

Bushnell, D. I. Native cemeteries and forms of burial east of the Mississippi. U.S. Bureau of American Ethnology, Bulletin, 71 (1920): 110-114.

Campbell, J. B. Campbell's abstract of Creek Indian census cards and index. Muskogee, Oklahoma, 1915.

Campbell, T. N. Medicinal plants used by Choctaw, Chickasaw and Creek Indians. Washington Academy of Sciences, Journal, 41 (1951): 285-290.

Caughey, J. W. McGillivray of the Creeks. Norman, 1938. 385 p.

Chalker, Russel M. Pioneer days along the Ocmulgee. Carrollton, Ga., author, 1970. 12, 251 p.

Chamberlain, A. F. Busk. U.S. Bureau of American Ethnology, Bulletin, 30, vol. 1 (1907): 176-178.

Chambers, Nella J. The Creek Indian factory at Fort Mitchell. Alabama Historical Quarterly, 21 (1959): 15-53.

Chambers, Nella Jean. Early days in East Alabama. Alabama Review, 13 (1960): 177-184.

Chappell, Gordon T. John Coffee: surveyor and land agent. Alabama Review, 14 (1961): 180-195.

Coleman, K. Federal Indian relations in the South, 1781-1789. Chronicles of Oklahoma, 25 (1947): 435-458.

Connelly, Thomas Lawrence. Indian warfare on the Tennessee frontier, 1776-1794: strategy and tactics. East Tennessee Historical Society's Publications, 36 (1964): 3-22.

Corbitt, D. C. Exploring the Southwest Territory in the Spanish Records. East Tennessee Historical Society's Publications, 38 (1966): 109-118.

Corbitt, D. C., tr. and ed. Papers from the Spanish archives relating to Tennessee and the Old Southwest. Translated and edited by D. C. Corbitt and Roberta Corbitt. East Tennessee Historical Society, Publications, 31 (1959): 63-82; 32 (1960): 72-93; 33 (1961): 61-78; 34 (1962): 86-105; 35 (1963): 85-95; 36 (1964): 70-80; 37 (1965): 89-105; 38 (1966): 70-82; 39 (1967): 87-102; 40 (1968): 101-118; 41 (1969): 100-116; 42 (1970): 96-107; 43 (1971): 94-111; 44 (1972): 104-113.

Corkran, David H. The Creek frontier, 1540-1783. Norman, University of Oklahoma Press, 1967. 15, 343 p. illus., maps.

Corry, J. P. Indian affairs in Georgia, 1732-1756. Philadelphia, 1936. 197 p.

Cotterill, R. S. The Southern Indians. Norman, 1954. 268 p.

Coulter, E. Merton. Madison Springs, Georgia watering place. Georgia Historical Quarterly, 47 (1963): 375-407.

Coulter, E. Merton. The Chehaw affair. Georgia Historical Quarterly, 49 (1965): 269-395.

Covington, James. English gifts to the Indians: 1765-1766. Florida Anthropologist, 13 (1960): 71-75.

Covington, James W. An episode in the Third Seminole War. Florida Historical Quarterly, 45 (1966/1967): 45-59.

Covington, James W. Federal relations with the Apalachicola Indians: 1823-1838. Florida Historical Quarterly, 42 (1963/1964): 125-141.

Covington, James W., ed. The Florida Seminoles in 1847. Tequesta, 24 (1964): 49-57.

Creek Nation, Laws, Statutes, etc. Laws of the Creek Nation. Edited by Antonio J. Waring, Jr. Athens, University of Georgia Press, 1960. 7, 27 p. (Georgia, University, Libraries, Miscellanea Publication, 1)

Crockett, David. Vie et mémoires authentiques. Paris, Club Français du Livre, 1961. 208 p. illus.

De Vorsey, Louis, Jr. Indian boundaries in Colonial Georgia. Georgia Historical Quarterly, 54 (1970): 63-78.

Debo, A. And still the waters run. Princeton, 1940. 417 p.

Debo, A. The road to disappearance. Norman, 1941. 399 p.

Debo, Angie. The location of the Battle of Round Mountain. Chronicles of Oklahoma, 41 (1963): 70-104.

DeJarnette, D. L. and A. T. Hansen. The archeology of the Childersburg Site, Alabama. Florida, State University, Department of Anthropology, Notes in Anthropology, 4 (1960): 1-65.

Doster, James F. Early settlements on the Tombigbee and Tensaw Rivers. Alabama Review, 12 (1959): 83-94.

Doster, James F. Land titles and public land sales in early Alabama. Alabama Review, 16 (1963): 108-124.

Doster, James F., ed. Letters relating to the tragedy of Fort Mims: August-September, 1813. Alabama Review, 14 (1961): 269-285.

Douglas, F. H. Three Creek baskets. Denver Art Museum, Material Culture Notes, 15 (1941): 66-69.

Dundes, Alan. A Choctaw tongue-twister and two examples of Creek word play. International Journal of American Linguistics, 30 (1964): 194-196.

Durham, Walter T. Kasper Mansker: Cumberland frontiersman. Tennessee Historical Quarterly, 30 (1971): 154-177.

Eakins, D. W. Some information respecting the Creeks. In H. R. Schoolcraft, ed. Information respecting the History, Condition, and Prospects of the Indian Tribes of the United States. Vol. 1. Philadelphia, 1851: 265-283.

Eggleston, G. C. Red Eagle and the wars with the Creek Indians of Alabama. New York, 1878. 346 p.

Everett, Mark Allen, et al. Light-sensitive eruptions in American Indians. Archives of Dermatology, 83 (1961): 243-248.

Fairbanks, C. H. Archeology of the funeral mound, Ocmulgee National Monument, Georgia. Washington, D.C., 1956.

Fairbanks, C. H. Creek and pre-Creek. In
J. B. Griffin, ed. Archeology of Eastern
United States. Chicago, 1952: 285-300.

Fairbanks, C. H. Some problems of the
origin of Creek pottery. Florida
Anthropologist, 11 (1958): 53-64.

Fairbanks, C. H. The protohistoric Creek
of Georgia. Southeastern Archaeological
Conference, News Letter, 3, no. 3
(1953): 21-22.

Fairbanks, Charles H. Excavations at
Horseshoe Bend, Alabama. Florida
Anthropologist, 15 (1962): 41-56.

Feest, Christian F. Lukas Vischers
Beiträge zur Ethnographie Nordamerikas.
Archiv für Völkerkunde, 22 (1968): 31-
66.

Fife, Sharon A. Baptist Indian church:
Thlewarle Mekko Sapkv Coko. Chronicles
of Oklahoma, 48 (1970/1971): 450-466.

Fink, Paul M. Jacob Brown of Nolichucky.
Tennessee Historical Quarterly, 21
(1962): 235-250.

Fischer, LeRoy H. Confederate Indian
forces outside of Indian Territory. By
LeRoy H. Fischer and Jerry Gill.
Chronicles of Oklahoma, 46 (1968): 249-
284.

Fleming, J. The Maskoke Semahayeta.
Union, 1836. 54 p.

Floyd, John. John Floyd at Fort Mitchell.
Alabama Historical Quarterly, 21 (1959):
11-13.

Foreman, Carolyn Thomas. Lee Compere and
the Creek Indians. Chronicles of
Oklahoma, 42 (1964): 291-299.

Foreman, Carolyn Thomas. The White
lieutenant and some of his
contemporaries. Chronicles of Oklahoma,
38 (1960): 425-440.

Foreman, Carolyn Thomas. The Yuchi:
children of the sun. Chronicles of
Oklahoma, 37 (1959): 480-496.

Foreman, G. The five civilized tribes,
147-219. Norman, 1934.

Foreman, G., ed. A traveler in Indian
Territory. Cedar Rapids, 1930. 270 p.

Foreman, Grant. The Five Civilized
Tribes; a brief history and a century of
progress. Muskogee, Okla., C. T.
Foreman, 1966. 58 p. illus.

Gaines, George S. Gaine's reminiscences.
Alabama Historical Quarterly, 26 (1964):
133-229.

Garvin, Russell. The free Negro in
Florida before the Civil War. Florida
Historical Quarterly, 46 (1967/1968): 1-
18.

Gatschet, A. S. A migration legend of the
Creek Indians. Philadelphia, 1884.
251 p.

Gatschet, A. S. Adjectives of color in
Indian languages. American Naturalist,
13 (1879): 475-485.

Gatschet, A. S. La langue maskŏki et ses
dialèctes. International Congress of
Americanists, Proceedings, 3, vol. 2
(1880): 742-758.

Gatschet, A. S. Tchikilli's Kasi'hta
legend in the Creek and Hitchiti
languages. Academy of Science of St.
Louis, Transactions, 5 (1888): 33-239.

Gatschet, A. S. Towns and villages of the
Creek Confederacy. Alabama Historical
Society, Publications, Miscellaneous
Collections, 1 (1901): 386-415.

Gatschet, Albert S. A migration legend of
the Creek Indians, with a linguistic,
historic, and ethnographic introduction.
Vol. 1. New York, AMS Press, 1969.
251 p.

Gibson, A. M. An Indian Territory United
Nations: the Creek Council of 1845.
Chronicles of Oklahoma, 39 (1961): 398-
413.

Gold, Robert L. The East Florida Indians
under Spanish and English control: 1763-
1765. Florida Historical Quarterly, 44
(1965/1966): 105-120.

Graebner, N. A. Pioneer Indian
agriculture in Oklahoma. Chronicles of
Oklahoma, 23 (1945): 232-248.

Graebner, N. A. The public land policy of
the five civilized tribes. Chronicles of
Oklahoma, 23 (1945): 107-118.

Griffin, William B. Spanish Pensacola,
1700-1763. Florida Historical Quarterly,
37 (1958/1959): 242-262.

Griffith, Lucille. South Carolina and
Fort Alabama, 1714-1763. Alabama Review,
12 (1959): 258-271.

Haas, M. R. A popular etymology in
Muskogee. Language, 17 (1941): 340-341.

Haas, M. R. Ablaut and its function in
Muskogee. Language, 16 (1940): 141-150.

Haas, M. R. Classificatory verbs in Muskogee. International Journal of American Linguistics, 14 (1948): 244-246.

Haas, M. R. Creek inter-town relations. American Anthropologist, n.s., 42 (1940): 479-489.

Haas, M. R. Dialects of the Muskogee language. International Journal of American Linguistics, 11 (1945): 69-74.

Haas, M. R. Geminate consonant clusters in Muskogee. Language, 14 (1938): 61-65.

Haas, M. R. Natchez and Chitimacha clans and kinship terminology. American Anthropologist, n.s., 41 (1939): 597-610.

Haas, M. R. Natchez and the Muskogean languages. Language, 32 (1956): 61-72.

Haas, M. R. On the historical development of certain long vowels in Creek. International Journal of American Linguistics, 16 (1950): 122-125.

Haas, Mary R. Historical linguistics and the genetic relationship of languages. In Theoretical Foundations. The Hague, Mouton, 1966: 113-153. (Current Trends in Linguistics, 3)

Haas, Mary R. The expression of the diminutive. In M. Estellie Smith, ed. Studies in Linguistics in Honor of George L. Trager. The Hague, Mouton, 1972: 148-152. (Janua Linguarum, Series Maior, 52)

Haekel, J. Mannerhäuser und Festplatzanlagen in Ozeanien und im östlichen Nordamerika. Baessler-Archiv, 23 (1940): 8-18.

Hagy, James William, ed. The lost archives of the Cherokee Nation. Edited by James William Hagy and Stanley J. Folmsbee. East Tennessee Historical Society, Publications, 43 (1971): 112-122; 44 (1972): 114-125.

Halbert, H. S. and T. H. Ball. The Creek War of 1813 and 1814. Chicago, 1895. 331 p.

Halbert, Henry S. The Creek War of 1813 and 1814. By H. S. Halbert and T. H. Ball. Edited by Frank L. Owsley, Jr. University, University of Alabama Press, 1969. 57, 331 p. illus., maps. (Southern Historical Publications, 15)

Hall, A. H. The Red Stick War. Chronicles of Oklahoma, 12 (1934): 264-293.

Hampton, James E. Pernicious anemia in American Indians. Oklahoma State Medical Association, Journal, 53 (1960): 503-509.

Harris, W. A. Here the Creeks sat down. Macon, 1958. 166 p.

Hatfield, Joseph T. Governor William Charles Cole Claiborne, Indians, and outlaws in frontier Mississippi, 1801-1803. Journal of Mississippi History, 27 (1965): 323-350.

Hatton, William. Some short remarkes on the Indian trade in the Charikees and in managment thereof since the year 1717. Edited by Rena Vassar. Ethnohistory, 8 (1961): 401-423.

Hawes, Lilla Mills, ed. The frontiers of Georgia in the late eighteenth century: Jonas Fauche to Joseph Vallance Bevan. Georgia Historical Quarterly, 47 (1963): 84-95.

Hawkins, B. H. A sketch of the Creek country. Georgia Historical Society, Collections, 3, no. 1 (1848): 19-85.

Hawkins, B. H. Letters. Georgia Historical Society, Collections, 9 (1916): 1-500.

Haynes, Robert V. Early Washington County, Alabama. Alabama Review, 18 (1965): 183-200.

Heath, Gary N. The first federal invasion of Indian Territory. Chronicles of Oklahoma, 44 (1966/1967): 409-419.

Hemperley, Marion R. Benjamin Hawkins' trip through Alabama, 1796. Alabama Historical Quarterly, 31 (1969): 207-240.

Hemperley, Marion R., ed. Benjamin Hawkins' trip across Georgia in 1796. Georgia Historical Quarterly, 55 (1971): 114-137.

Hemperley, Marion R., ed. Benjamin Hawkins' trip across western and northern Georgia, 1798. Georgia Historical Quarterly, 56 (1972): 415-431.

Henslick, Harry. The Seminole Treaty of 1866. Chronicles of Oklahoma, 48 (1970/1971): 280-294.

Hewitt, J. N. B. Notes on the Creek Indians. Ed. by J. R. Swanton. U.S. Bureau of American Ethnology, Bulletin, 123 (1939): 119-159.

Hodges, Bert.   Notes on the history of the Creek nation and some of its leaders. Chronicles of Oklahoma, 43 (1965): 9-18.

Hodgson, A.   Letters from North America, Vol. 1: 117-136.   London, 1824.

Hodgson, W. B.   The Creek Confederacy. Georgia Historical Society, Collections, 3, no. 1 (1848): 13-18.

Holland, James W.   Andrew Jackson and the Creek War.   University, University of Alabama Press, 1968.   47 p.   illus., maps.

Holland, James W.   Andrew Jackson and the Creek War: victory at the Horseshoe. Alabama Review, 21 (1968): 243-275.

Holmes, Jack D. L.   Alabama's forgotten settlers: notes on the Spanish Mobile District, 1780-1813. Alabama Historical Quarterly, 33 (1971): 87-97.

Holmes, Jack D. L.   Fort Ferdinand of the Bluffs; life on the Spanish-American frontier, 1795-1797. West Tennessee Historical Society, Papers, 13 (1959): 38-54.

Holmes, Jack D. L.   Law and order in Spanish Natchez, 1781-1798. Journal of Mississippi History, 25 (1963): 186-201.

Holmes, Jack D. L.   Spanish treaties with West Florida Indians, 1784-1802. Florida Historical Quarterly, 48 (1969/1970): 140-154.

Holmes, Jack D. L.   Spanish-American rivalry over the Chickasaw Bluffs, 1780-1795. East Tennessee Historical Society's Publications, 34 (1962): 26-57.

Holmes, Jack D. L.   The ebb-tide of Spanish military power on the Mississippi: Fort San Fernando de las Barrancas, 1795-1798. East Tennessee Historical Society's Publications, 36 (1964): 23-44.

Holmes, Jack D. L.   The Southern Boundary Commission, the Chattahoochee River, and the Florida Seminoles, 1799. Florida Historical Quarterly, 44 (1965/1966): 312-341.

Holmes, Jack D. L.   Three early Memphis commandants: Beauregard, Deville Degoutin, and Folch. West Tennessee Historical Society, Papers, 18 (1964): 5-38.

Holmes, Jack D. L., ed.   Fort Stoddard in 1799: seven letters of Captain Bartholomew Schaumburgh. Alabama Historical Quarterly, 26 (1964): 231-252.

Holway, Hope.   Ann Eliza Worcester Robertson as a linguist. Chronicles of Oklahoma, 37 (1959): 35-44.

Holway, Hope.   Union Mission, 1826-1837. Chronicles of Oklahoma, 40 (1962): 355-378.

Hood, Fred.   Twilight of the Confederacy in Indian Territory. Chronicles of Oklahoma, 41 (1963): 425-441.

Howard, James H.   The Southeastern ceremonial complex and its interpretation.   Columbia, 1968.   8, 169 p.   illus.   (Missouri Archaeological Society, Memoir, 6)

Howard, R. Palmer.   A historiography of the Five Civilized Tribes: a chronological approach. Chronicles of Oklahoma, 47 (1969): 312-331.

Howard, R. Palmer.   A historiography of the Five Civilized Tribes; a chronological approach.   Oklahoma City, Oklahoma Historical Society, 1969. 20 p.

Hryniewicki, Richard J.   The Creek Treaty of November 15, 1827. Georgia Historical Quarterly, 52 (1968): 1-15.

Hryniewicki, Richard J.   The Creek Treaty of Washington, 1826. Georgia Historical Quarterly, 48 (1964): 425-441.

Ivers, Larry E.   The battle of Fort Mosa. Georgia Historical Quarterly, 51 (1967): 135-153.

Jackson, Joe C.   Church school education in the Creek Nation, 1898 to 1907. Chronicles of Oklahoma, 46 (1968): 312-330.

Jackson, Joe C.   Summer normals in Indian territory after 1898. Chronicles of Oklahoma, 37 (1959): 307-329.

Jacobs, W. R.   Indians of the Southern Colonial frontier.   Columbia, S.C., 1954.

Jenkins, William H.   Alabama forts, 1700-1838. Alabama Review, 12 (1959): 163-180.

Jones, C. C.   Historical sketch of Tomo-chi-chi.   Albany, 1868.   133 p.

Jones, C. C.   Primitive storehouse of the Creek Indians. Smithsonian Institution, Annual Reports of the Board of Regents (1885): 900-901.

Jones, George Fenwick, ed. and tr. John Martin Bolzius reports on Georgia. Georgia Historical Quarterly, 47 (1963): 216-219.

Kansas City Star. Report on the Five Civilized Tribes 1897. Chronicles of Oklahoma, 48 (1970): 416-430.

Ketcham, H. E. Three sixteenth century Spanish chronicles relating to Georgia. Georgia Historical Quarterly, 38, no. 1 (1954): 66-82.

Kilpatrick, Jack Frederick. Muskhogean charm songs among the Oklahoma Cherokees. By Jack Frederick Kilpatrick and Anna Gritts Kilpatrick. Washington, D.C., Smithsonian Press, 1967. 4, 29-40 p. (Smithsonian Contributions to Anthropology, 2, no. 3)

King, Jerlena. Jackson Lewis of the Confederate Creek regiment. Chronicles of Oklahoma, 41 (1963): 66-69.

Klingberg, F. J., ed. The Carolina chronicle of Dr. Francis Le Jau, 1706-1717. California, University, Publications in History, 53 (1956): 1-228.

Krauss, Michael E. Proto-Athapaskan-Eyak and the problem of Na-Dene. International Journal of American Linguistics, 30 (1964): 118-131; 31 (1965): 18-28.

Lamplugh, George R. Farewell to the Revolution: Georgia in 1785. Georgia Historical Quarterly, 56 (1972): 387-403.

Lewis, Thomas M. N. Tribes that slumber; Indian tribes in the Tennessee region. By T. M. N. Lewis and Madeline Kneberg. Knoxville, University of Tennessee Press, 1958. 11, 196 p. illus., maps.

Lightfoot, B. B. The Cherokee emigrants in Missouri, 1837-1839. Missouri Historical Review, 56 (1961/1962): 156-167.

Loomis, Augustus W. Scenes in the Indian country. Philadelphia, Presbyterian Board of Publication, 1859. 283 p. illus.

Loomis, Augustus W. Scenes in the Indian Territory Kowetah Mission. Chronicles of Oklahoma, 46 (1968): 64-72.

Loughridge, R. M. and D. M. Hodge. English and Muskokee dictionary. St. Louis, 1890.

Mahon, John K. Military relations between Georgia and the United States, 1789-1794. Georgia Historical Review, 43 (1959): 138-155.

Mahon, John K. The treaty of Moultrie Creek, 1823. Florida Historical Quarterly, 40 (1961/1962): 350-372.

Mahon, John K. Two Seminole treaties: Payne's Landing, 1832, and Ft. Gibson, 1833. Florida Historical Quarterly, 41 (1962/1963): 1-21.

Marks, Laurence H. Fort Mims: a challenge. Alabama Review, 18 (1965): 275-280.

Martin, Martha Philips. Travel through Indian Country in the early 1800's; the memoirs of Martha Philips Martin. Edited by Harriet C. Owsley. Tennessee Historical Quarterly, 21 (1962): 66-81.

Mason, Carol Ann Irwin. The archaeology of Ocmulgee Old Fields, Macon, Georgia. Dissertation Abstracts, 24 (1963/1964): 3051-3052. UM 64-857.

Mason, Carol Irwin. Eighteenth century culture change among the Lower Creeks. Florida Anthropologist, 16 (1963): 65-80.

Mayes, Mayme B. Chief Joel B. Mayes of the Cherokee Nation. Chronicles of Oklahoma, 44 (1966/1967): 325-330.

McAlister, Lyle N. William Augustus Bowles and the State of Muskogee. Florida Historical Quarterly, 40 (1961/1962): 317-328.

McClary, Ben Harris. Nancy Ward: the last beloved woman of the Cherokees. Tennessee Historical Quarterly, 21 (1962): 352-364.

McDowell, William L., Jr., ed. Documents relating to Indian affairs, May 21, 1750-August 7, 1754. Columbia, South Carolina Archives Department, 1958. 22, 592 p. (Colonial Records of South Carolina, Series 2)

McDowell, William L., Jr., ed. Documents relating to Indian affairs: 1754-1765. Columbia, Published for the South Carolina Department of Archives and History by the University of South Carolina Press, 1970. 55, 657 p. illus. (Colonial Records of South Carolina, Series 2, 3)

McNeil, Kinneth. Confederate treaties with the tribes of Indian Territory. Chronicles of Oklahoma, 42 (1964): 408-420.

Milford, L. L. D.   Memoir or a cursory glance at my different travels. Ed. by J. F. McDermott. Chicago, 1956.   313 p.

Milford, L. L. D.   Mémoire ou coup-d'oeil rapide sur mes différens voyages et mon séjour dans la nation Crёck. Paris, 1802.   331 p.

Milfort, Louis. Memoirs; or, A quick glance at my various travels and my sojourn in the Creek Nation. Translated and edited by Ben C. McCary. Savannah, Ga., Beehive Press, 1972. 145 p. map.

Miner, Craig. The struggle for an East-West railway into the Indian Territory, 1870-1882. Chronicles of Oklahoma, 47 (1969): 560-581.

Morgan, L. H.   Systems of consanguinity and affinity. Smithsonian Contributions to Knowledge, 17 (1871): 291-382.

Morrell, L. Ross.   The Woods Island Site in Southeastern acculturation, 1625-1800. Tallahassee, 1965. 67 p. illus. (Notes in Anthropology, 11)

Motte, J. R.   Journey into wilderness. Gainesville, 1953.   361 p.

Murdock, Richard K.   The return of runaway slaves 1790-1794. Florida Historical Quarterly, 38, no. 2 (1959): 95-113.

Nunez, T. A.   Creek nativism and the Creek War of 1813-1814. Ethnohistory, 5 (1958): 1-47, 131-175, 292-301.

O'Donnell, J. H.   Alexander McGillivray: training for leadership, 1777-1783. Georgia Historical Quarterly, 49 (1965): 172-186.

O'Donnell, James H.   The Virginia Expedition against the Overhill Cherokee, 1776. East Tennessee Historical Society's Publications, 39 (1967): 13-25.

Olds, Dorris L.   Some highlights in the history of Fort St. Marks. Florida Anthropologist, 15 (1962): 33-40.

Olson, Gary D.   Thomas Brown, Loyalist partisan, and the Revolutionary War in Georgia, 1777-1782. Georgia Historical Quarterly, 54 (1970): 1-19, 183-208.

Opler, M. E.   The Creek "town" and the problem of Creek Indian political organization. In Edward H. Spicer, ed. Human Problems in Technological Change. New York, 1952: 165-182.

Osborn, G. C.   Relations with the Indians in West Florida during the administration of Governor Peter Chester, 1770-1781. Florida Historical Quarterly, 31 (1953): 239-272.

Owsley, Frank L., Jr.   Benjamin Hawkins, the first modern Indian agent. Alabama Historical Quarterly, 30 (1968): 7-13.

Owsley, Frank L., Jr.   British and Indian activities in Spanish West Florida during the War of 1812. Florida Historical Quarterly, 46 (1967/1968): 111-123.

Owsley, Frank L., Jr.   Jackson's capture of Pensacola. Alabama Review, 19 (1966): 175-185.

Owsley, Frank L., Jr.   The Fort Mims massacre. Alabama Review, 24 (1971): 192-204.

Owsley, Frank Lawrence, Jr.   The role of the South in the British grand strategy in the War of 1812. Tennessee Historical Quarterly, 30 (1971): 22-38.

Palmer, Edward.   Alabama notes; made in 1883-1884. Alabama Historical Quarterly, 22 (1960): 244-273.

Pardo, Juan.   Journals of the Juan Pardo expeditions, 1566-1567. Edited by Stanley J. Folmsbee and Madeline Kneberg Lewis. Translated by Gerald W. Wade. East Tennessee Historical Society, Publications, 37 (1965): 106-121.

Pate, James Paul.   The Chickamauga: a forgotten segment of Indian resistance on the southern frontier. Dissertation Abstracts International, 30 (1969/1970): 2445A.   UM 69-19,811.

Payne, J. H.   The green corn dance. Continental Monthly, 1 (1862): 17-29.

Peake, G. Ronald.   Oklahoma's "five tribes" Indians are improving their living conditions through public housing. Journal of Housing, 28 (1971): 430-432.

Peters, Thelma.   The Loyalist migration from East Florida to the Bahama Islands. Florida Historical Quarterly, 40 (1961/1962): 123-141.

Pickens, Donald K.   A note in Oklahoma history: Henry C. Brokmeyer among the Creek Indians. Chronicles of Oklahoma, 45 (1967): 73-76.

Pickett, A. J.   History of Alabama, Vol. 1: 74-127. Charleston, 1851.

Pope, G. A., Jr.   Ocmulgee Old Fields Creeks. Southeastern Archaeological Conference, News Letter, 3, no. 3 (1953): 20-21.

Pope, J. A tour through the southern and western territories of the United States. New ed., 52-66. New York, 1888.

Pope, John. A tour through the southern and western territories of the United States of North America. New York, Arno Press, 1971. 105 p.

Porter, Kenneth W. Billy Bowlegs (Holata Micco) in the Seminole Wars. Florida Historical Quarterly, 45 (1966/1967): 219-242.

Posey, Alexander. Journal of Creek enrollment field party 1905. Chronicles of Oklahoma, 46 (1968): 2-19.

Posey, Alexander Lawrence. The journal of Alexander Lawrence Posey, January 1 to September 4, 1897. Edited by Edward Everett Dale. Chronicles of Oklahoma, 45 (1967): 393-432.

Potter, E. An account of several nations of Southern Indians. Massachusetts Historical Society, Collections, ser. 1, 10 (1809): 119-121.

Potts, William S. An account of Alabama Indian Missions and Presbyterian churches in 1828 from the travel diary of William S. Potts. Edited by Joseph G. Smoot. Alabama Review, 18 (1965): 134-152.

Pound, M. B. Benjamin Hawkins--Indian agent. Athens, 1951. 280 p.

Quimby, G. I. and A. Spoehr. Historic Creek pottery from Oklahoma. American Antiquity, 15 (1950): 249-251.

Rainwater, Percy L. Indian missions and missionaries. Journal of Mississippi History, 28 (1966): 15-39.

Rampp, Lary C. Confederate Indian sinking of the J. R. Williams. Journal of the West, 11 (1972): 43-50.

Rea, Robert R. The trouble at Tombeckby. Alabama Review, 21 (1968): 21-39.

Read, W. A. Indian place names in Alabama. Louisiana State University, Studies, 9 (1937): 1-84.

Read, W. A. Indian stream-names in Georgia. International Journal of American Linguistics, 15 (1949): 128-132; 16 (1949): 203-207.

Reck, Georg Philipp von. Commissary Von Reck's report on Georgia. Translated by George Fenwick Jones. Georgia Historical Quarterly, 47 (1963): 95-110.

Reynolds, Thurlow W. Cherokee and Creek. Highlands, N.C., 1966. 87 p.

Rich, Lou. Wakulla Spring: its setting and literary visitors. Florida Historical Quarterly, 42 (1963/1964): 351-362.

Roberts, Frances C. Politics and public land disposal in Alabama's formative period. Alabama Review, 22 (1969): 163-174.

Romans, B. A concise natural history of East and West Florida. New York, 1775.

Roper, James E. Isaac Rawlings, frontier merchant. Tennessee Historical Quarterly, 20 (1961): 262-281.

Roper, James E. Marcus B. Winchester, first mayor of Memphis; his later years. West Tennessee Historical Society, Papers, 13 (1959): 5-37.

Russell, Orpha B. Notes on Samuel William Brown, Jr., Yuchi chief. Chronicles of Oklahoma, 37 (1959): 497-501.

Schmitt, K. Two Creek pottery vessels from Oklahoma. Florida Anthropologist, 3 (1950): 3-8.

Schmitt, K. and R. E. Bell. Historic Indian pottery from Oklahoma. Oklahoma Anthropological Society, Bulletin, 2 (1954): 19-30.

Sears, W. H. Creek and Cherokee culture in the 18th Century. American Antiquity, 21 (1955): 143-149.

Shoemaker, Arthur. The battle of Chustenahlah. Chronicles of Oklahoma, 38 (1960): 180-184.

Smith, Daniel M. James Seagrove and the mission to Tuckaubatchee, 1793. Georgia Historical Quarterly, 44 (1960): 41-55.

Smith, Raphael F. Hereditary methemoglobinemia: a family study with attention to the redox state of the myoglobin. By Raphael F. Smith, Thomas Wheeler, and Ashton Graybiel. Johns Hopkins Medical Journal, 126 (1970): 28-33.

Sonderegger, Richard Paul. The Southern Frontier from the founding of Georgia to the ending of King George's War. Dissertation Abstracts, 25 (1964/1965): 3546. UM 64-12,688.

Sosin, Jack M. The use of Indians in the War of the American Revolution: a reassessment of responsibility. Canadian Historical Review, 46 (1965): 101-121.

Spalding, Phinizy. South Carolina and Georgia: the early days. South Carolina Historical Magazine, 69 (1968): 83-96.

Speck, F. G. Ceremonial songs of the Creek and Yuchi Indians. Pennsylvania, University, University Museum, Anthropological Publications, 1 (1911): 157-245.

Speck, F. G. Notes on social and economic conditions among the Creek Indians of Alabama in 1941. América Indígena, 7 (1947): 195-198.

Speck, F. G. The Creek Indians of Taskigi town. American Anthropological Association, Memoirs, 2 (1907): 99-164.

Speck, F. G. The Negroes and the Creek nation. Southern Workman, 37 (1908): 106-110.

Spoehr, A. Changing kinship systems. Field Museum, Anthropological Series, 33 (1947): 153-235.

Spoehr, A. Creek inter-town relations. American Anthropologist, n.s., 43 (1941): 132-133.

Stephen, Walter W. Andrew Jackson's "forgotten army". Alabama Review, 12 (1959): 126-131.

Stewart, Martha. The Indian Mission Conference of Oklahoma. Chronicles of Oklahoma, 40 (1962): 330-336.

Sturtevant, William C. Creek into Seminole. In Eleanor Burke Leacock and Nancy Oestreich Lurie, eds. North American Indians in Historical Perspective. New York, Random House, 1971: 92-128.

Swan, C. Position and state of manners and arts of the Creek or Muscogee nation. In H. R. Schoolcraft, ed. Information respecting the History, Condition, and Prospects of the Indian Tribes of the United States. Vol. 5. Philadelphia, 1855: 251-283.

Swanton, J. R. A foreword on the social organization of the Creek Indians. American Anthropologist, n.s., 14 (1912): 593-599.

Swanton, J. R. An Indian social experiment and some of its lessons. Scientific Monthly, 31 (1930): 368-376.

Swanton, J. R. Animal stories from the Indians of the Muskhogean stock. Journal of American Folklore, 26 (1913): 193-218.

Swanton, J. R. Coonti. American Anthropologist, n.s., 15 (1913): 141.

Swanton, J. R. Early history of the Creek Indians and their neighbors. U.S. Bureau of American Ethnology, Bulletin, 73 (1922): 207-286.

Swanton, J. R. Ethnological value of the De Soto narratives. American Anthropologist, n.s., 34 (1932): 570-590.

Swanton, J. R. Indian place names. American Speech (Oct., 1937): 212-215.

Swanton, J. R. Indian recognition of return discharge in lightning. Journal of American Folklore, 69 (1956): 46.

Swanton, J. R. Modern square grounds of the Creek Indians. Smithsonian Miscellaneous Collections, 85, no. 8 (1931): 1-46.

Swanton, J. R. Myths and tales of the Southeastern Indians. U.S. Bureau of American Ethnology, Bulletin, 88 (1929): 1-86.

Swanton, J. R. Religious beliefs and medical practices of the Creek Indians. U.S. Bureau of American Ethnology, Annual Reports, 42 (1925): 473-672.

*Swanton, J. R. Social organization and social usages of the Indians of the Creek Confederacy. U.S. Bureau of American Ethnology, Annual Reports, 42 (1925): 23-472.

Swanton, J. R. The Creek Indians as mound builders. American Anthropologist, n.s., 14 (1912): 320-324.

Swanton, J. R. The green corn dance. Chronicles of Oklahoma, 10 (1932): 170-195.

Swanton, J. R. The interpretation of aboriginal mounds by means of Creek Indian customs. Smithsonian Institution, Annual Reports of the Board of Regents (1927): 495-506.

Swanton, J. R. The social significance of the Creek Confederacy. International Congress of Americanists, Proceedings, 19 (1915): 327-334.

Swanton, J. R. Tokulki of Tulsa. In E. C. Parsons, ed. American Indian Life. New York, 1925: 127-145.

Swanton, John R. Early history of the Creek Indians and their neighbors. New York, Johnson Reprint, 1970. 492 p. maps.

Tarvin, M. E. The Muscogees or Creek Indians from 1519 to 1893. Alabama Historical Quarterly, 17 (1955): 125-145.

Thomas, Daniel H. Fort Toulouse; the French outpost at the Alibamos on the Coosa. Alabama Historical Quarterly, 22 (1960): 137-230.

Thomas, Daniel H. Fort Toulouse--in tradition and fact. Alabama Review, 13 (1960): 243-257.

Thomason, Hugh M. Governor Peter Early and the Creek Indian frontier, 1813-1815. Georgia Historical Quarterly, 45 (1961): 223-237.

Tobler, John. John Tobler's description of South Carolina (1754). Translated and edited by Walter L. Robbins. South Carolina Historical Magazine, 71 (1970): 257-265.

Tresp, Lothar L., ed. and tr. August, 1748 in Georgia, from the diary of John Martin Bolzius. Georgia Historical Quarterly, 47 (1963): 204-216.

Underhill, Lonnie E. Hamlin Garland and the final council of the Creek Nation. Journal of the West, 10 (1971): 511-520.

Villiers du Terrage, M. de. Documents concernant l'histoire des Indiens de la région orientale de la Louisiane. Société des Américanistes, Journal, n.s., 14 (1922): 127-140.

Walker, William A., Jr. Martial sons: Tennessee enthusiasm for the War of 1812. Tennessee Historical Quarterly, 20 (1961): 20-37.

Watson, I. A. Creek Indian burial customs today. Chronicles of Oklahoma, 28 (1950): 95-102.

Wenhold, L. L. A seventeenth century letter of Gabriel Diaz Vara Calderón. Smithsonian Miscellaneous Collections, 95, no. 16 (1936): 1-14.

Willey, G. R. and W. H. Sears. The Kasita Site. Southern Indian Studies, 4 (1952): 3-18.

Willey, William J. The second federal invasion of Indian Territory. Chronicles of Oklahoma, 44 (1966/1967): 420-430.

Witthoft, J. Green corn ceremonialism in the eastern woodlands. Michigan, University, Museum of Anthropology, Occasional Contributions, 13 (1949): 52-70.

Woodward, T. S. Reminiscences of the Creek or Muscogee Indians. Montgomery, 1859.

Wright, Bessie L., ed. Diary of a member of the first mule pack train to leave Fort Smith for California in 1849. Panhandle-Plains Historical Review, 42 (1969): 61-119.

Wright, J. Leitch. Creek-American Treaty of 1790: Alexander McGillivray and the diplomacy of the Old Southwest. Georgia Historical Quarterly, 51 (1967): 379-400.

Wright, James L., Jr. William Augustus Bowles, Director General of the Creek Nation. Athens, University of Georgia Press, 1967. 8, 211 p. map.

Wright, M. H. American Indian corn dishes. Chronicles of Oklahoma, 36 (1958): 155-166.

Wright, Muriel H. Colonel Cooper's Civil War report on the Battle of Round Mountain. Chronicles of Oklahoma, 39 (1961): 352-397.

Wright, Muriel H. Seals of the Five Civilized Tribes. Chronicles of Oklahoma, 40 (1962): 214-218.

Young, Mary E. Indian removal and land allotment: the civilized tribes and Jacksonian justice. In Roger L. Nichols and George R. Adams, eds. The American Indian: Past and Present. Waltham, Xerox College Publishing, 1971: 132-145.

Young, Mary Elizabeth. Redskins, ruffleshirts and rednecks; Indian allotments in Alabama and Mississippi, 1830-1860. Norman, University of Oklahoma Press, 1961. 217 p. illus.

13-13 Cusabo

Anghiera, P. M. d'. De orbe novo, Vol. 2: 255-271. Ed. by F. A. MacNutt. New York, 1912.

Anonymous. Cusabo. U.S. Bureau of American Ethnology, Bulletin, 30, vol. 1 (1907): 373.

Anonymous. Edisto. U.S. Bureau of American Ethnology, Bulletin, 30, vol. 1 (1907): 414.

Anonymous. Etiwaw. U.S. Bureau of American Ethnology, Bulletin, 30, vol. 1 (1907): 443-444.

Gomara, F. L. de. Historia de las Indias. Madrid, 1749.

Hewatt, A. An historical account of the
rise and progress of the colonies of
South Carolina and Georgia, Vol. 1: 64-
73. London, 1779.

Hilton, W. A true relation of a voyage
upon discovery of a part of the coast of
Florida. South Carolina Historical
Society, Collections, 5 (1897): 18-28.

Lanning, J. T. The Spanish missions of
Georgia, 9-32. Chapel Hill, 1935.

Laudonnière, R. L'histoire notable de la
Floride. Paris, 1586.

Milling, C. J. Red Carolinians. Chapel
Hill, 1940. 438 p.

Mooney, J. The Siouan tribes of the East.
U.S. Bureau of American Ethnology,
Bulletin, 22 (1894): 5-101.

Oviedo y Valdez, G. F. de. Historia
general y natural de las Indias, Vol. 3:
624-633. Madrid, 1853.

Quattlebaum, P. The land called Chicora.
Gainesville, 1956. 153 p.

Sandford, R. The Port Royall discovery.
South Carolina Historical Society,
Collections, 5 (1897): 57-81.

Swanton, J. R. Early history of the Creek
Indians and their neighbors. U.S. Bureau
of American Ethnology, Bulletin, 73
(1922): 16-25, 31-80.

13-14   Hitchiti

Caldwell, J. R. The archeology of eastern
Georgia and South Carolina. In J. B.
Griffin, ed. Archeology of Eastern
United States. Chicago, 1952: 312-321.

Coulter, E. Merton. The Chehaw affair.
Georgia Historical Quarterly, 49 (1965):
269-395.

Covington, James W. Apalachicola Seminole
leadership: 1820-1833. Florida
Anthropologist, 16 (1963): 57-62.

Covington, James W. Federal relations
with the Apalachicola Indians: 1823-
1838. Florida Historical Quarterly, 42
(1963/1964): 125-141.

Gardner, William M. The Waddells Mill
Pond site. Florida Anthropologist, 19
(1966): 43-64.

Gatschet, A. S. A migration legend of the
Creek Indians, 77-85. Philadelphia,
1884.

Gatschet, A. S. Hitchiti. U.S. Bureau of
American Ethnology, Bulletin, 30, vol. 1
(1907): 551.

Gatschet, A. S. Tchikilli's Kasi'hta
legend in the Creek and Hitchiti
languages. Academy of Science of St.
Louis, Transactions, 5 (1888): 33-239.

Haas, Mary R. Historical linguistics and
the genetic relationship of languages.
In Theoretical Foundations. The Hague,
Mouton, 1966: 113-153. (Current Trends
in Linguistics, 3)

Pardo, Juan. Journals of the Juan Pardo
expeditions, 1566-1567. Edited by
Stanley J. Folmsbee and Madeline Kneberg
Lewis. Translated by Gerald W. Wade.
East Tennessee Historical Society,
Publications, 37 (1965): 106-121.

Smith, B. Comparative vocabularies of the
Seminole and Mikasuke tongues. In W. W.
Beach, ed. Indian Miscellany. Albany,
1877: 120-126.

Swanton, J. R. Animal stories from the
Indians of the Muskhogean stock. Journal
of American Folklore, 26 (1913): 214-
216.

Swanton, J. R. Early history of the Creek
Indians and their neighbors. U.S. Bureau
of American Ethnology, Bulletin, 73
(1922): 129-137, 141-143, 167-184.

Swanton, J. R. Myths and tales of the
Southeastern Indians. U.S. Bureau of
American Ethnology, Bulletin, 88 (1929):
87-117.

Swanton, J. R. Religious beliefs and
medical practices of the Creek Indians.
U.S. Bureau of American Ethnology,
Annual Reports, 42 (1925): 473-672.

Swanton, J. R. Social organization and
social usages of the Indians of the
Creek Confederacy. U.S. Bureau of
American Ethnology, Annual Reports, 42
(1925): 23-472.

Swanton, John R. Early history of the
Creek Indians and their neighbors. New
York, Johnson Reprint, 1970. 492 p.
maps.

13-15   Huma

Du Ru, Paul. Journal of Paul Du Ru,
missionary priest to Louisiana.
Translated, with introduction and notes,
from a manuscript in the Newberry
Library, by Ruth Lapham Butler.
Chicago, Printed for the Caxton Club,
1934. 10, 74 p.

Fischer, Ann. Field work in five
cultures. In Peggy Golde, ed. Women in
the Field. Chicago, Aldine, 1970: 265-
289.

Fischer, Ann. History and current status
of the Houma Indians. Midcontinent
American Studies Journal, 6 (1965): 149-
163.

Fischer, Ann. History and current status
of the Houma Indians. In Stuart Levine
and Nancy O. Lurie, eds. The American
Indian Today. Baltimore, Penguin Books,
1970: 212-235.

Harrington, M. R. Among Louisiana
Indians. Southern Workman, 37 (1908):
656-661.

Margry, P., ed. Découvertes et
établissements des Français dans l'ouest
et dans le sud de l'Amérique
septentrionale, Vol. 4: 174-177. Paris,
1880.

McWilliams, Richebourg Gaillard.
Iberville and the Southern Indians.
Alabama Review, 20 (1967): 243-262.

Parenton, V. and R. J. Pellegrin. The
"Sabines". Social Forces, 29 (1950):
148-154.

Quimby, G. I. The Natchezan culture type.
American Antiquity, 7 (1942): 255-275.

Shea, J. G., ed. Early voyages up and
down the Mississippi, 143-148. Albany,
1861.

Speck, F. G. A list of plant curatives
obtained from the Houma Indians of
Louisiana. Primitive Man, 14 (1941): 49-
73.

Speck, F. G. A social reconnaissance of
the Creole Houma Indian trappers of the
Louisiana bayous. América Indígena, 3
(1943): 134-146, 210-220.

Speck, F. G. and R. W. Dexter. Molluscan
food items of the Houma Indians.
Nautilus, 60 (1946): 34.

*Stanton, Max E. A remnant Indian
community: the Houma of southern
Louisiana. In J. Kenneth Morland, ed.
The Not So Solid South. Athens, Ga.,
Southern Anthropological Society, 1971:
82-92.

Swanton, J. R. Indian tribes of the Lower
Mississippi River Valley and adjacent
coast of the Gulf of Mexico. U.S. Bureau
of American Ethnology, Bulletin, 43
(1911): 285-292.

Swanton, John R. Indian tribes of the
Lower Mississippi Valley and adjacent
coast of the Gulf of Mexico. New York,
Johnson Reprint, 1970. 7, 387 p.
illus.

Thwaites, R. G., ed. The Jesuit Relations
and allied documents, Vol. 65: 146-155.
Cleveland, 1900.

13-16 Mobile

Bandelier, A. F., ed. The journey of
Alvar Nunez Cabeza de Vaca, 41-49. New
York, 1905.

Bass, A. James Mooney in Oklahoma.
Chronicles of Oklahoma, 32 (1954): 246-
262.

Bourne, E. G., ed. Narratives of the
career of Hernando de Soto, Vol. 1: 87-
98; Vol. 2: 16-21, 120-128. New York,
1904.

Dumont de Montigny. Mémoires historiques
sur la Louisiane, Vol. 1: 243-246.
Paris, 1753.

Gannon, Michael V. Altar and hearth: the
coming of Christianity, 1521-1565.
Florida Historical Quarterly, 44
(1965/1966): 17-44.

Gatschet, A. S. and C. Thomas. Mobile.
U.S. Bureau of American Ethnology,
Bulletin, 30, vol. 1 (1907): 916.

Gold, Robert L. Conflict in San Carlos:
Indian immigrants in eighteenth-century
New Spain. Ethnohistory, 17 (1970): 1-
10.

Hamilton, P. J. Colonial Mobile. 2d ed.
Boston, 1910. 594 p.

Lazarus, Mrs. W. C. Indians of the
Florida panhandle. Fort Walton Beach,
Fla., Temple Mound Museum, 1968. 5,
28 p. illus.

Lewis, T. M. N. A Florida burial.
Wisconsin Archeologist, n.s., 10 (1931):
123-128.

Margry, P., ed. Découvertes et
établissements des Français dans l'ouest
et dans le sud de l'Amérique
septentrionale, Vol. 5: 388-391. Paris,
1883.

McWilliams, Richebourg Gaillard.
Iberville and the Southern Indians.
Alabama Review, 20 (1967): 243-262.

Swanton, J. R. Early history of the Creek
Indians and their neighbors. U.S. Bureau

of American Ethnology, Bulletin, 73
(1922): 143-165.

Swanton, J. R.   Indian tribes of the Lower
Mississippi Valley and adjacent coast of
the Gulf of Mexico. U.S. Bureau of
American Ethnology, Bulletin, 43 (1911):
302-306.

Swanton, John R.   Early history of the
Creek Indians and their neighbors. New
York, Johnson Reprint, 1970. 492 p.
maps.

Swanton, John R.   Indian tribes of the
Lower Mississippi Valley and adjacent
coast of the Gulf of Mexico. New York,
Johnson Reprint, 1970. 7, 387 p.
illus.

Villiers du Terrage, M. de.   Documents
concernant l'histoire des Indiens de la
région orientale de la Louisiane.
Société des Américanistes, Journal,
n.s., 14 (1922): 127-140.

                    13-17   Monacan

Alexander, Edward P.   An Indian vocabulary
from Fort Christanna, 1716. Virginia
Magazine of History and Biography, 79
(1971): 303-313.

Alexander, Ralph W., Jr.   On the origin of
the Tutelo--an Eastern Siouan tribe. By
Ralph W. Alexander, Jr. and Georg K.
Neumann. Indiana Academy of Science,
Proceedings, 78 (1968): 88-92.

Alvord, C. W. and L. Bidgood.   First
explorations of the Trans-Allegheny
region by the Virginians. Cleveland,
1912. 275 p.

Anderson, J.   The newly discovered
relationship of the Tuteloes to the
Dakotan stock. American Philological
Association, Proceedings, 3 (1872): 15-
16.

Binford, L. R.   Comments on the "Siouan
problem". Ethnohistory, 6 (1959): 27-41.

Brickell, John.   The natural history of
North-Carolina. New York, Johnson
Reprint, 1969. 10, 14, 417 p. illus.,
map.

Bushnell, D. I.   Discoveries beyond the
Appalachian Mountains. American
Anthropologist, n.s., 9 (1907): 45-56.

Bushnell, D. I.   Indian sites below the
falls of the Rappahannock. Smithsonian
Miscellaneous Collections, 96, no. 4
(1937): 1-65.

Bushnell, D. I.   Monacan sites in
Virginia. Smithsonian Institution,
Explorations and Field-Work (1930): 211-
216.

Bushnell, D. I.   Native cemeteries and
forms of burial east of the Mississippi.
U.S. Bureau of American Ethnology,
Bulletin, 71 (1920): 122-131.

Bushnell, D. I.   The five Monacan towns in
Virginia. Smithsonian Miscellaneous
Collections, 82, no. 12 (1930): 1-38.

Bushnell, D. I.   The Manahoac tribes in
Virginia. Smithsonian Miscellaneous
Collections, 94, no. 8 (1935): 1-56.

Bushnell, D. I.   Virginia before
Jamestown. Smithsonian Miscellaneous
Collections, 100 (1940): 125-158.

Byrd, W.   The history of the dividing line
between Virginia and North Carolina.
Richmond, 1866. 2 v.

Coe, J. L.   The cultural sequence of the
Carolina Piedmont. In J. B. Griffin, ed.
Archeology of Eastern United States.
Chicago, 1952: 301-311.

Cringan, A. T.   Iroquois folk songs.
Annual Archaeological Report, being Part
of Appendix to the Report of the
Minister of Education, Ontario (1902):
137-152.

Dorsey, J. C.   A study of Siouan cults.
U.S. Bureau of American Ethnology,
Annual Reports, 11 (1890): 518-519.

Dorsey, J. C.   Preface. Contributions to
North American Ethnology, 9 (1893):
xviii-xxx.

Douglas, F. H.   The Virginia Indian
tribes. Denver Art Museum, Indian
Leaflet Series, 57 (1933): 1-4.

Feest, Christian F.   Virginia Indian
miscellany I. Archiv für Völkerkunde, 20
(1966): 1-7.

Frachtenberg, L. J.   Contributions to a
Tutelo vocabulary. American
Anthropologist, n.s., 15 (1913): 477-
479.

Griffin, J. B.   An interpretation of
Siouan archaeology in the Piedmont of
North Carolina and Virginia. American
Antiquity, 10 (1945): 321-330.

Griffin, J. B.   On the historic location
of the Tutelo and the Mohetan in the
Ohio Valley. American Anthropologist,
n.s., 44 (1942): 275-280.

Haas, Mary R. The last words of Biloxi. International Journal of American Linguistics, 34 (1968): 77-84.

Hale, H. The Tutelo tribe and language. American Philosophical Society, Proceedings, 21 (1883): 1-45.

Hendren, S. R. Government and religion of the Virginia Indians. Johns Hopkins University, Studies in Historical and Political Science, 13, nos. 11/12 (1895): 3-58.

Jefferson, T. Notes on the State of Virginia. Philadelphia, 1788. 244 p.

Kurath, G. P. The Tutelo fourth night spirit release singing. Midwest Folklore, 4 (1955): 87-105.

Kurath, G. P. The Tutelo harvest rites. Scientific Monthly, 76 (1953): 153-162.

Lawson, John. An account of the Indians of N. Carolina. In his The History of Carolina. Raleigh, Strother and Marcom, 1860: 277-390.

Lawson, John. An account of the Indians of N. Carolina. In Lawson's History of North Carolina. Richmond, Garrett and Massie, 1937: 179-259.

Maxwell, H. The use and abuse of forests by the Virginia Indians. William and Mary College Quarterly Historical Magazine, 19 (1910): 73-104.

Miller, C. F. Revaluation of the Eastern Siouan problem. U.S. Bureau of American Ethnology, Bulletin, 164 (1957): 115-212.

Miller, Carl F. Archeology of the John H. Kerr Reservoir basin, Roanoke River Virginia-North Carolina. Washington, D.C., Government Printing Office, 1962. 16, 447 p. illus., maps. (U.S., Bureau of American Ethnology, River Basin Surveys Papers, 25. U.S., Bureau of American Ethnology, Bulletin, 182)

Milling, C. J. Red Carolinians. Chapel Hill, 1940. 438 p.

Mooney, J. Monacan. U.S. Bureau of American Ethnology, Bulletin, 30, vol. 1 (1907): 930-931.

Mooney, J. Saponi. U.S. Bureau of American Ethnology, Bulletin, 30, vol. 2 (1910): 464-465.

Mooney, J. The Siouan tribes of the East. U.S. Bureau of American Ethnology, Bulletin, 22 (1894): 5-101.

Mooney, J. Tutelo. U.S. Bureau of American Ethnology, Bulletin, 30, vol. 2 (1910): 855-856.

Rights, D. L. The American Indian in North Carolina. Durham, 1947. 296 p.

Rights, D. L. The American Indian in North Carolina. Winston-Salem, 1957. 318 p.

Rioux, M. Persistence of a Tutelo cultural trait among the contemporary Cayuga. National Museum of Canada, Bulletin, 123 (1951): 72-74.

Robinson, W. Stitt. Tributary Indians in Colonial America. Virginia Magazine of History and Biography, 67 (1959): 49-64.

Sapir, E. A Tutelo vocabulary. American Anthropologist, n.s., 15 (1913): 295-297.

Smith, J. The generall historie of Virginia, New-England, and the Summer Isles, 129-148. Richmond, 1819.

Smith, John. Captain John Smith's history of Virginia; a selection. Indianapolis, Bobbs-Merrill, 1970. 22, 182 p.

Smith, John. The generall historie of Virginia, New-England, and the Summer Isles. Ann Arbor, University Microfilms, 1966. 96, 105-248 p. illus., maps.

Smith, John. Works, 1608-1631. Edited by Edward Arber. New York, AMS Press, 1967. 136, 984 p. illus.

Speck, F. G. Siouan tribes of the Carolinas. American Anthropologist, n.s., 37 (1935): 201-225.

Speck, F. G. The question of matrilineal descent in the southeastern Siouan area. American Anthropologist, n.s., 40 (1938): 1-12.

Speck, F. G. Tutelo rituals. Archaeological Society of North Carolina, Bulletin, 2, no. 2 (1935): 1-7.

Speck, F. G. and C. E. Schaeffer. Catawba kinship and social organization with a resume of Tutelo kinship terms. American Anthropologist, n.s., 44 (1942): 555-575.

Speck, F. G. and G. Herzog. The Tutelo spirit adoption ceremony. Harrisburg, 1942. 125 p.

Strachey, W. The historie of travaile into Virginia Britannia. London, 1849. 203 p.

Strachey, W. The historie of travell into Virginia Britania. Works Issued by the Hakluyt Society, Second Series, 103 (1953): 1-253.

Sturtevant, W. C. Siouan languages in the East. American Anthropologist, 60 (1958): 738-743.

Swanton, J. R. Early history of the Eastern Siouan tribes. In Essays in Anthropology Presented to A. L. Kroeber. Berkeley, 1936: 371-381.

Swanton, J. R. New light on the early history of the Siouan peoples. Washington Academy of Sciences, Journal, 13 (1923): 33-43.

Swanton, J. R. Siouan tribes and the Ohio Valley. American Anthropologist, n.s., 45 (1943): 49-66.

Talbot, W., ed. The discoveries of John Lederer. New ed. Rochester, 1902. 30 p.

Tooker, W. W. The Algonquian appellatives of the Siouan tribes of Virginia. American Anthropologist, 8 (1895): 376-392.

Tooker, W. W. The Algonquian names of the Siouan tribes of Virginia. New York, 1901. 83 p.

Willoughby, C. C. The Virginia Indians in the seventeenth century. American Anthropologist, n.s., 9 (1907): 57-86.

Wyth (White), J. Portraits to the life and manners of the inhabitants of that province in America called Virginia. New York, 1841. 15 p.

13-18   Mosopelea

Dorsey, J. O. and J. R. Swanton. A dictionary of the Biloxi and Ofo languages. U.S. Bureau of American Ethnology, Bulletin, 47 (1912): 1-340.

Griffin, J. B. The Fort Ancient Aspect. Ann Arbor, 1943. 407 p.

Griffin, James Bennett. The Fort Ancient aspect: its cultural and chronological position in Mississippi Valley archaeology. Ann Arbor, University of Michigan, 1966. 15, 376 p. illus. (Michigan, University, Museum of Anthropology, Anthropological Papers, 28)

Haas, Mary R. Swanton and the Biloxi and Ofo dictionaries. International Journal

of American Linguistics, 35 (1969): 286-290.

Haas, Mary R. The last words of Biloxi. International Journal of American Linguistics, 34 (1968): 77-84.

Holmer, N. M. An Ofo phonetic law. International Journal of American Linguistics, 13 (1947): 1-8.

Miller, C. F. Revaluation of the Eastern Siouan problem. U.S. Bureau of American Ethnology, Bulletin, 164 (1957): 115-212.

Sturtevant, W. C. Siouan languages in the East. American Anthropologist, 60 (1958): 738-743.

Swanton, J. R. A new Siouan dialect. In Putnam Anniversary Volume. New York, 1909: 477-486.

Swanton, J. R. Early history of the Eastern Siouan tribes. In Essays in Anthropology Presented to A. L. Kroeber. Berkeley, 1936: 371-381.

Swanton, J. R. New light on the early history of the Siouan peoples. Washington Academy of Sciences, Journal, 13 (1923): 33-43.

Swanton, J. R. Siouan tribes and the Ohio Valley. American Anthropologist, n.s., 45 (1943): 49-66.

Voegelin, C. F. Ofo-Biloxi sound correspondences. Indiana Academy of Science, Proceedings, 48 (1939): 23-26.

13-19   Natchez

Albrecht, A. C. Ethical precepts among the Natchez Indians. Louisiana Historical Quarterly, 31 (1948): 569-597.

Albrecht, A. C. Indian-French relations at Natchez. American Anthropologist, n.s., 48 (1946): 321-354.

Albrecht, Andrew C. The location of the historic Natchez villages. Journal of Mississippi History, 6 (1944): 67-88.

Anonymous. Mémoire sur la Louisiane, ou le Mississippi. Recueil A-Z, 2 (B) (1752): 123-152.

Baudry des Lozières, L. N. Voyage à la Louisiane. Paris, 1802. 382 p.

Berthond, A. M. A sketch of the Natchez Indians. Golden, 1886. 11 p.

Bossu, M. Nouveaux voyages aux Indes occidentales, Vol. 1: 37-79. Paris, 1768.

Bossu, M. Travels through that part of North America formerly called Louisiana, Vol. 1: 37-67. London, 1771.

Brain, Jeffrey P. The Natchez "paradox". Ethnology, 10 (1971): 215-222.

Brinton, D. G. On the language of the Natchez. American Philosophical Society, Proceedings, 13 (1873): 483-499.

Brinton, D. G. The Taensa grammar and dictionary. American Antiquarian and Oriental Journal, 7 (1885): 108-113.

Burgess, Charles E. The De Soto myth in Missouri. Missouri Historical Society, Bulletin, 24 (1967/1968): 303-325.

Bushnell, D. I. Native cemeteries and forms of burial east of the Mississippi. U.S. Bureau of American Ethnology, Bulletin, 71 (1920): 101-105.

Calhoun, R. D. The Taensa Indians. Louisiana Historical Quarterly, 17 (1934): 411-435, 642-679.

Charlevoix, P. F. X. de. Historical Journal. In B. F. French, ed. Historical Collections of Louisiana and Florida. Vol. 3. 1851: 140-170.

Charlevoix, P. F. X. de. History and general description of New France. Ed. by J. M. Shea. New York, 1866-1872. 6 v.

Chateaubriand, F. A. R. Les Natchez. Baltimore, 1932. 554 p.

Cushman, H. B. History of the Choctaw, Chickasaw and Natchez Indians. Greenville, 1899. 607 p.

Cushman, Horatio B. History of the Choctaw, Chickasaw and Natchez Indians. Edited by Angie Debo. New York, Russell and Russell, 1972. 503 p. illus.

Cushman, Horatio B. history of the Choctaw, Chickasaw and Natchez Indians. Edited by Angie Debo. Stillwater, Okla., Redlands Press, 1962. 503 p. illus.

Derbanne, François Dion Deprez. Natchitoches and the trail to the Rio Grande: two early eighteenth-century accounts by the Sieur Derbanne. Translated and edited by Katherine Briggs and Winston De Ville. Louisiana History, 8 (1967): 239-259.

Du Ru, Paul. Journal of Paul Du Ru, missionary priest to Louisiana. Translated, with introduction and notes, from a manuscript in the Newberry Library, by Ruth Lapham Butler. Chicago, Printed for the Caxton Club, 1934. 10, 74 p.

Dumont de Montigny. L'établissement de la province de la Louisiane. Société des Américanistes, Journal, n.s., 23 (1931): 273-440.

Dumont de Montigny. Mémoires historiques sur la Louisiane. Paris, 1753. 2 v.

Ethridge, A. N. Indians of Grant Parish. Louisiana Historical Quarterly, 23 (1940): 1108-1131.

Ford, J. A. Analysis of Indian village site collections from Louisiana and Mississippi. Louisiana, Department of Conservation, Anthropological Studies, 2 (1936): 1-285.

Foreman, G. The last trek of the Indians, 320-322. Chicago, 1946.

Gosselin, A. Les sauvages du Mississipi. International Congress of Americanists, Proceedings, 15, vol. 1 (1906): 31-51.

Griffin, James Bennett. The Fort Ancient aspect: its cultural and chronological position in Mississippi Valley archaeology. Ann Arbor, University of Michigan, 1966. 15, 376 p. illus. (Michigan, University, Museum of Anthropology, Anthropological Papers, 28)

Haas, M. R. Natchez and Chitimacha clans and kinship terminology. American Anthropologist, n.s., 41 (1939): 597-610.

Haas, M. R. Natchez and the Muskogean languages. Language, 32 (1956): 61-72.

Haas, Mary R. Historical linguistics and the genetic relationship of languages. In Theoretical Foundations. The Hague, Mouton, 1966: 113-153. (Current Trends in Linguistics, 3)

Haas, Mary R. The expression of the diminutive. In M. Estellie Smith, ed. Studies in Linguistics in Honor of George L. Trager. The Hague, Mouton, 1972: 148-152. (Janua Linguarum, Series Maior, 52)

Haas, Mary R. Tonkawa and Algonkian. Anthropological Linguistics, 1, no. 2 (1959): 1-6.

Haekel, J. Männerhäuser und Festplatzanlagen in Ozeanien und im östlichen Nordamerika. Baessler-Archiv, 23 (1940): 8-18.

Hart, C. W. M. A reconsideration of the Natchez social structure. American Anthropologist, n.s., 45 (1943): 374-386.

Haumonté, J. D., M. J. Parisot, and L. Adam. Grammaire et vocabulaire de la langue taensa. Paris, 1882. 11i p. (A famous forgery.)

Henshaw, H. W. and J. R. Swanton. Natchez. U.S. Bureau of American Ethnology, Bulletin, 30, vol. 2 (1910): 35-36.

Howard, James H. Bringing back the fire: the revival of a Natchez-Cherokee ceremonial ground. American Indian Crafts and Culture, 4, no. 1 (1970): 9-12.

Howard, James H. Bringing back the fire: the revival of a Natchez-Cherokee ceremonial ground. Cklahoma Anthropological Society, Newsletter, 18, no. 4 (1970): 11-17.

Humble, S. L. The Ouachita Valley expedition of DeSoto. Louisiana Historical Quarterly, 25 (1942): 611-643.

Imbelloni, J. Intorno ai crani "incredibili" degli Indiani Natchez. International Congress of Americanists, Proceedings, 22 (1926): 391-406.

Jennings, J. D. Prehistory of the Lower Mississippi Valley. In J. B. Griffin, ed. Archeology of Eastern United States. Chicago, 1952: 256-271.

Josselin de Jong, J. P. B. de. The Natchez social system. International Congress of Americanists, Proceedings, 23 (1928): 553-562.

Kenton, E., ed. The Indians of North America, Vol. 2: 425-450. New York, 1927.

*Le Page du Pratz. Histoire de la Louisiane. Paris, 1758. 3 v.

*Le Page du Pratz. The history of Louisiana. London, 1763. 2 v.

Le Petit, M. Relation des Natchez. Recueil de Voyages au Nord, 9 (1737): 1-79.

Lounsbury, F. G. Stray number systems among certain Indian tribes. American Anthropologist, n.s., 48 (1946): 672-675.

MacLeod, W. C. Natchez political evolution. American Anthropologist, n.s., 26 (1924): 201-229.

MacLeod, W. C. On Natchez culture origins. American Anthropologist, n.s., 28 (1926): 409-413.

Margry, P., ed. Découvertes et établissements des Français dans l'ouest et dans le sud de l'Amérique septentrionale, Vol. 5: 444-455. Paris, 1883.

Mason, Carol Irwin. Natchez class structure. Ethnohistory, 11 (1964): 120-133.

McWilliams, Richebourg Gaillard. Iberville and the Southern Indians. Alabama Review, 20 (1967): 243-262.

Mereness, N. D., ed. Travels in the American colonies, 47-49. New York, 1916.

Mooney, J. The end of the Natchez. American Anthropologist, n.s., 1 (1899): 510-521.

Morfi, J. A. de. Memorias for the history of the Province of Texas. Ed. by F. M. Chabot. San Antonio, 1932. 85 p.

Morice, A. G. Disparus et survivants. Société de Géographie (Québec), Bulletin, 20 (1926): 199-221.

Nash, Charles H. Chucalissa Indian Town. By Charles H. Nash and Rodney Gates, Jr. Tennessee Historical Quarterly, 21 (1962): 103-121.

Neitzel, Robert S. Archeology of the Fatherland site: the Grand Village of the Natchez. New York, American Museum of Natural History, 1965. 108 p. illus., maps. (American Museum of Natural History, Anthropological Papers, 51, pt. 1)

Neitzel, Robert S. The Natchez Grand Village. Florida Anthropologist, 17 (1964): 63-66.

Nuttall, T. A journal of travels into the Arkansa Territory, 268-282. Philadelphia, 1821.

Nuttall, Thomas. A journal of travels into the Arkansa Territory. Ann Arbor, University Microfilms, 1966. 12, 296 p. illus., map.

Oswalt, Wendell H. Other peoples, other customs; world ethnography and its history. New York, Holt, Rinehart and Winston, 1972. 15, 430 p. illus., maps.

Parish, J. C. The lake of the Taensa. Louisiana Historical Quarterly, 5 (1922): 201-207.

Phelps, Dawson A. The Natchez Trace; Indian trail to parkway. Tennessee Historical Quarterly, 21 (1962): 203-218.

Quimby, G. I. Natchez archaeology. Southeastern Archaeological Conference, News Letter, 3, no. 3 (1953): 22-24.

Quimby, G. I. Natchez social structure as an instrument of assimilation. American Anthropologist, n.s., 48 (1946): 134-137.

Quimby, G. I. The Natchezan culture type. American Antiquity, 7 (1942): 255-275.

Rainwater, Percy L. Conquistadors, missionaries, and missions. Journal of Mississippi History, 27 (1965): 123-147.

Ross, E. H. and O. A. Phelps, eds. A journey over the Natchez Trace in 1792. Journal of Mississippi History, 15 (1953): 252-273.

Shafer, Harry J. An evaluation of the Natchez occupation at the Fatherland Site. Journal of Mississippi History, 34 (1972): 215-235.

Shea, J. G., ed. Early voyages up and down the Mississippi, 76-86, 136-142. Albany, 1861.

Swadesh, M. Sociologic notes on obsolescent languages. International Journal of American Linguistics, 14 (1948): 226-235.

Swanson, Guy E. Rules of descent: studies in the sociology of parentage. Ann Arbor, University of Michigan, 1969. 5, 108 p. (Michigan, University, Museum of Anthropology, Anthropological Papers, 39)

Swanton, J. R. Animal stories from the Indians of the Muskhogean stock. Journal of American Folklore, 26 (1913): 192-209.

Swanton, J. R. Early history of the Creek Indians and their neighbors. U.S. Bureau of American Ethnology, Bulletin, 73 (1922): 312-316.

Swanton, J. R. Ethnological position of the Natchez Indians. American Anthropologist, n.s., 9 (1907): 513-528.

*Swanton, J. R. Indian tribes of the Lower Mississippi Valley and adjacent coast of the Gulf of Mexico. U.S. Bureau of American Ethnology, Bulletin, 43 (1911): 1-274.

Swanton, J. R. Myths and tales of the Southeastern Indians. U.S. Bureau of American Ethnology, Bulletin, 88 (1929): 213-266.

Swanton, J. R. Natchez. In J. Hastings, ed. Encyclopaedia of Religion and Ethics. Vol. 9. New York, 1917: 187-191.

Swanton, J. R. Social organization and social usages of the Indians of the Creek Confederacy. U.S. Bureau of American Ethnology, Annual Reports, 42 (1925): 23-472.

Swanton, J. R. Taensa. U.S. Bureau of American Ethnology, Bulletin, 30, vol. 2 (1910): 668-669.

Swanton, J. R. The language of the Taensa. American Anthropologist, n.s., 10 (1908): 24-32.

Swanton, J. R. The Muskhogean connection of the Natchez language. International Journal of American Linguistics, 3 (1924): 46-75.

Swanton, John R. Early history of the Creek Indians and their neighbors. New York, Johnson Reprint, 1970. 492 p. maps.

Thwaites, R. G., ed. The Jesuit Relations and allied documents, Vol. 65: 134-145; Vol. 68: 120-163. Cleveland, 1900.

Tonti, H. de. An account of Monsieur de la Salle's last expedition. New York Historical Society, Collections, 2 (1814): 217-341.

Tonti, H. de. Relation de la Louisiane, et du Mississippi. Recueil de Voyages au Nord, 5 (1734): 35-195.

Tooker, Elisabeth. Natchez social organization: fact or anthropological folklore? Ethnohistory, 10 (1963): 358-372.

Vinson, J. La langue taensa. Revue de Linguistique et de Philologie Comparée, 19 (1886): 147-169.

Walker, W. M. The Troyville mounds. U.S. Bureau of American Ethnology, Bulletin, 113 (1936): 1-73.

White, Douglas R. Natchez class and rank reconsidered. By Douglas R. White, George Peter Murdock, and Richard Scaglion. Ethnology, 10 (1971): 369-388.

Witthoft, J.   Green corn ceremonialism in
the eastern woodlands. Michigan,
University, Museum of Anthropology,
Occasional Contributions, 13 (1949): 70-
77.

13-20   Pamlico

Anonymous.   Moratoc. U.S., Bureau of
American Ethnology, Bulletin, 30, part 1
(1907): 942.

Barbour, Philip.   The earliest
reconnaissance of the Chesapeake Bay
area; Captain John Smith's map and
Indian vocabulary. Virginia Magazine of
History and Biography, 79 (1971): 280-
302.

Baxter, James Phinney.   Raleigh's lost
colony. New England Magazine, n.s., 11
(1894/1895): 565-587.

Binford, Lewis Roberts.   Archaeological
and ethnohistorical investigation of
cultural diversity and progressive
development among aboriginal cultures of
coastal Virginia and North Carolina.
Dissertation Abstracts, 25 (1964/1965):
6880-6881.   UM 65-5877.

Brickell, John.   The natural history of
North Carolina. Murfreesboro, N.C.,
Johnson, 1968.   14, 14, 424 p. illus.,
map.

Brickell, John.   The natural history of
North-Carolina. New York, Johnson
Reprint, 1969.   10, 14, 417 p. illus.,
map.

Butler, Lindley S.   The early settlement
of Carolina; Virginia's southern
frontier. Virginia Magazine of History
and Biography, 79 (1971): 20-28.

Butler, Lindley S.   The early settlement
of Carolina. Virginia Magazine of
History and Biography, 77 (1969): 20-28.

Dillard, Richard.   The Indian tribes of
eastern North Carolina. North Carolina
Booklet, 6 (1906/1907): 4-26.

Dunbar, Gary S.   The Hatteras Indians of
North Carolina. Ethnohistory, 7 (1960):
410-418.

Hariot, Thomas.   A briefe and true report
of the new found land of Virginia. New
York, Dover Publications, 1972.   15,
91 p. illus.

Hariot, Thomas.   A report of the new found
land in Virginia. New York, Da Capo
Press, 1971.   51 p.

Hariot, Thomas.   Thomas Hariot's Virginia.
By Theodore de Bry. Ann Arbor,
University Microfilms, 1966.   33 p.
illus., map.

Kuhm, Herbert W.   The Indians of Virginia.
Wisconsin Archeologist, n.s., 11
(1931/1932): 91-99.

Lawson, John.   An account of the Indians
of N. Carolina. In Lawson's History of
North Carolina. Richmond, Garrett and
Massie, 1937: 179-259.

Lawson, John.   An account of the Indians
of N. Carolina. In his The History of
Carolina. Raleigh, Strother and Marcom,
1860: 277-390.

McPherson, Elizabeth Gregory, ed.
Nathaniell Batts, landholder on
Pasquotank River, 1660. North Carolina
Historical Review, 43 (1966): 66-81.

Mook, Maurice A.   A newly discovered
Algonkian tribe of Carolina. American
Anthropologist, n.s., 45 (1943): 635-
637.

Mook, Maurice A.   Algonkian ethnohistory
of the Carolina Sound. Washington
Academy of Sciences, Journal, 34 (1944):
181-197, 213-228.

Mook, Maurice A.   The aboriginal
population of Tidewater Virginia.
American Anthropologist, n.s., 46
(1944): 193-208.

Mook, Maurice A.   The anthropological
position of the Indian tribes of
Tidewater Virginia. William and Mary
College Quarterly, n.s., 23 (1943): 27-
40.

Mooney, James.   Coree. U.S., Bureau of
American Ethnology, Bulletin, 30, part 1
(1907): 349.

Mooney, James.   Secotan. U.S., Bureau of
American Ethnology, Bulletin, 30, part 2
(1910): 494-495.

Mooney, James.   Weapemeoc. U.S., Bureau of
American Ethnology, Bulletin, 30, part 2
(1910): 926-927.

Quinn, David B.   Thomas Hariot and the
Virginia voyages of 1602. William and
Mary Quarterly, 3d ser., 27 (1970): 268-
281.

Sams, Conway Whittle.   The conquest of
Virginia; the forest primeval. New
York, G. P. Putnam's Sons, 1916.   23,
432 p. illus., maps.

Smith, John. Captain John Smith's history
    of Virginia; a selection. Indianapolis,
    Bobbs-Merrill, 1970. 22, 182 p.

Smith, John. The generall historie of
    Virginia, New-England, and the Summer
    Isles. Ann Arbor, University
    Microfilms, 1966. 96, 105-248 p.
    illus., maps.

Smith, John. Works, 1608-1631. Edited by
    Edward Arber. New York, AMS Press,
    1967. 136, 984 p. illus.

Speck, Frank G. Remnants of the
    Machapunga Indians of North Carolina.
    American Anthropologist, n.s., 18
    (1916): 271-276.

Speck, Frank G. The ethnic position of
    the Southeastern Algonkian. American
    Anthropologist, n.s., 26 (1924): 184-
    200.

Tyler, Lyon G., ed. Narratives of early
    Virginia, 1606-1625. New York, Charles
    Scribner's Sons, 1907. 15, 478 p. map.
    (Original Narratives of Early American
    History, 5)

White, John. Portraits to the life and
    manners of the inhabitants of that
    province in America, called Virginia. In
    Graphic Sketches from Old and Authentic
    Works Illustrating the Costume, Habits
    and Character of the Aborigines of
    America. New York, J. and H. G.
    Langley, 1841: illus.

Willoughby, Charles C. The Virginia
    Indians in the seventeenth century.
    American Anthropologist, n.s., 9 (1907):
    57-86.

13-21 Powhatan

Dunlap, A. R. A bibliographical
    discussion of the Indian languages of
    the Delmarva Peninsula. Archaeological
    Society of Delaware, Bulletin, 4, no. 5
    (1949): 2-5.

Barbour, Philip. The earliest
    reconnaissance of the Chesapeake Bay
    area; Captain John Smith's map and
    Indian vocabulary. Virginia Magazine of
    History and Biography, 79 (1971): 280-
    302.

Barbour, Philip L. Chickahominy place
    names in Captain John Smith's 'True
    Relation'. Names, 15 (1967): 216-227.

Beverley, R. The history and present
    state of Virginia. Chapel Hill, 1947.
    366 p.

Beverley, R. The history of Virginia.
    London, 1722. 284 p.

Beverley, Robert. The history and present
    state of Virginia. Edited by Louis B.
    Wright. Charlottesville, Dominion
    Books, 1968. 35, 366 p. illus.

Beverley, Robert. The history and present
    state of Virginia; a selection.
    Indianapolis, Bobbs-Merrill, 1971. 17,
    171 p.

Bibaud, F. M. Biographie des sagamos
    illustrés de l'Amérique Septentrionale,
    65-85. Montréal, 1848.

Binford, Lewis R. An ethnohistory of the
    Nottoway, Meherrin and Weanock Indians
    of southeastern Virginia. Ethnohistory,
    14 (1967): 104-218.

Binford, Lewis Roberts. Archaeological
    and ethnohistorical investigation of
    cultural diversity and progressive
    development among aboriginal cultures of
    coastal Virginia and North Carolina.
    Dissertation Abstracts, 25 (1964/1965):
    6880-6881. UM 65-5877.

Blume, G. W. S. Present-day Indians of
    tidewater Virginia. Archaeological
    Society of Virginia, Quarterly Bulletin,
    6, no. 2 (1951): 1-11.

Bozman, J. L. The history of Maryland,
    Vol. 1: 103-193. Baltimore, 1837.

Burk, J. D. The history of Virginia.
    Petersburg, 1822. 4 v.

Bushnell, D. I. Indian sites below the
    falls of the Rappahannock. Smithsonian
    Miscellaneous Collections, 96, no. 4
    (1937): 1-65.

Bushnell, D. I. Virginia before
    Jamestown. Smithsonian Miscellaneous
    Collections, 100 (1940): 125-158.

Bushnell, D. I. Virginia--from early
    records. American Anthropologist, n.s.,
    9 (1907): 31-44.

Clark, Wayne E. The Elkridge Site:
    initial excavation and interpretation.
    Marlyland Archeology, 6, no. 2 (1970):
    32-57.

Clayton, John. John Clayton's 1687
    account of the medicinal practices of
    the Virginia Indians. Edited by Bernard
    G. Hoffman. Ethnohistory, 11 (1964): 1-
    40.

Coates, James R.   Native Indians of the Old Dominion State. American Indian, 2, no. 4 (1945): 22-25.

Cooke, J. E. Virginia. 5th ed., 26-33. Boston, 1884.

Davidson, D. S.   Some string figures of the Virginia Indians. Indian Notes, 4 (1927): 384-395.

Douglas, F. H. The Virginia Indian tribes. Denver Art Museum, Indian Leaflet Series, 57 (1933): 1-4.

Feest, Christian F. Powhatan: a study in political organization. Wiener Völkerkundliche Mitteilungen, 13 (1966): 69-83.

Feest, Christian F. Virginia Indian miscellany I. Archiv für Völkerkunde, 20 (1966): 1-7.

Fewkes, V. J.   Catawba pottery-making. American Philosophical Society, Proceedings, 88 (1944): 69-124.

Fishwick, Marshall. William Berkeley: unappreciated patriot. West Virginia History, 23 (1961/1962): 195-204.

Forbes, J. D.   Anglo-Powhatan relations to 1676. Masterkey, 30 (1956): 179-183; 31 (1957): 4-7.

Garrow, Patrick H. An ethnohistorical study of early English Indian policy. Working Papers in Sociology and Anthropology, 2, no. 1 (1968): 35-45.

Geary, J. A.   Strachey's vocabulary of Indian words used in Virginia, 1612. Works Issued by the Hakluyt Society, Second Series, 103 (1953): 208-214.

Geary, J. A.   The language of the Carolina Algonkian Tribes. Works Issued by the Hakluyt Society, Second Series, 105 (1955): 873-900.

Gerard, W. R.   The Tapehanek dialect of Virginia. American Anthropologist, n.s., 6 (1904): 313-330.

Gerard, W. R.   Virginia's contributions to English. American Anthropologist, n.s., 9 (1907): 87-112.

Gibbon, John.   John Gibbon's manuscript notes concerning Virginia. Edited by Martha W. Hiden and Henry M. Dargan. Virginia Magazine of History and Biography, 74 (1966): 3-22.

Gilliam, C. E.   Powhatan Algonkian bird names. Washington Academy of Sciences, Journal, 37 (1947): 1-2.

Gilliam, C. E. Powhatan sun worship. Archaeological Society of Virginia, Quarterly Bulletin, 12, no. 1 (1957): 1-4.

Harrington, J. P. The original Strachey vocabulary of the Virginia Indian language. U.S. Bureau of American Ethnology, Bulletin, 157 (1955): 189-202.

Hassrick, R. and E. Carpenter. Rappahannock games and amusements. Primitive Man, 17 (1944): 29-39.

Hendren, S. R.   Government and religion of the Virginia Indians. Johns Hopkins University, Studies in Historical and Political Science, 13, no. 11/12 (1895): 3-58.

Hoffman, Bernard G.   An unusual example of Virginia Indian toponymics. Ethnohistory, 11 (1964): 174-182.

Holmes, W. H.   Stone implements of the Potomac-Chesapeake tidewater province. U.S. Bureau of American Ethnology, Annual Reports, 15 (1897): 3-152.

Hough, W. The Indians of the District of Columbia. Scientific Monthly, 32 (1931): 537-539.

Howe, H. Historical collections of Virginia, 135-141. Charleston, 1845.

Jefferson, T. Notes on the State of Virginia. Philadelphia, 1788. 244 p.

Johnston, James Hugo. Documentary evidence of the relations of Negroes and Indians. Journal of Negro History, 14 (1929): 21-43.

Kuhm, Herbert W. The Indians of Virginia. Wisconsin Archeologist, n.s., 11 (1931/1932): 91-99.

Lewis, C. M. and A. J. Loomie. The Spanish Jesuit mission in Virginia, 1570-1572: p. 231-272. Chapel Hill, 1953.

Lurie, N. O. Indian cultural adjustment to European. In J. M. Smith, ed. Seventeenth-Century America. Chapel Hill, 1959: 33-60.

Mason, O. T. Anthropological news. American Naturalist, 40 (1877): 624.

Maxwell, H. The use and abuse of forests by the Virginia Indians. William and Mary College Quarterly Historical Magazine, 19 (1910): 73-104.

McCary, B. C. Indians in seventeenth century Virginia. Williamsburg, 1957. 93 p.

McCary, B. C. The Kiskiack (Chiskiack) Indians. Archaeological Society of Virginia, Quarterly Bulletin, 13, no. 3 (1959): 7-12.

Michelson, T. The linguistic classification of Powhatan. American Anthropologist, n.s., 35 (1933): 549.

Mook, M. A. The ethnological significance of Tindall's map of Virginia, 1608. William and Mary College Quarterly Historical Magazine, n.s., 23 (1943): 371-408.

Mook, M. A. Virginia ethnology from an early relation. William and Mary College Quarterly Historical Magazine, n.s., 23 (1943): 101-129.

Mook, Maurice A. The aboriginal population of Tidewater Virginia. American Anthropologist, n.s., 46 (1944): 193-208.

Mook, Maurice A. The anthropological position of the Indian tribes of Tidewater Virginia. William and Mary College Quarterly, n.s., 23 (1943): 27-40.

Mooney, J. Chickahominy. U.S. Bureau of American Ethnology, Bulletin, 30, vol. 1 (1907): 259-260.

Mooney, J. Indian tribes of the District of Columbia. American Anthropologist, 2 (1889): 259-266.

Mooney, J. Pamunkey. U.S. Bureau of American Ethnology, Bulletin, 30, vol. 2 (1910): 197-199.

Mooney, J. Powhatan. U.S. Bureau of American Ethnology, Bulletin, 30, vol. 2 (1910): 299-302.

Mooney, J. Queene Anne, of the Pamunkeys. U.S. Bureau of American Ethnology, Bulletin, 30, vol. 2 (1910): 338.

Mooney, J. The Powhatan Confederacy. American Anthropologist, n.s., 9 (1907): 129-152.

Newport, C. A relatyon of the discovery of our river. American Antiquarian Society, Transactions and Collections, 4 (1860): 40-65.

Pollard, J. G. The Pamunkey Indians of Virginia. U.S. Bureau of American Ethnology, Bulletin, 17 (1894): 1-19.

Robinson, W. S. Indian education and missions in Colonial Virginia. Journal of Southern History, 18 (1952): 152-168.

Robinson, W. S. Tributary Indians in Colonial Virginia. Virginia Magazine of History and Biography, 67, no. 1 (1959): 49-64.

Robinson, W. Stitt. Tributary Indians in Colonial America. Virginia Magazine of History and Biography, 67 (1959): 49-64.

Rose, C. B. The Indians of Arlington. Arlington, Va., 1957. 30 p.

Rowell, M. K. Pamunkey Indian games and amusements. Journal of American Folklore, 56 (1943): 203-207.

Rozwenc, Edwin C. Captain John Smith's image of America. William and Mary Quarterly, 3d ser., 16 (1959): 27-36.

Sams, C. W. The conquest of Virginia: the first attempt. Norfolk, 1924. 547 p.

Sams, Conway Whittle. The conquest of Virginia; the forest primeval. New York, G. P. Putnam's Sons, 1916. 23, 432 p. illus., maps.

Semmes, R. Aboriginal Maryland, 1608-1689. Maryland Historical Magazine, 24 (1929): 157-172, 195-209.

Shackleford, George Green. Nanzatico, King George County, Virginia. Virginia Magazine of History and Biography, 73 (1965): 287-404.

Shiner, J. L. A Jamestown Indian site. Archaeological Society of Virginia, Quarterly Bulletin, 10 (1955): 14-15.

Silver, Shirley. Natick consonants in reference to Proto-Central Algonquian. International Journal of American Linguistics, 26 (1960): 112-119, 234-241.

Smith, Gerald Patrick. Protohistoric sociopolitical organization of the Nottoway in the Chesapeake Bay-Carolina Sounds region. Dissertation Abstracts International, 32 (1971/1972): 3135B-3136B. UM 71-30,690.

Smith, J. A true relation of Virginia. Ed. by C. Deane. Boston, 1866. 88 p.

Smith, J. The generall historie of Virginia, New-England, and the Summer Isles. New ed., 129-148. Richmond, 1819.

Smith, J. Works, 1608-1631. Rev. ed. Edinburgh, 1910. 2 v.

Smith, John.   Captain John Smith's history
   of Virginia; a selection. Indianapolis,
   Bobbs-Merrill, 1970. 22, 182 p.

Smith, John. The generall historie of
   Virginia, New-England, and the Summer
   Isles. Ann Arbor, University
   Microfilms, 1966. 96, 105-248 p.
   illus., maps.

Smith, John. Works, 1608-1631. Edited by
   Edward Arber. New York, AMS Press,
   1967. 136, 984 p. illus.

*Speck, F. G. Chapters on the ethnology of
   the Powhatan tribes. Indian Notes and
   Monographs, 1 (1928): 227-455.

Speck, F. G. The gourd lamp among the
   Virginia Indians. American
   Anthropologist, n.s., 43 (1941): 676-
   678.

*Speck, F. G. The Rappahannock Indians of
   Virginia. Indian Notes and Monographs, 5
   (1925): 25-83.

Speck, F. G. and C. E. Schaeffer. The
   deer and the rabbit hunting drive in
   Virginia and the Southeast. Southern
   Indian Studies, 2 (1950): 3-20.

Speck, F. G., R. B. Hassrick, and E. S.
   Carpenter. Rappahannock herbals, folk-
   lore and science of cures. Delaware
   County Institute of Science,
   Proceedings, 10 (1942): 1-55.

Speck, F. G., R. B. Hassrick, and E. S.
   Carpenter. Rappahannock taking devices:
   traps, hunting and fishing. Philadelphia
   Anthropological Society, Publications, 1
   (1946): 1-28.

Speck, Frank G. The ethnic position of
   the Southeastern Algonkian. American
   Anthropologist, n.s., 26 (1924): 184-
   200.

*Stern, T. Chickahominy. American
   Philosophical Society, Proceedings, 96
   (1952): 157-225.

Stern, T. Pamunkey pottery making.
   Southern Indian Studies, 3 (1951): 1-78.

Stewart, T. D. Excavating the Indian
   village of Patawomeke. Smithsonian
   Institution, Explorations and Field-Work
   (1938): 87-90.

Stewart, T. D. Further excavations at the
   Indian village of Patawomeke.
   Smithsonian Institution, Explorations
   and Field-Work (1939): 79-82.

Strachey, W. The historie of travaile
   into Virginia Britannia. London, 1849.
   203 p.

Strachey, W. The historie of travell into
   Virginia Britania. Works Issued by the
   Hakluyt Society, Second Series, 103
   (1953): 1-253.

Stuart, Meriwether. Textual notes on
   "John Gibbon's manuscript notes
   concerning Virginia". Virginia Magazine
   of History and Biography, 74 (1966):
   462-479.

Swanton, J. R. Newly discovered Powhatan
   bird names. Washington Academy of
   Sciences, Journal, 24 (1934): 96-99.

Tooker, W. W. The mystery of the name
   Pamunkey. American Antiquarian and
   Oriental Journal, 17 (1895): 289-293.

Tooker, W. W. The names Chickahominy,
   Pamunkey and the Kuskarawokes of Captain
   John Smith. New York, 1901. 90 p.

Tooker, W. W. The Powhatan name for
   Virginia. American Anthropologist, n.s.,
   8 (1906): 23-27.

Tyler, L. G., ed. Narratives of early
   Virginia. New York, 1907.

Tylor, E. B. Notes on Powhatan's mantle.
   Internationales Archiv für Ethnographie,
   1 (1888): 215-217.

Uhler, S. P. Pennsylvania's Indian
   relations to 1754. Allentown, 1951.
   144 p.

Wyth (White), J. Portraits to the life
   and manners of the inhabitants of that
   province in America called Virginia.
   New York, 1841. 15 p.

13-22   Seminole

Goggin, J. M. Source materials for the
   study of the Florida Seminole Indians.
   Florida, University, Anthropology
   Laboratory, Laboratory Notes, 3 (1959):
   1-19.

Jones, William K. General guide to
   documents on the Five Civilized Tribes
   in the University of Oklahoma Library
   Division of Manuscripts. Ethnohistory,
   14 (1967): 47-76.

N.Y.A. Project. Bibliography on Seminole
   Indians. Gainesville, 1940. 24 p.

Adams, George R. The Caloosahatchee
   massacre: its significance in the Second
   Seminole War. Florida Historical
   Quarterly, 48 (1969/1970): 368-380.

Anonymous. A sketch of the Indian tribes known under the appellation of Muskogees (Seminoles), etc. . . . Monthly Magazine of Religion and Literature, 1 (1840): 137-147.

Anonymous. Billy Bowlegs and suite. Gleason's Pictorial Drawing Room Companion, 3, no. 17 (1852): 257.

Anonymous. Improved sanitary and social conditions of the Seminoles of Florida. American Medical Association, Journal, 26 (1896): 683-684.

Anonymous. Los Indios Seminoles de Florida. Boletín Indigenista, 17 (1957): 140-144.

Anonymous. Notes on the passage across the Everglades. Tequesta, 20 (1960): 57-65.

Anonymous. The pole cat, or shell dance. Southern Literary Messenger, 3 (1837): 390-391.

Anonymous. William McIntosh, Creek chief. Alabama Historical Quarterly, 21 (1959): 73-75.

Antle, H. R. Interpretation of Seminole clan relationship terms. Chronicles of Oklahoma, 14 (1936): 343-348.

Antle, H. R. The legend of Abuska. Chronicles of Oklahoma, 20 (1942): 255-256.

Arnade, Charles W. Cycles of conquest in Florida. Tequesta, 23 (1963): 23-31.

Arnett, W. T. Seminole Indian clues for contemporary house form in Florida. Florida Anthropologist, 6 (1953): 145-148.

Ashcraft, Allan C. Confederate Indian Department conditions in August, 1864. Chronicles of Oklahoma, 41 (1963): 270-285.

Ashcraft, Allan C. Confederate Indian troop conditions in 1864. Chronicles of Oklahoma, 41 (1963): 442-449.

Bailey, Minnie Elizabeth Thomas. Reconstruction in Indian Territory, 1865-1877. Dissertation Abstracts, 29 (1968/1969): 198A. UM 68-8362.

Baillou, Clemens de. The diaries of the Moravian Brotherhood at the Cherokee Mission in Spring Place, Georgia for the years 1800-1804. Georgia Historical Quarterly, 54 (1970): 571-576.

Banks, Dean. Civil-War refugees from Indian Territory, in the North, 1861-1864. Chronicles of Oklahoma, 41 (1963): 286-298.

Bartram, W. Observations on the Creek and Cherokee Indians. American Ethnological Society, Transactions, 3 (1853): 3-81.

Bartram, W. The travels of William Bartram, naturalist's edition. New Haven, 1958. 788 p.

Bartram, W. Travels in Georgia and Florida, 1773-74. Ed. by F. Harper. American Philosophical Society, Transactions, n.s., 33 (1943): 126, 190, 209, 223-226.

Bartram, W. Travels through North and South Carolina. London, 1792.

Beauchamp, Green. Early chronicles of Barbour County. Alabama Historical Quarterly, 33 (1971): 37-74.

Bell, R. E. and D. A. Baerreis. A survey of Oklahoma archeology. Texas Archeological and Paleontological Society, Bulletin, 22 (1951): 7-100.

Bemrose, John. Reminiscences of the Second Seminole War. Edited by John K. Mahon. Gainesville, University of Florida Press, 1966. 115 p. map.

Bittle, George C. First campaign of the Second Seminole War. Florida Historical Quarterly, 46 (1967/1968): 39-45.

Bittle, George C. Florida frontier incidents during the 1850s. Florida Historical Quarterly, 49 (1970/1971): 153-160.

Bittle, George C. Richard Keith Call's 1836 campaign. Tequesta, 29 (1969): 67-72.

Bittle, George C. The Florida militia's role in the battle of Withlacoochee. Florida Historical Quarterly, 44 (1965/1966): 303-311.

Boyd, M. F. Asi-Yaholo or Osceola. Florida Historical Quarterly, 33 (1955): 249-305.

Boyd, M. F. Florida aflame. Tallahassee, 1951. 115 p.

Boyd, M. F. Historic sites in and around the Jim Woodruff Reservoir area, Florida-Georgia. U.S. Bureau of American Ethnology, Bulletin, 169 (1958): 195-314.

Boyd, M. F. Horatio S. Dexter and events leading to the treaty of Moultrie Creek with the Seminole Indians. Florida Anthropologist, 11 (1958): 65-94.

Boyd, M. F. The Seminole War. Florida
    Historical Quarterly, 30 (1951): 3-115.

Brooks, A. M. "Sylvia Sunshine." Petals
    plucked from sunny climes. 2d ed.
    Nashville, 1886. 495 p.

Buckmaster, Henrietta. The Seminole wars.
    New York, Collier Books, 1966. 153 p.
    illus.

Buice, Sammy David. The Civil War and the
    Five Civilized Tribes--a study in
    Federal-Indian relations. Dissertation
    Abstracts International, 31 (1970/1971):
    2815A-2816A. UM 70-23,966.

Buker, George E. Lieutenant Levin M.
    Powell, U.S.N., pioneer of riverine
    warfare. Florida Historical Quarterly,
    47 (1968/1969): 253-275.

Buker, George Edward. Riverine warfare:
    naval combat in the Second Seminole War,
    1835-1842. Dissertation Abstracts
    International, 31 (1970/1971): 1181A.
    UM 70-14,859.

Bullen, R. P. An archaeological survey of
    the Chattahoochee River Valley in
    Florida. Washington Academy of Sciences,
    Journal, 40 (1950): 100-125.

Bullen, R. P. Notes on the Seminole
    archaeology of West Florida.
    Southeastern Archaeological Conference,
    News Letter, 3, no. 3 (1953): 18-19.

Bushnell, D. I. Native cemteries and
    forms of burial east of the Mississippi.
    U.S. Bureau of American Ethnology,
    Bulletin, 71 (1920): 114-116.

Buswell, J. O. Seminole medicine. Florida
    Medical Association, Journal, 57 (Nov.
    1970): 36.

Buswell, James Oliver, III. Florida
    Seminole religious ritual: resistance
    and change. Dissertation Abstracts
    International, 33 (1972/1973): 988B-
    989B. UM 72-23,910.

Capron, L. Floridas "wild" Indians, the
    Seminole. National Geographic Magazine,
    110 (1956): 819-840.

Capron, L. Notes on the hunting dance of
    the Cow Creek Seminole. Florida
    Anthropologist, 9 (1956): 67-78.

*Capron, L. The medicine bundles of the
    Florida Seminole and the green corn
    dance. U.S. Bureau of American
    Ethnology, Bulletin, 151 (1953): 155-
    210.

Capron, Louis. First in Palm Beach.
    Tequesta, 25 (1965): 43-65.

Casey, R. R. Free kings of the
    Everglades. Southwestern Lore, 18
    (1952): 20-24.

Cavazos Garza, Israel. Las incursiones de
    los bárbaros en el noreste de México,
    durante el siglo XIX. Humanitas
    (Monterrey), 5 (1964): 343-356.

Chase, Charles Monroe. An editor looks at
    early-day Kansas; the letters of Charles
    Monroe Chase. Edited by Lela Barnes.
    Kansas Historical Quarterly, 26 (1960):
    118-151.

Church, A. A dash through the Everglades.
    Tequesta, 9 (1949): 15-41.

Coe, C. B. Koontee, the Seminole bread
    root. Scientific American Supplement
    (Aug. 20, 1898): 18929.

Coe, C. H. Red patriots. Cincinnati,
    1898. 298 p.

Coe, C. H. The parentage and birthplace
    of Osceola. Florida Historical
    Quarterly, 27 (1939): 304-311.

Cohen, M. M. Notices of Florida and the
    campaigns. Charleston, 1836. 240 p.

Cohen, Myer M. Notices of Florida and the
    campaigns. Gainesville, University of
    Florida Press, 1964. 49, 251 p.
    illus., map.

Cory, C. B. Hunting and fishing in
    Florida. 2d ed. Boston, 1896. 304 p.

Cory, Charles B. Hunting and fishing in
    Florida. New York, Arno Press, 1970.
    304 p. illus.

Cotterill, R. S. The Southern Indians.
    Norman, 1954. 268 p.

Covington, J. W. Cuban bloodhounds and
    the Seminoles. Florida Historical
    Quarterly, 33 (1954): 111-119.

Covington, J. W. The story of
    southwestern Florida. Vol. 1. New York,
    1957.

Covington, J. W., ed. A petition from
    some Latin-American fishermen, 1838.
    Tequesta, 14 (1954): 61-65.

Covington, James W. An episode in the
    Third Seminole War. Florida Historical
    Quarterly, 45 (1966/1967): 45-59.

Covington, James W. Apalachicola Seminole
    leadership: 1820-1833. Florida
    Anthropologist, 16 (1963): 57-62.

Covington, James W. Federal and state relations with the Florida Seminoles, 1875-1901. Tequesta, 32 (1972): 17-27.

Covington, James W. Federal relations with the Apalachicola Indians: 1823-1838. Florida Historical Quarterly, 42 (1963/1964): 125-141.

Covington, James W. Migration of the Seminoles into Florida, 1700-1820. Florida Historical Quarterly, 46 (1968): 340-357.

Covington, James W. The British meet the Seminoles; negotiations between British authorities in East Florida and the Indians, 1763-68. Gainesville, University of Florida, 1961. 66 p. illus., map. (Florida, State Museum, Contributions, Social Sciences, 7)

Covington, James W. The Indian scare of 1849. Tequesta, 21 (1961): 53-63.

Covington, James W. Trade relations between southwestern Florida and Cuba--1600-1840. Florida Historical Quarterly, 38, no. 2 (1959): 114-128.

Covington, James W., ed. The Florida Seminoles in 1847. Tequesta, 24 (1964): 49-57.

Craig, Alan K. Captain Young's sketch map, 1818. By Alan K. Craig and Christopher S. Peebles. Florida Historical Quarterly, 48 (1969/1970): 176-179.

Curtis, E. S. The North American Indian, Vol. 19: 8-11. Norwood, 1930.

Cushman, Joseph D., Jr. The Indian River settlement: 1842-1849. Florida Historical Quarterly, 43 (1964/1965): 21-35.

Davis, H. J. The history of Seminole clothing and its multi-colored designs. American Anthropologist, 57 (1955): 974-980.

Davis, H. N. Designs from the Seminoles [and] sewing art of the Seminoles. McCall's Needlework and Crafts Annual, 6 (1955): 61-63.

Debo, A. And still the waters run. Princeton, 1940. 417 p.

Densmore, F. Recording Indian music. Smithsonian Institution, Explorations and Field-Work (1931): 183-190.

Densmore, F. Recording Seminole songs in Florida. Smithsonian Institution, Explorations and Field-Work (1932): 93-96.

Densmore, F. Seminole music related to Cocopa. El Palacio, 32 (1932): 172-173.

Densmore, F. Seminole music. U.S. Bureau of American Ethnology, Bulletin, 161 (1956): 1-251.

Densmore, F. The Seminole Indian today. Southern Folklore Quarterly, 18 (1954): 212-221.

Dimock, A. W. and J. A. Dimock. Florida enchantments. New York, 1908.

Drew, F. Notes on the origin of the Seminole Indians of Florida. Florida Historical Quarterly, 6 (1927): 21-24.

DuBois, Bessie Wilson. Jupiter lighthouse. Tequesta, 20 (1960): 5-17.

Duncan, A. J. Report of A. J. Duncan, United States Indian Inspector, to the Honorable Secretary of the Interior, in regard to the reservation of lands for the use of the Seminole Indians of Florida. In Report of the Secretary of the Interior for the Fiscal Year Ending June 30, 1898. 1898: 204-242.

Dundes, Alan. Washington Irving's version of the Seminole origin of races. Ethnohistory, 9 (1962): 257-264.

Eby, Cecil D., Jr. Memoir of a West Pointer in Florida: 1825. Florida Historical Quarterly, 41 (1962/1963): 154-164.

Edwards, Newton. Economic development of Indian reserves. Human Organization, 20 (1961/1962): 197-202.

Ellis, L. B. The Seminoles of Florida. Gunton's Magazine, 25 (1903): 495-505.

Emerson, W. C. The Seminoles. New York, 1954. 72 p.

Erwin, A. T. and E. P. Lana. The Seminole pumpkin. Economic Botany, 10, no. 1 (1956): 33-37.

Fairbanks, Charles H. A Colono-Indian ware milk pitcher. Florida Anthropologist, 15 (1962): 103-106.

Fay, George E., ed. Charters, constitutions and by-laws of the Indian tribes of North America. Part VI: The Indian tribes of Oklahoma (cont'd.). Greeley, 1968. 5, 129 l. map. (University of Northern Colorado, Museum of Anthropology, Occasional Publications in Anthropology, Ethnology Series, 7) ERIC ED046556.

Fischer, LeRoy H. Confederate Indian forces outside of Indian Territory. By

LeRoy H. Fischer and Jerry Gill. Chronicles of Oklahoma, 46 (1968): 249-284.

Foreman, C. T. John Jumper. Chronicles of Oklahoma, 29 (1951): 137-152.

Foreman, C. T. The Jumper family of the Seminole nation. Chronicles of Oklahoma, 34 (1956): 272-285.

Foreman, G. Report of Cherokee deputation into Florida. Chronicles of Oklahoma, 9 (1931): iv.

Foreman, G. The five civilized tribes, 223-278. Norman, 1934.

Foreman, Grant. The Five Civilized Tribes; a brief history and a century of progress. Muskogee, Okla., C. T. Foreman, 1966. 58 p. illus.

Foster, L. Negro-Indian relationships in the Southeast. Philadelphia, 1935. 86 p.

Freeman, E. C. Culture stability and change among the Seminoles of Florida. International Congress of the Anthropological and Ethnological Sciences, Acts, 5 (1960): 248-254.

Freeman, E. C. Our unique Indians the Seminoles of Florida. American Indian, 2, no. 2 (1944/1945): 14-28.

Freeman, E. C. The Seminole woman of the Big Cypress and her influence in modern life. América Indígena, 4 (1944): 123-128.

Freeman, E. C. We live with the Seminoles. Natural History, 49 (1942): 226-237.

Freeman, Ethel C. Directed culture-change and selfdetermination in superordinate and subordinate societies. In International Congress of Anthropological and Ethnological Sciences, 7th. 1964, Moscow. Vol. 4. Moskva, Izdatel'stvo "Nauka", 1967: 85-90.

Freeman, Ethel Cutler. Lawlessness in an Indian tribe as a microcosm of a world trend. In International Congress of Anthropological and Ethnological Sciences, 8th. 1968, Tokyo and Kyoto. Proceedings. Vol. 2. Tokyo, Science Council of Japan, 1969: 191-193.

Freeman, Ethel Cutler. The happy life in the City of Ghosts: an analysis of a Mikasuki myth. Florida Anthropologist, 14 (1961): 23-36.

Freeman, Ethel Cutler. The least known of the Five Civilized Tribes: the Seminoles of Oklahoma. Florida Anthropologist, 17 (1964): 139-152.

Freeman, Ethel Cutler. Two types of response to external pressures among the Florida Seminoles. Anthropological Quarterly, 38 (1965): 55-61.

Gaillard, Frye. Seminoles of Florida. Indian Historian, 3, no. 4 (1970): 46-50.

Garbarino, Merwyn S. Big Cypress: a changing Seminole community. New York, Holt, Rinehart and Winston, 1972. 10, 132 p. illus.

Garbarino, Merwyn S. Decision-making process and the study of culture change. Ethnology, 6 (1967): 465-470.

Garbarino, Merwyn Stephens. Economic development and the decision-making process on Big Cypress Reservation, Florida. Dissertation Abstracts, 27 (1966/1967): 2578B-2579B. UM 66-13,983.

Garvin, Russell. The free Negro in Florida before the Civil War. Florida Historical Quarterly, 46 (1967/1968): 1-18.

Gatschet, A. S. A migration legend of the Creek Indians, 66-73. Philadelphia, 1884.

Gibson, A. M. An Indian Territory United Nations: the Creek Council of 1845. Chronicles of Oklahoma, 39 (1961): 398-413.

Giddings, J. R. The exiles of Florida. Columbus, Ohio, 1858.

Giddings, Joshua R. The exiles of Florida. Gainesville, University of Florida Press, 1964. 38, 346 p.

Giddings, Joshua R. The exiles of Florida. New York, Arno Press, 1969. 8, 338 p. illus.

Gifford, J. C. Billy Bowlegs and the Seminole War. Coconut Grove, 1925. 79 p.

Goggin, J. M. A Florida Indian trading post, circa 1763-1784. Southern Indian Studies, 1, no. 2 (1949): 35-37.

Goggin, J. M. Beaded shoulder pouches of the Florida Seminole. Florida Anthropologist, 4 (1951): 3-17.

Goggin, J. M. Osceola. Florida Historical Quarterly, 33 (1955): 161-192.

Goggin, J. M. Seminole archaeology in East Florida. Southeastern Archaeological Conference, News Letter, 3, no. 3 (1953): 16, 19.

Goggin, J. M. Silver work of the Florida Seminole. El Palacio, 47 (1940): 25-32.

Goggin, J. M. The present condition of the Florida Seminoles. New Mexico Anthropologist, 1 (1937): 37-39.

Goggin, J. M. The Seminole Negroes of Andros Island, Bahamas. Florida Historical Quarterly, 24 (1946): 201-206.

Goggin, J. M., et al. An historic Indian burial, Alachua County, Florida. Florida Anthropologist, 2, nos. 1/2 (1949): 10-25.

Goza, William. The Fort King Road--1963. Florida Historical Quarterly, 43 (1964/1965): 52-70.

Graebner, N. A. Pioneer Indian agriculture in Oklahoma. Chronicles of Oklahoma, 23 (1945): 232-248.

Graebner, N. A. The public land policy of the five civilized tribes. Chronicles of Oklahoma, 23 (1945): 107-118.

Greenlee, R. F. Aspects of social organization and material culture of the Seminole of Big Cypress Swamp. Florida Anthropologist, 5 (1952): 25-32.

Greenlee, R. F. Ceremonial practices of the modern Seminoles. Tequesta, 1, no. 2 (1942): 25-33.

Greenlee, R. F. Eventful happenings among the modern Florida Seminoles. Southern Folklore Quarterly, 9 (1945): 145-152.

Greenlee, R. F. Folktales of the Florida Seminole. Journal of American Folklore, 58 (1945): 138-144.

Greenlee, R. F. Medicine and curing practices of the modern Florida Seminoles. American Anthropologist, n.s., 46 (1944): 317-328.

Griffin, J. W. Some comments on the Seminole in 1818. Florida Anthropologist, 10, nos. 3/4 (1957): 41-49.

Griffin, J. W., ed. The Florida Indian and his neighbors: 45-54. Winter Park, 1949.

Groene, Bertram H. Lizzie Brown's Tallahassee. Florida Historical Quarterly, 48 (1969/1970): 155-175.

Hadley, J. N. Notes on the socio-economic status of the Oklahoma Seminoles. Comitato Italiano per lo Studio del Problemi della Popolazione, Pubblicazioni, ser. 3, 2 (1935): 133-159.

Hamlin, H. A health survey of the Seminole Indians. Yale Journal of Biology and Medicine, 6 (1933): 155-177.

Hammond, E. A., ed. Dr. Strobel reports on Southeast Florida, 1836. Tequesta, 21 (1961): 65-75.

Hammond, E. A., ed. Sanibel Island and its vicinity, 1833, a document. Florida Historical Quarterly, 48 (1969/1970): 392-411.

Harrington, M. R. Bad Injun boy--he fix 'em. Masterkey, 27, no. 5 (1953): 185.

Harrington, M. R. Funko the slave. Masterkey, 20 (1946): 169-170.

Harrington, M. R. Seminole adventure. Masterkey, 20 (1946): 157-159.

Harrington, M. R. Seminole oranges. Masterkey, 20 (1946): 112.

Harrington, M. R. Seminole surgeon. Masterkey, 27 (1953): 122.

Heath, Gary N. The first federal invasion of Indian Territory. Chronicles of Oklahoma, 44 (1966/1967): 409-419.

Henshall, J. A. Camping and cruising in Florida, 153-167. Cincinnati, 1884.

Henslick, Harry. The Seminole Treaty of 1866. Chronicles of Oklahoma, 48 (1970/1971): 280-294.

Hirschhorn, Howard H. Cerumen types and PTC-tasting in the Seminole Indians of Florida. American Journal of Physical Anthropology, n.s., 33 (1970): 107-108.

Holmes, Jack D. L. The Southern Boundary Commission, the Chattahoochee River, and the Florida Seminoles, 1799. Florida Historical Quarterly, 44 (1965/1966): 312-341.

Hood, Fred. Twilight of the Confederacy in Indian Territory. Chronicles of Oklahoma, 41 (1963): 425-441.

Hough, W. Seminoles of the Florida swamps. Home Geographic Monthly, 2, no. 3 (1932): 7-12.

Howard, James H. The Southeastern ceremonial complex and its interpretation. Columbia, 1968. 8,

169 p. illus. (Missouri Archaeological Society, Memoir, 6)

Howard, R. Palmer. A historiography of the Five Civilized Tribes: a chronological approach. Chronicles of Oklahoma, 47 (1969): 312-331.

Howard, R. Palmer. A historiography of the Five Civilized Tribes; a chronological approach. Oklahoma City, Oklahoma Historical Society, 1969. 20 p.

Hoxie, W. J. A Seminole vocabulary. Atlantic Slope Naturalist, 1 (1903): 64-65.

Hrdlička, A. The anthropology of Florida. Florida State Historical Society, Publications, 1 (1922): 1-140.

Huston, W. Los indios seminolas. Revista Geográfica Española, 7 (1940): 49-58.

Hutchinson, J. Painting among the Seminoles. American Artist, 30 (Apr. 1966): 52-57.

Irving, Washington. The Seminoles. Indian Historian, 2, no. 1 (1969): 35-37.

Kansas City Star. Report on the Five Civilized Tribes 1897. Chronicles of Oklahoma, 48 (1970): 416-430.

Kay, Russell. Tamiami Trail blazers: a personal memoir. Florida Historical Quarterly, 49 (1970/1971): 278-287.

Kersey, Harry A., Jr. A comparison of Seminole reading vocabulary and Dolch Word Lists. By Harry Kersey and Rebecca Fadjo. Journal of American Indian Education, 11, no. 1 (1971/1972): 16-18.

Kersey, Harry A., Jr. Ahfachkee day school. Teachers College Record, 72 (1970): 93-103.

Kersey, Harry A., Jr. Educating the Seminole Indians of Florida, 1879-1970. Florida Historical Quarterly, 49 (1970/1971): 16-35.

Kersey, Harry A., Jr. Educational achievement among three Florida Seminole reservations. By H. A. Kersey, Jr. and H. R. Greene. School and Society, 100 (1972): 25-28.

Kersey, Harry A., Jr. Improving reading skills of Seminole children. By Harry A. Kersey, Jr., Anne Keithley, and F. Ward Brunson. Journal of American Indian Education, 10, no. 3 (1970/1971): 3-7.

Kersey, Harry A., Jr. Training teachers in a Seminole Indian school--a unique

experience with the disadvantaged child. Journal of Teacher Education, 22 (1971): 25-28.

Knotts, Tom. History of the blockhouse on the Withlacooche. Florida Historical Quarterly, 49 (1970/1971): 245-254.

Krogman, W. M. The cephalic type of the full-blood and mixed-blood Seminole Indians. Zeitschrift für Rassenkunde, 3 (1936): 176-190.

Krogman, W. M. The physical anthropology of the Seminole Indians. Comitato Italiano per lo Studio del Problemi della Popolazione, Pubblicazioni, ser. 3, 2 (1935): 1-199.

Krogman, W. M. The racial composition of the Seminole Indians of Florida and Oklahoma. Journal of Negro History, 19 (1934): 412-430.

Krogman, W. M. The racial type of the Seminole Indians of Florida and Oklahoma. Florida Anthropologist, 1, no. 3/4 (1948): 61-73.

Krogman, W. M. Vital data on the population of the Seminole Indians. Human Biology, 7 (1935): 335-349.

Laumer, Frank. Encounter by the river. Florida Historical Quarterly, 46 (1967/1968): 322-339.

Laumer, Frank. Massacre! Gainesville, University of Florida Press, 1968. 20, 188 p. illus., maps.

Laumer, Frank. This was Fort Dade. Florida Historical Quarterly, 45 (1966/1967): 1-11.

Laxson, D. D. An historic Seminole burial in a Hialeah midden. Florida Anthropologist, 7 (1954): 111-118.

Laxson, D. D. Excavations in Dade and Broward counties 1959-1961. Florida Anthropologist, 15 (1962): 1-10.

Lollar, Wayne B. Seminole-United States financial relations, 1823-1866. Chronicles of Oklahoma, 50 (1972): 190-198.

Longacre, Robert E. Grammar discovery procedures; a field manual. The Hague, Mouton, 1964. 162 p. (Janua Linguarum, Series Minor, 33)

*MacCauley, C. The Seminole Indians of Florida. U.S. Bureau of American Ethnology, Annual Reports, 5 (1884): 469-531.

Madigan, La Verne. Most independent
people: a field report on Indian
Florida. New York, Association on
American Indian Affairs, 1959. 8 p.
map. (Indian Affairs, 31)

Mahon, John K. History of the Second
Seminole War, 1835-1842. Gainesville,
University of Florida Press, 1967. 12,
387 p. illus., maps.

Mahon, John K. The journal of A. B. Meek
and the Second Seminole War, 1836.
Florida Historical Quarterly, 38
(1959/1960): 302-318.

Mahon, John K. The treaty of Moultrie
Creek, 1823. Florida Historical
Quarterly, 40 (1961/1962): 350-372.

Mahon, John K. Two Seminole treaties:
Payne's Landing, 1832, and Ft. Gibson,
1833. Florida Historical Quarterly, 41
(1962/1963): 1-21.

Marchman, W. P. The Ingraham Everglades
exploring expedition, 1892. Tequesta, 7
(1947): 3-43.

Marmon, K. A. The Seminole Indians of
Florida. Riverside, California, Sherman
Institute, 1956. 20 p.

Mayberry, Ruben H. A survey of chronic
disease and diet in Seminole Indians in
Oklahoma. By Ruben H. Mayberry and
Robert D. Lindeman. American Journal of
Clinical Nutrition, 13 (1963): 127-134.

McAlister, Lyle N. William Augustus
Bowles and the State of Muskogee.
Florida Historical Quarterly, 40
(1961/1962): 317-328.

McCarthy, J. E. Portraits of Osceola and
the artists who painted them.
Jacksonville Historical Society, Papers,
2 (1949): 23-44.

McKenzie, B. and R. Fish. The Indian ball
game as played by the Seminoles. Indian
School Journal, 17, no. 2 (1916): 79-81.

McReynolds, E. C. The Seminoles. Norman,
1957. 412 p.

Mendez, A. F. Government medical service
to the Seminole Indians. Florida Medical
Association, Journal, 57 (1970): 28-32.

Mercer, H. C. Recent pile structures made
by Seminole Indians. American
Naturalist, 31 (1897): 357-359.

Mooney, J. Seminole. U.S. Bureau of
American Ethnology, Bulletin, 30, vol. 2
(1910): 500-502.

Moore-Willson, M. History of Osceola
County. Orlando, 1935. 59 p.

Moore-Willson, M. Seminoles. In J.
Hastings, ed. Encyclopaedia of Religion
and Ethics. Vol. 11. New York, 1921:
376-378.

Moore-Willson, M. The Seminole Indians of
Florida. Florida Historical Quarterly, 2
(1928): 75-87.

Moore-Willson, M. The Seminoles of
Florida. New ed. New York, 1914.
235 p.

Morice, A. G. Autres Muskokis. Société de
Géographie (Québec), Bulletin, 21
(1927): 211-231.

Motte, J. R. Journey into wilderness.
Gainesville, 1953. 361 p.

Munroe, K. A forgotten remnant.
Scribner's Magazine, 7 (1890): 303-317.

Munroe, K. Alligator hunting with the
Seminoles. Cosmopolitan, 13 (1892): 576-
581.

Neill, W. T. A note on the Seminole
burial from Hialeah, Florida. Florida
Anthropologist, 10, nos. 3/4 (1957): 11-
13.

Neill, W. T. Dugouts of the Mikasuki
Seminole. Florida Anthropologist, 6
(1953): 77-84.

Neill, W. T. Florida's Seminole Indians.
Silver Springs, 1952. 81 p.

Neill, W. T. Graters of the Mikasuki
Seminole. Florida Anthropologist, 7
(1954): 75-76.

Neill, W. T. Preparation of rubber by the
Florida Seminole. Florida
Anthropologist, 9 (1956): 25-28.

Neill, W. T. Sailing vessels of the
Florida Seminole. Florida
Anthropologist, 9 (1956): 79-86.

Neill, W. T. The calumet ceremony of the
Seminole Indians. Florida
Anthropologist, 8 (1955): 83-88.

Neill, W. T. The identity of Florida's
"Spanish Indians". Florida
Anthropologist, 7, no. 2 (1955): 43-57.

Neill, W. T. The site of Osceola's
village. Florida Historical Quarterly,
33 (1955): 240-246.

Neill, W. T. The story of Florida's
Seminole Indians. Silver Springs, 1956.
91 p.

Neill, Wilfred T. The story of Florida's Seminole Indians. 2d ed. St. Petersburg, Great Outdoors, 1964. 4, 128 p. illus., map.

New Orleans Correspondent. Billy Bowlegs at New Orleans. Harper's Weekly, 2, no. 76 (1858): 376-378.

Ober, F. P. Ten days with the Seminoles. Appletons' Journal, 14 (1875): 142-144, 171-173.

Olds, Dorris L. Some highlights in the history of Fort St. Marks. Florida Anthropologist, 15 (1962): 33-40.

Olson, Gary D. Thomas Brown, Loyalist partisan, and the Revolutionary War in Georgia, 1777-1782. Georgia Historical Quarterly, 54 (1970): 1-19, 183-208.

Osceola, B. Operations of the Seminole tribe of Florida as of January 1, 1959. Dania, Florida, 1959.

Ott, Eloise R. Fort King: a brief history. Florida Historical Quarterly, 46 (1967/1968): 29-38.

Owsley, Frank L., Jr. British and Indian activities in Spanish West Florida during the War of 1812. Florida Historical Quarterly, 46 (1967/1968): 111-123.

Owsley, Frank Lawrence, Jr. The role of the South in the British grand strategy in the War of 1812. Tennessee Historical Quarterly, 30 (1971): 22-38.

Panagopoulos, E. P. Chateaubriand's Florida and his journey to America. Florida Historical Quarterly, 49 (1970/1971): 140-152.

Peake, G. Ronald. Oklahoma's "five tribes" Indians are improving their living conditions through public housing. Journal of Housing, 28 (1971): 430-432.

Peithmann, I. M. The unconquered Seminole Indians. St. Petersburg, 1956. 95 p.

Peters, Thelma, ed. William Adee Whitehead's reminiscences of Key West. Tequesta, 25 (1965): 3-42.

Pierce, J. Notices of the agriculture, scenery, geology, and animal, vegetable and mineral productions of the Floridas, and of the Indian tribes. American Journal of Science, 9 (1825): 119-136.

Plato, Chris C. Polymorphism of the C line of palmar dermatoglyphics with a new classification of the C line terminations. American Journal of

Physical Anthropology, n.s., 33 (1970): 413-419.

Pollitzer, William S. Ancestral traits, parental populations, and hybrids. American Journal of Physical Anthropology, n.s., 30 (1969): 415-419.

Pollitzer, William S., et al. Indications of major genes for serum glucose and diabetes based on study of Seminole Indians. American Journal of Human Genetics, 22, no. 6 (1970): 28A.

Pollitzer, William S., et al. The Seminole Indians of Florida: morphology and serology. American Journal of Physical Anthropology, n.s., 32 (1970): 65-81.

Pollitzer, William S., et al. The Seminole Indians of Oklahoma: morphology and serology. American Journal of Physical Anthropology, n.s., 33 (1970): 15-29.

Porter, K. W. Farewell to John Horse. Phylon, 8 (1947): 265-273.

Porter, K. W. Florida slaves and free Negroes in the Seminole War, 1835-1842. Journal of Negro History, 28 (1943): 390-421.

Porter, K. W. John Caesar: Seminole Negro partisan. Journal of Negro History, 31 (1946): 190-207.

Porter, K. W. Negroes and the Seminole War, 1817-1818. Journal of Negro History, 36 (1951): 249-280.

Porter, K. W. Notes on Seminole Negroes in the Bahamas. Florida Historical Quarterly, 24 (1945): 56-60.

Porter, K. W. Origins of the St. John's River Seminole. Florida Anthropologist, 4 (1951): 39-45.

Porter, K. W. Osceola and the Negroes. Florida Historical Quarterly, 33 (1955): 235-239.

Porter, K. W. Seminole flight from Fort Marion. Florida Historical Quarterly, 22 (1944): 112-133.

Porter, K. W. Seminole in Mexico, 1850-1861. Chronicles of Oklahoma, 29 (1951): 153-172.

Porter, K. W. The Cowkeeper Dynasty of the Seminole nation. Florida Historical Quarterly, 30 (1952): 341-349.

Porter, K. W. The founder of the "Seminole Nation". Florida Historical Quarterly, 27 (1949): 362-384.

Porter, K. W. The Negro Abraham. Florida
    Historical Quarterly, 25 (1946): 1-43.

Porter, K. W. The Seminole in Mexico,
    1850-1861. Hispanic American Historical
    Review, 31 (1951): 1-36.

Porter, K. W. The Seminole Negro-Indian
    scouts, 1870-1881. Southwestern
    Historical Quarterly, 55 (1952): 358-
    377.

Porter, Kenneth W. Billy Bowlegs (Holata
    Micco) in the Civil War. Florida
    Historical Quarterly, 45 (1966/1967):
    391-401.

Porter, Kenneth W. Billy Bowlegs (Holata
    Micco) in the Seminole Wars. Florida
    Historical Quarterly, 45 (1966/1967):
    219-242.

Porter, Kenneth Wiggins. Thlonoto-sassa:
    a note on an obscure Seminole village of
    the early 1820's. Florida
    Anthropologist, 13 (1960): 115-119.

Potter, Woodburne. The war in Florida.
    Ann Arbor, University Microfilms, 1966.
    8, 184 p. maps.

Price, W. A. Dental-caries incidence in
    relation to nutrition among past and
    present Indians of Florida. Journal of
    Dental Research, 15 (1935): 179-180.

Rampp, Lary C. Confederate Indian sinking
    of the J. R. Williams. Journal of the
    West, 11 (1972): 43-50.

Rife, David C. Finger and palmar
    dermatoglyphics in Seminole Indians of
    Florida. American Journal of Physical
    Anthropology, n.s., 28 (1968): 119-126.

Roberts, A. H. The Dade massacre. Florida
    Historical Quarterly, 5 (1927): 123-138.

Sears, W. H. A-296--A Seminole site in
    Alachua County. Florida Anthropologist,
    12, no. 1 (1959): 25-30.

Sefton, James E. Black slaves, Red
    masters, White middlemen: a
    Congressional debate of 1852. Florida
    Historical Quarterly, 51 (1972/1973):
    113-128.

Seley, Ray B., Jr. Lieutenant Hartsuff
    and the Banana Plants. Tequesta, 23
    (1963): 3-14.

Self, R. D. Chronology of New Echota.
    Early Georgia, 1, no. 4 (1955): 3-5.

Sharppee, Nathan. Fort Dallas and the
    Naval Depot on Key Biscayne, 1836-1926.
    Tequesta, 21 (1961): 13-40.

Shoemaker, Arthur. The battle of
    Chustenahlah. Chronicles of Oklahoma, 38
    (1960): 180-184.

Simmons, W. H. Notices of East Florida.
    Charleston, 1822. 105 p.

Skinner, A. Notes on the Florida
    Seminole. American Anthropologist, n.s.,
    15 (1913): 63-77.

Skinner, A. The Florida Seminoles.
    Southern Workman, 40 (1911): 154-163.

Small, J. K. Seminole bread--the Conti.
    New York Botanical Garden, Journal, 22
    (1921): 121-137.

Smith, B. Comparative vocabularies of the
    Seminole and Mikasuke tongues. In W. W.
    Beach, ed. Indian Miscellany. Albany,
    1877: 120-126.

Smith, B. Comparative vocabularies of the
    Seminole and Mikasuke tongues.
    Historical Magazine, ser. 1, 10 (1866):
    239-243.

Smith, W. W. A lieutenant of the left
    wing. Sketches of the Seminole War.
    Charleston, 1836. 311 p.

Spoehr, A. Camp, clan, and kin among the
    Cow Creek Seminole. Field Museum,
    Anthropological Series, 33 (1941): 1-27.

Spoehr, A. "Friends" among the Seminole.
    Chronicles of Oklahoma, 19 (1941): 252.

*Spoehr, A. Kinship system of the
    Seminole. Field Museum, Anthropological
    Series, 33 (1942): 31-113.

Spoehr, A. Oklahoma Seminole towns.
    Chronicles of Oklahoma, 19 (1941): 377-
    380.

*Spoehr, A. The Florida Seminole camp.
    Field Museum, Anthropological Series, 33
    (1944): 117-150.

Sprague, J. T. The origin, progress, and
    conclusion of the Florida War. New
    York, 1848. 559 p.

Sprague, John T. The origin, progress,
    and conclusion of the Florida War.
    Gainesville, University of Florida
    Press, 1964. 30, 597 p. illus., map.

Stephan, L. L. Geographic role of the
    Everglades in the early history of
    Florida. Scientific Monthly, 55 (1942):
    515-526.

Stirling, G. Report on the Seminole
    Indians of Florida. Washington, D.C.,
    Applied Anthropology Unit, Office of
    Indian Affairs, 1936. 9 p.

Stirling, R. B.   Some psychological mechanisms operative in gossip. Social Forces, 34 (1956): 262-267.

Straight, W. M.   Josie Billie, Seminole doctor, medicine man, and Baptist preacher. Florida Medical Association, Journal, 57 (Aug. 1970): 33-40.

Straight, W. M.   Seminole Indian medicine. Florida Medical Association, Journal, 57 (1970): 19-27.

Strickland, Alice.   James Ormond, merchant and soldier. Florida Historical Quarterly, 41 (1962/1963): 209-222.

Strickland, Alice.   Ponce de Leon Inlet. Florida Historical Quarterly, 43 (1964/1965): 244-261.

Sturtevant, W. C.   A Seminole personal document. Tequesta, 16 (1956): 55-75.

Sturtevant, W. C.   Chakaika and the "Spanish Indians". Tequesta, 13 (1953): 35-73.

Sturtevant, W. C.   Notes on modern Seminole traditions of Osceola. Florida Historical Quarterly, 33 (1955): 206-217.

Sturtevant, W. C.   Osceola's coats? Florida Historical Quarterly, 34 (1956): 315-328.

Sturtevant, W. C.   R. H. Pratt's report on the Seminole in 1879. Florida Anthropologist, 9, no. 1 (1956): 1-24.

Sturtevant, W. C.   The medicine bundles and busks of the Florida Seminole. Florida Anthropologist, 7 (1954): 31-72.

Sturtevant, William C.   A newly-discovered 1838 drawing of a Seminole dance. Florida Anthropologist, 15 (1962): 73-82.

Sturtevant, William C.   Creek into Seminole. In Eleanor Burke Leacock and Nancy Oestreich Lurie, eds. North American Indians in Historical Perspective. New York, Random House, 1971: 92-128.

Sturtevant, William C.   Seminole men's clothing. In June Helm, ed. Essays on the Verbal and Visual Arts. Seattle, University of Washington Press, 1967: 160-174. (American Ethnological Society, Proceedings of the Annual Spring Meeting, 1966)

Sturtevant, William C.   Seminole myths of the origin of races. Ethnohistory, 10 (1963): 80-86.

Sturtevant, William C.   The Mikasuki Seminole: medical beliefs and practices. Dissertation Abstracts, 28 (1967/1968): 776B.   UM 67-11,355.

Swanton, J. R.   Coonti. American Anthropologist, n.s., 15 (1913): 141.

Swanton, J. R.   Early history of the Creek Indians and their neighbors. U.S. Bureau of American Ethnology, Bulletin, 73 (1922): 398-414.

Swanton, J. R.   Modern square grounds of the Creek Indians. Smithsonian Miscellaneous Collections, 85, no. 8 (1931): 1-46.

Swanton, J. R.   Religious beliefs and medical practices of the Creek Indians. U.S. Bureau of American Ethnology, Annual Reports, 42 (1925): 477-672.

Swanton, J. R.   Social organization and social usages of the Indians of the Creek Confederacy. U.S. Bureau of American Ethnology, Annual Reports, 42 (1925): 23-472.

Swanton, John R.   Early history of the Creek Indians and their neighbors. New York, Johnson Reprint, 1970. 492 p. maps.

Tebeau, C. W.   Florida's last frontier. Miami, 1957.

Tozier, M. M.   Report on the Florida Seminole. Washington, D.C., 1954. 25 p.

Tyler, Ronnie C.   The Callahan expedition of 1855: Indians or Negroes? Southwestern Historical Quarterly, 70 (1966/1967): 574-585.

U.S., Bureau of Indian Affairs, Seminole Agency.   The Seminole Indians of Florida. [n.p.] 1956. 18 p. illus.

Utz, Dora Doster.   Life on the Loxahatchee. Tequesta, 32 (1972): 38-57.

Vizcaya Canales, Isidro.   La invasión de los indios bárbaros al noreste de México, en los años de 1840 y 1841. Monterrey, N.L., 1968. 296 p. (Monterrey, Instituto Tecnologico y de Estudios Superiores de Monterrey, Publicaciones, Serie: Historia, 7)

Wallace, Ernest.   R. S. Mackenzie and the Kickapoos; the raid into Mexico in 1873. By Ernest Wallace and Adrian S. Anderson. Arizona and the West, 7 (1965): 105-126.

Wallace, Fred W. The story of Captain John C. Casey. Florida Historical Quarterly, 41 (1962/1963): 127-144.

Ward, M. M. The disappearance of the head of Osceola. Florida Historical Quarterly, 33 (1955): 193-201.

Webb, W. S. The Indian as I knew him. Ethnohistory, 2 (1954): 181-198.

Westfall, David N. Diabetes mellitus among the Florida Seminoles. By David N. Westfall and Arlan L. Rosenbloom. HSMHA Health Reports, 86 (1971): 1037-1041.

White, F. F. Macomb's mission to the Seminoles. Florida Historical Quarterly, 35 (1956): 130-193.

White, Frank L., Jr. The journals of Lieutenant John Pickell, 1836-1837. Florida Historical Quarterly, 38, no. 2 (1959): 142-171.

Wik, Reynold M. Captain Nathaniel Wyche Hunter and the Florida Campaigns, 1837-1841. Florida Historical Quarterly, 39 (1960/1961): 62-75.

Williams, J. L. The Territory of Florida, 209-278. New York, 1837.

Work, Telford H. Serological evidence of arbovirus infection in the Seminole Indians of southern Florida. Science, 145 (1964): 270-272.

Wright, J. Leitch. Creek-American Treaty of 1790: Alexander McGillivray and the diplomacy of the Old Southwest. Georgia Historical Quarterly, 51 (1967): 379-400.

Wright, Muriel H. Seals of the Five Civilized Tribes. Chronicles of Oklahoma, 40 (1962): 214-218.

Yonge, J. C. The white flag. Florida Historical Quarterly, 33 (1955): 218-234.

13-23 Timucua

Andrews, C. M. The Florida Indians in the seventeenth century. Tequesta, 1, no. 3 (1943): 36-48.

Arana, Luis Rafael. The Alonso Solana map of Florida, 1683. Florida Historical Quarterly, 42 (1963/1964): 258-266.

Arana, Luis Rafael. The exploration of Florida and sources on the founding of St. Augustine. Florida Historical Quarterly, 44 (1965/1966): 1-16.

Bartram, J. A description of East Florida. 3d ed. London, 1769. 40 p.

Bartram, W. The travels of William Bartram, naturalist's edition. New Haven, 1958. 788 p.

Bartram, W. Travels in Georgia and Florida, 1773-74. Ed. by F. Harper. American Philosophical Society, Transactions, n.s., 33 (1943): 193-194.

Basanier, M. L'histoire notable de la Floride. Paris, 1853. 223 p.

Bennett, Charles E., tr. and ed. A 16th century French "mug book" brings to light interesting comments on Florida history--Saturiba being featured. Florida Historical Quarterly, 39 (1960/1961): 260-265.

Bourne, E. G., ed. Narratives of the career of Hernando de Soto, Vol. 1: 22-30. New York, 1904.

Brinton, D. G. Notes on the Floridian peninsula: 111-138. Philadelphia, 1859.

Bullen, Ripley P. Southern limit of Timucua territory. Florida Historical Quarterly, 47 (1968/1969): 414-419.

Burrage, H. S., ed. Early English and French voyages, 120-128. New York, 1906.

Bushnell, D. I. Drawing by Jacques Lemoyne de Morgues of Saturioua, a Timucua chief. Smithsonian Miscellaneous Collections, 81, no. 4 (1928): 1-9.

Bushnell, D. I. Native cemeteries and forms of burial east of the Mississippi. U.S. Bureau of American Ethnology, Bulletin, 71 (1920): 116-122.

Celi, Francisco Maria. Tampa Bay in 1757: Francisco Maria Celi's journal and logbook. Edited by John D. Ware. Florida Historical Quarterly, 50 (1971/1972): 158-179, 262-277.

Connor, J. T. Jean Ribault. Florida State Historical Society, Publications, 10 (1927): 1-139.

Deagan, Kathleen A. Fig Springs: the mid-seventeenth century in North-Central Florida. Historical Archaeology, 6 (1972): 23-46.

Dickinson, J. God's protecting Providence. 7th ed. London, 1790. 136 p.

Dickinson, J. Narrative of a shipwreck in the Gulph of Florida. 6th ed. New York, 1803.

Douglass, A. E. A find of ceremonial weapons in a Florida mound. American Association for the Advancement of Science, Proceedings, 31 (1882): 585-592.

Douglass, A. E. Some characteristics of the Indian earth and shell mounds on the Atlantic Coast of Florida. American Antiquarian and Oriental Journal, 7 (1885): 74-82.

Ehrmann, W. W. The Timucua Indians of sixteenth century Florida. Florida Historical Quarterly, 18 (1940): 168-191.

Fraser, Douglas. Village planning in the primitive world. New York, George Braziller, 1968. 128 p. illus.

Gaffarel, P. L. J. Histoire de la Floride Française, 461-463. Paris, 1875.

Gannon, Michael V. Altar and hearth: the coming of Christianity, 1521-1565. Florida Historical Quarterly, 44 (1965/1966): 17-44.

Garcilaso de la Vega, el Inca. The Florida of the Inca. Translated and edited by John Grier Varner and Jeannette Johnson Varner. Austin, University of Texas Press, 1951. 45, 655 p. illus., map.

Gatschet, A. S. Volk und Sprache der Timucua. Zeitschrift für Ethnologie, 9 (1877): 245-260; 13 (1881): 189-200.

Gatschet, A. S. and R. de la Grasserie. Textes Timucua. Revue de Linguistique et de Philologie Comparée, 22 (1889): 320-346.

Gatschet, Albert S. The Timucua language. American Philosophical Society, Proceedings, 16 (1876/1877): 626-642; 17 (1877/1878): 490-504; 18 (1878/1880): 465-502.

Geiger, M. The Franciscan conquest of Florida (1573-1618). Catholic University, Studies in Hispanic-American History, 1 (1937): 1-319.

Gifford, J. C. Five plants essential to the Indians and early settlers of Florida. Tequesta, 4 (1944): 36-44.

Goggin, J. M. An introductory outline of Timucua archeology. Southeastern Archaeological Conference, News Letter, 3, no. 3 (1953): 4-15, 17.

Goggin, J. M. Space and time perspective in Northern St. Johns archeology, Florida. Yale University Publications in Anthropology, 47 (1952): 1-147.

Gold, Robert L. The East Florida Indians under Spanish and English control: 1763-1765. Florida Historical Quarterly, 44 (1965/1966): 105-120.

Granberry, J. Timucua I. International Journal of American Linguistics, 22 (1956): 97-105.

Grasserie, R. de la. Esquisse d'une grammaire du Timucua. Orléans [n.d.]. 44 p.

Grasserie, R. de la. Textes analysés et vocabulaire de la langue timucua. International Congress of Americanists, Proceedings, 7 (1888): 403-437.

Grasserie, R. de la. Textes en langue timucua. Paris, 1890. 27 p.

Grasserie, R. de la. Vocabulaire Timucua. Orléans, 1892. 16 p.

Griffin, J. W. and H. G. Smith. Nocoroco. Florida Historical Quarterly, 27 (1949): 340-361.

Hakluyt, R. Collection of the early voyages, travels, and discoveries of the English nation, Vol. 3: 612-616. London, 1810.

Harrison, B. Indian races of Florida. Florida Historical Quarterly, 3 (1924): 29-37.

Hrdlička, A. The anthropology of Florida. Florida State Historical Society, Publications, 1 (1922): 1-140.

La Roncière, C. G., ed. La Floride française. Paris, 1928. 139 p.

Lanning, J. T. The Spanish missions of Georgia, 9-32. Chapel Hill, 1935.

Laudonnière, R. History of Jean Ribault's first voyage to Florida. In B. F. French, ed. Historical Collections of Louisiana and Florida. New Series. Vol. 1. New York, J. Sabine, 1869: 177-362.

Laudonnière, R. History of the first attempt of the French to colonize the newly discovered country of Florida. In B. F. French, ed. Historical Collections of Louisiana and Florida. New Series. Vol. 1. New York, J. Sabine, 1869: 165-175.

Laudonnière, R. L'histoire notable de la Floride. Paris, 1586.

Le Moyne, J. Narrative. Boston, 1875.

Milanich, Jerald T. Excavations at the Richardson Site, Alachua County,

Florida: an early 17th century Potano Indian village (with notes on Potano culture change). Florida, Bureau of Historic Sites and Properties, Bulletin, 2 (1972): 35-61.

Milanich, Jerald T. Tacatacuru and the San Pedro de Mocamo Mission. Florida Historical Quarterly, 50 (1971/1972): 283-291.

Mooney, J. Timucuan family. U.S. Bureau of American Ethnology, Bulletin, 30, vol. 2 (1910): 752-754.

Moore, C. B. Certain sand mounds of the St. Johns River. Philadelphia, 1894. 2 v.

Ningler, L., ed. Voyages en Virginie et en Floride. Paris, 1927. 311 p.

Noble, G. Kingsley. On the genetic affiliations of Timucua, an indigenous language of Florida. Société des Américanistes (Paris), Journal, n.s., 54 (1965): 359-376.

Pareja, F. Arte de la lengua timuquana. Paris, 1886. 129 p.

Pareja, F. Cathecismo en lengua castellana y timuquana. Mexico, 1612. 160 p.

Pearson, Fred Lamar, Jr. Spanish-Indian relations in Florida: a study of two visitas, 1657-1678. Dissertation Abstracts, 29 (1968/1969): 1500A-1501A. UM 68-15,502.

Pearson, Fred Lamar, Jr. The Florencia investigation of Spanish Timucua. Florida Historical Quarterly, 51 (1972/1973): 166-176.

Pickett, A. J. History of Alabama, Vol. 1: 54-73. Charleston, 1851.

Ribault, J. Narrative. In B. F. French, ed. Historical Collections of Louisiana and Florida. Second Series. Vol. 2. New York, A. Mason, 1875: 170-182.

Romans, B. A concise natural history of East and West Florida. New York, 1775.

Smith, B. Documents in the Spanish and two of the early tongues of Florida. Washington, D.C., 1860. 12 p.

Smith, B. The Timuquana language. Historical Magazine, 2 (1858): 1-3.

Smith, R. M. Anthropology in Florida. Florida Historical Quarterly, 11 (1933): 151-172.

Sparke, J. The voyage made by Master John Hawkins. In E. J. Payne, ed. Voyages of the Elizabethan Seamen to America. Vol. 1. Oxford, 1893: 55-67.

Stirling, M. W. Florida cultural affiliations in relation to adjacent areas. In Essays in Anthropology Presented to A. L. Kroeber. Berkeley, 1936: 351-357.

*Swanton, J. R. Early history of the Creek Indians and their neighbors. U.S. Bureau of American Ethnology, Bulletin, 73 (1922): 320-387.

Swanton, J. R. Terms of relationship in Timucua. In Holmes Anniversary Volume. Washington, D.C., 1916: 451-463.

Swanton, J. R. The Tawasa language. American Anthropologist, 31 (1929): 435-453.

Ternaux-Compans, H. Recueil de pièces sur la Floride. Paris, 1841. 368 p.

Ware, John D. A view of Celi's Journal of Surveys and Charts of 1757. Florida Historical Quarterly, 47 (1968/1969): 8-24.

Wenhold, L. L., tr. A 17th century letter of Gabriel Diaz Vara Calderon, Bishop of Cuba. Smithsonian Miscellaneous Collections, 95, no. 16 (1936): 1-14.

Willey, G. R. Archeology of the Florida Gulf Coast. Smithsonian Miscellaneous Collections, 113 (1949): 1-624.

13-24 Tunica

Anonymous. Tunica. U.S. Bureau of American Ethnology, Bulletin, 30, vol. 2 (1910): 838-839.

Burgess, Charles E. The De Soto myth in Missouri. Missouri Historical Society, Bulletin, 24 (1967/1968): 303-325.

Bushnell, D. I. Drawings by A. DeBatz in Louisiana. Smithsonian Miscellaneous Collections, 85 (1927): 1-14.

Dumont de Montigny. L'établissement de la province de la Louisiane. Société des Américanistes, Journal, n.s., 23 (1931): 273-440.

Ford, J. A. Analysis of Indian village site collections from Louisiana and Mississippi. Louisiana, Department of Conservation, Anthropological Studies, 2 (1936): 1-285.

Gatschet, A. S. Sex-denoting nouns in American languages. American Philological Association, Transactons, 20 (1889): 159-171.

Gosselin, A. Les sauvages du Mississipi. International Congress of Americanists, Proceedings, 15, vol. 1 (1906): 31-51.

Gursky, Karl-Heinz. A lexical comparison of Atakapa, Chitimacha, and Tunica languages. International Journal of American Linguistics, 35 (1969): 83-107.

Haas, M. R. A grammatical sketch of Tunica. Viking Fund Publications in Anthropology, 6 (1946): 337-366.

Haas, M. R. The solar deity of the Tunica. Michigan Academy of Science, Arts and Letters, Papers, 28 (1942): 531-535.

Haas, M. R. Tunica dictionary. California, University, Publications in Linguistics, 6 (1953): 175-332.

Haas, M. R. Tunica. In F. Boas, ed. Handbook of American Indian Languages. Vol. 4. New York, 1941: 1-143.

Haas, M. R. Tunica texts. California, University, Publications in Linguistics, 6 (1950): 1-174.

Haas, Mary R. Historical linguistics and the genetic relationship of languages. In Theoretical Foundations. The Hague, Mouton, 1966: 113-153. (Current Trends in Linguistics, 3)

Haas, Mary R. Tonkawa and Algonkian. Anthropological Linguistics, 1, no. 2 (1959): 1-6.

Harpe, B. de la. Journal historique de l'établissement des Français à la Louisiane. Ed. by Beaurain. New Orleans, Paris, 1831.

Klingberg, F. J., ed. The Carolina chronicle of Dr. Francis Le Jau, 1706-1717. California, University, Publications in History, 53 (1956): 1-228.

Margry, P., ed. Découvertes et établissements des Français dans l'ouest et dans le sud de l'Amerique septentrionale. Paris, 1879-1888. 6 v.

Minturn, Leigh. A cross-cultural linguistic analysis of Freudian symbols. Ethnology, 4 (1965): 336-342.

Nash, Charles H. Chucalissa Indian Town. By Charles H. Nash and Rodney Gates, Jr. Tennessee Historical Quarterly, 21 (1962): 103-121.

Quatrefages, A. de, ed. Les voyages de Moncatch-Apé. Revue d'Anthropologie, 10 (1881): 593-634.

Quimby, G. I. The Natchezan culture type. American Antiquity, 7 (1942): 255-275.

Rainwater, Percy L. Conquistadors, missionaries, and missions. Journal of Mississippi History, 27 (1965): 123-147.

Rea, Robert R. Military deserters from British West Indies. Louisiana History, 9 (1968): 123-137.

Shea, J. G. Early voyages up and down the Mississippi, 77-81, 133-137. Albany, 1861.

Swanton, J. R. A structural and lexical comparison of the Tunica, Chitimacha, and Atakapa languages. U.S. Bureau of American Ethnology, Bulletin, 68 (1919): 1-56.

Swanton, J. R. Indian language studies in Louisiana. Smithsonian Institution, Explorations and Field-Work (1930): 195-200.

Swanton, J. R. Indian tribes of the Lower Mississippi Valley and adjacent coast of the Gulf of Mexico. U.S. Bureau of American Ethnology, Bulletin, 43 (1911): 306-336.

Swanton, J. R. Mythology of the Indians of Louisiana and the Texas Coast. Journal of American Folklore, 20 (1907): 285-289.

Swanton, J. R. The Tunica language. International Journal of American Linguistics, 2 (1921): 1-39.

Swanton, John R. Indian tribes of the Lower Mississippi Valley and adjacent coast of the Gulf of Mexico. New York, Johnson Reprint, 1970. 7, 387 p. illus.

Thwaites, R. G., ed. The Jesuit Relations and allied documents, Vol. 65: 127-135. Cleveland, 1900.

13-25 Tuscarora

Fenton, W. N. A calendar of manuscript materials relating to the history of the Six Nations. American Philosophical Society, Proceedings, 97 (1953): 578-595.

Pilling, J. C. Bibliography of the Iroquoian languages. U.S. Bureau of American Ethnology, Bulletin, 6 (1888): 1-208.

Anonymous. Presents for the Six Nations--
1815. Museum of the Fur Trade Quarterly,
4, no. 2 (1968): 6-8.

Anonymous. "The Indians in Virginia,
1689". Edited by Stanley Pargellis.
William and Mary Quarterly, 3d ser., 16
(1959): 228-243.

Barbeau, C. Marius. The language of
Canada: in the voyages of Jacques
Cartier (1534-1538). In Contributions to
Anthropology 1959. Ottawa, Queen's
Printer, 1961: 108-229. (Canada,
National Museum, Bulletin, 173)

Barbeau, M. Iroquoian clans and
phratries. American Anthropologist,
n.s., 19 (1917): 392-402.

Barnwell, J. The Tuscarora expedition.
Carolina Historical and Genealogical
Magazine, 9 (1908): 28-58.

Binford, Lewis R. An ethnohistory of the
Nottoway, Meherrin and Weanock Indians
of southeastern Virginia. Ethnohistory,
14 (1967): 104-218.

Binford, Lewis Roberts. Archaeological
and ethnohistorical investigation of
cultural diversity and progressive
development among aboriginal cultures of
coastal Virginia and North Carolina.
Dissertation Abstracts, 25 (1964/1965):
6880-6881. UM 65-5877.

Bland, E. The discovery of New Brittaine.
In A. S. Salley, ed. Narratives of Early
Carolina. New York, 1911: 1-19.

Brickell, J. The natural history of
North-Carolina. Dublin, 1737.

Brickell, John. The natural history of
North Carolina. Murfreesboro, N.C.,
Johnson, 1968. 14, 14, 424 p. illus.,
map.

Brickell, John. The natural history of
North-Carolina. New York, Johnson
Reprint, 1969. 10, 14, 417 p. illus.,
map.

Butler, Lindley S. The early settlement
of Carolina; Virginia's southern
frontier. Virginia Magazine of History
and Biography, 79 (1971): 20-28.

Butler, Lindley S. The early settlement
of Carolina. Virginia Magazine of
History and Biography, 77 (1969): 20-28.

Byrd, W. The history of the dividing line
between Virginia and North Carolina.
Richmond, 1866. 2 v.

Coe, Stephen Howard. Indian affairs in
Pennsylvania and New York, 1783-1794.
Dissertation Abstracts International, 30
(1969/1970): 649A-650A. UM 69-13,646.

Dillard, Richard. The Indian tribes of
eastern North Carolina. North Carolina
Booklet, 6 (1906/1907): 4-26.

Douglas, F. H. The Virginia Indian
tribes. Denver Art Museum, Indian
Leaflet Series, 57 (1933): 1-4.

Euler, Robert C. Ethnic group land rights
in the modern state: three case studies.
By Robert C. Euler and Henry F. Dobyns.
Human Organization, 20 (1961/1962): 203-
207.

Feest, Christian F. Lukas Vischers
Beiträge zur Ethnographie Nordamerikas.
Archiv für Völkerkunde, 22 (1968): 31-
66.

Fenton, W. N. Collecting materials for a
political history of the Six Nations.
American Philosophical Society,
Proceedings, 93 (1949): 233-237.

Fickett, Joan Gleason. The phonology of
Tuscarora. Studies in Linguistics, 19
(1967): 33-57.

Franklin, W. Neil. Act for the better
regulation of the Indian trade;
Virginia, 1714. Virginia Magazine of
History and Biography, 72 (1964): 141-
151.

Goldsborough, E. R. The aborigines of the
Lower Potomac River Valley. Pennsylvania
Archaeologist, 8 (1938): 27-36.

Graffenried, C. de. Manuscript. In W. L.
Saunders, ed. The Colonial Records of
North Carolina. Vol. 1. Raleigh, 1886:
905-986.

Hale, H. Indian migrations as evidenced
by language. American Antiquarian and
Oriental Journal, 5 (1883): 18-28.

Hewitt, J. N. B. Tuscarora. U.S. Bureau
of American Ethnology, Bulletin, 30,
vol. 2 (1910): 842-853.

Jack, Marvin. Indians in agriculture.
Indian Historian, 3, no. 1 (1970): 24-
26.

Johnson, E. Legends, traditions, and laws
of the Iroquois, or Six Nations, and
history of the Tuscarora Indians.
Lockport, 1881.

Johnson, Frank Roy. The Tuscaroras:
mythology, medicine, culture.
Murfreesboro, N.C., Johnson, 1967-1968.
2 v. illus., maps.

Johnston, James Hugo. Documentary evidence of the relations of Negroes and Indians. Journal of Negro History, 14 (1929): 21-43.

Landy, D. Tuscarora tribalism and national identity. Ethnohistory, 5 (1958): 250-284.

Lawson, John. An account of the Indians of N. Carolina. In Lawson's History of North Carolina. Richmond, Garrett and Massie, 1937: 179-259.

Lawson, John. An account of the Indians of N. Carolina. In his The History of Carolina. Raleigh, Strother and Marcom, 1860: 277-390.

Mohn, James F. Incidence of the blood group antigen Dia in the Tuscarora Indian of North America. By James F. Mohn, Reginald M. Lambert, and and Chester M. Zmijewski. Nature, 198 (1963): 697-698.

Mook, Maurice A. Algonkian ethnohistory of the Carolina Sound. Washington Academy of Sciences, Journal, 34 (1944): 181-197, 213-228.

Mooney, J. Nottoway. U.S. Bureau of American Ethnology, Bulletin, 30, vol. 2 (1910): 87.

Morgan, L. H. Systems of consanguinity and affinity. Smithsonian Contributions to Knowledge, 17 (1871): 291-382.

Morgan, L. H. The League of the Ho-De-No-Sau-nee or Iroquois. Ed. by H. M. Lloyd. New York, 1901. 2 v.

Olbrechts, F. M. De Pronominale Prefixen in het Tuscarora. In Donum Natalicium Schrijnen. Nimègue-Utrecht, 1929: 154-161.

Quinn, David B. Thomas Hariot and the Virginia voyages of 1602. William and Mary Quarterly, 3d ser., 27 (1970): 268-281.

Rights, D. L. The American Indian in North Carolina. Durham, 1947. 296 p.

Rights, D. L. The American Indian in North Carolina. Winston-Salem, 1957. 318 p.

Robinson, W. Stitt. Tributary Indians in Colonial America. Virginia Magazine of History and Biography, 67 (1959): 49-64.

Shy, John W. A new look at colonial militia. William and Mary Quarterly, 3d ser., 20 (1963): 175-185.

Smith, E. A. Comparative differences in the Iroquois group of dialects. American Association for the Advancement of Science, Proceedings, 30 (1881): 315-319.

Smith, E. A. The significance of flora to the Iroquois. American Association for the Advancement of Science, Proceedings, 34 (1885): 404-411.

Smith, Gerald Patrick. Protohistoric sociopolitical organization of the Nottoway in the Chesapeake Bay-Carolina Sounds region. Dissertation Abstracts International, 32 (1971/1972): 3135B-3136B. UM 71-30,690.

Uhler, S. P. Pennsylvania's Indian relations to 1754. Allentown, 1951. 144 p.

Wallace, A. F. C. Some psychological determinants of culture change in an Iroquoian community. U.S. Bureau of American Ethnology, Bulletin, 149 (1951): 55-76.

Wallace, A. F. C. The modal personality of the Tuscarora Indians. U.S. Bureau of American Ethnology, Bulletin, 150 (1951): 1-128.

Wallace, A. F. C. The Tuscaroras. American Philosophical Society, Proceedings, 93 (1949): 159-165.

Wallace, A. F. C. and W. D. Reyburn. Crossing the ice. International Journal of American Linguistics, 17 (1951): 42-47.

13-26   Yamasee

Arana, Luis Rafael. The Alonso Solana map of Florida, 1683. Florida Historical Quarterly, 42 (1963/1964): 258-266.

Arnade, Charles W. A letter to Merenciana, Indian cheftainess [sic]. Contributed by Charles W. Arnade and Louis Arana. Georgia Historical Quarterly, 45 (1961): 407-410.

Barcia Carballido y Zuñiga, A. G. Ensayo cronológica para la historia general de la Florida, 170-172. Madrid, 1723.

Barcia Carballido y Zuñiga, Andrés González de. Barcia's chronological history of the continent of Florida. Translated with an introduction by Anthony Kerrigan. Westport, Greenwood Press, 1970. 9, 426 p.

Barcía Carballido y Zuniga, Andrés Gonzalez. Barcia's chronological history of the continent of Florida. Translated with an introduction by Anthony Kerrigan. Gainesville, University of Florida Press, 1951. 60, 426 p.

Bartram, W. The travels of William Bartram, naturalist's edition. New Haven, 1958. 788 p.

Bartram, W. Travels in Georgia and Florida, 1773-74. Ed. by F. Harper. American Philosophical Society, Transactions, n.s., 33 (1943): 191-193.

Caldwell, J. R. The archeology of eastern Georgia and South Carolina. In J. B. Griffin, ed. Archeology of Eastern United States. Chicago, 1952: 312-321.

De Vorsey, Louis, Jr. Indian boundaries in Colonial Georgia. Georgia Historical Quarterly, 54 (1970): 63-78.

Franklin, W. Neil. Act for the better regulation of the Indian trade; Virginia, 1714. Virginia Magazine of History and Biography, 72 (1964): 141-151.

Geiger, M. The Franciscan conquest of Florida (1573-1618). Catholic University of America, Studies in Hispanic-American History, 1 (1937): 1-319.

Gold, Robert L. Conflict in San Carlos: Indian immigrants in eighteenth-century New Spain. Ethnohistory, 17 (1970): 1-10.

Gold, Robert L. The East Florida Indians under Spanish and English control: 1763-1765. Florida Historical Quarterly, 44 (1965/1966): 105-120.

Howard, James H. Altamaha Cherokee folklore and customs. By James H. Howard, in collaboration with Stewart R. Shaffer and James Shaffer. Journal of American Folklore, 72 (1959): 134-138.

Howard, James H. Medicines and medicine headdresses of the Yamassee. By James H. Howard and James Shaffer. American Indian Tradition, 8, no. 3 (1962): 125-126.

Howard, James H. The Yamasee: a supposedly extinct Southeastern tribe rediscovered. American Anthropologist, 62 (1960): 681-683.

Ivers, Larry E. Scouting the Inland Passage, 1685-1737. South Carolina Historical Magazine, 73 (1972): 117-129.

Ivers, Larry E. The battle of Fort Mosa. Georgia Historical Quarterly, 51 (1967): 135-153.

Jones, C. C. Historical sketch of Tomo-chi-chi, Mico of the Yamacraws. Albany, 1868.

Klingberg, F. J., ed. The Carolina chronicle of Dr. Francis Le Jau, 1706-1717. California, University, Publications in History, 53 (1956): 1-228.

Klingberg, Frank J. Early attempts at Indian education in South Carolina, a documentary. South Carolina Historical Magazine, 61 (1960): 1-10.

Klingberg, Frank J. The mystery of the lost Yamassee prince. South Carolina Historical Magazine, 63 (1962): 18-32.

Lanning, J. T. The Spanish missions of Georgia, 9-32. Chapel Hill, 1935.

Manucy, Albert. The man who was Pedro Menéndez. Florida Historical Quarterly, 44 (1965/1966): 67-80.

Milling, C. J. Red Carolinians. Chapel Hill, 1940. 438 p.

Mooney, J. Yamasee. U.S. Bureau of American Ethnology, Bulletin, 30, vol. 2 (1910): 986-987.

Palerm, A. San Carlos de Chachalacas. Cuadernos Americanos, 61, no. 1 (1952): 165-184.

Pearson, Fred Lamar, Jr. Spanish-Indian relations in Florida: a study of two visitas, 1657-1678. Dissertation Abstracts, 29 (1968/1969): 1500A-1501A. UM 68-15,502.

Rojas, Manrique de. Manrique de Rojas' report on French settlement in Florida, 1564. Translated by Lucy L. Wenhold. Florida Historical Quarterly, 38, no. 1 (1959): 45-62.

Shy, John W. A new look at colonial militia. William and Mary Quarterly, 3d ser., 20 (1963): 175-185.

Spalding, Phinizy. South Carolina and Georgia: the early days. South Carolina Historical Magazine, 69 (1968): 83-96.

Swanton, J. R. Early history of the Creek Indians and their neighbors. U.S. Bureau of American Ethnology, Bulletin, 73 (1922): 80-109.

Swanton, John R. Early history of the Creek Indians and their neighbors. New York, Johnson Reprint, 1970. 492 p. maps.

Zubillaga, F. La Florida. Rome, 1941. 473 p.

13-27 Yuchi

Anonymous. Timpoochee Barnard; Uchee
Indian leader. Alabama Historical
Quarterly, 21 (1959): 67.

Bauxar, J. J. Yuchi ethnoarchaeology.
Ethnohistory, 4 (1957): 279-302, 369-
464.

Beneviste, É. La négation en Yuchi.
Word, 6 (1950): 99-105.

Brannon, Peter A. Fort Mitchell Cemetery.
Alabama Historical Quarterly, 21 (1959):
68-71.

Covington, James W., ed. The Florida
Seminoles in 1847. Tequesta, 24 (1964):
49-57.

Crane, V. S. An historical note on the
Westo Indians. American Anthropologist,
n.s., 20 (1918): 331-337.

Eaton, John. Pipe stem dating and the
date for Silver Bluff, S.C. Florida
Anthropologist, 15 (1962): 57-62.

Elmendorf, William W. Item and set
comparison in Yuchi, Siouan, and Yukian.
International Journal of American
Linguistics, 30 (1964): 328-340.

Feest, Christian F. Virginia Indian
miscellany I. Archiv für Völkerkunde, 20
(1966): 1-7.

Foreman, Carolyn Thomas. The Yuchi:
children of the sun. Chronicles of
Oklahoma, 37 (1959): 480-496.

Gatschet, A. S. Some mythic stories of
the Yuchi Indians. American
Anthropologist, 6 (1893): 279-282.

Haas, M. R. The proto-Gulf word for
water. International Journal of American
Linguistics, 17 (1951): 71-79.

Haas, Mary R. Athapaskan, Tlingit, Yuchi,
and Siouan. In Congreso Internacional de
Americanistas, 35th. 1962, Mexico. Actas
y Memorias. Tomo 2. Mexico, 1964: 495-
500.

Hawkins, B. H. A sketch of the Creek
country. Georgia Historical Society,
Collections, 3, no. 1 (1848): 61-63.

Howard, James H. The Southeastern
ceremonial complex and its
interpretation. Columbia, 1968. 8,
169 p. illus. (Missouri Archaeological
Society, Memoir, 6)

Ivers, Larry E. The battle of Fort Mosa.
Georgia Historical Quarterly, 51 (1967):
135-153.

Juricek, John T. The Westo Indians.
Ethnohistory, 11 (1964): 134-173.

Lewis, Thomas M. N. Tribes that slumber;
Indian tribes in the Tennessee region.
By T. M. N. Lewis and Madeline Kneberg.
Knoxville, University of Tennessee
Press, 1958. 11, 196 p. illus., maps.

Mahan, Joseph Buford, Jr. Identification
of the Tsoyaha Waeno, builders of temple
mounds. Dissertation Abstracts
International, 31 (1970/1971): 2289A.
UM 70-21,213.

Mason, Carol Irwin. A reconsideration of
Westo-Yuchi identification. American
Anthropologist, 65 (1963): 1342-1346.

Mason, Carol Irwin. Comments on Mouse
Creek-Yuchi identification. American
Antiquity, 28 (1962/1963): 550-551.

Milling, C. J. Red Carolinians. Chapel
Hill, 1940. 438 p.

Neill, W. T. An historic Indian burial
from Columbia County, Georgia. Southern
Indian Studies, 7 (1955): 3-9.

Pardo, Juan. Journals of the Juan Pardo
expeditions, 1566-1567. Edited by
Stanley J. Folmsbee and Madeline Kneberg
Lewis. Translated by Gerald W. Wade.
East Tennessee Historical Society,
Publications, 37 (1965): 106-121.

Reck, Philipp Georg Friedrich von. Von
Reck's second report from Georgia.
Edited by George Fenwick Jones. William
and Mary Quarterly, 3d ser., 22 (1965):
319-333.

Russell, Orpha B. Notes on Samuel William
Brown, Jr., Yuchi chief. Chronicles of
Oklahoma, 37 (1959): 497-501.

Slay, James L. The settlement and
organization of Bradley County,
Tennessee. East Tennessee Historical
Society's Publications, 44 (1972): 3-16.

Speck, F. G. Ceremonial songs of the
Creek and Yuchi Indians. Pennsylvania,
University, University Museum,
Anthropological Publications, 1 (1911):
157-245.

Speck, F. G. Eggan's Yuchi kinship
interpretations. American
Anthropologist, n.s., 41 (1939): 171-
172.

*Speck, F. G. Ethnology of the Yuchi
Indians. Pennsylvania, University,

University Museum, Anthropological Publications, 1 (1909): 1-154.

Speck, F. G. Yuchi. U.S. Bureau of American Ethnology, Bulletin, 30, vol. 2 (1910): 1003-1007.

Swanton, J. R. Early history of the Creek Indians and their neighbors. U.S. Bureau of American Ethnology, Bulletin, 73 (1922): 184-191, 286-312.

Swanton, J. R. Identity of the Westo Indians. American Anthropologist, n.s., 21 (1919): 213-216.

Swanton, J. R. Social organization and social usages of the Indians of the Creek Confederacy. U.S. Bureau of American Ethnology, Annual Reports, 42 (1925): 23-472.

Swanton, John R. Early history of the Creek Indians and their neighbors. New York, Johnson Reprint, 1970. 492 p. maps.

Tobler, John. John Tobler's description of South Carolina (1754). Translated and edited by Walter L. Robbins. South Carolina Historical Magazine, 71 (1970): 257-265.

Wagner, G. Yuchi. In F. Boas, ed. Handbook of American Indian Languages. Vol. 3. Washington, D.C., 1934: 293-384.

Wagner, G. Yuchi tales. American Ethnological Society, Publications, 13 (1931): 1-357.

Wolff, H. Yuchi phonemes and morphemes. International Journal of American Linguistics, 14 (1948): 240-243.

Wolff, H. Yuchi text with analysis. International Journal of American Linguistics, 17 (1951): 48-53.

13-28   Lumbee

Ackley, Randall. Pembroke State University. Indian Historian, 5, no. 2 (1972): 43-45.

Barton, Lew. The most ironic story in American history. Pembroke, N.C., 1967. 17, 142 p. illus., map.

Baxter, James Phinney. Raleigh's lost colony. New England Magazine, n.s., 11 (1894/1895): 565-587.

Beale, Calvin L. American tri-racial isolates: their status and pertinence to genetic research. Eugenics Quarterly, 4 (1957): 187-196.

*Berry, Brewton. Almost White. New York, Macmillan, 1963. 11, 212 p.

Berry, Brewton. The myth of the vanishing Indian. Phylon, 21 (1960): 51-57.

Coates, James R. Native Indians of the Old Dominion State. American Indian, 2, no. 4 (1945): 22-25.

Dial, Adolph. The Lumbee Indians of North Carolina and Pembroke State University. By Adolph Dial and David K. Eliades. Indian Historian, 4, no. 4 (1971): 20-24.

Dillard, Richard. The Indian tribes of eastern North Carolina. North Carolina Booklet, 6 (1906/1907): 4-26.

Dunlap, A. R. Trends in the naming of tri-racial mixed-blood groups in the eastern United States. By A. R. Dunlap and C. A. Weslager. American Speech, 22 (1947): 81-87.

Estabrook, Arthur H. Mongrel Virginians; the Win tribe. By Arthur H. Estabrook and Ivan E. McDougle. Baltimore, Williams and Wilkins, 1926. 205 p. illus.

Evans, William McKee. To die game; the story of the Lowry Band, Indian guerillas of Reconstruction. Baton Rouge, Louisiana State University Press, 1971. 13, 282 p. illus., maps.

Frazier, Edward Franklin. The Negro family in the United States. Chicago, University of Chicago Press, 1939. 32, 686 p. illus.

Gaillard, Frye. Desegregation denies justice to Lumbee Indians. Indian Historian, 4, no. 3 (1971): 17-22, 43.

Gilbert, William Harlen, Jr. Memorandum concerning the characteristics of the larger mixed-blood racial islands of the eastern United States. Social Forces, 24 (1945/1946): 438-447.

Gilbert, William Harlen, Jr. Surviving Indian groups of the eastern United States. Smithsonian Institution, Annual Report of the Board of Regents (1948): 407-438.

Harper, Roland M. A statistical study of the Croatans. Rural Sociology, 2 (1937): 444-456.

Harper, Roland M. The most prolific people in the United States. Eugenical News, 23 (1938): 29-31.

Jenkins, Paul B. American Indian cross-bow. Wisconsin Archeologist, n.s., 8 (1928/1929): 132-135.

Johnson, Guy B. Personality in a White-Indian-Negro community. American Sociological Review, 4 (1939): 516-523.

Lawrence, Robert C. The state of Robeson. Lumberton, N.C., printed by J. J. Little and Ives, 1939. 8, 279 p.

Lowrey, Clarence E. The Lumbee Indians of North Carolina. Lumberton, N.C., 1960. 64 p. illus.

Makofsky, Abraham. Tradition and change in the Lumbee community of Baltimore. Dissertation Abstracts International, 32 (1971/1972): 4372B. UM 72-5749.

McMillan, Hamilton. Sir Walter Raleigh's lost colony. Rev. ed. Raleigh, N.C., Edwards and Broughton, 1907. 46 p.

McMillan, Hamilton. The lost colony found; an historical sketch of the discovery of the Croatan Indians. Lumberton, N.C., Robesonian Job Printing, 1898. 35 p.

McPherson, Orlando M. Report on the condition and tribal rights of the Indians of Robeson and adjoining counties of North Carolina. Washington, D.C., Government Printing Office, 1915. 252 p. illus., maps. (U.S., 63d Congress, 3d Session, Senate, Senate Document, 677. Serial Set, 6772)

Mooney, James. Croatan Indians. U.S., Bureau of American Ethnology, Bulletin, 30, part 1 (1907): 365.

Parsons, Elsie Clews. Folk-lore of the Cherokee of Robeson County, North Carolina. Journal of American Folk-Lore, 32 (1919): 384-393.

Peck, John Gregory. Education of urban Indians: Lumbee Indians in Baltimore. Chicago, University of Chicago, 1969. 11 p. (National Study of American Indian Education, Series II, 3) ERIC ED039977.

Peck, John Gregory. Urban station--migration of the Lumbee Indians. Dissertation Abstracts International, 33 (1972/1973): 1362B. UM 72-24,830.

Pollitzer, William S., et al. Hemoglobin patterns in American Indians. Science, 129 (1959): 216.

Price, Edward T. A geographic analysis of White-Negro-Indian racial mixtures in the eastern United States. Association of American Geographers, Annals, 43 (1953): 138-155.

Rights, Douglas L. The American Indian in North Carolina. 2d ed. Winston-Salem, J. F. Blair, 1957. 20, 298 p. illus., maps.

Sider, Gerald Marc. The political history of the Lumbee Indians of Robeson County, North Carolina: a case study of ethnic political affiliations. Dissertation Abstracts International, 32 (1971/1972): 4376B. UM 72-4038.

Speck, Frank G. Remnants of the Machapunga Indians of North Carolina. American Anthropologist, n.s., 18 (1916): 271-276.

Speck, Frank G. The Catawba nation and its neighbors. North Carolina Historical Review, 16 (1939): 404-417.

Weeks, Stephen B. Raleigh settlement on Roanoke Island: an historical survival. Magazine of American History, 25 (1891): 127-139.

Weeks, Stephen B. The lost colony of Roanoke: its fate and survival. American Historical Association, Papers, 5 (1891): 439-480.

Wooten, Sylvester Wendell. A comparison between Lumbee Indian commuting students, non-Indian dormitory students, and non-Indian commuting students in terms of their perceptions of the college environment. Dissertation Abstracts International, 33 (1972/1973): 1453A. UM 72-26,268.

13-29 Southeastern Mestizos

Ball, Bonnie S. Mystery men of the mountains. Negro Digest, 3, no. 3 (Jan. 1945): 39-41.

Ball, Bonnie S. The Melungeons: or, A vanishing race. Chillicothe, Ohio, Ross County Historical Society, 1960. 5 p. (Ohio Valley Folklore Research Project, Folk Publication, 57)

Ball, Bonnie S. Who are the Melungeons? Southern Literary Messenger, 3, no. 2 (June 1945): 5-7.

Beale, Calvin L. American tri-racial isolates: their status and pertinence to genetic research. Eugenics Quarterly, 4 (1957): 187-196.

Beale, Calvin L. An overview of the phenomenon of mixed racial isolates in

the United States. American
Anthropologist, 74 (1972): 704-710.

*Berry, Brewton. Almost White. New York,
Macmillan, 1963. 11, 212 p.

Berry, Brewton. America's mestizos. In
Noel P. Gist and Anthony Gary Dworkin,
eds. The Blending of Races. New York,
Wiley-Interscience, 1972: 191-212.

Berry, Brewton. The mestizos of South
Carolina. American Journal of Sociology,
51 (1945/1946): 34-41.

Berry, Brewton. The myth of the vanishing
Indian. Phylon, 21 (1960): 51-57.

Bond, Horace Mann. Two racial islands in
Alabama. American Journal of Sociology,
36 (1930/1931): 552-567.

Brewster, Paul G. The Melungeons: a
mystery people of East Tennessee.
Ethnos, 29 (1964): 43-48.

Burnett, Swan M. A note on the
Melungeons. American Anthropologist, 2
(1889): 347-349.

Butler, George E. The Croatan Indians of
Sampson County; their origin and racial
status. A plea for separate schools.
Clinton, N.C., Seeman Printery, 1916.
65 p. illus.

Carmer, Carl L. Stars fell on Alabama.
New York, Farrar and Rinehart, 1934.
14, 294 p. illus., map.

Coe, Samuel S. Chronicles of the Coe
Colony. With R. A. Adams. Kansas City,
Kan., S. S. Coe, 1930. 181 p.

Dane, J. K. The collective identity of
marginal peoples: the North Carolina
experience. By J. K. Dane and B. Eugene
Griessman. American Anthropologist, 74
(1972): 694-704.

Dromgoole, William Allen. The Malungeon
tree and its four branches. Arena, 3
(1890/1891): 745-751.

Dromgoole, William Allen. The Malungeons.
Arena, 3 (1890/1891): 470-479.

Dunlap, A. R. Trends in the naming of
tri-racial mixed-blood groups in the
eastern United States. By A. R. Dunlap
and C. A. Weslager. American Speech, 22
(1947): 81-87.

Estabrook, Arthur H. Mongrel Virginians;
the Win tribe. By Arthur H. Estabrook
and Ivan E. McDougle. Baltimore,
Williams and Wilkins, 1926. 205 p.
illus.

Foster, Laurence. Negro-Indian
relationships in the Southeast.
Philadelphia, University of Pennsylvania
Press, 1935. 86 p.

Frazier, Edward Franklin. The Negro
family in the United States. Chicago,
University of Chicago Press, 1939. 32,
686 p. illus.

Gilbert, William Harlen, Jr. Memorandum
concerning the characteristics of the
larger mixed-blood racial islands of the
eastern United States. Social Forces, 24
(1945/1946): 438-447.

Gilbert, William Harlen, Jr. Mixed bloods
of the Upper Monongahela Valley, West
Virginia. Washington Academy of
Sciences, Journal, 36 (1946): 1-13.

Gilbert, William Harlen, Jr. Surviving
Indian groups of the eastern United
States. Smithsonian Institution, Annual
Report of the Board of Regents (1948):
407-438.

Gregorie, Anne King. History of Sumter
County, South Carolina. Sumter, S.C.,
Library Board of Sumter County, 1954.
17, 553 p. illus., maps.

Hale, William Thomas. A history of
Tennessee and Tennesseans. Vol. 1. By
Will T. Hale and Dixon L. Merritt.
Chicago, Lewis, 1913.

Hames, Philip L. Roman survival
(pertaining to the Tennessee
Melungeons). By Philip L. Hamer.
Chillicothe, Ohio, Ross County
Historical Society, 1960. 3 p. (Ohio
Valley Folklore Research Project, Folk
Publication, 60)

Johnston, James Hugo. Documentary
evidence of the relations of Negroes and
Indians. Journal of Negro History, 14
(1929): 21-43.

McPherson, Orlando M. Report on the
condition and tribal rights of the
Indians of Robeson and adjoining
counties of North Carolina. Washington,
D.C., Government Printing Office, 1915.
252 p. illus., maps. (U.S., 63d
Congress, 3d Session, Senate, Senate
Document, 677. Serial Set, 6772)

Montell, William Lynwood. The Coe Ridge
Colony: a racial island disappears. By
Lynwood Montell. American
Anthropologist, 74 (1972): 710-719.

Montell, William Lynwood. The saga of Coe
Ridge: a study in oral history. By
Lynwood Montell. Knoxville, University
of Tennessee Press, 1970. 21, 231 p.
illus.

Olmsted, Frederick Law. A journey through
Texas, or, A saddle-trip on the
southwestern frontier. New York, Dix,
Edwards, 1857. 34, 516 p.

Olmsted, Frederick Law. The slave states.
Rev. and enl. ed. New York, G. P.
Putnam's Sons, 1959. 284 p. illus.

Pollitzer, William S. Ancestral traits,
parental populations, and hybrids.
American Journal of Physical
Anthropology, n.s., 30 (1969): 415-419.

Pollitzer, William S. Factors in the
microevolution of a triracial isolate.
By W. S. Pollitzer, R. M. Menegaz-Bock,
and J. C. Herion. American Journal of
Human Genetics, 18 (1966): 26-38.

Pollitzer, William S. Some interactions
of culture and genetics. American
Anthropological Association, Bulletin,
3, pt. 2 (1970): 69-86.

Pollitzer, William S. Survey of
demography, anthropometry, and genetics
in the Melungeons of Tennessee: an
isolate of hybrid origin in process of
dissolution. By William S. Pollitzer and
William H. Brown. Human Biology, 41
(1969): 388-400.

Pollitzer, William S. The physical
anthropology and genetics of marginal
people of the Southeastern United
States. American Anthropologist, 74
(1972): 719-734.

Price, Edward T. A geographic analysis of
White-Negro-Indian racial mixtures in
the eastern United States. Association
of American Geographers, Annals, 43
(1953): 138-155.

Price, Edward T. The Melungeons: a mixed-
blood strain of the southern
Appalachians. Geographical Review, 41
(1951): 256-271.

Price, Edward T. The mixed-blood racial
strain of Carmel, Ohio, and Magoffin
County, Kentucky. Ohio Journal of
Science, 50 (1950): 281-290.

Ramsey, Carolyn. Cajuns on the bayous.
New York, Hastings House, 1957. 300 p.
illus.

Shapiro, Harry L. The mixed-blood Indian.
In Oliver LaFarge, ed. The Changing
Indian. Norman, University of Oklahoma
Press, 1942: 19-27.

Shelby, Gertrude M. Po'buckra. By
Gertrude M. Shelby and Samuel G. Stoney.
New York, Macmillan, 1930. 5, 426 p.

Shepherd, Lewis. Romantic account of the
celebrated Melungeon case. Watson's
Magazine, 17, no. 1 (1913): 34-40.

Shugg, Roger W. Origins of class struggle
in Louisiana. Baton Rouge, Louisiana
State University Press, 1939. 10,
372 p. map.

Witkop, Carl J., Jr., et al. Hereditary
benign intraepithelial dyskeratosis: II.
Oral manifestations and hereditary
transmission. AMA Archives of Pathology,
7 (1960): 696-711.

Witkop, Carl J., Jr., et al. Sjögren-
Larsson syndrome and histinemia:
hereditary biochemical diseases with
defects of speech and oral functions.
Journal of Speech and Hearing Disorders,
28 (1963): 109-123.

Writers' Program, Tennessee. God bless
the devil! Liars' bench tales. James R.
Aswell, ed. Chapel Hill, University of
North Carolina Press, 1940. 11, 254 p.
illus.

Ethnonymy

Eastern United States Ethnonymy

An ethnonymy is a list of names of ethnic groups, together with alternate names and variant spellings. The ethnonymy on the following pages was prepared by the compilers of this bibliography to assist them in making decisions as to where to assign individual books, journal articles, etc. within the bibliography. Thus, it was designed primarily as a classificatory device for purposes unique to this bibliography. The basic ethnonymy was prepared before the compilation of this edition was begun, using as a base list the "Index of Tribal Names" compiled by Professor Murdock and published in the 1960 edition. The present compilers consulted a number of basic reference tools and added a large number of names of ethnic groups, reservations and reserves, and headings such as Pan-Indianism to this basic list. New names were also added as they were encountered in the literature. The resulting ethnonymy is comparatively extensive, but in reality contains a relatively small percentage of the total possible number of names found in the literature. However, the present list was generally sufficient for our needs in compiling this bibliography. We have supplied citations to a small number of reference works below which contain further listings and descriptions. The synonymy in Hodge (1907-1910) is particularly notable for the large number of variant names and spellings it gives, and should be the first source to be consulted for information on any name which is not in the present ethnonymy.

As noted in the General Introduction, there are now 269 individual ethnic group bibliographies in this work. In addition, there are bibliographies for each of the fifteen culture areas distinguished, as well as bibliographies for North America as a whole Pan-Indianism, Urban Indians, Canadian Indians, United States government relations with the Native Peoples, and Canadian government relations with the Native Peoples. Adding these together gives a grand total of 290 individual bibliographies, i.e. there are 290 possible places in which bibliographic citations on a particular ethnic group might be found. The ethnonymy acts as a locator device for finding the particular bibliography which might have the citations needed the user. The names in the ethnonymy are keyed to individual bibliographies by a four-digit code. The first two digits in the code refer to the culture area in which the group is located. The third and fourth digits in the code refer to the particular bibliography within the culture area to which citations on that particular ethnic group have been assigned. The two sets of digits have been separated by a hyphen for ease in reading. As an example, in the ethnonymy we may find the name and code "Navaho 15-21." This indicates that any bibliographic references to the Navaho which have been processed have been assigned to individual bibliography 15-21. This means that all bibliographic citations to the Navaho have been assigned to the twenty-first bibliography within culture area number 15, which on inspection turns out to be the Navajo bibliography within the Southwest culture area. Note that in this case, "Navaho" is a variant spelling of the name "Navajo." The latter name is the one used to denote this particular bibliography. Similarly, the name and code "Back River Eskimo 01-09" means that bibliographic citations on this group have been placed in the ninth bibliography within culture area number 1, which is the Netsilik Eskimo bibliography within the Arctic Coast area. Note that locating the name of an ethnic group in the ethnonymy does not necessarily mean that bibliographic references on that particular ethnic group will actually be found in the bibliography. The presence of a name in the ethnonymy simply means that *if* the compilers found a bibliographic reference on the Back River Eskimo, for example, they would include it in bibliography 01-09. If *no* references on the Back River Eskimo were located, none would be in bibliography 01-09.

The following ethnonymy contains the names and numerical codes for this volume only, that is, only those names and numerical codes applying to ethnic groups living in the Eastern United States will be found here. The first two digits of each numerical code will be one of three combinations: 10-, 12-, or 13-. These two-digit numbers refer to the Midwest, Northeast, and Southeast bibliographies respectively. The third and fourth digits of the numerical codes refer to the individual bibliographies within each of the three major divisions of this volume. Thus, 10-01 refers to the Fox bibliography, 12-05 refers to the Iroquois bibliography, and 13-19 refers to the Natchez bibliography.

The reference works which were found most useful in compiling the ethnonymy are listed below:

Canada, Department of Indian Affairs and Northern Development, Indian Affairs Branch. Linguistic and cultural affiliations of Canadian Indian bands. Ottawa, 1967.

Hodge, Frederick Webb, ed. Handbook of American Indians north of Mexico. Washington, D.C., Government Printing Office, 1907-1910. 2 pts. (U.S., Bureau of American Ethnology, Bulletin, 30). (SuDocs no. SI2.3:30) [reprint editions available]

Swanton, John R. The Indian tribes of North America. Washington, D.C., Government Printing Office, 1952. (U.S., Bureau of American Ethnology, Bulletin, 145) (SuDocs no. SI2.3:145) [reprint edition available]

U.S., Department of Commerce. Federal and State Indian reservations and Indian trust areas. Washington, D.C., 1974. (SuDocs no. C1.8/3:In2)

The following is a schedule of the code numbers of the individual bibliographies which will be found in each of the five volumes of the complete bibliography.

Volume 1, General North America, contains bibliographies for code numbers 01-00, 02-00, 03-00, 04-00, 05-00, 06-00, 07-00, 08-00, 09-00, 10-00, 11-00, 12-00, 13-00, 14-00, 15-00, 16-00, 16-01, 16-02, 16-03, 16-04, and 16-05.

Volume 2, Arctic and Subarctic, contains bibliographies for *all* code numbers beginning with 01-, 02-, and 11-.

Volume 3, Far West and Pacific Coast, contains bibliographies for *all* code numbers beginning with 03-, 04-, 05-, 06-, 07-, and 08-.

Volume 4, Eastern North America, contains bibliographies for *all* code numbers beginning with 10-, 12-, and 13-.

Volume 5, Plains and Southwest, contains bibliographies for *all* code numbers beginning with 09-, 14-, and 15-.

A

Abihka 13-12
Absentee Shawnee   10-08
Accohanoc   13-21
Accomac   13-21
Acolapissa   13-01
Acquera   13-23
Acuera   13-23
Adamstown Indians   13-29
Adshusheer   13-06
Agawam   12-12
Agua Dulce Indians   13-23
Aimiqta   10-04
Ais   13-05
Akawantcaka   13-25
Alabama   13-02
Alabama Creoles   13-29
Alabama-Coushatta   13-02
Alabama-Coushatta
  Reservation   13-02
Alabama-Quassarte   13-02
Albivi   10-02
Alibamu   13-02
Allegany Reservation   12-05
Altamaha Cherokee   13-08
Amimenipaty   12-02
Amonokoa   10-02
Andaste   12-01
Annamessicks   12-10
Apalachee   13-03
Apalachicola   13-14
Appomattoc   13-21
Äqkâmot   10-04
Aquackanonk   12-02
'Arabs'   12-13
Arendahronon   12-04
Arkansas Cherokee   13-08
Arrohattoc   13-21
Ashepoo   13-13
Ashipoo   13-13
Asomoche   12-02
Assunpink   12-02
Ataronchron   12-04
Ataronchronon   12-04
Atchatchakaneouen   10-05
Atchatchakangouen   10-05
Attignawantan   12-04
Attigneenongnahac   12-04
Attiwandaron   12-11
Attiwandaronk   12-11
Avoyel   13-19
Axion   12-02

B

Backhook   13-06
Bay of Quinte Mohawks   12-05
Bayogoula   13-01
Bear Island Indians   13-20
Big Cypress Reservation   13-22
Biloxi   13-04
Black Andersons   13-29
Black Minqua   12-01
Brass Ankles   13-29

Brighton Reservation   13-22
Brown People   13-29
Buckheads   13-29
Bushwackers   12-13

C

Cahokia   10-02
Cajuns   13-29
Calcefar   12-02
Caldwell   10-06
Calusa   13-05
Canadian Delaware   12-02
Canarsee   12-08
Canarsie   12-08
Canawese   12-10
Cape Fear Indians   13-06
Cape Indians   12-07
Capinans   13-16
Carmel Indians   13-29
Carmelites   13-29
Cat Nation   12-03
Catawba   13-06
Catawba, Santee   13-06
Catskill   12-02
Cattaraugus Reservation   12-05
Caughnawaga   12-05
Cayuga   12-05
Chackta   13-11
Chakchiuma   13-07
Chaouanons   10-08
Chatot   13-14
Chavises   13-29
Chawacha   13-01
Chawasha   13-01
Chehaw   13-14
Chepoussa   10-02
Cheraw   13-06
Cheroenhaka   13-25
Cherokee   13-08
Cherokee, Altamaha   13-08
Cherokee, Arkansas   13-08
Cherokee Band   13-19
Cherokee, Eastern   13-08
Cherokee, Oklahoma   13-08
Cherokee Reservation   13-08
Cherokee, Western   13-08
Chesapeake   13-21
Chiaha   13-14
Chickahominy   13-21
Chickamauga   13-08
Chickanee   13-06
Chickasaw   13-09
Chickasaw, Oklahoma   13-09
Chikohoki   12-02
Chillicothe   10-08
Chilucan   13-23
Chinko   10-02
Chiskiac   13-21
Chitimacha   13-10
Chitimacha Reservation   13-10
Choctaw   13-11
Choctaw, Mississippi   13-11
Choctaw, Northeastern   13-11
Choctaw, Oklahoma   13-11

Choctaw Reservation
  [Mississippi]   13-11
Choctaw, Southern   13-11
Choctaw, Tennessee   13-11
Choctaw, Western   13-11
Chonque   13-18
Choptank   12-10
Choula   13-07
Chowanoc   13-20
Christanna Indians   13-17
Citizen Band   10-06
Clappers   12-13
Clay-Eaters   13-29
Coe Clan   13-29
Coiracoentanon   10-02
Combahee   13-13
Conestoga   12-01
Congaree   13-06
Conoy   12-10
Coosa   13-12
Coosuc   12-12
Coranine   13-20
Corchaug   12-08
Coree   13-20
Coushatta   13-02
Cow Creek Seminole   13-22
Coweset   12-07
Coweta   13-12
Creek   13-12
Creek Band   13-19
Creek, Lower   13-12
Creek, Lower   13-22
Creek, Middle   13-12
Creek, Oklahoma   13-12
Creek, Upper   13-12
Creels   13-29
Creoles, Alabama   13-29
Creoles, Louisiana   13-29
Croatan   13-20
Croatan Indians   13-28
'Cubans'   13-29
Cusabo   13-13
Cuscarawaoc   12-10
Cuttatawomen   13-21

D

Delaware   12-02
Delaware, Canadian   12-02
Delaware, Indiana   12-02
Delaware, Ohio   12-02
Delaware, Oklahoma   12-02
Dominickers   13-29

E

Eastern Cherokee   13-08
Eastern Niantic   12-09
Eastern Pequot Reservation
  12-09
Eastern Shawnee   10-08
Edisto   13-13
Eno   13-06
Erie   12-03
Eriwonec   12-02

Esaw 13-06
Escamacu 13-13
Espeminkia 10-02
Etiwaw 13-13
Etocale 13-23

F

Fire Nation 10-06
Five Nations 12-05
Florida State Reservation
   13-22
Forest Potawatomi 10-06
Fox 10-01
Fox, Oklahoma 10-01
Fox, Tama 10-01
Fresh Water Indians 13-23
Frilot Cove 13-29

G

Gachwechnagechga 12-02
Ganawese 12-10
Gay Head Indians 12-07
Gibson 12-05
Goins 13-29
Golden Hill Reservation 12-09
Gouldstown 12-13
Grand River Iroquois 12-05
Grand River Tuscarora 13-25
Grigra 13-19
Guacata 13-05
Guale 13-26
Guatari 13-06
Guineas 13-29
Guyandot 12-04

H

Hackensack 12-02
Haliwa 13-29
Hammonasset 12-06
Hannahville Reservation 10-06
Hassanamisco Reservation
   12-07
Hassinunga 13-17
Hathawekela 10-08
Hatteras 13-20
Haverstraw 12-02
Hichiti 13-14
Hitchiti 13-14
Hollywood Reservation 13-22
Honies 12-13
Honniasont 12-01
Hook 13-06
Hopokohacking 12-02
Hostaqua 13-23
Hotcangara 10-09
Houma 13-15
Hughchee 13-27
Huma 13-15

Huron 12-04
Huron Potawatomi Band, Inc.
   10-06
Hyannis 12-07

I

Ibitoupa 13-07
Icafui 13-23
Illinois 10-02
Indiana Delaware 12-02
Indians, Adamstown 13-29
Indians, Agua Dulce 13-23
Indians, Bear Island 13-20
Indians, Cape 12-07
Indians, Cape Fear 13-06
Indians, Carmel 13-29
Indians, Christanna 13-17
Indians, Croatan 13-28
Indians, Fresh Water 13-23
Indians, Gay Head 12-07
Indians, Long Island 12-08
Indians, Person County 13-29
Indians, Prairie 10-00
Indians, Robeson County 13-28
Indians, Sampson County 13-29
Indians, Sand Hill 12-13
Indians, Southeastern 13-00
Indians, Summerwell 13-29
Indians, Sunset 13-19
Indians, West Hill 13-29
Iroquoians 12-00
Iroquois 12-05
Iroquois, Grand River 12-05
Iroquois, Oklahoma 12-05
Iroquois, Ontario 12-05
Issa 13-06
Issues 13-29
Iswa 13-06
Iyanough 12-07

J

Jackson Whites 12-13
Jeaga 13-05
Jece 13-05

K

Kahansuk 12-02
Kakinonba 13-02
Kanawha 12-10
Kansas Kickapoo 10-03
Kansas Potawatomi 10-06
Kansas Wyandot 12-04
Kasihta 13-12
Kaskaskia 10-02
Kaskinampo 13-02
Katenuaka 13-25
Kattera 13-17

Keating Mountain 12-13
Kecoughtan 13-21
Keshok 10-04
Keso 10-04
Keyauwee 13-06
Khionontaterrhonon 12-04
Kiawa 13-13
Kiawaw 13-13
Kickapoo 10-03
Kickapoo, Kansas 10-03
Kickapoo, Mexican 10-03
Kickapoo, Oklahoma 10-03
Kickapoo Reservation
   [Kansas] 10-03
Kilatika 10-05
Kispokotha 10-08
Kitchawank 12-06
Koasati 13-02
Koroa 13-24

L

Laster Tribe 13-29
Le Motte 10-04
Lenape 12-02
Lenni Lenape 12-02
Little Taensa 13-19
Long Island Indians 12-08
Lorette 12-04
Louisiana Creoles 13-29
Lower Creek 13-12
Lower Creek 13-22
Lumbee 13-28

M

Machapunga 13-20
Mahican 12-06
Mahocks 13-17
Malungeons 13-29
Mamekoting 12-02
Manabusho 10-04
Manahoac 13-17
Manhasset 12-08
Manokin 12-10
Manomoy 12-07
Manta 12-02
Mascouten 10-02
Mascouten 10-06
Massachusett 12-07
Massaco 12-06
Massapequa 12-08
Matinecoc 12-08
Matinecock Indian Village
   12-08
Mattapanient 12-10
Mattaponi Reservation 13-21
Mattapony 13-21
Mechkentowoon 12-06
Meearmeear 10-05
Meherrin 13-25
Meletecunk 12-02
Melungeons 13-29
Memankitonna 12-02
Mengakonkia 10-05

Menominee 10-04
Menomini 10-04
Menunkatuck 12-06
Mequachake 10-08
Meros 13-29
Merric 12-08
Meskwaki 10-01
Mesquakie 10-01
Mestizos 12-13
Mestizos, Southeastern 13-29
Metoac 12-08
Mexican Kickapoo 10-03
Miami 10-05
Miccosukee 13-22
Miccosukee Reservation 13-22
Michigamea 10-02
Middle Atlantic States 12-00
Middle Creek 13-12
Midwest 10-00
Mikasuke 13-22
Mikasuki 13-22
Mikasuki, Oklahoma 13-22
Mingo 12-05
Minisink 12-02
Minnesota Winnebago 10-09
Minqua 12-01
Minqua, Black 12-01
Minqua, White 12-01
Minsi 12-02
Mississippi Choctaw 13-11
Mobile 13-16
Mococo 13-23
Moctobi 13-16
Mohawk 12-05
Mohawk, Saint Regis 12-05
Mohawks of the Bay of Quinte 12-05
Mohegan 12-09
Mohican 12-06
Moingwena 10-02
Monacan 13-17
Monahassano 13-17
Moneton 13-17
Monomoy 12-07
Montauk 12-08
Montauk Indian Village 12-08
Moors 12-13
Moraoughtacund 13-21
Moratoc 13-20
Moratok 13-20
Moravian of the Thames 12-02
Mosilian 12-02
Mosopelea 13-18
Mountain People, Ramapo 12-13
Moyawance 12-10
Mucoço 13-23
Mugulasha 13-01
Muklasa 13-02
Mummapacune 13-21
Munceys of the Thames 12-02
Munsee 12-02
Munsee Delaware of Kansas 12-02

Munsee, Wisconsin 12-02
Muskhogeans 13-00
Muskogee 13-12
Musquaki 10-01

N

Nacotchtank 12-10
Nahyssan 13-17
Naniaba 13-16
Naniba 13-16
Nansemond 13-21
Nantaughtacund 13-21
Nanticoke 12-10
Nantuxet 12-02
Napissa 13-07
Napochi 13-01
Naraticon 12-02
Narragansett 12-09
Nashua 12-12
Natchez 13-19
Natick 12-07
Nause 12-10
Nauset 12-07
Navasink 12-02
Nebraska Winnebago 10-09
Nehantic 12-09
Nentego 12-10
Nesaquake 12-08
Neshamini 12-02
Neusiok 13-25
Neutral 12-11
New York Tuscarora 13-25
Newichawanoc 12-12
Niantic 12-09
Niantic, Eastern 12-09
Niantic, Western 12-09
Nipmuc 12-07
Nochpeem 12-06
Nontuc 12-12
Northeast 12-00
Northeastern Choctaw 13-11
Nottaway 13-25

O

Ocale 13-23
Ocaneechi 13-17
Occaneechi 13-17
Oçita 13-23
Oconee 13-14
Ofo 13-18
Ohio Delaware 12-02
Ohopesha 10-04
Oil Spring Reservation 12-05
Oka 12-05
Okahoki 12-02
Okalusa 13-01
Okelousa 13-01
Oklahoma Cherokee 13-08
Oklahoma Chickasaw 13-09
Oklahoma Choctaw 13-11
Oklahoma Creek 13-12
Oklahoma Delaware 12-02

Oklahoma Fox 10-01
Oklahoma Iroquois 12-05
Oklahoma Kickapoo 10-03
Oklahoma Mikasuki 13-22
Oklahoma Potawatomi 10-06
Oklahoma Sauk 10-07
Oklahoma Seminole 13-22
Oklahoma Seneca 12-05
Oklahoma Seneca-Cayuga 12-05
Oklahoma Shawnee 10-08
Oklahoma Wyandot 12-04
Okmulgee 13-14
Onatheaqua 13-23
Onawmanient 13-21
Oneida 12-05
Oneida Reservation 12-05
Oneida, Wisconsin 12-05
Oneidas of the Thames 12-05
Onondaga 12-05
Onondaga Reservation 12-05
Ontario Iroquois 12-05
Ontponea 13-17
Oshkosh 10-04
Osochi 13-14
Ossipee 13-18
Outagami 10-01
Ozinies 12-10

P

Pamacocack 12-10
Pamlico 13-20
Pamunkey 13-21
Pamunkey Reservation 13-21
Parry Island Potawatomi 10-06
Pascagoula 13-16
Paspahegh 13-21
Pasquotank 13-20
Passayonk 12-02
Pataunck 13-21
Patchoag 12-08
Patchogue 12-08
Patuxent 12-10
Paugusset 12-06
Pawokti 13-02
Pea Ridge Group 13-29
Pedee 13-06
Peedee 13-06
Pennacook 12-12
Pensacola 13-16
Peoria 10-02
Pepicokia 10-05
Pequot 12-09
Perquiman 13-20
Person County Indians 13-29
Peshtiko 10-04
Petun 12-04
Piankashaw 10-05
Piankatank 13-21
Picquintanacsuak 12-10
Pineys 12-13
Piqua 10-08
Piscataway 12-10
Pissasec 13-21
Piwaqtinet 10-04

Pocomtuc 12-12
Pocumtuc 12-12
Podunk 12-06
Pohoy 13-23
Pompton 12-02
Pondshiners 12-13
Pools 12-13
Poospatuck Reservation 12-08
Pooy 13-23
Poquonock 12-06
'Portuguese' 13-29
Posoy 13-23
Potano 13-23
Potapaco 12-10
Potawatomi 10-06
Potawatomi, Forest 10-06
Potawatomi, Kansas 10-06
Potawatomi of Huron, Michigan 10-06
Potawatomi, Oklahoma 10-06
Potawatomi, Parry Island 10-06
Potawatomi, Prairie 10-06
Potawatomi Reservation [Kansas] 10-06
Potawatomi Reservation [Wisconsin] 10-06
Potawatomi, Walpole Island 10-06
Potawatomi, Wisconsin 10-06
Potawatomie of the Woods 10-06
Poteskeet 13-20
Potomac 13-21
Powhatan 13-21
Prairie Indians 10-00
Prairie Potawatomi 10-06

Q

Quabaug 12-07
Quinebaug 12-07
Quinipissa 13-01
Quinnipiac 12-06
Quiripiac 12-06

R

Ramapo Mountain People 12-13
Ramps 13-29
Rappahannock 13-21
Raritan 12-02
Reckgawawanc 12-02
Red Earth People 10-01
Red Legs 13-29
Redbones 13-29
Renaview 13-29
Robeson County Indians 13-28
Rockaway 12-08

S

Sabine 13-15
Sac 10-07
Sac and Fox Reservation [Iowa] 10-00
Sac and Fox Reservation [Kansas-Nebraska] 10-00
Sac and Fox Reservation [Oklahoma] 10-00
Saint Regis Mohawk 12-05
Saint Regis Mohawk Reservation 12-05
Sampson County Indians 13-29
Sand Hill Indians 12-13
Sanford Community 13-06
Santee 13-06
Santee Catawba 13-06
Saponi 13-17
Sara 13-06
Saraw 13-06
Saturiba 13-23
Saturiwa 13-23
Sauk 10-07
Sauk, Oklahoma 10-07
Sawokli 13-14
Schaghticoke Reservation 12-09
Secacawoni 13-21
Secatoag 12-08
Secatogue 12-08
Secotan 13-20
Secowocomoco 12-10
Seminole 13-22
Seminole, Cow Creek 13-22
Seminole, Oklahoma 13-22
Seneca 12-05
Seneca, Oklahoma 12-05
Seneca-Cayuga, Oklahoma 12-05
Setauket 12-08
Setauket Indian Village 12-08
Sewee 13-06
Shackaconia 13-17
Shackamaxon 12-02
Shakitok 10-04
Shakori 13-06
Shantok 12-09
Shantuck 12-09
Shateras 13-17
Shawnee 10-08
Shawnee, Absentee 10-08
Shawnee, Eastern 10-08
Shawnee, Oklahoma 10-08
Shetinasha 13-10
Shinnecock 12-08
Shinnecock Reservation 12-08
Shoccoree 13-06
Shunien 10-04
Shununiu 10-04
Sicaog 12-06
Siconesse 12-02
Sintsink 12-06
Sissipahaw 13-06
Siwanoy 12-06

Six Nations 12-05
Six Nations Reserve 12-05
Sixtown 13-11
Skaruren 13-25
Slaughters 12-13
Smilings 13-29
Souhegan 12-12
Southeast 13-00
Southeastern Indians 13-00
Southeastern Mestizos 13-29
Southern Choctaw 13-11
Squahkeag 12-12
Squawkeag 12-12
Stegaraki 13-17
Stockbridge 12-06
Stockbridge-Munsee Reservation 12-06
Stono 13-13
Stukanox 13-17
Suali 13-06
Sugeree 13-06
Summerwell Indians 13-29
Sunset Indians 13-19
Surruque 13-23
Susquehanna 12-01
Susquehannock 12-01

T

Tacatacuru 13-23
Taensa 13-19
Taensa, Little 13-19
Tallapoosa 13-12
Tama Fox 10-01
Tamali 13-14
Tamaroa 10-02
Tamathli 13-14
Tangipahoa 13-01
Tankiteke 12-06
Tanxitania 13-17
Tanxnitania 13-17
Taposa 13-07
Tapouaro 10-02
Tappan 12-02
Tassenocogoula 13-19
Tauxenent 13-21
Tawasa 13-02
Tegninateo 13-17
Tekesta 13-05
Tennessee Choctaw 13-11
Tequesta 13-05
Thames Moravian 12-02
Thames Munceys 12-02
Thames Oneidas 12-05
Timucua 13-23
Tionontati 12-04
Tiou 13-24
Tioux 13-24
Tirans 12-02
Tobacco 12-04
Tocobaga 13-23
Tocwogh 12-10
Tohome 13-16
Tohontaenrat 12-04
Tonawanda Reservation 12-05
Tunica 13-24
Tunxis 12-06

'Turks' 13-29
Tuscarora 13-25
Tuscarora, Grand River 13-25
Tuscarora, New York 13-25
Tuscarora Reservation 13-25
Tuskegee 13-02
Tuskeruro 13-25
Tutelo 13-17
Twightwees 10-05
Tyendinaga 12-05

U

Uchi 13-27
Uçita 13-23
Unalachtigo 12-02
Unami 12-02
Upper Creek 13-12
Ushpee 13-18
Ushpi 13-18
Utina 13-23

V

Van Guilders 12-13

W

Waccamaw 13-06
Wachuset 12-12
Walpole Island Potawatomi 10-06
Wamesit 12-12
Wampanoag 12-07
Wando 13-13
Wangunk 12-06
Waoranec 12-02
Wapoo 13-13
Wappinger 12-06
Waranawonkong 12-02
Warrasqueoc 13-21
Warrennuncock 13-06
Washa 13-01
Wateree 13-06
Wawarsink 12-02
Wawyachtonoc 12-06
Waxhau 13-06
Waxhaw 13-06
Wea 10-05
Weanoc 13-21
Weapemeoc 13-20
Wecquaesgeek 12-06
Wendat 12-04
Wenro 12-04
Wenrohonron 12-04
Wenrohonronon 12-04
Wenrôtronon 12-04
Weromo 13-29
Werowocomoco 13-21
Wesorts 12-13
West Hill Indians 13-29
Westenhuck 12-06

Western Cherokee 13-08
Western Choctaw 13-11
Western Niantic 12-09
Western Pequot Reservation 12-09
Westo 13-27
White Minqua 12-01
Whonkenti 13-17
Whonkentia 13-17
Wiananno 12-07
Wiccomiss 12-10
Wicocomoco 13-21
Wicocomoco 12-10
Wicomese 12-10
Wiekagjoc 12-06
Wimbee 13-13
Win 13-29
Winnebago 10-09
Winnebago, Minnesota 10-09
Winnebago, Nebraska 10-09
Winnebago Reservation [Nebraska] 10-09
Winnebago Reservation [Wisconsin] 10-09
Winnebago, Wisconsin 10-09
Winyaw 13-06
Wisconsin Munsee 12-02
Wisconsin Oneida 12-05
Wisconsin Potawatomi 10-06
Wisconsin Winnebago 10-09
Woccon 13-06
Wyandot 12-04
Wyandot, Kansas 12-04
Wyandot, Oklahoma 12-04
Wyandotte 12-04

X

Xuala 13-06

Y

Yacomanshaghking 12-02
Yadkin 13-06
Yamacraw 13-26
Yamasee 13-26
Yazoo 13-24
Yellowhammers 13-29
Yeopim 13-20
Yesan 13-17
Youghtanund 13-21
Yowani 13-11
Yuchi 13-27
Yui 13-23
Yustaga 13-23

General Ethnic Map of Native North America

1	TSETSAUT		
2	BELLABELLA		
3	BELLACOOLA		
4	CHILCOTIN		
5	LILLOOET		
6	COWICHAN		
7	KLALLAM	71	QUERES
8	QUILEUTE	72	TANO
9	QUINAULT	73	TEWA
10	TWANA	74	JEMEZ
11	SNUQUALMI	75	TAOS
12	THOMPSON	76	KIOWA APACHE
13	NICOLA	77	HIDATSA
14	SANPOIL	78	MISSOURI
15	SPOKAN	79	WINNEBAGO
16	KALISPEL	80	SOUTHAMPTON ESKIMO
17	COEUR D'ALENE	81	PENNACOOK
18	WALLAWALLA	82	MASSACHUSET
19	CAYUSE	83	MOHEGAN
20	UMATILLA	84	METOAC
21	TENINO	85	NANTICOKE
22	MOLALA	86	POWHATAN
23	WISHRAM	87	TUSCARORA
24	KLIKITAT	88	PAMLICO
25	CHEHALIS	89	CUSABO
26	KWALHIOQUA	90	APALACHEE
27	CHINOOK	91	ALABAMA
28	TLATSKANAI	92	CHANCHIUMA
29	TILLAMOOK	93	TUNICA
30	ALSEA	94	BILOXI
31	SIUSLAW	95	ACOLAPISSA
32	COOS	96	HUMA
33	CHASTACOSTA	97	CHITIMACHA
34	TOLOWA	98	KARANKAWA
35	TAKELMA	99	TARAHUMARA
36	KLAMATH	100	CHINIPA
37	ACHOMAWI	101	GUASAVE
38	YANA	102	HUICHOL
39	SHASTA	103	TAMAULIPECO
40	KAROK	104	JANAMBRE
41	CHIMARIKO	105	HUAXTEC
42	HUPA	106	TOTONAC
43	YUROK	107	CHINANTEC
44	WIYOT	108	ZAPOTEC
45	WAILAKI	109	TEQUISTLATECO
46	YUKI	110	HUAVE
47	WINTUN	111	CHIAPANEC
48	POMO		
49	WAPPO		
50	OLAMENTKE		
51	COSTANO		
52	SALINA		
53	TUBATULABAL		
54	KAWAIISU		
55	CHUMASH		
56	GABRIELINO		
57	LUISEÑO		
58	CAHUILLA		
59	KAMIA		
60	COCOPA		
61	YUMA		
62	MARICOPA		
63	HALCHIDHOMA		
64	MOHAVE		
65	HAVASUPAI		
66	HOPI		
67	ZUNI		
68	MANSO		
69	ACOMA		
70	ISLETA		